UNDERSTANDING THE UK ECONOMY

KT-443-162

MACMILLAN TEXTS IN ECONOMICS

Macmillan Texts in Economics is a new generation of economics textbooks from Macmillan developed in conjunction with a panel of distinguished editorial advisers:

David Greenaway, Professor of Economics, University of Nottingham
Gordon Hughes, Professor of Political Economy, University of Edinburgh
David Pearce, Professor of Economics, University College London
David Ulph, Professor of Economics, University College London

PUBLISHED

Public Sector Economics: Stephen J. Bailey
Understanding the UK Economy (4th edition): edited by Peter Curwen
Business Economics: Paul R. Ferguson, Glenys J. Ferguson and R. Rothschild
Environmental Economics: Nick Hanley, Jason F. Shogren and Ben White
International Finance: Keith Pilbeam
The Economics of the Labour Market: David Sapsford and Zafiris Tzannatos

Macmillan Texts in Economics

If you would like to receive future titles in this series as they are published, you can make use of our standing order facility. To place a standing order please contact your bookseller or, in case of difficulty, write to us at the address below with your name and address and the name of the series. Please state with which title you wish to begin your standing order. (If you live outside the United Kingdom we may not have the rights for your area, in which case we will forward your order to the publisher concerned.)

Customer Services Department, Macmillan Distribution Ltd,
Houndmills, Basingstoke, Hampshire, RG21 6XS, England

UNDERSTANDING THE UK ECONOMY
Fourth Edition

Edited by

Peter Curwen

Contributors

Keith Hartley and Nick Hooper
Paul Marshall

MACMILLAN

First edition 1990
Reprinted 1990
Second edition 1992
Third edition 1994
Fourth edition 1997

Published by
MACMILLAN PRESS LTD
Houndmills, Basingstoke, Hampshire RG21 6XS
and London
Companies and representatives
throughout the world

ISBN 0–333–68525–3

A catalogue record for this book is available
from the British Library.

This book is printed on paper suitable for recycling and
made from fully managed and sustained forest sources.

10   9   8   7   6   5   4   3   2   1
06 05 04 03 02 01 00 99 98 97

Copy-edited and typeset by Povey–Edmondson
Tavistock and Rochdale, England

Printed in Malaysia

Dedicated to the memory of
Thelma Curwen
1920–96

Contents

List of Figures

List of Tables

List of Abbreviations

ACAS	Arbitration, Conciliation and Advisory Service
ACT	Advance Corporation Tax
AD	Aggregate Demand
AFBD	Association of Futures Brokers and Dealers
AIM	Alternative Investment Market
AMS	Aggregate Measure of Support
APACS	Association for Payment Clearing Services
APC	Average Propensity to Consume
ATM	Automated Teller Machine
BBC	British Broadcasting Corporation
BES	Business Expansion Scheme
BIS	Bank for International Settlements
BoP	Balance of Payments
BPM	Balance of Payments Manual
BSA	Building Society Association
BTEC	Business and Technician Education Council
CA	Community Action
CAP	Common Agricultural Polcy
CBI	Confederation of British Industry
CBoT	Chicago Board of Trade
CCC	Competition and Credit Control
CCT	Compulsory Competitive Tendering
CD	Certificate of Deposit
CET	Common External Tariff
CFSP	Common Foreign and Security Policy
CGBR	Central Government Borrowing Requirement
CGT	Capital Gains Tax
CP	Community Programme
CPAG	Child Poverty Action Group
CR	Concentration Ratio
CRT	Composite Rate Tax
CSE	Consumer Subsidy Equivalent
CSE	Certificate of Secondary Education
CSO	Central Statistical Office
CTT	Capital Transfer Tax
CVD	Countervailing Duty
DCE	Domestic Credit Expansion
DES	Department of Education and Science
DHSS	Department of Health and Social Security
DIB	Defence Industrial Base
DIY	Do It Yourself
DM	Deutsche Mark
DSO	Direct Service Organisation
DSS	Department of Social Security
DTI	Department of Trade and Industry
EA	Employment Action
EAGGF	European Agricultural Guarantee and Guidance Fund
EAP	Enlarged Access Policy
EAS	Enterprise Allowance Scheme
EC	European Community
ECB	European Central Bank
ECJ	European Court of Justice
ECU	European Currency Unit
EDI	Electronic Document Interchange
EEA	Exchange Equalisation Account
EEC	European Economic Community
EER	Effective Exchange Rate
EFF	Extended Fund Facility
EFL	External Financing Limit
EFTA	European Free Trade Association
EFTPOS	Electronic Funds Transfer at Point of Sale
ELs	Eligible Liabilities
EMCF	European Monetary Co-operation Fund
EMI	European Monetary Institute
EMS	European Monetary System
EMTNs	Euromedium-term Notes
EMU	Economic and Monetary Union

EPU	European Political Union		IMD	Institute for Management Development
ERI	Effective Exchange Rate Index		IMF	International Monetary Fund
ERM	Exchange Rate Mechanism		IMRO	Investment Management Regulatory Organisation
ESA	European System of Accounts			
ESCB	European System of Central Banks		IPD	Interest, Profits and Dividends
ET	Employment Training		IPR	Intellectual Property Right
EU	European Union		ISDA	International Swap Dealers Association
FCIs	Financial Companies and Institutions			
FES	Family Expenditure Survey		ITO	Industry Training Organisation
FIMBRA	Financial Intermediaries and Brokers Regulatory Association		JA	Jobstart Allowance
			JG	Jobfinder's Grant
FIS	Family Income Supplement		JM	Jobmatch
FMI	Financial Management Initiative		JP	Jobsearch Plus
FRN	Floating-rate Note		JRS	Job Release Scheme
FSBR	Financial Statement and Budget Report		JTS	Job Training Scheme
			LA	Local Authority
GAB	General Agreements to Borrow		LASFE	Local Authority Self-financed Expenditure
GATS	General Agreement on Trade in Services			
			LAUTRO	Life Assurance and Unit Trust Regulatory Organisation
GATT	General Agreement on Tariffs and Trade			
			LCE	London Commodity Exchange
GCSE	General Certificate in Secondary Education		LDC	Less-developed Country
			LDE	London Derivatives Exchange
GDFCF	Gross Domestic Fixed Capital Formation		LDMA	London Discount Market Association
			LEC	Local Enterprise Company
GDP	Gross Domestic Product		LFS	Labour Force Study
GEMM	Gilt-edged Market Maker		LFW	Learning for Work
GGE	General Government Expenditure		LIBOR	London Inter-bank Offered Rate
GGFD	General Government Financial Deficit		LIF	Low Income Families
GNP	Gross National Product		LIFFE	London International Financial Futures Exchange
GNVQ	General National Vocational Qualification			
			LSE	London Stock Exchange
HBAI	Households Above Average Income		LTOM	London Traded Options Market
HMSO	Her Majesty's Stationery Office		MA	Modern Apprenticeships
HP	Hire Purchase		MCA	Maximum Commissions Agreement
IBA	Independent Broadcasting Association		MCA	Monetary Compensatory Amount
			MERM	Multilateral Exchange Rate Model
IBB	Invest in Britain Bureau		MIPs	Mortgage-interest Payments
IBELs	Interest Bearing Eligible Liabilities		MIRAS	Mortgage-interest Relief at Source
ICCs	Industrial and Commercial Companies		MFA	Multi-fibre Arrangement
			MLR	Minimum Lending Rate
IDC	Industrial Development Certificate		MMC	Monopolies and Mergers Commission
IEA	Institute of Economic Affairs			
IFA	Independent Financial Adviser		MoD	Ministry of Defence
IFS	Institute for Fiscal Studies		MPC	Marginal Propensity to Consume
IGA	Inter-government Agreement		MPW	Marginal Propensity to Withdraw
IICP	Interim Indices of Consumer Prices		MSC	Manpower Services Commission
ILO	International Labour Office			

MTFS	Medium-term Financial Strategy	RPI	Retail Prices Index
MTN	Multilateral Trade Negotiation	RPIX	Underlying Retail Prices Index
NAFTA	North American Free Trade Association	RPM	Resale Price Maintenance
		RSA	Regional Selective Assistance
NAIRU	Non-accelerating Inflation Rate of Unemployment	RSSL	Recruitment Subsidy for School Leavers
NBFI	Non-bank Financial Intermediaries	SB	Supplementary Benefit
NCT	New Control Total	SDR	Special Drawing Right
NCVQ	National Council for Vocational Qualifications	SEA	Single European Act
		SEAQ	Stock Exchange Automated Quotation
NDP	Net Domestic Product		
NES	New Earnings Survey	SEM	Single European Market
NHS	National Health Service	SERPS	State Earnings Related Pension Scheme
NI	National Income		
NICs	National Insurance Contributions	SFA	Securities and Futures Authority
NNDI	Net National Disposable Income	SFES	Small Firms Employment Subsidy
NNP	Net National Product	SFF	Supplementary Financing Facility
NSB	National Savings Bank	SIB	Securities and Investments Board
NVQ	National Vocational Qualification	SMU	Support Measurement Unit
NWS	New Worker's Scheme	SNA	System of National Accounts
OECD	Organisation for Economic Co-operation and Development	SRO	Self-regulatory Organisation
		TB	Treasury Bill
OEIC	Open-ended Investment Company	TDI	Total Domestic Income
OFGAS	Office of Gas Supply	TEC	Training and Enterprise Council
OFT	Office of Fair Trading	TES	Temporary Employment Scheme
OFTEL	Office of Telecommunications	TESSA	Tax Exempt Special Savings Account
OMO	Open-market Operation	TFE	Total Final Expenditure
ONS	Office for National Statistics	TFW	Training for Work
OPEC	Organisation of Petroleum Exporting Countries	TIFFE	Tokyo International Financial Futures Exchange
OTC	Over the Counter	TPI	Tax and Price Index
PAYE	Pay As You Earn	TRS	Transitional Reduction Scheme
PDI	Personal Disposable Income	TSA	The Securities Association
PEP	Personal Equity Plan	TSB	Trustee Savings Bank
PFI	Private Finance Initiative	TUPE	Transfer of Undertakings Regulations
PIA	Personal Investment Authority	TWS	Travel to Work Scheme
PIBS	Permanent Interest Bearing Shares	UAA	Utilised Agricultural Area
PPP	Purchasing Power Parity	USM	Unlisted Securities Market
PPS	Perpetual Preferred Stock	VAT	Value Added Tax
PRT	Petroleum Revenue Tax	VER	Voluntary Export Restraint
PSBR	Public Sector Borrowing Requirement	VSTF	Very-short-term Financing Facility
PSDR	Public Sector Debt Repayment	WEF	World Economic Forum
PSE	Producer Subsidy Equivalent	WiE	Workforce in Employment
PW	Project Work	WIRS	Workplace Industrial Relations Survey
R&D	Research and Development		
RDG	Regional Development Grant	WP	Workstart Pilot
REG	Regional Enterprise Grant	WT	Work Trials
RER	Real Exchange Rate	WTO	World Trade Organisation

YC	Youth Credits	YTS	Youth Training Scheme
YES	Youth Employment Subsidy	YWS	Young Worker's Scheme
YOP	Youth Opportunity Programme		

Countries are sometimes abbreviated in tables and figures, and the following abbreviations are used:

The macroeconomic model uses the following abbreviations:

Austria	A	C	Consumption
Belgium	B	E	Expenditure
Denmark	DK	I	Investment (or Income)
Finland	FIN	G	Government spending
France	F	M	Imports
Germany (united)	D	O	Output
Greece	GR	T	Taxation
Ireland	IRL	X	Exports
Italy	I	Y	Income
Japan	JAP		
Luxembourg	L		
Netherlands	NL		
Portugal	P		
Spain	E		
Sweden	S		
United Kingdom	UK		
United States	USA		
West Germany	WG		

Preface to the First Edition

We very much hope that the justification for writing a book of this kind is self-evident. If this is not the case, then we simply wish to point out that economic literacy remains at far too low a level in the UK. In seeking to enhance this literacy we like to think that this book will be of interest to a very wide-ranging audience, but we recognise that, in practice, almost all those who read it will be studying a parallel course in economic principles, either at A-level or as undergraduates, or will already be acquainted with economic issues either through their work or their reading of the financial press. We hope that the book is sufficiently challenging to interest readers who are already conversant with economics, but not so challenging as to prevent readers who are not conversant with economic theory from following the discussion.

We have tried to strike an acceptable balance between analysis and description. It is obviously necessary, in a book of this kind, to describe how the UK functions at the present time, and also how it has functioned in the past where this has been different. It is, however, unilluminating simply to explain what is done in policy terms without simultaneously explaining why, and the reasons why are also to be found in the book where appropriate. It should be noted that the kinds of models to be found in textbooks may often fail to explain why many policies are being pursued, because the real world may be evolving very rapidly and be using fairly crude rules of thumb whilst coming to terms with these changes. It is accordingly our intention to concentrate upon the real world, and to give short shrift to textbook models which cannot shed much light upon it.

Most readers familiar with economics will have been taught the subject as a succession of separate boxes labelled 'employment', 'inflation', and so on. There is, as a consequence, a preference for applications to be organised into similar boxes, to be dipped into one by one as appropriate. We do not care for this approach because, first, it fails to emphasise the fundamental linkages between the various parts of the economy; secondly, it fails to deliver a satisfactory historical perspective; and thirdly, it permits the authors covering the content of separate boxes to offer a subjective interpretation of events which conflicts with that to be found in other boxes. Rather oddly, some books consider this latter point to be a virtue, and express distaste for the imposition of monolithic structures. Our view is that this very much a vice, and indicative of lack of editorial control. This book is accordingly approached from precisely the opposite viewpoint – namely, that individual authors should work to a carefully predetermined structure and that stylistic differences should be kept to a minimum. In particular, each author has been asked to set out the pros and cons of every policy debate without prejudice. This does not mean that the authors do not have strong preferences concerning the conduct of policy, nor indeed that they have refrained from expressing them, but rather that they do not seek to persuade by omitting to mention what the counter-arguments are.

The issue concerning the need to provide a framework which integrates individual sections has been difficult to resolve. One innovative feature in this respect is the introductory chapter which seeks to provide both a philosophical basis and an historical perspective for all that follows. A second innovation is to set the discussion of fiscal and monetary policy at the end of the book, in Chapter 12, so that it draws together the macroeconomic threads from previous chapters, with Chapters 11 doing the same for the microeconomic threads. The early chapters presume least prior knowledge, but when necessary they are extensively cross-referenced to later points in the text where the missing information is to be found. Issues which can be broadly be said to concern welfare have been allocated a chapter of their own (Chapter 10), rather than ignored altogether or dispersed in brief and unrelated sections throughout the text.

Certain themes inevitably appear under several chapter headings – for example, the development of the Single European Market (SEM). Generally speaking they are left dispersed, but cross-referenced to other parts of the book where the same themes recur. However, in certain cases – for example, agriculture – it has made more sense to collect the themes together under one heading in order to avoid duplication and the loss of continuity in the discussion. For these reasons, the structure of the book may at first sight appear unusual, but we firmly believe that it does, in fact, make better sense then the structures to be found in other texts, and we leave it to the readers to judge for themselves (and hopefully to let us know their opinions on the matter in due course).

While the book is essentially about the UK economy, it has a stronger international flavour than is commonly associated with books on this topic. This reflects a whole host of developments, such as the Single European Market and deregulation in general, which are making it increasingly inappropriate to view policy within the physical confines of the UK alone. Since this is very much a feature of ongoing policy we have deliberately set up our discussion so that it offers clear pointers towards the future, and we have chosen to compensate for this by saying much less than is usual about the more distant past.

In our opinion the election of the current government was a significant watershed in policy terms, for reasons set out in the Introduction. Each chapter is accordingly structured to say relatively little about the period before 1969; to provide a fairly detailed review of the decade 1969–79; and to focus primarily upon the decade 1979–89 and especially how it has compared with the decade that preceded it.

All this places great demands upon the handling of data. We have tried to introduce as much data as possible, and to locate it all within the appropriate context rather than relegate it to appendices. Equally, we recognise that tabular material can be boring – and, at times, a poor means of communication – so where appropriate other methods of presentation have been used. A point to be emphasised is that data are expressed in the form normally used by government and reported in the media. Thus, for example, the Public Sector Borrowing Requirement (PSBR) is not simply stated as an absolute number but as a percentage of gross domestic product GDP. Much of the data is adjusted for inflation, and whenever space permits the comparable data for other countries are also included.

The contributors to this book (other than the editor) have been chosen because they are knowledgeable in their fields. However, too much knowledge can be a vice as well as a virtue when it comes down to the need to compress a great deal of information into a small space, and the authors are commended to you not so much because they are 'specialists' but because they have proved in their previously published work that they have the facility to communicate to the target audience for this book. We hope that it makes enjoyable reading. No doubt you will let us know if that is not the case. One way or the other the editor is more than happy to accept responsibility for the entire finished product, although individual authors are responsible only for the chapters which bear their name.

Finally I would like to thank Gorden Hughes and the other five anonymous reviewers for their thorough dissection of the text in its varying stages of completion. There is a myth – propagated, one suspects, by those who write only short articles – that textbooks are not refereed adequately, but that has been far from the reality in this particular case. Whilst some suggestions for improvements have been set aside for this edition, it is anticipated that they will be incorporated in the second edition. Any restructuring of the text in subsequent editions will be determined entirely by the suggestions of users, and these are accordingly welcomed by the editor.

PETER CURWEN

Preface to the Second Edition

Armed with reviews and a large number of questionnaires completed by teachers, we have set out to revise the text significantly for this second edition. While not every suggestion for improvement has been adopted on this occasion, we are already considering how best to manage the book's evolutionary path.

It is important to begin by clearing up one particular misunderstanding. Although it is hoped that many readers will be able to enjoy the text without having previously learned economics in a formal way, we anticipated that most readers would use this book in conjunction with a basic text on economic theory, thereby allowing us to concentrate upon its applications in the real world. The text contains such models as are essential to assist both the general reader and students of economics who are reading ahead of their main text to understand the issues which we address, which can be very complicated, but it is simply impractical to try to combine detailed theory and applications in a single text.

We have attempted to keep the text as up to date as is humanly possible. To this end we have introduced a large amount of new data, particularly in the form of Figures, whilst removing a much smaller amount which appeared in the first edition. We believe that this database provides a truly comprehensive overview of the workings of the UK economy. In recognition of recent developments we have included a good deal of additional material on the European Community, and have sought wherever possible to draw comparisons between the performance of the UK and other member states.

The editor has chosen in this edition to take over responsibility for writing all of the first nine chapters in the book, two of which have been divided compared to the first edition as a result of the addition of much new material. This should ensure greater uniformity of approach, and also ease the burden of revision for future editions. The new material is generally intended to introduce developments which have taken place over the past two years, but completely new sections have also been added where it was thought that it would enhance the discussion in a material way. For example, there is a new section devoted to the housing market in Chapter 3, which is accompanied by a fuller discussion of the link between wealth, consumption and saving, and Chapter 2 contains a completely new version of the overall model of the economy.

It is hoped that these, and other, improvements have enhanced the usefulness of the text for a wide variety of readers. As before, the text has been thoroughly reviewed in draft form in order to ensure that this is so, and we would like to thank the reviewers for their extensive and helpful comments.

PETER CURWEN

Preface to the Third Edition

Only two years have passed since the publication of the second edition, but events have, as ever, refused to stand still, necessitating some significant revisions to parts of the text. Looking back at what was written two years ago, the analysis appears to have held up well and we see no need to retract anything of substance, but there can be no doubt that two years of recession oblige us to rethink the probable course of the UK economy during the rest of the decade.

When the second edition was at final proof stage it proved necessary to insert a substantial section relating to the Maastricht Treaty. At the time it was assumed that it would be signed and sealed before 1992 was out, with member states if anything moving closer together in the narrow band of the Exchange Rate Mechanism (ERM). In the event, the outcome has been rather different, so this edition contains a good deal of analysis of what went wrong and where it is taking the UK.

In this, and other respects which reflect, for example, the official creation of the Single Euro-pean Market on 1 January 1992, the text is increasingly seeking to examine the role of the UK as part of a wider political/economic system. Nevertheless, the UK has recently been affected by the consequences of some of its own peculiar structures, and of these the housing market is clearly the most prominent. For this reason, the discussion of the role of the housing market has been greatly extended in this edition.

In most other respects the primary task has been, as usual, to update the database so that it provides a meaningful picture of the current state of the economy; in effect, that prevailing at the end of 1992 or some months into 1993, but any significant turns in events at the end of 1993 have also been integrated into the text. We therefore trust that this new edition will continue to provide teachers and students alike with an invaluable insight into the workings of the UK economy.

PETER CURWEN

Preface to the Fourth Edition

There has been a three-year rather than a two-year gap between this and the preceding edition, and hence there has been somewhat more updating to be done than previously. Like most revised texts, this book has tended to grow modestly larger with each successive edition. It is always easier to add new information than to declare old information to be redundant. This caused the individual chapters to become somewhat unwieldy at the time of the third edition, so for this edition they have mostly been divided into two, roughly equal, parts. However, this has had very little effect upon the overall coverage of the book, and should not cause confusion for those used to previous editions.

Chapter 1 remains as before. The old Chapters 2 and 3 have been divided such that the latter third of Chapter 2 plus the initial third of Chapter 3 now become Chapter 3 in this edition, with the remainder of the old Chapter 3 becoming a new Chapter 4. The old Chapter 4 has been divided down the middle to form two new Chapters, 5 and 6. The old Chapter 5 has also been divided, but in this case it is the central part of the old Chapter 5 on taxation which becomes the new Chapter 7, and the remainder which forms the new Chapter 8.

Both the old Chapters 6 and 7 have been divided in two to form two new chapters, creating new Chapters 9 to 12 inclusive. However, as the old Chapters 8 and 9 were relatively short, they have not been divided and become new Chapters 13 and 14. The old Chapter 10 has been divided in two, forming new Chapters 15 and 16. The major structural revision is in respect of the old Chapter 11 on industry and policy. Here, in addition to a basic division to form new Chapters 17 and 19, a relatively small part of the old chapter has been lifted

out to form, much extended, a completely new Chapter 18 on privatisation. Finally, the old Chapter 12 has become a truncated Chapter 20 in order to reduce the complexity of the discussion.

The new structure is intended to offer coverage at the rate of roughly one chapter a week for a full-year course, or two a week for a semester. We decided not to extend the book by adding any further new chapters at this stage, preferring an incrementalist approach with successive editions, but we feel sure that readers will be more comfortable with the new chapter size.

In addition to the creation of a new chapter, new material has been added where desirable, and in particular the continued development of the European Union, not least its expansion in size, is reflected in an increased emphasis upon events outside the UK.

In political terms, a general election is due fairly soon after this book is published. There is widespread agreement about the probability of a change of government, although it remains unclear whether the winner will obtain an absolute majority or be forced to rule by coalition. Clearly, a change in government has implications for the content of a book such as this, and the authors have sought to signal and/or discuss probable changes in policy direction. However, it is looking increasingly likely that comparatively little will be affected by a switch to a Labour government, so we remain unconcerned that this edition will become dated any quicker than its predecessors.

It is, perhaps, worth noting in conclusion that, although the text is critical of many of the policies pursued over the past decade and a half, the authors remain firmly of the belief that the UK economy is overall much stronger than it was in 1979. Most of the text is given over to a discussion of the factors underpinning the size of the national 'cake'. However, considerable space is also given over to a discussion of the way in which the 'cake' is divided up, which is widely believed to be done less equally today compared to 1979. The task facing an incoming Labour government, should that eventuality arise, will be to find a means of simultaneously making the 'cake' bigger and dividing it up more equally. We hope to report on its progress in the next edition.

PETER CURWEN

Acknowledgements

The authors and publishers wish to thank the following for permission to use copyright material:

Bank of England for Tables 4.6, 4.8, 5.3, 6.2, 9.3, 9.6, 13.9 and Figures 3.2, 3.18, 3.21, 5.2, 6.2, 6.3, 9.3, 9.4, 9.5, 10.3, 10.4, 14.2.

Barclays Bank for Figure 2.6

Council of Mortgage Lenders for Table 6.1.

Financial Times for Tables 6.5, 12.4 and Figures 6.1, 12.1.

Her Majesty's Stationery Office for Tables 12.6, 14.5.

Information Division, HM Treasury, for Table 4.1 and Figure 4.2.

Noel Alexander Associates for Tables 5.4, 6.4.

Office for National Statistics for Tables 2.1, 2.2, 2.3, 2.4, 2.6, 2.7, 3.1, 3.2, 3.3, 3.6, 4.4, 4.5, 4.7, 7.5, 8.1, 8.2, 8.6, 9.1, 9.4, 11.4, 13.1, 13.4, 13.5, 13.6, 14.1, 15.2, 15.5; and Figures 2.5, 3.5, 3.6, 3.7, 3.8, 3.9, 3.17, 4.3, 4.4, 4.5, 4.12, 7.1, 7.2, 8.1, 8.5, 9.1, 9.2, 9.7, 11.1, 13.1, 13.2, 13.3, 13.9, 14.1, 14.3, 14.5, 15.3, 15.4, 17.3, 19.1, 20.1, 20.5.

Office for Official Publications of the European Communities for Tables 4.5, 8.3, 8.7, 8.8, 9.5, 12.2, 19.1.

Organisation for Economic Co-operation and Development for Table 4.2 and Figure 3.16.

The Economist for Figures 5.1, 6.6

Every effort has been made to trace all the copyright-holders, but if any have been inadvertently overlooked the publishers will be pleased to make the necessary arrangements at the first opportunity.

Chapter 1

History and Politics

Peter Curwen

■ 1.1 Introduction

Our purpose in this chapter is to set the scene for the detailed analysis of the UK economy which is the subject matter of this book.

Economics has become increasingly technical, in an attempt to build ever more sophisticated models which tend to lose touch with the behaviour of economic agents in the real world. This, in its turn, has tended to detract from the need to study the historical and political context within which policy-making actually takes place. This book, however, is entirely about the real world, and therefore requires the reader to have at least a rudimentary understanding of economic history and political systems. This chapter sets out to provide this understanding and may, therefore, readily be omitted by those already well-versed in these fields.

Economic ideas, in common with those in many other disciplines, tend to pass through the successive phases of **revolution** and **evolution.** The revolutionary phases are often associated with a particular event, such as the publication of a book, although the seeds of the ideas may have been sown a great many years earlier awaiting the ideal moment for germination. Furthermore, it is

not altogether easy to pinpoint when a revolution is set in motion since there is inevitably a great deal of inertia before revolutionary ideas gain widespread acceptance. The subsequent discussion is concerned primarily with the Keynesian and monetarist revolutions. The former is generally associated with the publication of the *General Theory* in 1936, but for our purposes is more sensibly seen in policy terms as underpinning the significant changes which took place between 1944 and 1949. The monetarist revolution flowered during the 1970s and came of age in the UK during the early years of the period of Conservative rule commencing in 1979, and it is partly for this reason that 1979 is treated as the watershed year for the text as a whole.

The evolutionary phase of Keynesianism lasted broadly from 1950 to 1970, at which point events (discussed below) conspired to bring about its steady decline prior to its official replacement by monetarism. Monetarism, on the other hand, barely had the chance to evolve at all before significant aspects were consigned to virtual oblivion, leaving the UK in a kind of policy limbo – part-monetarist, part-Keynesian and part whatever seemed to be a good idea at the time to deal with short-term problems.

1

It is important to appreciate, to begin with, that there are two quite divergent ways of looking at those economic models which are put into practice. The first, clearly enunciated by Keynes himself and generally favoured by the intellectual circles in which he moved, is that the ideas of economists and political philosophers are the **driving force behind the implementation of policy.** Support for this viewpoint can be found in the influential doctrine of *laissez-faire* during the nineteenth century, and subsequently in the writings of Keynes himself. The opposing doctrine is that economists have a barely detectable influence on society as a whole, since the popularity of particular ideas ultimately depends upon their compatibility with economic and political circumstances at the time. In other words, the broad direction in which economic policy moves is determined by the ways in which **interest groups in society respond to changing economic opportunities,** and economic models are chosen because they lend intellectual support to the behaviour of those groups.

The debate between these two schools of thought will, naturally, never be satisfactorily resolved because it is hard to see how either case can be 'proved' to everyone's satisfaction. An interesting current illustration of this debate relates to the case of privatisation, where it is possible to argue, on the one hand, that the policy was adopted as a result of ear-bending in influential Conservative circles by the Institute of Economic Affairs and other like-minded groups and, on the other, that once the decision had been taken to reduce the role of government and to cut public expenditure, asset sales were simply one available means to achieve these goals.

A variety of economic models is analysed in the chapters which follow. However, it is at best unhelpful simply to model the economy at a specific point in time as though it can be divorced from the historical and political context which shaped it over a period of many decades. Indeed, it is possible to argue that many of the key influences moulding the way the economy behaves today have their origins well back into the nineteenth century, but a shortage of space does not permit us to examine these other than in a fairly cursory way.

■ *1.2* The Neo-classical World

At the end of the nineteenth century the **forces of the market-place** still largely held sway over economic life. Certainly, government had been taking on board ever wider responsibilities which needed to be financed through taxation, but macroeconomic management of the kind practised after 1945 was incompatible with the prevailing 'neo-classical' orthodoxy.

This held true, for example, with respect to unemployment. The mechanisation of agriculture at the turn of the century forced large numbers of people off the land and into towns and cities. There were, understandably, difficulties in absorbing this inflow of labour into the industrial workforce, and the prevailing orthodoxy therefore needed to explain the adjustment process whereby the level of employment would be restored to equilibrium. The line taken by the neo-classical school was that, in a competitive market system such as characterised the UK economy at the time, the **equilibrium condition was one of full employment.** In other words, any imbalances between the supply of, and demand for, a factor of production such as labour could only be temporary, since any imbalance between the two would automatically trigger forces in the market-place which would bring them back into balance. The forces in question were **changes in relative prices,** such that if there was excess demand for a factor of production its price (its wage in the case of labour) would be driven upwards until the point was reached at which potential purchasers would be induced to switch over from demanding the new, relatively expensive, factor of production, to others which in the process had become relatively cheap. Likewise, the price of a factor of production in excess supply would be driven steadily downwards, until a level was reached at which all that was being supplied at that price level was purchased.

Given its resurgence in the modern context of **supply-side economics,** it is important to appreciate what interpretation this line of argument placed upon the concept of full employment. What the neo-classical model was effectively saying was that if the market for labour was left to its own devices, a wage rate would be established such that anyone who was willing to work would have a job to go to, and employment would in that sense be permanently 'full'. By implication, all unemployment could be treated as **voluntary** because the individuals in question must either be unwilling to work at **any** wage rate, or willing to work, but only at a wage rate higher than what the market was prepared to pay. There would always be enough potential jobs to employ everyone willing to work, it was simply a question of finding the market-clearing wage. However, if some individuals chose not to accept that wage, then clearly they were preventing the market from functioning smoothly, in which case they were themselves the **cause** of the problem of unemployment. Since they were the cause, and a cure was readily available were they willing to accept a reduction in their target wage rate, it could not by implication be anyone else's responsibility to deal with unemployment. Hence there was no need for governments to intervene in the labour market.

1.2.1 Real and Money Magnitudes

Within the neo-classical model a crucial distinction was made between **real** and **money** magnitudes. The total **volume** of labour – or of any other factor of production – in employment at any one time was regarded as a real magnitude, governed by the price of one factor relative to that of others. If all other things remained equal, and if a unit of labour cost £1 whilst a unit of machinery cost £2, then labour was half the price of capital and would be employed in preference to capital. This would be wholly unaffected by a doubling of the **general price level,** with the prices above rising to £2 and £4 respectively, since labour would remain one-half of the price of capital per unit employed, and indeed this would hold true were prices in general to rise by a multiple of 100 or 1000 times. The **volume** of labour would remain constant while the monetary **value** of labour used would vary enormously.

It followed that there was no direct link between the general level of prices and the level of employment. Nevertheless, there had to be a reason why the general price level showed considerable volatility over time, and the reason was called the **Quantity Theory of Money.** The original, or 'old' version of the Quantity Theory was formulated within the context of a monetary system called the gold standard. This meant that the total amount of money available was directly related to the available stock of gold – originally on a one-to-one basis but, subsequent to the widespread adoption of the principle of credit creation, in a fixed proportionate relationship. Hence, if more gold was put into circulation, but no more real goods and services, prices in general would be driven upwards in order to ensure that the available stock of money would remain just sufficient, **and no more**, to purchase the available stock of goods and services. This applied equally well in reverse, with prices falling when the output of goods and services increased but no new supply of gold became available.

1.2.2 Mass Unemployment

The return of the labour force from active military duty after 1918 coincided with a sharp downturn in economic activity resulting from a combination of matters such as an overvalued exchange rate, ageing technology and increased world-wide competition. Industries such as coal mining suffered badly. Motive power was switching from coal to oil, and deep-mining in Britain was very expensive compared to the costs of newly-opened mines elsewhere. The coal mine owners sought to resolve the problem by forcing their coal miners to take a reduction in their wages. However, the miners resisted, going on strike in 1921 and triggering the General Strike of 1926. They were ultimately defeated (hindered, in part, by the lack of a welfare system to fall back on in hard times), but many mines were nevertheless forced to shut down. This was paralleled in other industries and, as a result there was widespread unemployment in the UK at a time when other economies were booming.

Although the depression which began in the UK in 1919 was by no means typical (the overvalued currency was a critical factor not found elsewhere), it did provide food for thought for many economists brought up in the neo-classical orthodoxy, amongst them John Maynard Keynes. The neo-classical model was steadily amended and refined, and within Keynes's *Treatise on Money*, published in 1930, one can detect a distinct step forward along the evolutionary path of the existing orthodoxy at precisely the point in history when events conspired to expose the model's inadequacies, for in 1929 there occurred the Wall Street Crash.

Unfortunately, the response of most governments after the Great Crash was to do all the wrong things. In particular, America rapidly introduced an era of trade protectionism to which other countries responded in kind, with the result that the total volume of world trade fell sharply. It has also been argued by writers such as Milton Friedman that the American Federal Reserve System deliberately engineered a shortage of liquidity, thereby making it very difficult for debtors to obtain the money they needed to settle their debts. Irrespective of the causes, the effects were straightforward enough. Unemployment rose sharply throughout the Western World, the impact falling particularly upon towns and regions overdependent upon traditional industries such as ship-building.

In the face of mass unemployment the neo-classical orthodoxy effectively broke down. To argue that millions of people could be got back to work simply by lowering the wage rate, thereby restoring equilibrium in the labour market, seemed futile in the extreme. But on the subject of what else could be done the model was largely silent. The time was at last ripe for the seed of revolution to grow.

■ *1.3* The Keynesian Revolution

This revolution is associated with the work of Keynes, and in particular with the ideas expressed in the *General Theory of Employment, Interest*

and Money, published in 1936. The *General Theory* is a book of baffling obscurity – which some argue was deliberate in order to get the central, simpler propositions accepted while the arguments raged about interpreting the complexities. The standard textbook version essentially dates back to the model introduced after the Second World War, and it is certainly only fair to argue that Keynes himself, who died in 1946, would have made significant alterations to his text had he lived longer. Nevertheless there can be little dispute about his main lines of attack upon the neo-classical orthodoxy.

In the *General Theory*, Keynes set out to demonstrate that the level of National Income – and hence effectively of output and employment – was determined by the **interaction of changes in both real and monetary variables**, and also that there was a direct link between decisions taken by **individual households and firms** and the effect upon the **economy as a whole**. The cornerstone of Keynes' work was the rejection of the reasoning which led in the neo-classical model to the automatic restoration of full employment, the creation of an alternative theory which in the general case would generate less than full employment, and the use of that theory to explain how unemployment could be cured.

One of the main innovations of the Keynesian model was its stress upon the role of **expectations in the face of uncertainty**. Keynes felt that decisions with respect to the expansion or curtailment of output were to a considerable degree dependant upon the prevailing set of expectations about the future held by households and firms. In the event, for example, that firms in general did not expect an early recovery from a period of recession, their natural reaction would be to hold back from producing output which they did not expect to be able to sell, and to lay off workers whom they could no longer gainfully employ. The consequence of such a policy would be a significant reduction in the amount of money which households had to spend since, insofar as it existed, State assistance was not as rewarding as full-time employment. The consequent cut-back in consumption spending would adversely affect retail outlets, which in turn would reduce orders from wholesalers, and the latter would cut back orders from manufacturers.

The curtailment of output and employment undertaken in the expectation of the fall in demand for goods and services would thus itself create the expected circumstances of reduced consumption. In other words, expectations have an in-built tendency to be **self-fulfilling, and** in so doing they inevitably help to generate a further set of **similar expectations**. The confirmation of a firm's expectations that it would not be able to sell what it produced would thus probably cause the firm to curtail output and employment still further. The link between decisions taken by households and firms, and their consequences for the economy as a whole were, therefore, plain to see.

This line of reasoning tended to imply that the level of employment was affected by the prevailing set of expectations. But there seemed little enough reason to suppose that the prevailing state of expectations would always be such as to secure full employment. The neoclassical model argued that full employment could always be restored by reducing the wage rate. But suppose the wage rate was indeed to fall as it recommended. The result would logically be a reduction in the amount of money available for current consumption, which in turn would lead inevitably to a reduction in sales and profits. The Keynesian model argued that firms would respond by **cutting** output and employment. Since this was exactly the opposite conclusion to that postulated in the neo-classical model, the inevitable conclusion was that full employment could not, in fact, be restored through changes in relative prices.

The one undisputed fact of the early 1930s was that the Great Crash and its aftermath had resulted in depressed expectations. It was not that the firms did not want to expand on an individual basis, but if one firm produced more output, created new jobs and paid out more in wages at a time when other firms did not follow suit, then almost all of the extra wages would be spent on the output of other firms rather than that of the firm paying out the wages, thereby inevitably driving it into bankruptcy. Of course, if all firms chose to expand simultaneously there would be

enough extra wages in circulation to keep them all in business, but that could only happen if their expectations were simultaneously to improve, and in the climate of the 1930s that was simply not going to happen.

It followed logically from this that full employment could be restored if either households unilaterally decided to spend more money – for example, by running down accumulated savings – or firms decided to invest in more capital machinery. But if neither group was willing to behave in this way, the needed improvement in the climate of expectations would have to be engineered by some other party. Clearly, the only other party capable of achieving this was the **government.**

The implication was that full employment could be restored only if the government created a demand for goods and services. This, however, flew straight in the face of the neo-classical orthodoxy and, somewhat curiously, given the part played by Keynes in this tale, the UK government was particularly disinclined to accept the need for increased government spending.

☐ *1.3.1 A Matter of Debt*

But what other objections, apart from a simple-minded belief in the neo-classical model, were there to increased government spending? The answer was that increased spending not covered by increased taxation meant that the indebtedness of the government would have to increase. In general, public expenditure was not expected, unlike private investment, to be self-financing over time. Hence balancing the fiscal books was held to be the soundest way to behave.

In advocating government spending in excess of tax revenue, Keynes was not, however, suggesting that borrowing to get the economy on the move again was to be regarded as anything other than a temporary measure. The idea was that once public spending and the consequent increase in income and employment had generated more optimistic expectations, the simultaneous expansion of private sector organisations would once again be restored as the driving force behind economic activity, thereby allowing the government to cut back its own operations and to use revenue from the newly-expanded tax base to redeem at least part of the outstanding debt.

In fairness to Keynes, it should be said that his view of the world was one in which a group of public-spirited intellectuals would operate economic policy with wisdom, discretion and foresight. His was not a world of fiscal profligacy; debt was perfectly sensible so long as there was an intention to repay, to balance the books over the longer haul. But spending other people's money proved to be more enjoyable than spending one's own, especially as it helped to keep politicians in elected office, so acceptance of the belief that there was nothing particularly immoral about debt *per se* was turned around and used in evidence against him. Politicians in office all agreed that debt **ought** to be repaid, but they could not see any political advantage in doing so, especially as the interest payments might fall due during another political party's period in office.

In practice, it is probably fair to argue that it was the Second World War, rather than the *General Theory*, which accounted for the demise of neo-classicism in the UK. Elsewhere the Nazis in Germany were behaving in a thoroughly Keynesian way by the mid-1930s, and the New Deal was implemented in the USA, albeit with far less effect because the desire to help the disadvantaged had to compete with the desire not to run budget deficits. However, unemployment remained extremely high in the UK, especially on a regional basis (thereby providing further 'evidence' of labour market inflexibility), until the government was forced, despite itself, to re-arm. Even then it was well into 1941, the second year of the War, before all of the unemployed could be absorbed into 'productive' work.

☐ 1.3.2 The New Order Cometh

By the end of the Second World War the Keynesian revolution had inexorably entered into its 'orthodoxy' phase, common to all advanced Western economies for roughly 25 years. Not surprisingly, the sacrifices of the war years served to speed up enormously the process of social change.

Under no circumstances was there to be a re-run of the 1930s, which meant that a clear priority had to be given to the eradication of unemployment. On the whole, the expectation was that, once the economy was restored to a peacetime footing, there would be considerable problems in switching the labour force into civilian occupations. The concept of **full** employment was not, therefore, an immediate objective. The *White Paper on Employment* in 1944 talked in terms of something less ambitious, but for once the reality was an improvement upon the expectation. Naturally, the initial period of postwar reconstruction was bound to generate exceptionally high levels of demand in the short term. But the maintenance of demand in the longer term would obviously need the government to play a more active role via **demand management,** which would have the characteristics established in the Keynesian model, namely short-term, counter-cyclical fiscal policy. Monetary policy would also need to be short-term and counter-cyclical, but would have little to do bar keeping down the interest rate in order to cheapen the cost of borrowing for investment.

But the Keynesian revolution was not simply an issue of macroeconomic objectives and instruments. It was an era in which voters turned away from markets, which were perceived as **efficient** but **inequitable,** in order to create a fairer and more just society. Although Churchill, who had led the wartime government was a Conservative, there was nevertheless a massive swing towards the Labour Party, which by that time had almost completely displaced the Liberals. The era of the **Welfare State** had arrived.

■ 1.4 Efficiency versus Equity

The postwar years have been characterised by contradictions within the processes of macroeconomic control, but one must not lose sight of the underlying debate about the role of market mechanisms. The Keynesian model effectively discarded the view that a modern advanced economy could be left to its own devices, and ushered in the era of the **mixed economy.** But there are clearly an enormous variety of ways in which one can draw boundaries between private and public sectors, and a great deal therefore hinges on the balance between **efficiency and equity at the microeconomic level**. At the end of the day there are very few goods and services that cannot be supplied efficiently by the market mechanism – in the sense of maximising output for given inputs – but the amounts of goods and services produced, and their allocation between households, may be considered inequitable from a wider social perspective. One may naturally respond by arguing that concentration upon the issue of equity does not of itself necessitate any conflict with the objective of maximum efficiency, and indeed it is clear that the introduction of the Welfare State presupposed that no serious conflict would occur.

However, efficiency in the market is dependent upon the profit motive, and the profit motive has accordingly to be subjugated to the wider **public interest** if equity issues are to be given greater priority. This line of argument can best be clarified by a concrete example. Before the Second World War the health service largely required payment to be made at the point of consumption. Its size, therefore, depended upon people's willingness and ability to pay, but insofar as there was a demand for the service it could be provided very efficiently. The National Health Service (NHS) was introduced because this level of provision was felt to be both inadequate and inequitable, but equity – or so it was thought – could be maximised only by providing health care free at the point of consumption. Theoretically, there was no reason why this expanded provision could not be delivered as efficiently as before, but logically this would be true only if the motivation towards efficiency was generated as strongly by the pursuit of the public interest as by the pursuit of profit. At the time this was taken for granted, because it was felt that there as a consensus within society that the public interest should transcend private interests. In setting up the NHS, in expanding education and welfare services and in taking industries into public ownership, very little thought was thus given to the issue of objectives and how best to achieve them.

In retrospect this was, at best, unfortunate, but it reflected the widely held view at the time that a transfer of ownership from private to public sector would be sufficient to guarantee an improvement in performance. For example, there was bound to be a better relationship between managers and workers in an industry once it had been transferred to public ownership, since the owners would no longer be seeking to squeeze every drop of profit out of the workers. There would be no more General Strikes, no more trouble in the coal industry, the long-term future of which would now be assured. Regrettably, hardly anyone observed that the coal-miners themselves had no greater personal stake in the industry post-nationalisation than had existed previously. Indeed, if anything, they had even less of a stake since wages and jobs were no longer directly related to the profitability of the industry. It would thus be in their personal interest to try to raise their wages even if it resulted in the industry making losses. They might well prefer not to take this action because, for example, there was a government in power which had their wholehearted support. But if another, less appealing, government took power, or if the economic environment became so problematic that any government would be forced to try to control wages, then confrontation would almost inevitably occur. In such a situation it would be vital for someone to re-establish control, whether by management or ultimately by government. Yet to **re-establish** control there needed to be an **effective** system of control established in the first place, which even a cursory glance at the statutes governing the nationalised industries or the NHS demonstrates not to have been the case.

A further aspect of the **efficiency versus equity** debate to which insufficient attention is paid relates to the distributions of income and wealth, and their implications for tax regimes. So far we have discussed the Keynesian orthodoxy largely from the expenditure side, but if public spending is to rise appreciably then it will be necessary to raise taxes, in which case one needs to stress the issue of **whom or what to tax,** and how onerously the individual taxes are to be applied. Once one starts out with the premise that a greater degree of equity is needed, it follows logically that the primary purpose of taxation, other than simply to finance expenditure, is to **redistribute**. This requires a strong element of progressivity to be present, most obviously in the income tax and wealth tax schedules. But this in turn has implications for efficiency, since it affects the incentives to work and to take risks.

One further point is worth emphasising at this stage, before we return to the historical narrative. No matter what macroeconomic control system is adopted, it must send out both explicit and implicit signals at a microeconomic level. In a market system the signals are primarily in the form of **changing prices**, and this will remain true of many goods and services which are publicly provided even though the prices in question are not market prices. The **absence** of a price – as in the provision of health care – sends out an equally strong signal. When one compares different societies with roughly equal wealth, one should **expect** to find different consumption patterns. This is because a good may be taxed or subsidised in one society where in the other society it is not. If, for example, mortgages and pension contributions are subject to tax relief, one should hardly be surprised to discover that the most popular forms of wealth are houses and pensions.

To summarise this part of the argument, what we are saying is that the macroeconomic model, whether Keynesian or otherwise, requires one to look deeply into its microeconomic implications, and this is why in later chapters we will be looking at tax regimes, industrial policy, welfare provision and other related matters.

▌ 1.5 Employment, Trade and Inflation

As we have indicated above, the primary focus of the Keynesian model was upon the level of unemployment. However, it followed logically that if there was insufficient demand for private sector goods and services, and a consequent falling off in the level of employment, then the new jobs created by public spending in order to maintain full employment would tend to be in the public sector

– that is, in central and local government and the nationalised industries. And if the prevailing orthodoxy held that any shortcomings in the operations of private sector bodies needed to be remedied by government in order to promote the cause of **social justice** (and sometimes **efficiency**), then the mix of the mixed economy was logically going to become weighted increasingly towards the public sector and away from the private sector. But the Keynesian model did not of itself imply a significant long-term shift, since public expenditure was meant to come to the fore only during recessions. When the economy was booming it could even be necessary for the public sector to be cut back in order to dampen down excess demand in the private sector.

So why did the upsurge in public spending happen in every major European economy? One obvious reason was that elected politicians saw themselves as elected to change things for the better, and this was bound to cost money. Furthermore, a consensus about the desirability of improving equity and welfare was incompatible with sharp cuts in public spending, since no element of such spending could be cut without causing someone somewhere to lose his or her job. Yet if the government could not bring itself to make meaningful cuts, the political opposition had little choice, if it wanted to get elected, other than to differentiate its product by promising to spend even more, and to resist any cuts which were on the agenda.

This argument had particular implications for employment policy. In principle, the objective of giving everyone a job could be fulfilled independently of locational issues. In other words, if an industry shut down in the North and another simultaneously expanded in the South, full employment could be maintained by moving the redundant workers to the new location. However, this inevitably meant both short-term hardship for those required to move and probably long-term decline in the areas where firms shut down. In countries such as West Germany these consequences did not trouble politicians overmuch, but in the UK they were considered to be unacceptable, and steps were taken, even by Conservative governments ostensibly dedicated to free-market principles, to prevent them – through, for example, the rescue of lame-duck industries.

The according of primacy to the objective of full employment also created other kinds of difficulty. The maintenance of high levels of demand in order to sustain full employment had implications for other important policy objectives, in particular for inflation and for the external trading position as reflected in the balance of payments. The existence of inflation and of deficits in the balance of payments needed to be examined from the point of view both of cause and of cure. Unfortunately, the Keynesian model had nothing useful to say about inflation because it had been formulated during an historical period when prices were tending to fall rather than to rise, and there seemed to be no obvious reason in theory why the demand for labour could not be expanded to absorb the available supply without bidding up its price.

Nevertheless, inflation did exist throughout the 1950s and 1960s, albeit at a fairly modest level, so in many ways the simplest thing was to do very little about it and to hope that it would go away. Every now and again prices would rise unusually sharply, and something would need to be done about it, but on the whole there were more important things to worry about. In particular, high levels of demand tended to be associated with high levels of imports, the more so as the UK became increasingly unable to compete internationally with respect to her manufactured goods.

Now a balance-of-payments (BoP) deficit can be dealt with in a number of different ways:

1. the **domestic economy can be deflated** (expenditure reducing) so that there is less demand to spill over into imports;
2. the **price of imports can be raised,** and that of exports lowered, via an alteration in the exchange rate (expenditure switching);
3. **artificial restraints on trade** can be introduced, such as tariffs and quotas on imports or subsidies to exports.

In the event, the remedy mentioned in 3 was available on only a short-term emergency basis, because the UK was a member of the GATT (General Agreement on Tariffs and Trade) which

required free trade to be pursued whenever possible. Solution 2 was available within the terms and conditions of the adjustable-peg exchange rate regime introduced in 1944 at Bretton Woods. Unfortunately, it was considered to be a sign of failure for a country to lower its exchange rate, and so it was a policy to be avoided except as a last resort for fear that the government so doing would lose votes. But this left only solution 1, although its implementation meant that the level of aggregate demand would have to be cut back, thereby adversely affecting output and employment.

Given the higher priority assigned to full employment than to the external balance, this could obviously be tolerated only for the minimum period compatible with restoring the balance of payments into better shape, whereupon demand would need to be expanded again in order to restore full employment. However, since this procedure had done nothing to deal with the underlying causes of the problem – namely an uncompetitive economy – but only with its symptoms in the form of a balance of payments deficit, the symptoms were obviously going to recur once the economy was back at full employment again. A succession of periods of demand expansion to create jobs followed by demand reduction to control imports thus became the dominant characteristic, known as **stop–go,** of UK economic policy during the 1950s and 1960s.

1.5.1 Fiscal Versus Monetary Policy

As we have indicated, the level of aggregate demand was largely manipulated via **fiscal means,** and monetary policy had relatively little to do. However, its assigned role – namely, low interest rates to foster investment – was somewhat incompatible with a world in which inflation was a persistent phenomenon, since rising prices implied the need to raise interest rates to deter consumption financed by credit.

In the USA during the late 1950s, Professor Milton Friedman at Chicago University and others began publishing material which indicated that the **money supply** was the all-important aggregate on which the authorities would have to concentrate their attention if they wished to have any meaningful control over economic activity. Friedman argued, in particular, that the role of monetary policy during the Great Depression had been widely misunderstood. The orthodox version of events held that the US monetary authorities had pursued aggressively expansionary monetary policies between 1929 and 1933, but that these policies had proved ineffectual. Friedman, on the other hand, contended that the monetary authorities had pursued highly **deflationary** policies. According to his research, the quantity of money in the United States fell by one third during the course of the Depression, thereby providing clear evidence that monetary policy was extremely effective in regulating the level of economic activity rather than the reverse.

At the heart of Friedman's work lay the **New Quantity Theory** which represented a modernised version of the neo-classical model, linking the money supply to **money national income** (the volume of (real) output at current prices). In his model, most commonly known as **Monetarism,** real output resulted from decisions taken primarily by households and firms in the private sector, and could not be adjusted by demand management. Since real magnitudes were ultimately unaffected by the supply of money, the latter was directly linked **only to the rate of inflation,** and became its **primary cause.**

However, the fact was that in trying to elevate inflation to become the primary focus of economic policy, Friedman's time had not yet arrived, particularly where the UK was concerned, although his ideas caught on more quickly elsewhere. Just as the Keynesian revolution had to wait for the neo-classical orthodoxy to break down in the face of mass unemployment, so the monetarist revolution had to wait upon a breakdown of the Keynesian orthodoxy. But for the moment at least, the Keynesian facade seemed impregnable. Quite simply, in an atmosphere of **you've never had it so good,** one does not seriously question the view that the prevailing orthodoxy had helped to bring this about. True, the UK economy had grown slowly by comparison with most other comparable countries, but growth was rapid by comparison with previous periods in the UK. True, there were periodic balance of payments crises which deflected the economy off course, and inflation was also ever-present. But jobs were freely available for those who wanted to work, and most people's standard of living was rising steadily. It was not a time for revolution, even in ideas.

The issue of inflation remained largely ignored, both in academic and political circles. This passive view of the problem was reinforced when, in 1957, A. W. Phillips published an article discussing what henceforth became universally known as the **Phillips Curve.** The Phillips Curve suggested that inflation need not be considered as an independent problem, but its real importance lay in the fact that up until that point in time the Keynesian model had contained no theory of inflation. Given that inflation was treated with rather more indifference than it merited, this missing link had not prevented the model from operating to most people's satisfaction. Nevertheless, the apparent message of the Phillips Curve that there was a **predictable trade-off** between employment and inflation (thereby offering, in effect, a **menu of choices** between combinations of employment and inflation) appeared greatly to simplify economic policy. The government simply had to choose the particular **level of aggregate demand** which would generate the **target level of employment,** and a predetermined amount of inflation would simultaneously be generated. The price level could, therefore, be relegated to a lowly place in the pecking order of economic objectives, since in choosing the target value for the primary objective one could not be thrown off course by an unforeseen rate of inflation as one could by the balance of payments.

Unfortunately, at the end of the 1960s the situation began to deteriorate alarmingly. The rate of inflation began to rise sharply, and to register a value well above what had been predicted on the basis of the Phillips Curve. At first the authorities understandably treated this as an aberration, arguing that the original relationship between unemployment and inflation would shortly be restored. But when employment was allowed to rise slightly to help rein back inflation, it did not have the desired effect, and a new phenomenon appeared known as **stagflation** – namely, rising prices at the same time as rising unemployment. This phenomenon clearly needed to be explained within the context of the Keynesian model, but the model was found wanting. After 25 years its Achilles heel had been exposed. By a quirk of history, it was precisely at this point in time, at the beginning of the 1970s, that the exchange rate mechanisms introduced at Bretton Woods also began to break down, to the point at which the UK felt obliged, in 1972, to move over to a **floating rate** (albeit a **managed** one). This meant that balance-of-payments crises could now be dealt with via the exchange rate rather than via deflation (given the political will to accept currency depreciation), and thus allowed more freedom for demand to be managed in order to maintain full employment. But raising demand at a time when inflation was roaring ahead was not really a sensible option, and the quadrupling of oil prices by OPEC helped send the inflation rate soaring to 24 per cent in 1975, as well as causing significant damage to the balance of payments. The Labour government in power at the time was unable to cope with these pressures, particularly as foreign currency reserves were inadequate for the purpose, and turned for help to the International Monetary Fund (IMF), a body which was sympathetic to the monetarist doctrines now coming into vogue. The price exacted in return for assistance was that the UK economy would have to be subjected to a dose of monetarism, with tight control over the money supply and a tight fiscal policy keeping demand in check.

It was rather ironic that a Labour Government should be the **first to apply monetarist doctrines**, since its underlying philosophy was hardly right-wing. Nevertheless, it was as much imposition as choice at the time (or at least that was how the government excused its behaviour) and an inevitable effect was what, from the government's point of view, was a highly undesirable further upturn in unemployment. Indeed, the attempt to impose fiscal discipline, and to control inflation via a prices and incomes policy, ultimately led to the **winter of discontent** and to the government's

downfall. It was replaced in 1979 by the first Thatcher government, which unlike its predecessor **deliberately chose** to make a version of monetarism the key plank of UK economic policy.

◼ *1.6* The Brief Reign of Monetarism

As previously indicated, the Keynesian orthodoxy collapsed in the face of a persistent rate of inflation well above the rate predicted by the Phillips Curve, and into the vacuum created by the failure of the model stepped the **monetarist revolution**. It is important to remember that monetarism was a reworking of the neo-classical model rather than a totally new approach, and that it was **not invented after 1970**. As with the Keynesian model, it had been advocated for many years prior to that, but few people were altogether persuaded by it. In particular, it must be borne in mind that its underlying philosophy placed particular emphasis upon **markets**, and played down very heavily the role of government as prime mover in the economy.

It would be fair to argue that the Conservative government under Edward Heath was sympathetic to the doctrine of the free market, but at the end of the day it did not have the conviction to let markets have their head. Indeed, it is an interesting aspect of the Heath government that it took Rolls-Royce and British Leyland **into** public ownership rather than let them be destroyed by the forces of the market, thereby demonstrating that expediency was often a stronger factor than polemic in political manifestos. The Thatcher government was different in that it set out determinedly to apply monetarism as a philosophy, relying heavily upon the evidence that the lax monetary policy introduced during the Heath Government's term of office had been responsible for the inflationary boom of the early 1970s. However, what the Thatcher government did not at first realise was just how difficult this was going to be. Because monetarism is about markets, it is clearly much more than simply a statement about the money supply and the macroeconomy, and in that respect it becomes difficult to form a judgement as to its success or failure since some parts of the philosophy may work quite well whereas others may need to be discarded as unworkable. Whether what remains at the end of this process is still monetarism is, therefore, highly debatable, and we need to shed some light on this issue below.

Viewed in terms of macroeconomic policy, monetarism is fairly straightforward. It contends that the price level is the most important economic objective because real variables such as employment can best be stimulated in the context of a non-inflationary environment. However, whereas zero (or near-zero) rates of inflation assist in the generation of employment through their positive impact upon the prospects of the private sector, demand management is either self-defeating (because public spending simply displaces private spending – 'crowding out') or a recipe for accelerating inflation. The only way to control the price level is via the money supply. Hence it follows that the growth of the money supply should be geared to the expected growth rate of real output, which thereby makes it possible to buy any extra output at the **existing** level of prices. The balance of payments can be left to its own devices by allowing the exchange rate to float freely, thereby ensuring a tendency for it to self-equilibrate.

However, certain points follow logically from the above. First, governments must resist the temptation to create money by **spending more than they earn** and thereby creating a borrowing requirement, so fiscal policy must be viewed from the point of view of its consequences for the money supply. Fiscal conservatism means balancing government spending against taxation, but since markets are much better at determining what people want to consume than the bureaucrats in local and central government, public spending must be kept under tight control. This in turn will permit taxes to be cut, which will leave more of their incomes in people's pockets and provide the incentive for them to work harder, thereby generating economic growth. This growth will eventually provide new jobs in areas of the economy where there is genuine private demand, represented by direct spending by consumers, rather

than an artificial demand generated by government spending designed, for example, to keep technologically backward and internationally uncompetitive industries in business.

This approach is generally known as **supply-side economics** because it rests upon the assumption that **supply must be created before demand** if there is to be non-inflationary growth within the economy (see Chapter 3 for a fuller discussion of these matters). At the microeconomic level, the philosophy has far-reaching effects. Individual households and firms must be made to stand on their own feet, to succeed or fail as the market for what they provide dictates. Those who fail may need to be helped by the government within reason, but not to the point at which failure seems to be a soft option. In particular, employment is dependent upon the forces of the market. Jobs may need to be preserved by workers taking wage cuts and/or retraining, or they may need to move to where the work is (possibly on their bicycles). If institutions such as trade unions are less than keen about these developments then their power to prevent them must be destroyed, and that applies to professional bodies as well as to craft unions.

Not surprisingly, these doctrines seem firmly rooted in the neo-classical orthodoxy where the individual is responsible for his or her own predicament, and it is not the job of government to provide relief. In other words, the postwar swing from efficiency to equity must be put into reverse gear. Efficiency is once again to be king, and those who are productive will be allowed to enjoy the fruits of their labour. To be rich is no longer socially unacceptable; to be poor is unnecessary, so poverty must be pushed back into decent obscurity.

∎ 1.7 The Thatcher Years, 1979–90

At a good many points in the body of the text we will have cause to note that the Thatcher years in office are open to a variety of interpretations. Mrs Thatcher was not afraid of controversy, and the very fact that she sought to revitalise the economy by attacking those groups which she felt had traditionally held back progress was bound to engender very strong feelings among those affected by her decisions. Some controversies were driven by theoretical considerations, for example the renewed debate about the theoretical underpinnings of both the Keynesian and monetarist models. Others were concerned with the use and alleged abuse of statistical data generated both by the government and by other sources. Yet others had to do with her style of government.

On the theoretical front we have already referred to the debate between demand-siders and supply-siders, but there has also been a reinterpretation of the Keynesian model in order to make it more compatible with the observed phenomena of the 1970s and the 1980s. The adherents of this approach are usually known as new, neo- or radical Keynesians. In addition, there has arisen a school of thought known as 'New Classical Economics', which has much in common with monetarism but which differs with respect to, for example, the role of expectations. It is fair to say that most economists take an eclectic view of the proceedings, accepting parts, but not all, of any one viewpoint. However, one consequence is that the government receives conflicting advice, particularly where it is sought internally from the likes of the Treasury as well as from outsiders such as the 'seven wise (wo)men', and it has become increasingly difficult to divine which model – if any – of the economy it is trying to implement. Accepting for the moment that economic policy may, therefore, be driven as often by short-term expediency as by the logic of a specific model, it is nevertheless desirable to provide a brief summary of recent experience.

One unchanging point of reference, explored fully in Chapter 20, has been the priority accorded to the **control of inflation**. In the early Thatcher years, this was seen as the task assigned to the money supply, but that has now altered insofar as control of the money supply is widely (but by no means universally) seen as a failure. Indeed, the government itself declared, in June 1989, that it no longer intended even to compile the money supply measure, known as M3, favoured during the early 1980s. For some time now, the govern-

ment has relied upon the **interest rate** as its primary means of regulating demand, a policy which, as is noted at many points in this text, has met with mixed success, although it may anyway be argued that there is no unanimity about the meaning of the term 'success'. For example, it is possible to argue simultaneously that the UK's growth record during the 1980s was good because it remained high by international standards for many years, and that it was bad because the level of output barely rose above the level achieved at the time the Conservative government first took office. Equally, the inflation rate did fall to well below 5 per cent at one stage during the 1980s, the soaring money supply notwithstanding, and it is currently comfortably below that figure, but it has never shown any sign of getting down to below 1 per cent and has generally remained above that of some of the UK's keenest competitors such as Germany, Japan and the USA.

The Thatcher government certainly achieved its aim of fiscal conservatism for a period during the late-1980s, turning the inherited borrowing requirement into a debt repayment. However, there remains a body of opinion which believes that such behaviour was inappropriate, and it is significant to note that this did not result from the intended reduction in government spending combined with a lesser reduction in taxation. Rather, in absolute terms, even after allowing for inflation, government spending rose in almost every year, with tax revenue rising even faster in the mid-1980s due to the phenomenon known as **fiscal drag** (all of which matters are discussed in detail in Chapter 6). The fiscal position also deteriorated sharply in the early 1990s.

The **exchange rate**, in particular, presents ambiguities. The one certainty is that it was never permitted to float as freely as it should in a basic monetarist model – which allows the advocates of such a model to contend that it has never been properly tested. There was an increasingly acrimonious debate about whether the UK should become a fully committed member of the European Monetary System (EMS) (see Chapter 10) – and indeed, more widely, about the UK's role in Europe particularly in relation to the Maastricht Treaty.

At the microeconomic level there was a real attempt to deregulate markets and to transfer assets from the public to the private sector – indeed the UK is generally acknowledged to be the world leader in privatisation, although Americans might remark that it would have been better not to have created so many areas that needed to be deregulated in the first place. However, asset sales were likened in some quarters to 'selling the family silver', and it is also the case that some of the worst rigidities (such as are manifested in the housing market) were not addressed at all successfully. Indeed, for many the overriding impression given by the Thatcher government was its interventionist and centralising stance in a wide variety of markets, and particularly in relation to the local authorities. At heart this reflects one of the most awkward realities of economic life – namely, the fact that, since free markets are subject to abuse, the more free the markets are supposed to be the more they need to be regulated. This issue is addressed at various points in the text, for example with respect to financial markets in Chapter 5, and particularly in Chapter 19.

At the macroeconomic level, as already indicated, the Thatcher government came to suffer from a shortage of instruments to control the economy, and hence it came to overuse – and arguably abuse – those that were favoured. Here again it is much easier to explain where the government went wrong than to provide a convincing alternative approach.

As has been noted above, the Keynesian model broke down in the face of exceptionally high levels of inflation. It can just as easily be argued, however, that the most telling indictment of monetarism was its failure to reduce unemployment to acceptable levels. The fact that during the Keynesian orthodoxy governments chose to live with permanently rising prices, and that during the monetarist orthodoxy they chose to live with heavy unemployment, may be put down to the forces of democracy – at the end of the day the electorate must vote for one particular party – but even democracy can be made to mean all things to all men, and it is possible to argue that votes are not so much cast in favour of policy packages as against alternatives which are viewed as wholly

unacceptable. Some reflections on political processes are contained in the section which follows, and also in Chapter 18. For the moment, it is necessary only to note that the movement away from any kind of established orthodoxy and towards what may best be termed pragmatism may be the only way forward. As will constantly be reiterated in the course of the text, the world's economies are evolving very rapidly, and the model of last year's behaviour may provide a poor guide to the current year, let alone to the future. In the UK, the Keynesian orthodoxy lasted for three decades whereas the monetarist experiment lasted for well under one decade. For the moment revolution is unfashionable and evolution is the name of the game.

∎ 1.8 Enter (and Depart?) Mr Major

Mr Major took over from Mrs Thatcher at a time when she had become increasingly seen as a divisive factor within the Conservative Party. However, unlike his predecessor he was no visionary, and indeed the party was looking for a different type of leadership when he was elected. He has shown, as in relation to the exchange rate, not merely a tolerance for U-turns in policy but a regrettable tendency to claim credit for the very consequences which he had previously been trying hard to avoid. Attempts to persuade commentators that there is a consistent set of policies worthy of the term 'Majorism' have been greeted with amused disbelief. His hold on the party was much more tenuous than that of Mrs Thatcher in her early years in office and, indeed, he was fortunate to survive a fundamental loss of confidence in his leadership, in part stemming from internal divisions over Europe, at the end of 1995.

Assuming he loses the next election, he will probably be remembered for very little. This is not entirely his fault, as he has had to preside over a frequently disunited party, has been opposed by a resurgent Labour Party and has had to endure a severe recession which has brought to the surface a 'feel-bad' factor, among other things. Also, no one went to war with Britain except over fish. Nevertheless, insofar as this book is particularly concerned with the past two decades, one of its objectives must be to assess his successes and his failures, and the lessons to be learned from the latter.

■ *1.9* The Political Context

It is a reasonable expectation of a so-called 'democracy' that its citizens will consider it to be their right – and possibly their duty – to exhort the government to adopt this or that economic strategy. However, what they often fail to appreciate is that in order to deliver economic policies one must first create a **political system** with that end in mind, and since there are many ways of devising such a system, its precise form is ultimately of great consequence. One simple point to make in this context is to ask whether the 'Thatcher revolution' would have occurred in any of the other major industrial countries had it not occurred in the UK – to which the answer must be a firm negative because it was critically dependent upon the political context of the UK. In retrospect, there can be no doubt that Mrs Thatcher had a more profound impact than President Reagan. However, as we shall argue below, the odds were stacked in her favour before she began.

A crucial – though by no means unique – feature of the UK political system is that it involves a race to be 'first past the post' between a very small number of very strong contenders and a number of 'also-runs'. Each constituency race produces a single Member of Parliament who may well fail to be supported by a majority of those casting their vote, let alone of those eligible to vote. Hence this system permits of a government being formed by a political party irrespective of whether it has been supported by more voters than any other alternative party, let alone all other parties in aggregate. Once a government has been formed, the level of electoral support is normally a non-issue until the electoral term is over, although by-elections are traditionally viewed as an opportunity to voice a protest against government policy

and hence can lead, as in recent times, to a progressive reduction in the government's majority (the Conservatives hold the dubious record of losing the last 14 successive by-elections).

On occasion, the combination of a strong opposition party and the also-rans may muster enough MPs to outvote the government. Even when it applies, the opposition parties are generally less than fully united in their political goals. The style of political debate is inevitably highly adversarial, but this should not be allowed to conceal the key point that when the fire and fury has died down, and the vote is taken, **a government with an absolute majority of MPs is always the official winner provided its own MPs vote with it.** From this it follows that **a government with a clear majority has more to fear from its own backbenchers than from the opposition parties** (which is unfortunate if, for example, they are divided over the issue of the UK's role in Europe).

Clearly, this system delivers extraordinary powers to a majority government, or perhaps more strictly, to the Cabinet of such a government and even more so, perhaps, to its leader. Constitutionally, the monarchy has no power of veto, nor does the House of Lords (the upper chamber) which can only debate and recommend alterations to legislation which the government can reject out of hand. A simple majority of one seat in the House of Commons is thus technically sufficient (provided, of course, every MP is available to vote) to permit the government to steamroller through any legislation that it wishes, irrespective of whether or not it was mentioned in the campaign manifesto issued to voters.

In principle, individual MPs can refuse to vote in accord with their party line, but the rules disallowing the use of private monies to 'buy votes' effectively mean that a prospective MP can only get elected by subsuming his or her individuality to the party image (few voters know who their MP is, or even the name of their constituency). For this reason, an MP who rejects a 'three-line whip', instructing them to vote in a pre-determined way, can expect to lose the support of the party machine and later, if not sooner, lose his or her seat. It follows that, especially when a party has a small overall majority, MPs habitually toe the line rather than bring down the government, possibly provided it makes some minor concessions to those whose consciences are troubling them.

As a consequence, backbench MPs normally have little effective power over economic policy, whereas a small section amongst them, appointed to the Cabinet, have a great deal. Furthermore, a Prime Minister, elected from within the ranks of MPs and hence inseparable from the party in power, can exercise even more power by using the threat of dismissal from the Cabinet to force recalcitrant members to do what he or she wishes.

This ability to steamroller policy through Parliament is both a virtue and a vice. It obviously permits of very strong government, and there can be no doubt that voters prefer a government with a clear sense of purpose and a determination to put it into practice, to one which is constantly vulnerable to losing on a vote of confidence. But such power can easily be abused (and there is anyway no demonstrable relationship between the size of majorities and the success of government policy), and it follows that if the opposition cannot bring a government to heel, that task must fall to the government's own backbenchers. It is slightly ironic, therefore, that the latter can do little unless the government's majority is small, but where that is the case and backbenchers are willing to put their careers on the line on a point of principle, they can cause endless problems for their own party as Mr Major discovered in 1995. We will have more to say about this in the context of the vote on the Maastricht Treaty in Chapter 10.

With a general election pending at the time of publication, it is worthwhile to consider briefly the probability of a new majority government. Given the predicted electoral swing to Labour, they might well be expected to achieve this. However, the so-called 'cube law' of elections, which meant historically that if two parties were level-pegging, each 1 per cent of the vote would deliver an additional 3 per cent of the seats (that is, roughly 18), and which accounted in good part for the electoral swings needed to produce both Conservative and Labour majority governments, has progressively broken down to the point at which it will no longer apply in 1997 (it barely applied in 1992 when the Conservatives got 54.9 per cent of the combined Conservative and Labour vote and 55.6 per cent of Conservative plus Labour seats).

This reflects the progressive tendency for supporters of a particular party to cluster in cities or the countryside, in the process reducing the number of genuinely marginal seats. The reason why the Conservatives won so convincingly during the 1980s can therefore be ascribed predominantly to the Labour Party's continuing attempts to shoot itself in the foot with the likes of pre-election victory rallies. This problem has been addressed by shifting the Labour Party towards the centre ground, but this also means that the major parties come increasingly to resemble one another. Furthermore, it tends to boost the electoral chances of a party which appeals to local and regional interests, as in Scotland, thereby reducing the prospects of an overall majority (for a useful summary of these and related matters, readers are recommended to consult a series of five weekly articles in *The Economist*, commencing 14 October 1995).

☐ *1.9.1 Other Political Systems*

We will return subsequently to comment upon the performance of government in the UK, but first it is salutary to compare the above analysis to political systems elsewhere. In the USA, which also has a two-main-party, first-past-the-post system, the President is not, however, the leader of the party in power in the House of Representatives (often called 'the House'), but elected independently, and may well belong to the other party. If the House is unsympathetic he may, therefore, find it very difficult to get his Bills enacted. He, in his turn, has considerable power to veto Bills emanating from the House, so one rebuff may well be repaid in kind. The upper chamber (the Senate) is a powerful body in its own right, and may well be controlled by the opposite party to the House. A President, House and Senate (which together constitute the Congress) may periodically, though by no means invariably, belong to the same party, but this does not guarantee complete co-operation. This is partly because election is as much a function of the wealth and prestige of the individual as of the party machine, and hence individual Representatives and Senators quite frequently vote against their own party line. All this prevents the accumulation of too much power in **too** few hands, as was precisely the original intention when the system was created, but it is not exactly designed to deliver priorities, such as cuts in government spending, since every politician, irrespective of party, in an area adversely affected by such cuts will automatically vote against the strategy. One has only to survey the partial shutdown of the US government at the end of 1995 to understand the system's drawbacks.

In continental Europe there is widespread **proportional representation** (seats allocated in proportion to votes cast). This effectively prevents any one party from getting an absolute majority over all others, which on the face of it should lead to weak government. On the other hand it follows that, as a general rule, a coalition must reach agreement on priorities which are common to all parties if it wishes to avoid government by crisis, and the important policies may, therefore, get carried out with all-party support even when there is fundamental disagreement about other matters. The obvious drawback is that these shared priorities invariably sit somewhere near the political centre, and if voters are unhappy about that they can express their disapproval only by voting for someone or something on the extreme of the political spectrum (fascist or communist). As has also been demonstrated, for example in Italy very recently, there is some tendency for corruption to creep in by way of payment for political favours.

If, on the other hand, the UK government thinks that the electorate want, for example, privatisation or a poll tax, then they can be delivered by the system. Critics complain that this is all very well and good, but that it enables the government to deliver such policies **irrespective of whether** they are wanted by the electorate. On the other hand, it is reasonable to argue that a party with 100 plus seats in Parliament is itself a coalition of interests, so its leaders cannot single-mindedly pursue, say, a very right or left wing path without running into severe internal dissent.

Furthermore, it must never be forgotten that governments are by no means all-powerful, and may be forced to take involuntary actions. This may arise simply because the UK is not a particularly big player on the world stage and cannot, therefore, be insulated from the forces which buffet the world economy. No matter how healthy the underlying economy, the UK cannot expect to grow much if at all – at a time when other advanced economies are sliding into recession. More generally, the government may find itself in a losing battle with the forces of the market-place. The government may, for example, wish to see the exchange rate rise, but if the foreign exchange market wishes to see the exchange rate fall that may well prove to be the ultimate outcome.

To sum up this brief discussion, the overall picture with respect to the UK is that it has a political system with enormous potential power to direct economic policy. The system could accordingly result in enormous swings in the direction of policy as each successive government seeks to undo what its predecessor has done, but this does not necessarily happen because many priorities are shared, and the external environment may not permit it. It should also be remembered that for a government to spend its time in office removing its predecessor's legislation from the statute book is not merely very unconstructive, but may leave little time to enact new policies. In any event, many policies which the political system requires the opposition party to oppose may privately be approved of, and others may simply be too expensive to implement. For example, no future government could possible afford to repurchase the shares of privatised companies even if, as is unlikely, they were prepared to devote scarce parliamentary time to that end. Finally, as previously noted, the probable disappearance of majority government will constrain future governments in ways which Mrs Thatcher never had to contend with. We will probably, for better or for worse, never see her likes again.

Chapter 2

Introduction to the Macroeconomy

Peter Curwen

■ 2.1 Introduction

In the course of this book we will be examining a great many facets of the aggregate economy. Certain of these require detailed consideration, and hence have an entire chapter given over to their analysis. Others, however, require less detailed treatment, and it is our primary purpose in this and the subsequent chapters to bring them together at the earliest stage in the overall discussion. Although this necessarily means that these chapters are less cohesive than those which follow, they are essential pieces of the complete macroeconomic jigsaw puzzle. Indeed, one of the primary purposes of these chapters is to provide an overview of the entire jigsaw which must, of necessity, be put together in accordance with the picture on the lid. Unfortunately, as we shall soon discover, the picture on the lid is out of focus, so we can never be entirely sure that each piece is in its proper place!

The schematic figures which follow may well appear complex at first sight, especially to those with no prior experience of modelling the economic system of the UK. Nevertheless, it is worth observing that the 'Treasury' model which the government uses for forecasting purposes contains literally hundreds of equations, and there will, no doubt, be a number of readers who feel that our schematics are too simplistic. However, the recent record of both the Treasury and most other models in forecasting such variables as the level of unemployment and the rate of inflation has been less than inspiring, so it is debatable whether there is any correlation between accuracy and the number of variables in the model.

The most obvious reason for recent difficulties in forecasting is that the behaviour of economic agents such as households and firms is constantly evolving, while forecasts are necessarily based primarily upon measures of behaviour in past periods. It is one of the particular objectives of this book to explore the reasons for what, in certain cases, have been quite fundamental changes in behaviour since 1979.

In the sections which follow we will be making use of the conventional distinction between **instruments**, **targets** and **objectives** of policy. It should, however, be noted that these will be treated in a more flexible manner than is the custom in introductory textbooks. The evolution of the UK economy over the past decade has turned many relationships upon their head, and engendered much controversy about the linkages, and especially the causality implied by these linkages, between different parts of the economic system. For example, it is clear that under certain circumstances both the interest rate and the exchange rate can be used as instruments – that is, as levers which, when pulled, set in train a sequence of changes in other variables, acting as intermediate targets, which ultimately cause changes in policy objectives.

However, interest rates and exchange rates are closely inter-related, as discussed below, so it is evident that one must be regarded as the instrument and the other as the target. Which is which depends upon how one sets up the system, so it is possible to argue that 'one model's instrument is another model's target'.

■ 2.2 The Internal Sector

The internal sector is modelled in **Figure 2.1**. It is essentially a Keynesian version of the model, with the alternative version operating via the money supply discussed separately below. There are three objectives in the model; the rate of economic growth, the level of employment and the rate of inflation. The route to all of these objectives passes through the box marked 'aggregate demand'.

It is accordingly important to consider whether an increase or decrease in aggregate demand will cause all three objectives to move simultaneously in the desired direction. Unhappily, this is not the case in practice. Whereas an increase in aggregate demand (AD) can be expected to increase the level of employment, at least in the short term, it almost always also causes the rate of inflation to rise (the Phillips Curve relationship – see **p. 102**).

Clearly, therefore, there are **trade-offs** between objectives in the model. Now it may be observed that, if one objective can be satisfied only at the expense of a second when a single pathway is followed through the model, this drawback can largely be avoided where it is possible to deal with the second objective by following a route which does not pass through the AD box. It is possible, for example, to hold down prices during a period of buoyant demand by recourse to a prices and incomes policy (see **pp. 527–8**). Regrettably, this has never proved to be successful other than in the short term, and while it is possible to argue that the Thatcher government operated an unofficial policy in the public sector during the 1980s, and that Mr Major did so subsequently, such a policy does not officially exist and has as a consequence been left off **Figure 2.1**.

Given the trade-off between objectives, it is necessary for the government to decide upon a **rank ordering** of priorities – which objective is most important, which least – and to determine the **desired value** for each objective. It is to be noted that we do not seek at this juncture to specify what these might be. Whereas, for example, many textbooks tend to talk in terms of 'full' employment, we do not do so here because the precise meaning of this term has for many years been a matter of considerable controversy (see Chapter 13).

A further reservation is in order. It is evident that there is a consensus about the desirability of maintaining a 'high' level of employment in the UK, as indeed there is about maintaining a low rate of inflation. Nevertheless, the attainment of these objectives can often prove to be less of a benefit than it appears to be at first sight. For example, a reduction in the price of raw materials which are imported represents 'good news' for a manufacturing nation such as the UK, since it helps to hold down costs, and hence inflation. It follows, however, that it must be very damaging to less-developed nations which export those materials. Such countries may subsequently prove unable to repay their international debts, which may partly be owed to the UK government and partly to UK banks (see **pp. 260–2**). Thus, if there is a default on the debt, any initial benefits derived from lower import prices are partly or wholly wiped out by subsequent losses. Such considerations are, for example, of considerable impor-

Figure 2.1 *The Internal Sector: Demand*

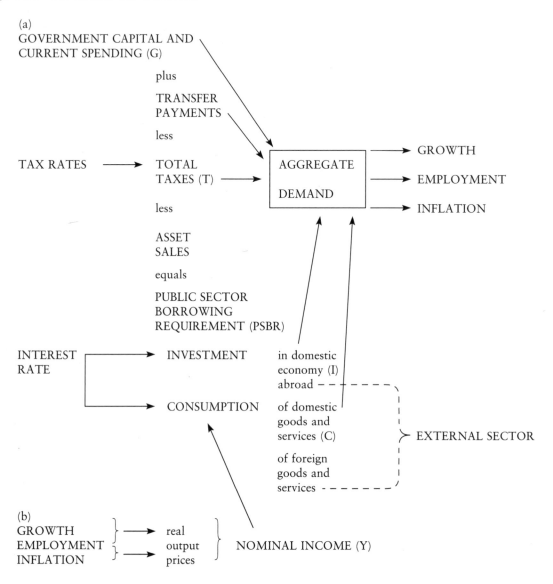

tance in the context of the Common Agricultural Policy.

Figure 2.1 indicates that there are a variety of pathways through the AD box. In a Keynesian world, the government concentrates upon its fiscal position $(G - T)$ since it has direct control over its own spending whereas it can influence consumption and investment decisions only indirectly. Particular expenditures and tax rates are thus the preferred instruments of policy, but it is

to be noted that C and I are also affected by changes in the structure of interest rates. The use of the interest rate is a monetary rather than a fiscal policy, and it follows that both monetary and fiscal policies are normally used in tandem, although there is constant controversy concerning the optimum balance between the two.

Two other matters are worthy of note. In the first place, the internal sector cannot be divorced from the external sector, which is analysed below.

Possible linkages via consumption and investment are indicated in **Figure 2.1**. Secondly, the Public Sector Borrowing Requirement (PSBR) is an important magnitude which is created by the formula: government expenditure **plus** transfer payments **less** total taxes **less** asset sales (for a detailed analysis, see **pp. 199–203**). It is accordingly possible to treat it as an aspect of fiscal policy. However, it is also possible, as discussed below, to treat it in the context of changes in the money supply.

Section (b) of **Figure 2.1** serves two purposes. In the first place, it serves to clarify the important distinction between the **real** and **nominal** approaches to measuring economic activity. Growth and employment are physical measures, expressed as volumes, which are 'real' in the sense that they are measured independently of the prices at which they are sold. When a volume measure is multiplied by current prices it is converted into a money value, its 'nominal' counterpart. Hence the value of economic activity at current prices, or nominal income, changes either because more activity (growth) is taking place at unchanged prices, because the same activity is taking place at higher prices or because both output and prices are changing simultaneously.

Secondly, **Figure 2.1** serves to remind the reader of the feedback mechanisms which are ever-present in the model. As shown by the arrow at its foot, the level of consumption is itself determined in good part by the level of nominal income. Hence, when the level of consumption changes, it changes the level of nominal income as shown by the pathway through **Figure 2.1**, which in turn causes the level of consumption to change, which subsequently causes the level of nominal income to change and so forth (the multiplier mechanism as set out below).

2.3 Money Supply and the Supply Side

As discussed in Chapter 1, the prevailing view that the UK economy is driven by demand in accordance with the Keynesian model became very unfashionable during the late 1970s, and was replaced by the view that the regulation of demand would more appropriately be conducted via control of the money supply. The controversy this engendered is set out more fully in Chapter 20, and need not concern us in detail here. What we do need to bear in mind is that a primary objective of economic policy during the 1980s was to reduce inflation, and that it was argued that this could best be achieved via a restrictive policy towards money supply growth.

This is illustrated in **Figure 2.2** where the direct link runs from aggregate demand to inflation, whereas the link from aggregate demand to growth and employment is shown as a broken line indicating that aggregate demand was not, in general, being manipulated in order to affect these variables. Given the perceived direct link between the money supply and aggregate demand, it is evident that the money supply now becomes an intermediate target of policy. As such, it needs to be regulated via policy instruments such as open market operations, or other instruments such as credit controls or monetary base control. It is, however, also determined in part by the size of the PSBR insofar as this has implications for the way in which it is financed – that is, whether the method of financing creates new money or transfers existing money between the private sector, banks and government.

In other words, the fiscal stance that determines the PSBR has some bearing upon the money supply, as has the rate of interest which represents the cost of issuing or redeeming government securities (for example, via an open market operation). A sharp change in the size of the PSBR necessitates an adjustment to the structure of interest rates. When the interest rate changes, it either attracts or deters a flow of short-term international capital ('hot money'). This, in turn, affects the money supply, since if international capital flows into the UK then foreign borrowers must first convert it into sterling, whereas if it flows out then UK residents must first turn sterling into foreign currencies. Both flows necessarily affect the amount of sterling held in the UK, although it is possible to neutralise any inflows by converting them into holdings of government securities (**sterilisation**).

Figure 2.2 *Money Supply and the Supply Side*

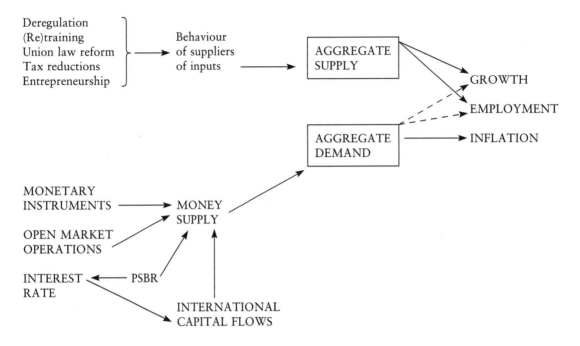

It should be noted that, once the primary purpose of managing aggregate demand is to restrain prices, it is possible to achieve this objective using **any** form of demand management, whether fiscal or monetary. In this respect, therefore, the box marked aggregate supply can just as easily be superimposed upon **Figure 2.1**, although it should be borne in mind that the general thrust of the Keynesian model is to enlarge aggregate demand, whereas its role would have to switch to restraining AD if the objective was the control of inflation.

Furthermore, one obvious difficulty with this approach to policy-making is that there is no longer a direct link between **aggregate demand** and **growth/employment**. Hence these objectives must be regulated by instruments on the **supply side** of the economy – that is, via the box marked aggregate supply.

Supply-side economics had its roots in the work of J. B. Say (1767–1832) who is best known for coining the expression **supply creates its own demand** (Say's Law). Say's basic argument was

> It is important not to confuse control over the money supply with supply-side economics. The money supply is concerned with the control of aggregate demand, whereas supply-side economics is concerned with the control of aggregate supply. However, it follows that the two will tend to be used in tandem.

that if there was an increase in the numbers of those seeking work then competition among the suppliers of labour would drive down the real (inflation-adjusted) wage to the point at which employers would be willing to buy any available labour that had not already chosen to be self-employed. In the process of using these labour inputs to make products, payments would have to be made for both labour and other inputs in the form of wages, interest and so forth. The value of output is thus exactly matched by an equal value of factor payments sufficient to buy everything that has been produced.

We have discussed in Chapter 1 the historical reasons for the apparent breakdown in this argument because of real wage inflexibility in the context of the post-1919 depression, and the emergence of the Keynesian model which effectively turned the argument on its head by holding that the macroeconomy should be driven by changes in aggregate demand. However, shifting the aggregate demand curve to the right, while the aggregate supply curve remains unchanged, will cause the aggregate price level to rise sharply unless the aggregate supply curve is effectively horizontal – that is, unless more labour will be forthcoming at the existing real wage.

One can appreciate the possibility of a more or less horizontal supply curve under conditions of severe recession, but it is clearly far less plausible in the context of a prosperous economy where the bulk of the labour supply is already in employment, where the labour force is immobile or where the real wage is unattractive due, for example, to high levels of state benefits. If any, or all, of these conditions hold true then shifting the aggregate demand curve to the right will generate higher prices at the same time as higher output.

There are clearly two possible ways to deal with this problem. In the first place, an attempt can be made to suppress the inflationary pressure directly via a prices and incomes policy. The history of this approach is set out in detail in Chapter 20, and it is fair to conclude that it is more likely to be effective in the short term than in the medium/long term. Hence, in the long term the more sensible approach would appear to be to transfer aggregate demand to the task of controlling the price level (whether via Keynesian or Monetarist measures) and to assign to aggregate supply the task of stimulating output.

It is evident that, if aggregate supply can be increased while holding aggregate demand broadly constant, then not only will output and employment rise but some downwards pressure will be exerted upon the price level. Naturally, from a practical viewpoint, it may be argued that aggregate demand can not readily be held back in the face of rising aggregate supply, at least in the context of the UK economy, but so long as supply moves first and demand is not permitted to out-run it subsequently, it is possible to create the combination of growing output and very modest inflation. This may, under certain circumstances, require strict control over aggregate demand by the government. In this context, control over the money supply is one option for controlling aggregate demand. If this is considered to be ineffective, an alternative instrument such as the interest rate will need to be used in its stead. On the other hand, as very recent experience has shown, it may only be necessary to generate a 'feel-bad' factor. It is important to bear in mind at this juncture that aggregate supply is ultimately dependent upon supply at the microeconomic level. The bottom line is accordingly that individuals must be given **incentives to work harder and more productively** and to behave in an **entrepreneurial manner**. This can happen only if markets are allowed to operate as freely as possible; hence, the main task of government is to create an environment in which effort is rewarded rather than to take decisions on behalf of individuals. From this it follows that the government should reduce its share of total expenditure and so reform the fiscal system that the total tax burden is reduced and disincentive effects are kept to a minimum.

Lower tax rates encourage saving, investment work effort and risk-taking. Consumption, leisure, the use of tax shelters and the black economy cease to be as attractive as previously. As supply increases in response, the consequent rising incomes, profits and wealth provide an increase in the tax base which returns to the Treasury the revenue lost as a result of the tax rate reductions. Savings also rise, thereby providing additional finance for investment.

At least, that is the theory. It is often objected that work effort and saving are unresponsive to reductions in tax rates. Further, that the 'substitution effect' will come into play whereby, if it is possible to earn a given net-of-tax sum with less work effort once tax rates are lowered, then less work will be done. However, whereas this could be true for individuals, it could not be true in the aggregate since if everyone worked less hard, total output and incomes would fall and people would have to work harder to restore their pre-tax incomes to their previous level.

The impact upon work effort may be difficult to measure directly. One way in which workers have traditionally responded to what they perceive as an insufficient net-of-tax reward for work effort has been to work more slowly, absent themselves, take longer vacations and move jobs more frequently. In other words, it may be that the supply-side effects will show up as much in the **quality of work** as in the number of hours worked.

It is, however, slightly ironic that, at least in the medium term, it is incumbent upon the government to take a great deal of (often legislative) action in order to get the supply side of the economy to work better. Thus, for example, the failure of the private sector to deal adequately with the training of the labour force has left the government with much of the responsibility for improving the quality of the labour supply. Equally, deregulation of markets has generally brought regulation hard on its heels. There is a wide range of governmental initiatives which may reasonably be considered as supply-side measures, and it is not possible to comment on them all in detail at this juncture. It should, however, be noted that some are directed at removing the **unemployment trap** – that is, the tendency for certain people to find themselves no better off financially when in employment than when unemployed; some at encouraging workers to price themselves back into jobs, mainly by curbing the power of the trade unions to push up wages; some to improve the quality of the labour force; and some to transfer activity back from the unofficial (black) economy to the official economy.

It is extremely difficult to judge whether these measures have been successful, as few unambiguous econometric studies have as yet been published. Obviously, such indicators as the rate of growth offer some support for the efficacy of supply-side measures, and there is widespread agreement that the labour market works rather better than it did in 1979. However, whether reductions in direct tax rates have achieved anything much is open to doubt, particularly since, as demonstrated in Chapter 7, the aggregate tax burden remains rather high.

■ 2.4 The External Sector

Let us now turn to the external sector, which is illustrated in **Figure 2.3**. This part of the model introduces additional complications, since it is evident that all kinds of external difficulties can arise if policy is directed exclusively at resolving internal problems. We can begin by noting that aggregate demand is increased by exports of goods and services, and reduced by imports of goods and services which form part of aggregate consumption in the internal sector. In this respect exports can be subsidised, as in the case of agriculture, as a component of a fiscal policy, whereas imports can be altered via the use of tariffs and quotas (which are not marked in **Figure 2.3** as they are currently of little significance – but see the discussion of the General Agreement on Tariffs and Trade on **pp. 302–8**).

More significantly, given international agreements to restrict subsidies and tariffs, both imports and exports can be affected by alterations in the **exchange rate**, which itself responds to imbalances in trade flows. However, the use of this instrument was severely constrained during the period when the UK was a member of the Exchange Rate Mechanism of the European Monetary System (see **pp. 280–4**), and at that time the exchange rate was more appropriately thought of as an **objective** rather than as an **instrument** of policy.

This can be clarified as follows. Consumption spending rises in the UK, creating additional demand of which part leaks out into imports. In order to purchase these it is necessary to change sterling into the currency of the seller, which causes the exchange rate to fall against that currency. It is a matter of necessity, from a book-keeping perspective, that the balance of payments accounts sum to zero (see **pp. 209–12**), so a current account deficit must be exactly counterbalanced by a net inflow of capital. For the most part, this inflow will need to be attracted in the short term by offering higher rates of interest compared to those prevailing in other major financial centres, so a worsening current account deficit will normally result in an increase in interest rates in the UK.

Figure 2.3 *The External Sector*

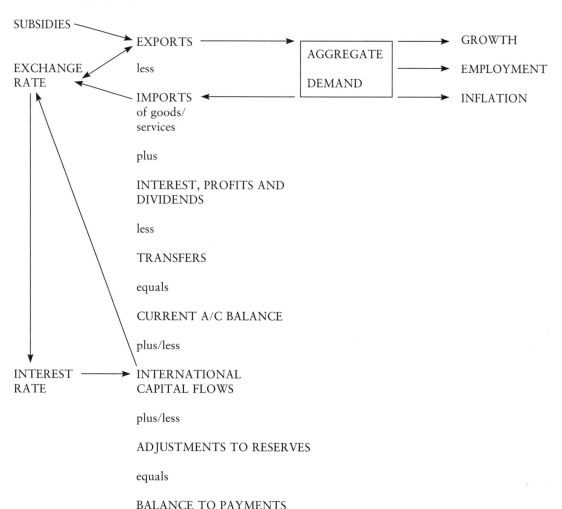

As a consequence of the capital inflow, the exchange rate is prevented from falling, and, in the context of the Exchange Rate Mechanism, from breaching the lower limit permitted for sterling. This lower limit accordingly represents the minimum value for the objective while the change in the interest rate which prevented it from being breached represents the instrument.

Where there are no set bounds for the exchange rate, as is currently the case in principle, the exchange rate reverts back to its status as instrument with a view to promoting exports and restraining imports. This allows the interest rate to continue to be used as an instrument, but with a view to controlling domestic demand rather than capital flows. Insofar as the interest rate can be relieved of its role in the external sector, it removes one of the major dilemmas of economic policy, namely how to achieve a structure of interest rates that is simultaneously appropriate for both internal and external equilibrium.

For a country with an ongoing current account deficit such a structure is almost impossible to achieve where the exchange rate is an objective, since this necessitates high interest rates and these in turn result in reduced investment, low rates of growth and rising unemployment. The promotion of growth and employment necessitates a policy of low interest rates, which deters capital inflows and exerts downwards pressure upon the exchange rate. However, this is not the whole story since the exchange rate itself affects the rate of inflation. When the exchange rate falls this causes import prices to rise, which eventually feeds through to domestic prices. If the exchange rate can be prevented from falling by maintaining high interest rates, the implication is that import prices will not rise. On the other hand, high interest rates cause the cost of housing to rise, which is also inflationary!

It is the role of the government to juggle these various considerations and to decide accordingly what are to be instruments, targets and objectives. On the whole, the postwar UK governments have not been notably successful in performing this juggling act.

■ 2.5 The Multiplier

One further factor now needs to be taken into account. Let us suppose that we begin with government expenditure raised by £133 in order to lift the economy out of recession. This will have the effect, according to official estimates, of raising GDP in the UK by roughly £100 because some of this initial expenditure will leak out into imports and some will immediately return to the Treasury as expenditure taxes. Bear in mind that our concern here is exclusively with the **domestic** effects of spending, and that we are operating **at**

the **margin** – that is, tax allowances have been used up so **all** extra income is subject to taxation.

What happens next is depicted in **Figure 2.4**. As can be seen, the value of domestic output grows by £100 which in turn raises total factor incomes by £100. The major part of this is personal incomes, and of this a part is saved and a part goes in income taxation and national insurance. The residual part is profit, which is partly distributed and partly undistributed. Profit is also subject to taxation. At the margin, deductions from income are quite high in aggregate, and if combined with personal and corporate saving result in the withdrawal of £68 of the extra £100 of income. Of the remaining £32, one quarter will disappear in the form of expenditure taxes and imports, resulting in an increase in the value of UK output of £24. This then raises incomes a second time by £24, and so forth.

Each time the sequence is repeated, the value of UK output goes up by 24 per cent. Thus, we get the sequence as follows:

$$£100 + £24 + £5.8 + £1.4 + £0.3 + \ldots = £132$$

The **multiplier** is the relationship between the **eventual increase** in GDP of £132 and the **initial increase** in GDP of £100, which in this case has a value of 1.32. A short cut to this figure is to use the formula:

$$\text{Multiplier} = 1 \div \text{the marginal propensity to withdraw (MPW)}$$

The MPW is a technical term for the marginal rate of deductions of all kinds in one full circuit of

Figure 2.4 *The Multiplier*

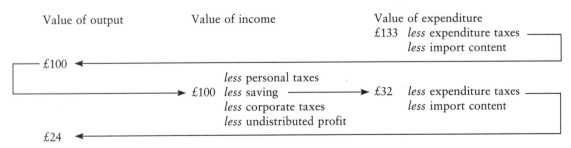

Figure 2.4, and is thus equal in this case to 76 per cent. Hence $1/0.76 = 1.32$.

The above is a much simplified version of the full multiplier equation expressed in the Treasury and other econometric models. Nevertheless, it is sufficiently accurate to bring out the basic point that the UK fiscal multiplier is actually much smaller than is popularly supposed.

■ *2.6* Crunchy Numbers

In what follows there is a great amount of data, wherever possible the most up-to-date available as at October 1996. Much of this data comes from the Office for National Statistics (ONS) formerly the Central Statistical Office (CSO). Over the past decade, ONS statistics have become less reliable, primarily because the abolition of exchange controls has made it much more difficult to keep track of money moving in and out of the UK, because statisticians have failed to keep pace with the shift from manufacturing to services and because the government has reduced the range of numbers it collects, partly to save money and partly to ease the burden of paperwork for business.

As a result, the current figures published each month or quarter are subject to significant errors. In many cases, the practice is to insert a 'balancing item' or 'statistical adjustment', which means that the money is known to exist, but for the time being (and perhaps for ever) it cannot be attributed to any particular category in a set of accounts. As time passes, missing money tends to turn up and it becomes possible to attribute unattributed money to specific categories. Hence, if we look back to 1979, we have a very good idea what was happening at the time, but we do not know very accurately what is happening right now even though that is precisely what we need to know if we are to manage the economy intelligently.

No doubt, by the time the next edition of this book comes out, the data in this edition will have been substantially revised, and it may be an interesting exercise for readers to look back to the previous edition and to compare the data for the years up to 1993. Above all else, the reader should treat almost all of the monthly data reported in the media with great caution since it is habitually inaccurate or distorted by non-recurrent items. Unfortunately, financial markets tend to be driven by the latest data, but the reader is advised to take a more sanguine view.

■ *2.7* Introduction to National Income Accounting

It is possible to use some simple national income accounting to bring out a proposition of considerable importance to our later discussion. As a matter of definition, total spending on domestic goods and services (E) must consist of private sector final consumption (C) **plus** private sector investment (including houses) (I) **plus** government spending (G) **plus** spending on domestic goods by foreigners (exports (X)) **less** spending on imports (M). Thus:

$$E = C + I + G + X - M$$

In its turn, C is assumed to take place out of net-of-tax income $(Y - T)$, and income that is not spent must, by definition, be saved (S). Thus:

$$C = Y - T - S$$

But Y and E are simply two alternative ways of measuring economic activity, as demonstrated in the sections which follow. Thus:

$$E = Y, \text{ and hence by substitution}$$
$$Y = [Y - T - S] + I + G + X - M$$

Thus, through rearrangement:

$$Y - Y + T + S - G - X + M = I$$

Cancelling the Ys, and further rearranging the other elements gives:

$$S + [T - G] + [M - X] = I$$

In other words, **investment** in the UK economy must be **financed** either by domestic savings (S), a budget **surplus** (T greater than G) or by running a balance of payments **deficit** (M greater than X). In the latter case, this arises because the counterpart to such a deficit is an **inflow of capital** of equal size.

One element of this equation may appear to be puzzling, namely the assertion that a budget surplus can finance investment. Let us assume that the external sector is in balance ($X = M$). If we also assume that savings are zero ($Y = C + T$), then some of the claims on income are transferred to the government in the form of taxes, and the only way in which the above equation can balance, which it must as a matter of definition, is if the government does not use up all of its claims on income – that is, T is greater than G – but makes some of them available for investment purposes.

■ *2.8* The National Accounts

□ *2.8.1 The Basic Building Blocks*

The concept of 'aggregate economic activity' is clearly of fundamental importance for our understanding of how the economy works. Before any action is taken, the government needs to know what state the economy is in, and it needs to know retrospectively what difference was made by undertaking a particular course of action. In order to do these things we need a set of national accounts, and this is provided by the Office for National Statistics. It appears each year as the *UK National Accounts*, which is always referred to as the *Blue Book*.

During the period between *Blue Books,* the ONS produces either monthly or quarterly data which appear in a variety of publications such as *Economic Trends,* the *Monthly Digest of Statistics* and *Financial Statistics,* and there are also periodic press releases. Unfortunately, the data appear under a wide array of definitions, so there is no choice but to explain below what all the terms mean that the reader may come across in his or her reading, even though it may seem at times that they are infinite in number.

As with any system of accounts, the *Blue Book* records flows of **money**. The value of a transaction can be approached in one of three ways, namely: the amount of money that the buyer gives

up in order to obtain a good or service (**expenditure**); the amount of money received by the seller (the value of **output** or **product**); the amount of money received in various forms by all those who contributed to the value of the end-product (**income**). These three figures must be equal **by definition**, since there is clearly only one sum of money involved in any given transaction.

If the value of all domestic transactions is aggregated together we get the variable known as **Gross Domestic Product** (GDP). This accordingly comes in three variants, namely GDP(E) where 'E' stands for expenditure; GDP(O) where 'O' stands for output; and GDP(I) where 'I' stands for income. It is important to bear in mind that the accounts are ultimately concerned with **final products** – for example, the sale of a desk in a shop to an end-user. However, there are a string of transactions prior to the final sales which might, for example, run as follows: raw materials sold to producer of semi-finished product; semi-finished product sold to producer of the finished product; finished product from factory sold to wholesaler, sold from wholesaler to retailer and sold from retailer to customer. It would be seriously misleading to add together all of these transactions and to call them 'economic activity' since there would be elements of double, triple, quadruple and so on counting involved. It is necessary, therefore, to use a **value-added** principle in counting. Beyond the raw material stage we add only the value added by each further stage en route to the end-user. In other words, we take the value of a transaction and **subtract** from it the value of the immediately preceding transaction in the above-mentioned sequence.

What we end up with is the value of the final transaction at the price ruling at the time it takes place. This is known as the **nominal** or **money** value of the transaction. However, if precisely the same transaction takes place at a different point in time, it is possible that the value of the transaction will be different because there has been a change in the price. In other words, the value of economic activity can go up over time because **more** goods and services are being sold at **constant** prices; because the **same number** of goods and services are being sold at **higher** prices; because **slightly**

more goods and services are being sold at **slightly higher** prices; and so forth. In order to isolate the change in the **volume** of sales it is necessary to strip away the effect of rising prices by **deflating** the nominal value such that it leaves us with an inflation-adjusted magnitude. This so-called **real** value is thus measured in **constant-price** terms. It is necessary to select a base year for this purpose, which for most variables in this book, and in particular the *Blue Book*, is 1990.

Measuring changes in the volume of output over time is a critical matter since this is the concept known as **economic growth**. Obviously, therefore, the particular sequence of prices used to deflate money GDP is of some importance but, as we will discover below, there are many price indices which could be used for this purpose, and the reader must be careful to check which deflator is being used if data are to be truly compatible.

It is also the case that GDP and other measures of economic activity can be recorded in several ways. GDP at **market prices** is final output valued at the market prices at which it is sold. This is usually a greater magnitude than the sum of production costs (value added) because the government levies taxes such as value added tax (VAT) at the point of sale. In some cases the rate of VAT is zero, so no differences will arise, and in some cases market prices are reduced below production costs because of subsidies paid by the government to producers. Hence, we also need to take account of GDP at **factor cost**, which is equal to GDP at **market prices** minus total **indirect taxes** and plus **subsidies**. In the national accounts, the sum of indirect taxes and subsidies is termed **Net Indirect Taxes**.

GDP, as the name suggests, is concerned solely with measuring the monetary flows generated by economic activity within the boundaries of the UK. However, UK residents may receive income from abroad, and there may be flows of money to foreigners as a result of domestic UK economic activity. GDP thus needs to be adjusted if it is to measure the total income available to UK citizens, which is called **Gross National Product** (GNP) and which is equal to GDP **plus Net Property Income from Abroad**.

Account must also be taken of the fact that part of the UK's stock of physical capital is used up over the course of a year. Buildings and machines may wear out through use (depreciation) or they may become outmoded by a technologically superior product and hence fall in value even though physically intact (obsolescence). **Capital Consumption** of these kinds must be replaced if the economy is to maintain its capacity to produce. When capital consumption is deducted from economic activity measured **gross** the residual is termed **net**, and GNP thereby becomes **Net National Product** (NNP) whereas GDP becomes **Net Domestic Product** (NDP). These net figures express the value of resources generated in the course of a year which can be used either for consumption or to renew the stock of physical capital via investment. When NNP is expressed at factor cost, it is customary to call it **National Income** (NI).

As noted previously, all three measures of economic activity must be equal by definition. However, in practice, in the case of each measure there are data limitations and measurement difficulties such that the estimates never do coincide exactly despite their conceptual equivalence. For this reason, the ONS produces a definitive estimate known as GDP(A) where 'A' stands for average. For the period since the latest base year, GDP(A) is the unweighted arithmetic average of GDP(E), GDP(O) and GDP(I). If each of the measures of GDP is subtracted from GDP(A) it gives rise to a **statistical discrepancy**, which is itemised in the accounts in order to bring all of the individual definitions into line.

No matter how accurately economic activity is measured, it is necessarily a flawed measure insofar that it can only take account of transactions where a monetary flow is recorded – in other words, market-based activities. Where a transaction occurs, but no monetary flow is thereby generated, the transaction will not appear in the national accounts. Thus, for example, the accounts ignore the activities of housewives, all do-it-yourself and all voluntary work. In the case of all illegal activity, and also where, for example, someone employed in the official economy is 'moonlighting', there actually is a monetary flow when a transaction occurs, but it is not declared to the authorities and hence does not appear in the national accounts. Such unrecorded flows are called the **black economy**. Hence, the national accounts understate substantially the true value of all economic activity, but provided the unrecorded part remains roughly the same proportion of the total then the rate of growth of recorded activity will still be correct. Problems could arise, however, if, for example, reductions in tax rates caused unofficial activity to appear in the official market and to become recorded, since this would give the impression that growth had accelerated when in reality it remained unchanged.

2.8.2 Measures at Market Prices: Effects of Introducing the Community Charge

GDP estimates for the years 1989–92 are affected by the abolition of domestic rates and the introduction of the Community Charge, commencing in Scotland in April 1989. In the national accounts, domestic rates are classified as a tax on expenditure on housing services, and are therefore included in consumers' expenditure at market prices. However, the Community Charge, until its demise in April 1993, is classified as a separate category of transfer, which is treated as a deduction from income in calculating personal disposable income. It follows that the Community Charge is not part of consumers' expenditure. Estimates of consumers' expenditure and of GDP at current market prices from 1989–92 are, therefore, marginally lower than they would have been if the Community Charge had not replaced domestic rates. GDP at current factor cost is unaffected. Estimates at constant prices of consumers' expenditure and GDP are also unaffected (see *Economic Trends*, August 1989).

2.8.3 The Expenditure Approach

The calculation of GDP, GNP and NI using the expenditure approach involves the measurement of all categories of expenditure in the economy. The sum of consumers' expenditure, investment (called gross domestic fixed capital formation in the national accounts), additions to work in progress and general government final consumption is equal to **Total Domestic Expenditure**. If exports of goods and services are added to this we arrive at **Total Final Expenditure** (TFE). However, not all of this expenditure is upon domestically produced goods and services, so in order to arrive at GDP it is necessary subsequently to deduct expenditure on imports.

It is conventional to value expenditure at the prices actually paid, which yields an estimate of GDP at market prices. If indirect taxes are subsequently deducted and subsidies added in, the end-result becomes GDP at **factor cost**. The further addition of net property income from abroad results in **GNP** at factor cost. Finally, the deduction of estimated capital consumption results in **NNP** at factor cost which is known as **National Income** (**expenditure based**).

These relationships are set out for 1995 in **Table 2.1** which contains *Blue Book* estimates for 1995 GDP which, when measured at current market prices, was worth £700 billion. Much the largest component of total expenditure, at 64 per cent of GDP, consisted of consumers' expenditure. To this needs to be added government expenditure (21 per cent) and investment expenditure (16 per cent) in order to arrive at the share of GDP which is 'domestic'. The contribution of the external sector is counted net (−1 per cent) as the difference between exports and imports.

GDP at factor cost was valued at £604 billion after adjusting for the net impact of expenditure taxes and subsidies of £96.6 billion. Net indirect taxes thus accounted for 13.8 per cent of GDP at market prices.

The transition to GNP at factor cost requires the addition to GDP of net property income from abroad of £9.5 billion. In turn, GNP is reduced to NNP by the subtraction of £73 billion of capital consumption. This is the expenditure estimate of National Income which can be converted to the 'average' estimate through the statistical discrepancy or expenditure adjustment.

Table 2.1 *1995 National Product Expenditure-based, at Current Prices (£ bn)*

	Consumers' expenditure	447.2
plus	General government final consumption	149.5
plus	Investment expenditure	
	of which:	109.3
	Gross domestic fixed capital formation (105.4)	
	Value of physical increase in stocks and work in progress (3.9)	
equals	Total domestic expenditure	706.0
plus	Exports of goods and services	197.6
minus	Imports of goods and services	−203.1
equals	Gross domestic product (GDP) at market prices	700.5
minus	Taxes on expenditure	−103.6
plus	Subsidies	7.0
equals	Gross domestic product (GDP) at factor cost	603.9
plus	Net property income from abroad	9.5
equals	Gross national product (GNP) at factor cost	613.4
minus	Capital consumption	−72.9
equals	Net national product (NNP) at factor cost or national income (expenditure estimate)	540.5
plus	Statistical discrepancy (expenditure adjustment)	0.4
equals	Net national product (NNP) at factor cost or national income (average estimate)	540.9

Source: UK National Accounts 1996, Table 1.2.

□ *2.8.4 The Income Approach*

Table 2.2 shows the alternative way of calculating 1995 GDP and NI in terms of income. Total Domestic Income is the sum of all incomes from employment, incomes from self-employment, gross trading profits of companies, the gross trading surplus of public corporations and general government enterprises, rent and other (imputed) incomes. If the nominal increase in the value of stocks of raw materials and products is subtracted from TDI, the residual becomes GDP (income based) and measures the income arising from economic activity during the year in question.

In order to reconcile the income-based measure of GDP with that based upon expenditure, a statistical adjustment or residual error term is added, as noted previously. The resultant figure is measured at factor cost because it is literally a method of deriving GDP through the summation of incomes paid to factors of production. Further adjustments in order to calculate GNP, NNP and NI are exactly the same as for the expenditure-based estimate.

In 1995, Total Domestic Income before deducting stock appreciation amounted to £609.3 billion, of which the largest share (62 per cent) consisted of income from employment valued at

Table 2.2 *1995 GDP Income-based at Current Factor Cost (£ bn)*

Factor Incomes		
Income from employment		377.9
Income from self-employment[1]		67.7
Gross trading profits of companies[1]		91.0
Gross trading surplus of public corporations and general government enterprises		5.2
Rent[2]		62.8
Imputed charge for consumption of non-trading capital		4.7
Total domestic income[1]		609.3
minus	Stock appreciation	−4.9
equals	GDP (income-based)	604.4
plus	Statistical discrepancy (income adjustment)	−0.1
equals	GDP, at factor cost, average estimate	604.3
plus	Net property income from abroad	9.5
minus	Capital consumption	−72.9
equals	NNP at factor cost or national income (average estimate)	540.9

Notes:
[1] Before providing for (deducting) stock appreciation and depreciation.
[2] Before providing for depreciation.
Source: UK National Accounts 1996, Table 1.4.

£378 billion. After subtraction of £4.9 billion of stock appreciation from TDI we get an estimate of 1995 GDP at factor cost. This is fractionally different from the equivalent figure using the expenditure approach, so a statistical discrepancy or income adjustment of £0.1 billion is needed to produce the estimated GDP(A) of £604.3 billion. The addition of net property income from abroad and the subtraction of capital consumption from GDP(A) produces the same figure for national income as in **Table 2.1**.

It is interesting to note that, although income from employment remained the largest component of GDP (I), its share has been falling progressively during the 1990s. In 1991, it was 66.6 per cent, somewhat lower than its peak value of 72 per cent in 1975 but nonetheless indicative of the fact that those in work had done very well for

themselves during the late 1980s. However, in 1995Q3 the share was down to 61.8 per cent, the lowest figure recorded since records began in 1955. In contrast, the share enjoyed by company trading profits had risen from 11.6 per cent in 1992 to 15.3 per cent in 1995Q3.

☐ *2.8.5 The Output Approach*

As output has to be produced before either incomes are paid out or those incomes are spent, the calculation of output is the first of the various estimates of economic activity to be published. It is customary to publish data on GDP(O), on a provisional basis, at quarterly intervals roughly three weeks after the end of the relevant quarter.

Table 2.3 GDP at Constant Factor Cost: Output Based Measure, Index Numbers of Output by Sector (1990 = 100)

	1990 weight in total output	1979– 1980[2]	1981– 1982[2]	1983– 1984[2]	1985– 1986[2]	1987– 1988[2]	1989	1990	1991	1992	1993	1994	1995
Agriculture, forestry and fishing	19	75.3	84.6	97.0	95.4	92.8	96.7	100.0	101.5	106.0	98.2	98.0	98.6
Energy and water supply	22	80.2	81.6	87.8	90.8	97.7	97.3	100.0	105.7	107.4	111.8	113.1	116.7
Manufacturing	232	86.7	77.7	80.7	85.1	92.7	100.2	100.0	94.6	94.0	95.3	99.3	101.5
Total production	278	84.4	79.7	83.4	89.1	96.0	100.3	100.0	96.3	96.2	98.3	103.2	105.9
Construction	72	67.5	62.9	71.2	74.5	88.6	97.6	100.0	92.0	87.9	87.2	90.5	89.6
Services: Distribution, hotels, etc.	143	73.3	70.6	76.2	83.6	94.2	100.8	100.0	96.1	95.2	99.9	103.4	104.5
Transport and communication	84	72.7	71.9	79.9	82.0	91.9	99.1	100.0	98.2	99.8	104.8	112.2	118.5
Government and other	211	–	–	90.2	93.2	97.7	99.4	100.0	100.8	101.4	102.5	103.8	105.3
Financial and business	193	–	–	77.2	84.8	93.8	97.8	100.0	99.7	98.1	100.7	105.7	110.2
Total services	631	76.0	76.6	81.2	87.0	95.0	99.3	100.0	99.1	98.8	101.6	105.8	107.4
GDP (output based)[1]	1 000	77.7	76.7	81.1	86.9	95.0	99.4	100.0	97.9	97.4	99.6	103.7	106.2

Note:
[1] Adjusted for the statistical discrepancy this yields the index of the output of goods and services.
[2] Two-year averages.
Source: UK National Accounts (ONS, 1996), Table 1.6. Economic Trends. UK Economic Accounts.

Data are derived from estimates of physical output and survey returns from producers, and are subject to considerable revision, partly in the light of subsequent and more detailed estimates of income and expenditure.

It is not customary to express output data in money terms, but rather in the form of a series of index numbers, as in **Table 2.3** which contains not only the series for GDP(O), spanning the period 1979–95, but also the series for various sub-categories of GDP(O). In the left hand column the total output in 1990 is assigned a weight of 1000, and each sub-category or part thereof is assigned a proportion of the total weight according to the proportion of GDP(O) that it contributed in 1990. Thus, it can be seen that the services sectors, with a weight of 631, accounted for 63.1 per cent of 1990 GDP(O), whereas the production industries accounted for 27.8 per cent and the manufacturing industries for only 23.2 per cent. However, this is not all that unusual for a major advanced economy; only in Japan among the Group of 7 do the services sectors constitute less than 60 per cent of output.

It can be seen from **Table 2.3** that the services sectors rode out the 1980–81 recession without much difficulty, although distribution was hit fairly hard as one might have expected. In contrast, both manufacturing and construction fell back heavily. Interestingly, the 'other services' sector grew at the same rate as manufacturing from 1981 to 1990, despite their sharply contrasting experiences during 1979–81, and construction grew at an even faster rate than all service sectors.

From 1985 to 1990 in particular there was a boom in construction, and distribution and transport also grew unusually rapidly. Manufacturing (which peaked in 1989) also performed creditably. In contrast, the energy and water supply sector, which had made progress right through the 1980–81 recession on account of the discovery of North Sea oil, made comparatively little progress from 1986 to 1990, only to move forward again strongly during the 1990–92 recession. It can be seen from the weights that the agriculture, forestry and fishing sector barely affects total output (although it has a disproportionate effect upon policy making – see **pp. 309–22**). It performed

Table 2.4   *UK GDP by Industry,[1] 1992 (£ bn)*

Industry Category	Net Output
Agriculture, forestry and fishing	11.9
Energy and water supply	15.8
Mining/quarrying	14.6
Manufacturing	131.7
Construction	31.8
Distribution, hotels and catering; repairs	84.7
Transport and communication	50.8
Banking, finance, insurance, business services and leasing[2]	110.7
Ownership of dwellings (rent)	47.4
Public administration, national defence and compulsory social security	39.5
Education and health services	73.0
Other services	23.3
Total	635.2
Adjustment for financial services[3]	−30.8
GDP (income-based)	604.4
Statistical discrepancy (income component)	0.1
GDP at factor cost (average estimate)	604.3

Notes:
[1] The contribution of each industry to the GDP (its value-added), net of stock appreciation but before providing for (deducting) capital consumption.
[2] Including net interest receipts by financial companies.
[3] The same as net interest receipts by financial companies.

Source: UK National Accounts 1996, Tables 2.1 and 2.2.

particularly poorly from 1984 to 1988, but has subsequently done much better.

The 1990–92 recession took its greatest toll of construction followed by manufacturing. In the former case it is the only sector yet to recover all of the ground lost since 1990 (with implications for the employment of unskilled labour). In the case of agriculture, progress was initially made but real output is now back below its 1990 level. Manufacturing only managed to exceed its 1990 real output during 1995, whereas transport and communications, together with energy and water supply, have rebounded most strongly. Overall, real GDP just about recovered its 1990 level in 1993, but has subsequently moved forward quite rapidly.

It is obviously possible to put a value upon the output of a given year, as is done for 1995 in **Table 2.4**. This has to be done on a **value-added** basis, as noted earlier, and this in turn requires that the data be collected on a factor cost basis which is recorded net of stock appreciation but before deducting capital consumption.

The level of disaggregation in **Table 2.4** is greater than in **Table 2.3**. Both contain a composite category for the energy and water supply industries, which in 1995 was worth £15.8 billion and which represented 2.6 per cent of GDP(A).

This can be compared with agriculture, forestry and fishing with its slightly smaller net output of £11.9 billion. In fact, this comparison is deceptive because oil and gas are sold in the free market whereas agricultural products are heavily subsidised, so the real contribution of the agricultural sector is much less than it appears to be on the basis of **Table 2.4**.

The contribution of financial services to GDP(A) is brought out clearly in **Table 2.4**. The figure of £110.7 billion includes net interest receipts which need to be subtracted lower down **Table 2.4** because they do not contribute directly to net output. On a grossed-up basis, the gap between the contributions of financial services and manufacturing is no longer all that large, and it can be expected to narrow further in due course.

Table 2.5 serves to emphasise yet further the evolving nature of the UK economy. As can be seen in column (2), construction and services substantially outgrew production during the period 1980–95, with agriculture, forestry and fishing also performing well (but only at the beginning and end of the period). After adjusting for the relative importance of the various sectors, as signified by column (1), it is possible to calculate, in

Table 2.5   *GDP, Growth of Output by Sector, 1980–95*

	(1) 1995 Weight in Total Output[1]	(2) Percentage Change from 1980 to 1995	(3) Contribution to Change in Output 1980 to 1995 $((1) \times (2))$	(4) Percentage Share of Total Change
Agriculture, forestry and fishing	1.9	41.3	78.5	2.6
Production	27.8	20.8	578.2	18.4
Construction	7.2	35.0	252.0	8.0
Services	63.1	35.3	2227.4	71.0
Total Index of Output	100.0	31.4	3136.1	100.0

Note:
[1] Expressed as % of total weights in Table 2.3.

Source: UK National Accounts 1996, Table 1.6.

column (4), the percentage share of the total change in output between 1980 and 1995 contributed by each sector. As can be seen, the services sectors played a dominant role, with the production industries lagging far behind.

2.8.6 Real National Income 1979–95

The purpose of this section is to examine briefly real national income data spanning the full term of Conservative rule. This is presented, with the omission of certain intermediate years, in **Table 2.6**. This table culminates with an index of GDP(A) at factor cost. As can be seen, real GDP(A) fell back during 1980–81. It had regained its 1979 level by 1983, and significant gains were made in every year from 1982 to 1989 with a further small gain in 1990. It suffered a severe setback in 1991 and a further modest one in 1992, before resuming its growth in 1993. In 1994 it surpassed its 1990 level and is currently one-third higher than in 1979.

Overall, therefore, real GDP improved during eight of the ten years comprising the 1980s, and the overall improvement, even allowing for the prior recession, was roughly twenty three per cent. Some leeway was subsequently lost, but one conclusion, which is often played down by those on the political left, is inescapable: **the UK is significantly wealthier overall (by about one-third) than it was when Mrs Thatcher was first elected** (although the benefits have not been evenly spread among different groups in society). The main driving force was clearly real consumption, although real investment performed very creditably from 1981 to 1989. In contrast, general government final consumption was very subdued, demonstrating that the 1980s were years in which the government largely turned its back on Keynesian demand management.

2.8.7 Exports and Imports

Our discussion in this section is essentially concerned with matters internal to the UK, but it is

worth picking up from **Table 2.6** a few pointers to the subject matter of the later chapters on international trade. As can be seen, the volume of exports remained almost static during the 1980–81 recession, in which respect it must be remembered that export demand is determined by spending power in other economies, which did not collapse anything like as steeply as in the UK at this time. Furthermore, North Sea oil moved into excess supply and the UK was able to become a net exporter.

The effects of that recession on UK demand are clearly seen when one examines the real value of imports, which fell during 1980 and 1981. However, by 1983, imports had regained all of the lost ground as the economy moved out of recession. In 1984 export and import demand were in approximate balance, and continued to be so until 1987, after which the growth of imports sharply outstripped that of exports until recession set in again at the end of the decade. One of the most remarked-upon features of the 1990–92 recession, which differed from prior experience, was the fact that import demand was higher in 1992 than in 1990. Exports predictably held up as companies looked outside the depressed home market for sales, and the September 1992 devaluation also served to narrow the gap between exports and imports.

2.9 Sectoral Surpluses and Deficits

Although this text is concerned primarily with the period since 1979, it can be illuminating to examine certain longer-term trends. This is true, for example, in the case of sectoral surpluses and deficits. There are basically four of these, covering the personal, public, overseas and company sectors, although there is also a sub-set of the latter which covers only those companies deemed to be industrial and commercial (ICCs – the others are financial companies and institutions (FCIs)). The overseas sector account tracks the direction in which money flows, and hence is a mirror image of the current account surplus or deficit. In other

Table 2.6 *UK Real Domestic Product by Category of Expenditure at 1990 Prices,*[1] *1979–95 (£ bn)*

	1979	1981	1983	1985	1987	1988	1989	1990	1991	1992	1993	1994	1995
Consumers' expenditure	247.2	247.4	261.2	276.8	311.2	334.6	345.4	347.5	339.9	339.7	348.0	356.9	364.0
General government final consumption	99.3	101.3	104.3	105.2	107.9	108.6	110.1	112.9	115.8	115.7	116.0	118.2	119.7
Gross domestic fixed capital formation	75.8	64.9	71.8	81.6	92.3	105.2	111.5	107.6	97.4	96.0	96.6	99.4	99.3
Value of increase in stocks and work in progress	4.0	−3.9	1.6	1.3	1.7	5.1	2.7	−1.8	−4.6	−1.7	0.3	2.9	3.3
Exports of goods and services	95.1	94.2	95.7	109.2	120.6	121.2	126.8	133.2	132.2	137.4	142.5	155.6	166.9
Imports of goods and services	−89.7	−84.0	−94.0	−106.0	−122.1	−137.4	−147.6	−148.3	−140.3	−149.9	−154.4	−162.7	−169.1
GDP (expenditure-based) at market prices	433.4	418.0	440.9	468.1	511.6	537.2	548.9	551.1	540.3	537.5	549.0	570.3	584.0
Statistical discrepancy	−0.5	−2.4	−1.1	–	–	–	–	–	–	–	–	–	0.3
GDP (average estimate) at market prices	–	–	–	–	–	–	–	–	–	–	–	–	–
Factor cost adjustment	−56.9	−54.1	−56.6	−60.3	−67.8	−71.5	−72.7	−72.2	−71.4	−71.0	−71.8	−73.9	−75.5
GDP at factor cost	376.0	364.1	384.3	407.8	443.8	465.7	476.2	478.9	468.9	466.4	477.2	496.4	508.8
Index of GDP at factor cost, 1990 = 100	78.5	75.4	80.2	85.2	92.7	97.2	99.4	100.0	97.9	97.4	99.6	101.3	106.2

Notes:
[1] For the years before 1983, totals differ from the sum of their components.
Source: UK National Accounts 1996, Table 1.3; *Economic Trends.*

words, a deficit on the current account of the balance of payments shows up as a sectoral surplus because money flows in to finance it and vice versa.

It is for this reason that, starting in 1970, the modest deficit of the **overseas sector** at the time turned rapidly into a sizeable surplus at the time of the first oil price rise, only to settle back to zero at the end of the decade. At the beginning of the 1980s, on the back of North Sea oil, it dropped sharply into deficit, only to rise back to zero by the mid-1980s and to rise further to a substantial surplus which peaked in 1989, as shown in **Figure 2.5**. It has subsequently remained in surplus, other than briefly in 1994, but at somewhat reduced levels which reflect the recessionary conditions either in the UK or later in continental Europe.

At the beginning of the 1970s, the **public sector** was in surplus, but by the mid-1970s it had collapsed back into massive deficit. Subsequently, the situation improved somewhat, although substantial deficits remained the order of the day until 1985. During the years which followed, as we will discover in detail in Chapters 7 and 8, the fiscal position improved dramatically, but as shown in **Figure 2.5**, the customary deficit reappeared in no uncertain fashion after 1990, hitting bottom in 1994Q1 at nearly £14 billion. Things are slowly getting better, but for the moment most of the other sectors have to remain in surplus to counter-balance this huge deficit.

Throughout the entire period, the **personal sector** exhibited an almost exactly opposite pattern. It remained in surplus from 1972 to 1986, although from 1981 to 1988 the trend was almost continuously downwards, amounting in all to a change of nearly 10 per cent of GDP. The opposite turnaround for the public sector, commencing in 1975, was actually larger than this, but took longer to be achieved, and like that sector the personal sector has recently moved significantly into reverse gear, commencing in 1992, as shown in **Figure 2.5**. We will be discussing this pattern in detail in the sections which follow.

From 1970 to 1982, the **ICC** sector balance exhibited relatively little variability, oscillating regularly from a small positive to a small negative percentage of GDP. However, in 1982, it rose to

4.4 per cent of GDP, and in 1983 began a decline which accelerated after 1986. By 1989 the total turnaround represented 10 per cent of GDP, but as shown in **Figure 2.5**, this sector has spent the past six years repairing its balance sheets and succeeded in returning into surplus in 1993. The overall company sector has generally moved in parallel, with FCIs modestly in surplus in 1989 and modestly in deficit in 1990. However, as noted below, the pattern changed dramatically in 1992 when FCIs produced a big surplus whereas the ICCs ran an even bigger deficit.

The various sectoral lines converged in 1986, which had not happened since the early 1970s. At that time, the collapse of the public sector's financial position was mirrored by a major upturn for the personal and, temporarily, the overseas sector. However, in 1986, every sector was, most unusually, in the throes of a massive uni-directional movement, from early 1980s surplus into deficit or vice versa. This sequence came to an end in 1988–89, and a pattern has reappeared noticeably similar to that seen after the lines previously converged in the early-1970s. On the face of it, a further period of convergence is now underway, with the various lines possibly meeting in 1997–98.

In the sections which follow we will be examining the personal and company sectors in more detail. However, the discussion of the public and overseas sectors is more sensibly held over to the later chapters dedicated to fiscal policy and trade respectively.

☐ *2.9.1 Personal Sector*

It is of great interest to examine why the personal sector moved from a position of surplus to a position of deficit late in 1987 and back into surplus at the end of 1990. As noted above, the decline in the financial surplus of the personal sector commenced at the beginning of the 1980s, so it is the experience of the early 1990s which stands in sharp contrast to that of the first decade of Conservative rule. In order to clarify what happened we need to refer to **Table 2.7** which identifies the major changes since 1986.

Figure 2.5 *Financial Surplus/Deficit,[1] by Sector (£ bn Quarterly, 1988–96)*

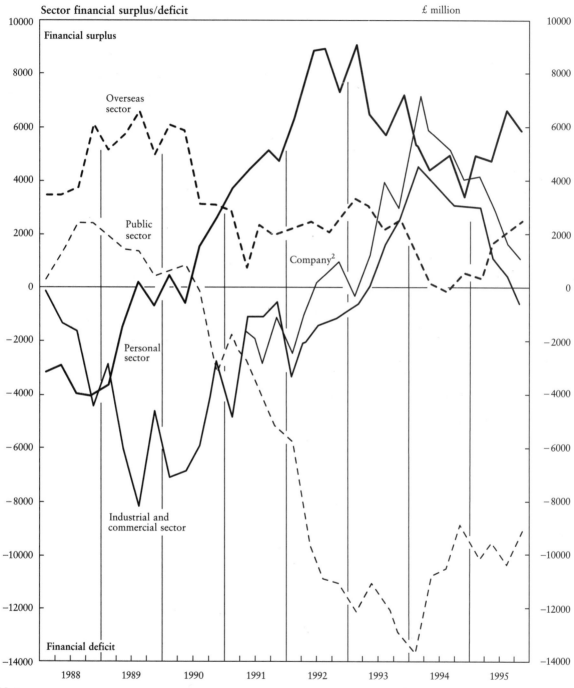

Note:

[1] This balance is equal to saving *plus* capital transfers *less* GDFCF *less* increase in value of stocks and work in progress.

[2] ICC plus financial companies and institutions.

Source: Economic Trends, Table 2.9.

Table 2.7   *Personal Sector: Financial Account, Main Changes 1986–95 (£ bn)*

	1986 −87[1]	1988 −89[1]	1990	1991	1992	1993	1994	1995
Loans for house purchase	−28.2	−42.0	−33.2	−25.9	−18.3	−16.2	−19.1	−15.1
UK company securities	−8.5	−19.2	−11.2	−5.5	−0.3	−10.2	−3.2	−13.8
Sterling bank lending	−7.2	−12.8	−8.2	−2.3	−0.3	+1.1	−3.4	−6.8
Unit trust units	+2.7	+0.3	0	+1.0	−0.3	+6.0	+6.2	+3.9
Deposits with building societies	+12.7	+18.7	+17.9	+17.3	+10.8	+9.7	+8.4	+14.2
Sterling bank deposits	+8.2	+19.2	+15.9	+6.5	+5.5	+1.9	+2.6	+13.1
National Savings	+2.5	−0.1	+0.8	+2.2	+5.0	+3.0	+4.6	+3.3
British Government securities	+1.3	−2.6	−1.0	+1.4	−1.0	+3.8	+1.2	−0.9
Life assurance and pension funds	+20.3	+25.2	+27.7	+28.6	+27.5	+29.0	+27.8	+33.0

Note: [1] Average of two years.

Source: Financial Statistics, UK Economic Accounts, Table A21.

As usual, a key element relates to the housing market. The table shows that the build-up of debt primarily took the form of loans for house purchase, which peaked at an astonishing annual £40+ billion in 1988–89 at a time when house prices were rising rapidly. The recent price falls went hand-in-hand with a massive reduction in such loans, on a scale which has dwarfed most of what has happened elsewhere in the account. However, there has in aggregate also been a substantial movement out of direct holdings of company securities, most notably in the three years following the 1987 crash and in 1993 and 1995. It is evident that, privatisation issues notwithstanding, the personal sector has lost its enthusiasm for direct holdings of equity.

On the other hand, it has continued to pump massive amounts of money into life assurance and pension funds, with no discernible cyclical effect, which means that the personal sector, although it generally fails to appreciate this, has an ever-larger but increasingly less-direct interest in the stock market. On the other hand, until fairly recently, personal investment in unit trusts struggled to regain its pre-1987 momentum. The period from 1987 to 1990 also witnessed a run-down in personal holdings of government securities, although this partly reflected the paucity of supply as a result of repayments of the National Debt. The Debt has once again risen rapidly, and

personal holdings have begun to follow suit, particularly when the government has expressly targeted the sector for such sales as in 1993.

Very large sums of money have been lodged in building society accounts, partly as a result of liquidating other assets. Such accounts are interest-bearing, as for the moment are bank accounts of various kinds which in aggregate were roughly as popular in the late 1980s. As interest rates declined during the 1990s, the attraction of such accounts declined in tandem, with the banks suffering even more than the building societies. To some extent, these monies ended up in higher-yielding National Savings and in unit trusts.

Overall, therefore, the picture until 1992 was one of the personal sector maintaining its liquidity, cutting back on mortgage debt and, as shown by the data on bank lending, cutting back hugely on its loans from banks at high rates of interest. This was a recipe for prolonged recession, but since the end of 1992 the personal sector surplus has been heading back towards balance, albeit at a cautious pace.

☐ 2.9.2 Company Sector

The most remarkable feature of the period 1986–89 was the collapse in the financial health of the company sector, with an almost equally remarkable improvement since then which has yet to run its full course. In 1989 as a whole (**Figure 2.5** plots quarterly data), ICCs ran up a deficit of £20.5 billion, a threefold increase on 1988 and one to be followed by a £21.5 billion deficit in 1990. Surprisingly, however, this was not reflected in the balance sheets of most large corporations which were sufficiently strong to be able to sustain dividend growth. In fact, large companies continued to pay out dividends well in excess of what was warranted by their income growth, a policy which makes some sense as a smoothing device through the economic cycle but which obviously causes short-term problems. As the Bank of England noted at the time, the ratio of dividends to post-tax profits reached 'an almost unprecedented' 62 per cent in the final quarter of 1989. Needless to say, this strategy was partly reversed in subsequent years, although it has by no means died the death especially where companies, as in the electricity sector, are under threat of takeover.

In 1983, the ICCs' net borrowing requirement stood at a mere £1.0 billion. By 1996 it had risen to £10.6 billion, but this was insignificant compared to the leap to £28.2 billion in 1987 followed by £50.1 billion in 1988 and £52.5 billion in 1989 (see *Economic Trends*, Table 2.12). During the three years 1987 to 1989, investment abroad was running at a level in excess of £10 billion per year and, more notably, investment in UK company securities soared from £5.1 billion in 1987 (the year of the crash) to £15.1 billion in 1988 and £16.4 billion in 1989. Once the acquisition of financial assets is added in, the resultant gross borrowing requirement roughly trebled between 1987 and 1989.

It is almost facile to argue that this trend clearly could not be sustained in the face of a deepening recession commencing in 1990. This shows up in the data, although there are the usual caveats which arise because account has to be taken of an often large and variable balancing item (unidentified flows), and of an expansion in the size of the ICC sector as a result of privatisation. Furthermore, it is possible to argue that the onset of the deficit reflected the confidence of the sector rather than the reverse. Fixed investment rose from £36.0 billion in 1987 to £43.6 billion in

1988 and to £52.5 billion in 1990, since when it has declined modestly (see *Economic Trends Annual Supplement*, Table 1.14). ICCs seemed to be quite happy to finance this by bank and other borrowing, which had soared to nearly £70 billion by 1989, thereby raising noticeably their 'gearing' (ratio of debt to equity).

Obviously, it had become difficult to raise much finance via an issue of ordinary shares in the aftermath of the 1987 crash, but ICCs did not seem to have taken much account of the possibility (probability?) that interest rates might rise and cause the interest charges on their borrowing to become over-burdensome. Another interesting feature of this period is that increasing reliance was placed upon innovatory financial instruments such as interest rate swaps. Further features of the late 1980s were the sharp upturn in the acquisition of UK company securities, which indicated much increased activity in the merger/takeover market, and the high level of overseas investment, especially in the USA, which greatly exceeded the acquisition of ICCs by foreign companies at this time. It is notable that 80 per cent of all takeover bids in 1989 were conducted in cash, which understandably made it necessary to resort to bank borrowing.

The net borrowing requirement peaked at £17.9 billion in the third quarter of 1989. Since then, apart from the £16.8 billion recorded in the final quarter of 1990 following on from unusually small totals in 1990Q2 and Q3, the quarterly figures have mostly fallen below £10 billion and throughout 1994 below £1 billion, although the 1995 quarterly figures all fell between £5 billion and £10 billion. Although other forms of borrowing have remained buoyant, it is especially notable that bank borrowing fell from **minus** £1.4 billion in 1991 to **minus** £11.3 billion in 1993, only returning to positive territory in 1994Q4. Equally, investment in UK company securities fell to a negligible £2.3 billion in 1990, reflecting the demise of the mega-bid, and subsequently showed no signs of returning anywhere near to late-1980s levels until 1995Q1. Investment abroad also collapsed, bottoming out at £1.7 billion in 1990 and showing only modest growth beyond that point. In other words, the corporate sector well and

Figure 2.6   *Financial Crisis and Credit Crunch*

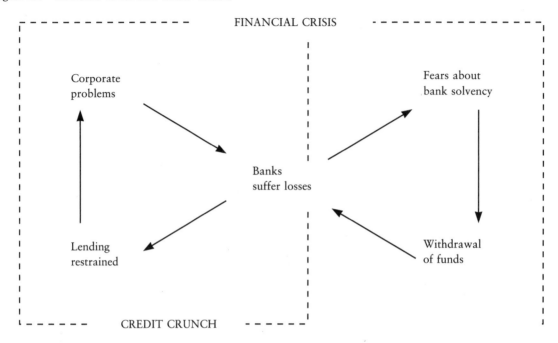

Source: Adapted from *Barclays Bank Review* (November 1990).

truly battened down the hatches, and concentrated wholeheartedly upon restoring battered balance sheets before re-emerging in 1995 to cast its eyes over the likes of the electricity companies. For the most part, this was a successful strategy, although company failures have remained a regular feature.

☐ 2.9.3 Credit Crunch

A **credit crunch** exists when financial intermediaries, and especially banks, become unwilling to lend to the private sector. They may try to widen the gap between the interest rate at which they borrow and the rate at which they lend, as was generally the case throughout the 1990–92 recession. For example, in early 1991 there were four reductions in base rates but the overdraft rate to personal customers went up. Alternatively, intermediaries may toughen the criteria to be met before a loan is sanctioned. If crunch becomes crisis, lending may dry up altogether.

In **Figure 2.6** the left-hand triangle represents a credit crunch, whereas the full figure represents a financial crisis. In the heyday of Keynesian demand management, the expansionary phase of the business cycle was set off via a loosening of fiscal policy. This did not happen during the 1980s, however, when as previously noted the upswing was based primarily upon the free availability of credit. This was similar to what happened in the nineteenth century when there was a series of booms and recessions driven by the behaviour of the financial markets. A credit crunch presupposes a prior boom based upon credit. The indebtedness of the personal and company sectors grows sharply and bank lending becomes increasingly directed towards more speculative types of activity, such as junk bond financed management buy-outs and property development, where returns are potentially very high.

When the slow-down inevitably arrives, there is a rash of company failures, which in turn damages the banks' balance sheets when the loans are written off. This causes the banks' credit ratings to be lowered and hence raises the cost of finance. The banks not merely respond by raising charges for their other lending in order to recover their own higher costs, but also widen the spread between borrowing and lending rates. They also dispose of their collateral when payments secured by that collateral cease to be made, and shut down companies which, in better times, they would have been willing to tide over a bad patch. This may cause their own credit ratings to be further downgraded.

The step from credit crunch to financial crisis requires that depositors become afraid that their deposits will be put at risk by the banks' problems, and consequently withdraw their funds, thereby precipitating a run on the banks. In practice, deposit insurance can be expected to prevent this latter step, especially if combined with assurances by the authorities that they will maintain the liquidity of the system.

It is accordingly more appropriate to ask whether there was a credit crunch in the early 1990s. Certainly, the banks pulled in their horns

and took a very tough line with companies that got into trading difficulties during the recession. The banks were much criticised in the media for their apparent indifference to the suffering of both entrepreneurs and mortgagees in difficulties as a result of job loss, but the banks unashamedly took the view that someone other than, of course, the top managers responsible for strategy, should bear the brunt for the banks' mistakes during the credit boom of the late 1980s.

Corporate failures accordingly rose sharply, although it should be borne in mind that when company formation is unusually rapid, as it was during the mid-1980s, the failure rate can be expected to rise as soon as recession strikes. There are a number of different sources of data on this issue, such as Dun and Bradstreet and the British Chambers of Commerce, but the data tell a uniform story in spite of differing definitions, as shown in **Figure 2.7** which illustrates what happened as the recession set in.

Company insolvencies rose steadily from 1980 to 1985, by which time the overall number had

Figure 2.7　*Company Insolvencies*

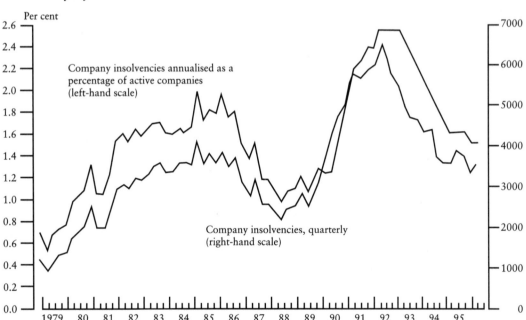

Source: Bank of England Quarterly Bulletin (February 1993).

roughly doubled. They then fell back sharply to the level of 1982 between 1986 and 1988 and, after marking time in 1989, they began to rise very sharply in 1990. This possibly arose because the introduction of wrongful trading provisions aimed at protecting creditors in the Insolvency Act 1986 may have led some firms to opt for insolvency earlier than in the 1980–81 recession, but it also has to be recognised that the number of small firms had grown significantly during the 1980s. The 1992 figure was roughly three times that of 1989.

The rate of increase, at roughly 65 per cent, was highest in 1991, but it still registered a further rise in 1992 despite the odd 'green shoot'. At the time, failures were located primarily in the South-East outside London, Scotland and the South-West, indicating a high failure rate among companies formed in the late 1980s boom.

During the 1980s, company formation comfortably outnumbered failures, although the ratio of six to one in 1988 had fallen to two to one by 1992. The urge to behave entrepreneurially nevertheless remained strong, although new company formation was clearly linked to the loss of employment during the recession.

The relatively unhelpful attitude of the banks, which they preferred to refer to as relatively realistic, inevitably affected the rate of company formation. However, there has been no tendency for failures to outnumber formations. It is accordingly reasonable to conclude that the potential credit crunch was averted although for a time, until interest rates began to fall, it was a close-run thing.

Since the end of 1992 the situation has improved considerably (see *Bank of England Quarterly Bulletin,* August 1995, pp. 274–5). However, although a further modest improvement overall was evident in 1995, this was not the case for larger companies, especially if located in London and Scotland. The significance of the slowing down in the reduction in insolvencies is difficult to pin down for the time being, but it is at least possible to argue that there should be a long-term decline in insolvencies if inflation remains low.

Bibliography

Cornelius, M. and Wright, K. (1995) 'Company Profitability and Finance', *Bank of England Quarterly Bulletin* (August).

Smith, J. and Sterne, G. (1994) 'Personal and Corporate Sector Debt', *Bank of England Quarterly Bulletin* (May).

Chapter 3

Income and Wealth

Peter Curwen

■ *3.1* Income and Wealth

Before proceeding any further, it is important to clear up a misunderstanding which, to judge by their utterances over the years, is particularly prevalent among politicians but which is also made too little of in introductory textbooks, and which concerns the distinction between the concepts of **income** and **wealth**. Income is a **flow** – that is, it appears in a series of instalments over time, for example weekly, monthly or yearly. Most income is **earned**, and consists primarily of payments in return for labour inputs, that is, wages and salaries as shown in **Table 2.2**. However, it may also be **unearned**, in the form, for example, of rent, interest and dividends. Some also appears as transfer payments, for example payments to the unemployed.

Wealth, on the other hand, is a **stock**, and is measured at a particular point in time. Wealth may either be **physical**, taking the form of assets which can be handled, for example a house or its contents, or **financial**, for example cash in the bank or building society, stocks and shares. It must be counted net of liabilities – for example, a person's wealth tied up in a house is equal to the current market value of the property less any outstanding mortgage.

This is less straightforward than it looks. In the first place, it is evident that income can be converted into wealth via the act of **saving**, and for most people their wealth originates in setting aside some part of their income flow. However, where, for example, a person takes out a repayment mortgage, part of the monthly outgoing is a payment of interest while another part is a repayment of capital. The latter part therefore constitutes an addition to that person's wealth, although in practice most people tend to think of mortgage payments as spending rather than saving. Equally, wealth can create a flow of unearned income, either because a property which is let out produces rent, a bank account yields interest or a share yields a dividend.

Further ambiguities arise where, for example, a person buys a car. Strictly speaking a car is a form of physical wealth, but unlike a house it can be expected to self-destruct within, say, fifteen years (although a 'classic' car is an exception), and hence tends to be viewed by purchasers as a form of expenditure. The same may be said of clothing and household appliances, and the key issue is ultimately how the Inland Revenue view such assets for tax purposes since some kind of arbitrary decision has to be made for official purposes.

Trickier problems arise in respect of **pension** rights. Employees' contributions to a pension fund are often deducted at source, and are effectively a form of compulsory saving in order to acquire a stock of wealth which the employee cannot access prior to retirement, subsequent to which there is generally a lump-sum payment followed by a flow of unearned income in the form of a pension which continues for an indeterminate number of years. For this latter reason it is extremely difficult to say how much wealth any single individual has tied up in a pension right.

Trickier still is **human capital**. In effect, if a person borrows money to finance his or her education, then the knowledge gained is a form of wealth that can generally be expected to result in a flow of income in future years which exceeds what would have been available in the absence of that knowledge. Thus the loan finances the creation of wealth which subsequently generates incremental income that can be used to repay the loan.

For these and other reasons, hardly anyone has any real idea how much wealth he or she owns, though people are obviously well informed about their incomes. Interestingly, when one considers the widespread usage of the term **rich**, the word could equally well apply to a person who has a huge income and no assets as to a person who has virtually no income but a great deal of wealth (for example, a widow on a pension living in a big house free of mortgage). These usages are by no means interchangeable, as politicians constantly need reminding, and this not merely causes endless problems for tax/benefit policy, as in the case of local taxation (see **pp. 181–3**), but there is an issue of wider significance because it becomes unclear to what extent spending decisions are driven by considerations of income and/or wealth. Given that housing constitutes such a large part of most people's stock of wealth, it follows that the state of the housing market is closely tied to patterns of spending in the modern economy. In effect, as discussed below, wealth provides the collateral security that facilitates over-consumption – failing all else, if debt piles up as a result of over-indulgence with credit cards, it is generally possible to sell off property and settle debts with the proceeds before a new property is acquired.

We have previously noted, in **Table 2.7**, the ways in which the personal sector has switched its resources around over the past decade. Another way of examining this issue is in terms of the composition of the net wealth of the personal sector, as shown in **Table 3.1** (see also *Bank of England Inflation Report*, May 1995, p. 24). Once

Table 3.1 *Composition of the Net Wealth of the Personal Sector, UK (%)*

	1971	1981	1991	1994
Life assurance and pension funds	15	16	27	33
Dwellings (net of mortgage debt)	26	36	37	28
Stocks, shares and unit trusts	23	8	8	10
National Savings, notes and coin and bank deposits	13	10	9	9
Shares and deposits with building societies	7	8	8	8
Non-marketable tenancy rights	12	12	8	7
Other fixed assets	10	10	5	5
Other financial assets net of liabilities	−6	–	−2	–
Total (= 100%) (£ billion at 1994 prices[1])	1172	1416	2529	2551

[1] Adjusted to 1994 prices using the consumers' expenditure deflator.
Source: Social Trends, 26, Chart 5.20.

again, it is worth making the point that the real wealth of the personal sector has almost doubled since 1979 (although the gains have not been equally distributed), and also noting that the relative preference for different forms of wealth has changed quite materially.

3.2 Personal Income, Consumption and Saving

☐ 3.2.1 Consumption Rules OK?

Before we turn to analyse the database a few introductory words are in order. Consumption holds the key to the behaviour of the UK economy. Adam Smith, who should be mentioned in all self-respecting books on political economy, knew all about this two centuries ago. 'Consumption is the sole end and purpose of all production', he wrote in *The Wealth of Nations*. Elsewhere, he noted that England was 'a nation that is governed by shopkeepers'. Perhaps what he should have said is that England is a nation of **shoppers**. The British do not habitually take to the streets to protest, nor indeed to vote in local elections. They know that, irrespective of who governs them, the shops will be full, and that they can express their position in society through what they buy. It should not be forgotten that Britain has an amazingly efficient system of retail distribution – just compare it with that of Japan, a country which is more efficient at **making** things but hopelessly inefficient at **distributing** them (it even has a law preventing the spread of department stores). However, the Japanese are hardly likely to agree with Adam Smith's assertion that 'The interest of the producers ought to be attended to, only so far as it may be necessary for promoting that of the consumer'.

If readers have seen old newspapers they will know that their primary function was to spread information about what was on offer. It is, therefore, hardly surprising that the demand side of the economy came to dominate economic thought, as in the work of Keynes, rather than the supply side. When Macmillan expressed the opinion that the British had 'never had it so good', he was being

deadly serious – governments are elected in Britain by looking after the interests of consumers. What consumers want (the 'feel-good' factor) is low interest rates, rising real incomes and house prices but not rising prices elsewhere in the economy. On the other hand, despite a widespread belief to the contrary, the fact that so many people are unemployed seems to have had remarkably little effect upon voting patterns since 1979 although the **duration** and **unpredictability of unemployment** has recently come to the fore as a major contributor to the current 'feel-bad' factor which will undoubtedly affect voting patterns in 1997.

It has not traditionally been especially difficult for the government to generate the urge among consumers to go shopping, as Chancellor Lawson discovered in the late 1980s. Nor is it normally easy to destroy their confidence to the extent that they lose the desire to shop. However, it can be done, as recent experience testifies. In the sections which follow we will have much more to say on these matters.

☐ 3.2.2 Personal Income

Personal income consists of wages and salaries, employers' national insurance contributions, current grants from general government and other personal income. In total these constitute much the largest element of national income. However, the term 'personal' is somewhat ambiguous in that it refers not merely to individuals but to incorporated businesses, private non-profit-making bodies and life assurance and pension funds. The latter three elements are largely excluded in data for 'household' incomes, but in making this distinction there are particular difficulties with, for example, the earnings of entrepreneurs who are, in effect, individual person and business rolled into one. Measured at current prices, personal income has risen continuously since 1979, and its annual rate of growth has averaged roughly ten per cent.

Personal income net of income taxes, social security contributions and transfer payments is called **personal disposable income** (PDI). While

PDI is understandably more volatile than pre-tax income, given that tax regimes can be altered at specified points in time, the longer-term trends are very similar and exhibit an almost identical rate of growth. The individual components of pre-tax personal income can mostly be measured quite accurately (±3 per cent or less) and the same is true for income tax and social security contribu-

Figure 3.1   *Personal Income, 1981–95, Quarterly at 1990 Prices*

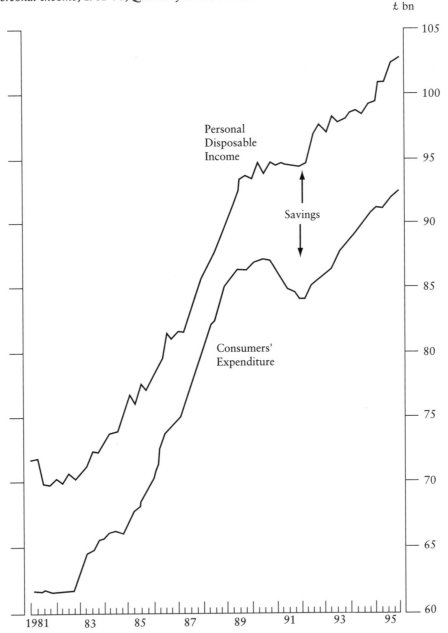

£ bn

Personal
Disposable
Income

Savings

Consumers'
Expenditure

Source: Economic Trends, Table 2.5, Annual Supplement Table 1.6.

tions. However, the subtraction of the latter from the former inevitably renders PDI less accurate than either (± between 3 and 10 per cent).

Figure 3.1 plots PDI in real (inflation-adjusted) terms from 1981–95. As can be seen, it started to rise quite rapidly as the economy came out of recession in 1982. It slowed down abruptly at the onset of the next recession, remained more or less constant for a period of two years, and since the beginning of 1992 has risen patchily. It is accordingly evident that in terms of their spending power, most people in the UK did very well during the Thatcher years, but that the 1990s have so far been a disappointment.

☐ 3.2.3 Consumers' Expenditure

Consumers' expenditure represents the consumption not merely of households but of the other non-household parts of the personal sector. Nevertheless, household consumption constitutes 90 per cent of the total, and it is reasonable to treat the former as a close approximation of the other. Consumers' expenditure is plotted in real terms in **Figure 3.1**, where the quarterly data are seasonally adjusted. This is necessary because consumption always surges in the final quarter of each year due to Xmas shopping, and the unadjusted data give the false impression that this heralds an ongoing upturn in expenditure.

As can be seen, consumers' expenditure rose even more rapidly than PDI during the second half of the 1980s, in the process squeezing the residual which represents savings. However, it came to a virtual standstill before the recession really set in, only to collapse back at the end of the decade, in the process driving many consumer good companies to the wall. It bottomed out at the end of 1991 at the level of three years previously, and subsequently began to climb continuously at roughly the long-term trend rate, albeit not at the rate customary during the mid-1980s (see *Bank of England Inflation Report*, February 1990, p. 20). One important observation, to which we will return, is that even in the recession an excessive amount of consumption took the form of imported products. In very recent times,

Figure 3.2   *Consumption as a Percentage of GDP*[a]

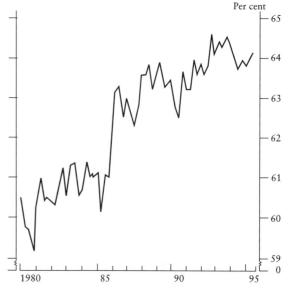

(a)   At current market prices

Source: Bank of England Inflation Report, February 1996, Chart 3.4.

consumption has been boosted by the fact that half of the gross spending on the National Lottery (the part not given out as prizes) is included in consumption.

An alternative way of expressing the data on consumption is as a percentage of GDP, as in **Figure 3.2**. This brings out even more clearly than **Figure 3.1** the consequences of the surge in real consumption during the latter part of the 1980s followed by the effects of the recession. It is too early to say whether the ratio will settle around a new equilibrium of 64–65 per cent, but the pattern of **Figure 3.1** provides some support for this possibility.

Figure 3.3 breaks consumption down into a number of selected categories on an inflation-adjusted basis. Between 1971 and 1996, total real consumers' expenditure rose by roughly 80 per cent. In spite of this, beer consumption fell slightly and tobacco consumption fell by 30 per cent. Expenditure on food rose very slightly in real terms, which is not unexpected given that people do not tend to eat all that much more as

Figure 3.3   *Consumers' Expenditure at Constant Prices, by Selected Item, UK, 1975–95*

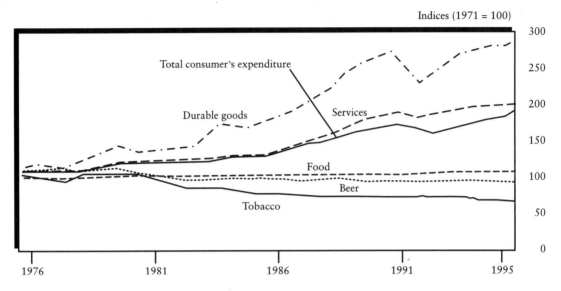

Source: *Economic Trends, Annual Supplement*, Table 1.7.

they get richer (low income elasticity), especially if it is fashionable to be slim. On the other hand, real expenditure on durable goods rose sharply during the 1980s and, having been badly affected by the recession, has risen again almost to three times its 1971 level. In 1995, 97 per cent of households had a colour television (74 per cent in 1981), but the black and white set, owned by 20 per cent in 1981, had virtually disappeared by 1995; 89 per cent a washing machine (78 per cent in 1981); 88 per cent a deep freezer/fridge freezer (only 49 per cent in 1981); 91 per cent a telephone (75 per cent in 1981); 50 per cent a tumble drier (23 per cent in 1981); 77 per cent a video; 67 per cent a microwave; ; 47 per cent a CD player; 24 per cent a home computer; and 19 per cent a dishwasher (all of the latter being (almost) unknown in 1981). Furthermore, the fact that over 90 per cent of households with dependent children possess a colour TV, washing machine, deep freezer and video recorder demonstrates that even the relatively poor are not denied the use of modern durable goods (see also *The Economist*, 1996).

From the mid-1980s onwards, real consumption of services also began to soar. This was predict-able in that the market for available durable goods was reaching saturation (although, for example, households began to acquire a TV for every adult and every child). Services temporarily stalled in the recession, but have subsequently resumed their steady upwards progress, reaching a level twice that of 1971 by 1995.

Table 3.2 indicates how these trends have affected the spending patterns of UK households. Food has become proportionately much less important (the Common Agricultural Policy notwithstanding), and there have been significant reductions in alcohol, tobacco (pre-1990), clothing (pre-1990) and fuel and power (post-1985). Transport has become more important, although it reached a peak in 1989 and has subsided back to the proportion customary in the late 1980s. Housing has shot up to record proportions after a sharp drop between 1989 and 1990 (caused by the fact that whereas domestic rates were previously included, the community charge (and council tax) was not) due in part to the Conservative government's switch to market-driven rents. However, it is the somewhat catch-all 'other goods, services and adjustments' where

Table 3.2 *Share of Total Household Expenditure at Current Prices, UK*

	1976	1981	1985	1987	1989	1991	1993	1995
Food	19.2	16.3	14.4	13.2	12.2	12.4	11.7	11.1
Alcoholic Drink	7.6	7.3	7.4	6.7	6.2	6.6	6.1	6.0
Tobacco	4.1	3.6	3.3	2.9	2.6	2.7	2.7	2.7
Clothing and footwear	7.7	6.7	7.0	6.8	6.2	5.9	5.9	5.9
Housing	13.6	14.9	15.4	15.2	15.3	14.5	15.7	16.5
Fuel and power	4.7	5.1	4.9	4.2	3.6	4.0	3.7	3.4
Household goods and services	7.6	6.9	6.7	6.7	6.7	6.4	6.5	6.3
Transport and communication	15.4	17.2	17.4	17.9	18.6	17.6	17.6	17.7
Recreation, entertainment and education	9.2	9.4	9.4	9.4	9.6	9.8	10.2	10.7
Other goods, services and adjustments	10.8	12.5	14.1	17.0	19.0	20.1	19.9	19.7
Total	100.0	100.0	100.0	100.0	100.0	100.0	100.0	100.0

Source: UK National Accounts, Table 4.7.

the increase is most marked, although it has not changed much since 1989. For example, the practice of eating out has become much more common over the past two decades, but the biggest change of all has been the practice of taking foreign holidays.

It is also worth noting that attention in the media is addressed to trends in **retail sales** as a guide to trends in consumers' expenditure, since the former are published on a provisional basis much earlier than the latter. However, it must be borne in mind that, for example, whilst food represents roughly 12 per cent of consumers' expenditure, it represents roughly 40 per cent of retail sales which exclude energy, rent and rates and other services. Hence, in the short term, retail sales may prove a very unreliable guide to trends in the larger aggregate.

As can be seen from **Table 3.3**, PDI is, by definition, either **consumed** or **saved**. The proportion saved (the **saving ratio**) is specified in **Table 3.3**, and it follows that the proportion consumed, known technically as the average propensity to consume (APC), is given by the formula '1 − saving ratio'. This fell below 90 per cent during the recession, which taking the official data at face value appears not to have happened

since the late 1970s (see *Social Trends*, 26, Chart 6.20). It should be borne in mind that, because consumption is determined by PDI rather than gross income, savings tend to fall somewhat when the tax and national insurance burdens rise. Between 1983 and 1987, for example, total deductions rose from 21.20 to 21.45 per cent of total income, whereas the saving ratio fell sharply other than in 1984, the only year in which total deductions fell as a proportion of gross income. While this relationship must be treated with caution, it does suggest that when the government removes demand from the economy via taxation, consumption steps into the breach to maintain demand.

During the late 1980s, consumers' expenditure rose faster than PDI. It appears to have been the case that consumers not merely spent the whole of their PDI but borrowed in order to finance yet more consumption. As the subsequent discussion on saving indicates, such behaviour may not repeat itself for a long time to come, but the Chancellor, in his Spring 1993 Budget, announced that taxes would rise sharply, commencing in the 1994–95 financial year, and once again consumption appears to have been maintained in part by running down savings.

Table 3.3 *Personal Income, Expenditure and Saving, 1985–95 (£ bn)*

	1985	*1987*	*1989*	*1991*	*1992*	*1993*	*1994*	*1995*
Wages and salaries	169.1	200.4	248.5	290.3	300.9	308.2	318.7	331.7
Employers' contributions	26.5	29.4	34.4	40.2	41.2	43.6	46.3	46.1
Current grants	46.8	52.5	56.8	69.3	80.0	88.4	92.6	96.5
Other personal income	62.6	78.9	103.9	116.7	125.8	131.9	139.3	158.9
Total personal income	305.0	361.2	443.6	516.5	547.9	572.1	596.9	633.2
Less deductions:								
Taxes on income	37.7	43.4	53.6	63.4	65.2	63.6	68.2	74.7
Social security contributions	24.2	28.6	32.9	36.4	37.0	39.5	41.9	44.3
Miscellaneous current deductions	1.7	2.1	2.4	2.7	2.5	2.9	2.9	2.8
Community charge	–	–	0.6	8.1	7.9	8.0	8.4	9.0
Personal disposable income (PDI)	241.4	287.1	354.1	405.8	435.3	458.1	475.5	502.4
Less consumers' expenditure	217.9	267.5	330.5	365.0	383.5	406.4	427.3	447.2
Balance: personal saving	23.5	19.6	23.6	40.8	51.8	51.7	48.2	55.2
Saving ratio %[1]	9.7	6.8	6.6	10.1	11.9	11.3	10.1	11.0

Note:
[1] Saving as % of PDI.
Source: Monthly Digest of Statistics, Table 1.5; UK National Accounts 1996, Table 4.1.

☐ *3.2.4 Saving*

National Saving is the sum of private (personal and company) saving and public saving. **Personal saving** is the difference between PDI and consumers' expenditure. In principle, it is equal to personal investment plus the personal sector's acquisition of financial assets **net** of personal borrowing. **Company saving** is the residual income of companies net of tax, profits remitted abroad, transfers and payments of interest and dividends. Company expenditure on durable goods in the form of fixed investment and stocks is **not** deducted from their income in measuring company saving, but depreciation is. **Public saving** is the difference between the public sector's current receipts and current expenditure, and is broadly equivalent to public sector net investment **less** public sector borrowing (or **plus** public sector debt repayment).

The discussion of saving in the media is concerned primarily with the personal sector, although as we will note later, this is somewhat misguided. Unfortunately, personal sector saving is a very unreliable statistic (potentially up to 20 per cent inaccurate in either direction) as it is the difference between two somewhat inaccurate figures for PDI and consumers' expenditure respectively. Furthermore, the distinction between consumption expenditure on durable goods and saving can be a fine one. Whereas, for example, the purchase of a car is treated as current consumption in the statistics, many purchasers would see the accumulation of a deposit and the repayment of the residual purchase price as an act of **saving**. On occasion, the ONS redefines consumption as saving (for example, DIY expenditure in 1984), and more generally the saving ratio tends to be retrospectively adjusted in each year's 'Blue Book'. The ratios recorded during the 1970s have been particularly reduced – with, for example, a downgrading of each of the previous seven years ratios by almost 1 per cent in the 1987 'Blue Book'.

A further consideration obscures the meaning of saving, namely that whereas personal payments into a private pension fund are counted as saving, contributions to the government's pension and social security schemes are not. Obviously, if the latter were not deducted from gross income, both PDI and the saving ratio (including such payments) would be considerably larger. Finally, as noted earlier, it is evident that, whereas interest payments on a mortgage constitute consumption, that part of the monthly repayment which expunges part of the capital owed to the lender must transfer wealth to the borrower, and in that sense is clearly an act of saving.

In many ways, it is surprising that the saving ratio is treated with the reverence it is accorded in the media. As shown in Cullison (1990), the official saving ratio in the USA, which is considerably lower than in the UK, is widely regarded as a nonsense, with estimates of the true rate varying from twice the official rate to an astonishing six times the official rate.

Figure 3.4 *The Personal Savings Ratio, 1958–95 (%)*

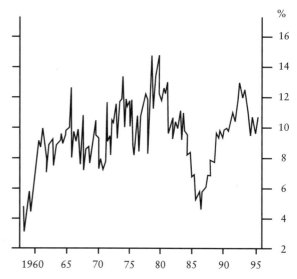

Source: Bank of England Quarterly Bulletin. Economic Trends, Table 2.5.

As noted in *Barclays Bank Review* (February 1990, p. 17) the ratio derived from identified financial transactions is almost twice as high as the official ratio. When it comes to saving, therefore,

Table 3.4 *Composition of Consumer Credit, UK, 1984–95 (% and £ bn)*

	1984	1986	1988	1990	1992	1993	1993	1994	1995
Bank credit card lending	14.8	17.2	15.8	17.1	18.7	20.0	–	–	–
Credit cards	–	–	–	–	–	–	20.1	20.4	21.2
Bank loans[1]	63.2	61.6	64.8	64.0	62.7	58.5	–	–	–
Banks[2]	–	–	–	–	–	–	78.4	77.0	76.5
Finance houses[3]	9.9	11.9	10.9	10.4	9.5	–	–	–	–
Other specialist lenders	–	–	–	–	–	–	12.6	14.1	15.5
Insurance companies	3.1	2.6	2.3	2.3	2.7	3.0	2.8	2.2	1.8
Retailers	9.0	6.6	5.6	4.7	5.0	5.1	4.9	4.8	4.1
Building societies	0.0	0.0	0.6	1.5	1.4	1.5	1.5	1.9	1.8
Credit outstanding at the end of year (= 100%) (£ bn)	22.3	30.2	42.5	52.6	53.0	52.5	53.3	58.2	65.1

Notes:
[1] Banks and all other institutions authorised to take deposits under the Banking Act 1987.
[2] Finance houses and other credit companies.
[3] Including share of credit cards.

Source: Financial Statistics, Table 3.2B.

the most sensible approach is, as usual, to take a long-term series defined on a consistent basis, so that there is a clear view of the trend even if not of the absolute magnitudes.

Figure 3.4 illustrates the official net personal saving ratio from 1958 to 1995. It is interesting to note that after a surge in 1960, it moved steadily upwards, on average, until 1980, peaking at this time at roughly 15 per cent. From 1980 to 1988 it was more or less downhill all the way, with the ratio bottoming out in 1988 at less than 5 per cent. The onset of recession witnessed a steady, quite rapid climb back to 13 per cent in 1992Q2, a pattern heavily reminiscent of the early 1960s, followed by a sharp decline back to 9.4 per cent in 1994Q2. Since then, it has fluctuated between 9.2 and 10.5 per cent. This raises the issue as to what can reasonably be regarded as a 'typical' rate of personal saving. The evidence of the 1960s and 1970s indicates a 'typical' pattern fluctuating in the region of 10 per cent, but the period since 1979 has yet to see any sign at all of an equilibrium being restored in the region of that or any other number.

It is evident that there was at least one big difference between the 1980–81 recession and that of 1990–92, namely the saving ratio at the commencement of each period. This is unsurprising when one considers the changes in the personal sector's balance sheet during the 1980s. As we have noted, net wealth is much higher in relation to income compared to a decade ago and, more importantly, the personal sector is loaded up with liabilities which, being financial, are not subject to asset price inflation.

Between 1982 and 1989, total credit outstanding (in addition to mortgage liabilities) in Britain rose in money terms from £15 billion to £45 billion, and to well over £30 billion in inflation-adjusted terms. **Table 3.4** disaggregates the problem from 1984 to 1995. It is slightly difficult to interpret since the finance houses disappeared from the table in 1992 and in 1993 the table was significantly reformatted. However, it would appear that prior to the onset of recession, there was little variability in the sources of credit. The building societies were allowed to enter the market through a change in the law, but had very little

impact. The main loss of market share affected retailers as more and more customers switched to national credit cards, although their absolute level of business remained high. Post-1992 the banks continud to lose customers as did retailers and insurance companies. Credit card borrowing increased in popularity, but an influx of new companies diverted demand away from the banks.

In money terms, total credit remained virtually static throughout the recession, implying a reduction in real terms. However, this disguises somewhat the fact that the balance between new borrowing and repayment of debt had begun to alter significantly, and by the middle of 1992, as shown in **Figure 3.5**, there was actually a net repayment of debt, albeit briefly, which may not seem particularly strange until one puts it into the context of

Figure 3.5　*Net consumer credit*[1]

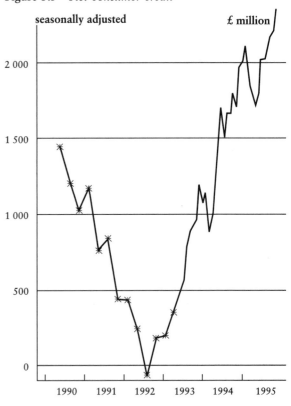

Note: [1] Quarterly data until April 1993, three month summation thereafter.
Source: Economic Trends, February 1996, Chart 3.

the rampant consumerism of the previous decade. Just how dramatic the turnaround has been is well illustrated by the data on retail sales, as shown in **Figure 3.6**. To say that the 'shop till you drop' philosophy had gone out of fashion would clearly be an understatement. Furthermore, although retail sales had recovered by the end of 1992, they remain highly volatile, and indeed collapsed again at the end of 1994 and in mid-1995.

The debt burden is depicted in **Figure 3.7**, which illustrates how unusual the behaviour of consumers was in the early 1990s – it was previously seen a full two decades earlier in a very different inflationary context. This is particularly evident when the burden of interest payments is taken into account. Unlike in the early 1970s, the low inflation (and hence low interest rate) environment of the early 1990s produced a hugely geared effect of debt repayment upon interest

charges. Clearly, therefore, this is one area where the UK economy is not beating to the drum of history.

3.2.5 Why the Saving Ratio Varies Over Time

At this juncture it may be useful to pull together the strands of the previous discussion in order to analyse why the saving ratio may vary over time. It is useful to start with the relationship between inflation and consumption/saving behaviour. The traditional view was that once people came to realise that the value of money would be adversely affected by inflation, they would rush out to spend it as quickly as possible. This view was broadly supported by behaviour during the overseas hyper-inflations of the prewar period, but the relatively modest price rises manifested in the UK since 1970 appear to have stimulated more mixed behaviour, with the saving ratio rising during the high (by UK standards) inflation of the 1970s, then falling with more modest inflation in the 1980s. There are a number of ways of explaining this, and their relative merits are unlikely ever to be satisfactorily distinguished since they are, in any event, significantly interdependent.

For example, if a person sets out to maintain the **real**, rather than the **nominal** value of his or her savings, he or she will be obliged to increase the nominal value of those savings at the same rate as prices are rising. Furthermore, since high rates of inflation generally go hand in hand with rising unemployment, people who fear that they may lose their jobs may try to build up a pool of savings in order to cushion their potential loss of income. Equally, if prices of consumer goods are rising so rapidly that people feel that they will never be able to afford to buy them, they may decide to give up trying to do so and save instead.

The role of interest rates in all of this is hard to divine. Since interest rates, in nominal terms, tend to rise with inflation, the sacrifice in terms of interest foregone when buying consumer goods must itself be rising. However, the real rate of interest was negative during the mid-1970s at a time of very high nominal rates, and positive in the

Figure 3.6 *Volume of Retail Sales*

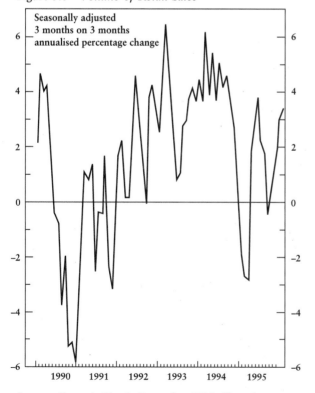

Source: Economic Trends, December 1995, Chart 2.

Figure 3.7   *Personal Sector Debt Burden*

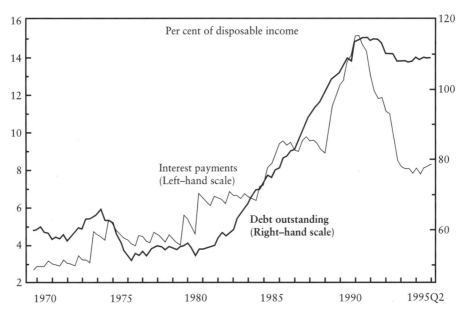

Source: Financial Statement and Budget Report 1996–97, Chart 3.7.

mid-1980s at a time of much lower nominal rates. One could accordingly have expected savings to be higher rather than lower in the later period (assuming, of course, that savers were not suffering in the 1970s from **money illusion** – the illusion that nominal and real rates are the same). In fact, correlating savings against real rates of interest appears to indicate a rather weak relationship. This may, in turn, reflect the fact that financial deregulation has made it increasingly easy for people to borrow, and hence the principle that one has to save before one buys a costly item (even a house) has steadily been eroded. Rather perversely at first sight, people may continue to put increasingly large sums of money into life assurance and pension funds and simultaneously borrow to finance current consumption. Savings are defined net of borrowing, so increased borrowing reduces the saving ratio. However, the borrower is unlikely to view borrowing as dissaving. Indeed, pension fund contributions may well be compulsory rather than voluntary, and hence be dismissed as having no direct bearing on decisions about current consumption. In 1980, after adjusting for contributions to life insurance and pension funds, the personal sector still placed 30 per cent of its savings on a discretionary basis, whereas by 1986 this latter figure had become negative.

A broader view of these factors may be termed the **wealth effect**. Over the long haul – and indeed in most individual years – the value of property has tended to rise faster than prices in general. Equally, the value of company shares has easily outstripped inflation over the past decade, and more recently, though not previously, post-tax rates of interest have also outstripped inflation. As a result, people who own assets (currently, in practice, the majority of households) will tend to feel wealthier as time passes, and hence feel less need to convert current income into wealth via saving. This will also reflect the increased probability of inheritance.

One could also reasonably expect consumers to smooth their spending over the business cycle, maintaining it in recessions while boosting it very modestly in booms. This would cause saving to be pro-cyclical, falling in recessions and rising in booms. Unfortunately, this does not accord with

UK experience since as we have already noted, the saving ratio was extremely high in 1980–81 and rose sharply during the recent recession after falling right back during the mid-1980s boom.

This ties in with our previous point, since it is clear that the period of falling house prices, both in nominal as well as real terms, during the early 1990s must have affected people's perceptions about their wealth and the long-term security provided by their assets. As a result, they evidently chose to save much more to provide security against the possibility of rainier days ahead. This was also supported by several other factors. For example, the sharp rise in unemployment at the end of the 1980s introduced an added element of uncertainty, more especially because it struck not only at the relatively unskilled in the North but at the relatively skilled in the South where house prices were falling most rapidly. A further consideration was the dawning realisation that with so many people living to a grand old age, and needing to be looked after at enormous expense in nursing homes, inheritances could melt away to nothing much at all. Finally, it is important to remember that the saving ratio is calculated net of liabilities, and there was a sharp contrast between the huge growth in liabilities in the mid-1980s and the much reduced level of borrowing commencing at the end of the decade. In effect, it was as much a case of people borrowing less as of people saving more, in response to the factors described above.

A final factor relates to the **age structure of the population**. The bulk of savings are accumulated by people between the ages of 45 and 65. Younger people have heavy outgoings incurred in setting up homes and raising families, whereas the elderly earn little and may need to eat into past savings as noted above. The high birth rate immediately after the Second World War has produced an exceptionally large generation which is now entering its period of high savings, and this is likely to buoy up savings during the 1990s.

All the above inevitably sows the seeds of doubt about our ability to forecast trends in saving. Nevertheless, it is also important not to interpret saving purely within the context of the personal sector. The Bank of England, utilising a somewhat different approach to the calculation of savings from that used previously, aggregated the savings of the personal sector, company sector and public sector, all expressed as a percentage of GDP at factor cost. From this it would appear that the decline in personal saving was offset by an increase in company saving from 1979 to 1988, whereas the saving of the public sector remained consistently negative until 1987. As a result, total savings at current prices showed a remarkable degree of stability from 1980 to 1988. However, calculations done by Eurostat and the OECD indicate that there was a fairly sharp drop in gross national saving in 1986 and a further drop after 1990. This particularly reflected the fact the public sector returned to deficit, since the personal sector tended to move the other way. The evidence suggests that although the private sector saves more when the public sector saves less, the compensation is by no means total. According to the OECD (see *OECD Economic Outlook*), the UK sits at the bottom of their members' league table, at around 15 per cent as compared to the 20+ per cent common throughout the European Union. One minor consolation is that the overall reduction of roughly 5 per cent since 1970 has taken place throughout the EU as well as in the UK, reflecting the widespread problem of public sector indebtedness, so the UK's relative position has not changed (see also Jenkinson, 1996).

The government has been somewhat ambivalent about the necessity to offer incentives to savers, although pressure from the media was such as to induce a 'Savers' Budget' in 1990. It is somewhat ironic that the government has subsequently found it difficult to induce people to go out and **spend** in more recent times as an antidote to recession.

■ 3.3 The Housing Market

It has become increasingly apparent over the past decade and a half that the workings of the housing market play an extremely important role in the conduct of economic policy. The liberalisation of financial markets in the early 1980s led to much increased competition between banks, building societies and other intermediaries to make loans secured against housing. These, as the banks had belatedly discovered, were much less risky than lending to sovereign states.

The effects of liberalisation were to weaken prudential controls in the housing market. Prior to the 1980s, owner-occupation was subsidised, firstly insofar as tax relief was given on mortgage interest payments (up to a loan limit of £25 000, which in the mid-1970s bought a substantial house anywhere outside London), and secondly because houses were not subject to capital gains tax. Not surprisingly, owner-occupation was very popular, as shown in **Figure 3.8**. However, most of the money provided in the mortgage market originated in retail (High St) deposits in building society branches, and there were accordingly periodic famines and few feasts. As a result, mortgages were rationed and this made it almost impossible for borrowers to over-extend themselves. Large deposits were required, and a loan of 2.5 times income, or even less, was the norm.

Once capital controls were dismantled in 1979, and wholesale finance became available in a more competitive market, prospective borrowers found it progressively easier to demand reduced deposits and much higher income multiples (generally taking into account second incomes as well). As a result, total mortgage debt in Britain, already high in 1982 (at 32 per cent of GDP) soared to 60 per cent of GDP by 1990, by far the highest ratio of the major economies. Only in the USA, where all mortgage debt is tax-deductible, did anything like such a surge take place. In Germany, by way of contrast, where home loans cannot exceed 60 per cent of the value of a property and where interest payments attract no tax relief, mortgage debt actually fell as a proportion of GDP.

The owner-occupied stock of dwellings shown in **Figure 3.8** represented roughly 68 per cent of the total stock in 1995, growing at the expense primarily of the public rental sectors. An important factor in this respect was the legislation giving local authority/new town tenants the right to buy their properties at heavily discounted prices (see *Social Trends, 26,* Chart 10.7), resulting in a steady 100 000 to 200 000 properties being transferred every year after 1981, although sales have slowed noticeably since 1991.

Figure 3.8　*Stock of Dwellings by Tenure, UK, 1971–94 (million)*

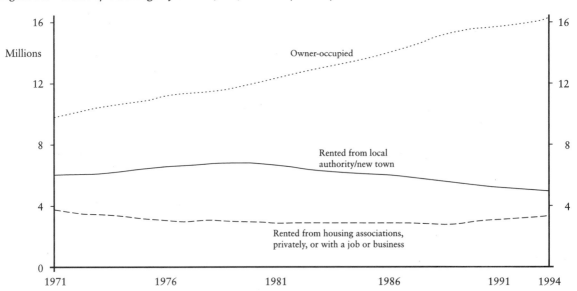

Source: Social Trends, 25 (1995 edn), Chart 10.1; *Social Trends,* 26 (1996 edn), Chart 10.3.

Table 3.5 *The UK Housing Market*

If we compare the housing market and the housing finance system in the UK with those of other advanced economies, several features stand out (see also *Bank of England Quarterly Bulletin*, February 1991, pp. 56–66). These features have become less prominent over the past five years as the housing market has adjusted to its difficult trading conditions and problems of bad debts.

- mortgage lending is relatively long-term;
- unusually small deposits are required;
- income multipliers are relatively high;
- the private rental sector is relatively regulated;
- house prices on average run further ahead of retail prices;
- personal savings are relatively low;
- mortgage debt is high relative to GDP;
- equity withdrawal via a remortgage is relatively easy;
- mortgages are subsidised, which is uncommon;
- there is relatively little tax on capital gains.

The US housing market bears the closest resemblance to that of the UK, but things are quite different in Germany and Japan. In the latter countries, for example, it is not customary to lend more than 60 per cent of the value of a property, so it is not surprising that their inhabitants save much more than their counterparts in the UK, who expect to borrow at least 90 per cent of a new property.

In the case of Japan, the high rate of savings also reflects an acute shortage of building land which results in such high property prices that first-time buyers are frequently unable to enter the market until they are relatively old, if at all. It is also a demonstrable proposition that countries such as Japan, Germany and France, with the least developed systems of housing finance, have the highest personal saving ratios.

As it happens, even at its current historically-high level, owner-occupancy in the UK is only slightly higher than in the USA, Japan and Canada, and well below that in Ireland, Norway, Spain and Greece (see *Social Trends*, 26, Chart 10.4). However, during the 1980s one unpleasant side-effect of an otherwise generally popular rise in owner-occupancy was that it was becoming increasing burdensome in terms of mortgage interest tax relief, as shown in **Figure 3.9**. Furthermore, the strong demand for owner-occupied houses drove up house prices, at times so rapidly that they outstripped retail prices by a comfortable margin. The period to 1989 could truly be said to be characterised by the phenomenon of **asset price inflation**. However, a point which it is worth bearing in mind in this regard is that the inflation of house prices has always been much more closely related to the inflation of land values, since prime residential building land is very scarce, than to the inflation of building costs.

The tendency for house prices to rise over time, in both nominal and real terms, is common to all advanced economies (see Cutler, 1995), and reflects growing populations, rising real incomes and inelastic supply. However, the added element in the case of the UK was that during the latter part of the 1980s the slackening of prudential controls quite simply got out of hand. Not only did 100 per cent mortgages become commonplace (although a building society was typically only responsible for the first 80 per cent and an insurance company for the rest), but sums in excess of the buying price were also happily advanced on the grounds that house prices would rapidly catch up (see Cutler, 1995, Chart 7). The Department of the Environment calculated in 1989 that 36 per cent of first-time buyers had mortgages in excess of the value of their property. The effects of this can be seen in a number of ways, of which the most significant is shown as **Figure 3.10**.

Figure 3.9　*Total Cost of Mortgage Interest Tax Relief,[1] UK*

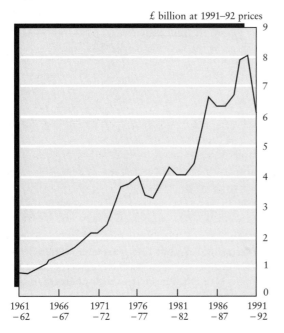

£ billion at 1991–92 prices

Note:
[1] Includes expenditure on option mortgage scheme.
Source: Social Trends, 23 (1993 edn), Chart 8.22.

Figure 3.10　*Personal Sector: Income and Capital Gearing*

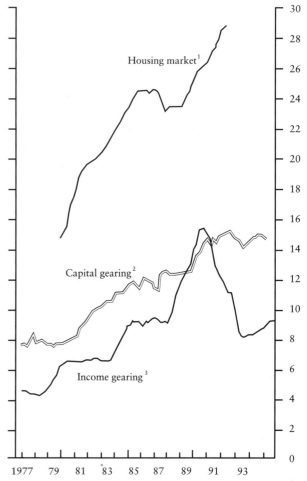

Notes:
[1] Stock of lending to persons for house purchase as a proportion of the value of owner-occupied housing stock.
[2] Borrowing from banks and building societies as a proportion of net personal sector financial and physical assets.
[3] Ratio of gross interest payments to PDI.
Source: Compiled from the *Bank of England Quarterly Bulletin* (various).

Figure 3.10 illustrates two aspects of the personal sector's capital gearing. The first of these covers bank and building society lending as a proportion of total net personal assets, which roughly doubled in the course of the 1980s. As the economy moved out of recession in 1983, real personal disposable income began to grow rapidly, and this provided the leverage for households to opt for owner occupancy and to attempt to move up the housing ladder by borrowing ever-larger sums. The number of house transactions began to rise inexorably towards two million per year, as shown in **Figure 3.11**, but there were also more people chasing each property which drove up prices. This can be seen in **Figure 3.10** as a sharp increase in the value of the owner-occupied housing stock represented by lending rather than paid-up capital.

There was a parallel increase in income gearing, which measures the ratio of gross interest payments to PDI. However, the real explosion did not

take place until 1987, at which time house prices began to rise so rapidly that they eventually doubled in nominal terms throughout almost all of the UK, although the process effectively rolled out of London and the South East towards other

Figure 3.11 *House Transactions (millions) in England and Wales*

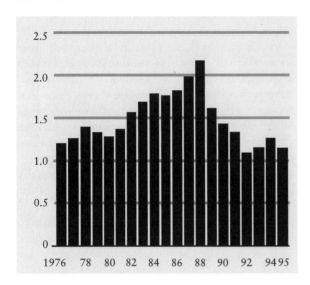

Source: Economic Trends, Table 5.6.

areas. This can be seen in **Figure 3.12** which illustrates nominal and real house price growth. The nominal increase in 1987–88 was about the same as in 1979–80, and somewhat less than in 1973–74, but these were periods of much higher general inflation such that real house prices in 1987–88 rose faster than at any time other than in 1973–74.

The effects show up in **Figure 3.10** as a dramatic rise in the housing market capital gearing line, but more notably in the income gearing line because interest rates rose sharply in belated recognition of the fall-out from this enormous increase in personal wealth. We have already noted in our previous discussion of consumption that the surge in wealth, and effectively in collateral, appears to have triggered over-consumption and an associated collapse in saving, leading to the appearance of a huge personal sector financial deficit. This also reflected the phenomenon of **equity withdrawal**. The sale of inherited houses to release cash was nothing new, but it was progressively dawning on householders that the constantly rising value of their homes was providing a

Figure 3.12 *Real and Nominal House Price Growth*

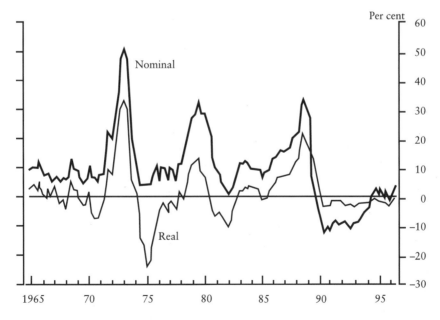

Source: Complied from the *Bank of England Quarterly Bulletin*.

cushion of equity between the market price and the outstanding mortgage which could be released by taking out a second mortgage. This desire to release liquidity was happily met by an endless stream of financial intermediaries which could not envisage the possibility of losing money since, after all, nominal house prices had never been known to fall. As a result, even more liquidity was released in addition to that released via inheritance, and yet more was released because when people moved house they typically did not reinvest all of their untaxed capital gains net of expenses, but rather increased their mortgages to reflect their higher incomes and pocketed the difference in cash. During the 1980s, the annual amount of equity withdrawal at 1990 prices was £9.5 billion, over ten times higher than during the 1970s (see Cutler, 1995, p. 264).

This phenomenon was very important because it provided the wherewithal for a very high level of consumption (particularly, as it happens, of imports), much of it associated with housing. This level of consumption was not sustainable in relation to net incomes, but the ready provision of credit, combined with increased collateral in the form of property, temporarily relieved most households of the worry traditionally associated with high levels of indebtedness. In this respect there was a link with the interest rate since that determined the servicing cost of the increased debt, and an important consideration at the time was that, as shown in **Figure** 20.2, interest rates were on a downwards trend from 1985 onwards, and had been brought down to an exceptionally low level in nominal terms in the aftermath of the stock market crash of October 1987.

Cheap mortgages naturally fuelled the desire to buy houses, and this can be seen clearly in **Figure 3.13** which plots the relationship between house prices and earnings. This relationship has a 'norm' to which it can be expected to revert in the medium term, although recent reductions in

Figure 3.13   *House Price: Earnings Ratio*[1]

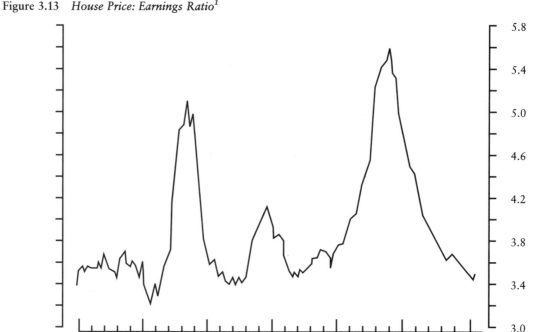

Note: [1] Department of Environment house price index ÷ average earnings.
Source: Compiled from the *Bank of England Quarterly Bulletin* and FSBR 1996–97, Chart 3.9.

the tax relief on interest payments may well have lowered the norm relative to the period pre-1979. The data suggest that this norm was traditionally in the region of 3.2 to 3.5. The peak value in 1989 was roughly 5.5, and, with hindsight, it is obvious that this was unsustainable. However, the more interesting phenomenon was the extraordinary collapse which began in 1989 and which turned the corner in mid-1996.

A major contributory factor was the doubling of the nominal interest rate from 7.5 per cent in 1988 to 15 per cent in 1990, since this hugely increased mortgage repayments as a proportion of net income. This shows up in respect of the income gearing line in **Figure 3.10** which rose above 14 per cent, over twice the level prevailing even in the early 1980s let alone the 1970s. In this context, it has to be said that the interest rate is a rather blunt weapon as an instrument for domestic demand management. Raising interest rates is unlikely to deter consumption unless it forces up monthly mortgage repayments to the point at which householders' pips squeak loudly, and even that may act with a lagged effect because so many

mortgages are currently readjusted only once a year. It also has to be said that the use of penal interest rates to regulate new mortgage borrowing serves to punish all other debtors at the same time.

The collapse in the housing market was indeed dramatic. At the end of 1989 the housing stock was worth, depending upon who you ask, in excess of £1000 billion, but one year later £100 billion of this had evaporated and this reduction has been continuing until very recently. However, the debt secured on domestic property has to be taken into account. According to the Halifax, for example, the net equity fell from £760 million in 1989 to £600 million in 1995, while the Nationwide estimate for 1995 is £490 million. Since these are at current prices, the real value of the net equity in 1989 has fallen much further, possibly by as much as one-half overall.

The situation after 1989 can be viewed from a variety of perspectives, as in **Figures 3.10, 3.11** and **3.12. Figure 3.11** shows that the number of house transactions fell back in 1992 to half the level prevailing in 1989. It is, however, **Figure 3.12**

Figure 3.14 *Percentage Deviation of Regional House Prices from the National Average Since 1983*

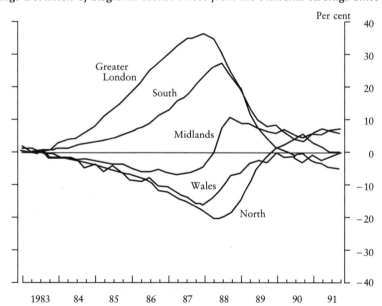

Source: Bank of England Quarterly Bulletin, Department of the Environment.

which illustrates the most extraordinary aspect of what happened, namely the unprecedented fall in **nominal** house prices which on average have fallen by 12 per cent from their peak. Furthermore, this fall was neither modest nor short-lived, as nominal prices have struggled for years to regain their 1989 levels. It is also notable that real house prices fell by a much lesser amount, and by less than in 1975 and 1981, because of the modest rates of inflation after 1990.

We have already observed that the surge in house prices rolled outwards from London. It is unsurprising, therefore, that the effects were somewhat dampened by the time the outermost regions of the UK were reached. At the time, this was perceived as something of a misfortune in these areas, but the subsequent impact of the collapse in demand was also disproportionately felt in those regions where the rises had been largest, and was of much less consequence elsewhere. This can be seen most clearly in **Figure 3.14** which expresses regional variations in house prices relative to the UK average. At the end of 1987 the gap between London and the North had become enormous, in the process making it financially impossible for anyone to move in a southerly direction. By the end of 1990, regional house prices had converged back to roughly the relative relationship previously seen in 1984. The nominal reductions this implied in London, and especially in East Anglia, were commonly of the order of 30 per cent, although as a consequence much property was withdrawn from the market to await better times.

For most households, the combination of an increasingly expensive mortgage and, for those who had entered the market when prices were at their highest in 1988–89, a house worth less than was owed to the mortgagee, was basically an inconvenience which forced a cut-back in consumption. They paid their monthly instalments and stayed put. For many, however, the situation was the recipe for disaster. If they could not afford the monthly repayments, perhaps as a result of unemployment, the arrears mounted up very quickly. This can be seen in **Table 3.6** which indicates that the number of loans in arrears by 6–12 months tripled between 1989 and 1992, and

the number in arrears by over 12 months rose more than ten-fold during the same period, although this reflected in part the reduction in interest rates over the period since it takes more months to repay an outstanding balance when the monthly instalment falls. On the other hand, many mortgagors had their arrears 'capitalised', thereby causing the arrears to disappear. Unsurprisingly, faced with the possibility that some mortgagors were unlikely to be able to repay anything of significance for the foreseeable future, most lenders opted for repossession, with the number of cases tripling in 1990 alone.

As noted, provided there is an ability to pay mortgage instalments, the fact that a property is worth less than the outstanding mortgage is not of itself an immediate problem for the householder. However, on a sufficient scale it is a problem for the economy as a whole because of the immobility it engenders, given a reluctance on the part of lenders to permit negative equity to be transferred from one property to another. The precise extent of negative equity is difficult to calculate, but by March 1993 the Bank had revised the total upwards to 1.8 million on the grounds that house prices had continued to fall sharply, and the total value of negative equity was estimated to be of the order of £12 billion, with one in three households with mortgages in the South East suffering. The Woolwich Building Society simultaneously estimated the number of households in negative equity at 1.6 million.

The government understandably felt under pressure to relieve these problems, but had no desire to do so in a manner that would once again run the risk of setting off the spiral of rising house prices and over-consumption. In November 1991, for example, a scheme was launched to make empty repossessed houses available to the homeless through housing associations. This was followed by a scheme to allow householders threatened by repossession to remain in their homes while paying rent rather than a mortgage. In December 1991, home-buyers were given an eight-month holiday from stamp duty on properties worth up to £250 000, and the government agreed to pay social security benefits designed to cover mortgage interest payments direct to the

Table 3.6 *Mortgage Lenders:*[1] *Number of Mortgages, Arrears and Possessions, UK (thousands)*

		Loans in arrears at end-period		Properties taken into possession in period
	Number of mortgages	By 6–12 months	By over 12 months	
1971	4506	17.6	..	2.8
1976	5322	16.0	..	5.0
1980	6210	15.5	..	3.5
1981	6336	21.5	..	4.9
1982	6518	27.4	5.5	6.9
1983	6846	29.4	7.5	8.4
1984	7313	48.3	9.5	12.4
1985	7717	57.1	13.1	19.3
1986	8138	52.1	13.0	24.1
1987	8283	55.5	15.0	26.4
1988	8564	42.8	10.3	18.5
1989	9125	66.8	13.8	15.8
1990	9415	123.1	36.1	43.9
1991	9815	183.6	91.7	75.5
1992	9922	205.0	147.0	68.5
1993	10 137	164.6	151.8	58.5
1994	10 375[2]	133.7	117.1	49.2
1995	–	108.0	89.0	49.4

Notes:

[1] Council of Mortgage Lenders estimates as at 31 December in each year. Estimates only cover members of the Council, but these account for more than 90 per cent of all mortgages outstanding.

[2] 30 June.

Source: Social Trends, 26 (1996 edn), Chart 10.7 updated.

lenders in order to prevent householders from 'squandering' the money on other things. However, these and other schemes, including the raising of the threshold to £60 000 before stamp duty became liable in the Spring 1993 Budget, ultimately made little difference.

The housing market has taken much longer to recover than was expected, and indeed was indicated by prior experience. In one obvious sense at least, affordability is no longer the issue in the housing market since it is beginning to resemble the situation last seen in the early 1970s. For example, **Figure 3.10** shows that income gearing, responding to a steady reduction in interest rates, is now back at the level of the mid-1980s, and the house price/earnings ratio has only recently bottomed out. As a result, a single adult aged 18–39 with a 90 per cent mortgage would have needed to pay out 65 per cent of average take-home earnings on mortgage interest payments in 1990, but only 20 per cent in 1995. However, this is not necessarily good news for all segments of the housing market since many first-time buyers can afford to ignore flats and terraced property and enter the market with the purchase of a semi-detached house.

The main problem must logically be one of confidence, reflecting in good part the experience of millions of households, both first and second hand, of unemployment during the early 1990s, together with the growing expectation that employment in the future will be less likely to be permanent. Confidence is slowly returning, but there was only a modest upturn in house prices in 1996, if only because supply tended to rise initially to meet demand. Meanwhile, the number of repossessions has remained at much the same level as in 1994 and 1995, according to the Council of Mortgage Lenders, although the number of households in negative equity, which turned up again to anything from the 1.15 million cited by the Woolwich (after allegedly falling below 1 million at the end of 1994) to the 1.7 million cited by the Nationwide, has begun to fall quite rapidly. According to the Nationwide, price falls in the North West shifted the burden of negative equity away from the South East but, on a more positive note, it also estimated in 1996 that the overall amount of negative equity had fallen to £8.3 billion, and some of that is undoubtedly covered by money tied up in endowment policies. The fact that the problem has taken so long to go away despite falling interest rates reflects, in part, the penalties exacted upon those in arrears, the recent reduction in mortgage tax relief to 15 per cent and the cut in housing benefits for those on income support during the first nine months of unemployment or sickness.

Householders are unlikely ever to forget completely the lesson that nominal house prices can fall as well as rise, and are likely to remain deterred by the scale of repossession for the foreseeable future. Furthermore, low nominal interest rates are nevertheless positive in real terms, more likely to rise in future than to fall, and little offset by tax relief. It is also worth noting that Personal Equity Plans and TESSAs currently provide alternative ways of accumulating tax-relieved assets, so housing is likely to be seen increasingly in terms of its value in use rather than its value as an investment. The notion of affordability looks quite different when placed in this context, but precisely what this implies for the conduct of economic policy remains to be seen.

However, two logical consequences are clearcut. In the first place, there is a strong correlation between housing transactions and consumer spending on durables. When people move house they typically spend several thousand pounds renovating fixtures and fittings. True, there is an incentive to engage in home improvements if people do not intend to move, but with house prices only rising slowly there is no longer much investment potential in such behaviour compared to the 1980s. Secondly, the so-called 'enterprise culture' is dependent upon housing equity as collateral to underwrite otherwise risky start-up loans. During the 1980s, VAT registrations rose by 5 per cent for every 10 per cent rise in house prices. It follows from the above discussion, therefore, that it will be difficult to restore the enterprise culture to full flower until such time as house prices pick up further and, more generally, that the 'feel-bad factor' is not merely deep-rooted but unresponsive to conventional ideas about the 'affordability' of property.

☐ *3.3.1 Housing and Inheritance*

During the 1980s, the idea took root that, with so many households owning property, in many cases outright, inheritance would provide the pool of capital that younger generations would otherwise have to accumulate the hard way via saving. The precise sums involved were poorly understood, but were assumed to be enormous and, indeed,

the extent of equity withdrawal in the housing market appeared to underpin this belief.

In practice, however, things were not quite what they seemed. According to Department of the Environment data (see Frosztega and Holmans, 1993) the total amount inherited by individuals in 1989–90, net of tax and expenses but excluding house sales prior to old people going to live with relatives or in residential and nursing homes, was £11.3 billion a year of which £4.9 billion came from dwellings. This represented less than 1 per cent of total marketable wealth. Furthermore, only a small percentage of inheritances exceeded £100 000 and more than half were worth less than £10 000, partly because of multiple beneficiaries.

Given the relatively advanced age at which people typically die, it is unsurprising that the median age at which inheritance was received was 47, at which age almost all inheritors already (part-)owned their own houses, so the inherited money was typically saved or invested, spent or used for home improvements. Using inheritances to 'trade-up' to better property was fairly unusual.

Unfortunately, even this limited largesse 'cascading down the generations' is fast disappearing in order to pay for long-term care for the elderly. In 1990, the National Health Service and Community Care Act was passed. The key provision, implemented progressively since 1993, is the Care in the Community system which set out to permit disabled people to remain living in their own homes rather than being transferred to hospital wards. This was expected to be much cheaper than the alternative of providing long-term hospital beds.

However, the Act distinguished between 'medical care' and 'social care' which is concerned with daily living costs. Medical care is free on the National Health Service whereas social care is not. Thus, when an elderly person is no longer capable of living at home, and is transferred into a nursing or residential home that person must, if so able, pay personally for the care provided. Originally, anyone with an annual income, inclusive of pensions and social security benefits, in excess of £3000, and who possessed wealth valued in excess of £8000, had to contribute towards the cost of care, which could often exceed £300 per week, on a sliding scale. The Spring 1995 Budget lifted the wealth threshold to £10 000 for part-contribution and £16 000 for full contribution, with the calculation of wealth including the value of a property, so it is obvious that once a person enters into residential care the majority of any potential inheritance will be rapidly wiped out. In the longer term, therefore, the cascading effect of wealth accumulated in housing will be somewhat, and possibly much, reduced.

■ 3.4 Investment

□ 3.4.1 Investment Defined

The term **investment** is used by the general public to refer to the acquisition of certain physical and financial assets. For our purposes, however, the purchase of an asset such as a painting or putting money into a building society account must be regarded as an act of **saving**. When we refer to investment, we mean that an addition has been made to the stock of productive capital machinery known as **fixed capital formation**. The existence of this capital stock is what enables the economy to produce output both in the current and in future periods.

Total investment, or **Gross Domestic Fixed Capital Formation** (GDFCF), consists of **replacement** investment and **net** investment. Replacement investment is simply that investment needed to make good any reductions in the capital stock due to depreciation and obsolescence. Net investment is any investment over and above that needed to keep the capital stock constant, and hence results in an increase in that stock. In general, net investment is the driving force behind economic growth and improved productivity. Nevertheless, this can be attributed in part to replacement investment insofar as this is technically superior to the capital stock which is being replaced.

Table 3.7 sets out the path of GDFCF as a proportion of GDP over the period from 1979 to

Table 3.7   *Investment (GDFCF) by Type of Asset and by Sector as % of GDP, at Market Prices, 1979–95*[1]

	1979	1981	1983	1985	1987	1989	1990	1991	1992	1993	1994	1995
GDFCF as % of GDP	18.6	16.2	16.0	17.0	17.8	20.4	19.5	17.0	15.7	15.0	15.0	15.0
GDFCF excluding dwellings as % of GDP	14.8	13.0	12.5	13.6	13.9	16.0	15.6	13.8	12.5	11.9	11.8	11.9
Private sector investment as % of GDP	13.0	11.5	11.4	13.4	14.9	17.5	16.3	13.3	12.8	12.4	12.4	12.5
General government investment as % of GDP	2.6	1.8	1.9	1.9	1.8	1.9	2.3	2.1	2.1	1.8	1.9	1.8
Public corporation investment as % of GDP	2.9	2.7	2.6	1.7	1.1	1.1	0.9	0.7	0.8	0.8	0.7	0.7
Stocks and work in progress as % of GDP	1.1	−1.1	0.5	0.2	0.3	0.5	−0.3	−0.9	−0.3	0.1	−0.5	−0.5

Note:
[1] For the years before 1983, totals may not equal the sum of their components, because of the method used in rebasing to 1985 prices.

Source: Economic Trends, Annual Supplement, Tables 1.3 and 1.8.

Figure 3.15   *Investment as a Proportion of GDP¹*

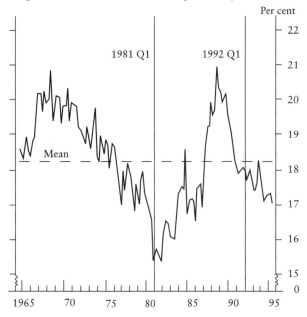

Note: ¹ At constant market prices.

Source: Bank of England Inflation Report, February 1996, Chart 3.8.

1995, but omitting certain intermediate years. In absolute terms, the growth of GDFCF during the period up to 1989 was superficially impressive, but the economy was growing rapidly during part of this period and this renders much of this improvement illusory when taken in relation to the growth in real GDP. Only in the late 1980s did the ratio of GDFCF to GDP rise noticeably above the mean average since 1965, as shown in **Figure 3.15,** and it has fallen back below that average since 1990. It is important to note, however, that investment throughout the G10 countries has fallen by an average of 3 percentage points since the mid-1970s (see *Bank of England Quarterly Bulletin*, February 1996, p. 54), which is very similar to the UK experience.

So far, investment performance since the recession has been muted compared to what happened after 1981, and also compared to the US experience since 1990. It has been suggested (see *Bank of England Inflation Report*, May 1995, p. 26) that this is because, in the 1980s, 'firms used bank borrowing to supplement their own internal funds

[whereas] during the current recovery, many companies have preferred to use undistributed profits to pay back the resulting debt rather than invest'. Nevertheless, in its *Inflation Report* of February 1996 (p. 24) the Bank expressed some puzzlement as to why there had been no improvement even by the end of 1995, given that companies were by then flush with cash. It has been remarked elsewhere that part of the problem relates to the fact that real interest rates remain relatively high in the UK, and that the City's demands for high short-term profits represents an insurmountable hurdle for many otherwise viable long-term investments. A somewhat more positive interpretation relates to the effects of information technology leading to quality improvements in investment not picked up in official statistics (for a detailed analysis of this issue see *Financial Times*, 31 July 1995). However, the very fact that investment surged so much during the late 1980s compared, for example, to the USA (see *The Economist*, 22 April 1995, p. 29), arguably much reduced the need to invest heavily for some time. If this is indeed the case, investment should show some improvement during the latter half of the decade.

Investment in **physical assets** can take a wide variety of forms. Officially these are categorised as private dwellings, other building and work, vehicles, ships and aircraft and plant and machinery. The first of these is the odd man out because a house used for personal rather than business purposes cannot contribute to output, although the money spent on its purchase clearly contributes to aggregate demand. Hence it is sensible to concentrate upon the ratio relating GDFCF **minus** expenditure on dwellings to GDP, which constitutes the second row of **Table 3.7.** Here the picture is fairly similar. In 1984, the ratio rose back to the level prevailing during the late-1970s, and subsequently moved sharply upwards to peak in 1989 at 16.0 per cent. Since then, it has also fallen back to levels not seen since 1979.

Other notable features of **Table 3.7** are the comparative buoyancy of general government investment in recent years, and the declining importance of the public corporations as a result of the programme of privatisations. This programme boosted private sector investment, which ended the decade well above its starting level before subsiding during the recession.

It should be recognised that technological progress has become so rapid that simple maintenance of the real level of GDFCF is insufficient to maintain the UK's ability to compete. It will be necessary, during the latter half of the decade, to do rather better than to return to the level of real GDFCF prevailing in 1989 if the level of investment is to be seen as sufficient to ensure real growth in future years.

□ 3.4.2 The Pattern of Investment

The pattern of investment is revealed in the bottom row of **Table 3.7** and the whole of **Table 3.8**. What was discovered in **Table 3.7** was the dominant role played by private sector investment, and **Table 3.8**, which divides total GDFCF into its component parts, indicates the destination of that investment over the period beginning in 1979. Initially, investment in other new buildings and work was the largest sector, just ahead of investment in plant and machinery. In 1985 their positions reversed, and again in 1989, since which

time the 1979 pattern has reasserted itself. Investment in plant and machinery has constituted a roughly constant percentage of GDFCF since 1989, which is to the good since it is a major contributor to economic growth. Unfortunately, however, elsewhere in the G7 investment is biased more heavily towards plant and machinery than in the UK, and this is likely to prove detrimental to the UK in the longer term.

Investment in new buildings and work has constituted an unusually large proportion of GDFCF since 1990, largely at the expense of investment in dwellings. In the light of our previous discussion on housing, the decline in the ratio of investment in dwellings to GDFCF during the late 1980s may come as something of a surprise. However, if this is broken down into private and public sector elements the picture is quite different. In real terms, for example, public sector investment in dwellings remained remarkably constant from 1984 to 1989, and hence declined quite rapidly in relation to a fast-growing GDP.

Private investment in dwellings, on the other hand, was 20 per cent higher in real terms in 1989 compared to 1984, and over the decade as a whole some £100 billion was invested in private dwell-

Table 3.8 *Investment by Type of Asset as % of GDFCF, 1979–95[1]*

	1979	1981	1983	1985	1987	1989	1990	1991	1992	1993	1994	1995
Investment in dwellings as % of GDFCF	26.6	23.8	25.7	22.6	23.6	22.2	19.9	18.4	19.1	20.1	20.2	20.1
Investment in other new buildings and work as % of GDFCF	31.1	33.3	33.7	32.5	34.2	33.7	36.4	38.5	38.8	37.5	36.6	35.7
Investment in plant and machinery as % of GDFCF	29.5	31.9	30.6	33.2	31.5	34.0	34.2	34.9	34.0	33.6	34.0	35.2
Investment in vehicles, ships and aircraft	14.6	11.1	10.6	11.6	10.7	10.1	9.5	8.2	8.1	8.8	9.2	9.0

Note:
[1] For the years before 1986, totals may not equal the sum of their components, because of the method used in rebasing the original data to 1985 prices.

Source: Economic Trends, Annual Supplement (1995), Table 1.8.

Figure 3.16 *Growth Rates and Investment Ratios, OECD, 1979–90*

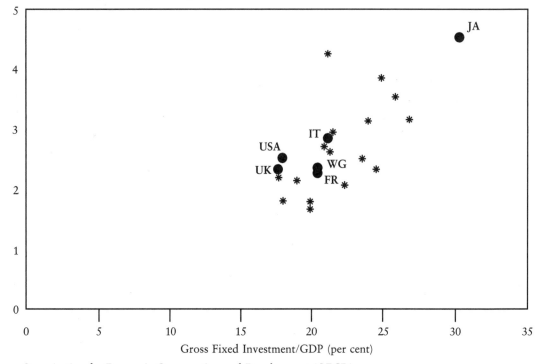

GDP Growth (average annual percentage rate)

Gross Fixed Investment/GDP (per cent)

Source: Organisation for Economic Co-operation and Development (OECD).

ings, representing 40 per cent of total investment in plant and machinery. It would doubtless have been better for the economy if the balance had been more in favour of the latter. As it happens, that is what happened after 1989 as falling nominal house prices eroded the desirability of house purchase at a time when the public sector was also running in low gear.

Fluctuations in the level of investment have a considerable impact upon the business cycle. Over time, the level of investment determines the rate of growth of the capital stock, and this is a major determinant of the rate of growth of real income. **Figure 3.16** shows that during the 1980s the UK grew on average at the same rate as France and West Germany, but needed two percentage points less investment to do so. While this does not provide a full excuse for having such a low level of investment by international standards, it does suggest that the UK's performance has converged upon that of other major EU economies.

It is often argued, with some justice, that the **quality** of investment is a critical issue. For this reason, UK investment has been viewed as of questionable value because much more of it has traditionally been devoted to the defence industries compared to Japan and West Germany, and these industries have not been viewed as particularly beneficial for growth, exports and jobs. Equally, the poor performance of parts of the nuclear industry in which huge sums were invested, and the money wasted on prestige products such as Concorde, have provided ammunition for critics of British investment performance. Nevertheless, the 1980s do not appear to conform with this stereotype, and it would appear that investment in, for example, West Germany, was overall rather less efficient.

Government policy has had some part to play in this turnaround. Fiscal policy changes no longer make it worthwhile for companies to invest mainly to save tax rather than to enhance the capital stock and improve efficiency. In addition, the low level of corporation tax helps to make the UK a particularly attractive destination for investment by foreigners, and such investment tends to be highly efficient and productive. On the other hand, a problem still remains in that pension funds, the major shareholders in the UK, continue to exert pressure for distribution of dividends at times when it would be preferable for at least a part of this money to be retained for reinvestment.

□ 3.4.3 Business Investment

Business investment is investment which takes place in the trading sector of the economy. This necessarily excludes private investment in dwell-ings and also in practice excludes general govern-ment investment. On the other hand, it includes the public corporations (but not NHS Trust hos-pitals), and in particular nationalised industries, which supply goods and services in the same way as private corporations.

A sub-category within business investment is **manufacturing** investment. Business investment currently accounts for roughly two thirds of GDFCF, and manufacturing investment for roughly one quarter of business investment. As is customary, the longer-term trend is best repre-sented by expressing business investment as a percentage of GDP as in **Figure 3.17**.

During the 1970s business investment adjusted for inflation was fairly static, and this resulted in a steady decline in the ratio to GDP from 1977 onwards because GDP was growing. Investment

Figure 3.17   *Business investment–GDP ratio*[1]

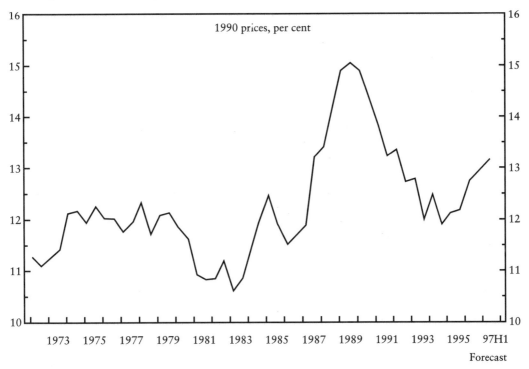

Note: [1] Business investment includes public corporations (except National Health Trust Hospitals) and investment under the Private Finance Initiative.

Source: Financial Statement and Budget Report 1996–97, Chart 3.12.

fell back so sharply in 1980–81 that the ratio worsened despite falling GDP, but equally surged faster than GDP from 1982 to 1985 causing the ratio to rise. During 1986–87 business investment did not keep up with GDP even though it was itself at record levels in real terms, but as GDP growth fell away at the end of the decade the continued growth of investment caused the ratio to climb above 15 per cent, well above the trend line. This could not be expected to last for long, and there was subsequently a three-year decline back towards the longer-term trend level. The forecast is for an improvement, and as **Figure 3.17** indicates, the 1990s are almost certain to be significantly better than the 1970s.

The initial surge in the mid-1980s resulted from the bringing forward of investment to avoid changes in the tax system intended to discourage forms of investment undertaken primarily in order to obtain tax breaks. The longer surge at the end of the decade suggested that the message was at last getting through to business that sustained investment is a pre-condition for sustained growth. This is especially important given that the traditional driver of growth via domestic consumption expenditure has gone out of fashion.

Manufacturing investment accounted for roughly one-third of business investment in the period to 1970. Subsequently it fell back to roughly one-quarter. The void was filled by investment in financial services and, to a far lesser degree, investment in retail and wholesale distribution. From the late 1980s onwards, there was a surge in investment in the energy and water sectors subsequent to their privatisation. There is an element of deception in the substantial switchover from manufacturing to service sector investment, insofar as manufacturing companies tended increasingly to sub-contract maintenance, finance, recruitment, training and other services. Nevertheless, it is evident that the UK has a comparative advantage in the provision of services (at least until competitors catch up) rather than in the provision of manufactures, although it would be highly inadvisable for this to induce over-investment in services and under-investment in manufacturing.

☐ 3.4.4 Saving and Investment

Up until the 1980s the link between saving and investment was very strong. Countries such as Japan and West Germany, which saved a relatively high proportion of their GDP, also invested heavily, whereas the opposite was true for the USA and UK. As we noted previously, saving by the household sector can be absorbed by government or by companies overseas, and the removal of exchange controls after 1979 broke the link between domestic saving and domestic investment – but not completely.

During the latter part of the 1980s, the surge in investment in the UK could be accommodated by international borrowing without being constrained by a shortfall of domestic saving, but most domestic saving in OECD countries (61 per cent from 1980 to 1987) ended up as domestic investment. This proportion was 30 per cent lower than in the 1960s, and a larger reduction was felt by Community members except that in their case the reduction was from 74 per cent down to only 36 per cent. The tendency to rely upon overseas saving is thus not limited to the UK, although the UK is certainly more vulnerable than most to any shortfall in overseas saving given the inadequate level of domestic saving.

■ 3.5 Stocks

Fixed investment does not include investment in stocks or inventories. The scale of investment in stocks is small in comparison with GDFCF. Nevertheless, it is important both because it reflects changes in the level of demand and also causes such changes to occur.

Although stocks play no part in the provision of services, they are clearly vital in overcoming imbalances between the supply and demand for raw materials and semi-finished and finished manufactures. When sales rise relative to production, this causes stocks to be run down, which acts as a signal to producers to increase output if the increased demand is expected to continue. Conversely, a rise in stocks relative to production, unless it is planned by producers in anticipation of a higher level of future sales, signals a reduction in demand and the need to cut back production if demand is expected to remain low. As the economy slides into recession, producers cut back severely and rely upon their cushion of stocks to meet demand. Destocking accordingly speeds up the rate of decline of output, and the phenomenon is very clear in the major postwar recessions, with destocking cutting output by over 3 per cent in 1974–75 and by 2.5 per cent in 1980 alone. However, the reduction was much milder in 1990, as destocking only appears to have continued for one year (mid-1989 to mid-1990) compared to all of 1980 and half of 1981 and to all of both 1974 and 1975. The reason for this is that there was relatively little stockbuilding in the pre-recession period.

If GDP is growing erratically then this will cause the accumulation or run-down of stocks to be erratic in its turn, and this will then feed through to cause further erratic movements of GDP. This pattern is clearly seen during the 1970s, and can usefully be analyzed in terms of the **stock–output ratio**.

During the 1970s, as shown in **Figure 3.18**, the stock–output ratio for the manufacturing sector exhibited a procession of peaks and troughs, culminating in an unusually high peak at the end of the decade. During the period 1976–79, stock-building was positive, encouraged by negative real interest rates and a tax regime favourable towards stockholding. However, when in 1980 real interest rates rose sharply and demand collapsed, stocks were reduced sharply in order to maintain cash flow. The reduction in tax relief on stocks in 1981, combined with high real rates of interest and improvements in stock-control methods throughout the decade, served to stabilise stockbuilding at a modest positive rate which, given the rather

Figure 3.18 *UK Stock–Output Ratio*[1]

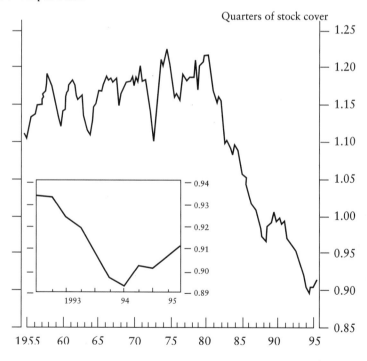

Note: [1] Levels of stocks outstanding relative to quarterly GDP in 1990 prices; includes alignment adjustment.
Source: Bank of England Inflation Report, February 1996, Chart 3.11.

faster rise in GDP, triggered a decline in the stock–output ratio which only came to an end in the case of manufacturing in 1994, although the retail sector responded to growth in consumer demand after 1985 by restocking at a rapid pace and has remained as a fairly constant ratio to GDP ever since.

Overall, UK stockholding remains higher than is customary for major competitors, although there is not much fat left to trim. It would appear that improved information systems have enabled firms to recognise that stocks are building up at an early stage, and that they are able to cut back on their orders in good time. However, this process itself exerts a depressive effect upon GDP growth, and there can be no doubt that a sharp upturn in stockbuilding in the manufacturing sector is a necessary pre-condition if growth is to be resumed at the rate of the late 1980s. For the moment, the jury is out.

■ 3.6 Capacity Utilisation

Figure 3.19 is based on the responses to the Confederation of British Industry (CBI) survey of business conditions and expectations. It shows the percentage of firms answering 'No' to the question: 'Is your present level of output below your capacity output level?'. The degree of capacity utilisation revealed by the answers to this question provides a very good indication of the strength of aggregate demand in the economy. In 1979, 50 per cent of firms surveyed reported full capacity working. This represented the highest negative response since the 1970–73 boom as shown in **Figure 3.19**, although it hardly suggested an economy working flat out. The rapid decline in the degree of capacity utilisation in 1980 was the sharpest recorded in any single year from 1970 to date, and also the lowest absolute level of capacity utilisation with 85 per cent of firms reporting below-capacity output.

By 1985, capacity working had regained the 1979 level, and this was followed by further growth of demand which produced the highest level of capacity utilisation, at 70 per cent, since 1970. The level of capacity utilisation in 1989 indicated a very high level of aggregate demand in the economy, and hence the likelihood of both increasing inflationary pressure and a worsening balance of trade deficit.

Figure 3.19 *Capacity Utilisation (%)*

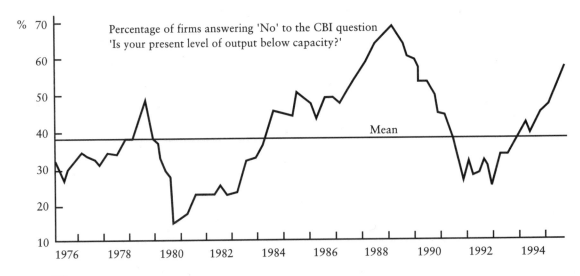

Source: CBI.

These duly materialised, with inflation rising just as it had after the previous cyclical peaks in 1973 and 1979. It is possible to argue that improvements in management such as 'just-in-time' delivery, sub-contracting and outsourcing, and on the supply side in general, made it possible to run the economy nearer to capacity during the 1980s compared to previous decades without causing the economy to boil over, but the situation in 1989 was unsustainable on any measure as indeed it had been in 1979 at a time when there was even less slack in the labour market than in 1989.

The downturn in 1979–80 was short but severe. The more recent downturn was more gradual but longer-lasting, with the response rate in **Figure 3.19** falling back from 70 per cent to 30 per cent prior to levelling off at the end of 1991. This was followed by a period of 'bouncing along the bottom', but the subsequent upturn was much sharper than either post-1975 or 1980 such that capacity constraints are now once again an issue.

However, unlike previously, this has yet to trigger higher inflation. This may result from the fact that companies take more account of labour as against machinery when estimating capacity. It is also fair to say that capacity is increasingly less relevant as a national concept; it is more a question of 'access' to capacity irrespective of where it may be located.

A final comment relates to the relationship between capacity utilisation and unemployment (see Brittan, 1995). There is some evidence that a given level of capacity utilisation has been associated with increasingly more unemployment over the past three decades. However, there is as yet no unequivocal explanation as to why this has occurred.

■ 3.7 Company Profitability

Figure 3.20 presents a long-term view of companies' pre-tax profitability, adjusted also to take

Figure 3.20 *Companies' Real Rates of Return on Capital, Pre-tax, 1973–96*

Source: Bank of England Quarterly Bulletin (August 1993), Chart 5.6; FSBR 1996–97, Chart 3.11.

account of the North Sea oil sector after the mid-1970s. The profitability of all industrial and commercial companies (ICCs) sagged fairly continuously from 1962 to 1970, and as can be seen it fell abruptly from 1973 to 1975 as costs rose sharply as a consequence of rising oil and other commodity prices. From this point on there was nowhere to go but up – though not for long as there was a further sharp downturn after 1978 which, in the case of non-oil ICCs, depressed profitability below even the level prevailing in the mid-1970s.

The excellent profitability of the oil sector produced a somewhat better result for ICCs as a whole, and as the economy grew rapidly out of the recession profitability grew alongside GDP. The improved climate for profits in turn fostered investment even though borrowing costs remained high, and additional investment helped to sustain profitability. By the late 1980s the situation appeared to be much healthier than it had been for two decades, but the onset of recession

caused profitability to slump once again during 1990.

For ICCs as a whole the reduction in profitability in 1990–91 was as severe as in 1980–81, although the non-oil sector did not perform significantly worse this time around. As a result, profitability did not fall back as much as might have been expected, before beginning to rise again in 1992 more or less continuously to 1996.

It is not particularly easy to interpret the overall picture. One of the main thrusts of the Thatcher government was to improve the workings of the economy, as discussed below. This included reductions in corporate taxation and the removal of distortions in the tax system that encouraged investment for short-term financial gain rather than for the long term. The power of organised labour was also eroded. Despite these changes profitability fell back after 1989 in a similar manner to that in previous recessions, so these measures either had a limited impact upon profitability or they

Figure 3.21 *Cross-country Profitability*

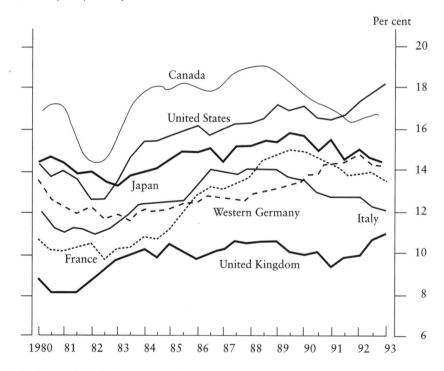

Source: Bank of England Quarterly Bulletin, August 1994.

were offset by other supply-side problems as yet unaddressed. Certainly, the endemic problem of productivity gains showing up as increases in real wages rather than as rising profits continues to cause concern, although the fact that the rate of return stabilised in 1992 must be attributed, at least in part, to the containment of labour costs earlier in the recession.

The fact that profitability did not ultimately fall back to the levels seen during the 1980–81 recession can be attributed, firstly, to the fact that levels of, and growth in, productivity were much higher entering the 1990s recession than a decade earlier; secondly, to the fact that UK industry was more competitive than in the early 1980s; and thirdly, to the fact that UK export markets were stronger and capacity utilisation higher (Bank of England, 1993, p.362).

Profitability in the UK has been consistently poor by the standards of comparable economies, as shown in **Figure 3.21**, although the data may exert a downwards bias in the case of the UK (Bank of England, 1993, p. 300). Nevertheless, the relatively rapid growth of UK profitability in the mid-1980s served to reduce the gap for a while, although this shows up more clearly for manufacturing rather than for business as a whole. The gap appears to have opened up again at the turn of the decade, but the onset of growth in the UK at a time of recession elsewhere in the EU saw it close down somewhat, commencing in 1992, other than in relation to the USA. A significant factor was the departure of the UK from the Exchange Rate Mechanism, since by 1990, whereas domestic margins were on a modestly rising trend, export margins had collapsed. Set at 1986Q1 = 100, export margins had fallen to 95 in mid-1990 as the exchange rate became progressively uncompetitive, but they surged immediately to 107 after 'White' (or 'Black') Wednesday, reaching 112 during 1995.

Bibliography

Bank of England (1992) 'Negative Equity in the Housing Market', *Bank of England Quarterly Bulletin* (August).

Bank of England (1993) 'Company Profitability and Finance', *Bank of England Quarterly Bulletin* (August).

Boleat, M. *et al.* (1991) *The State of the Economy 1991* (London:Institute of Economic Affairs).

Breedon, F. and M. Joyce (1992) 'House Prices, Arrears and Possessions', *Bank of England Quarterly Bulletin* (May).

Brittan, S. (1995) 'Capacity Limits Job Expansion', *Financial Times* (6 April).

Chrystal, A. (1992) 'The Fall and Rise of Saving', *National Westminster Bank Quarterly Review* (February).

Cornelius, M. and K. Wright (1995) 'Company Profitability and Finance', *Bank of England Quarterly Bulletin* (August).

Cullison, W. (1990) 'Is Saving Too Low in the United States?', *Economic Review* (May/June).

Cutler, J. (1995) 'The Housing Market and the Economy', *Bank of England Quarterly Bulletin* (August).

Eltis,W. (1991) 'United Kingdom Investment and Finance', Chapter 3 in M. Boleat *et al.*, *The State of the Economy 1991* (London: IEA).

Feldstein, M. and P. Baccheta (1989) 'National Saving and International Investment', *National Bureau of Economic Research Working Paper 3164*.

Financial Statement and Budget Report 1996–97. HC 30. November 1995.

Frosztega, M. and Holmans, A. (1993) 'Inheritance of House Property', *Economic Trends*, 481 (November).

Jenkinson, N. (1996) 'Saving, Investment and Real Interest rates', *Bank of England Quarterly Bulletin* (February).

Lee, C. and W. Robinson (1990) 'The Fall in the Savings Ratio: the Role of Housing', *Fiscal Studies* (February).

Lipsey, R. and I. Kravis (1987) 'Is the US a Spendthrift Nation?', *National Bureau of Economic Research Working Paper 2274*.

Smith, J. (1994) 'Personal and Corporate Sector Debt', *Bank of England Quarterly Bulletin* (May).

Social Trends, 26, 1996.

The Economist (1995) 'The Wheels of Investment Start to Turn' (22 April).

The Economist (1996a) 'Consumers Like the Rest of Us'(24 February).

The Economist (1996b) 'America's Power Plants' (8 June, p.118).

Wright, K. (1994) 'Company Profitability and Finance', *Bank of England Quarterly Bulletin* (August).

Chapter 4

Growth, Productivity and Inflation

Peter Curwen

■ *4.1* Growth

For a country to grow richer in a strictly material sense, it must first of all grow. In other words, it is the increase in the **volume** of goods and services (real GDP) which economic growth represents that underpins the improvement in a country's material standard of living over time. Since living standards are more meaningful when expressed in terms of individuals, real GDP **per head** is often preferred. It should, however, be noted that there are quite a number of qualifications to be made when linking growth to living standards – for example, if the extra goods and services are all exported, domestic consumption will not be affected, and the fruits of growth may not be distributed at all equally such that some individuals may become worse off even when the economy is growing rapidly. Furthermore, whilst certain activities conferring 'economic well-being' such as gardening are excluded from official figures, other activities which reduce well-being such as damaging the environment are included (see, for example, comments on the 'genuine progress indicator' in *The Economist*, 30 September 1995, p. 63). Nevertheless, provided population growth does not outstrip economic growth – fortunately not the case in advanced societies – the only certain

way for individuals to become steadily richer is for economic growth to be the rule rather than the exception.

It must also be remembered that growth is **compound**. In other words, if there is 10 per cent growth for three years, the index of real GDP will not rise in the sequence 100 : 110 : 120 : 130 but in the sequence 100 : 110 : 121 : 133. Whereas this makes little difference in any single year, it makes an enormous difference over several decades. At 10 per cent compound, real GDP doubles in 7.5 years, triples four years later and is four times as large less than three years after that. At a growth rate of 5 per cent it takes 33 years to raise real GDP by a factor of 5, whereas at a growth rate of 10 per cent it takes only 17 years.

This is why Japanese growth rates have traditionally been regarded with envy, but a word of caution is nevertheless necessary. If GDP is initially very low, high growth rates make little absolute difference. Thus, if a country with a GDP of £10 billion doubles its GDP, the absolute difference is only equivalent to a 10 per cent growth rate for a country with an initial GDP of £100 billion. By and large, mature advanced economies do not, therefore, grow at all rapidly. Now that Japan falls into this category, it also struggles to grow noticeably faster than comparable large economies. The key issue about growth is, accordingly, not why the UK grows slowly but why it has traditionally grown **more slowly than comparable economies.**

It is important to emphasise that the UK economy does grow in the majority of years, and hence that in the aggregate the citizens of the UK have become progressively better off, in terms both of income and of wealth. For whatever reason, some critics like to refer to the 'good old days' of the 1960s or 1970s, but although growth may at the time have been relatively rapid by recent standards, households were, on average, considerably less well-off than today.

However, even after setting aside the issue as to how to measure GDP itself, it should be noted that it is by no means a straightforward matter to decide exactly what the word 'growth' means. For example, the customary method is to choose a fixed base year for valuing GDP at the prices then prevailing, and to deflate the values of GDP in subsequent years by a suitable price deflator in order to establish a sequence of figures for 'real GDP'. This has the virtue of simplicity and long-established use, and results in a measure which is the sum of its parts. However, this method is very sensitive to the choice of base year because certain sectors, such as computers, represent a volatile share of GDP as time passes, and when the base date is rolled forward for, say, five years, the entire historic series of growth has to be adjusted to take account of the changed shares of sectors in GDP. Unfortunately, it is by no means obvious how to choose a better methodology (but see Steindel (1995) for a full discussion of the issues).

Equally, it is far from obvious how you get more of it. It is relatively easy to identify a number of factors which fast-growing economies have in common, but relatively difficult to identify which are causal factors in growth and which are the effects of growth, not to mention their relative importance. Not surprisingly, traditional models emphasise the virtues of investment, financed by internal saving, and the virtues of technological change, although it remains difficult to explain why this should be faster at certain times compared to others. It is also important to take account of human capital derived from education and training. However, there are those who believe these factors to be overstated (see *The Economist*, 1995c) on the grounds that a country starting from a point where education and training is very poor should be able to profit vastly more from improved education and training than advanced countries, which does not appear to be the case. Furthermore, the highly educated and trained tend to gravitate towards advanced countries where they expect to be better rewarded. In the specific context of the UK, the failings of the educational system are well-known and undoubtedly contributed to the relatively poor growth of the 1960s and 1970s (see Oulton, 1995, pp. 60–62). This has been remedied to some extent over the past decade, but there is still disagreement as to whether investment should be directed primarily towards primary, secondary or tertiary sectors.

There is also some dispute concerning technological change, which in principle is readily fostered by buying new technology in the open market but which in practice may prove to be difficult to introduce. In recent times, the so-called 'endogenous growth' models have come to the fore as a result of their popularity in certain political circles. These models emphasise technological change, the means by which it is promoted and the means by which it is diffused within an economy. Nevertheless, it has to be borne in mind that governments now have their fingers in so many economic pies that they are constantly affecting decisions to save, invest and innovate, albeit inadvertently, and hence that they are as likely to be damaging growth by their actions as promoting it.

When comparing advanced economies it is difficult to claim that any among them is seriously disadvantaged in terms of access to advanced knowledge. Furthermore, the context of a free market in international flows of finance, relatively low barriers to trade and a settled political environment, provides support for the view that it is institutional factors such as the education and training systems, the organisation of the labour market and the government's own policies which underpin faster growth in certain advanced economies compared to others.

☐ *4.1.1 Long-term Growth*

It is useful to begin by taking a long-term perspective, as is done in **Figure 4.1** which presents the data on an annualised basis from 1956 including forecasts for 1996 and 1997. The three recessions since 1974 stand out starkly in relation to the previous two decades. The most recent, with very little growth in 1990 followed by a reduction in GDP in 1991 and 1992, like its predecessor, also stands out in relation to other OECD countries (see *OECD Economic Indicators*, 57, Annex Table 1) in terms of its severity. The USA, which is following the same cyclical pattern (see below) only suffered a modest drop in GDP in 1991 before re-emerging into a period of strong growth. The EU as a whole, in contrast, started subsiding in 1988, reaching negative territory in 1993 before rebounding modestly. It follows, therefore, that taking the period starting in 1990 leaves the UK trailing somewhat in terms of average annual growth, although the situation has improved markedly over the past year or two. Furthermore, the most notable feature of the recent recovery commencing in 1992Q2 is that it has shown a remarkably smooth profile of output growth whereas the previous recoveries in real GDP commencing in 1981 and 1975 were much more volatile measured on a quarterly basis (see *Bank of England Inflation Report*, November 1995, p. 19).

An alternative version of the history is illustrated in **Figure 4.2** where the data have been used to calculate overlapping six-year period growth rates, rather than annual growth rates, in order to facilitate comparison with the high-growth period in the mid-1980s (here taken as 1981–87). **Figure 4.2** shows that during the 1950s and 1960s, successive six-year periods had annual growth rates contained largely in the 2.5 to 3.5 per cent range. Nevertheless, the sharp improvements in the mid-1960s and late 1960s, and then again in 1973, are of particular interest in relation to the period post-1985, both in terms of the fact that they were short-lived and that each peaked at a successively lower level. Essentially, it was downhill all the way from 1965 to 1985, spanning the term of office of several governments of quite different political hues. The strength of the upturn after 1985 is comparable only to that during the early postwar recovery phase, but its starting point was a far lower rate of growth than at any point during the intervening period.

Figure 4.1   *GDP – Factor Cost (annual Change – %)*

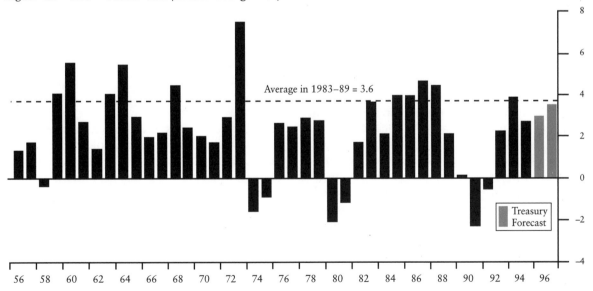

Source: Office for National Statistics.

Figure 4.2 *Average Growth for Six-year Periods, 1949–54 to 1983–87 (%)*

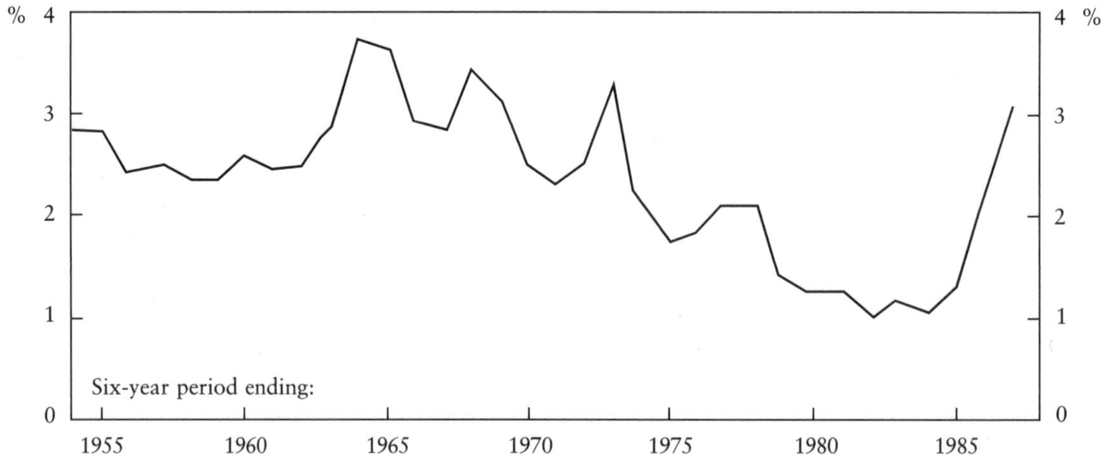

Source: Treasury Economic Progress Report, 196 (June 1988).

Taking the period 1960–87 as a whole, the UK's performance was poor by comparison with other advanced economies with the exception of the USA. During most of the 1960s it was worse even than that of the USA, although it was quite good compared to previous decades and better than the two subsequent decades. The downwards trend from 1974 to 1979 was by no means unique to the UK as 'shocks' such as oil price rises affected other advanced economies to much the same extent, but that simply meant that the UK continued to grow relatively slowly (although the USA did even worse).

The big difference occurred after 1981 since the UK started to grow strongly whereas other advanced economies, with the exception of Japan, continued to perform badly by their own standards. As a result, the UK shot up the growth league. Nevertheless, the previous long period of relatively slow growth had placed the UK in the invidious position of getting progressively wealthier at a time when many comparable countries were becoming much wealthier than the UK. Even in 1966, only the USA had a higher level of GDP per head. At that time Japan was a long way behind, but by 1980 Japan had joined the increasingly long list of countries with a higher GDP per head than the UK. After two decades of falling

behind, it obviously needed more than a short burst of relatively rapid growth for the UK to recover all of the lost ground. Nevertheless, at least the fatalistic view commonly voiced during the 1970s that the process of relative decline was irreversible, had been shown to be demonstrably false.

■ 4.2 Productivity

In order for real GDP to grow year on year, we strictly need only to keep increasing the size of the labour force and to maintain output per person employed at a constant level. However, if the labour force is not growing at all, or very slowly, what is needed is to make each worker more **productive**. Productivity is thus of crucial importance, and it is in respect of **productivity** that a 'miracle' is alleged to have taken place in the UK during the 1980s.

But did it? A major difficulty lies in deciding exactly what the word 'productivity' means. As indicated above, most of the discussion centres around **labour** productivity as measured by **output per person employed** (or output per head). It can also be measured as output per person hour, although this produces an almost identical trend in practice. One could also refer to output per unit of capital, or **capital** productivity, but the most commonly utilised alternative is known as **total factor productivity** which is defined as output per unit of average input, where average input is a weighted average of capital (roughly 30 per cent) and labour (roughly 70 per cent) and where account is taken not merely of increases in the quantity of capital and labour but of improvements in quality, reductions in inefficiency and better techniques. Labour productivity, for example, can be responsive to changes in the quality of the capital stock, to the way work is organised and to the industrial relations climate.

On a more technical note, it has been observed that whereas official UK statistics on productivity are derived by dividing manufacturing output by the number of persons producing it, other OECD countries prefer to use as the numerator 'manufacturing value added at constant prices' (either single or double deflated) (for details see Wells, 1994, pp. 186–7). There is also some disagreement concerning the measurement of numbers employed. There are accordingly many sceptics who believe that official data overstate growth rates in the UK since 1979. With such caveats in mind, what is the overall picture presented by the official data?

Table 4.1 is concerned with labour productivity over the period 1960–88, divided into three subperiods and covering manufacturing industry as well as the whole economy. The most notable feature is the significant reduction in productivity during the 1970s compared to the 1960s, and the rather modest improvement during the bulk of the 1980s. Once again, the poor performance of the UK compared to the other major economies during the 1960s is plain to see, especially with respect to manufacturing. During the 1970s the general level of performance was much inferior, but the UK nevertheless managed to fall even further behind in manufacturing. In the words of Crafts (1993, p.49):

In sum, the evidence is that a good deal of the relatively slow growth of the UK during [1950–73] was due to an environment which permitted or even encouraged the survival of the inefficient and created a situation where the bargaining power of those seeking to block productivity-enhancing change was often considerable.

Figure 4.3 illustrates the relationship between output and labour productivity during the period 1975 to 1986, based upon 1980 = 100. **Figure 4.3**

Table 4.1   *Output Per Person Employed, Average Annual Percentage Changes*

Whole Economy	1960–70	1970–80	1980–88
UK	2.4	1.3	2.5
US	2.0	0.4	1.2
Japan	8.9	3.8	2.9
Germany	4.4	2.8	1.8
France	4.6	2.8	2.0
Italy	6.3	2.6	2.0
Canada	2.4	1.5	1.4
G7 average	3.5	1.7	1.8

UK data from ONS. Other countries' data from OECD except 1988 which are calculated from national GNP or GDP figures and OECD employment estimates.

Manufacturing Industry	1960–70	1970–80	1980–88
UK	3.0	1.6	5.2
US	3.5	3.0	4.0
Japan	8.8	5.3	3.1
Germany	4.1	2.9	2.2
France	5.4	3.2	3.1
Italy	5.4	3.0	3.5
Canada	3.4	3.0	3.6
G7 average	4.5	3.3	3.6

UK data from ONS. Other countries' data from OECD, except France and Italy which use IMF employment data. 1988 data for France and Italy cover first three quarters only.

Source: Reproduced from *Treasury Economic Progress Report*, 201 (April 1989).

Figure 4.3   *Output and Productivity,[1] UK, 1975–86 (1980=100)*

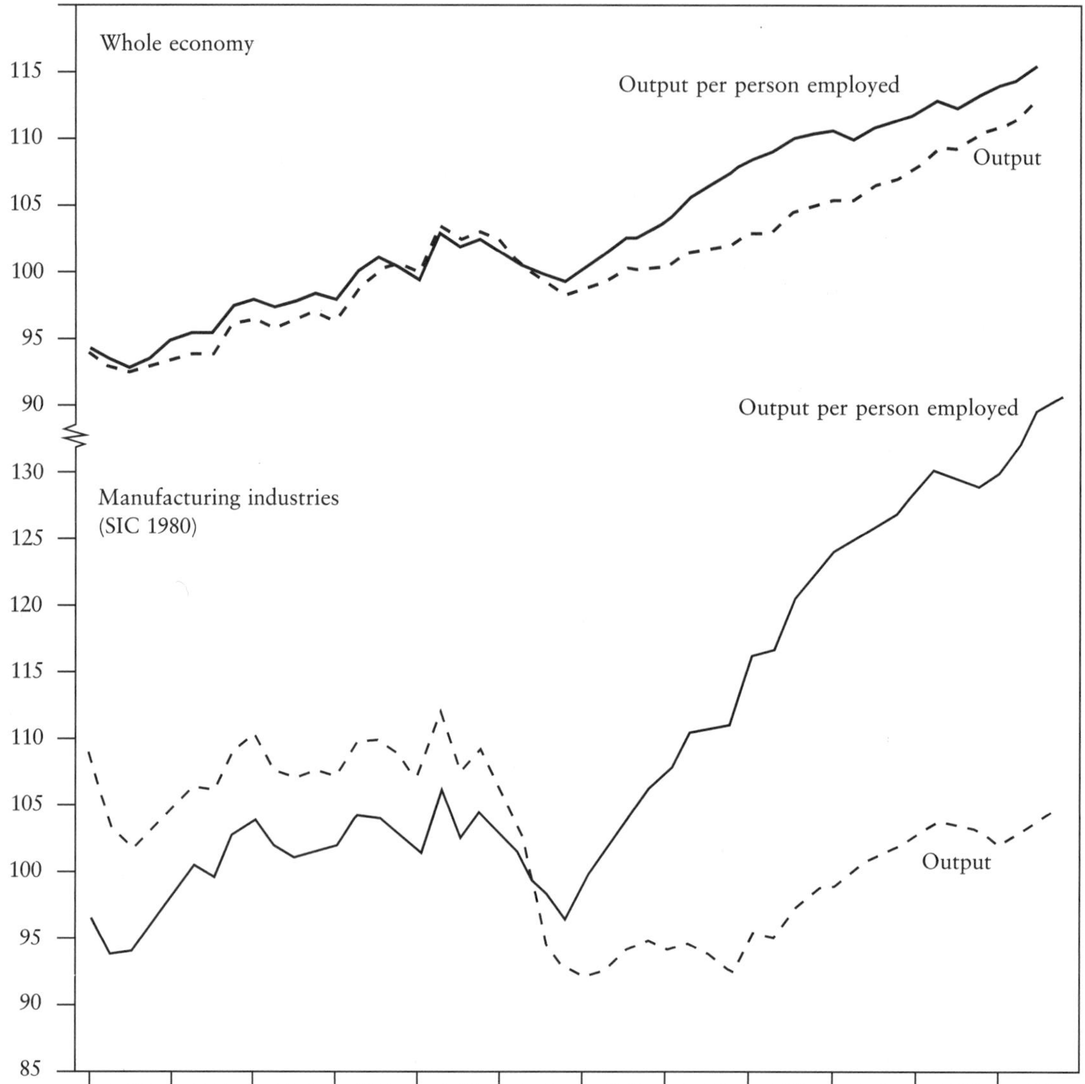

Note: [1] Seasonally adjusted.
Source: Labour Market Trends.

brings out very clearly the contrast between the 1970s and the 1980s. In the manufacturing sector, real output hobbled along during the second half of the 1970s, with productivity following an almost identical trend but below that of output. The sheer inefficiency of labour use in manufacturing is scarcely credible in the light of the more recent discovery that UK workers are not necessarily bone idle by choice but can be motivated to work as productively as the Germans and Japanese.

The situation for the rest of the economy was scarcely much better. However, the effects of the 1980–81 recession are interesting in that, as discussed in Chapter 2, output and employment collapsed in manufacturing but not in the rest of the economy. Indeed, employment in manufacturing collapsed so fast that productivity responded quite quickly and was back to its pre-recession level during 1981. Output in manufacturing barely budged from its nadir until 1983, and was still well below its pre-recession level even in 1986.

Elsewhere in the economy the situation was less serious in that the fall in output was short-lived, but it still took several years for output to regain its pre-recession level because few jobs had been shed and productivity growth was consequently sluggish. Not so in manufacturing. With hundreds of thousands of jobs lost, productivity took off at a rate which previously would have come to a grinding halt in no time at all. However, on this occasion it did not falter, as shown in **Figure 4.4** which is based upon 1990 = 100. From 1985 to the end of 1988 output in manufacturing rose by 20 per cent. Unemployment had ceased to grow much by 1985, and began to fall in 1986, so labour productivity only just kept ahead of output during this period. Elsewhere in the economy, output continued to grow steadily, albeit much more slowly than in manufacturing, and as employment picked up the consequence was that labour productivity ceased to grow at all from the end of 1986.

Figure 4.4   *Output and Productivity,[1] UK, 1987–95 (1990 = 100)*

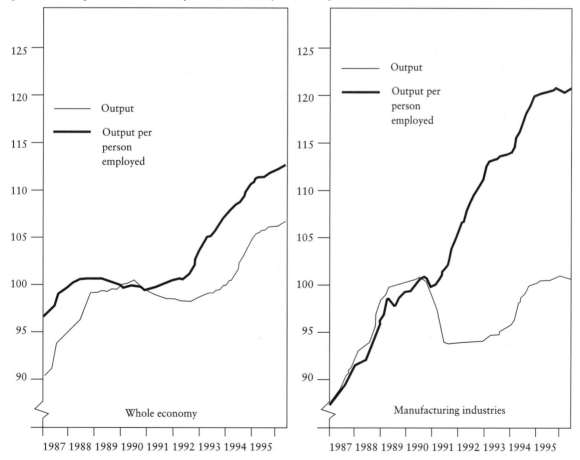

Note: [1] Seasonally adjusted.
Source: Labour Market Trends, Table 1.8.

By 1989 the party was over and the hangover began. Not surprisingly, it was much more painful in manufacturing although, as noted elsewhere, the pain was shared more equally by the service sectors than in 1980–81. Whereas output was falling only modestly in the economy as a whole during 1989–91, it was collapsing fairly rapidly in manufacturing. Towards the end of 1991 the situation stabilised, but output fell overall in 1992 for the third year running, the first time this had happened since 1930–32. Output only regained a clear upward trend in mid-1993.

Nevertheless, as shown clearly in **Figure 4.4**, the fall in employment in the economy as a whole, but more especially in manufacturing, combined with these output trends to create an upturn in productivity. In the case of manufacturing this was roughly as fast as during the period 1985 to 1989, such that an overall improvement exceeding 30 per cent had been achieved by the end of 1992. This has led Eltis and Higham (1995, p. 72) to claim that 'the UK appears to have closed about three quarters of the West European productivity gap in manufacturing industry that existed in 1979 when French and German manufacturing productivity were (respectively) one third and one half above that in the UK'.

In looking across both **Figure 4.3** and **Figure 4.4**, it is possible to understand why there is so much acrimonious debate about whether one should examine the period from 1979 onwards or that from 1981 onwards. A peak to trough (1979–91) perspective can be made to provide a severe indictment of government policy towards the manufacturing sector. On the other hand, a trough to peak (1981–88) perspective can be used to support the resurrection of UK manufacturing hypothesis, which can be supported even more satisfactorily when the data on output per person employed are used.

It may be noted that, both within the manufacturing sector and elsewhere in the economy, the performance of different sub-sectors has been very variable. This may have resulted in an understatement of productivity. The current weights are based on 1990, which means that the shrinkage of declining sectors is given too much weight and the expansion of other sectors too little.

Furthermore, recent data on output per head have not reflected the greater incidence of part-time working and variations in overtime work.

The OECD provides data on productivity in the business sector (this is frequently revised when it appears in each successive *OECD Economic Outlook*). As this is more broadly defined than manufacturing, it provides a kind of halfway house between manufacturing and the whole economy. As shown in **Table 4.2**, in respect of **labour** productivity the picture is the now familiar one, namely a poor performance throughout the 1960s and 1970s, followed by a performance surpassed only by Japan and France among the G7 from 1979 to 1993. In respect of **capital** productivity, the UK was the only major economy to show a gain during the 1979–93 period, albeit only modestly into positive territory, whereas during the 1960s and 1970s the UK had performed in line with the OECD average. In respect of **total factor productivity**, the performance during 1979–93 was comparable with that of Japan and much better than the other G7 economies, although some smaller EU countries did somewhat better, notably Ireland.

4.2.1 Why Did Productivity Improve?

It is widely accepted that the 1980s recovery had little to do with investment. One alternative possibility is that improvements in productivity are related to plant closures. If the effect of the 1980–81 recession was to close down a large proportion of the least-efficient plants in the UK, then that alone could account for much of the subsequent improvement in productivity as output became increasingly concentrated in efficient plants (and utilised the most-efficient workers). Unfortunately, the evidence on this topic is ambiguous. A reasonable interpretation would appear to be that the rate of scrapping of the capital stock accelerated sharply at the beginning of the 1980s, and continued at levels some 50 per cent higher than in previous years.

This sounds impressive, but given that scrapping accounted previously for roughly 2 per cent

Table 4.2   *Productivity in the Business Sector, Percentage Changes at Annual Rates*

	Total Factor Productivity[1]			Labour Productivity[2]			Capital Productivity		
	1960[3]–73	1973–79	1979–93[4]	1960[3]–73	1973–79	1979–93[4]	1960[3]–73	1973–79	1979–93[4]
United States	1.6	−0.4	0.4	2.2	0	0.8	0.2	−1.3	−0.5
Japan	5.6	1.3	1.4	8.3	2.9	2.5	−2.6	−3.4	−1.9
Germany[5]	2.6	1.8	1.0	4.5	3.1	1.7	−1.4	−1.0	−0.6
France	3.7	1.6	1.2	5.3	2.9	2.2	0.6	−1.0	−0.7
Italy	4.4	2.0	1.0	6.3	2.9	1.8	0.4	0.3	−0.7
United Kingdom	2.6	0.6	1.4	3.9	1.5	2.0	−0.3	−1.5	0.2
Canada	1.9	0.6	−0.3	2.9	1.5	1.0	0.1	−1.1	−2.8
Total of above countries[6]	2.9	0.6	0.8	4.3	1.4	1.5	−0.5	−1.5	−0.8
Belgium	3.8	1.4	1.4	5.2	2.7	2.3	0.6	−1.9	−0.7
Ireland	3.6	3.0	3.3	4.8	4.1	4.1	−0.9	−1.2	0.2
Netherlands	3.5	1.8	0.8	4.8	2.8	1.3	0.8	0	−0.2
Norway[7]	2.3	1.4	0	3.8	2.5	1.3	0	−0.3	−1.9
Portugal	5.4	−0.2	1.6	7.4	0.5	2.4	−0.7	−2.5	−0.8
Spain	3.2	0.9	1.6	6.0	3.2	2.9	−3.6	−5.0	−1.5
Total of 21 OECD countries	2.9	0.6	0.9	4.4	1.6	1.6	−0.7	−1.7	−0.9

Notes:

[1] TFP growth is equal to a weighted average of the growth in labour and capital productivity. The sample-period averages for capital and labour shares are used as weights.

[2] Output per employed person.

[3] Or earliest year available, i.e. 1961 for Australia, Greece and Ireland; 1962 for Japan, the United Kingdom and New Zealand; 1964 for Spain; 1965 for France and Sweden; 1966 for Canada and Norway and 1970 for Belgium and the Netherlands.

[4] Or latest available year, i.e. 1991 for Norway and Switzerland; 1992 for Italy, Australia, Austria, Belgium, Ireland, New Zealand, Portugal and Sweden and 1994 for the United States, western Germany and Denmark.

[5] Western Germany.

[6] Aggregates were calculated on the basis of 1992 GDP for the business sector expressed in 1992 purchasing power parities.

[7] Mainland business sector (i.e. excluding shipping as well as crude petroleum and gas extraction).

Source: OECD Economic Outlook, 57, Annex Table 59.

of the capital stock each year, the acceleration accounted for only roughly 1 per cent extra each year for possibly six years. This additional 6 per cent of scrapped capital would indeed have boosted productivity, but not significantly, especially when account is taken of the fact that, during the 1980–81 recession, plant closures were not concentrated among the least-productive plants, but involved many larger plants with above-average productivity.

It is more plausible to argue that the shock effect of the 1980–81 recession, both for management and workers, accounts for the productivity gains of the 1980s. During the 1970s, labour was hoarded and hence productivity was depressed. The effect of North Sea oil upon the exchange rate, rendering UK companies increasingly un-competitive, effectively forced them to improve productivity or go under, and this caused over two million workers eventually to lose their jobs. The government's deflationary policies, its attack upon restrictive labour practices (a factor parti-cularly emphasised by Oulton – see, for example, Oulton, 1995, pp. 68–70) and the withdrawal of many subsidies combined to force a reappraisal of work organisation that rapidly paid dividends. It is, however, slightly ironic that the government never intended the recession to be so severe, yet if it had been as mild as elsewhere in Europe the transformation of UK productivity would almost certainly not have occurred.

This line of argument also implies, however, that the easy productivity gains have been rea-lised, and that unless there are continuing high levels of investment and training there will be severe difficulties in engineering further produc-tivity 'miracles'. In this context, there is the per-formance of manufacturing output to consider. As can be seen in **Table 4.3**, the productivity improvement in the UK up to 1987 was, according to the OECD, entirely the effect of labour shed-ding whereas in the USA, and especially in Japan, it reflected primarily increases in output. Only in West Germany was the situation at all compar-able to that in the UK, although the critical dif-ference, as ever, shows up in the final column. In the UK, the productivity gains reappeared as high-er real earnings. In the USA real earnings actually

fell, and in Japan they absorbed only one quarter of productivity gains.

A re-run of this phenomenon clearly offers no long-term solution to the UK's problems. As shown in **Figure 4.4**, the situation improved a good deal between 1986 and 1990, with manufac-turing output growing rapidly. However, the on-set of recession produced a pattern very similar to that of 1980–81. The present situation is never-theless better than a decade ago in three respects. In the first place, overseas investors in the form of, for example, Japanese car-makers, have de-monstrated that they can achieve levels of output and productivity comparable to best practice overseas. Secondly, there is little expectation of another dramatic surge in real earnings. Finally, the post-recession rise in output has not, as in previous cases, been driven almost exclusively by consumption, which has remained depressed until very recently, but in part by the buoyancy of exports and in part by the resilience of the services sectors. Nevertheless, productivity levels still lag those in many advanced other economies, so con-tinued rapid expansion in manufacturing output is a pre-condition for catching up some of the ground lost in the past, and most recently in 1991–92. While the exchange rate is more compe-titive than in 1992, the lingering recession in other major markets bar the USA indicates that the path ahead will not be smooth.

Pessimists tend in particular to point to the 'burden' of the UK's relatively small manufactur-ing sector. However, the USA, which has an even smaller manufacturing sector in relation to GDP, produces not merely far more output per manu-facturing worker than the UK but considerably more than Japan and Germany, so all is not yet lost, especially if highly productive manufacturing facilities continue to be set up in the UK by over-seas companies. It is also salutary to remember that the impression of Japanese invincibility is based upon the productivity performance of its internationally-traded manufactures such as cars, steel and consumer electronics. Turn, however, to brewing or food manufacturing and the story is quite different, partly because the Japanese dis-tribution and retailing sytems which employ rela-tively high numbers of workers are highly

Table 4.3 *Manufacturing Industry, 1979–87*

| | Output per Worker | % Change in | | |
		Employment	Output	Real Earnings[1]
USA	29.8	−6.3	21.6	−3.9
Japan	52.2	6.7	62.4	13.4
W. Germany	16.5	−7.5	7.6	10.4
UK	37.8	−27.5	0.0	25.8

Note:
[1] Hourly earnings deflated by consumer price index.
Source: OECD.

inefficient by US and UK standards. Japanese agriculture, in particular, is desperately inefficient and far more heavily subsidised even than that of the EU.

☐ 4.2.2 Competitiveness

Of late, there has been increasing attention paid to the notion of 'competitiveness'. The official UK government definition is:

> the degree to which a country can, under free and fair market conditions, produce goods and services which meet the test of international markets, while simultaneously maintaining and expending the real incomes of people over the long term. (Cm 2563, p. 9)

However, objective measurement of this concept is quite another matter. According to the Institute for Management Development's (IMD) *World Competitiveness Yearbook 1996*, the UK ranks 19th in the world (see *Financial Times*, 28 May 1996; 30 May 1996). The most popular measure is, however, the 'world competitiveness scoreboard', which until 1996 was prepared by the World Economic Forum (WEF) in conjunction with IMD, which defines competitiveness as 'the ability of a country or company to, proportionately, generate more wealth than its competitors in world markets'. The scoreboard is a weighted index based upon statistical data supplemented by an opinion survey of international executives. Countries in 1995 were ranked according to 378 criteria aggregated as domestic economic strength; government; finance; infrastructure; management; science and technology; and people. In 1994, the UK's ranking was 14, but in 1995 its ranking fell to 18 out of 48.

The UK's best rankings were 8 in internationalisation and 9 in finance, and its rank was 16 or above in 5 of the 8 categories. However, its worst performance was a ranking of 24 in 'people' (education, skills and worker attitude). What made all of this rather suspicious are factors such as the drop in the UK's 'management' ranking from 13

in 1994 to 20 in 1995. One wonders how such a dramatic change could have occurred in the space of a single year, especially in terms of something normally viewed as essentially stable such as the quality of management.

For 1996, the WEF altered its methodology (causing IMD to produce separately its own league table) to place more emphasis upon free market policies (see *The Times*, 30 May 1996, p. 29; *The Economist*, 30 June 1996, p. 86). The biggest weights among the reduced total of 155 indicators were given to openness to international trade; the depth of financial markets; the flexibility of the domestic labour market; and quality of government. As a result, the UK's ranking rose to 15 (not strictly comparable with the previous year's 18), above both Germany and France. The UK's ranking was 4 in hiring and firing and 5 in restructuring the workforce, but 44 for its ability to supply skilled labour and 35 for its education system.

The Labour Party has taken to using a ranking according to GDP per head and refers to the 'world prosperity league table' (see *The Economist*, 8 June 1996, pp. 28–9), presumably because these show the UK's competitiveness in decline since 1979. As usual, these measures are highly vulnerable to the accusation of 'selective methodology', and competitiveness has arguably become little more than a useful concept for political point scoring.

Certainly, it may be observed that the UK attracts a disproportionate share of the world's inward investment, which is somewhat curious if the economy is as uncompetitive as it is alleged. Equally, it is curious that the exchange rate is largely disregarded as a source of competitiveness and, insofar as it is valued, it is on account of its stability. Evidently, the UK should be left in peace to devalue since it is thereby damaging its competitiveness!

Possibly the most interesting aspect of the debate about competitiveness is that the compilation of league tables suggests that competitiveness is a zero-sum game with one country only able to improve its competitiveness at the expense of another. However, Paul Krugman in particular (see, for example, *Foreign Affairs*, April 1994) argues that it is fallacious to talk of countries competing in the same way as companies. This is not to say that countries do not compete, since in practice variations in exchange rates necessarily affect an individual country's ability to export. On the other hand, whereas companies which cannot compete go bust, this does not happen to countries, primarily because most businesses serve wholly or largely the domestic market.

Furthermore, the so-called 'law of comparative advantage' ensures that a country can always trade something profitably even if it is less efficient in everything that it does than another country. At the end of the day, a country becomes wealthier if it improves its domestic productivity, and the fact that another country improves its productivity at a faster rate does not damage that conclusion. Naturally, the fact that absolute improvements in the standard of living are relatively modest by the standards of competitors can be — and in the case of the UK most certainly has been and still is — a source of national angst, but it would be at best unwise to conclude from this that one's competitors are thereby the 'economic enemy'.

■ 4.3 Is There a Business Cycle?

During the Vietnam War era of 1961–69, the US economy grew continuously for 106 months compared to the average in previous expansions of 35 months. Before turning down in 1990, the US economy logged up over 90 months of expansion, the longest ever in peacetime. It would appear to be the case that expansions have become longer and downswings shorter and shallower — the average US downswing now appears to last less than a year. Evidence from Britain, Germany and Japan suggests that the severity of cyclical swings has been much reduced since 1975.

There are a number of possible reasons for the relative stability of the cycle:

- Manufactured products exhibit a strong cyclical effect, in good part because of variability in investment and stocks: services, however, are less volatile, partly because they can not be stored. Advanced economies have switched pro-

gressively from manufacturing to the provision of services.
- Government spending, which acts counter-cyclically, has grown as a proportion of GDP. Automatic stabilisers have also become more important.
- Stock control methods have become more sophisticated, with the result that stockbuilding has less impact upon the cycle.
- Improved financial management, as manifested after the October 1987 crash, has tended to avert panic responses to severe malfunctions in the world economy which serve only to make the problem worse.

With respect to the long expansion of the 1980s, it would appear that this was assisted by the modest levels of inflation affecting most countries compared to the 1970s. Governments tend to respond to a sharp rise in prices by pressing on the monetary brake, and this has frequently brought an upswing to a grinding halt during past cycles. In addition, the collapse of the oil price in 1986 gave a boost to the major advanced economies just as the expansion was running out of steam.

One of the curiosities of recent experience is that there no longer appears to be a synchronised cycle for all major advanced economies. Both the UK and USA lapsed into recession in the middle of 1990, at a time when Japan and Germany (on the back of reunification) were still buoyant. As a result, international trade did not collapse and the world economy as a whole remained comparatively prosperous for such a late phase in a major expansion.

Subsequently, the situation reversed itself, with first the USA, having adopted a very low interest rate policy, and subsequently the UK, pulling off the bottom and growing again at precisely the time when Japan and most of the EU were suffering sharp reductions in output. The fall-out from this unsynchronized behaviour was severe, and in particular will lead to the probable downfall of many governments. The strains within the EU, as discussed in Chapter 11, resulted both in devaluations and in the UK's departure from the ERM. Furthermore, there has been a general upsurge in protectionist sentiment.

It is difficult to know whether the major economies will move back into line again this side of the millennium. Unfortunately, the world economy performs badly when the major economies are pulling in opposite directions, not least because this produces widely divergent views about the appropriate path for interest rates and exchange rates, so the restoration of a synchronised cycle would be highly beneficial.

■ 4.4 Inflation

Since the late 1940s, the UK economy has experienced a succession of severe macroeconomic problems punctuated by short periods of more favourable economic performance. The same problems have recurred, often simultaneously, although at particular times one has tended to be dominant. These problems have encompassed a low or non-existent growth rate; high unemployment; persistent inflation; balance of trade deficits; and fiscal deficits. Since the early 1970s, the dominant problem has most frequently been that of persistent inflation, since even when, as is true currently, inflation is relatively low and set to remain that way for a while, there is far from widespread confidence that this will remain the case for very long. In 1975, at the height of the oil crisis, the annualised rate of inflation exceeded 24 per cent, a higher rate than at any other time this century and one rarely seen in other advanced economies. That was an experience which no one wishes to repeat, and the period since 1979 has been dominated by the desire to prevent not merely its recurrence but the recurrence of double-digit inflation. In this respect, it is fair to say that West Germany has been even more concerned about the problem than the UK, but this reflects the fact that the Germans had suffered a hyper-inflation earlier in the century which put the British experience of the 1970s in the shade.

□ 4.4.1 Measurement of Inflation

The term inflation refers to a rise in the general level of prices in the economy, or in an average measure of prices in the economy, rather than to the behaviour of the price of an individual good or service. Inflation becomes a serious problem when the general level of prices rises **persistently** and unpredictably. The rate of inflation is calculated using an index of the general price level, or some other relevant concept of prices, and the index is constructed as a **weighted average** of the relevant prices. The issue of relevant prices highlights the fact that different groups of people are interested in the behaviour of different sets of prices; for example, a manufacturer will be concerned about the rate of increase of fuel and raw materials, while a consumer will be more interested in retail prices. For this reason the ONS publishes several different price indices or measures of inflation.

The most widely used of these is the **Retail Prices Index** (RPI) which is a weighted average of prices for a basket of some 600 goods and services consumed by a 'typical' household. The total weights of 1000 are distributed so as to reflect the pattern of spending as revealed by the Family Expenditure Survey (FES), and a new set of weights is introduced at the beginning of each year (see *Employment Gazette* June 1992, pp. 304–6). Over time, the weights assigned to different groups of goods and services can vary considerably, and it is also necessary periodically to alter the main categories of weights in order to reflect major changes in spending patterns. In January 1987, a significant amendment was made to the categories which had been in force since 1974 in order to take account of such items as holiday expenditure and the cost of financial services. Important subsequent amendments were, in February 1993, the inclusion of foreign holidays and, in April 1993, the replacement of the Community Charge by the Council Tax. In March 1995, 31 items were added to the basket and 4 removed. The most important addition was the cost to homeowners of keeping their houses in good condition, which is assumed to be in proportion to the price of the house. This resulted in house prices feeding directly into the RPI as well as mortgage interest payments. Also added were annual credit card fees and contact lenses, whereas cabbage greens and calculators were

Figure 3.17   *Structure of the RPI*

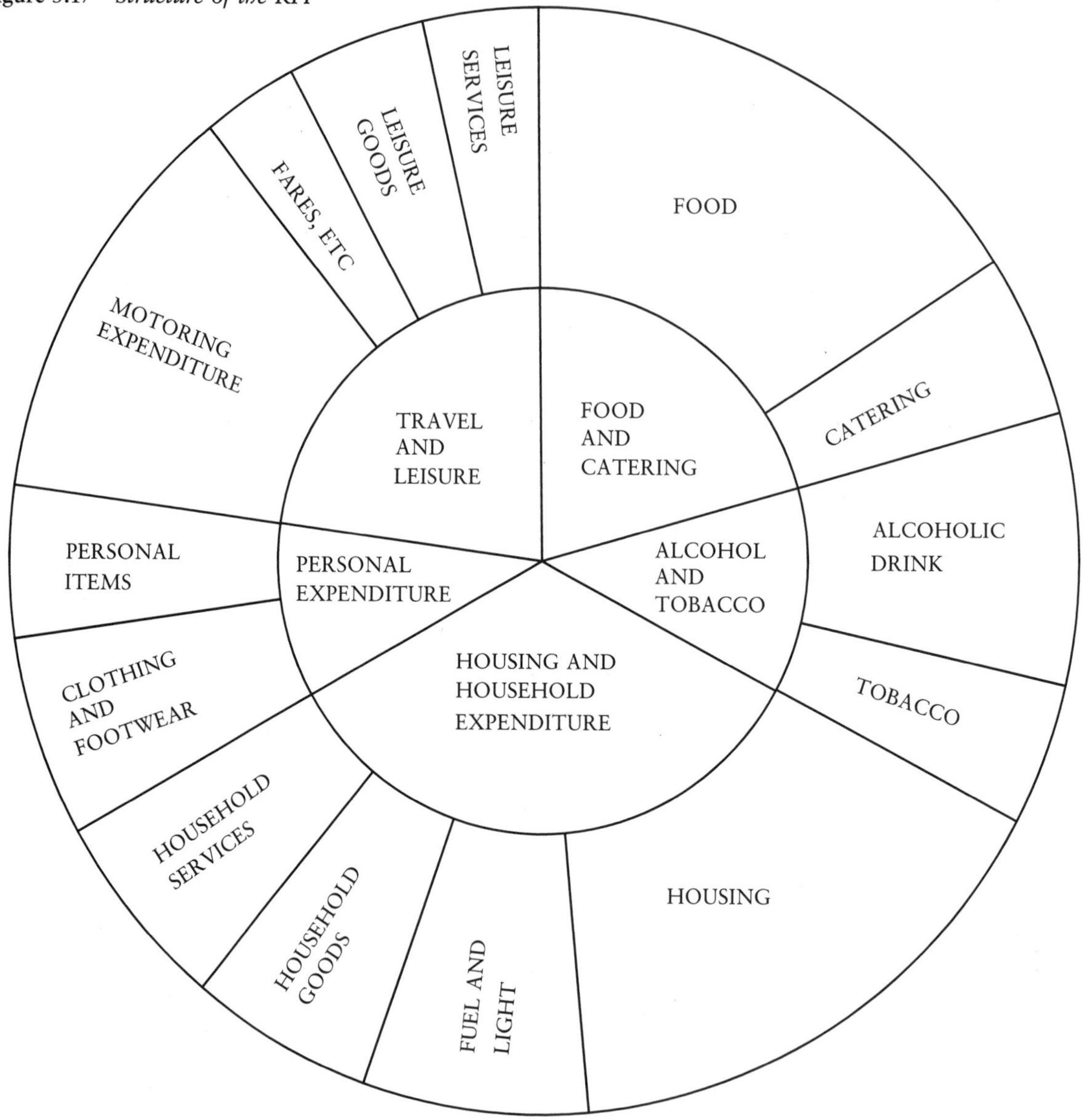

Source: Office for National Statistics

deleted. In March 1996, the additions included Dr Martens; aerobic classes; funerals; muesli; condoms; microwave-ready meals; camcorders; and computer disks, while the deletions included lard; tinned rice pudding; net curtain material; fan belts; and mackerel.

The three largest categories in May 1996, as shown in **Figure 4.5**, were housing (187), motor-ing expenditure (125) and non-seasonal food (117). These weights exclude the spending of high income earners and of pensioner households, the latter having their own independent RPI which is used, for example, to index-link pensions.

The RPI for the period since 1975, based upon 1985 = 100 is shown in **Table 4.4**. However, inflation is commonly expressed as a rate of change,

Table 4.4   *Assorted Price Indices (1985 = 100)*

Year	General Index of Retail Prices		Tax and Price Index		Producer Price Index				GDP Deflator[1]	
					Materials and Fuel		Manufactured (Home Sales)			
1975	36.1	(24.1)[2]	37.7	(25.3)[2]	40.0	(11.7)[2]	37.9	(23.1)[2]	37.6	(27.6)[2]
1976	42.1	(16.5)	45.0	(19.4)	49.9	(24.7)	44.0	(16.1)	42.9	(14.1)
1977	48.8	(15.7)	51.6	(14.7)	57.5	(15.2)	52.0	(18.2)	48.2	(12.4)
1978	52.8	(8.2)	53.1	(2.9)	59.6	(3.7)	57.1	(9.8)	53.9	(11.8)
1979	59.9	(13.4)	59.5	(12.1)	67.3	(12.9)	63.3	(10.8)	60.8	(12.8)
1980	70.7	(18.0)	69.8	(17.3)	73.0	(8.4)	72.2	(14.1)	72.3	(18.9)
1981	79.1	(11.9)	80.1	(14.8)	79.7	(9.2)	79.1	(9.6)	79.9	(10.5)
1982	85.9	(8.6)	88.0	(9.9)	85.5	(7.3)	85.2	(7.7)	85.2	(6.6)
1983	89.8	(4.6)	91.5	(4.0)	91.4	(6.9)	89.8	(5.4)	90.1	(5.8)
1984	94.3	(5.0)	95.0	(3.8)	98.9	(8.2)	95.0	(5.8)	94.5	(4.9)
1985	100.0	(6.1)	100.0	(5.3)	100.0	(1.1)	100.0	(5.3)	100.0	(8.0)
1986	103.4	(3.4)	101.9	(1.9)	92.4	(−7.6)	104.2	(4.2)	102.6	(2.5)
1987	107.7	(4.2)	104.5	(2.6)	94.0	(1.7)	108.1	(3.7)	107.6	(5.0)
1988	113.0	(4.9)	107.6	(2.9)	96.8	(3.0)	112.7	(4.3)	114.1	(6.0)
1989	121.8	(7.8)	115.2	(7.1)	101.2	(4.5)	118.0	(4.7)	122.9	(7.7)
1990	133.3	(9.5)	125.3	(8.8)	100.3	(−0.9)	124.9	(5.8)	132.5	(7.8)
1991	141.1	(5.9)	132.2	(5.5)	98.6	(−1.7)	131.6	(5.4)	140.2	(5.8)
1992	146.4	(3.7)	135.9	(2.9)	98.1	(−0.5)	135.7	(3.1)	146.6	(4.6)
1993	148.7	(1.6)	137.7	(1.3)	102.6	(4.6)	141.0	(3.9)	151.7	(3.5)
1994	152.4	(2.4)	141.6	(2.9)	105.6	(2.9)	144.7	(2.6)	154.3	(1.7)
1995	157.7	(3.5)	147.3	(4.0)	115.6	(9.5)	150.6	(4.1)	158.1	(2.0)

Notes:
[1] GDP at current factor cost ÷ GDP at constant factor cost.
[2] Figures in brackets represent the percentage change from the previous year.
Source: Economic Trends; Labour Market Trends.

which is set out on an annual basis in the brackets. Thus, for example, the annual rate for calendar 1995 can be calculated from **Table 4.4** by the formula 157.7 **less** 152.4 **divided by** 152.4 **times** 100 per cent, which equals 3.5 per cent. When this is repeated on a monthly basis the resulting pattern is as shown in **Figure 4.6**. It is especially interesting to note the pattern described by the sequence **abcd** and by **aefghi. Abc** is virtually a linear sequence, with **d** further below **c**, and while **aefghi** is curvilinear it, like **abcd**, is constantly downward sloping. This would suggest that inflation has been on a downward path since the first oil shock in 1974, the sharp upturns in 1979–80 and 1988–90 notwithstanding. There should ac-

cordingly be a further point **j** appearing even lower than **i** in due course, although achieving that will certainly be a challenge.

The RPI measures only the prices of final goods and services. It thus excludes the prices of intermediate products, but includes the effects of alterations in indirect taxes and in excise duties. There are obviously other ways of going about the measurement of inflation, and a number of other measures in common usage are set out in **Table 4.4**. The **Tax and Price Index** (TPI) has been published since August 1979. The general idea was to take account of changes in income taxes and National Insurance contributions (NICs) which were expected to fall, thereby leav-

Figure 4.6   *RPI (%)*

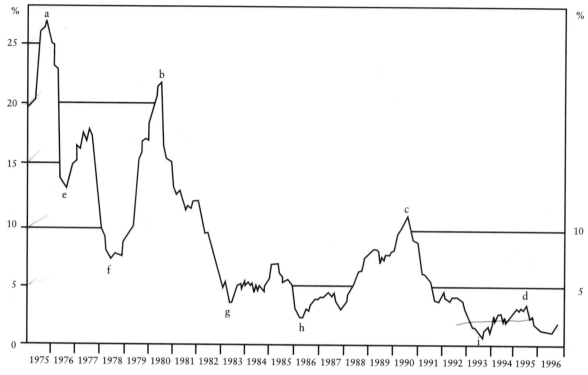

Source: *Labour Market Trends.*

ing households with more real spending power than appeared to be the case after adjusting gross incomes for changes in the RPI. This was expected to exert downward pressure on wage demands. However, as it turned out, the TPI promptly rose more rapidly than the RPI as a result of the 1980 Budget, and was put into abeyance, a position it has continued to occupy ever since although the TPI has risen somewhat more slowly than the RPI since April 1983. The **Producer Price Index**, previously known as the Wholesale Price Index, is divided into an index covering the prices of materials and fuel and an index covering the prices of home sales of manufactured products ('factory gate' prices). These indices respond to inflationary pressures earlier than the RPI, and hence can be useful in providing prior warning of an upsurge in retail prices. As shown in **Table 4.4**, the RPI shadows factory gate prices fairly closely in most years, whereas the index for materials and fuel is relatively volatile and is the

more likely to show reductions. A combination of falling input prices and rising output prices is evidence of a sharp rise in profit margins.

Although these are the only price indices which are widely reported in one or other of their variants, some of the adjustment from nominal to real magnitudes is done using so-called 'price deflators'. The best-known of these is the index of total home costs, commonly referred to as the **'implicit' price deflator**, which is also recorded in **Table 4.4**. This index measures the change of all prices in the economy as reflected in changes in the cost of producing all of the components of GDP.

As with so many other things, data on inflation must be treated with caution because inadequate account is taken of **changes in quality over time**. Companies are constantly turning out goods that are lighter, faster, more energy-efficient and more reliable than their predecessors. For example, one can buy a video for much the same price as five years ago even though it will have many additional features. Basic office computers keep falling in price, but simultaneously become more powerful. A plane ride to the Costa Del Sol may appear to be an unchanging commodity, but as any passenger will know, modern jets are faster and more comfortable than those they replaced. As was noted in *The Economist* (1994b), comparing the price of light in 1800 with its present-day equivalent produces an over-statement of the true price change by an astonishing factor of 1000. This may be unusually large, but the upwards bias in the price of computers is generally agreed to be in the region of 15 per cent a year.

According to the Chairman of the US Federal Reserve, US inflation is systematically overstated by 1 per cent per annum. This figure may or may not apply to the UK, but a combination of quality improvements and, increasingly, discounts off list prices are by no means insignificant.

All of the main measures of inflation tell much the same story in the longer term, but monthly and quarterly data can deviate quite appreciably (which is why one should not pay too much attention to them). Since the recorded figures for short-term inflation do have a significant impact upon financial markets, there is political capital to be made out of the exclusion from the RPI of any components which are rising undesirably fast from the government's point of view. In this respect, for example, controversy has surrounded the **treatment of housing costs** in the RPI.

The key point to bear in mind is that inflation can be **persistent** only if something is persistently causing prices to rise – in other words it is **recurrent**. Wages, for example, tend to rise continuously. Interest rates, or rates of tax, on the other hand, tend to change on a periodic, one-off basis. Because the RPI is a rolling twelve-month index, an increase in, say, VAT in March 1997 will appear in the index [March 1997 – March 1996/ March 1996] but not in the corresponding index for the previous month, and will therefore cause the RPI to rise in March 1997. However, in March

Figure 4.7 *Housing, Selected Components of the RPI (January 1987 = 100)*

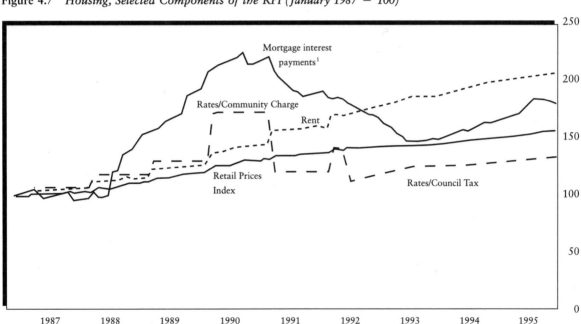

Note: [1] Mortgage interest payments included in the RPI as a proxy for owner-occupiers' shelter costs.
Source: *Social Trends*, 23 (1993 edn), Chart 8.15, updated to illustrate trend.

1998, assuming VAT remains **unchanged** in the interim, the 1997 increase in VAT will have shifted in the formula [March 1998 – March 1997/March 1997] in such a way as to cause the RPI to **fall** in March 1998. In effect, the RPI is as much dependent upon what happened to prices a year previously as upon what happens in the current month. Because of the formula it means, for example, that a series of interest rate reductions will cause the RPI to fall back very sharply, but the effect will wear off a year later unless they fall further in the interim – which logically cannot go on for ever.

As noted previously, housing constitutes the biggest single element in the RPI, and can therefore have a significant distorting effect in the short term. As can be seen in **Figure 4.7**, this did not happen prior to 1988, but became very important subsequently, especially when, on the advice of the Retail Prices Index Advisory Committee, the Community Charge was substituted for domestic rates in the RPI at the time the Charge was introduced. From the beginning of 1986 to June 1990, the RPI rose by 32 per cent whereas the rent index rose by 45 per cent and the rates/Community Charge index rose by 95 per cent (mostly between March and April 1990). The index of mortgage interest payments rose by 132 per cent over the same period, and in every month from May 1988 to June 1990, due partly to increasing mortgage balances related to house price inflation.

These developments sparked off a furious debate about the 'proper' way to measure inflation (and brought about the publication of an extensive report on inflation in each edition of the *Bank of England Quarterly Bulletin*). As a result, it has become customary to distinguish the official **headline** and **underlying** RPIs from others proposed by non-governmental sources. However, it is possible to devise a variety of underlying rates, depending upon what is excluded from the headline RPI. The exclusion which defines the underlying rate as officially published is mortgage interest payments (MIPs), thereby generating the index known as **RPIX**, but to this may be added local taxation and/or petrol and/or VAT and/or excise duties (generating so-called **core** rates which tend,

in practice, to follow the same trend as the underlying rate). The most-used among these is RPI minus mortgage interest payments, council tax, VAT, excise duties, car purchase tax, vehicle excise duty, insurance tax and airport tax, known as **RPIY**. RPIY is equivalent to an index of prices faced by suppliers rather than consumers. The ONS also publishes RPI minus housing, for which the Bank of England has its own variants known as HARP and THARP.

The point of the exercise is to strip out those factors in the headline rate which can potentially cause sharp one-off effects capable of disguising the underlying trend (see *Bank of England Inflation Report*, February 1994, p. 7). If all one-off factors are excluded one is left primarily with wage effects – in other words, underlying inflation cannot be reduced to zero unless wages, on average, more or less stop rising. An additional rationale for stripping out MIPs is that if it becomes necessary to raise interest rates in order to restrain inflationary pressures, this has the perverse short-term effect of raising the headline rate of inflation.

The relationship between the headline rate, RPIX and RPIY, which is illustrated in **Figure 4.8** spanning 1990–96, is obviously dependent upon these one-off effects. From 1987 to 1990 these essentially had the effect of boosting the headline rate, but not RPIX or RPIY, because of sharp rises in interest rates and local taxation. The standard rate of VAT was raised in April 1991, but this coincided with a steady downwards trend in interest rates, as noted previously, and with reductions in local taxation and nominal oil prices. As a consequence, the headline rate fell below RPIX and RPIY in mid-1991, and remained below them until the end of 1993. Subsequently, it remained above them until February 1996. The 'mortgage war' set in motion during the latter part of 1995, combined with the disappearance of some of the one-off rises in indirect taxes from the price indices, had the effect of closing down the gap between the various measures which had opened up in 1994, and in February 1996 the RPI both fell to a 15–month low and dropped below RPIX. Nevertheless, it is worth remarking that, in the same month, RPIX had been below 4 per cent

Figure 4.8   *Inflation During the 1990s*

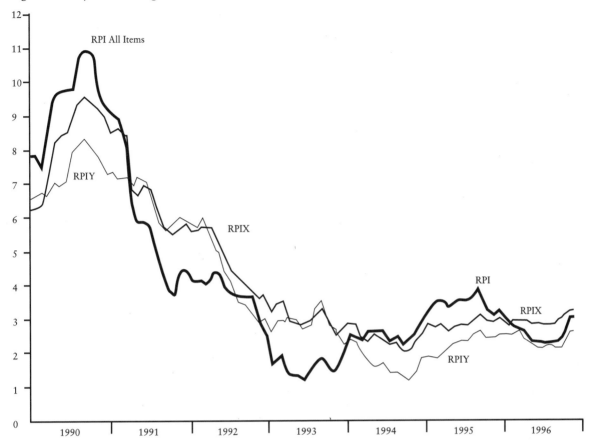

Source: Labour Market Trends, Table 6.1.

for forty consecutive months, the longest period of low inflation during peacetime since the 1930s.

Given the volatility of these transient elements in the inflationary mix, one can appreciate the Bank of England's preference for RPIY as an indicator of the true extent of inflationary pressure in the economy, although RPIX has been the steadiest measure during the 1990s.

That the headline and underlying rates periodically cross paths is somewhat ironic because, when the headline rate was higher at the turn of the decade, it was argued that wage negotiations should be tied to the underlying rate on the grounds that companies should not be expected to compensate workers for changes external to the corporate sector such as higher interest rates.

In the month to January 1993, the headline rate dropped by 0.9 per cent and RPIX fell by 0.5 per cent, the biggest fall since records began in 1975, only to be followed by an 0.6 per cent drop three months later and a further 0.5 per cent in the month to October. Little wonder, then, that many commentators took the view that inflation had been permanently tamed, even though the long-term historical record would suggest otherwise. From a political perspective, there was much to be gained from being able to switch attention from the problem of inflation to that of lack of jobs. In the UK since 1945, no government had been re-elected after presiding over a significant increase in the rate of inflation during its term of office. However, given the fact that so many people remained fearful of losing their jobs, it seemed to be appropriate for attention to be diverted, albeit temporarily, to creating jobs even at the expense of a modest increase in inflation.

☐ *4.4.2 Inflation Targeting*

Inflation targeting has been around since October 1992. It can be justified on two main grounds. First, it is seen as a better way of establishing common expectations among wage bargainers and within financial markets than through setting a target for the growth of broad money. Second, it establishes a commitment on the part of the authorities to maintain stable prices.

The government's base target currently remains, as originally, to keep RPIX within a 0 to 4 per cent band. However, the then Chancellor, Lamont, subsequently added his intent to push the rate down into the lower half of the range by the end of the term of office, and later added his aspiration to reduce the rate to 2 per cent or less in the long term. Chancellor Clarke, in his June 1995 Mansion House speech, stated his intention to keep RPIX below 2.5 per cent if the Conservatives were to be re-elected. There is accordingly some ambiguity about which target is the most important. Furthermore, one must be careful to distinguish the latter, which involves a permanent cap of 2.5 per cent, from any aspiration to keep RPIX to an average not exceeding 2.5 per cent over the economic cycle, which would be easier to achieve since it would be compatible with higher inflation at the peak of the cycle.

Judging by the UK's postwar record, the achievement of these aspirations would be no mean feat, and would leave little leeway to adjust for supply side 'shocks' should any transpire. It is also the case that RPIX is not necessarily the best inflation measure to be used for this purpose – certainly, it does not find much favour with the Bank of England. On a more positive note, we have observed in our prior discussion that quality improvements are equivalent to a minimum 1 per cent reduction in prices – in other words 1 per cent recorded inflation is tantamount to price stability. It should also be taken into account that

zero inflation does not permit nominal interest rates to fall below the rate of inflation – that is, for real interest rates to become negative as might be desired when emerging from recession – since this would imply lenders paying borrowers to borrow. Nevertheless, this is not to suggest that an underlying rate much, if at all, above 4 per cent is desirable, since the drawbacks are severe in terms of lost growth and jobs in the long term.

Inflation targeting is not unique to the UK; there are formal targets in, for example, Canada, Finland, New Zealand and Sweden, and more general medium-term targets (which can play a secondary role to exchange rate targets) in, for example, France and Germany (see Haldane, 1995; *The Economist*, 1995b). Some countries target the headline rate, others something approximating to RPIX. The advantages of targets are seen as enhancing the credibility of macroeconomic policy; easing the conduct of monetary policy; and making governments more accountable. Unfortunately, they do not appear in practice to have done much to lower inflationary expectations, at least not in the UK.

There are those who argue that an inflation target is less useful than a target for nominal GDP (see *The Economist*, 1993). Such a target effectively trades inflation for growth on a one-for-one percentage basis. For the moment, at least, the authorities remain unpersuaded of the latter's virtues.

There are even those who are unsure why the authorities worry so much about inflation in the first place. One interesting study which tries to shed some light on this matter is by Barro (1995) in which he attempts to assess whether inflation damages economic growth (see also *The Economist*, 1995a). If inflation is plotted against growth across a wide range of countries the resultant diagram appears to show no clear pattern at all. Barro's study covered more than one hundred countries, rich and poor, over the period 1960 to 1990, and concluded that an increase in inflation of one per cent would reduce the rate of growth by between 0.02 and 0.03 per cent per year.

For a country suffering massive inflation, the lost growth cost of that inflation would appear to be substantial, whereas it would appear to be negligible for a country reducing its inflation from, say, 8 per cent to 3 per cent. In any event, the relationship is statistically unreliable when restricted to countries in such a position. Furthermore, to reduce inflation to 3 per cent is itself costly in terms of the need to cut output and jobs, albeit temporarily. On the other hand, taken over sufficiently long periods, the effects would be cumulative and hence more significant, and Barro's estimates are in any event towards the bottom end of the range of estimates made by others.

☐ 4.4.3 International Perspectives

It is understandable that, in addressing the problem of inflation, individual countries tend to judge their performance either against a norm based upon historical experience or, less frequently, against an ideal set well below that norm. As a result, relatively little attention is paid to what is happening in other advanced economies even though, logically, some of the forces operating to raise prices in the UK will be operating in exactly the same way elsewhere. In other words, in judging just how much attention should be paid to the problem of inflation relative to, say, unemployment, it is useful to know how inflation-prone the UK really is by international standards.

The factor common to the experience of every country during the 1970s was the behaviour of the price of **crude oil**. In real terms, this rose by a factor of four in 1974 as a consequence of the formation of the OPEC cartel (known as the first 'oil shock'). The fact that the real price of oil subsequently held steady for nearly five years largely explains why inflation rates began to fall in oil-importing countries (which at that time included the UK). In 1979 there was a second 'oil shock' which was proportionately less severe but nevertheless quite sufficient to trigger an upturn in inflation throughout the world, as shown in **Figure 4.9**. Combined with increases in the prices of other commodity imports, the effects were quite severe, but once again the real price of oil stabilised, after falling sharply in 1985 due to the collapse of OPEC, at a level somewhat below that of the late 1970s, and apart from a

Figure 4.9 *Consumer Price Indices, Selected Countries, 1978–85 (%)*

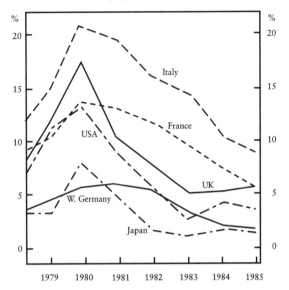

Source: OECD *Main Economic Indicators.*

Figure 4.10 *Change in Consumer Prices, EU Comparision, 1981–91*

Average annual percentage increase

	%
United Kingdom	6.0
Belgium	4.1
Denmark	5.0
France	5.3
Germany (Fed. Rep.)	2.3
Greece	18.5
Irish Republic	6.0
Italy	8.5
Luxembourg	4.0
Netherlands	2.2
Portugal	16.2
Spain	8.4

Source: Social Trends, 23 (1993 edn), Chart 6.11.

sharp blip at the time of the Gulf War it has shown no further tendency to rise and is now trading in real terms at prices similar to the early 1970s.

For comparative purposes, it is best to have recourse to the standardised data produced by the OECD, and these are illustrated in **Figures 4.9** and **4.10**. Care is needed because the choice of period is important. **Figure 4.10** produces data on inflation for the 12 Community member states during the (Thatcher) decade 1981–91. As can be seen, the UK fared a bit worse than average, but whereas the media were prone to make invidious comparisons with West Germany (as was) and the Netherlands, one can see that the Greeks, Portuguese and Italians were inclined to think the UK had the problem under reasonable control.

Figure 4.9 concentrates upon the period 1978–85 in order to make the point that the initial response of the Thatcher government to its inherited problems, including big hikes in indirect taxes, combined with the OPEC oil price rise mentioned above, precipitated a sharp bout of inflation. Although the increase was unusually

sharp, the subsequent reduction was also unusually sharp because of the way in which the RPI formula works in response to one-off price rises, as noted above.

Table 4.5 covers the past decade with a bigger sample set including the 15–member EU, the USA and Japan. The sharp drop in the price of oil in 1985 helped to pull down the inflation rate worldwide, with all countries bar Greece and Spain converging for the first time in over a decade, and West Germany actually enjoying falling prices. In the period post-1986 the UK, which was right in line with the EC-12 average in 1985 and 1986, once again performed badly and indeed had become the worst performer among the larger economies, including Italy, by 1990. As before, the cyclical peak partly reflected the increase in indirect taxation, in this case the rise in the standard rate of VAT to 17.5 per cent in 1991. However, it then converged rapidly on rates elsewhere, falling below the EU-12 average in 1992 and performing better than all the major EU economies in 1993, including Germany which, post-unification with the East, was now struggling to control inflation.

Table 4.5   *Consumer Price Indices. All Items. International Comparison, Percentage Changes on a Year Earlier*

	United Kingdom	Austria	Belgium	Denmark	Finland	France	Germany (West)	Greece	Irish Republic
1985	6.1	3.3	4.9	4.7	6.3	5.9	2.2	19.3	5.4
1986	3.4	1.7	1.3	3.6	3.6	2.7	−0.3	23.0	3.8
1987	4.2	1.4	1.6	4.1	3.4	3.1	0.2	16.4	3.2
1988	4.9	1.9	1.2	4.5	5.1	2.6	1.3	13.5	2.1
1989	7.8	2.6	3.1	4.8	6.6	3.7	2.8	13.7	4.1
1990	9.5	3.2	3.4	2.6	6.1	3.4	2.7	20.4	3.2
1991	5.9	3.3	3.2	2.4	4.2	3.0	3.5	19.5	3.1
1992	3.7	4.1	2.4	2.1	2.6	2.5	4.0	15.9	2.1
1993	1.6	3.6	2.8	1.3	2.2	2.1	4.1	14.4	1.4
1994	2.4	3.0	2.3	2.0	1.1	1.7	3.0	10.9	2.4
1995	3.4	2.3	1.5	2.1	1.0	1.6	1.9	9.3	2.6
1996[1]	2.4	1.5	2.0	2.0	0.7	2.4	1.5	9.2	2.0

Notes:
[1] latest month
[2] EU15

Source: Business Monitor MM23, Labour Market Trends, Table 6.8.

By 1993, a distinct convergence is evident, precisely in line with the expectations associated with the move towards full Economic and Monetary Union (see also Connock, Gilly and Hillier, 1995, p. 49). However, the position over the past year has given grounds for concern that a further bout of divergence has been set in train (see *Bank of England Quarterly Bulletin*, November 1995, p. 336).

It is evident from the above that the UK is one of the more volatile advanced economies when it comes to inflation (although the use of the headline rate rather than RPIX or RPIY is a significant factor here), but there is also evidence that it **can** perform as well – that is, there do not appear to be any fundamental structural reasons why the UK is an unusually inflation-prone economy.

On a final point, Eurostat has been asked to produce comparable 'harmonised' consumer price indices for member states (which, for example, treat housing costs identically). This is being done in two stages, with the results of stage I, the Interim Indices of Consumer Prices (IICP) published at the beginning of 1996 (see *Bank of Eng-*

land Inflation Report, May 1996, p. 7). Stage II indices will be released in 1997.

☐ 4.4.4 Analytic Considerations

We do not propose, in the sections that follow, to go into a detailed analysis of inflation. In the first place, we have yet to investigate such matters as unemployment and trade deficits, and it is more sensible to bring everything together in Chapter 20. Secondly, it is simply not the purpose of this book to replicate the abstractions of more theoretical texts. We do not, therefore, intend to conduct an in-depth analysis of Phillips Curves at this point. If, however, we examine **Figure 4.11** it is evident that the original Phillips Curve trade-off between inflation and unemployment has not been seen again since the 1960s. For our purposes, the interesting empirical question is why the sequence unwound as it did from 1980 to 1986, and why, after improving markedly from 1986 to 1988, it then underwent a loop very similar to that commencing in 1978 but almost upside

Table 4.5 *continued*

Italy	Luxembourg	Netherlands	Portugal	Spain	Sweden	EU12 average	USA	Japan
9.2	4.1	2.3	19.6	7.8	7.4	6.1	3.5	2.0
5.8	0.3	0.2	11.8	8.8	4.2	3.5	1.9	0.6
4.8	−0.1	−0.4	9.4	5.2	4.2	3.3	3.7	0.1
5.0	1.5	0.9	9.6	4.8	5.8	3.6	4.1	0.7
6.3	3.3	1.1	12.8	6.8	6.4	5.1	4.8	2.3
6.5	3.7	2.6	13.2	6.7	10.5	5.7	5.4	3.1
6.4	3.1	3.9	10.9	6.0	9.4	5.0	4.2	3.3
5.1	3.1	3.9	9.1	5.9	2.2	4.3	3.1	1.7
4.2	3.6	2.1	6.5	4.6	4.6	3.4	3.0	1.3
4.0	2.2	2.7	5.2	4.7	2.2	3.2	2.6	0.7
5.2	2.0	2.0	4.1	4.7	2.5	3.1^2	2.6	−0.2
4.6	1.5	2.0	2.9	3.5	1.3	2.7^2	2.9	0.3

down. Because at this juncture we have yet to discuss concepts such as the 'natural' rate of unemployment (discussed in Chapter 13), we must accordingly conduct the discussion in fairly general terms.

It is evident that inflation is a **multi-causal phenomenon**. No doubt monetary policy has had a part to play, as discussed in Chapter 20. Undoubtedly, trade union militancy is a factor which must, at times, be taken into account, and the external sector, the subject of Chapters 9 and 10, cannot be ignored.

What cannot be disputed is that in the early postwar period the UK was uncompetitive. Attempts to deal with this problem were legion, but generally unsuccessful, in part because of the resistance of the workforce which was highly unionised compared to competitor countries. In good part, the pressure to introduce reforms floundered because governments of all political persuasions were locked into the belief that they had to maintain high levels of employment. This meant running the economy with high levels of demand, since this was adjudged an easier way to keep people in jobs than by increasing supply. However, it is evident that expanding demand in the face of fixed supply is an excellent recipe for the creation of inflationary pressure.

Some of this excess demand usually leaks out into the external sector, and results in balance of payments crises. In effect, **these provide an alternative manifestation of an inflationary crisis**, and hence are unlikely to disappear without triggering a resurgence of inflation unless something has been done to control the latter in the meantime. Certainly, the traditional expedient of lowering the exchange rate simply served initially to raise import prices, and fed through into domestic inflation as companies adjusted their prices to take account of increased costs. This process represented 'cost-push' rather than 'demand-pull' pressures, as textbooks were wont to label them.

Figure 4.11   *The Phillips Curve*

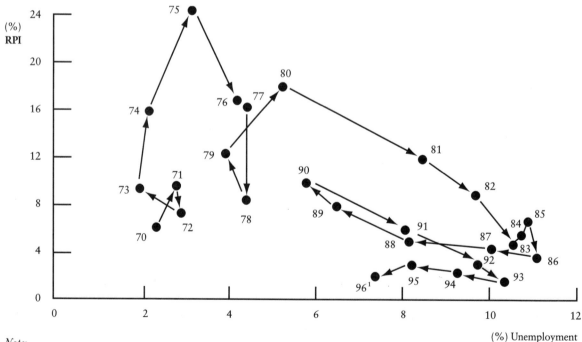

Note:
[1] Author's estimate.
Source: Labour Market Trends.

Cost-push pressures also arise if either wages rise **independently** of demand or companies increase their profit margins **independently** of demand. In either case, the key issue is whether the government is willing to **validate these pressures** by recourse to an accommodating fiscal and monetary stance. During the heyday of the Keynesian model, governments were rarely willing to tolerate cuts in output and jobs – and if at all, only in the short term. Starting in the period after 1976, but more notably after 1979, governments adopted a tougher stance. Such an about-turn in policy may at first be treated with scepticism, but if adhered to the message will eventually get through, as it did during 1980–81. Nevertheless, it was far costlier than expected – or intended – in terms of the number of workers who lost their jobs in the process of persuading employers and employees that the government was serious about controlling inflation.

Inflationary pressures which arise for reasons outside the direct control of the government are more problematic. If, say, the prices of imported commodities rise, then the standard of living of UK residents must necessarily decline. If the labour market is competitive, this will result in a reduction in wages, keeping total costs, and hence prices, unchanged. However, wages will probably not fall, in which case there is renewed inflationary pressure, and either the government reins back demand and uses job losses to suppress inflation or it accommodates the pressure and prices escalate. In the latter case, the tough stance is merely delayed in practice since the government will be forced to act once the inflationary pressure becomes severe.

The inflationary pressure described here is cost-push – that is, it occurs on the supply side of the economy – but its effects are clearly dependent upon the demand-side response by government. Given the above, it is a touch unfortunate that the UK government changed its stance from tough to accommodating during the so-called 'Lawson boom' in the latter part of the 1980s, with the consequences evident in **Table 4.5**. Nevertheless, this permits us to adopt a more optimistic view about future developments since politicians appear to have learnt from this experience.

One further point needs emphasising very strongly. It is clearly fallacious to argue that inflation cannot be reduced unless the economy stops growing, or that growth cannot be resumed until inflation is suppressed. As the data below show clearly, periods of rapid productivity growth are periods when unit costs rise very little, if at all, in the high-growth sectors (predominantly manufacturing). Where inflation emerges is in those sectors where productivity growth is low or non-existent, but which obtain roughly the same increase in wages on grounds of 'comparability'. Nevertheless, it is clearly impractical and inequitable to lock all of the gains from productivity within the manufacturing sector.

What governments must guard against are attempts by workers to protect themselves against any erosion in their standards of living which arises for **external reasons** such as higher oil prices. As we remarked earlier, there is scant sympathy in the UK for the view that when imported commodities go up in price this often represents the only means by which workers in much poorer societies can improve **their** standard of living.

□ *4.4.5 Inflation Since 1980*

It is possible to analyse what has happened since 1980 in the manufacturing sector. The ongoing rise in labour costs, which has always been a characteristic of the UK economy, was in every year from 1981 to 1992 compensated by some improvement in productivity, most obviously in the periods when the economy was emerging from recession. As a result, at least in manufacturing, unit labour costs rarely contributed significantly to any rise in output prices.

During this period, input prices also rarely fed through to the shops to any significant degree. Their influence was particularly benign in 1990–92 (see **Table 4.6**), at least prior to the depreciation of sterling in October 1992. Bought-in services were a more significant influence post-1988, responding to the growth in employment opportunities, but the effects of the recession began to

Table 4.6   *Contributions[1] to Output Prices in Manufacturing[2] from Changes in Cost Components (%)*

	Labour productivity (increase−) (1)	Labour costs (2)	Unit labour costs (3)=(1 + 2)[3]	Input prices (4)	Bought-in services[4] (5)	Margins (residual) (6) = (7−(3 + 4 + 5))[3]	Output prices (7)
1991	−0.7	3.5	2.9	−0.7	2.5	0.4	4.9
1992	−2.1	2.7	0.5	−0.7	1.2	1.2	2.3
1993Q2	−3.2	2.4	−0.8	1.4	−0.2	2.0	2.3

Notes:
[1] Calculated for each component as the twelve-month growth rate scaled by weights derived from 1984 input–output tables as follows:

unit labour costs	0.44
input prices	0.33
bought-in services	0.22

[2] Excluding food, drink and tobacco.
[3] Figures may not add up to totals because of rounding.
[4] Proxied by unit labour costs in the service sector.

Source: Bank of England Quarterly Bulletin (August 1993) p. 319.

show up clearly in the data for 1992 as job losses became severe in the services sector.

During the mid-1980s, a major contributory factor was clearly domestic profit margins. These rose exceptionally sharply in 1986, although this was evidently a one-off phenomenon. It has been argued that manufacturing companies basically apply a mark-up to their expected long-run costs, which does explain the rise in margins in 1986 when oil-related import prices fell sharply, but the relationship is much more ambiguous in other years. It is evident that, whereas companies were constrained in their ability to put up their prices because of competitive pressures in the early 1980s, they felt able to take advantage of their improved competitiveness in subsequent years. It is also evident that as spare capacity was used up, there was a tendency to take advantage of the shortage of supply by raising margins.

Margins in manufacturing understandably suffered during the recession, and there appeared to be some evidence that UK companies had begun to emulate their Japanese and German rivals in their willingness to cut margins in order to maintain competitiveness. Profit margins were so poor in the early 1980s that it is hard to castigate

companies for taking advantage of the window of opportunity to restore them in later years. The fact that margins fell throughout 1992 was thus a good omen, given that so much of the manufacturing sector sells in competitive international markets. With Japan and Germany in recession, the need was to remain competitive, taking advantage of the sterling depreciation, and in particular to raise productivity and reduce unit labour costs.

The fact that these rose so far during 1990 and 1991 was troubling, although this was more a case of poor productivity than of excessively high wage costs by 1980s' standards. This shows up in **Table 4.7**, which also illustrates the point that the record across the economy as a whole was inferior to that in manufacturing, where most (measurable) productivity gains are located, throughout the period from 1981 to 1994. In most advanced countries, Japan excepted, service-sector inflation has traditionally exceeded inflation in manufacturing. As previously noted, the prices of, for example, electrical goods may actually fall, but this is most unusual in respect of services. Service-sector inflation is relatively high because wages roughly keep pace with those in manufac-

Table 4.7 *Index of Wage Costs Per Unit of Output[1] (%)*

	Manufacturing	*Whole economy*
1980	22.9	21.9
1981	8.1	9.6
1982	4.6	5.2
1983	1.2	3.8
1984	3.0	6.5
1985	5.1	5.4
1986	4.0	4.6
1987	2.3	5.1
1988	2.7	7.1
1989	4.4	9.9
1990	6.7	9.7
1991	5.7	7.1
1992	0.8	3.9
1993	−0.2	0.0
1994	0.1	−0.4
1995	3.0	1.1

Note:
[1] % change from a year earlier.

Source: Labour Market Trends, Table 5.8.

turing but productivity growth is slower; because services cannot be stockpiled leading to price reductions in order to clear stocks; because as incomes rise consumers demand improved services; because consumers are less likely to switch doc-

tors than tins of beans; and, in particular, because most services are protected from the forces of international competition. For these reasons the objective of zero inflation is more meaningful when applied to the manufacturing sector rather than to the service sector.

These factors are clearly not confined to the UK, and although the UK's record was much worse than the average for the major six economies in 1990 and 1991, it was considerably better in 1992 and 1993. The deterioration in Japan and Western Germany has been especially noteworthy.

Table 4.8 indicates fairly clearly that cost pressures have re-emerged over the past two years, both in terms of wages and other inputs. It is particularly interesting to examine the path of earnings, which is shown for manufacturing industries in Britain over the past decade in **Figure 4.12**. The pattern for the whole economy is, in practice, very similar, albeit set mostly at a somewhat lower level. The apparently uniform upper limit for the data throughout the period can be contrasted with what happened previously. The average earnings index fell progressively from a starting point of 15 per cent in the 12–month period ending in January 1981 to just under 10 per cent in the 12–month period ending in January 1983. At this point the index stabilised, and that for the whole economy remained absolutely

Table 4.8 *Rates of Change of Manufacturers' Costs. Year-on-year (% change)*

	1993	*1994*	*1995*
Costs			
Unit wage costs	−0.2	–	3.0[1]
Materials and fuels (including semi-manufactured imports)	4.5	2.6	9.6
Imports of finished manufactures	8.5	3.9	8.4[1]
Services	2.9	3.5	1.9
Output prices[2]	3.9	2.5	4.2

Notes:
[1] 1995 is the average of 11 months data.
[2] Domestic sales.

Source: Bank of England Inflation Report (February 1996) Table 5B

constant at 7.5 per cent for nearly three years. Starting in mid-1987, the latter index climbed to a new equilibrium in the 9–10 per cent band where it remained until the Spring of 1991. Meanwhile, the manufacturing earnings index fluctuated remarkably little. Indeed, given the rapid growth in the economy, its consistency was quite remarkable and, for that matter, much remarked upon.

However, this rapid growth did affect wages and salaries per unit of output which, given the consistency of earnings, effectively presented a mirror image of the trend in output per head, as can clearly be seen in **Figure 4.12**. The exceptionally strong growth in output per head, which emerged from negative territory in 1980, came to a halt at the end of 1983, and was followed by a decline lasting two years. However, within the space of one year the situation had so reversed itself as to cause wages and salaries per unit of output to fall briefly below zero. They stayed comfortably below 5 per cent until 1989, at which point output per head fell sharply, itself entering negative territory in 1990 by which time wages and salaries per head had touched 10 per cent for the first time in a decade.

At this juncture, concerns resurfaced about **stagflation** (rising prices in conjunction with rising unemployment). Given that competitor countries were keeping a tight grip on their unit labour costs at the time, the fear was increasingly voiced that there would be a rerun of the late 1970s. However, events turned out very differently, as shown in **Figure 4.12**. There are, in practice, three key determinants of wage inflation, namely the rate of price inflation, the level and rate of change of unemployment and the level of profits. At the end of 1990, these impacted upon pay negotiations in such a way as to achieve something not seen for a decade, namely a fall in the average earnings index – and one, note, that **began almost exactly where the previous one finished off.**

Since 1990 the rate of price inflation has remained below its level at that time. This is partly accounted for by the fact that the average earnings index has remained well below its level during the 1980s, although it temporarily showed some signs of rising back to that level at the end of 1994. Productivity peaked in mid-1993 and then fell sharply, but the fact that it has fallen back to zero early in 1996 is potentially ominous.

Figure 4.12   *Earnings and Output per Head: Manufacturing Industries – Increases over Previous Year, Great Britain (%)*

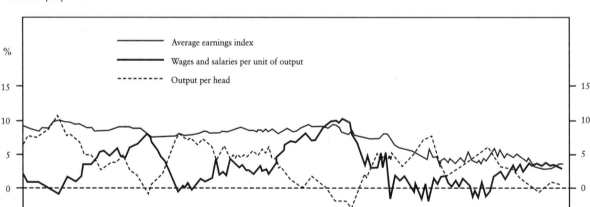

Source: Labour Market Trends.

Fortunately, given the behaviour of earnings, wages and salaries per unit of output have yet to climb above the 5 per cent mark.

A minor digression is warranted at this point in order to reflect upon the anonymous comment that 'When I first started working, I used to dream of the day when I might be earning the salary I'm starving on today'. This requires us to examine the behaviour of earnings adjusted for inflation (using the tax and price index). As can be seen in **Figure 4.13**, real earnings have generally been quite buoyant since 1980. Although money earnings were rising at a constant rate until 1990, their real counterparts were highly volatile, reflecting the pattern shown in **Figure 4.6**. The 'Lawson boom' period in the mid/late-1980s was particularly notable, but with the TPI rising sharply at the end of the decade real earnings fell back to earth. After a further mini-boom as the TPI subsided, the decline in the rate of increase of money earnings once again brought real earnings growth back through zero during 1995.

Whether expressed in money or real terms, earnings were surprisingly subdued as the economy moved out of recession. It has been argued that this reflects the fact that earnings usually pick up most quickly in the South-East, which on this occasion bore most of the brunt of recession; that large numbers of the unskilled unemployed held down wages; that male unemployment was high, holding back full-time male wages; and that institutional arrangements were changed (for example, via Restart) to induce the unemployed to take low-paid jobs

Taking the period since 1980 as a whole, it is abundantly clear that, on average, employees have enjoyed substantial improvements in their real earnings, and to talk in a general way about workers 'suffering' under the Conservatives is clearly nonsense. However, the average does not tell us anything about the distribution of earnings, which we must accordingly turn to in Chapter 15.

☐ *4.4.6 Is Inflation Dead?*

The comments on earnings above certainly suggest that there is unlikely to be a surge in inflation driven by rising wage costs in the near future. A further notable feature is that, from 1988 to 1994,

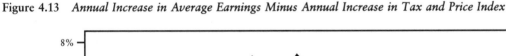

Figure 4.13 *Annual Increase in Average Earnings Minus Annual Increase in Tax and Price Index*

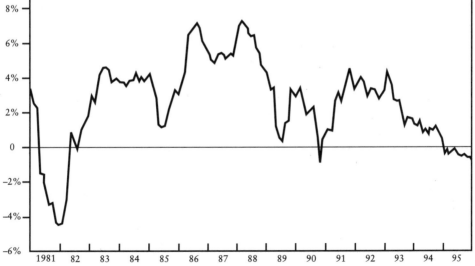

Source: Office for National Statistics.

commodity prices including oil, fell steadily causing real prices to fall by one-third. In 1993, *The Economist* all item commodity price index, adjusted for inflation, was one-third of its level in 1980, and indeed lower than at any previous time during the century. It seems unlikely that this can continue indefinitely into the future, and indeed commodity prices showed much more buoyancy commencing at the end of 1993 although they collapsed back during 1995 to levels not seen for 30 years. Furthermore, non-oil commodities currently only represent some 9 per cent of imports compared to 17 per cent in 1973, so they have much less impact. In any event, the key issue is, of course, whether increases will be passed on to the consumer which shows no sign of happening for the time being.

A further factor is that nominal interest rates are currently so low that they are, by implication, much more likely to rise than to fall in the future. Equally, there is some anxiety on the part of householders to see inflation rise in order to provide relief from debts including negative equity, not to mention a (privately-held) desire on the part of a large number of EU governments to see inflation wipe out some of the debts which stand in their path to full monetary union.

Finally, we have deliberately said very little about the money supply, firstly because it is discussed in detail in a later chapter, and secondly because it is not currently fashionable to worry about it as a causal factor in inflation given a weakening of the link between narrow money and inflation during 1994 and 1995 and a decline in narrow money velocity on a scale not seen for decades. This led the Bank of England to state in the February 1996 *Inflation Report* (p. 8) that 'at present, the growth in MO is unlikely to be signalling higher inflation'. However, the growth of 'broad' money has recently accelerated beyond the upper limit of its 3–9 per cent monitoring range, and this is seen in some quarters as a sure indicator of higher inflation in due course.

Bibliography

Barro, R. (1995) 'Inflation and Economic Growth', *Bank of England Quarterly Bulletin* (May).

Blackaby, D. and L. Hunt (1990) 'An Assessment of the UK's Productivity Record in the 1980s: Has There Been a "Miracle"?', *Economics* (Autumn).

Brittan, S. (1994) 'Competitiveness Rides Again', *Financial Times* (21 April).

Brittan, S. (1995) 'Time to Bury Those League Tables', *Financial Times* (25 May).

Competitiveness: Helping Business to Win. Cm 2563. May 1994 (London: HMSO).

Competitiveness: Forging Ahead. Cm 2867. May 1995 (London: HMSO).

Connock, M., A. Gully and H. Hillier (1995) 'Macroeconomic Convergence in Europe: A Review of the Maastricht Conditions', *The Review of Policy Issues*, 1 (4).

Crafts, N. (1993) *Can De-Industrialisation Seriously Damage Your Wealth?* (London: Institute of Economic Affairs).

Craven, B. and R. Gausden (1991) 'How Best to Measure Inflation? The UK and Europe', *The Royal Bank of Scotland Review* (June).

Eltis, W., D. Fraser and M. Ricketts (1992) 'The Lessons from the Superior Economic Performance of Germany and Japan', *National Westminster Bank Quarterly Review* (February).

Eltis, W. and D. Higham (1995) 'Closing the UK Competitiveness Gap', *National Institute Economic Review*, 154 (November).

Feinstein, C. and R. Mathews (1990) 'The Growth of Output and Productivity in the UK: the 1980s as a Phase of the Post-war Period', *National Institute Economic Review* (August).

Gilbert, C. (1990) 'Primary Commodity Prices and Inflation', *Oxford Review of Economic Policy* (Winter).

Haldane, A. (1995) 'Inflation Targets', *Bank of England Quarterly Bulletin* (August).

Hall, S., M. Walsh and T. Yates (1996) 'How Do UK Companies Set Prices?', *Bank of England Quarterly Bulletin* (May) pp. 180–92.

Kaletsky, A. (1996) 'How Labour Would Try to Change the Ways of Business', *The Times* (18 April).

Layard, R. and S. Nickell (1989) 'The Thatcher Miracle?', *American Economic Review, Papers and Proceedings* (May).

MacFarlane, H. and P. Mortimer-Lee (1994) 'Inflation Over 300 Years', *Bank of England Quarterly Bulletin* (May).

Muellbauer, J. (1991) 'Productivity and Competitiveness', *Oxford Review of Economic Policy*, 7 (3).

Nickell, S. (1990) 'Inflation and the UK Labour Market', *Oxford Review of Economic Policy* (Winter).

O'Mahoney, M. (1995) 'International Differences in Manufacturing Unit Labour Costs', *National Institute Economic Review*, 154 (November).

Oulton, N. (1990) 'Labour Productivity in UK Manufacturing in the 1970s and in the 1980s', *National Institute Economic Review*, 151 (May).

Oulton, N. (1995) 'Supply Side Reform and UK Economic Growth: What Happened to the Miracle?', *National Institute Economic Review*, 154 (November).

Oulton, N. and M. O'Mahoney (1994) *Productivity and Growth: A Study of British Industry, 1954–86* (Cambridge: Cambridge University Press).

Roberts, P. (1989) 'Supply-side Economics', Chapter 3 in J. M. Buchanan *et al.* (eds), *Reaganomics and After* (London: Institute of Economic Affairs).

Steindel, C. (1995) 'Chain-Weighting: The New Approach to Measuring GDP', *Current Issues in Economics and Finance*, 1 (3) (Federal Reserve Bank of New York).

The Economist (1992) 'Zero Inflation', (7 November).

The Economist (1993) 'Economic Straightjackets' (30 October).

The Economist (1994a) 'A Cruise Around the Phillips Curve' (19 February).

The Economist (1994b) 'The Price of Light' (22 October).

The Economist (1995a) 'The Cost of Inflation' (13 May).

The Economist (1995b) 'What Happened to Inflation?' (16 September).

The Economist (1995c) 'How Does Your Economy Grow?' (30 September).

van Ark, B. (1992) 'Comparative Productivity in British and American Manufacturing', *National Institute Economic Review* (November).

Wells, J. (1994) 'Not Very Productive', *New Economy*, 1 (3).

Chapter 5

The Banking System

Peter Curwen

■ 5.1 Introduction

The UK financial services sector (wholesale and retail) generates roughly 6.5 per cent of UK GDP. It is responsible, for example, for 75 per cent of the world's secondary trading in international bonds; 60 per cent of its international bond issues; 60 per cent of its foreign equities turnover; and 27 per cent of its foreign exchange turnover. As this suggests, the overall financial system in the UK is the most sophisticated in Europe and bears comparison only with that of the USA, albeit on a much smaller scale overall. For this reason, it is necessary to divide it up for analytical purposes into that part which comes under the heading of 'banking' and that part best described as 'non-banking'. Until fairly recently, this distinction would have been clear-cut and uncontroversial. As we shall see in what follows, the traditional distinction has become increasingly blurred of late, particularly in the light of the change in status of certain former building societies. To begin with, however, we need to examine certain aspects of their behaviour which are common to all financial intermediaries.

■ 5.2 Financial Intermediation

In a primitive economic world those who have saved part of their income and who wish to **on-lend their savings** (the ultimate lenders), will meet together with those who wish to **borrow** for various reasons (the ultimate borrowers) and arrange a mutually agreeable price for the transfer of funds between them. However, in a sophisticated world such transfers are beset with difficulties; the lenders and borrowers may be geographically dispersed, the amounts which lenders wish to make available may not match the amounts which borrowers wish to borrow and the term to maturity of funds on offer may not match borrowers' requirements. In principle, the price charged for transfers of funds – **the interest rate** – can be adjusted to overcome most of these difficulties, but in many cases a mutually agreeable interest rate will not be forthcoming, and the transfers will not take place even though lenders wish to lend and borrowers wish to borrow. Financial intermediaries are needed to overcome this problem.

Any lender who has decided to hold a portfolio of financial assets has to balance a number of considerations in deciding which assets to hold. In the first place, he or she is concerned with the **risk** element in the loan, which arises either because he or she may need cash prior to an asset's redemption date or because even if an asset can be redeemed before maturity this may involve a partial loss. Furthermore, if relatively small sums are involved, these can generally be turned into only one or two different types of asset, thereby preventing the lender from holding a sufficiently diversified portfolio of assets to protect against a particularly bad performance or outright default by one type of asset held. Secondly, the lender is unlikely to want to lend for long periods, partly because it constrains the ability to spend as the opportunity arises. Finally, the individual lender is unlikely to be well-informed. It may prove a time-consuming and expensive process to find a borrower willing to match the characteristics of the loan, and indeed the lender may ultimately fail to do so.

It is equally true that potential borrowers may be unable to find lenders willing and able to match their requirements, which often include a desire to borrow for long periods of time. At the end of the day these considerations, combined with the fact that the lender obviously wants to maximise the interest rate whilst the borrower wants to minimise it, severely constrain the volume of funds transferred directly between individuals.

It is also necessary to take account of **liquidity considerations**. Liquidity is concerned primarily with the speed with which any financial instrument can be turned into cash, or wholly liquid, form. But it is also important that the value of the instrument is preserved in the process. It is possible to sell most financial instruments in the open market for cash, but there is no guarantee that the exact face-value of the instrument will be repaid to its holder unless it is held to maturity. If it is sold prior to maturity, then its face-value will be determined by the face-value of newly-issued instruments having the same characteristics with respect, for example, to yield, maturity and risk. An early sale of any instrument may thus result in either a capital gain or a capital loss. Conventionally, any instrument issued with an original life-span of no more than 91 days is considered to be liquid, and this term also applies to any instrument which, irrespective of its original term to maturity, has less that 91 days left to maturity.

These matters can be addressed by an intermediary. The **law of large numbers** operates such that, whereas some liabilities to depositors need to be kept in cash or near-cash form to meet daily cash withdrawals, the rest can be on-lent to borrowers as long-term lending. As a consequence, the intermediary, unlike an individual, can create a balance sheet with its liabilities in relatively liquid forms and its assets (representing its claims on those to whom it lends) in relatively illiquid forms. Because it handles large numbers of loans, an intermediary must expect some borrowers to default. However, such defaults are very unlikely to put the intermediary at risk of going out of business. Hence, whereas the ultimate lender, in lending directly to one or a few individuals, faces the possibility of a total default, he generally runs the risk of losing no more than a small proportion of his funds if the intermediary he deposits them with gets into difficulties. Furthermore, the rate of interest can be adjusted to take account of different degrees of risk when lending to different intermediaries.

It is important to note from this discussion that when funds are deposited with an intermediary the money is not, in the majority of cases, on-lent in exactly the same form to the ultimate borrower. Instead, the process of **funds transformation** takes place whereby the intermediary creates liabilities, in the form of claims against itself by the ultimate lender, having different characteristics to its assets in the form of its own claims against the ultimate borrowers. Sometimes one intermediary may on-lend to another, with the result that funds transformation takes place on more than one occasion as funds flow through the financial system, and in the process the ultimate lender becomes increasingly separated from the ultimate borrower.

In summary, the process of intermediation is as beneficial to lenders as it is to borrowers. On the one hand, as discussed above, the lender faces a reduced risk; he can withdraw his money on demand or by giving relatively short periods of notice; he has to choose between only a small number of intermediaries; and he effectively obtains a share in a much more diversified portfolio than he could hold as an individual. On the other hand, the borrower knows where to go to get funds, and there are more funds available.

One final point which should be noted is that, whereas in principle the use of an intermediary might be expected to cause interest rates paid to depositors to fall, and those charged to borrowers to rise (since the intermediary exists to make a profit by selling its services), this may well not happen in practice. The depositor faces a reduced risk of default, and therefore should accept a lower reward for the risk-taking element of the loan, so that even after adding the intermediary's mark-up the cost to the borrower may be lower than for a direct transfer from the ultimate lender.

◼ 5.3 Classifying Financial Intermediaries

The range of financial intermediaries in the UK is unusually varied. The first task, is, therefore, to determine the most coherent way to arrange them in classes for further analysis. There are two main considerations here. In the first place, monetary controls operate through intermediaries, and it would seem helpful to divide up intermediaries into those that are affected by controls (particularly over the money supply) and those that are not. In this respect, it was traditionally argued that intermediaries which can create credit (**banks**) should be distinguished from those which cannot create credit (**non-banks**).

The second consideration is that it is necessary to lay down in law what, for example, is or is not a bank so that appropriate prudential supervision can be exercised by the Bank of England (see discussion of the Banking Act 1987 below). Historically, these considerations did not create particular difficulties, but the 1980s witnessed much blurring of traditional distinctions between intermediaries, partly as a result of attempts to regulate particular institutions in the pursuit of money supply control. In September 1983, the Bank of England introduced a new classification system

for banks which created three categories of 'British bank'. The first category comprises the **retail banks**, as listed below. The second, categorised as **other British banks**, comprises primarily the subsidiaries of the clearing banks, while the third category comprises the **British merchant banks**. All other banks are categorised as **overseas banks**.

The banks can also be divided into those which conduct business primarily in the **retail** market – that is, branch banks handling vast numbers of small accounts – and those which conduct **wholesale** business involving small numbers of very large transactions. The retail banks are mostly British, whereas the wholesale banks are mostly foreign. Most banks fall partly into both categories, so their classification is determined by their predominant form of business. The **discount houses** retain a separate classification.

However, many intermediaries are not banks as defined above. Whereas these can be lumped together as **non-bank financial intermediaries** (NBFI), some closely resemble banks in that they take in deposits, often via branch networks, while others conduct their business in quite different ways. **Table 5.1** shows the full classification.

We now need to examine, albeit briefly, the individual components of the UK financial sector. At the heart of the sector lies the Bank of England, so we will start by discussing its role, subsequently moving on to look at the banks, both retail and wholesale, and the non-bank financial intermediaries (in the chapter which follows). We will then examine the capital market where equities and bonds are traded, before completing the discussion with an overview of how the sector has evolved in recent years and the changes that can be expected to take place in the near future.

◼ 5.4 The Bank of England

The Bank of England (the Bank) is the central bank of the UK. It started life as a joint stock company in 1694, and in return for a large loan to the government was put in a privileged position which enabled it to become the largest private bank. It was subsequently authorised to hold the gold reserves of the banking system. In 1844 note

Table 5.1 *Financial Intermediaries: Classification in 1996*

Banks	
Retail Banks:	London clearing banks (5)
	Scottish clearing banks (3)
	Northern Ireland banks (4)
	Abbey National plc
	Co-operative Bank plc
	Yorkshire Bank plc
	Girobank plc
	Direct Line Ltd
	Cheltenham & Gloucester plc[1]
	Bank of England Banking Department
Wholesale banks:	Other British banks
	British Merchant Banks
	Overseas banks
Discount houses	
Non-bank financial intermediaries	
Other	Building societies
Deposit-takers:	National Savings Bank
	Finance Houses
Other NBFI:	Insurance companies
	Pension funds
	Investment trusts
	Unit trusts

Note:
[1] Wholly-owned by Lloyds Bank.

issuing powers were terminated other than via the Bank, which gradually became a monopoly supplier (other than in Scotland and Northern Ireland). It also increasingly stood prepared to maintain liquidity in the banking system. While not technically a public sector body until the passing of the Bank of England Act 1946, it had long been under the control of the Treasury (Chancellor of the Exchequer). It still retains today the residual part of its private sector clientele. It is managed by a Court of Directors, headed by the Governor, who are appointed by the Crown.

Since 1844 the Bank's balance sheet has been somewhat artificially divided into two halves, namely the **Issue Department** which is concerned with the issue of notes by the Bank, and the **Banking Department** which is concerned with everything else. Issue Department liabilities consist of notes in circulation, and its assets consist of an equivalent amount of government and other securities. Banking Department liabilities consist of public deposits (accounts of the government), bankers' deposits and reserves and other accounts. Bankers' deposits are either **operational** and used for inter-bank clearing, to equalise cash-flows between banks and the government or to pay for the purchase of notes and coins, or **non-operational** cash-ratio deposits to comply with banking regulatory requirements. Banking Department assets consist of government securities, advances and other accounts, and premises, equipment and other securities which are primarily in the form of commercial bills.

5.4.1 Functions of the Bank of England

The 1946 Bank of England Act defines the constitutional relationship between the Bank and the government as follows:

> The Treasury may from time to time give such directions to the Bank as, after consultation with the governor of the Bank, they think necessary in the public interest

For its part:

> the Bank, if they think it necessary in the public interest, to request information from and make recommendations to bankers, and may, if so authorised by the Treasury, issue directions to any banker.

The Act makes no specific reference to the Bank's duties and responsibilities because they were considered to be well-established by custom and practice. Overall, the Bank performs a wide variety of functions. It:

- is responsible for the issue of notes and coins;
- acts as banker to the central government;
- acts as banker to the banking sector;

- manages the Exchange Equalisation Account (EEA);
- advises the government on, and on behalf of the government carries out, its monetary policy;
- is responsible for the precise timing of interest-rate changes;
- supervises the banking sector.

According to the Bank's Governor (George, 1996, p. 92), three core purposes can be discerned from the above, namely:

- maintaining the integrity and value of the currency;
- maintaining the stability of the financial system, both domestic and international;
- seeking to ensure the effectiveness of the UK's financial services.

These days, notes and coins are the proverbial 'small change' of the financial system, and are produced to meet demand rather than to implement policy. As banker to the government the Bank handles the daily net balances of government departments, financing them when they show a deficit and converting any surplus into repayments of debt. The balance sheet item 'public deposits' is normally kept as small as possible in order to minimise the need to issue – and pay interest on – new national debt. The Bank is responsible not only for debt transactions that arise in the present period, but also for managing all the outstanding debt from previous periods. This requires a continuous stream of transactions in both the bill market and in the market for longer-dated government securities, known as **gilt-edged** (or gilts for short). Most government debt instruments can be freely traded on the Stock Exchange and money markets, and can therefore be controlled for policy purposes in the manner set out below.

All clearing banks keep an account at the Bank through which pass the daily transfers of funds between public deposits and the accounts of the banks' customers, and also the daily transfers of funds from one bank to another for bank clearing purposes (plus the occasional purchase of notes and coins). These transfers utilise the bankers' operational balances at the Bank, which do not

need to be particularly large as all daily cash flows are netted out.

The **Exchange Equalisation Account** contains the UK's gold and foreign currency reserves. These reserves are used periodically for intervention purposes in order to maintain the value of the exchange rate for sterling in accordance with the wishes of the government. If sterling is considered to be too high the Bank will sell sterling and buy foreign currencies. Sterling required for this purpose is obtained from the National Loans Fund which forms part of the public deposits. The Bank accordingly needs to keep accounts with a large number of overseas central banks.

Altogether, the Bank operates in three separate markets – **gilt-edged**, **discount** and **foreign exchange**. These operations collectively constitute the government's **monetary policy**. The Bank has always had the right to use its expertise to give advice to the government concerning the conduct of monetary policy, but it is nevertheless only the **government's agent**, and it is the Chancellor of the Exchequer, acting via the Treasury, who has ultimate responsibility for such policy. Confusion may arise in this respect because it is inevitably reported in the media that the Bank has taken particular actions in the gilt-edged or currency markets, but in so doing it is simply following instructions. Market interventions are, however, best performed at particular times and on a particular scale, and the Bank has considerable discretion in this respect since the Chancellor cannot be expected personally to keep the markets under continuous scrutiny.

The Bank's freedom of manoeuvre has been enhanced in recent years through its publication of a quarterly report on the UK's inflation prospects which is not subject to censorship by the Treasury. Furthermore, the monthly meetings between the Governor and the Chancellor are reported in the media, with the result that enormous attention is directed towards any difference in views between the two, even if the Chancellor necessarily has the last word under the current system. However, even if instructed to change interest rates by the Chancellor, it is ultimately up to the Governor as to the precise timing of such a change.

This is in good part because the Bank has such an important role to play in the gilt-edged market. The Bank not merely issues gilts on behalf of the government, but underwrites the issues in that any unsold gilts are bought-in by the Issue Department for future resale. It buys and sells on a daily basis in order to ensure that there is a receptive market for large-scale holders of gilts, especially insurance companies and pension funds that may wish to adjust their portfolios. The Bank's operations also inevitably affect gilt-edged prices, and hence long-term interest rates. Until recently this was considered of great importance, because sales of gilts reduce the liquidity of the private sector and hence help to control the money supply.

The final, but increasingly vital, role of the Bank is to **supervise the banking sector** (and indirectly, in practice, other financial intermediaries). With such vast sums at stake confidence is all-important, and it is the Bank's job to set the rules and ensure fair play. It was not customary to question the Bank's ability to achieve this in the banking sector, although recent events such as the BCCI scandal have cast a cloud over the Bank's reputation in this respect. However, the increasing sophistication and diversity of non-banking activity did oblige the Bank to permit other regulatory bodies to take over some of its responsibilities, for example the Securities and Investments Board (SIB) under the terms of the Financial Services Act 1986 (see **pp. 155–6**).

Banking supervision was first formalised under the Banking Act 1979 which allowed the Bank to authorise recognised banks and licensed deposit takers (which offered a narrower range of services). However, the collapse of Johnson Matthey Bankers in September 1984 set in train a reappraisal which resulted in the passing of the **Banking Act 1987**, which now treats all banks as a uniform category. In order for a bank to be authorised, it is required in particular that every director, controller and manager shall be a fit and proper person to hold his position; that the business of the bank be conducted prudently, especially in respect of capital adequacy, liquidity, and bad and doubtful debt provision; that proper systems of accounting and control are

maintained; and that net assets are at least ECU 5 million. If necessary, required standards can be adjusted in individual cases. The Bank can object to takeovers and mergers involving banks. The Bank must be notified if a bank becomes over-exposed (borrowing in excess of 10 per cent of bank capital) to an individual borrower. A Board of Banking Supervision has been set up to give guidance on the development of the supervisory system.

In May 1993 it was revealed that the Bank had been clandestinely supervising a lifeboat operation at the end of 1991, which cost it £115 million in indemnities and subsidies given to bigger banks to persuade them to lend to a few small (unnamed) banks in difficulties. It was public knowledge that the Bank had cleared up the mess surrounding the National Mortgage Bank, had stepped in to save City Merchants Bank and had actively intervened when the local authorities withdrew funds from smaller banks during the fallout from the BCCI affair. Nevertheless, the fact that some 40 small banks had been in difficulties, and that perhaps five had to be saved from bankruptcy, came as something of a surprise to the financial markets.

Traditionally, monetary policy was heavily dependent upon **liquidity ratio controls**. This is no longer the case, and since 1982 no such controls have been enforced by the Bank. Individual banks are expected to maintain what they themselves consider to be a prudent level of liquidity, but the Bank requires that banks maintain systems for keeping proper checks on liquidity, and reserves the right to check up that this is the case.

In 1988 the Bank issued a consultative paper which contained a new set of tough proposals concerning bank liquidity. However, banks objected to being told what type of assets they had to hold, particularly since the Bank wanted them to include low-yielding Treasury bills. In addition, foreign banks complained that they were already subject to liquidity controls in their home countries. As a result, the Bank dropped the proposals in April 1990 on the grounds that the banking system was too diverse to be subjected to a common liquidity regime, and that the EU might soon be proposing its own regime.

The **Financial Services Act 1986** also led to a more formal regulation of the wholesale money markets. To become an approved institution a bank must pass a 'fit and proper' test covering ability to manage and capital adequacy, and agreement to abide by the 'London Code of Conduct'. The Bank also runs the scheme which insures depositors against the failure of an authorised bank.

In October 1990 the Bank issued a set of procedures which it wished banks to adopt when dealing with companies in a liquidity crisis. In particular, it encouraged creditor banks 'jointly (to) ensure that (a troubled company) has sufficient liquidity to continue trading until a considered view of its prospects can be reached'. The Bank was, however, at pains to emphasise that its purpose was to remind banks of traditional procedures rather than to recommence the policies of intervention forsaken during the 1980s.

5.4.2 Should the Bank be Independent?

As noted previously, the Bank is essentially an arm of government, and as such is one of the least independent central banks in the developed world. During the past several years many voices have been raised in favour of granting more independence to the Bank. Such independence has two dimensions, namely political and economic. Political independence denotes that decisions can be made without interference by the government, and by implication that appointments to the governing board are not politically motivated. Economic independence denotes that monetary policy can be executed without fear of offsetting behaviour by the government.

The main justification for independence is that it will provide credibility to programmes for restraining inflation. Monetary stability is seen as a central purpose for the Bank, and the Governor sees the role of the Bank as follows (George, 1996, p. 92).

Above all, this involves securing price stability as a precondition for achieving the wider eco-

nomic goals of sustainable growth and employment. We pursue this core purpose by influencing decisions on interest rates . . . by implementing agreed policy through our market operations and our dealings with the financial system; and by maintaining confidence in the note issue.

The Bank's role is linked to the Maastricht Treaty provisions for full monetary union (see **pp. 285–7**) which required that a European Central Bank (ECB) be set up that is constitutionally independent of member states and legally obliged to maintain price stability within the EU. Given the necessity for the ECB to operate via national central banks, it follows that they must themselves be independent prior to a member state embracing full monetary union. Specifically, to be compatible with the Maastricht Treaty, a central bank must be prohibited from taking instructions from the government; it must be prohibited from purchasing debt instruments directly from the government and from providing credit facilities to the government; and its governor's term of office must last for at least five years;

At the time of writing, the UK has withdrawn from the Exchange Rate Mechanism and opted out of any formal obligation to proceed to full monetary union, hence there is considerable reluctance on the part of the government to loosen the apron strings which tie the Bank to the Treasury. The government is aware, for example, that this would remove any possibility of using inflation as a surrogate tax to supplement revenue when the borrowing requirement becomes excessive.

Alesina (1989) ranked central banks according to an index of independence, taking into account characteristics such as the formal institutional relationship between the government and the central bank, the presence of government officials on the bank's board and the existence of rules forcing the central bank automatically to print money to finance budget deficits. The study demonstrated that over the period 1973 to 1986 the least independent central banks were in Italy and Spain (which was, however, granted considerably more autonomy in May 1994), whereas the most independent were in Switzerland and West Germany. Britain was included amongst those central banks with only a modicum of independence. Subsequent work, notably by Alesina and Summers (1993), has examined the relationship between independence, inflation and unemployment, as shown in **Figure 5.1**.

As can be seen, there was a close correlation between the index of independence and the rate of inflation, although this has weakened since 1988 suggesting that independence is by no means a necessary condition for success in suppressing inflation (as in respect of the UK and France). Furthermore, unemployment also tended to be low in highly independent banks, but the overall correlation was much weaker as was also the case for the link between independence and growth. This suggests that inflation is affected by expectations as to whether the central bank means what is says when it adopts a tough anti-inflationary stance, or whether it is expected to be told to relax its stance by politicians anxious to protect jobs.

After summarising the empirical studies, Pollard (1993, p.34) notes that there is a problem of causality since, for example, 'countries with an aversion to inflation may formalize this through the creation of an independent central bank'.

Given the position of Britain in **Figure 5.1**, it is understandable that there is a credibility problem in respect of monetary policy. The government's view is currently that the high level of home ownership makes changes in interest rates too sensitive an issue to be divorced from government control, and Blake and Westaway (1993) argue that there is little benefit in having an avowedly independent bank that is continuously at odds with the government's own policies.

■ 5.5 Banks in the UK

As previously discussed, there are two ways in which the banking sector can usefully be divided up for analytic purposes – namely, British/overseas and retail/wholesale. **Table 4.2**, parts (a) and (b), sheds considerable light on why these distinctions are useful. As shown in part (a), the total deposit liabilities of banks in the UK at the end of

Figure 5.1 *Central Bank Independence and Inflation/Unemployment*

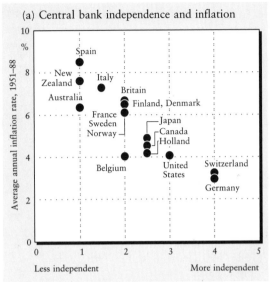

(a) Central bank independence and inflation

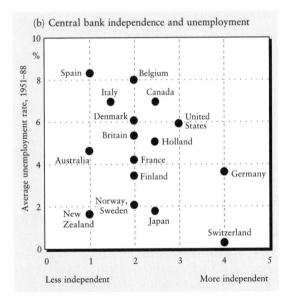

(b) Central bank independence and unemployment

Source: The Economist, 25 January 1992.

1995 were £1765 billion. Of this total, £1621 billion was recorded separately either as sterling or foreign currency liabilities, whereas the rest was in a mixture of currencies. To those unfamiliar with the Eurocurrency markets (discussed below), it may come as a surprise to note that

Table 5.2 (a) *Banks in UK,[1] Deposit Liabilities at 30 December 1995*

	Sterling deposit liabilities (a)		Foreign currency deposit liabilities (b)		Total deposit liabilities
	£ bn	%[2]	£ bn	%	£ bn[3]
Retail banks	411.1	74.7	139.6	25.3	637.4
British merchant banks[4]	21.8	58.6	15.4	41.4	43.0
Other British banks	37.4	77.4	10.9	22.6	59.6
American banks	23.6	17.4	112.0	82.6	142.9
Japanese banks	31.1	14.5	182.9	85.5	217.4
Other overseas banks[5]	134.0	20.8	511.6	79.2	665.4
Total	659.0	40.4	972.4	59.6	1765.7

Notes:
[1] As a result of the changes in the monetary sector culminating in the conversion of the Abbey National Building Society into a bank on 12 July 1989, the term 'monetary sector' was replaced by 'banks in the United Kingdom' or simply 'banks'.

[2] Expressed as percentage of (a) + (b) only.

[3] Including items in suspense and transmission, capital and other funds.

[4] Members of British Merchant Banking and Securities Houses Association (formerly the Accepting Houses Committee).

[5] Including consortium banks listed separately prior to August 1987.

Source: Calculations based on Bank of England data.

(b)

	% Banks in the UK sterling deposits	% Banks in the UK foreign currency deposits	% Banks in the UK total deposits[1]
Retail banks	62.4	14.4	36.1
Wholesale banks	37.6	85.6	63.9
British banks	71.4	17.1	41.9
Overseas banks	28.6	82.9	58.1

Note:
[1] Excluding items in suspense and transmission, capital and other funds.

Source: Calculations based on Bank of England data.

roughly 60 per cent of the £1621 billion was in the form of non-sterling deposits.

The proportions are in practice somewhat variable, because they are a snapshot of the picture on one particular day which may be unrepresentative of the days which both precede and follow it. One reason for this is that wholesale banking tends to respond to demand – in other words, if there is a potential borrower for a very large sum of foreign currency at a particular point in time, the wholesale banks will go out and attract deposits of the same magnitude. One must also bear in mind that the valuation of foreign currency deposits varies according to movements in the exchange rate. It is thus quite possible to find the ratio between sterling and non-sterling deposits registering a much lower order of magnitude.

This ratio disguises the fact that the retail banks, which are primarily British banks with branch networks, conduct much more of their business in sterling than the wholesale banks. As shown in part (**b**) of **Table 5.2**, 62.4 per cent of sterling deposits were held by retail banks, whereas wholesale banks took 71.4 per cent of foreign currency deposits. Since the wholesale banks are mostly subsidiaries of foreign banks, it follows that the latter must take in the majority of all deposits and, as shown in **Table 5.2 (b)**, the proportion was roughly 58 per cent of the total. Here again, the distinction between British banks taking in most of the sterling deposits, and overseas banks taking in an even bigger proportion of the foreign currency deposits, is particularly notable.

□ 5.5.1 Retail Banks

The retail banks comprise primarily the clearing banks in England and Scotland and the Northern Ireland banks. There are also Abbey National, Yorkshire Bank, Co-op Bank, the Girobank and Direct Line which provide very similar services. The odd man out is the Bank of England Banking Department, which gets included in the statistics despite its quite different role discussed above.

The typical retail bank is a clearing bank which provides services to individuals and firms through a branch network. The traditional side of the business is represented by current (sight) and deposit (time) accounts, provision of cheque books, clearing of cheques, overdraft facilities and personal loans, small currency transactions and a wide range of financial advice. In the 1980s there has been considerable innovation in the way that traditional services are provided, such as cheque-guarantee cards, automated teller machines, Eurocheques and, most recently, new lines of business have been developed such as large-scale mortgage lending, managed unit trusts and share dealing services.

All retail banks publish balance sheets to a set pattern, and their combined balance sheet as at 31 December 1995 is set out in **Table 5.3**. Retail banks do an increasing amount of wholesale business, as discussed below, but this is not distinguished separately in the balance sheet. The balance sheet ultimately represents a trade-off between a number of contradictory forces. On the one hand, retail banks are, with minor exceptions, obliged to make profits for shareholders, and high rates of return can be earned only by lending for fairly long periods of time and by taking a certain amount of risk. On the other hand, account holders constantly require cash to be made available, and other low-return assets may need to be held either for prudential reasons in order to avoid a possible loss of confidence by depositors or because it is so required by the Bank of England.

The balance sheet, both liabilities and assets, is divided into sterling and foreign currency categories. **Sterling deposits** are heavily dominated by the sight and time deposits of individuals and companies in the UK. Traditionally, the latter paid interest while the former did not, but sight deposits remained in the majority because they offered instant access whereas time deposits required notice of withdrawal. However, factors such as the provision of interest-bearing instant-access accounts by building societies eventually persuaded large numbers of depositors that only minimum sums should be kept in bank current accounts, and the banks were forced to respond by offering to forgo charges on such accounts provided, typically, they were kept in credit. As a result, time deposits lost their appeal, and sight deposits once again became equally popular.

In 1987 the Midland Bank introduced a Vector account which paid interest on accounts held in credit, but attracted few customers because interest earned was largely offset by account charges. The decision by Lloyds Bank in October 1988 to offer all of its customers an interest-bearing current account came as a considerable surprise, but once the Midland, Barclays, Royal Bank of Scotland and TSB followed suit, this process became unstoppable. Indeed, in January 1989, Barclays went one stage further by abolishing charges for

Table 5.3   *Retail Banks: Balance Sheet*

	31/12/88 (£ mn)	31/12/90 (£ mn)	31/12/92 (£ mn)	31/12/95 (£ mn)
Sterling Liabilities				
Notes Issued	1 407	1 678	2 084	2 576
Deposits: UK banks	20 165	27 830	31 383	48 233
UK public sector	4 185	4 550	4 233	7 235
UK private sector	137 362	218 053[5]	237 471	299 478
Overseas	17 609	26 730	22 386	27 399
Certificates of deposit[1]	11 965	21 354	22 732	28 765
Other Currency Liabilities				
Deposits: UK banks	6 373	6 903	11 268	14 341
Other UK	6 883	10 371	15 402	23 019
Overseas	26 437	37 346	60 419	80 422
Certificates of deposit[1]	3 549	6 690	13 666	22 160
Sterling and Other Currencies[2]	47 038	64 609	70 965	84 051
TOTAL LIABILITIES[3]	282 974	426 114	492 009	637 679
Sterling Assets				
Notes and Coins	3 375	3 926	4 293	5 329
Balances with Bank of England[4]	749	1 032	829	1 200
Market loans: Secured money with LDMA	5 220	7 375	4 947	4 420
Other UK banks	17 639	31 748	43 743	58 372
UK banks CDs	4 201	8 469	9 161	13 300
UK local authorities	738	226	297	318
Overseas	3 573	5 258	7 265	12 464
Bills: Treasury bills	1 502	2 469	1 762	9 900
Eligible local authority bills	388	31	24	–
Eligible bank bills	6 060	10 064	7 997	9 809
Other	137	150	217	334
Advances: UK public sector	702	527	348	524
UK private sector	147 920	234 239[5]	248 871	300 732
Overseas	5 284	4 599	2 380	3 101
Banking Dept. leading to central government (net)	956	1 657	1 227	−1 801
Investments: British government stocks	3 547	3 226	2 571	12 353
Others	5 122	10 785	17 839	30 670
Other Currency Assets				
Market loans and advances: UK banks	10 007	9 395	16 911	18 536
UK bank CDs	178	736	729	951
UK public sector	–	18	2 575	5
UK private sector	7 648	10 980	12 541	18 139
Overseas	30 391	38 020	53 437	61 823
Bills	436	1 153	3 540	2 732
Investments	6 198	11 675	20 499	46 500
Miscellaneous (all currencies)	20 999	28 355	28 016	27 967
TOTAL ASSETS	282 974	426 114	492 009	637 679

Notes:
[1] And other short-term paper issued.
[2] Items in suspense and transmission, capital and other funds.
[3] Of which eligible liabilities amounted to £160 billion at end-1988; £249 billion at end-1990; £258 billion at end-1992; £328 billion at end-1995.
[4] Including cash ratio deposits.
[5] These figures were affected significantly by the reclassification of existing business with Abbey National Group at 1 July 1989. This added roughly £30 billion to UK private sector sterling deposits, sterling advances and eligible liabilities.

Source: Bank of England.

transactions on current accounts such as standing orders and cheques. The distinction between sight and time deposits will eventually appear to be no more than an historical anachronism, especially when it is borne in mind that the retail banks' wholesale business largely comprises interest-bearing sight deposits.

Wholesale deposits have fixed terms to maturity varying from days to years, and are paid a market-determined rate of interest which may therefore differ considerably from interest rates paid to individuals. Whereas wholesale deposits are still fairly modest, it must be recognised that there is intense competition for retail deposits and the retail banks, like all other intermediaries, can no longer rely on a sufficiently large inflow of retail deposits to meet their needs for on-lending particularly in, for example, the mortgage market.

Certificates of Deposit (CDs) are fixed-term deposits that are exchanged for a certificate issued by the bank which can be traded in the open market. Hence, although the deposit itself cannot be withdrawn before maturity, the original depositor can get at his cash much earlier by selling his CD, although he may well be obliged to sell it for less than its face value if interest rates have risen.

The large item **sterling and other currencies** includes items in suspense because, for example, of uncertainty about ownership, items being transferred between accounts and finally the capital injected into the banks by shareholders **plus** liabilities to bond holders. It is also the custom to itemise 'eligible' liabilities. These comprise all sterling deposits from non-bank sources with an original maturity of no more than two years; net interbank lending in sterling; sterling CDs issued **less** sterling CDs held; any net deposit liabilities in sterling to overseas offices; and any net liabilities in currencies other than sterling **less** 60 per cent of the net value of transit items. Eligible liabilities were first introduced in 1971 for the purposes of monetary control, and since August 1981 all banks with eligible liabilities in excess of £10 million must hold 0.35 per cent of their eligible liabilities in the form of non-interest-bearing balances at the Bank of England. Although these

were originally intended to operate as a cash-ratio monetary control mechanism, they currently serve only to provide the Bank of England with a free source of income to pay for its functions as the central bank.

Overall, the preponderance of instant-access or short-notice deposits means that retail bank liabilities are exceptionally liquid, and this inevitably has to be reflected in their asset portfolios. The liquid assets category includes, first, notes and coins (till money) plus balances at the Bank of England which are partly involuntary to finance the Bank, and partly voluntary to facilitate inter-bank clearing. Sterling market loans represent short-term money market lending, whether to the discount houses; the inter-bank market; another bank in return for that bank's CD; local authorities; or overseas individuals and banks. Of these, inter-bank lending is by far the most important, although it is only in recent years that it has become so dominant. It represents transfers from banks which temporarily have an excess of liquidity to those which are temporarily short of funds (an especially useful practice in the days when monetary controls operated on bank liquidity, although this is no longer of any relevance). There is a speculative element, insofar as any bank which expects interest rates to rise can borrow for long periods in the hope that the money can be on-lent for an initial short period at current interest rates, and then re-lent subsequently for successive periods at higher rates, thereby earning a speculative profit. If interest rates are expected to fall, successful speculation would require the bank to borrow short, and subsequently to re-borrow more cheaply, while lending long at current rates.

Eligible bank bills are also prominent in the balance sheet. An eligible bill is one which the Bank of England will buy, via the discount houses, in order to make good a shortfall of cash in the banking sector. Only the bills issued by private companies, called **commercial bills**, which have been 'accepted' (guaranteed to be redeemed at face value) by major banks that fulfil specified requirements laid down by the Bank of England acquire the status of eligible bank bills. The government's own bills (Treasury bills) are obviously also eligible, as are certain bills issued by local authorities.

It is worth noting that when a bank buys a bill it is not redeemed at face value plus interest by its issuer, but rather the bank buys the bill at a discount to its face value and when it matures its issuer redeems it at face value. The difference between the price paid and the face value can then be divided by the price paid in order to convert the discount into a conventional rate of interest. Any discounted bill can be rediscounted any number of times – that is, it can be resold at a different price to another party who subsequently is paid the bill's face value if it is held to maturity. By rediscounting bills a bank can, therefore, hold a portfolio of bills some part of which matures on any given day of the year.

The bulk of bank lending to private individuals and firms is represented by UK **private sector advances**. Public sector advances are normally insignificant because lending to the government and local authorities is largely via discounting their bills, money market loans and the purchase of long-dated government securities (gilt-edged). Private sector advances are linked to bank base rates where modest sums are involved, but large loans are commonly linked to the central money market interest rate known as the London Inter-Bank Offered Rate (**LIBOR**). It is important also to note that, traditionally, the pattern of private sector sterling deposits and advances was one where the deposits of individuals were recycled into loans to firms. In 1978, individuals deposited three times as much as they borrowed. By 1988 these deposits had trebled, but their borrowing had risen nearly tenfold, and marginally exceeded these deposits. Since 1983 they have borrowed more than firms in aggregate.

Banking Department lending to central government represents the net contribution to the retail banking sector of the Banking Department of the Bank of England. As it retains certain long-standing private individual accounts these do need to be itemised as retail bank assets, but the major part, which represents transactions with government departments, is something of an anachronism in the balance sheet. This item is quite often negative, which simply means that government departments have more money on deposit than they are borrowing at that point in time.

Foreign currency assets are almost entirely in the form of inter-bank lending within the UK and of lending to overseas residents, companies and especially banks. It may finally be noted that the fixed assets of retail banks, in the form primarily of property, are not separately itemised because of their relatively modest value.

In conclusion, we may note that the pattern of the retail banks' balance sheet is constantly evolving. In particular, the difficulty of attracting adequate retail funds has driven banks into the wholesale markets where interest rates are linked to LIBOR, and this has to be balanced by increased LIBOR-linked lending. The problem is accentuated by the need to pay interest on sight deposits which were traditionally a free source of funds. Furthermore, the retail banks are obliged to hold some non-interest earning assets in the form of bankers' balances. These factors, combined with a very expensive branch network and with severe losses on many of their loans have understandably made considerable inroads into their profitability, and they have increasingly seen the solution as a movement away from traditional banking services and towards other financial services – that is, banks as financial supermarkets.

5.5.2 Domestic and International Debts

Retail banks have acquired an unenviable reputation for losing money. It all began when they decided that sovereign states would not default on their debts. Unfortunately, the rulers of many of these states decided that they could do as they pleased, which in many cases was not to repay. Then the banks decided that property lending must be sound because it was secured by real assets, which in many cases subsequently proved to be unsaleable except at bargain basement prices. As a result they advanced money for highly-leveraged management buy-outs in the expectation that the junk bonds (very high yielding but risky) they obtained in return would indeed yield a high return once the company taken over was broken up and resold. In many cases, wrong again. This led them to engage in devices to abolish risk such as swaps (discussed below), only to discover that they **shifted risk** – in the case of local authority swaps onto themselves – but they did not **abolish** it. Finally, they decided to create financial services empires by buying estate agency chains – just in time for the housing market to collapse – and insurance companies.

It was clear by the early 1980s that a good deal of the money lent to LDCs would never be repaid even if these countries did not officially renege on their debts (see **pp. 260–3**). However, banks which had become heavily involved in this lending, possibly because of the fanciful idea that sovereign country debt was more secure than lending to households and firms, because it gave a measure of status to a bank to be the banker to a sovereign state, and because the monopoly of knowledge that banks had about borrowers (and about the risk of making a loan) had become freely available to competitors via computers, were unwilling to write the debt off their balance sheets for fear that it would expose their inadequate capital structure. Initially, the common practice was to convert short-term loans into long-term loans, and to set aside some of the profits earned on other business into a reserve fund to cover international bad debts. Where possible, the capital base of a bank was replenished by an additional issue of equity and it was possible to offset some losses against tax liabilities.

In 1987 the international banks, following the example set in America, decided to bite the bullet and write a significant part of the debt off their balance sheet. Nevertheless, it remained understandably difficult for banks to raise new capital in the markets, especially in the aftermath of the October 1987 crash. In 1989, Lloyds' cover for problem country debts was raised to 47 per cent, well above that for the other three which stood at between 31 and 22 per cent in 1988. Since that time, all of the banks have seen fit to make additional provisions, so that there will soon be no further need to make major provisions against defaulting sovereign debt.

Unfortunately, as previously mentioned, there were plenty of other non-performing loans to take

their place. They stemmed primarily from increased participation in highly-leveraged transactions and increased exposure to the property sector. These appeared to be commercially sound in the boom conditions of the late 1980s, but rebounded on the banks with the arrival of high interest rates and recession. This can be seen in **Figure 5.2**, which covers the period to 1991.

In retrospect, it is difficult to understand how the banks could have mismanaged their affairs so badly. For example, whereas it is theoretically possible to make a loss in the life and pensions business if too many customers die at the wrong time or surrender their policies, if expenses go out of the control or if investment returns deteriorate, it had always been difficult to do so in the past. Nevertheless, the TSB paid £227 million for Target Life in August 1987 only to end up selling it for a loss in excess of £200 million to Equity and Law in January 1991. It then followed this up by shutting down its centralised mortgage lending arm

Figure 5.2 *Provisions and Write-offs in Large British Banks*[1]

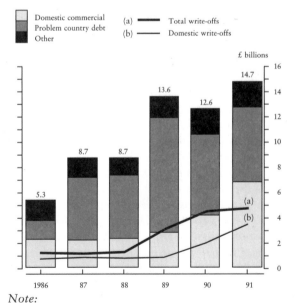

Note:
[1] Barclays, Lloyds, Midland, National Westminster, Bank of Scotland, Royal Bank of Scotland, Standard Chartered, TSB.

Source: Bank of England Quarterly Bulletin.

Mortgage Express (the third largest of its kind established in 1986) in April 1991 because it was unsaleable.

Estate agencies have also taken their toll. In March 1993, for example, Abbey National put its 355 branch Cornerstone network, in which it had invested £226 million since 1987, up for sale for roughly £35 million, but attracted no bids. Meanwhile TSB admitted to huge losses on its chain as did Lloyds in respect of its Black Horse Agencies. However, this problem has not been confined to the banks, with Nationwide BS dumping its 304 branches for a nominal £1, the Alliance & Leicester announcing in February 1996 its desire to dispose of its 70 branches and even the insurers Sun Alliance indicating a desire to follow suit. The banks, building societies and insurers spent in aggregate roughly £2 billion building up chains, but the total losses are anyone's guess.

□ 5.5.3 Retail Banks in Transition

Retail banks responded in a number of ways in order to restore their battered profit margins. For example:

- They widened interest rate margins on loans and charged higher fees for services.
- They shed staff and cut branch networks.
- They found themselves conserving capital in the face of weak demand for loans.
- They disposed of unprofitable subsidiaries.
- They engaged in takeovers/mergers

The consequences for bank workforces were fairly predictable in that the banks had to slash their branch networks and their staff. In 1984, there were 14 360 bank branches in Britain, but only between 8000 and 9000 are expected to survive to the end of the decade. Some 13 000 banking jobs were shed in 1990; 26 000 in 1991 and 30 000 in 1992. Overall, the five years to 1994 saw the number of jobs fall from 355 000 to 288 000 (officially – the BIFU union puts the reduction at 110 000 jobs). According to a report issued in November 1995, a further 100 000 jobs, representing more than a third of those remaining, will

disappear during the rest of the decade, and even this may prove to be conservative given the pace of takeover activity. Indeed, Barclays announced the loss of 1000 branch jobs and 500 regional office jobs in March 1996; Yorkshire Bank the loss of 300 headquarter staff and Lloyds/TSB the loss of 500 administrative jobs in April 1996; and NatWest the intention to shut 300 branches over four years with the potential loss of 10 000 jobs, in July 1996.

Banks have also had to rethink their global strategies. As retail banks have discovered, often to their cost, banking remains largely a domestic business, and cultural, tax and regulatory obstacles have so far prevented the creation of a single market in the EU despite the directives discussed below. The banks' attitude to their US operations has been particularly ambivalent. At the end of the 1980s, such large losses were being sustained that withdrawal was the key concern, with Barclays completing its withdrawal in May 1992. However, with bad debts mounting up at home, US subsidiaries once again began to look attractive. For example, Royal Bank of Scotland, which began with the purchase of Citizens Financial Group in 1988, completed its acquisition programme with the Old Stone Federal Savings Bank in mid-1994. In March 1994, National Westminster (now NatWest Group) bought Citizens First Bancorp, followed by Central Jersey Bancorp in July. However, it subsequently sold off its US retail subsidiary NatWest Bancorp in September 1995 for £2.6 billion on the grounds that it was too small to compete successfully.

Given the domestic emphasis of their business, it was inevitable that some of the retail banks would look to amalgamating their businesses with those of other financial intermediaries, either via a takeover or a merger. The amalgamation of banks within the British banking sector itself has always been fraught with regulatory difficulties. When, for example, the Midland Bank went up for auction in 1992, the highest bid was tendered by Lloyds, but that of the Hong Kong and Shanghai Bank proved more acceptable to both the Office of Fair Trading and the European Commission. On the other hand, no difficulties were raised when Lloyds bid for the TSB Group, thereby creating LLoyds/TSB at the very end of 1995 (for details of mergers involving building societies see **pp. 137–9**). The retail banking sector will be enlarged through the conversion of building societies following the example of Abbey National. The most significant among these will be that of Halifax/Leeds. Once that goes through there will be three large banks – Barclays, NatWest and Lloyds/TSB – and three medium-sized banks – Midland, Abbey National and Halifax – dominating the UK retail banking sector.

A particularly interesting phenomenon is the creation of **bancassurers** – subsidiaries of banks (and building societies) selling life and pensions products through their retail branches. This obviously avoids the need to incur overheads in respect of a separate sales organisation. Abbey National, for example, bought Scottish Mutual Assurance for £285 million in 1992, and in the face of a market depressed by the pension mis-selling scandal, nevertheless managed to virtually double its new business in 1995. NatWest and the TSB (as was) also run life arms, and in January 1996 Midland bought Commercial Union's remaining 20 per cent stake in Midland Life and became the latest retail bank to own a fully independent life business.

A rather more awkward fact of life for retail banks is that their tribulations tend to create more problems for the future. For example, when in the early 1990s the retail banks were mostly downgraded from AAA status by the main credit rating agencies, their borrowing costs rose as a consequence. With many blue chip companies achieving a higher rating in their own right, they could save money by going directly to the money markets rather than by operating through the banks.

The reputation of the banks has been particularly damaged by a stream of adverse publicity, related in particular to accusations that they have profited from falling base rates by failing to pass on the benefits to small-business customers. A Bank of England study published in January 1993 refuted these particular claims, but was widely regarded as a whitewash.

In June 1993, for example, National Westminster introduced penal charges on current account holders who overdraw substantially without authority, thereby temporarily opting to penalise their most unprofitable customers. With retail banks allegedly losing money on 80 per cent of their current accounts, the burning issue has long been just how far they are willing to go to court further unpopularity in order to restore their finances. The answer, if the decision to clear cheques in three days rather than four, initiated in June 1994, is anything to go by, is not much further. Fortunately for them, the retail banks' financial situation has improved so much, with the addition of £3.5 billion to an already strong capital base in 1995 alone (*Financial Times*, 16 March 1996) that they can now afford to behave in a more 'user-friendly' manner.

5.5.4 Basel (Basle) Capital Convergence Accord

In July 1988 the Governors of the Group of Ten central banks signed the Basel Capital Convergence Accord, thereby making banking the first industry to be regulated on a world-wide basis. The central purpose of the Accord (which is not, however, legally binding) is to force all international banks to comply with minimum capital requirements, and thereby to **ensure fair competition between them**. So far the Accord only covers credit risk but, while it is true that non-repayment of domestic and international loans has been the biggest risk faced by banks, other sources of risk such as those associated with exchange rate and interest rate variability need to be added to the Accord and are currently under discussion as noted below.

The Accord essentially lays down a definition of **capital** and a formula for working out how much of it banks must have, depending upon the **riskiness** of their assets. The definition was complicated by different practices in different countries, but needed to identify capital **permanently available to meet losses**. In the UK, banks are financed with both equity and debt, but German banks have very little of the latter. Equally, US banks issue 'perpetual preferred stock' (PPS) which is neither one nor the other. In the event, a compromise was reached whereby **at least 50**

per cent of capital must be tier 1 or 'core' capital, comprising equity, disclosed reserves and PPS (but only if it is non-cumulative, meaning that failure to pay dividends in one year must not create an obligation to make them up in later years). Tier 2 includes long-term debt and other debt instruments

The other complication concerned the 'risk weighting' of assets. Risk assets comprise all bank assets, including off-balance sheet commitments, weighted according to their riskiness. The UK, as a full member of the OECD, is deemed to be a low-risk borrower, as are other OECD members (with the possible exception of Turkey) plus Saudi Arabia. Bank lending to other countries is deemed to be at greater risk. All commercial lending is deemed to be at equal risk, irrespective of the size of the borrowing company, in order to avoid vast numbers of individual decisions about credit worthiness.

Every bank had until 1991 or early 1993 to meet its minimum **'risk asset ratio'**, which could be imposed at a level higher than that of the Accord if individual countries so wished. The Accord itself requires that capital must be equivalent to at least 8 per cent **of a bank's risk-weighted assets**, together with a minimum tier 1 ratio of 4 per cent. These ratios are sometimes known as the BIS (Bank for International Settlements) ratios. The Bank of England decided, however, not to leave matters to chance and to a last-minute cleaning-up of banks' balance sheets, and accordingly announced in November 1988 that UK banks would have to meet the Accord stipulations by the end of 1989, well in advance of most other signatories.

In practice, UK banks have had little difficulty in meeting their ratios via retained earnings and modest rights issues. Oddly enough, it is the big Japanese city (commercial) banks which have got problems. At the end of the 1980s, 9 out of the biggest 10 banks in the world and 23 out of the biggest 30 were Japanese. Several were bigger, in market capitalisation terms, than the entire British banking industry. They were permitted to count 45 per cent of the investment gains on shareholdings as capital, and the booming Tokyo Stock Market was viewed as an effective guaran-

tor that their ratios would be easy to safeguard. The enormous fall in the Nikkei index during 1990 proved how vulnerable they were in reality.

There is still room for improvement in implementing the ratio. It is argued that the necessity to retain capital equal to 8 per cent of commercial loans compared to zero for cash, 10 per cent for Treasury bills and 20 per cent for gilts has undesirably distorted lending away from the former category. It is also alleged that it makes little sense to treat all commercial loans as equally risky since this may incline banks to divert scarce capital away from blue-chip companies to others where the capital is, in reality, much more at risk. Also, the fact that loans secured on residential property require only half as much capital as commercial loans will inevitably make it harder to suppress asset price inflation.

At the end of April 1993 the Basel Committee recommended that from January 1994 banks should set aside less capital when they have arrangements with other banks for netting out liabilities. It also recommended that, commencing in 1997, banks should set aside extra capital to cover the market risks they run in respect of operations in foreign exchange, securities and derivatives markets, and yet more capital to cover their interest rate risks. This was met with widespread protests since it appeared to require more or less a doubling of bank capital ratios for what were generally regarded as manageable risks.

In April 1994, it was proposed that if banks did not care for the new rules then they could apply to use their own in-house techniques of risk management instead. The banks remained unhappy with this and the matter was thrown back into the melting pot in September 1995. However, the argument is not, for once, being conducted in a climate of crisis. Outside Japan, tier 1 ratios are almost universally well above 4 per cent, even in a country like France which has to carry the burden of hopeless cases such as Crédit Lyonnais, and are often, as in the UK, in the region of 8 per cent. If anything, the fear is that banks will embark upon another of their spending sprees which have caused so much damage since the mid-1970s (for a discussion of possible future developments see *The Economist*, 25 May 1996, pp. 114–15).

□ 5.5.5 The Single Market

As with other parts of the financial system, the banks have had to come to terms with a stream of EU directives (for a full list see Molyneux, 1994). A first step was taken in 1977 with the adoption of the **First Banking Co-ordination Directive** which required all 'credit institutions' to be authorised and monitored. The **Second Banking Co-ordination Directive** followed in 1989, and came into force on 1 January 1993. This provided a passport for credit institutions to supply certain services throughout the EU once authorised in the home state.

On 3 January 1991, the Bank of England adopted two directives which govern banks' capital and the size of their balance sheets. The directives also affect building societies, but in that case implementation is the responsibility of the Building Societies Commission. The **Solvency Ratio Directive** lays down a formula for calculating how large a balance sheet a credit institution can run, based on the riskiness of its assets and the size of its capital. It sets a minimum ratio of capital to assets of 8 per cent. The **Own Funds Directive** states how a credit institution's capital is to be calculated. These directives came into force on 1 January 1993. The two directives were essentially a reiteration of the Basel capital adequacy provisions, and hence did not require major policy changes since the banks were already operating under the Basel provisions.

The **Large Exposures Directive** came into effect on 1 January 1994, and harmonises the rules which cover the exposures of credit institutions to individual borrowers or groups of connected clients. Finally, the **Capital Adequacy Directive** became effective on 1 January 1996. This applies risk-based capital requirements to non-bank investment firms. Banks have to carry capital on their 'trading books' calculated in the same manner as securities firms.

As Molyneux has observed (1994, p. 40), despite the existence of these directives there are three serious impediments holding back the creation of a Single Market in financial services, namely:

- Member states have considerable freedom to claim an exemption on the grounds of the so-called 'general good' opt-out;
- tax obstacles largely frustrate cross-border provision;
- EU law is 'flexibly' transposed into national law.

□ 5.5.6 Wholesale Banks

As shown in **Table 5.2 (a)**, at end-1995 the total deposit liabilities of the wholesale banks amounted to some £1128 billion, of which some £1040 billion was held at overseas banks. Collectively, therefore, wholesale banks greatly outweigh retail banks, but as there are 600 or so such banks currently in operation in the UK, their individual portfolios are on average much smaller than those of the typical retail bank.

Wholesale banks concern themselves with small numbers of large-scale transactions. Deposits of less than £100 000 are unlikely to be accepted, and these deposits are often parcelled up into even larger loans. Deposits are not normally withdrawable on demand, so there is no need to keep anything like the same degree of cash and near-cash reserves as retail banks. Furthermore, it is possible to supplement liquidity by borrowing in the interbank market or through issuing certificates of deposit. Because each deposit is in a specific currency (mostly non-sterling – see **pp. 147–9** for a discussion of the Eurocurrency markets), and the depositor can specify the term to maturity, wholesale banks need to find borrowers who want the same currencies for as near as possible the same periods of time. A perfect match between assets and liabilities is, however, rarely possible because of the preference among lenders to lend for periods of time which are shorter than the periods over which borrowers prefer to borrow, and there are obvious problems in matching currencies. The characteristic transaction of a wholesale bank is, therefore, quite different from that of a retail bank, but this has led to the main retail banks setting up wholesale banking subsidiaries in order to diversify their pattern of business, so there are in practice more links between the two banking sectors than may at first seem apparent.

British Merchant Banks

The British Merchant banks are distinguished from other British wholesale banks by virtue of their membership of the British Merchant Banking and Securities Houses Association. Their former name of 'accepting houses' arose from the traditional practice of 'accepting' commercial bills, which effectively guarantees repayment in full upon maturity and hence both makes the bills easier to market and reduces the discount which needs to be offered. Some bills are retained for their own portfolios, but this type of agency business is no longer all that important.

Currently banking activity is almost entirely wholesale rather than retail. The total deposit liabilities are modest by wholesale banking standards, and are generally divided between sterling and foreign currencies in approximately a 60:40 ratio. Both deposits originating overseas and from the inter-bank markets (UK banking sector) have become increasingly prominent. Assets are correspondingly distributed, with the bulk of sterling assets in the form of loans to the UK inter-bank market and advances to UK borrowers, and the greater part of foreign currency assets in the form of lending abroad, especially to foreign banks. Lending to non-bank customers is relatively unimportant and, as indicated above, very little cash is held.

British merchant banks are also significant providers of financial services. Many undertake responsibility for all the administrative aspects of issuing new equity; provide a wide range of banking services for companies and some wealthy individuals; act as management consultants with respect to, for example, mergers and takeovers; and provide portfolio management services for pension funds and, in certain cases, unit trusts and investment trusts.

Other British Banks

The typical other British bank, so categorised because whereas it is registered in the UK it does most of its business with overseas clients, is considerably smaller than the typical British merchant bank. Of the 200 or more such banks, the core group comprises long-standing institutions originally set up to facilitate retail banking in British colonies. This has understandably not been a growth area for some time, and this category now includes a number of the smaller UK banks which offer a restricted range of services, including some which, although not officially merchant banks, provide almost identical services. Since the Banking Act 1979 took them within its provisions, many former finance houses have also operated in this category, competing directly with organisations listed separately under the heading.

The total deposit liabilities of other British banks are no longer greater than those of the British Merchant banks, and there are considerable similarities in the respective balance sheets. Other British banks do not, however, hold many acceptances.

□ 5.5.7 Overseas Banks

A number of American and European banks have had a London office for many decades in order to provide services for their customers while in the UK. However, the number of overseas banks has grown enormously over the past two decades, initially as a result of the growth of Eurocurrency markets, and more recently as a result of financial deregulation.

As shown in **Table 5.4**, there were 541 overseas banks in London in 1995, a gain of roughly 160 since 1980. The invasion was originally spearheaded by American banks, although their numbers peaked in 1983 and are now fewer than those of Japanese banks which have more than doubled since 1980, with departures commencing only in 1990. The past three years have seen the fastest overall influx since the early 1980s, which suggests that the much predicted demise of London as a result of continental competition has been postponed, especially since this influx has mostly originated in Europe.

As shown in **Table 5.2(a)**, whereas in 1995 the American banks alone still had deposit liabilities of £143 billion, equal to 175 per cent of the

Table 5.4 *Foreign Banks in London*

	US			Europe			Japan			Arab			Others			Summary		
	Total	Out	In	Total	Out	In	Total	Out	In	Total	Out	In	Total	Out	In	Total	Out	In
1980	71	2	1	141	3	21	24	0	0	19	0	1	128	3	12	383	8	35
1981	73	1	3	147	2	8	25	0	1	23	0	4	131	5	8	399	8	24
1982	77	0	4	153	0	6	29	0	4	26	0	3	144	1	14	429	1	31
1983	76	2	1	165	3	15	31	0	2	28	0	2	145	2	3	445	7	23
1984	75	1	0	168	6	9	35	0	4	35	0	7	146	2	3	459	9	23
1985	70	7	2	169	0	1	38	0	3	34	2	1	143	5	2	454	14	9
1986	68	3	1	184	3	18	40	0	2	34	2	2	136	8	1	462	16	24
1987	64	5	1	190	5	11	46	0	6	33	1	0	131	6	1	464	17	19
1988	59	8	3	201	5	16	50	0	4	36	1	4	132	3	4	478	17	31
1989	57	4	2	204	6	9	50	0	0	35	1	0	136	1	5	482	12	16
1990	53	4	0	207	10	13	51	2	3	34	1	0	133	6	3	478[1]	23	19
1991	49	5	1	209	8	10	54	1	4	36	0	2	146	1	14	494	15	31
1992	45	5	1	202	12	5	52	2	0	40	1	5	155	2	11	494	22	22
1993	49	0	4	208	12	18	52	0	0	40	1	1	165	2	12	514	15	35
1994	49	2	2	215	2	9	52	1	1	37	3	0	168	5	8	521	13	20
1995	51	2	4	228	7	20	52	0	0	38	1	2	172	5	9	541	15	35
Total		51	30		84	189		6	34		14	34		57	110		212[2]	397

Notes:

[1] Comparable figures for Paris and Frankfurt were 277 and 247 respectively.

[2] Many of these departments were due to mergers of foreign banks.

Source: Noel Alexander Associates.

combined liabilities of British merchant banks and other British banks, this represented only 67 per cent of the liabilities of the Japanese banks which are mostly comparative newcomers to London. The Japanese banks in 1988 had deposit liabilities virtually equal to those of the retail banks and it was thought that they would soon overtake them, but in the event the sterling liabilities of the retail banks shot up as did deposits at other (non-American) overseas banks. The latter currently exceed the deposits of Japanese banks by a wide margin. As **Table 5.4** indicates, this has resulted from the huge influx of European banks (82 net between 1979 and 1989), with a significant surge after the Single European Act in 1986.

The Eurocurrency markets are discussed separately below, and it is necessary to note at this stage only that the enormous growth in **international money** (for example, dollars traded outside America) was particularly centred in London, so all the important overseas banks necessarily had to open an office there to participate on any scale in these markets. American banks, in particular, were drawn to London by a desire to avoid the much tighter regulations in their domestic markets. Because American and Japanese banks have been at the forefront of developments in electronic banking, they have been particularly well placed to take advantage of the recent deregulation of financial services, and their recent movement into, for example, the mortgage market has had profound effects upon traditional practices in the UK. No doubt overseas banks will steadily encroach upon other areas of business, such as corporate finance, and given that their deposits are backed by the vastly greater assets of the parent companies, they look set to play an increasingly dominant role.

As shown in **Table 5.2 (a)**, the overseas banks do the vast bulk of their business in **foreign currencies**. Their deposits, predictably, largely come from overseas, and mostly from parent organisations. Around one third of their sterling deposits also come from overseas, and most of what remains is borrowed in the UK inter-bank markets which also provide over 15 per cent of foreign currency deposits. On the assets side of the balance sheet there are minimal amounts of cash and balances held at the Bank of England, but massive amounts of foreign currency lending to overseas residents, a great deal of which is routed via overseas banks. Inter-bank lending is very important, both in sterling and foreign currencies. As with other categories of wholesale banks, almost exactly the same amount is borrowed from the inter-bank markets as is lent to them. Apart from the modest net effect of retail bank operations in the inter-bank markets, it is simply a matter of definition that total lending must be equal to total borrowing, and the very large sums being transferred represent either portfolio adjustments by individual banks (for example, adjustment of maturity profiles) or simply opportunities which individual banks have to borrow from other banks with no immediate customers and to on-lend at a profit. Because wholesale banking is in aggregate so much larger than retail banking, the small proportion of assets held in sterling still represents a far from modest amount of lending. Whereas they are clearly more than happy to compete for sterling business in the UK, they do not as yet show any real interest in operating outside London, and this is why one gets the impression, even in the largest provincial cities, that the UK retail banks are the only major banking intermediaries.

☐ 5.5.8 The Discount Market

The discount market is a money market, the membership of which was until recently restricted to the eight discount houses which were members of the London Discount Market Association (LDMA), of which seven currently remain in business. The nature of their business can be clearly seen in the LDMA balance sheet which consists almost exclusively of sterling liabilities, mostly in the form of funds borrowed 'at call' (recallable without notice) and overnight. These funds, as we have seen, represent the most liquid asset bar cash itself in the retail banks' balance sheet. On the assets side of the balance sheet are to be found very little bar sterling-denominated short-term assets.

The functions of the discount market are to make a market in bills of all kinds, to give the banking sector a means by which they can replenish their cash holdings virtually on demand and to assist in the financing of short-term trade debts through the purchase of discounted commercial bills from banks and their customers. The discount houses are also committed to tender for the whole of every issue of Treasury Bills (TBs) in order to guarantee that government departments can pay their way, but they can be outbid, and indeed holdings of TBs have fallen to quite modest levels.

The LDMA, in essence, exists to maintain liquidity in the financial system. There are vast amounts of short-term instruments in existence, and the LDMA effectively guarantees that they can be bought and sold freely, thereby greatly reducing the need for cash holdings. At the end of daily cheque clearing, for example, some banks will have cash surpluses which can earn interest, albeit at very low rates, by being placed in the discount market, while the others can find on the spot the cash which is needed to settle deficits.

The discount market also has an important role to play in the conduct of monetary policy. Every day, money flows between government departments and the clearing banks via accounts held at the Bank of England. On any given day this may result in a very large net cash flow in one direction or the other. If government departments have drawn heavily on cash held at the clearing banks, the banks will have to go immediately to the discount market to replenish their cash holdings. With cash in short supply, short-term interest rates will have to rise rapidly to attract sufficient cash into the market. Conversely, if the clearing banks are flush with cash, which is then deposited in the discount market, the LDMA will have to bid for short-term assets, causing their prices to rise and their yields to fall.

If short-term interest rates become very volatile, this will quickly be transmitted to longer-term interest rates and to the exchange rate. In order to avoid this, the Bank of England stands ready to smooth cash flows between government departments and the clearing banks. If the banks have too much cash the Bank will mop it up by selling eligible bills to the LDMA, and if there are cash shortages the Bank will buy eligible bills in return for cash. This is called an **open-market operation** (OMO). While it is the case that the Bank of England is willing on occasion to deal directly with financial intermediaries other than the LDMA, it is formally the case that only the LDMA may go to the Bank for funds when they cannot be obtained from any other source.

An OMO in the discount market therefore provides the means whereby the Bank can influence short-term interest rates. Since August 1981 the procedure has been as follows. When cash is in short supply the Bank will invite the LDMA to sell eligible bills. If their selling price is acceptable to the Bank it will buy the bills and relieve the cash shortage. However, if the price is unacceptable, it will ask the LDMA to re-offer at a different price, thereby raising or lowering the interest rate as appropriate. The same procedure can be used if the Bank offers to sell eligible bills in order to mop up surplus cash.

If the Bank was, exceptionally, to refuse to buy bills at any price offered by the discount houses, then it would leave them with no option but to ask for a 'lender-of-last-resort' loan from the Bank, and the Bank would be able to charge any interest rate that it wished as a condition for making the cash available. The significance of this procedure is that the money markets cannot know for certain, in advance of the Bank's response to an offer to buy or sell eligible bills, what the Bank's views are about the appropriate level for short-term interest rates. The money markets are constantly nudging short-term interest rates up and down, but the Bank can signal its desire either to see these rate movements go beyond the limits set by the market, or the restoration of rates previously prevailing. By behaving in this way the Bank does not seek to dominate the markets on a continuous basis, as was the practice throughout most of the period prior to 1981, but rather to give clear guidance to the markets as and when it is considered to be appropriate.

Bibliography

Alesina, A. (1989) 'Politics and Business Cycles in Industrial Democracies', *Economic Policy* (April).

Alesina, A. and Summers, L. (1993) 'Central Bank Independence and Macroeconomic Performance: Some Comparative Evidence', *Journal of Money, Credit and Banking* (May).

Baimbridge, M. and B. Burkitt (1995) 'Reflections on Central Bank Independence', *The Review of Policy Issues*, 1 (3).

Bank of England (1993) 'Cross-border Alliances in Banking and Financial Services in the Single Market', *Bank of England Quarterly Bulletin* (August).

Blake, A. and P. Westaway (1993) 'Should the Bank of England be Independent?', *National Institute Economic Review* (February).

Briault, C., A. Haldane and M. King (1996) 'Central Bank Independence and Accountability: Theory and Evidence', *Bank of England Quarterly Bulletin* (February).

Colwell, R. (1991) 'The Performance of Major British Banks, 1970–90', *Bank of England Quarterly Bulletin* (November).

Dale, R. (1994) 'Regulating Investment Business in the Single Market', *Bank of England Quarterly Journal* (November).

David, P. (1994) 'International Banking', *The Economist* (30 April).

Dowd, K. (1995) 'Central Bank Independence and Inflation: An Alternative View', *The Review of Policy Issues*, 1 (3).

Dowd, K. (1996) 'Should the Bank of England Be Abolished?', *The Review of Policy Issues*, 2 (1).

Fraser, I. and P. Mortimer-Lee (1993) 'The EC Single Market in Financial Services', *Bank of England Quarterly Bulletin* (February).

George, E. (1996) 'The Bank of England: How the Pieces Fit Together', *Bank of England Quarterly Bulletin* (February).

Healey, N. (1996) 'What Price Central Bank Independence?', *The Review of Policy Issues*, 2 (2).

Healey, N. and P. Levine (1992) 'Unpleasant Monetarist Arithmetic Revisited: Central Bank Independence, Fiscal Policy and European Monetary Union', *National Westminster Quarterly Bank Review* (August).

Molyneux, P. 'Europe's Single Banking Market and the Role of State Autonomy', *The Review of Policy Issues*, 1 (1).

Pollard, P. (1993) 'Central Bank Independence and Economic Performance', *Federal Reserve Bank of St Louis Quarterly Review* (July/August).

The Economist (1993) 'The Sum, Not the Parts' (11 December).

The Economist (1994a) 'A New Broom for Europe's Capital Markets' (5 November).

The Economist (1994b) 'So Much for the Cashless Society' (26 November).

The Economist (1995) 'Too Much of a Good Thing' (27 May).

Unger, B. (1992) 'World Banking', *The Economist* (2 May).

Wood, G., T. Mills and F. Capie (1993) *Central Bank Independence: What Is It and What Will It Do For Us?* (London: Institute of Economic Affairs).

Chapter 6

The Financial System

Peter Curwen

■ 6.1 Introduction

This chapter is concerned with all aspects of the financial system bar the banks. However, the separation between banks and non-banks is becoming increasingly artificial, and many of the comments in the latter part of this chapter necessarily refer to the financial system as a whole.

An interesting illustration of how rapidly things are changing in the world of financial services can be seen in the case of Marks and Spencer, the most famous clothing and food retailer in the UK. M&S moved into financial services in the mid-1980s in an attempt to resolve the problem that it did not want to accept credit cards but its customers did. M&S accordingly decided to launch its own charge card, thereby avoiding the payment of commission, and it has acquired some 4 million card-holders. It has marketed an increasing range of other financial services to these card-holders, commencing with personal loans (originally, but no longer, to finance M&S purchases) and branching out into unit trusts, personal equity plans, life insurance and pensions. These services are highly profitable, but M&S has steered clear of mortgages in order to avoid the possibility of becoming associated with repossession.

It is fortunate for the 'traditional' financial intermediaries that there are very few companies like M&S, and that others which have dabbled in financial services in the past have been largely unsuccessful. Nevertheless, far more people enter chain stores than banks and building society branches every day, so it is far from surprising that the public finds it convenient to shop for financial services at the same time as socks and suits. One other important factor, in the light of recent scandals concerning the mis-selling of services in order to obtain huge up-front commissions, is that a company like M&S can afford to sell services using salaried personnel.

It is important to remember, therefore, in reading the sections that follow, that a financial intermediary is defined by what it does rather than by what it calls itself or by the nature of the umbrella organisation of which it is a part.

■ 6.2 Non-bank Financial Intermediaries

□ 6.2.1 Building Societies

The building societies began life as terminating societies, which lasted as long as it took to build houses for all of the members. Over time they became permanent, and came to monopolise a particular form of financial service. Modern so-

133

cieties are **mutual organisations**, which bring together the generally modest savings of large numbers of individuals and parcel them up into a much smaller number of mortgages. Savers' accounts are known as **shares** and **deposits**. Shareholders do not, however, share in a society's profits, but by virtue of being society members can vote at annual general meetings on such issues as conversion to banking status (see below). Interest rates are slightly lower on deposit accounts, which have the balancing advantage of priority in repayment if a society goes bankrupt. This is not generally thought to be much of a risk, so there are understandably many times as many shareholders as depositors.

During the 1970s the societies faced little competition from the banks, which thought mortgage lending to be too long-term; did not enjoy the composite tax rate arrangement which cheapened the cost of funds to societies; had, unlike the societies, to build a profit margin into the interest rate charged; and had their aggregate lending constrained by monetary controls. The societies chose to avoid competition amongst themselves by operating an **interest rate cartel**, and mortgage lending was heavily constrained by the inflow of retail funds in the absence of access to wholesale markets.

None of these considerations any longer apply. Building societies both compete amongst themselves for business, and are under attack not merely from the 'clearing' banks, but also from the foreign banks and the mortgage corporations which keep down costs by having no branch network. When funds were in short supply, large-scale borrowing attracted an interest rate penalty. Currently, the larger the loan the cheaper it tends to be, as funds from the wholesale markets appear to be almost limitless. Faced with bank encroachment upon their traditional business, the societies have responded by encroaching on the business of the banks and insurance companies.

Table 6.1 provides an interesting historical snapshot of the building society sector. The number of societies has dropped dramatically since 1960, and although the rate of reduction has necessarily slowed down, the process of merger is still continuing. Assets accordingly became concentrated in the hands of a relatively small number of societies, many of which were huge by historical standards. As the number of societies shrank, they snapped up sites in every High Street in the land, a process which peaked in the mid-1980s when there were twice as many branches as a decade earlier. This process is now beginning to reverse itself as societies seek to economise on their operations and to merge their operations, but the really big reductions, as in 1989 with the Abbey National, result from the transfer of societies to the banking sector.

These operational changes also cut back the number of shareholders, which peaked at 44 million in 1988. This is rather astonishing given the size of the population, but many people hold

Table 6.1   *Building Society Statistics (End-year)*

	1960	1970	1975	1980	1985	1990[1]	1993[1]	1994[1]
Number of societies	726	481	382	273	167	117	101	96
Number of branches	N/A	2 016	3 375	5 684	6 926	6 055	5 654	5 566
Number of shareholders (mn)	3.9	10.3	17.9	30.6	40.0	37.0	37.8	38.2
Number of depositors (mn)	0.6	0.6	0.7	0.9	2.1	4.3	5.5	5.5
Number of borrowers (mn)	2.4	3.7	4.4	5.4	6.7	6.7	7.2	7.4
Number of advances in year (mn)	0.4	0.6	0.8	0.9	1.7	1.4	1.0	1.1
Volume of advances in year (£ bn)	0.6	2.0	4.9	9.5	26.5	43.1	33.2	36.8

Note:
[1] Excluding Abbey National plc.

Source: Housing Finance (formerly the *BSA Bulletin*) (August 1993).

accounts at several societies. In a given year only a fraction of these accounts are active, and many lie dormant for years on end, but the number of active accounts has nevertheless risen sharply since the passing of the Building Societies Act 1986. The number of borrowers has grown more steadily (adjusting for sectoral transfers), but whereas the amount borrowed only rose by a factor of less than 5 during the highly inflationary 1970s because inflows to societies were limited, it trebled during the first half of the 1980s alone in the face of much tougher competition from other lenders. This reflected much sharper increases in house prices than in retail prices in general, together with an enormous influx of money into the mortgage market. Had it not been for the exclusion of Abbey National, the sums advanced would probably have doubled again by the end of the decade.

Not surprisingly, this was financed mainly from share and deposit account liabilities. These stood at £50 billion in 1980, and at the time this represented over 90 per cent of total liabilities. By 1988 deposit liabilities stood at £151 billion, but even so this represented less than 80 per cent of the total. This is accounted for by the fact that in 1979 wholesale borrowing from the money markets was non-existent, yet in 1992 a total of £47.6 billion was being borrowed, representing some 18 per cent of the total. One can anticipate the continuance of this reduction in reliance upon retail deposits into the future.

The asset side of the balance sheet is dominated by mortgage lending (see **Table 6.2**), the traditional business of the societies. In future years we are going to see the long-term effects of the relaxed personal lending rules set out in the Building Societies Act 1986. Immediately after the Act there was a portfolio adjustment. Over £1 billion of local authority investments were sold off, and after a significant build-up of British government securities between 1980 and 1983, these were also heavily depleted between 1986 and 1989.

The liquidity of the societies is hard to explain. The Chief Registrar of Friendly Societies used to require that cash plus investments be maintained at a minimum of 7.5 per cent of total assets. As the balance sheet shows, it is the custom for the

societies to keep well in excess of that amount. Historically, it was just about possible to argue that, if inflows dried up, commitments to mortgage lending could be maintained by running down these reserves, but with wholesale funding now freely available that hardly any longer seems necessary.

Building Societies Act 1986

As most deposits are effectively withdrawable upon demand, whereas mortgages are mostly granted for 25 years, the **liquidity mismatch** between assets and liabilities is very striking. However, the average life of a mortgage is in reality only 7 years (which partly explains the belated enthusiasm for mortgage lending by the banking

Table 6.2 *Building Societies, Assets and Liabilities, 31 December 1995[1]*

	£ mn	%
Assets		
Commercial[2]	240 925	81.1
Cash and bank deposits	30 068	10.1
British government stock	4 140	1.4
Other investments	2 591	0.9
Other liquid assets	11 437	3.9
Other public sector debt	3 342	1.1
Other assets	4 486	1.5
Total	296 989	100.0
Liabilities		
Shares and deposits	211 567	71.2
Wholesale	53 942	18.2
Other liabilities and reserves	31 792	10.6
Total	296 989	100.0

Notes:
[1] From July 1989 figures exclude Abbey National plc.
[2] Of which 218 090 are Class 1 assets, namely advances to individuals secured on land for the residential use of the borrower which must also be first charges on the property.

Source: Bank of England Quarterly Bulletin (February 1996) Table 5.2.

sector); there is a constant inflow of capital and interest repayments; very little bad debt; and almost all borrowing and lending is at floating interest rates, so there is always a margin between them to cover expenses and leave room for profit.

The Building Societies Act 1986 has operated since January 1987, and has subsequently been amended to relax its rules which, while allowing societies to move some way from their traditional business both in terms of methods of raising finance and of disposal of funds, are nevertheless regarded as overly restrictive. For example, the original 20 per cent limit on the amount of funding to be raised from wholesale sources was doubled with effect from 1 January 1988. The Building Societies Commission set a lower limit for each individual society.

One of the most important new powers gained by societies in the 1986 Act was the ability to undertake limited unsecured lending. Three classes of commercial asset were introduced. Up to 15 per cent of commercial assets can be in the form of class 3 assets (unsecured advances, investment in land and investment subsidiaries), but only provided societies have commercial assets in excess of £100 million. This has permitted qualifying societies to issue credit cards, to provide overdrafts and to provide unsecured loans for non-housing-related purposes.

There was also a provision in the Act for designating bodies with wide powers in which societies may invest which has been used on several occasions. From 1 July 1989, appropriate mortgage companies were designated as suitable for investment or support by a society. These may buy, administer or sell the existing mortgage books of other lenders as well as making mortgage loans on their own account. Furthermore, since 1 January 1988, societies have been permitted to establish subsidiaries to operate in other EU member states.

The review of building society powers completed in June 1988 resulted in their being able to offer a wide range of banking and housing-related services; to take up to a 100 per cent stake in life assurance companies and up to a 15 per cent stake in general insurance companies; to undertake fund management; and to take up to

100 per cent stakes in stockbrokers. Because building societies cannot easily issue shares, they have to raise capital by increasing their retained earnings which makes it difficult to finance acquisitions and other forms of expansion. Legislation was accordingly introduced in June 1991 permitting societies to issue **Permanent Interest Bearing Shares** (PIBs) which, like non-voting shares, would yield interest rather than dividends, and the Leeds Permanent made the first issue only a few days later. In June 1994, the Leeds Permanent was also the first society to undertake mortgage lending through a mortgage-backed loan facility (securitisation).

Nevertheless, the fact that societies do not have to distribute dividends to shareholders has been highly beneficial in recent times when, like the banks, they have had to make provisions for bad loans. In practice, the societies rarely commit themselves to provide more than 80 per cent of the value of a property in the form of a mortgage, leaving the residual part to be provided by an insurance company via a mortgage indemnity policy, but house prices have fallen so far in some instances that societies have suffered losses. When the insurance companies responded to their own losses by raising their charges, the societies successfully pressed the government in April 1993 to accede them the right to set up their own insurance companies and, in July 1994, societies were permitted to write their own house structure and contents insurance. The Woolwich and Halifax promptly set up as 'bancassurers', transferring life insurance business from their existing tied insurance companies and selling it direct from their branches.

With some societies eager to expand their range of financial services even faster than the rate at which the rules evolved, the issue inevitably arose as to whether any of them might wish to convert to banking status. The government adopted a neutral stance, and introduced draft rules governing conversion on 28 July 1988. The Abbey National, the second largest society at that time, obtained the necessary majority to convert in April 1989. Support for conversion by Abbey members was so high that other societies were thought to be almost certain to follow suit. In the event, however, no other societies rushed out to follow the Abbey's example, in good part because they were now permitted to do so many new things under their own relaxed rules. This was probably just as well, because at the time they did not show themselves to be particularly astute in expanding into new spheres of operation. This was especially true in respect of their acquisition of estate agency chains. In 1991, Cheltenham & Gloucester withdrew from estate agency, nursing big losses. In late 1994, the Nationwide sold its 304 estate agency branches for £1, which still proved to be anything but a bargain for the buyer, and in 1995, Bristol & West closed agency branches and put the rest up for sale as did the Alliance & Leicester. In March 1996, the Woolwich sold Chestertons Residential for £8 million having paid £20.75 million for it in 1991 although it retained its own-brand agency.

However, with home ownership at a historic high, and with building societies becoming increasingly indistinguishable from banks, at least in the minds of the general public, the concept of mutuality in the context of a national market was seen in many quarters as no more than an historic anachronism. The societies were making profits, but it was unclear what purpose these were supposed to serve. Clearly, therefore, a further shake-up of the sector could be expected even though societies were protected from wholesale takeover by stringent voting rules, and was duly triggered by the £1.8 billion bid by Lloyds Bank for the Cheltenham and Gloucester (C&G), accepted by its members in April 1995. Their enthusiasm was in no small way stimulated by the fact that they were entitled to a significant pay-out, as shown in **Table 6.3**. In the case of the Abbey National conversion, fairly modest numbers of free shares were distributed, but the C&G offer was in cash. The decision not to refer the takeover to the Monopolies and Mergers Commission was taken in September 1995.

In May 1995, the Abbey National offered £1.35 billion to acquire National & Provincial, the ninth largest society at that time. Not to be outdone, the members of the Halifax (largest) and Leeds Permanent (fifth largest) promptly agreed to a merger, following its clearance by the High Court in March, to be followed by a stock market flotation in 1997. In January 1996, the Woolwich (third largest at that time) announced its intention to convert, probably in the autumn of 1997, and this was followed, at the beginning of February 1996, by the announced intention of the Alliance & Leicester to convert in the spring of 1997. In April 1996, the Bank of Ireland announced the takeover of Bristol & West in the summer of 1997 (for details of timetables see *Financial Times*, 7 May 1996).

Among the other large societies, the Britannia, although committed to mutuality, announced its intention to pay profits back to members rather than convert. Qualifying members can expect to receive between £10 and £500 per year, commencing 1997. The Coventry, in contrast, announced in March 1996 its intention to cut mortgage rates while improving rates for savers in order to extend the benefits of mutuality.

An interesting twist on conversion was provided by the Northern Rock in April 1996 when it announced that it intended to float on the stock exchange in Autumn 1997, but that it intended to retain a link with its mutual roots by creating a charitable body, the Northern Rock Foundation which would receive 5 per cent of annual pre-tax profits

On those occasions when bad debts have appeared to threaten the viability of smaller societies, their larger brethren have been happy to step in and take them over, thereby expanding their branch networks and market shares. Whereas such mergers can be expected to continue, bad debts have been a factor in discouraging conversion which would make societies answerable for such debts to shareholders.

In March 1996, the government proposed that building societies which announced plans to merge would be given up to one year's protection from predatory bids to prevent deals being disrupted (*Financial Times*, 19 March 1996) and that building societies could pursue a broader range of activities so long as their principal purpose was providing residential mortgages funded substantially by individual savers (see *Financial Times*, 11 March 1996). It also announced that continental European banks would be allowed to take over

Table 6.3 *Building Society Windfalls From Conversion*[1]

Society	Bonus	Paid	Details
C&G	Average £2000 + cash; max. £14 000	10 August 1995	Borrowers and those investing after 31 December 1992 excluded.
National & Provincial	Abbey National shares worth at least £500	Summer 1996	Fixed sum for all investors and borrowers. Investors for over 2 years at qualifying date get a variable sum. Maximum of £4750
Halifax/Leeds	Halifax plc shares worth at least £600	Early 1997	Investors and borrowers with Halifax and Leeds get fixed sum at flotation. Investors for over 2 years at time also get a variable sum
Woolwich	Woolwich plc shares	Autumn 1997	Fixed number for borrowers and investors on 31 December 1995 remaining to flotation plus more if on books at 31/12/94
Alliance & Leicester	250 Alliance plc shares worth £1000 on average	Spring 1997	Fixed number for all borrowers and investors on 31 December 1995
Northern Rock	Shares worth £1000 on average	Autumn 1997	Not known
Bristol & West	Bank of Ireland shares worth £250	Summer 1997	Investors for over two years at takeover to get £500 plus variable sum

Note:
[1] These windfalls are subject to tax: in the case of the C&G, the cash sums are subject to capital gains tax; in the other cases, when the free shares are sold the proceeds will be subject to capital gains tax.

UK building societies. A further relaxation of building society rules, in the form of the right to make unsecured loans to business, was announced in April 1995. This formed the first part of the latest Treasury review of societies' powers which will include the right to raise 50 per cent of funds in the wholesale markets with up to 25 per cent of lending not needing to be related to residential housing. These relaxations will obviously reduce the need for societies to convert. It is interesting that although conversion releases even more constraints on societies, it will probably make only modest differences in the medium term. Certainly, the Abbey National, which interestingly refuses to call itself a bank, still obtains 80 per cent of its pre-tax profits from retail lending.

The other recent developments on the residential market front have been the announcement by the Prudential in October 1995 that it intended to enter by the end of 1996, utilising the telephone and a direct sales force; an increase in remortgages, facilitated by cheap rates and/or cashbacks, from 11 per cent to 28 per cent of the market in the two years to September 1995, demonstrating that mortgages were becoming consumer goods bought on price rather than brand loyalty; the first interest-free mortgage (for 6 months only) offered by the West Bromwich in April 1996; and the lowest loan rate for over 30 years, at 6.49 per cent, offered by the Nationwide in July 1996.

Cross-border Activity

The implementation of the Single European Market has made little progress with respect to the integration of housing finance systems in the EU. Levels of owner-occupancy are highly variable in member states, and the legal procedures, institutions and financial instruments are often incompatible. As a result, the creation of a mortgage directive is unlikely to be realised. However, the Second Banking Coordination Directive, published at the end of 1988, permitted mortgage lenders to operate outside their home country in the same way as they operate at home.

The 'mutual recognition of techniques' has so far failed to lead to a plethora of cross-border activity. Part of the difficulty lies in the necessity to establish a subsidiary elsewhere in the EU before conducting business there. The most active society in recent times has been the Woolwich, which established an Italian subsidiary at the end of 1990 and purchased a French subsidiary in 1991. In November 1993, the Bradford and Bingley was the first society to set up as a Bauspakasse in Germany, and the Halifax opened for business in Spain at roughly the same time. With no brand image to fall back on, and a tiny presence in their respective markets, caution remains the order of the day.

☐ *6.2.2 Insurance Companies*

The business of life insurance is often conducted by large composite insurers which also incur general risks such as damage to house and car. Our concern here is primarily with **life insurance**, which may also be provided by specialist insurance companies. The business of life insurance has little to do with liquidity. The commonest form of policy is where the individual makes regular monthly payments which entitle him or her to a lump sum at a specific future date (an **endowment**). If the endowment is 'with profits', then bonuses will be added in line with the profitability of the company. If the policy holder dies before the policy matures, then a lump sum will be paid to the next-of-kin or specified beneficiary.

An endowment may alternatively be purchased via a single, large, lump-sum down-payment. Special forms of endowment are increasingly linked to mortgages, either 'low cost' endowments or mortgage protection policies which simply guarantee to repay the outstanding mortgage upon the death of the mortgagee (term insurance). Unit-linked endowments are also increasingly available, with several companies giving up traditional endowments altogether because of their difficulty in maintaining bonuses, and indeed there is the now customary proliferation of new forms of life insurance in this exceptionally competitive market. Endowments can be, and frequently are, cashed in before maturity, although this generally results in a repayment of less than the total amount paid in, since insurance brokers are frequently paid the first year's premium as a fee for arranging the endowment.

Life insurance companies hold roughly half of their long-term assets in the form of UK and overseas equities, and the rest mostly comprises gilts and UK land, property and ground rents. Equities are even more prominent in the assets structure of pension funds, because fixed-yield assets would not keep pace with commitments to make payments based upon rapidly-rising incomes. These institutions clearly, therefore, play a dominant role in the equity and gilt-edged markets.

As noted in the preceding chapter on the retail banks, the bancassurers are taking over substantial parts of the market in life and pension products at the expense of the stand-alone insurance companies. In particular, Standard Life, the UK's largest life company, suffered badly when its agreement to supply all pensions and investment products to the Halifax was terminated. In March 1996, the Halifax consolidated its position by taking over Clerical Medical for roughly £800 million. Pressures in the market were also reflected by the merger between Royal Insurance and Sun Alliance which made its stock market debut in July 1996 and which is expected to lead to the loss of 5000 jobs, and the takeover of United Friendly by Refuge Assurance in August which is expected to lead to the loss of up to 1800 jobs and the closure of 100 branches. Between

1991 and 1996, the life and general insurance industry lost 16 000 jobs, but mergers, buy-outs, improved technology etc are predicted to lead to further losses of up to 100 000 jobs over the next five years.

The insurance companies are often less than astute investors on behalf of their policy holders. In May 1991, for example, the Prudential Corporation decided that it was 'emotionally unsuited' to being a residential estate agent, and completed the sale of its 500-branch operation which it had built up a total cost of £338 million. Total receipts from branch sales were £30 million. General Accident did equally badly with its ill-fated acquisition of its New Zealand subsidiary, NZI Corporation, and in March 1996 Sun Alliance announced the sale of its loss-making Chancellors agencies acquired for £26 million in 1989.

The life insurance companies have cause to be very grateful for the decision to introduce personal pensions, discussed below, since it provided them with a huge source of new business. This has, however, led to accusations of mis-selling, and they have been asked to re-examine their policies to see if policy-holders would have been better off remaining in their previous schemes. So far, the insurance companies have shown a remarkable unwillingness to deal with the issue! It is to be expected that they have learned their lesson from the 1980s, namely that it is not easy to cross-sell life insurance and other similar policies with the products of other types of financial intermediary. Nevertheless, as evidenced by the acquisition of a banking licence by Scottish Widows and others in 1995, and by the Prudential's announcement in October 1995 that it intended to enter the retail deposit and residential mortgage markets by the end of 1996 (that is, to become a bank), the logic being that when endowments mature they can be recycled to mortgages via Prudential savings accounts, the insurance companies clearly intend to play their part in the restructuring of the personal financial services sector.

The advent of the Single European Market has not been favourable for UK insurers. Since the 1970s, insurers have been permitted to set up subsidiaries throughout the Community, but whereas UK insurers have been discouraged from investing elsewhere in the EU by relatively tough regulatory regimes, their relatively well capitalised German and French equivalents have moved into the UK market and eroded their market share. This has largely been achieved via take-overs, for example of Cornhill by Allianz of Germany and of Sun Life by UAP of France, although, in June 1994, Commercial Union helped redress the balance by purchasing Groupe Victoire. It is argued that the tax regime in each country favours the particular products that are popular there, so there is no point in setting up a new operation selling products that are popular in other member states.

On 1 July 1994, the personal insurance market was officially opened up under the terms of the third life directive except in certain states with temporary exemptions. This permits companies to sell their products on the basis of regulations in their home states and to set their own rates for different classes of policy, and UK insurers such as Scottish Amicable and Equitable Life promptly started up European operations. However, getting customers to buy unfamiliar types of policy from unfamiliar companies is likely to be a long-winded affair even if UK insurers are amongst the most innovative in the EU.

Lloyd's of London

The cornerstone of the UK's insurance market is Lloyd's of London. Traditionally, one had to be very rich to join a syndicate and become a 'name' since 'names' were subject to 'unlimited liability'. From 1967 to 1987 Lloyd's made substantial profits and the risk attached to unlimited liability seemed of little account. As a result, large numbers of modestly wealthy middle class individuals signed up as 'names'. However, this proved to be a case of very bad timing.

Lloyd's is very slow to declare its results because syndicates cannot close their accounts for any year in whch there are unknown ouststanding claims. Heavy and unremitting pollution claims from the USA, together with a series of severe natural disasters and events such as the explosion on the Piper Alpha platform in the North Sea, have plunged Lloyd's into the red since 1988 to an extent that can ultimately only be guessed at. Losses for the 1990 year alone, announced in June 1993, amounted to £2.9 billion, the largest ever. Many outstanding claims relate to policies written decades ago to cover pollution and diseases unforeseeable at the time (such as asbestosis). As a result a 'name' may ultimately be liable for hundreds of times the original investment.

Many, if not most, 'names' responded by taking legal action, claiming that Lloyd's had been lax in its regulation of the market and that 'names' were victims of negligence. As the cases came progressively to court, most of the judgements came down in favour of the 'names'. In its turn, Lloyd's instigated wide-ranging reviews of its procedures, to include the issue of 'unlimited liability', and proposed a once-and-for-all settlement of all outstanding claims. However, these moves have failed to satisfy a large proportion of the 'names', some of whom would remain bankrupt even after the settlement. The market was opened to corporate capital with limited liability in order to offset the huge loss of capital consequent upon any settlement and the desertion of the market by individual 'names', but it is possible that the reputation of Lloyd's has been severely damaged and, indeed, that it may not even survive in its present form for much longer.

Pension Schemes

A **pension** cannot be paid out to anyone other than the person in whose name the monthly payments are made, irrespective of who pays the premiums, nor in part to anyone other than his or her spouse or children upon the death of the pensioner. Most pension schemes involve payments both by the individual and the company he or she works for. Until recently, this has meant that if the individual moved jobs the pension in the old job would be frozen until retirement, and the individual would have to start up a new one with the new employer. In certain circumstances, however, pensions are now 'portable' between jobs. The self-employed must buy personal pensions for themselves, and it is now possible for individuals to top up existing pension rights by buying additional personal pensions.

Pension, or superannuation, funds make payments for as long as a pensioner lives after reaching pensionable age. In certain cases these payments were index-linked before 1990. Thus, while life insurance is primarily a means of buying protection (for dependents) in the event of early death, a pension fund exists to cover the risk of living too long without an income. The popularity of life insurance and pension funds has traditionally been fostered by the existence of tax concessions both to individuals and to companies. Tax relief on life insurance premiums was, however, discontinued in the 1985 Budget.

The **State Earnings Related Pension Scheme** (Serps) was once compulsory for all, and financed, at least in principle, by National Insurance Contributions (NICs). In 1985, the decision was taken to allow people to opt out by contracting a personal pension for themselves. This was expected to reduce the burden on the National Insurance Fund, although this was to be more than offset by the 5.8 per cent NICs' rebate, the special incentive of 2 per cent of relevant earnings payable until April 1993 and tax relief on the employee's part of the rebate. It is estimated that at least 50 per cent of personal pension plans are financed in this way, and high rates of surrender and high expense ratios among intermediaries have caused the government to announce a restructuring of the rebate system in April 1996.

It was estimated that 500 000 people would immediately take out personal pensions, with numbers eventually peaking at 1.75 million, but by April 1990, 4 million personal pensions had been taken out. As a result, the net cost to the Exchequer was estimated by the comptroller and auditor-general to reach an eventual figure of £5.9 billion at April 1988 prices (the time when the new pensions were first introduced). In 1990–91, the net cost was estimated at £1.8 billion, equivalent to a 1.5p rise in the rate of income tax.

One serious misjudgement, apart from the cost, was to allow those who opted out of Serps to rejoin at any time they chose. The nature of the rebates made it exceptionally attractive to opt out when employees were in their twenties, and to opt back in 20 years later – hence the large numbers who chose to opt out. The government was accordingly stuck with the problem of how to keep the cost to the Exchequer under control without simply inducing everyone to opt back into Serps.

There are two obvious ways to reduce the burden of state pensions as the population ages over the next two decades. The projections are set out in **Figure 6.1**. The first is to recognise that pensioners as a whole are no longer the poorest group in society and hence to target the basic state pension at those who need it most, and the second is to raise the age at which it becomes payable. Women are anyway more expensive in pension terms because they live longer on average, and this is exacerbated if they also retire earlier. This was recognised in the case of occupational pensions as a consequence of the Barber and subsequent cases taken before the European Court of Justice (see *Financial Times*, 29 September 1994). In the case of state pensions, the decision was made to phase in equality of retirement age at 65 between 2010 and 2020 (for details see Secretary of State for Social Security, 1993).

By tying state pension increases to prices rather than earnings in 1988, the projected cost of state pensions in 2030 will be 'only' £34.7 billion and less thereafter. Unfortunately, this will be insufficient to provide even a minimal standard of living for the retired who are dependent upon state pensions alone. The debate over pensions is therefore far from resolved, not least because it remains wholly unclear why everyone should be forced to retire at precisely the same age.

☐ 6.2.3 Unit Trusts

Direct investment in equities has never been popular among individuals in the UK. This is partly because it is not possible to obtain a diversified porfolio of shares if there is only a modest amount of capital to invest. Unit trusts and investment trusts pool the savings of large numbers of individuals, and by giving them a share in a diversified portfolio of assets this reduces the risk element in equity-related saving. Nevertheless, as with any equity-linked portfolios, those of trusts can fall heavily in value when the Stock Exchange is depressed.

In the case of unit trusts there is a legally binding trust deed. A trustee, normally a large financial intermediary, holds the trust's assets on behalf of unit-holders, and the trust is independently managed by another company within the terms of the trust deed. Units can be bought and sold only with the trust itself. New units are created as desired, and old ones eliminated when units are sold back to the trust. The trust repays such units by disposing of investments. There has recently been considerable dispute about the rules for calculating the purchase and sale price of units, and it is permissible for a unit trust to refuse to repurchase under specified circumstances.

The period from 1980 to 1987 was a very successful one for unit trusts. The value of annual gross sales soared from little more than £1 billion to in excess of £15 billion in 1987, and although there was a good deal of repurchasing, net investment was significantly positive in every year and total unit trust funds rose to roughly £40 billion. In 1985 there were 2.5 million holdings, but by

Figure 6.1 *UK Pensions: Social Security Cost if Benefits are Linked to RPI*

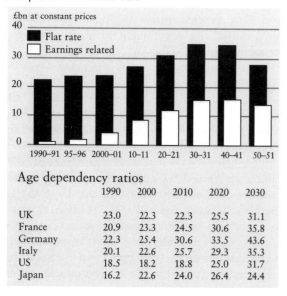

Age dependency ratios

	1990	2000	2010	2020	2030
UK	23.0	22.3	22.3	25.5	31.1
France	20.9	23.3	24.5	30.6	35.8
Germany	22.3	25.4	30.6	33.5	43.6
Italy	20.1	22.6	25.7	29.3	35.3
US	18.5	18.2	18.8	25.0	31.7
Japan	16.2	22.6	24.0	26.4	24.4

Source: Financial Times, 28 June 1993.

1987 this had increased to 5 million holdings. Annual net investment has remained positive until the present day although it was close to zero in 1990 and 1992. From its 1987 peak, the number of unit holders fell continuously to total 4.35 million by the end of 1992. However, the introduction of unit trust Personal Equity Plans (PEPs), together with a sharp reduction in interest rates which enhanced the attractiveness of equity linked investments, led to a revival in holdings which rose back to 5 million by the end of 1993. Funds under management also rose to a record £95.5 billion.

Although funds were comfortably above their levels five years previously, this was not entirely good news for investors since 6 per cent front-end sales charges plus 1 per cent annual charges ate into capital gains and the bid/offer spread amounted on average to a further 6 per cent of the price. When the government lifted controls on charges in 1979, it was in the expectation that competition would drive them down, whereas in practice they were often twice as high over a 20-year period by 1990. As a first step to improve this situation, the Securities and Investments Board introduced new regulations in November 1994 which permitted trusts to levy an exit charge when an investor sells units instead of a front-end charge. In addition, the SIB's list of approved securities and derivatives was replaced by a duty on managers to ensure that the markets where they invest meet certain criteria.

With three times as many trusts in existence compared to a decade ago, the customer is understandably rather bewildered. The number of management companies has nevertheless fallen, but as there is a clear advantage for larger groups in terms of costs there are likely to be ongoing mergers among management companies.

Given the buoyancy of the stock market, the collapse of unit trust sales in early 1995 came as something of a surprise. Roughly half of all unit trust sales in 1994 were linked to PEPs, and these did quite badly, so there was a clear tendency to switch money into building society accounts. However, the combination of a rising stock market, falling interest rates and the arrival of tax-efficient PEPs investing in corporate bonds presaged a revival of the market which reached a record net figure of £1.36 billion in March 1996 (see *Financial Times*, 23 April 1996). At this point £120 billion was invested by 6.2 million unit holders.

Whether the industry will survive in its present form is now doubtful since in May 1996, the government announced that mergers between unit trusts and the conversion of unit trusts into Open Ended Investment Companies (OEICs) would be free from 0.5 per cent stamp duty. OEICs have the advantage that their products can be marketed abroad more easily because investors can buy and sell at one price (see *Financial Times*, 11 May 1996).

☐ 6.2.4 Investment Trusts

Investment trusts are much the smallest group of NBFIs in terms of assets. They operate rather differently from unit trusts in that they are public companies rather than legal trusts, and sell shares in the trust itself. The money received is then invested in other equities and securities. Their own shares are quoted in the Stock Exchange and can be fully traded. In 1994, £250 million was invested by 80 000 regular savers.

☐ 6.2.5 National Savings Bank (NSB)

The NSB, which had its origins in the need for wartime financing and which is now under the control of the Department of National Savings, is important primarily as a route for channeling private sector savings directly into the hands of the government. In this way the PSBR can be financed without the need to issue an equivalent amount of marketable debt instruments. National Savings were unpopular in the decades prior to 1975, but it has subsequently been possible to widen their appeal by deliberately making them attractive compared to deposits at banks and building societies. This is done primarily either through index-linking, which guarantees that a specified real rate of interest, adjusted for inflation, is earned, or through a reduction in the tax burden to be borne by such savings.

☐ 6.2.6 Finance Houses

The finance houses are no longer of much importance in the financial system because there has been a tendency for the largest houses to convert into banks, included statistically in the 'other British banks' category. Funds are raised in the wholesale markets and by issuing bills. They are used to provide loans to individuals (to be repaid in instalments) and to private companies, together with leasing finance whereby a finance house buys a machine or factory and leases it to a company. This type of business is also done by retail banks, but many finance houses have special relationships with large manufacturers and retail chains.

■ 6.3 Money Markets

☐ 6.3.1 A Brief History

We have already referred, when discussing individual groups of financial intermediaries, to the existence of money markets, and it is now necessary to say something about these markets in general, and specifically about those of them not previously mentioned.

The movement of huge sums of short-term funds around the financial system is historically a relatively new phenomenon. Up until the early 1960s, organisations acquired short-term funds either from the commercial banks in the form of overdrafts and loans or as trade credit from suppliers. The banks' ability to lend was itself determined largely by the value of retail deposits, and they did not complete amongst themselves as their interest rates were uniformly linked to the central Bank Rate. Furthermore, direct controls on lending were frequently imposed by the Bank of England.

However, commencing in the early 1960s, large amounts of dollars began to be deposited in London (see discussion of Eurocurrency markets below), and these deposits were totally independent of the existing banking system. They could, there-

fore, be handled by any institution willing to make a sufficiently attractive offer to depositors, and they could be handled flexibly because they did not fall within the compass of existing monetary controls. As a result, large numbers of foreign banks came to London, each intent on grabbing as big a share of the business as possible, and this in turn meant that competition for deposits was so intensive as to exclude the possibility of interest rate cartels. Once in the UK, they also began to compete for sterling deposits, previously the exclusive preserve of the UK banks, which were obliged to match their interest rates.

The Bank of England acknowledged the desirability of competition on an equal footing between institutions when it introduced the Competition and Credit Control (CCC) document in 1971. This detached bank interest rates from Bank Rate, which was abolished, and allowed each bank to set its own **base rate**. The replacement of Bank Rate by the market-determined **Minimum Lending Rate** (MLR) was, however, more apparent than real in practice, as the government found it increasingly difficult to forgo the use of the interest rate as a major instrument of monetary control. Furthermore, base rates have tended to fall back into line. However, this disguises the fact that whereas retail banking is still operated as a virtual cartel, wholesale banking is not. If one has a large sum of money to sell then it can be offered around to the highest bidder. One interesting consequence is that **asset management** whereby, as discussed above, financial intermediaries and especially banks must maintain part of their asset portfolio in liquid forms, becomes matched by **liability management** whereby liquidity can be supplemented via borrowing in the money markets. Precisely the same argument applies for governments and commercial organisations. Cash, which does not earn interest, can no longer be left lying idle, even overnight. It is hardly surprising, therefore, that retail banking, where small accounts are handled at considerable expense, is increasingly viewed as simply a means whereby a captive audience is acquired for the sale of profitable financial services, and the primary concerns of liquidity, risk and profitability are juggled in the money markets.

☐ *6.3.2 Types of Money Market*

The primary money market is the **discount market**. This has already been discussed, and nothing further needs to be added at this juncture. In addition to the discount market there are currently six other significant sterling money markets known, collectively as the **'parallel' or secondary markets**. These are the inter-bank market; the certificate of deposit market; the sterling commercial paper market; the local authority market; the finance house market; and the inter-company market. They are called 'sterling markets' to distinguish them from the Eurocurrency market discussed below.

The inter-bank market has also been mentioned previously. It is the largest parallel market and, as the name indicates, is the market in which **banks lend to one another**. After a period of rapid growth it went into a sharp decline in 1991, partly as a reflection of concerns about the credit quality of banks and partly as a result of the growth of derivatives markets. Having started in 1955, the local authority market is the oldest, and is where local authorities issue their own debt instruments which are sold to banks and other investor. Loans are unsecured, so the reputation of the borrower is all-important. Until recently local authorities, with their right to levy local taxes, were regarded as low-risk borrowers, but the dubious practices of certain authorities have altered that somewhat. The inter-company market, which began in 1969, is where **large companies lend directly** to one another. It is a low-key affair because there are alternative ways to lend with security at much the same rates of interest. The finance house market is also fairly insignificant because of the transfer of many of the largest houses to the banking sector. The sterling CD market, started in 1968, consists of a **primary** market in which new CDs are issued, and a **secondary** market in which they are subsequently bought and sold, thereby enhancing their liquidity and hence desirability. The market has grown rapidly, but it is totally dwarfed by the foreign currency CD market.

It is not always possible to distinguish to which market a particular transaction should be assigned, since many types of intermediary operate in several of them simultaneously. Supervision is accordingly exercised largely over participants' banking activities although, as discussed above, the Bank of England is involved in the discount market on a daily basis. In the parallel sterling markets **supervision is light**. Participants are expected to join the Sterling Brokers Association and adhere to the Bank's issued code of practice. The Bank also checks on the various instruments issued to ensure that they are of the highest quality. This lightness of touch has provided a suitable environment for rapid growth, but the Bank must occasionally wonder why it fosters markets which make its monetary controls much harder to implement.

☐ *6.3.3 Financial Futures and Options*

So far, we have been exclusively concerned with transactions involving a current payment in exchange for the current delivery of some kind of asset such as a share or bond. However, a large number of contracts involve either the delivery of an asset at some **future date** in exchange for a payment made **in the present**, or the purchase of the right to buy or sell (or to decline to buy or sell) an asset at some **future date** at a price **agreed when taking out the option**. The former are traded on the London International Financial Futures and Options Exchange (LIFFE/LTOM) and are known as **financial futures**, and might involve, for example, a contract to buy an amount of gilts in three months' time at a current price which reflects the expectations of the parties to the contract about the future trend of interest rates. Currencies can also be traded in this way. The latter are also traded on LIFFE/LTOM and are known as **traded options** (as distinct from the similar but less-commonly purchased **traditional** options). These involve the outlay of a modest sum today for the rights to buy or sell in the future at an agreed price, known as 'calls' and 'puts' respectively. If the market price moves in such a way as, for example, to rise above the agreed price for a call option, then the option will be enforced by the buyer. Where the writer of the option (the seller) does not have the asset to hand it will have to be purchased in the market and immediately resold at a loss (which is partly offset because the seller has received the price of the option in cash). If, however, the market price has fallen below the price agreed at the time of buying the option (in other words, the asset can be bought more cheaply in the open market) then the option will be allowed to lapse, and the writer of the option gets to keep the money paid for the option **less** trading costs.

Financial futures and traded options clearly involve risks for both buyer and seller. Almost invariably, **one must gain at the expense of the other**. However, there is a sound rationale behind this kind of behaviour. When a buyer agrees to buy an asset at some future date he runs the risk that he could have bought it more cheaply in the future compared to the present. On the other hand, he avoids the risk that he would have had to pay well above the agreed price. Traded options are thus a mechanism for **financial leverage**. In other words, in return for the downpayment of a modest sum, a buyer of call options is guaranteed the chance to make a profit by buying and instantly reselling a very expensive portfolio of assets which he could not have afforded to pay for in full at the time of buying the option. Equally, the most he can lose is the total cost of the options should he decline to take them up, even if the price of the asset has fallen disastrously in the meantime.

Traded options also provide a hedge against share movements which would be disadvantageous to a shareholder. Thus, for example, a shareholder whose shares have risen sharply in value can protect at least part of the capital gain by taking out an option conferring the right to sell the shares at a price of his or her choosing. If this happens to be the current share price then the maximum loss is the cost of taking out the options **plus** trading costs, irrespective of how much the shares subsequently fall in value.

It was intended that LIFFE and LTOM would merge in April 1991, with the International Petroleum Exchange, the London Metal Exchange and the London Commodity Exchange (LCE – until 1 July 1993 known as the FOX) eventually joining LIFFE/LTOM to form an overall exchange capable of challenging the pre-eminent position of Chicago. Little progress was initially made with this scheme although LIFFE/LTOM did eventually merge together in March 1992.

LIFFE is the dominant partner in LIFFE/LTOM and itself accounts for two thirds of aggregate turnover on the derivative exchanges as shown in **Figure 6.2**. The 1990 Budget was a big boost for trading in derivatives because it permitted institutions to avoid paying tax on any of their transactions without having to prove that they were not 'trading' in the market. Turnover soared in 1991 and reached a peak in the first quarter of 1994, since when the situation has stabilised somewhat. The largest contracts are still traded using 'open

Figure 6.2 *Aggregate Turnover on the London Derivatives Exchanges*

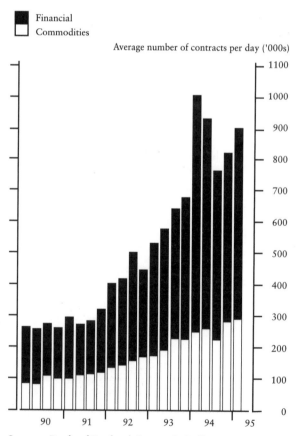

Average number of contracts per day ('000s)

■ Financial
□ Commodities

Source: Bank of England Quarterly Bulletin.

outcry' on the Stock Exchange floor, but there has been some movement towards screen-based trading. This may help to bring back retail clients who constitute only 30 per cent of business compared to 70 per cent in Chicago, but fees remain high and it is the usual Catch 22 situation in which fees cannot come down until trading volume picks up, but trading volume will not pick up until fees come down.

During 1995, LIFFE forged alliances with the Chicago Board of Trade (CBoT) and the Tokyo International Financial Futures Exchange (TIFFE). In the same month as the latter, November 1995, the merger of LIFFE and LCE was announced, to take place in July 1996. Effectively, LIFFE is taking over the LCE and the combined exchange will use its name. These link-ups reflect the fact that the exchanges are increasingly dominated by the interests of the larger banks and securities houses whose interests span both financial and commodities markets; the need to economise on the cost of trading on multiple exchanges; and evidence of a slowdown in trading because the market for basic bond futures contracts is near saturation.

1995 was seen as a disappointment for LIFFE as trading volumes were down relative to the admittedly exceptional 1994, partly in response to the Barings crisis. However, LIFFE was still the world's biggest market for interest rate and currency swaps, and had the busiest month in its history in February 1996 as well as its second busiest day (after 2 March 1994) on 20 February 1996. Interestingly, the sharpest growth was seen in trading in German government bond futures, although this could disappear once full EMU takes effect (see *Financial Times*, 21 March 1996, p. 23).

☐ *6.3.4 Eurocurrency Markets*

The size of the Eurocurrency markets in the UK, as indicated in **Table 5.2** (**p. 118**), is much larger than one might expect. Eurocurrency transactions are **wholesale** borrowing and lending in a currency other than that of the country in which the transactions take place. Thus Eurosterling

can be transacted anywhere other than in the UK, and Eurodollars anywhere other than in the USA and so forth. The term 'Eurocurrency' is, therefore, something of a misnomer since it can involve non-European currencies and be transacted outside Europe. It arose because, as previously stated, the markets began with dollars deposited in Europe. At present London is the biggest Eurocurrency market, accounting for approximately 20 per cent of all transactions by value.

There is normally a lower limit of $1 million set for each transaction, and also often an upper limit since loans are unsecured whereas much of the lending is very short-term loans in the form of Eurocommercial paper (the total market for which rose from $4 billion in early 1986 to $45 billion in early 1988), and especially of Eurobonds which are largely fixed-interest securities or floating-rate notes (FRNs) denominated in a Eurocurrency. FRNs are attached to LIBOR in the UK, and may be convertible to equity. They are issued by multinational firms, foreign governments, local authorities and public corporations. There is also a great deal of inter-bank lending. Eurobonds are not usually traded on the Stock Exchange, but rather certain international banks and security houses 'make a market'. There are sufficient market-makers to ensure that Eurobonds can be freely traded at competitive prices.

Consequences

The Eurocurrency markets have, as noted above, been an important source of funds for inter-bank lending. This has had the effect of bringing together banks throughout the world into an informal network, and there can be no doubt that international liquidity has been enhanced in the process. However, it is clear that there are dangers in moving around vast sums of money without there being any institution in overall control of proceedings. This can arise firstly with respect to individual banks. Eurocurrencies tend to travel through a succession of banks on their route between ultimate lender and ultimate borrower. An individual bank cannot, therefore, know to what extent its lending may end up with any particular borrower, and therefore how vulnerable it is to that borrower's financial health.

Secondly, from the point of view of sovereign states, it is clear that domestic monetary policy may be rendered ineffectual by the Eurocurrency markets. The movement of 'hot money' has, for example, recently been of considerable concern to the UK government. It should be noted, in particular, that interest rate differentials between countries are critical in determining the direction of flow of hot money, and hence that no individual country can set its interest rate structure in isolation. The loss of control implied by these developments is inevitably a considerable irritant to banks and governments alike, but attempts to regulate Eurocurrency markets would simply result in their replacement by other markets not subject to the new regulations.

Growth in the largest market, for Eurocommercial paper, has gone into reverse over the past year, reflecting the maturity of the market, slower economic growth, a reduction in longer-term interest rates and a fall-off in the credit quality of issuers. Overcapacity has led to the withdrawal of several banks, leaving roughly ten active dealers. Euromedium-term notes, on the other hand, have become increasingly popular as shown in **Figure 6.3**. Over the past two years outstanding issues have risen threefold, and the large building societies have become prominent issuers of EMTNs.

The primary eurobond market is currently thriving, with $348 billion of eurobonds issued in the first half of 1996, more than 50 per cent up on the same period in 1995 (see *Financial Times*, 1 July 1996.

ECU Securities

In 1981 a market developed for Eurobonds denominated in European Currency Units (ECUs – see **pp. 000–00**). As shown in **Figure 6.4**, the market built up rapidly in 1985, then subsided. An initial problem was the absence of any parallel market in short-term (up to six-month) ECU bills. The market picked up again in 1988, as the Single

Figure 6.3   *Stock of Outstanding Euronotes*

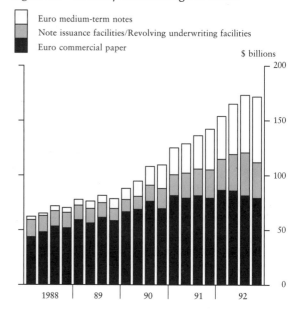

Source: Bank of England Quarterly Bulletin.

Figure 6.4   *ECU Primary Bond Market – Historical Evolution (Ecu Billions)*

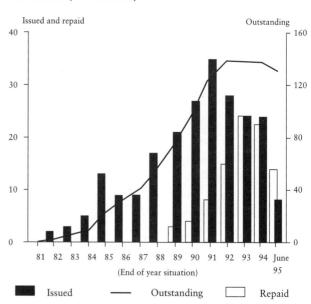

Source: European Commission.

European Market began to exert an influence. In August 1988, the UK government launched a series of ECU Treasury bill tenders, partly as a preemptive measure to concentrate the ECU markets in London.

These and other issues were hugely successful. By the end of 1990 there were $60 billion of fixed-rate ECU bonds outstanding in the international bond market, making it the fifth-ranking currency by value of outstanding bonds. At the end of the 1980s a number of central banks, including the Bank of England, began to use the ECU markets for their own reserves management operations. As a result issuance surged to ECU 27.5 billion in 1991. The Bank of England also began issuing ECU Treasury notes (for details of the development of the ECU markets see Bank of England (1992)). ECU denominated securities were particularly attractive to the Japanese who preferred them to bonds issued in individual currencies on the grounds that they combined relatively high yields with relatively low risk. A futures contract in ECU Bonds was also been launched by LIFFE/LTOM and in France.

With the single European currency increasingly on the minds of investors, it seemed that the ECU would be playing an ever-greater role in the international securities markets. However, the rejection of the Maastricht Treaty by Denmark in 1992 caused a crisis in the ECU bond market, with dealing suspended temporarily in July. The market may never recover fully from this shock.

■ 6.4 Capital Markets

When companies need more medium- and long-term capital than is available from retained profits, and when the government cannot cover its expenditure from its tax revenue, they make up the shortfall by recourse to the capital markets. These thus encompass both the **institutions** which

Figure 6.5 *The Capital Markets*

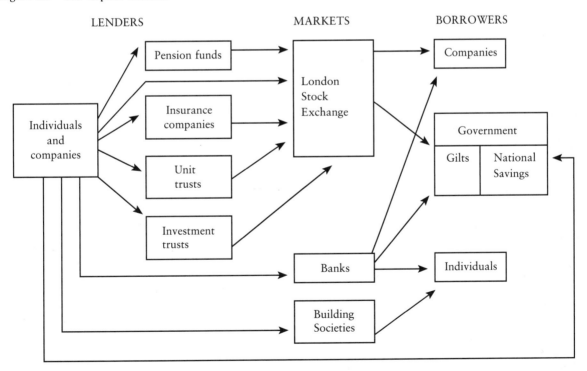

provide medium- and long-term finance, illustrated in **Figure 6.5**, and the **forms of financial instrument** which are traded there.

6.4.1 'Big Bang' and its Aftermath

The term 'Big Bang' is the colloquial name for the **deregulation of the Stock Exchange** in October 1986. A variety of circumstances conspired to bring it about at that particular point in time. Historically, there were two major groups of participants in the Exchange. The first, the **stock-brokers**, acted on behalf of clients, both personal and institutional, who paid a commission for stockbroking services. Brokers primarily traded equity, but also gave advice on portfolios. In order to obtain shares the brokers had to go to a **jobber** who acted as a **market maker** – that is, he held a portfolio of shares which he bought and sold on his own account. Since jobbers could not deal directly with the general public, they were independent of the brokers in a so-called 'single capacity' system. The Stock Exchange's own rules enforced the system, the main attractions of which were superficially that there were always jobbers willing to trade and that, since the brokers had nothing personally to gain by using one jobber rather than another, they would get the best deal they could for their clients.

However, the system had two particularly serious defects. In the first place, the scale of commissions paid to brokers was fixed by the Exchange. An institution buying shares worth £10 million thus had to pay virtually the same rate as a personal investor buying shares worth £1000. Secondly, the Stock Exchange would not allow individual member firms to grow at the expense of others.

In 1983, under pressure from the government, the Stock Exchange agreed to **forgo fixed commissions and single capacity trading** as from 27 October 1986. Commencing in March 1986, any Stock Exchange firm could be **wholly taken over by outsiders**. This also held true in the gilt-edged market which had previously been dominated by only two firms of jobbers.

As Big Bang approached there was a mad rush to organise the new 'dual-capacity' market-making firms which stood ready to deal directly with investors, to trade on their own account and to make markets in as many shares as they wished. Brokers and jobbers were taken over by UK and foreign banks, thereby **destroying the historic distinction between banking and security trading** in the UK. The number of trained personnel was understandably totally inadequate, and vast sums of money were offered to attract qualified staff.

One significant problem related to **technology**. Very few old-style jobbers had modern electronic dealing rooms, so there was also a mad scramble to obtain new premises and to get them wired up. The system for transmitting data throughout the Exchange, known as SEAQ (Stock Exchange Automated Quotation System), was only just about up and running in time for Big Bang. Once the electronics were in place, the Stock Exchange floor suffered a virtual mass desertion.

For a year, all went very well. The stock market boomed and the volume of business rose to new heights. However, in October 1987 there was a market collapse which made even the Wall Street Crash of 1929 look insignificant. The authorities in the UK and elsewhere reacted positively on this occasion, making large amounts of liquidity available to prevent market makers going to the wall, and in the event remarkably little damage was done. The real economy carried on working pretty much as before. The enormous cuts in the capitalisation of firms did not make any real difference because, at the end of the day, share prices simply reflect the use of capital which has already been invested. One thing that understandably was affected was the amount of new equity capital which could be raised, because that is not normally allowed to exceed a given proportion of the value of existing capital. The issue of 'rights' (see below) came to a grinding halt, and was slow fully to recover.

Equally, on paper, investors became less wealthy, which might have caused them to cut consumption and save more with consequent effects upon GDP. However, this did not take place. What happened is that many personal and institutional investors stayed out of the equity market until early 1991, and the daily volume of shares traded fell well below 1987 levels. As a result, many market makers and brokers struggled to break even, and there were eventually extensive redundancies in the City. Personal investors switched back to the building societies which regained much of the mortgage market share previously lost to the banks.

As can be seen in **Table 6.4**, twice as many foreign securities houses set up shop in London in 1986 compared to 1984 and 1985, and even more in 1987. This increase in capacity neatly coincided with the cyclical downturn after the October 1987 crash, and caused the members of the Stock Exchange to lose £27 million in 1987 and £265 million in 1988. Subsequently, market activity peaked and the LSE returned to profit in 1989, but the volume of trading in UK and foreign equities, government securities and other fixed income stocks struggled to rise above levels prevailing before the crash.

What is surprising is not the reduction in the number of new entrants in 1988 and 1989, but rather that there were as many as there were and that they exceeded the negligible number of departures. Those departures, either of UK or overseas houses, as did occur received much publicity, but they were in fact atypical. This was not, however, merely the triumph of hope over experience, since the LSE managed to replace much of its sagging domestic business with trading in international securities. In 1991, there were twice as many entrants as departures, creating a record number of participants, but even though there were as many entrants again in 1992, the number of departures was extraordinarily high, with Japanese houses departing for the first time. Since then, departures have continued to be relatively frequent, especially in respect of Europe, but the inflow has risen to record levels so 1992 may well prove to have been a 'blip' in an otherwise inexorable rise in numbers.

Table 6.4   *Foreign Securities' Houses in London*

	US			Japan			Europe			Other			Summary		
	Total	*In*	*Out*	*Total*	*In*	*Out*	*Total*	*In*	*Out*	*Total*	*In*	*Out*	*Total*	*In*	*Out*
1980	43	4	1	21	1	0	13	3	0	27	1	0	104	9	1
1981	45	2	0	23	2	0	13	0	0	30	3	0	111	7	0
1982	47	2	0	25	2	0	15	2	0	31	1	0	118	7	0
1983	52	5	0	25	0	0	17	2	0	33	2	0	127	9	0
1984	51	0	1	27	2	0	17	1	1	35	3	1	130	6	3
1985	51	0	0	29	2	0	17	1	1	37	3	1	134	6	2
1986	52	1	0	34	5	0	18	1	0	39	5	3	143	12	3
1987	54	2	0	41	7	0	21	3	0	39	1	1	155	13	1
1988	54	0	0	41	0	0	24	3	0	37	2	4	156	5	4
1989	55	1	0	42	1	0	23	1	2	38	1	0	158	4	2
1990	54	2	3	44	2	0	28	5	0	34	1	5	160	10	8
1991	55	2	1	47	3	0	27	5	6	40	8	2	169	18	9
1992	53	5	7	45	1	3	24	5	8	43	7	4	165	18	22
1993	60	8	1	48	3	0	22	8	10	43	4	4	173	23	15
1994	64	8	4	49	1	0	22	4	4	53	14	4	188	27	12
Total		42	18		32	3		44	32		56	29		174	82

Source: Noel Alexander Associates.

6.4.2 New Issue and Secondary Markets

There are two markets. The first, called the **new-issue or primary market**, is where new securities are offered to investors. The second, called the **secondary market**, is where existing securities are traded. The securities traded fall into two basic categories. Equity, or shares, are issued by companies and pay dividends, usually half-yearly, which are variable and linked to profitability. Most shares carry voting rights at the annual general meeting, although these are rarely exercised in practice. The value of a share is also variable, being determined by the forces of supply and demand, and a shareholder may, therefore, make either a capital gain or loss over time. Interest-bearing securities (stocks) come in a variety of forms. They are mostly issued by the government in the form of **gilts**. Those issued by companies are called **debentures**. There is also an active market in **Eurobonds** as outlined earlier. Stocks almost universally become redeemable at a specific future date, and yield a fixed rate of return. However, some are convertible into equity, and others are in the form of floating-rate notes, or are index-linked to guarantee their return in real rather than money terms. Stocks may also be subject to capital gains and losses as interest rates vary if sold before maturity.

The secondary market is essential if the primary market is to operate successfully. In other words, stocks and shares are regarded as liquid assets by investors even though they are frequently held for long periods of time by the original purchaser, and it is essential that there is a mechanism for rapid trading. The London Stock Exchange lies at the centre of the capital markets, but it is by no means necessary to use its services in order to raise longer-term capital. This is related to the role of financial intermediaries which hold the bulk of all stocks and shares in the UK. Whereas it is quite easy for individuals to deal in shares, personal portfolios are still, despite privatisation, very modest. In the UK, most investors prefer to save with pension funds, insurance companies and unit trusts where there have normally been tax

advantages whereas there are none for personal shareholdings other than special concessions for privatisation issues and where shares are transferred into Personal Equity Plans.

6.4.3 Raising Funds

In order to raise funds on the Stock Exchange a company must 'go public' and obtain a 'quotation'. This is an expensive affair, and a company is usually expected to show evidence of a respectable trading record over a period of years. Where a company is too new, operates in a very risky sector or cannot afford the costs of a full listing, it traditionally went to the **Unlisted Securities Market (USM)**. The **Over the Counter** (OTC) market, established in January 1987, was shut down at the end of 1990. However, shares were relatively difficult to trade in the USM as there were few market makers and big differences in buy and sell prices, and there was a significant decline in the amount of money raised in the last four years as shown in **Figure 6.6**.

When the USM was established, a five-year trading record was required before companies

Figure 6.6   *The USM*

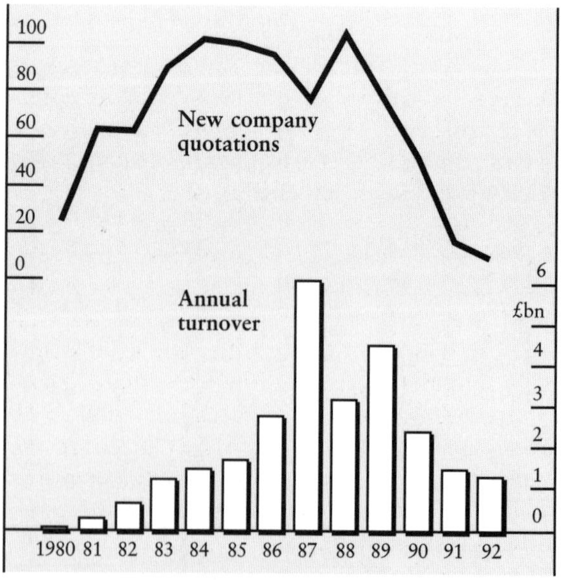

Source: The Economist, 6 March 1993.

could obtain a full listing as against three years for the USM. In 1991, these became three and two years respectively, and many companies responded by waiting until they could go directly to a full listing. As a result, the Stock Exchange decided at the end of 1992 to scrap the USM by 1995, with new members permitted to join only until June 1993. The 308 members would be allowed to transfer cheaply to the full market. However, this decision did nothing to resolve the fundamental problem of lack of liquidity in the market for small companies' shares In February 1995, the LSE published detailed rules for a replacement of the USM, to be known as the **Alternative Investment Market** (AIM). Operational from mid-June, AIM set out to attract growth companies with little or no track record but requiring capital for expansion or product development, and private or family controlled companies which do not need money but see a quotation as a means of raising their profile and enhancing liquidity in their shares. Prospectuses need only meet minimum EU rules. After 6 months, AIM was trading 121 companies (see *Bank of England Quarterly Bulletin*, February 1996, p. 26), and numbers subsequently picked up further and reached 200 by mid-1996. However, as the year progressed concerns were expressed over the rate of admissions, rising prices of new issues and the diligence of advisers and brokers (see *Financial Times*, 9 July 1996).

Where a full listing on the Stock Exchange is required, but the value of the new issue is modest, it is customary to opt for a 'public placing' whereby the issuing house (usually a merchant bank) places up to 75 per cent of the shares directly with institutional clients, the remainder being made available on the Exchange. Not surprisingly, shares issued in this way tend to end up concentrated in a very few hands. For larger issues an Issue by Prospectus or an Offer for Sale is normally required, with up to half the shares being sold to institutions, the difference being that in the latter case the issuing house first acquires the shares and then sells them to the public (favoured where the company is obscure but the issuing house is well known).

These methods are expensive because a prospectus has to be drawn up containing a full financial history of the company. The issue must be advertised nationally, and the issuing house and other advisors paid a commission. If oversubscribed, a system of allocation will have to be chosen and implemented. In the great majority of cases, the issue will be underwritten for a further fee as a precaution against an undersubscription, the underwriter then being obliged to purchase the outstanding shares. An Offer for Sale may be either at a fixed price, or less commonly by tender at (or above) a predetermined minimum price. The latter prevents the shares being seriously underpriced with attendant capital gains for 'stags' who immediately resell, but will almost certainly leave virtually all of the shares with the institutions.

Occasionally there are 'scrip' issues whereby, perhaps to make each share cheaper and hence more marketable, the number of shares may, for example, be doubled and their price halved. This does not raise any new capital as such, unlike a **rights** issue which is where existing shareholders are offered the right to buy additional newly-issued shares. If they do not wish to acquire the extra shares then the rights can be sold on the Stock Exchange. Strictly speaking, the price of the old shares should fall to bring into line the higher total number of shares and the higher total capitalisation of the company. Rights issues are popular with companies themselves because all the company has to do is send a circular to existing shareholders, who also benefit because there are no brokerage charges to pay but who may find their shareholdings diluted if they cannot afford to take up their rights.

The Stock Exchange in London (LSE) is the world's third largest, although it is dwarfed by total turnover in New York and Tokyo. More importantly, however, the LSE is the world's biggest foreign equity market where two-thirds of reported trading of equities outside their country of origin takes place. The advantage of the LSE lies in its low trading costs and in its structure, with market makers taking positions between buyers and sellers, and thereby providing superior liquidity for large wholesale trades.

The existence of **SEAQ International** has been important in this respect. This is a lightly regulated, computerised arena in which more than 50 large securities firms, mostly British, American and Japanese, trade huge blocks of shares among themselves and with institutions. SEAQ was founded in June 1985, and currently accounts for anything between 10 and 60 per cent of the turnover in the stocks of other European countries.

However, in 1993, the LSE's reputation was badly dented when it was forced to give up on Taurus, its attempt to bring its paper-based share settlement system into the modern world. This system update was necessitated by competition from cheaper electronic trading systems in the UK and from continental bourses eager to win back trading in their shares that had migrated to London. In the former case, the LSE now faces competition from Tradepoint, which set out initially to trade in the largest 400 shares. An important aspect is its order- driven system of dealing whereby orders from buyers are automatically matched with sellers after they have inputted the prices at which they are willing to deal. This contrasts with the quote-driven system of SEAQ where market makers act as intermediaries, sometimes buying on their own account and sometimes passing stock straight on to a seller.

It is also significant that whereas SEAQ serves to post market makers' prices and to report the trades, it does not execute them. Hence, if it fails to perform its tasks efficiently, it could be displaced by other information gatherers such as Reuters. It is for this reason that it was intended to replace SEAQ by a more modern system called SEQUENCE in mid-1996. This will provide a limited facility for order-matching to compete with Tradepoint and Reuter's Instinet, as well as SEATS which already provides an electronic order board for shares with just a single market maker.

On the international front, the increased liquidity on foreign bourses such as France's CAC and Germany's IBIS threatens to repatriate trade in those countries' shares. Furthermore, the French stock market abolished stamp duty on share transactions for foreign investors in 1994. Whereas market making was dominant up to 1990, executing orders for clients has recently

come to the fore, and this can now be done much more easily outside the LSE.

☐ 6.4.4 Gilt-edged Securities

The issue of **gilts** is the responsibility of the Bank of England, and the total value outstanding grew rapidly as a result of new borrowing by the government in the majority of postwar years. However, in the Autumn Statement of November 1988 the Chancellor declared that he would 'fully fund' the Public Sector Debt Repayment (PSDR), the effect of which was to withdraw £9 billion of gilts from the market during the financial year 1988–89. This not merely had the effect of altering considerably the shape of the yield curve which relates short-term to long-term yields, but caused problems for institutions such as pension funds which like to hold long-dated assets that match their long-dated liabilities. Indeed, given a shortage of alternative long-dated securities denominated in sterling offering an attractive rate of return, institutions turned increasingly to invest in foreign bonds. The Chancellor followed this up in December by announcing that, commencing in January 1989, the Bank of England would conduct reverse gilts auctions, concentrating on short-dated gilts.

There were no new issues of gilts during 1990. In the light of the shrinking market, a reduction in the number of actively traded stocks was brought about in 1990 by inviting investors in small, less-liquid issues to convert into larger, more liquid issues. Somewhat surprisingly, the number of market makers (GEMMs) remained constant at 19 throughout 1990, the first full year post-Big Bang not to have seen any withdrawals (there are 19 in 1993).

In January 1991, faced with the certainty of the reappearance of the PSBR in 1991–92, the Treasury began issuing new gilts. Subsequently, the rapid growth of the PSBR caused new issues to escalate to such a degree that fears were expressed about the Bank of England's ability to dispose of all that were on offer. So far it has been successful in that regard, but there was temporarily very little excess demand for several of the issues in 1993.

■ 6.5 Investor Protection

In the run up to Big Bang it became clear that deregulation on the intended scale could have highly adverse effects upon investors. The government therefore appointed Professor Gower to look into the issue of investor protection, and his Report was published in 1984. Gower raised a good many objections to existing practices, which were generally based upon the principle of letting the professionals look after their own because only they were competent to do so. With more and more cases of practices such as insider dealing coming to light, and wholly inconsequential punishments being meted out by the professionals, the government decided to build many of Gower's criticisms into a Financial Services Act which became law in 1986.

□ 6.5.1 Financial Services Act 1986

The Financial Services Act is intended as a **system of regulation covering the entire investment sector**, from the largest bank to the smallest investment advisor. It is intended to ensure that financial services are provided only by those who are fit and proper to do so, that legitimate complaints can be laid before the relevant authorities and that compensation is available where appropriate. Over the past decade the regulatory framework has been painfully pieced together. At its centre lies the Securities and Investments Board (SIB) whose powers are delegated to it by the Treasury. The SIB is a private company, financed by levies on its members. The main responsibility of the SIB is to oversee the Self Regulatory Organisations (SROs) of which there were originally five (now three).

AFBD	Association of Futures Brokers and Dealers
FIMBRA	Financial Intermediaries, Managers and Brokers Regulatory Association
IMRO	Investment Management Regulatory Organisation
LAUTRO	Life Assurance and Unit Trust Regulatory Organisation
TSA	The Securities Association

The TSA and AFBD were later merged to form the

SFA	The Securities and Futures Authority

FIMBRA, LAUTRO and most of IMRO were also merged to form the

PIA	Personal Investment Authority

The SIB's first task was to draw up its rule-book. Each SRO then had to draw up its own rulebook which had to be at least as rigorous as that of the SIB. All investment businesses have to register with a SRO of their choosing, or may opt to be regulated directly by the SIB. Failure to register is a criminal offence. The SIB can investigate any alleged malpractice, and apply sanctions as appropriate, and in certain circumstances bring legal proceedings.

The key elements of all rule-books are that:

1. clients' money must be kept separate from that of investment businesses;
2. written contracts must be provided to clients specifying agreed services;
3. there must be 'polarisation' (see below);
4. investigations of clients' needs must be undertaken and best possible advice given in the light of their findings;
5. clients should be advised to go elsewhere if expertise is lacking;
6. an established complaints procedure must be followed.

Polarisation requires all registered bodies to state clearly whether they are acting as a salesman or agent for the services of only one intermediary or as independent advisers choosing the best services from all those on offer. There is no middle ground. If a bank elects to be an independent adviser then it cannot recommend its own services although a client can expressly ask for them.

Polarisation has caused particular controversy because of differences between the amount of information on commissions which has to be disclosed to clients by salesmen in each category.

The compensation scheme has operated since August 1988. It pays out a maximum of £50 000 to any investor who loses money when a registered firm goes into liquidation, although the PIA ombudsman can recommend larger payments.

The extent of regulation is a critical issue. On the one hand, too much regulation drives business away to less-regulated markets elsewhere in the EU. On the other hand, too little regulation fosters abuse and fraud. The SIB came up with the 'new deal', comprising 10 principles (**tier 1** introduced in July 1990) and 40 'core rules' (**tier 2**, introduced in January 1991) all written in clear, straightforward English. The principles are along the lines of 'a firm should observe high standards of integrity and fair dealing'. The core rules are designed to draw a clear distinction between business carried out between professionals and the sale of investment products to the general public.

Unfortunately, the key to the regulatory edifice lies in the SRO's 'third-tier' rules which are by no means simple and easy to comprehend. In any event, interpreting simple rules is much harder than writing them, and the notes and appendices tend to be longer than the rule-book itself. Life was made slightly easier by the fact that on 1 April 1991 the TSA and AFBD merged to form the **Securities and Futures Authority** (SFA), which left only 4 SRO rule-books.

6.5.2 Disclosure of Life Assurance Commissions

Polarisation emphasised the distinction between independent financial advisers (IFAs) and tied agents (or, as they prefer to be known, appointed representatives) selling the products of one company. IFAs were to rely upon commissions for their income. As some life companies could be tempted to bias proceedings by offering excessive commissions, a maximum commissions agreement (MCA) was introduced by LAUTRO. The Office of Fair Trading promptly struck this down

as anti-competitive, causing commissions to rise by 20 to 30 per cent. This did at least keep some agents as IFAs, given that direct-selling life assurance companies had previously managed to induce large numbers of IFAs to become their tied agents by offering commissions well in excess of the MCA.

The trouble was that the remaining IFAs were told to disclose more about their commissions to clients, which they could fudge as IFAs but did not need to do at all as tied agents, so virtually every bank and building society ceased to be an IFA. This caused FIMBRA's income to fall drastically and it got into financial difficulties. The IFA share of the life and pensions market fell below 40 per cent, yet the SIB had originally set out to ensure that there would be a strong independent sector. However, the trend moved back towards IFAs as problems of monitoring tied agents increasingly surfaced.

Disclosure has become a critical issue. A personal pension plan can carry as many as seven different layers of charges and first-year payments in endowments mostly go as commission. IFAs were originally subject under SIB rules to 'soft' disclosure of commissions. That is, at the time of sale the client had to be told the method by which the IFA was paid for its services. The insurance company provided details of the commission after the sale takes place, hidden among the small print. Tied agents did not need to disclose commissions. The playing field was not level, and the client rarely got to know the truth.

In March 1991, the SIB announced a new review of the regulatory system, with especial emphasis upon disclosure. The Financial Services Act was supposed to usher in a new era of clearly defined relationships. This proved to be optimistic because, in March 1992, the SIB rejected calls for the full disclosure of commission at point of sale, and opted instead for investors to be told the surrender values of their policies during their first five years. The pay-out figures used for these calculations were standard industry-wide projections provided by LAUTRO rather than individual company performance figures, and did not enlighten the investor. As a consequence, the Office of Fair Trading issued a report in March 1993 which recommended more extensive changes as shown in **Table 6.5**.

In July 1993, the SIB was instructed by the Treasury to produce new regulations which, operative from July 1994, would require sales agents and advisers automatically to give customers written information about commissions in terms of cash before the customer signed a proposal form for any life product. The customer would also need to be handed a document spelling out details of the product.

6.5.3 The Personal Investment Authority

Early in 1992 Sir Kenneth Clucas proposed in a report to the SIB that a single body incorporating FIMBRA, LAUTRO and parts of IMRO be created, to be known as the **Personal Investment Authority** (PIA). Many banks and building societies initially refused to join, primarily because they feared that they would be forced to increase substantially their contributions to the Investors Compensation Scheme to cover defaults among small independent intermediaries (which might anyway vote not to liquidate FIMBRA). The life insurance companies then responded that they would not join unless the banks also joined. However, the restructuring went ahead and the SIB

Table 6.5 *Disclosure Regimes*

Information disclosed	At Present	SIB proposal	OFT proposal
Reduction in yield	✓	✓	✓
Wealth warnings	✗	✓	✓
Adviser's status	✗	✓	✓
Five-year surrender values	✗	✓	✓
Later surrender values	✗	✗	✓
Independent adviser's commission	✗	✗	✓
Companies' total charges	✗	✗	✓
Tied agents' commission	✗	✗	✗

Source: Financial Times, 19 March 1993.

fixed a deadline of end-September 1994 for independent financial advisers to choose between registering with the PIA; applying to be regulated directly by the SIB or a recognised professional body; stating that they were joining a network of advisers or setting up a 'tie' with a life company; or signalling their intention to leave the investment business. By the deadline, some 4300 of the former 5300 FIMBRA members had applied to join the PIA.

6.5.4 Failure of Regulation

Despite the reduction in the number of SROs, the various bodies constantly squabbled about their respective roles and blamed each other for breakdowns in the system. One notable example was the failure of IMRO in the years up to 1991 to prevent the disappearance of some £440 million of pension assets mainly from a fund management company controlled by the late Robert Maxwell. More recently, the widespread mis-selling of personal pensions exposed serious deficiencies in regulation. With respect to the SIB, it was noted in particular that it could not determine the scope of an SROs activities and could not direct member firms to any particular SRO, thereby permitting them to shop around for the weakest regulator. Furthermore, it had no direct enforcement powers over any firms as was demonstrated when it issued guidance to the PIA concerning how its members should decide which customers merited compensation for mis-sold pensions. On appeal, the High Court held that the SIB had no direct power over SROs, that it possibly had no indirect powers and that all it could do was revoke an SRO's authorisation. However, the SIB itself took the view that this was too destructive to be a valid option.

In January 1996, recognising that remedial action needed to be taken, especially in the light of the problems encountered with the compensation scheme in 1995 and continuing disagreements between the SIB and the SROs, the government announced that regulatory responsibility for insurance (including Lloyd's) remaining with the DTI would pass to the Treasury as part of a regulatory shake-up (a form of second 'big bang') to take place after the next election. All of the main regulatory bodies would be rolled up into the SIB (in line with proposals already tabled by the Labour Party).

There are other intimations of regulatory tightening. For example, the PIA announced in April 1996 that 120 000 pension and investment advisers would have to sign individual contracts and be personally liable to fines or even expulsion from the industry, commencing in 1997 (see *Financial Times*, 19 April 1996), and in August 1996, the SFA announced that in the year ending March 1996 fines exceeded £1 million for the first time. In the aftermath of Barings, it also stated that in future the burden of proof would be shifted such that regulated companies would have to prove that they did not break the rules rather than the SFA having to prove that they did.

▌ 6.6 Financial Intermediation in the Future

Let us turn, by way of summary, to pick out from the above discussion the most important themes which will determine how the financial system will evolve during the remainder of this century.

⬚ 6.6.1 Deregulation and Regulation

A particularly interesting issue is the balance between **deregulation** and **regulation**. Historically, the financial system in the UK was heavily regulated by the government acting through the Bank of England. In addition, specific kinds of financial assets and liabilities were favoured by tax concessions to lenders and/or borrowers. As a result, certain parts stagnated. This imbalance was recognised in the UK when the present government came to power and, starting with the abolition of exchange controls in 1979, it set in train a process of freeing up the system. Most of the monetary controls were subsequently terminated or put into abeyance; public corporations were sold, partly to small shareholders; the Financial Services Act

1986 and Building Societies Act 1986 became law; the Stock Exchange was reformed via Big Bang; portable pensions were introduced as were personal equity plans, and so on.

However, these processes have been incomplete and the government has been forced to recognise that free-for-alls in financial markets are a recipe for widespread abuse, and hence **deregulation has dragged regulation in its wake**. Whereas the Financial Services Act and Building Societies Act, for example, have allowed NBFIs to provide services previously forbidden to them, they have also made it necessary to set up regulatory bodies to ensure that the new services are provided by fit-and-proper intermediaries, and that the new rules are obeyed to the letter. This in turn has caused many disputes about what kinds of regulatory bodies are needed, and how they should be financed. It must be recognised that financial markets always have been regulated in the sense that, for example, the Stock Exchange imposed a rulebook upon its members, but this kind of self-regulation is bound to be treated with considerable scepticism by outside parties who read about scandals and their resolution behind closed doors. However, it is clear that other existing bodies such as the Bank of England and the Monopolies and Mergers Commission do not have the resources to cope with the huge increase in regulatory work, and hence other bodies have had to be created. The full current framework for financial regulation in the UK is set out in **Figure 6.7**.

Matters came to a head in the aftermath of the scandals associated with Barlow Clowes, Robert Maxwell and mis-selling of personal pensions. It was alleged that there are too many regulators, that the regulatory system did too little to deter illegal activities and that the system was too costly to operate. In particular, it was alleged that self-regulation was such a failure that statutory regulation would be preferable. The reality is that, while these criticisms were all partly true, they represented much less of a problem than the fact that the regulatory system had a poor record in detecting improper behaviour and an even worse record in bringing about successful prosecutions. The Conservative government initially showed little inclination to act on these failings, but it

Figure 4.10 *The Framework for Financial Regulation in the UK*

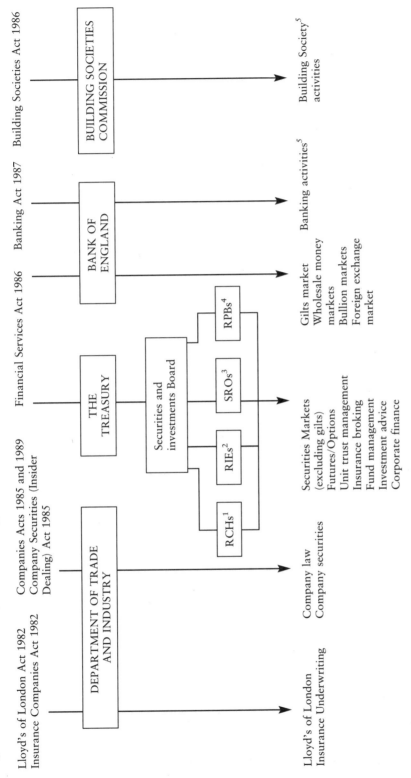

Notes:
1 RCHs = Recognised clearing houses.
2 RIEs = Recognised investment exchanges.
3 SROs = Self regulatory organisations.
4 RPBs = Recognised professional bodies.
5 The investment business of banks and building societies is supervised within the Securities and Investments Board regime.

Source: D. Goacher (mimeo).

(and the Labour Party) now recognise that a fairly radical shake-up of the system is necessary, and as noted above, the initial steps have been taken to get it introduced. An important question, as yet unanswered, concerns the length of time it will take these new arrangements to settle down. The fall-out from Big Bang took almost a decade to settle, but at least this time around there is much more experience from which to draw appropriate lessons for the future.

☐ 6.6.2 Innovation

Nevertheless, it is only to be expected that further amendments and fine-tuning will be forthcoming in the years to come. Indeed, this is almost inevitable in the face of ever more rapid **innovation** in financial markets. Regulations can ultimately be applied only to cover existing practices, and it is clear that a rule-book set up to cover practices existing even in 1990 will be looking out of date by 2000. Financial innovation is driven by a variety of forces, including most obviously changes in monetary control systems; the desire to avoid regulation; vast increases in the total sums being transacted; a wider variety of both lenders and borrowers; and increasing sophistication on the part of both in specifying their needs.

We have already referred to the rapid growth of Eurobonds. It is worth noting that, hand in hand with these, it is increasingly common to find transactions in the **swaps** market. According to the International Swap Dealers Association (ISDA) the nominal principal involved in interest rate and currency swaps was in excess of $2000 billion in mid-1993. Despite their superficial complexity, at the heart of any swap lies simply an agreement between two institutions receiving or paying interest income to exchange payments or receipts. For example, if one bank has borrowed in dollars at a fixed rate, and a second bank has borrowed in yen at a floating rate, each then agrees to meet the interest payments of the other. Their decisions are influenced by different expectations concerning the future path of both the currencies and the interest rates in question. Whole sequences of swaps can be placed end-on-end in a single programme. However, most swaps currently involve simple swaps in dollars between fixed-rate and floating-rate notes. Currency swaps carry more risk than interest rate swaps because both exchange rates and interest rates may move adversely at the same time. Banks accordingly run a 'swaps book' in which swaps are matched up, thereby limiting their exposure to exchange rate or interest rate movements.

☐ 6.6.3 The Swaps Debacle

In 1989, a case was bought before the High Court by a district auditor who, on checking the books of a London borough, Hammersmith and Fulham, uncovered £6 billion of interest rate swaps and was unsure of their legality. On 1 November, the High Court ruled that not only were the swaps *ultra vires* (that is, the council had no legal powers to engage in swaps) but that any interest rate management contacts with any council were illegal and unenforceable.

Some 78 banks had traded swaps and options with local authorities. All the outstanding contracts were frozen at the time of the judgement, and the banks stood to lose at least £500 million. On appeal, the Court of Appeal ruled unanimously that legality depended upon the objective of the council official at the time of the deal. If the objective was money management, then the deal was in order since this was a proper function of a local authority. If it was to make a profit, it was *ultra vires*.

On further appeal, the House of Lords ruled on 14 January 1991, again unanimously, that the Court of Appeal was wrong and annulled not merely Hammersmith's swaps but over one thousand other local authority swaps dating back to 1982. The banks were appalled. After all, both the Bank of England and the Audit Commission had sanctioned swaps as tools for managing interest rate risk. The banks and the Bank appealed to the government to introduce retrospective legislation to validate the illegal transactions, but the government refused. The banks were recommended to issue writs for repayment. These were expected to recover about £125 million and, with the Treasury meeting 35 per cent of the residual losses through tax repayments, the banks were expected to suffer a net loss of £275 million.

A series of out-of-court settlements commenced in February 1992, with six test cases settled for undisclosed sums by June. However, the first case to be argued in the High Court resulted in a ruling in February 1993 that Islington Council should repay £1 million to Westdeutsche Landesbank. The High Court also ruled that restitution could be applied to swap agreements that had already been closed. In March, Islington decided to appeal, but lost its case in December. Kleinwort Benson also won a second case against South Tyneside Council, and it became increasingly clear that councils would have to repay substantial sums in out-of-court settlements.

6.6.4 Disintermediation

It is important to note that much innovative activity such as swaps is **off-balance sheet**. In other words, the bank concerned in a transaction does not lend to the borrower funds which the bank has itself previously borrowed, which would cause both transactions to appear on its balance sheet, but rather acts as the agent organising a loan directly between ultimate lender and ultimate borrower. The process in which funds flow from lender to borrower other than via the banks is known as **disintermediation**, and has obvious consequences for monetary controls which are intended to operate via regulations imposed upon specified intermediaries (traditionally banks).

It also involves the process known as **securitisation**, whereby conventional bank or building society lending is replaced by other forms of financial instruments. A Eurobond, for example, is a 'securitised' debt, which means that it is sold by a borrowing institution to a lender without the money being either lent to, or by, a bank. The purchaser may subsequently resell the debt in the secondary Eurobond market, and the debt may be resold any number of times before maturity. The obvious consequence of securitisation is that the issuer of the security has no real idea who actually holds it as an asset at any given time. However,

securitised debt is set to become increasingly popular as top quality borrowers such as 'blue chip' companies take advantage of the fact that they can actually borrow more cheaply in their own names than through the intermediation of a bank, the credit rating of which may have suffered as a result of bad debts.

On the face of it, financial innovation should permit independent groups of intermediaries to carve out their own market niches, and indeed specialist intermediaries are often successful as niche operators. However, a successful niche operator with a limited capital base is sooner or later going to attract the attention of an intermediary in another part of the system which has spare capital and limited capacity to expand in its major lines of business. Historically, the process of merger and takeover between different kinds of intermediary was heavily restricted, but in a deregulated environment the key issue is simply whether the merged company will be a fit-and-proper operator in every market in which it wishes to operate. The process of merger and takeover may allow an intermediary to reduce the risk inherent in its exposure to a single or very small number of markets. It may provide a short cut, via merger with another intermediary overseas, to becoming an international as against a national operator. There are also going to be circumstances in which a company outside the financial system will want to merge with a financial intermediary, especially if it wants, for example, to provide credit facilities to its customers.

It is unclear where the adjusments implied by the above will end. It is certain that for many companies the process of merger will prove to be an unhappy and costly business, and parts of the merged organisations may subsequently need to be shut down or resold. It was clear at the time of Big Bang, for example, that there were too many players and too little talent in almost every part of the equity and bond markets. The crash of October 1987 caused the process of readjustment to be speeded up, but it is by no means complete as yet. The link between economic efficiency and concentration in the financial markets cannot be determined by historical precedent. There is much evidence of a 'clash of cultures' when different kinds of intermediary are brought together. At the end of the day, the authorities must also form a judgement both about their ability to oversee the system and also the compatibility of different kinds of financial system with the pursuit of their major objectives.

☐ 6.6.5 Internationalisation

One of the trickier issues is raised by the **internationalisation** of the financial system. Predominantly national intermediaries still dominate the UK retail markets, particularly the building societies, but the process of merger and take-over is gradually becoming more international in scope. Big Bang specifically encouraged the inflow of foreign capital, but it would be wrong to suppose that this can be interpreted as a completely laissez-faire attitude on the part of the authorities. They have indicated that there are distinct limits beyond which internationalisation will not be permitted to go, although they are evidently prepared to accept the takeover of a clearing bank such as the Midland provided the acquirer is a well-established denizen of the City.

☐ 6.6.6 New Technology

To be a major international intermediary it must be possible for the head office to know what is going on in the farthest-flung outposts of the company. This has increasingly been made possible by the introduction of **new technology**, and especially of computers, which can communicate information instantaneously over vast distances. However, the introduction of computers has had much more widespread effects, because it has permitted an individual intermediary to handle an enormously increased range of data, and therefore made it possible for it to compete in many more markets than in previous periods when a lack of skilled manpower could not produce enough detailed information for rational decisions to be made. Dealing with a multiplicity of currencies is no longer more than a technicality, and the full spread of interest rates can be arrranged on a

screen at the touch of a button. Much of the software is marketed commercially, so it is not even necessary for organisations to develop their own software before joining in a new market. It should, however, be borne in mind that computers cannot think for themselves, so if information is mistakenly or fraudently inserted, serious consequences can easily arise involving losses on a scale which would have been spotted much more quickly in less-sophisticated systems.

Dealing in equities and gilts is almost totally dependent upon modern technology, but this technology barely touches upon the everyday lives of individuals. However, automated teller machines (ATMs) are now in widespread usage, and NatWest, for example, spent £1 billion in order to create a computerised system which would allow it to deal with deposits, cash dispensing and account information at branches entirely through machines.

EFTPOS (electronic funds transfer at point of sale) has become popular very quickly. EFTPOS is a system whereby, for example, a supermarket uses an individual's debit card to debit his or her purchases direct to a bank account, thereby rendering unnecessary the use both of cash and cheques. By the end of 1990, 45 per cent of adults in Britain owned a debit card, and figures from the Credit Card Research Group in 1994 revealed that a credit card and a debit card each existed for every two members of the entire population. Elsewhere in Europe fewer cards typically exist per head of population, but these are almost all debit cards (whereas in the USA they are almost all credit cards). Interestingly, total spending per head of population using both types of card is remarkably similar in advanced economies at £1000 to £1200 per year.

Given the pattern elsewhere in Europe, it was predicted that Switch and Visa cards would be used ten times as often as credit cards by the year 2000. According to the Association for Payment Clearing Services (APACS) in August 1996 (see *Financial Times*, 17 August 1996), the volume of transactions by debit cards rose to over 1 billion in 1995, an increase of 25 per cent over 1994. Debit card transactions are expected to double by the year 2000, with debit card use becoming increasingly more common compared to credit cards. APACS predicts that there will be roughly 11 billion automated, paper or card transactions by 2000, and the numbers of cheques and paper credits, which both peaked in 1990 at 3.9 billion and 390 million respectively, are undoubtedly declining in use at a sharp rate, with cheque use down to 1.8 billion transactions in 1995. However, the banks have struggled to make a profit from issuing debit cards which are far more costly for retailers than cheques, and the latter are still used as often as they were ten years ago. Cash, meanwhile, continues to account for roughly 77 per cent of all transactions, although its use declined steadily during the period 1985–93 before rising again after 1994.

In January 1991, the big five clearing banks announced that they had agreed upon a scheme that would eliminate paper for corporate customers and replace it with electronic messages. Inter-bank electronic document interchange (EDI) enables companies to make payments by sending messages directly from their computers to their bank. The bank then transfers the funds and notifies the recipient electronically. There are those who claim that transacting using electronic money (e-money) over the Internet is the next stage for individuals, once security procedures have been strengthened (*The Economist*, 1995), but this is not imminent on any significant scale.

Alternatively, the new millennium may usher in widespread use of the 'electronic purse' which, in the guise of Mondex, a joint venture between NatWest and the Midland, that went online in Swindon in July 1995. The basic idea is that individuals and businesses transfer cash value from bank accounts onto a plastic 'smart' card which carries a computer chip. The card can then be used to make transactions of any value provided both parties carry a card and card reader. UK banks and retailers stand to gain enormously because processing notes and coins is estimated to cost the better part of £5 billion a year. The 'smart' card will also resolve the problem of counterfeit money and theft, in the latter case by providing a facility to 'lock up' cash deposits electronically. A national launch is pencilled in for 1997. In June 1996, Visa International an-

nounced that it would statrt trials of a Visa Cash card in conjunction with five UK banks in 1997. So far, M&S has declined to participate.

Other innovations already in common usage are electronic gadgets which allow an individual sitting at home to access his bank account or a share dealing service via a telephone link, with the information shown on a home computer screen. In the 1980s, most experiments with 'home banking' failed because they were too sophisticated. The Bank of Scotland led the way in 1985, and other banks followed with systems using home computers, specially-designed terminals or voice- or tone-activated systems. However, it rapidly became clear that whereas most customers were happy with the idea of using the phone, they wanted a person rather than a machine at the other end of the line. The Midland Bank accordingly set up Firstdirect in 1989 as a retail bank with staff but without branches. All transactions are done over the telephone on a 24–hour a day basis, and no computer is required by the customer. Cash is withdrawn from ATMs. Other banks subsequently gave up on computerised systems and substituted people, although some residual electronic services remain in use.

Firstdirect has been sufficiently successful to cause other banks belatedly to respond, although not by setting up a service to replace branches but by adding a more limited telephone facility to their existing branch structures. This is likely to add to costs unless some branches are simultaneously shut down or automated, but there is a general reluctance to follow the example of Firstdirect in case it also gets overtaken by new technology.

The market for Internet banking is poised to grow sharply by the year 2000, with 154 banks having established a Web site by mid-1996 (*Financial Times*, 12 August 1996). Costs for Internet banking only run to 20 per cent of income compared to a normal 60 per cent on average, which is a massive incentive for banks to experiment with the Internet, although services remain unsophisticated for the time being.

These developments represent progress towards a cashless society, but as noted above there remains, and will remain for the foreseeable future, very large numbers of the 'unbanked'. Furthermore, the use of ATMs requires relatively large amounts of cash to be held, so what is being replaced is not so much cash as cheques which, as noted above, makes the banks happy as cheques are expensive to process. However, they are relatively cheap to use for customers in many circumstances where modern technology is being charged for at what, bearing in mind that the technology was supposed to reduce costs, are extortionate rates.

■ 6.7 Conclusion

It is clear from this discussion that the circumstances of the financial markets post-Big Bang are somewhat different from those anticipated in 1986. At the time, there was an almost universal belief that the markets would be transformed by the quest for globalisation, and that in order to compete a financial supermarket would have to be created.

This would require the elimination of the weakest players from the markets, leaving the survivors with profitable businesses with significant shares of each market. The reality has been a fascinating illustration of the forces of competition, which in this case are dependent upon information flows. The quest for globalisation was based upon the assumption that the market players with the most sophisticated, and by implication most expensive, communications would have an advantage over the less-well-capitalised players. To the discomfiture of those companies that spent vast sums of money following the path mapped out by this line of reasoning, it proved possible for all the players, even those operating on a small scale and with relatively little capital, to access the necessary information on equal terms. Furthermore, it has become possible for customers to shop around at the touch of a button on a computer screen. They are largely indifferent from whom they buy, so they may simply opt continuously for the cheapest (and probably not very profitable) bargain such as is offered by a basic share dealing only service. Alternatively, they may be willing to pay a premium for high quality advice, but if this fails to

meet expectations they can readily transfer his allegiance elsewhere.

Building up allegiance is largely a matter of personal relationships and trust. This is why, following American precedents, department stores like M&S began to offer a limited range of financial services. Most department stores have long offered store cards and personal finance. Given the ongoing rather poor image of banks, it is none too surprising that many people are at least as happy to deal with M&S. In any event, it is evident that most functions performed by clearing banks can be done satisfactorily by a different type of financial intermediary such as a building society, and indeed the two are becoming indistinguishable in the eyes of those who buy retail services.

It is also probable that many of the new ventures in financial services by non-financial companies will be at least as successful as diversification by existing financial intermediaries. As has been recounted at various stages in the preceding analysis, there is a good deal of licking of wounds going on, and the financial sector is still some way from reaching a post-Big Bang equilibrium. The winners have undoubtedly been the stockholders and estate agents who were bought out by financial intermediaries for highly inflated prices in the belief that there would be lots of synergy to tap. Some of these fortunate sellers have recently been able to buy back their old companies for a fraction of their selling price. If there is one lesson to be learned above all others, it is that there is no substitute for local knowledge of the customer.

Bibliography

Bank of England (1992) 'Ecu Securities Markets', *Bank of England Quarterly Bulletin* (May).

Bank of England (1993) 'Cross-border Alliances in Banking and Financial Services in the Single Market', *Bank of England Quarterly Bulletin* (August).

Beck, B. (1996) 'The Economics of Ageing', *The Economist* (27 January).

Callen, T. and J. Lomax (1990) 'The Development of the Building Societies' Sector in the

1980s', *Bank of England Quarterly Bulletin* (November).

Curwen, P. and K. Paul (1994) 'Lloyd's of London', *Business and the Contemporary World*, VI (3).

Davis, E. (1991) 'The Development of Pension Funds – An International Comparison', *Bank of England Quarterly Bulletin* (August).

Fraser, I. and P. Mortimer-Lee (1993) 'The EC Single Market in Financial Services', *Bank of England Quarterly Bulletin* (February).

Hutton, B. (1994) 'Ringing in the Revolution', *Financial Times* (15 January).

Ingham, H. and S. Thompson (1993) 'Structural Deregulation and Market Entry: The Case of Financial Services', *Fiscal Studies*, 14 (1).

Lapper, R. (1994) 'Hard Work to be Free and Single', *Financial Times* (1 July 1994, p. 19).

Peet, J. (1992) 'Financial Centres: Rise and Fall', *The Economist* (27 June).

Secretary of State for Social Security (1993) *Equality in State Pension Age*. Cm 2420 (London: HMSO).

The Economist (1994) 'Electronic Money' (26 November).

Unger, B. (1992) 'World Banking', *The Economist* (2 May).

Chapter 7

Taxation

Peter Curwen

■ 7.1 Introduction

Our purpose in Chapters 7 and 8 is to describe the components of the UK fiscal system and to provide an up-to-date statistical analysis of taxation, government expenditure, borrowing and debt. We do not seek to discuss the operation of fiscal policy instruments as such, which is left to the concluding chapter because it is unhelpful to discuss fiscal policy independently of monetary policy. Furthermore, it is impractical to discuss the use of policy instruments until all of the relevant policy objectives have been thoroughly reviewed, and their inter-relationships assessed.

Our first task, which occupies this chapter, is to examine the available data on taxation.

■ 7.2 The Overall Tax Burden

Between 1948 and 1985, in money terms, the gross receipts from taxation rose by 3200 per cent. Starting from 1948 it took 14 years to double tax revenue. It doubled again in eight years, and again in five. This acceleration was clearly associated with a sharp rise in the rate of inflation, especially in the mid-1970s. However, prices rose by a total of only 1200 per cent during the equiva-

lent period, which means that gross tax receipts more than doubled in real terms. As the population has remained fairly constant, the gross real burden of taxes **per capita** has also clearly more than doubled.

However, individuals are less interested in their total tax bill than in the **proportion of their total earnings which is taxed away**. It is accordingly sensible to stick to the definitions which match up with the government's expenditure data and to express the tax burden in the form of total taxation as a percentage of GDP. Interestingly, this has shown no long-term continuous tendency to rise because GDP has risen significantly, although the trend line has been anything but smooth.

Taxation as a percentage of GDP fell from 1948 to 1960, admittedly from the high percentage required for postwar reconstruction. However, it was back to the 1948 level by 1970. Having fluctuated somewhat during the 1970s, it rose sharply after the election of the Conservative government in 1979, as shown in **Figure 7.1**. The tax burden stabilised somewhat at the end of the 1980–81 recession, briefly fell sharply and stabilised again during the period 1985–86 to 1990–91 when the two measures used in **Figure 7.1** became effectively one and the same. A further sharp fall then ensued during 1990–91 and 1991–92. As is clearly

Figure 7.1   *Taxes and Social Security Contributions*

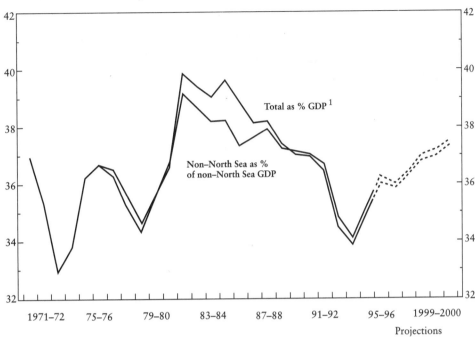

Note:
[1] On a national accounts accrual basis.
Source: FSBR 1996–97, p. 72.

shown in **Figure 7.1, it took from 1979–80 to 1992–93 for the tax burden to fall back below that prevailing at the time the first Thatcher government was elected. Furthermore, the trend line has turned up again since 1993–94 in no uncertain fashion.**

☐ *7.2.1 The Marginal Rate of Tax*

The tax burden is normally defined in terms of the **average** rate of tax – that is, total tax divided by total GDP. Given the existence of tax allowances, it is evident that the rate levied on an **extra** £1 of income, the **marginal** rate of direct tax (including social security contributions), will be **higher than** the average rate of direct tax. Suppose, for example, an employer wishes to pay an extra £1 to a worker. In every case he must himself pay 10p in National Insurance Contributions (NICs). The employee may, or may not, pay 10p in NICs

(because they are levied only up to a maximum income, see **p. 174**) and will pay either 20p, 23p or 40p in income tax. Out of what is left, the employee will subsequently incur VAT, excise duties and other indirect taxes.

Thus out of every additional £1 earned, a higher rate income tax payer will initially pay 40p (income tax) but the employer will also pay NICs of 10p – a total tax rate of 50p. For a standard rate payer it will be either 23p + 10p (employer NICs) +10p (Employee NICs) = 43p or, if employee NICs do not apply, 33p. The Labour Party promise to uncap NICs – that is, to make the 10p apply in all cases. Under such circumstances, we get 60p for the higher rate payer and 43p for the standard rate payer. And this, remember, only relates to **direct** tax. When what remains is spent, all kinds of additional **indirect** taxes are incurred.

The Labour Party argues that uncapping NICs will yield sufficient extra revenue to finance improved child benefits and state pensions, but this is most unlikely to occur. In 1978–79, the last Labour government's final financial year in power, with higher rates of income tax **alone** rising to 83 per cent, the highest-paid 1 per cent of the working population contributed 11 per cent of all income tax and the highest-paid 10 per cent contributed 34 per cent. In 1989–90, with the higher rate set at 40 per cent, the highest-paid 1 per cent contributed 15 per cent and the highest-paid 10 per cent contributed 42 per cent. The most recent equivalent contribution figures are 17 per cent and 45 per cent respectively. It is widely recognised that, when higher rates of income tax go up, almost everyone in a position to do so **looks for ways to avoid (and possibly to evade) tax**, so the tax burden will simply be redistributed back from the highest paid to the lowest paid and **little or no extra spending will be financed**.

Opinion polls consistently reveal that UK residents **prefer** more public spending to tax cuts. But for four successive elections they just as consistently **voted** for Conservative governments which promised tax **reductions**. Readers may draw their own conclusions.

■ *7.3* Fiscal Drag

It may come as something of a surprise, in view of the sharp reduction in the marginal rates of income tax in recent years, that the burden of taxation has responded so little. This can primarily be explained by the phenomenon of **fiscal drag** which arises because, whereas the Rooker–Wise–Lawson amendments to the 1977 Finance Bill provided that tax allowances be raised in line with inflation unless the Budget specifically provided otherwise, the index used to adjust for inflation is for **prices** rather than **incomes**.

When the economy is growing strongly, incomes tend, on average, to grow noticeably faster than prices. Hence, even if tax allowances are adjusted to compensate for rising prices, an increasingly larger proportion of total earned income is subjected to tax. In 1987–88 this caused tax revenue to be some £2 billion higher than forecast, and this was comfortably exceeded in 1988–89. As a rule of thumb, each 1 per cent rise

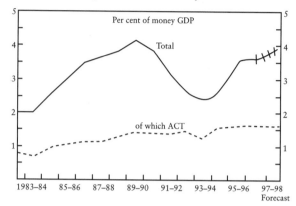

Figure 7.2   *Corporation Tax Receipts*

Source: FSBR 1993–94, Chart 6.1; FSBR 1996–97.

in real income increases the average personal tax rate by between 1.5 and 1.75 per cent.

Though not technically fiscal drag, precisely the same effect will occur for corporate taxation when profits are rising much faster than GDP, as can clearly be seen in **Figure 7.2**. Equally, spending tends to rise with real incomes, with the result that indirect tax receipts rise sharply.

During the recession commencing in 1990, fiscal drag operated in reverse, with incomes rising more slowly for the employed, large numbers losing their jobs, falling profits and a collapse in household spending. The consequent rapid erosion of the tax base made it very difficult for the government to maintain tax revenue. The only way to compensate for this was to reduce tax thresholds (allowances), but this was politically unacceptable. For obvious reasons, governments of all hues must rely upon fiscal drag to eliminate the Budget deficit during the latter part of the decade, although it cannot expect drag to operate as forcefully as it did in the 1980s.

■ *7.4* International Comparisons

The ONS calculates the tax and social security burden for OECD member countries on a standardised international definition used by the OECD. This reveals, firstly, that in 1994 the overall tax burden in the UK as a percentage of **GNP** at market prices was in the lower half of the list of the 20 most advanced economies, well below the Nordic countries and comfortably below the rest of the EU, albeit appreciably above the USA, Japan and Australia. **Table 7.1** illustrates the position in 1983, 1988 and 1993, the latest year for which confirmed data are available. As can be seen, the UK fell rapidly down the rank order during this decade, although this had less to do with a falling ratio as such, at least prior to 1990, than with the general tendency for the ratios to rise elsewhere.

Clearly, therefore, the UK is **not over-burdened by 'deductions' relative to most other industrialised countries.** As it happens, many of the misconceptions about the burden of taxation arise because of a failure to distinguish between the burden of deductions and the burden of taxation *per se*. In practice, there are very different balances between what are officially called 'taxes' as against 'social security contributions' in different countries. For example, the (direct + indirect) tax burden in the UK is reasonably high whereas social security contributions are relatively low. Equally, the balance between direct and indirect taxation is highly variable between countries, as shown in **Table 7.2**.

Table 7.1 *Taxes and Social Security Contributions as a % of GDP at Market Prices by Rank[1]*

	1983 Percentage and Rank		1988 Percentage and Rank		1993 Percentage and Rank	
Sweden	49.8	2	54.8	1	49.9	1
Denmark	46.5	4	51.7	2	49.9	1
Netherlands	46.0	6	47.6	4	48.0	3
Italy	35.8	12	36.7	13	47.8	4
Norway	46.6	3	47.8	3	45.7	5
Finland	37.6	8	43.3	8	45.7	5
Belgium	46.4	5	46.4	5	45.7	5
Luxembourg	50.8	1	43.9	6	44.6	8
France	43.6	7	43.8	7	43.9	9
Austria	41.1	10	42.0	9	43.6	10
Greece	33.9	13	34.9	14	41.2	11
Germany	37.4	9	37.7	11	39.0	12
Ireland	36.4	11	39.1	10	36.3	13
Canada	32.9	14	34.0	15	35.6	14
Spain	27.5	18	32.8	16	35.1	15
UK[2]	37.3	8	37.1	12	33.6	16
Switzerland	31.6	15	32.6	17	33.2	17
USA	28.1	17	29.5	20	29.7	18
Japan	27.0	19	30.3	19	29.1	19
Australia	28.6	16	30.6	18	28.7	20

Notes:
[1] Calculations based on OECD Revenue Statistics.
[2] Includes the Community Charge.
Source: Economic Trends (Nov. 1993), p. 19.

Table 7.2 *Taxes and Social Security Contributions as % of GNP at Current Market Prices 1993*

	Direct Taxes		Indirect Taxes		Social Security
	Households	Companies	Total	of which VAT	
UK	9.7	2.5	14.2	[6.6]	6.1
Greece	3.5	2.6	19.9	[8.5]	12.3
France	7.2	2.1	14.8	[7.6]	19.8
Japan	7.4	4.2	7.9	[1.5]	9.6
Germany	10.2	1.6	13.3	[7.6]	16.7
USA	11.1	3.0	9.0	[0.0]	8.3
Netherlands	13.4	3.5	13.0	[7.0]	18.7
Sweden	19.6	2.4	16.3	[8.8]	14.3
Denmark	28.8	2.7	18.2	[10.2]	1.7

Source: Data derived from OECD statistics.

Unfortunately, what this means in policy terms is that there is equal ammunition (a) for those who believe that taxation should be set at the lowest possible level in a free society and (b) for those who believe that the UK can afford to increase public expenditure, financed out of taxation, without raising the tax burden above that commonly ruling elsewhere in the EU, or indeed in Europe generally.

■ 7.5 The Tax System

□ 7.5.1 Introduction

The tax system in the UK is somewhat out of line with that typically found elsewhere in the OECD. This is partly because, for example, it was only in the UK, between 1955 and 1985, that the importance of income tax, measured as a percentage of GDP, fell rather than rose. However, the UK has been typical in its increased emphasis upon National Insurance Contributions (or their equivalent) which, though not technically a tax, has precisely the same effect as income tax upon disposable income.

The UK tax system has been developed in an **evolutionary** rather than a **revolutionary** manner since 1948. Although no Chancellor has chosen to institute a major programme of tax reform (unless, as some believe, Nigel Lawson is to be regarded as the exception in this respect), the long-term consequence of continuous small adjustments has been to alter the relative importance of different taxes quite dramatically (Keen, 1991). The preference for evolution is unsurprising from a political perspective since it has been calculated that, as a rule of thumb, tax reform is politically acceptable only if the beneficiaries outnumber the losers by a ratio of four to one. Furthermore, it is much easier to sweeten a reform that hurts the pockets of a large number of voters by giving them back bigger sums via tax cuts elsewhere in the system, and this can be done only if tax revenue is buoyant. In any event, the Inland Revenue are never keen on major administrative changes. The structure of the tax system since 1948 is set out in **Table 7.3**. The sections which follow review the individual components of the UK tax system. So far as the period from 1985 to 1995 specifically is concerned, the evolution of the system can be summarised as follows:

- The Conservative government concentrated upon reducing the marginal rates of direct tax, although it achieved this in relation to income tax and not in relation to National Insurance Contributions.

Table 7.3   *The Structure of the UK Tax System since 1948*

Ongoing Taxes	New Taxes	Repealed Taxes
Beer duty	Selective employment tax (1967)	Profits tax (1965)
Customs and protective duties	Capital gains tax (1967)	Selective employment tax (1972)
Hydrocarbon oil duty	Corporation tax (1967)	Purchase tax (1973)
Income tax	Car tax (1973)	Estate duty (1974)
Local authority rates	Value added tax (1973)	Capital transfer tax (1976)
National Insurance	Capital transfer tax (1974)	Community Charge (1993)
Stamp duty	Petroleum revenue tax (1978)	Car tax (1993)
Tobacco duty	Inheritance tax (1986)	
Vehicle licences	Community Charge (1989)	
Wine and spirits duties	Council tax (1993)	
	Air passenger duty (1994)	
	Insurance premium tax (1994)	
	Landfill tax (1995)	

- It succeeded in widening the tax base through, for example, imposing increasingly heavy taxation on the use of company cars, reductions in the real value of a mortgage subject to tax relief, and reductions in the rate at which relief is available to be set against mortgages and the married couple's allowance.
- It shifted the burden of taxation towards indirect tax, mainly by raising the basic rate of VAT to 17.5 per cent, by its extension to cover domestic fuel, and by the imposition of tax upon air passengers, insurance premiums and landfill.
- It twice reformed local taxation, on the second occasion by moving back towards where it began.

☐ 7.5.2 Taxes on Income

Income Tax

Income tax remains the most important element of the tax system, but its importance has declined since 1979. In general, income tax is charged **on all income that originates in the UK** (including, since 1987, the earnings of overseas entertainers and sportsmen), and on **all income arising abroad of people resident in the UK.**

However, every taxpayer is entitled to a **personal allowance** to set against his or her gross taxable income (which is itself taken net of any pension fund contributions). There is currently a separate allowance for the single and for the married (but see discussion of personal allowances reform below). This is generally referred to as the **standard rate tax threshold**. It may also be supplemented by a whole variety of other allowances, of which the most common is tax relief for interest paid on mortgages (at 15 per cent in 1996–97). Currently this is almost always paid direct (at source) by the Inland Revenue to the building society or bank acting as mortgagee, with the mortgagor paying a net-of-tax relief monthly figure (the MIRAS system), so it does not normally affect an individual's tax code. Tax relief may also be given for such things as covenants, or for payments under the Business Expansion

Scheme (BES). Once all allowances have been deducted, the residual sum becomes the **taxable income.**

Historically, income tax was designed to be **progressive** – that is, to take a higher proportion of income in tax as income rises. This was based upon the principle of **ability to pay**, and provided the main mechanism whereby the redistribution of spending power between households could be effected. Progressivity was thought to require a significant number of different tax rates, although in practice there is progressivity if there is a single tax threshold below which the tax rate is 0 per cent and above which it is positive. During the early postwar period the standard rate rose sharply, and was held at over 40 per cent throughout the period from 1948 to 1968, although until 1971 two-ninths of earned income was exempt from tax so that the effective rate was lower than the nominal rate.

The higher rates were ultimately raised to punitive levels, and predictable consequences followed. During the 1970s everyone in a position to do so earned 'income' in the form of legitimate tax-relieved 'perks', and taxable income fell to half the total income declared to the Inland Revenue. Furthermore, a good deal of income was undeclared (the black economy). But with the tax base shrinking in leaps and bounds, the only way to maintain total tax revenue was assumed at the time to be to raise tax rates even higher, setting off the vicious circle yet again.

The disincentive effects of high tax rates on hard work understandably did nothing for economic growth, and in recognition of this the standard rate had been brought down to 33 per cent by the beginning of the Conservative government's term of office. The government declared its intention of bringing down the basic rate as part of the MTFS, and managed to reduce it steadily to 25 per cent by 1988–89. In so doing, it reduced both the rewards of non-declaration relative to the drawback of a possible prison sentence, and the benefits of perks compared to cash. At the same time, many perks were either abolished (for example, tax relief on life insurance premiums) or were held roughly constant in money terms thereby reducing their real value (for example, mortgage interest relief). As a result, taxable income rose to two-thirds of total income by 1987–88.

The possibility of moving to a 25 per cent standard rate, which the government had declared to be its ultimate goal but which was widely regarded at the time as little more than a pipedream, arose as a result of the immense fiscal drag in 1987–88. Chancellor Lawson was very keen to emulate the USA which had already moved to a two-rate system of 15 per cent and 34.7 per cent (adjusted for local income tax), in the process abolishing a whole host of tax reliefs as a quid pro quo. The Chancellor had always been ambivalent about perks, inventing new ones such as the Business Expansion Scheme whilst abolishing existing ones. However, he found himself able in the Budget of 1988 not merely to fund higher levels of spending and to reduce the PSBR, but also to produce his own two-rate structure with the standard rate set at 25 per cent and the higher rate set at 40 per cent (compared to the five higher rates ranging from 40 per cent to 60 per cent only the previous year). Furthermore, he did not need to eat heavily into perks. The basic rate was further lowered to 24 per cent in the 1995 Budget and to 23 per cent in the 1996 Budget.

Compared to other major industrialised countries, the standard rate tax threshold in the UK still remains low (at £4045 for a single person in 1997–98), and the standard rate itself is almost the highest. However, the top rate is lower than all except that of the USA (although it bites at the very low threshold of £25,500 of taxable income), and there is a 20 per cent rate on a modest amount of taxable income. This was introduced in the 1992 Budget, encompassing the first £2000 of taxable income, and extended to £3900 in the 1995 Budget. There is, therefore, still considerable scope for further rate reductions, but fiscal drag will be needed to provide the means to achieve them. Indeed, in his 1988 Budget speech, Nigel Lawson stated that the objective was to be a standard rate of 20p, and that rate was introduced on a supplementary basis in the manner indicated above as a token of the Conservative government's desire to meet the 20p standard rate objective at some time during its term in office.

Three further issues need to be carefully noted. In the first place, the sharp reduction in the top rate of tax inevitably transferred huge sums of money to the highest income earners without offsetting reductions in perks, whereas the minor reduction in the standard rate made little difference to the bulk of the working population. This inevitably made the distribution of post-tax income less equal. Against this can be set the benefits of a simplified tax structure and the hoped-for incentive effect on work effort and entrepreneurial activity. Secondly, the very high levels of consumer spending during 1988, and their consequences for overheating and inflation, made Lawson wary of anything that smacked of fiscal giveaways in his 1989 Budget, and his successors, Major and Lamont, chose to proceed very cautiously even in the face of a deepening recession. Clarke, responsible for the 1995 and 1996 Budgets, might have been expected to be more openhanded, given an impending election no later than 1997, but had insufficient room to manoeuvre given the lack of buoyancy in tax revenues, and had to content himself with a 1 per cent reduction in the basic rate on both occasions. Thirdly, the creation of a 20 per cent band has been accompanied by a reduction first to 20 per cent and then, in the 1995 Budget, to 15 per cent, in the tax relief available on mortgage interest payments, tax credits and tax relief for married couples, so successive Chancellors have certainly not treated the objective of a 20 per cent standard rate simply as an exercise in transferring large sums into people's pockets.

Nevertheless, the 1991 Budget undoubtedly represented a move back towards more progressivity in the income tax structure. In particular, the abolition of tax relief on mortgage interest payments at the higher rate of tax imposed additional burdens only upon high-income households. The more recent introduction of a lower tax rate has benefited primarily low earners, and the freezing of the higher rate threshold in 1993–94 also had a rebalancing effect.

A final comment relates to the so-called 'black economy'. It is estimated that the black economy in the UK generates over £60 million a year, with the poorest 20 per cent of the population financing one-third of their spending from income which they do not declare to the Inland Revenue. Were this to be taxed at the rates prevailing for declared income, there would be an additional £25 billion of revenue available to the government (although, naturally, not all black market activity would take place if it had to be declared).

7.5.3 Independent Taxation for Married Couples

Recent changes in the structure of income tax have altered it to a greater degree, and at a faster rate, than at any other time since 1945. Nevertheless, these changes still represent tinkering rather than true reform. There is little sign of the latter on the horizon, but one issue is worthy of mention, namely that of independent taxation for married couples. The pre-1990 system of taxing husband and wives treated a married woman's income in law as if it belonged to her husband, a procedure dating back to the time when it was uncommon for wives to earn outside the home. This gave rise to dissatisfaction because such a high proportion of married women were in employment outside the home. Furthermore, the married man's allowance, originally intended to compensate for the added burden of supporting non-earning members of a household, had become something of an anomaly in a world of two-income households where the working wife was given an additional single person's allowance in her own right. As a consequence, a household containing a married couple where both were working was in receipt of 2.5 times as much in allowances as a single person household. Even more anomalous was the fact that if the wife alone was at work she was entitled to the full set of allowances, whereas if the husband alone was at work he was entitled only to the married man's allowance.

Green Papers, published in 1980 and 1981, considered how to eradicate these anomalies, and in his Budget speech in 1988 the Chancellor announced that, from 6 April 1990, husbands and wives would be taxed independently on their income and chargeable capital gains. This has meant that (a) husband and wife become independent taxpayers, each with his or her own allowances to set against income from whatever source, and each responsible for dealings with the Inland Revenue; (b) every taxpayer receives the single person's allowance; (c) in addition, a married couple receives the difference between the current single allowance and the married allowance, which since 1993–94 can be set either against the income of husband or wife or shared equally between them (although this attracts only a 15 per cent rate of relief); (d) special arrangements apply for those aged over 65; (e) a husband and wife's capital gains are taxed independently, with each entitled to a single person's exempt allowance; (f) the existing exemptions from capital gains tax and inheritance tax on transfers of capital between husband and wife continue as before.

7.5.4 National Insurance Contributions

NICs were introduced as a universal tax in 1948. Unusually for the UK tax system they are a hypothecated tax, which means that they exist to finance specific items of expenditure, in particular retirement pensions and unemployment and sickness benefit. Originally, NICs were levied at a flat rate which was regressive in its impact. Benefits were related to contributions, but this became impractical as benefits grew rapidly because flat-rate NICs would have had to be levied at a level which would have borne down too heavily on the poor. Earnings-related NICs were therefore introduced in 1961 on a partial basis, and this became the only form of NICs after 1975.

An annual review of NICs is required by the provisions of the Social Security Act 1975. It is necessary to comment briefly on this because from the taxpayer's point of view both income tax and NICs have the same effect since they are deducted at source on Pay As You Earn (PAYE), which applies to all except the self-employed in the UK. Although the income tax structure was simplified in the 1988 Budget, the structure of NICs retained the perverse principle that once a threshold was triggered the relevant rate was applied not only to income between the thresholds but to all income, thereby generating very high marginal rates at the threshold points.

The reform of NICs introduced in the 1989 Budget took effect in October 1989. This simplified the system in that those with earnings below £62 per week in financial year 1997–98 continue to pay nothing, while those with earnings at or above £62 pay 2 per cent on the first £62 and 10 per cent on the rest up to the upper earnings limit of £465 per week.

Removal of all except a very modest NICs' liability on the first £62 of weekly earnings undoubtedly benefits the low paid (and helps to offset fiscal drag), but it remains the case that the lower earnings limit is indeed very low (below that for income tax) and also that, once earnings rise above £465 per week, the combined rate of income tax plus NICs falls back at the margin from 33 per cent to 23 per cent as shown in **Figure 7.3**. This can hardly be called a progressive structure, and it must also be borne in mind that it is only those whose incomes are high enough to provide spare cash who can afford to spend

Table 7.4 *NICs, 1997–98*

Weekly Earnings	*Percentage NIC Rate*	
	Employees	*Employers[1]*
Below £62	0	0
£62 to £109	⎧ 2% of £62	3.0
£110 to £154	⎜ plus	5.0
£155 to £209	⎨ 10% of earnings	7.0
£210 to £465	⎜ between £62	10.0
Above £465	⎩ and £465	10.0

Notes:
[1] Rates apply to all earnings.
[2] If contracted out, rate on earnings between lower and upper earnings limits reduced by 1.8% for employees and 3% for employers.

Source: FSBR 1996–97, p. 105, updated in 1996 Budget.

money in tax-deductible ways (by taking out a £30 000 mortgage, for example). Furthermore, employee benefits do not attract NICs. Despite the 1989 reform, the employer continues to pay NICs on all employee earnings at the rates shown in **Table 7.4**.

The government has come under pressure to make employee NICs open-ended in terms of income, which would have the effect of a permanent marginal rate of deduction of either 33 per cent or 50 per cent on taxable income alone. This is Labour policy, but has so far been ignored by Conservative Chancellors. Instead, in the 1991 Budget, Chancellor Lamont made employers pay NICs on the benefit of cars provided for the private use of employees, based on the scale charges set for income tax. Employees are, however, exempted.

☐ *7.5.5 Corporation Tax*

During the 1970s, corporation tax, which is levied on company profits, had much in common with income tax. On the face of it the marginal rate was high, but deductible allowances were so extensive, particularly those concerned with capital investment, that large companies were able to

Figure 7.3 *Marginal Deduction Rates, 1997–98[1]*

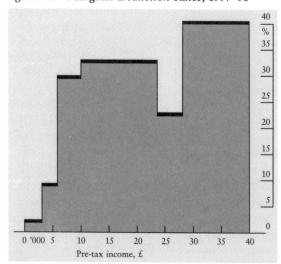

Note:
[1] Income tax and NICs for married man.
Source: FSBR 1997–98.

adjust their balance sheets so as to incur little or no tax liability.

As a result, Nigel Lawson reformed the tax in 1984 by phasing out many of the allowances and by simultaneously cutting the tax rate progressively from 52 per cent to 35 per cent. The matching rate for small companies earning profits below £100 000 per annum was initially set at 29 per cent (to match the existing income tax standard rate), and was reduced to 25 per cent for the financial year 1988–89. By international standards, company taxation in the UK thereby became modest.

However, care must be taken to **adjust for the phasing out of capital allowances**, and for the **failure to inflation-adjust** those that remained. Furthermore, the abolition of tax relief on the increase in the value of stocks due to inflation, which did not seem controversial at the time because inflation had fallen rapidly, temporarily became a problem once again when inflation rose towards the end of the decade. Hence, as we have seen in **Figure 7.2**, many companies actually found themselves paying more tax than before even though the rate was much lower.

With the onset of recession in 1990, the need for a Budget to assist businesses resulted in the retrospective reduction in the rate of corporation tax in the 1991 Budget to 34 per cent for the 1990–91 financial year and to 33 per cent for 1991–92, at which rate it has subsequently remained. In addition, companies were to be allowed to carry back trading losses for three years instead of one year, and the profits threshold for the small companies' corporation tax rate of 25 per cent was raised, reaching £300 000 in 1996–97 during which financial year the rate fell to 24 per cent. From April 1997, the rate will be 23 per cent.

The remaining allowances of any consequence are concerned with **depreciation provisions**. These exist in order to permit companies to build up a stock of money (often itself confusingly called 'capital') which can be used to replace their worn-out or obsolete physical capital stock. Since money set aside for this purpose is needed merely to keep the company in business as a going concern, it is clearly not 'profit' and should not be taxed as such. There are basically two ways of calculating how much money can be set aside

each year without incurring a tax liability on the equivalent amount of gross profit. The first is the straight-line method whereby a given proportion of the original capital cost is set aside each year, for example 15 per cent each year for four years. Alternatively, the declining-balance method is used whereby a specified proportion of the original outlay is set against tax liability in Year 1, and the same proportion of the residual amount is written down in Year 2 and so on. This has the effect of setting aside the largest absolute amount of tax liability in Year 1, and successively smaller absolute amounts in successive years. It is up to the tax authorities to determine which depreciation method is to be applied. Historically, when inflation was unusually high, adjustments also needed to be made for the fact that the replacement cost of a unit of capital was much higher than the original cost, but this is no longer considered to be necessary.

Prior to 1984 it was customary to allow a very high proportion of all capital expenditure to be set against corporation tax liability in the year of purchase, but since 1986 these provisions have been made much less generous in view of the much lower rates of tax. Each year 25 per cent of the cost of plant and machinery can in principle be set against corporation tax liability on a declining-balance basis while only 4 per cent of the cost of industrial or agricultural buildings and hotels can be written down on a straight-line basis each year since buildings last much longer than machines. Short-life machinery and plant may be wholly written down over its lifetime. These provisions are universal because it would be far too difficult and expensive to deal with companies on an individual basis. However, it remains possible for the government to make exceptions, usually in the context of **regional policy**.

Corporation tax is levied on all profits, whether retained within the company or distributed to shareholders. However, if a company wishes to distribute profits in the form of dividends, then these are paid in a net-of-tax form. The company is obliged to pay the tax liability arising on the gross dividends at an agreed rate of **income tax** on behalf of the shareholders. This is collected by the tax authorities in advance of the time when dividends are paid out and is therefore known as advance corporation tax (ACT). ACT is strictly not a corporation but an income tax. The shareholder receives his dividend together with a 'tax credit' which he can pass on to the Inland Revenue in order to show that the tax liability on his dividend has already been discharged (although he will have to pay extra tax if his marginal rate is 40 per cent). Any shareholders exempt from income tax can claim a refund. At present a company subtracts the ACT payment from the total corporation tax liability on its profits, and the outstanding sum is paid over at the end of the relevant financial year in the form of **mainstream** corporation tax.

The low rate of corporate income tax is, as discussed elsewhere, one of the reasons why inward investors are attracted to the UK. There is one lower rate in the EU, Sweden's 28 per cent, and the French rate is 33.33 per cent but elsewhere rates climb as high as Germany (58.95 per cent) and Italy (52.2 per cent). It is also of interest that the rate in the USA is an effective 40 per cent and in Japan 51.6 per cent.

□ 7.5.6 North Sea Taxes

North Sea taxation consists of royalties, petroleum revenue tax (including advance payments) and corporation tax from North Sea oil and gas production (before ACT set-off). In 1984–85 these amounted to £12 billion, but in 1986–87 there was a very sharp fall to £4.8 billion, a figure which was halved again by 1989–90. The recent further decline indicates how unimportant this element of the tax system has become.

Royalties are levied on the production of oil and gas fields on an individual basis. However, in order to induce oil companies to explore for oil and gas in less accessible – and hence more costly – tracts of the North Sea, the Conservative government first abolished royalties on newly-developed fields in the central and northern sectors in 1982, and in the 1988 Budget subsequently abolished royalties on post-1982 oil and gas fields in the Southern Basin and onshore areas. The latter development was primarily intended to stimulate gas production.

As a consequence, North Sea taxation became almost entirely dependent upon profit-related taxes. Prior to the 1993 Budget, petroleum revenue tax (PRT) was charged at a rate of 75 per cent on profits (net of royalties) from the production, as opposed to the refining, of oil and gas under licence in Britain and on its Continental Shelf. Various allowances could be set against PRT, in particular certain costs incurred in oil exploration. Corporation tax was payable on profits in the usual way, but was levied on profits net of royalties and PRT.

The PRT rate on existing oilfields has been reduced to 50 per cent, and it has been abolished altogether for new fields as part of the 1993 Budget, but by simultaneously disallowing offsetting exploration costs it was expected that PRT would start contributing once again to receipts.

Events in the North Sea, such as the Piper Alpha fire, and the instability of oil prices due to the Gulf War, had an erratic effect upon North Sea production. Also, the effect of much increased investment in the North Sea caused profitability to fall, and as a consequence PRT needed to be repaid in 1991–92. North Sea revenues currently represent less than 1 per cent of total tax revenue – a far cry from the 9 per cent which they represented at their peak in 1984–85.

□ 7.5.7 Customs and Excise Duties

Customs duties are charged on imported goods in accordance with the Common Customs Tariff of the European Community. This exempts community goods imported from other EU member states, and provides a uniform EU-wide tariff barrier against goods from elsewhere in the world. Special arrangements apply for agricultural products in accordance with the Common Agricultural Policy (CAP). As these duties are an EU, rather than a purely national policy, their proceeds are transferred to Brussels to help finance the EU.

Excise duties, on the other hand, are not concerned with controlling trade flows but purely with raising revenue from goods and services which are either in inelastic demand (their consumption varies less than in proportion to price) or anti-social, or both. They apply to oils used for road fuel (and for other uses at a reduced rate); to alcoholic drinks (taxed largely in accordance with alcoholic strength); to tobacco products (in accordance with number, price or weight); to betting; and to gambling machine and casino licences. Road usage is additionally taxed through vehicle licences.

These duties are very unpopular, but have the virtue (from the Chancellor's viewpoint) that consumers are really aware only of how much they are going up and not of how much has cumulatively been levied in the past. Each increase therefore causes great aggravation at the time, but very rapidly gets forgotten as consumers get used to the new levels of prices, which are anyway constantly adjusting for other reasons. Furthermore, as they are levied in incremental amounts expressed in pence, their incidence is very erratic. VAT receipts automatically rise in money terms when product prices rise, but excise duties do not and therefore can – and often do – fail to keep pace with inflation. Surprisingly, some products, such as whisky, are currently very cheap by historical standards once inflation is taken into account, partly as a result of a move to uniform taxation of alcohol content.

Alcohol and tobacco products bear VAT on the total cost after levying excise duties – that is the tax is taxed! In the case of cigarettes, EU harmonisation proposals (see below) resulted in a specific tax of 3p per cigarette **and** a special ad valorem tax of 21 per cent of retail price. As a result, nearly 80 per cent of the retail price of a packet of cigarettes consists of tax of one kind or another whereas it is only roughly one third for a pint of beer.

In recent years, increasing attention has been paid to the wider social costs associated with the misuse of alcohol, tobacco and vehicles by individuals, but there has been no real attempt to force a radical reduction in consumption via the price mechanism. This may partly reflect the desire to maintain revenue, since sharp increases in prices may, at least temporarily, cause demand (and hence revenue) to fall disproportionately. Perhaps more importantly, excise duties feed straight through to the rate of inflation, control of which is the primary macroeconomic objective.

One innovation, in the 1988 Budget, was the introduction of a reduced rate of duty on unleaded petrol which (allegedly) causes less pollution than its leaded equivalent. A more surprising move came in the form of the first cut in spirit duties for 100 years as part of the 1995 Budget, although it had anyway become very difficult to raise duties on alcohol because of enormous legal and illegal importation of relatively cheap alcoholic products from France. Nevertheless, the 1994 Budget did recognise the heavy social costs imposed by smoking and driving by introducing an annual uplift of tax in real terms by 3 per cent on most tobacco products and by 5 per cent on fuel oil.

☐ *7.5.8 Taxes on Wealth*

For the most part, income has to be **earned**. By saving part of this income, a pool of wealth can be accumulated. However, a very large proportion of the total pool of wealth currently results from capital gains (especially rising house values) and from inheritance, neither of which requires much effort to acquire. Thus, in principle, one would expect wealth to be taxed much more harshly than income on grounds of equity.

There are, however, a number of practical difficulties. Much wealth is, for example, tied up in physical assets (houses, businesses, farms, and so forth) and to pay a wealth tax in cash could require a part of these assets to be sold. This could be very damaging to efficiency (for example, farms could become progressively smaller). Equally, the incentive for an entrepreneur to build up a business would be much reduced were it to be necessary for the business to be sold off by his or her heirs in order to pay wealth taxes, since it is reasonable to suppose that the entrepreneur is often driven by a desire to build up a business dynasty. Furthermore, it is inequitable and impractical to force widows to sell up their family homes upon the death of their husbands. As a result, wealth taxes have never accounted for more than a very small proportion of total tax revenue.

Inheritance Tax

It is possible to value assets on an annual basis and to tax their value on an ongoing basis. Annual wealth taxes are levied elsewhere in Europe, but have never been implemented in the UK. Instead, wealth is liable to tax only upon its **transfer from one individual to another**, whether in the form of a gift during the donor's lifetime, or upon the donor's death. This is administratively convenient since estates must be valued for probate purposes when a person dies.

Inheritance taxes have been levied in the UK since 1894. Until 1974 they were known as Estate Duty (or death duty) and applied only to transfers at death. The Labour government introduced Capital Transfer Tax (CTT) in 1974 in order to incorporate certain lifetime gifts. These were accumulated over time, with the tax rate being applied to each gift being determined by the cumulative total. However, transfers of property between husbands and wives, both during life and at death, were tax-exempt, together with gifts and bequests to charity. Tax-exempt thresholds also applied to transfers upon death, and to gifts both to individuals and in total during any one year.

In practice, CTT proved to be scarcely more punitive than its predecessor because of the widespread exemptions and the low rates levied on lifetime gifts. When elected in 1979, the Conservatives nevertheless set about 'drawing the teeth' of CTT by raising thresholds, lowering rates and reducing aggregation periods during which lifetime gifts were accumulated (those made pre-1979 being exempt). In 1986, CTT was renamed Inheritance Tax. The period of accumulation was reduced from 10 to seven years and the rate of tax was lowered. Anyone making a 'potentially exempt transfer', and living for a further seven years, could subsequently expunge that transfer from their cumulative lifetime total of taxable gifts. If that person lived on for between four and seven years, a proportion of the tax would become payable, ranging from 100 per cent for deaths occurring within three years of making a gift to 20 per cent in the seventh year.

Between 1979 and 1988, prices in general less than doubled. However, the tax threshold for inheritance tax (CTT) rose from £25 000 in 1979 to £110 000 in the Budget of 1988, representing a more than doubling in real terms. Furthermore, the multiple rate structure of previous years was abolished, and a single rate of 40 per cent introduced. The threshold and rate changes in 1988 had little effect upon modest estates, but reduced the tax bill on an estate of £1 million by £145 000 (and by even more where legitimate tax shelters had been used). The 1997–98 threshold stands at £215 000. Owner-occupied farmlands and interests in un-incorporated businesses are also tax-exempt.

In 1965, annual wealth taxes and capital transfer taxes accounted for 1.6 per cent of the total tax revenue of OECD countries, with the UK well above that figure. In 1985, the OECD average was down to 0.7 per cent with the UK below average at 0.5 per cent where it has approximately remained ever since. Only some 4 per cent of inherited estates currently attract a tax liability. It is therefore fair to conclude that, whilst becoming wealthy is problematic (although becoming progressively easier as houses are inherited), staying wealthy is no problem at all.

Capital Gains Tax (CGT)

This tax is levied on the difference between the purchase and sale price of any asset. This price difference might occur entirely because of inflation, and capital gains tax has accordingly been index-linked since 1982 so that only **real gains** are currently taxed. Were there no CGT, it would pay those with spare income to invest it almost entirely in assets with potential for capital gains rather than in those which accrue interest or other forms of unearned income.

It has to be said that this tends to occur anyway because a large variety of assets are exempt from CGT, including principal private residences (but not second houses), agricultural property, winnings from the football pools and other forms of gambling, motor cars, National Savings instruments and so forth. Furthermore, there is a threshold below which gains are tax-exempt, and a provision to set losses against gains before tax liability is assessed.

Before April 1988 the tax threshold stood at £6600, and the tax at 30 per cent. However, the tax was based on any assets acquired since 1965, and the high threshold existed partly to adjust for the fact that gains between 1965 and 1982 were not index-linked. In April 1988, the threshold was reduced to £5000, and is £6500 in 1997–98. Gains are currently taxed at the individual's highest income tax rate. However, any gains accruing prior to April 1982 are wholly tax-exempt. Fewer than 100 000 people currently pay capital gains tax.

The similar tax treatment of earned income and capital gains is at variance with the traditional view that earned income is morally superior to unearned income, and should accordingly be less-heavily taxed. However, the widespread exemptions allowed under CGT have made rather a mockery of this principle, and the Conservative government effectively wished it to be known that for tax purposes 'income' is simply income irrespective of source (it was anyway never exactly clear whether a capital gain was wealth or unearned income, although CGT has been listed here as a tax on wealth for convenience). This view is also consistent with the change made in March 1987 for companies since which time their gains have been taxed at normal corporation tax rates.

Stamp Duty

Transfers or sales of property (other than of stocks and shares) above a value of £60 000, are subject to stamp duty of 1 per cent on the entire purchase price. Transfers of stocks and shares are subject to stamp duty of 0.5 per cent, regardless of the amount. There is no stamp duty on transfers of property other than land and buildings.

□ 7.5.9 *Taxes on Expenditure*

Value Added Tax (VAT)

VAT is the most wide-ranging tax on expenditure, and has been in force since the UK joined the EEC in 1973. It is levied in one instalment directly by the retailer upon the customer. The standard rate of VAT was raised sharply to 15 per cent in 1979 as part of the switch by the first Thatcher government from direct to indirect taxation (initially with predictably inflationary consequences). It was raised to 17.5 per cent in April 1991 as a quid pro quo for the £140 per head reduction in the Community Charge. There is also a zero rate. These rates are not uniform throughout the EU, and this is therefore one of the areas where harmonisation has yet to be achieved. However, this represents a highly elusive goal in practice because of the enormous problems which would need to be overcome if it became necessary to switch some of the burden of taxation back onto income taxes.

VAT is collected at each stage in the production and distribution of goods and services by taxable persons (running a business with a turnover in excess of £47 000 per annum in fiscal year 1996–97). The burden of the tax is ultimately borne by the consumer as part of the final purchase price, but the tax is built up in stages. When a taxable person purchases taxable goods or services (say at £10), the supplier adds VAT to the supply price. This is called the taxable person's input tax (£1.75). When the taxable person subsequently adds value to the good or service, and sells it on to another taxable person, he adds VAT to the price charged (say at £20 which includes the input tax). This is known as the output tax (£3.50). Since the input tax has already been paid by the original supplier, it is necessary only for the taxable persons to pay over to the Customs and Excise the difference between the output tax and the input tax, or in other words the tax on the **value which has been added to the good or service**. Since the final price in our example is £23.50 of which £3.50 is tax, the taxable person has added £10 to the supply price of £10 and paid a second instalment of £1.75 in tax.

There will normally be several such instalments before the final customer is reached, once account is taken of both wholesalers and retailers. VAT is further complicated by the fact that not all goods and services are taxable. This arises primarily because everyone pays 35p in tax on a taxable item costing £2.35 irrespective of income, so the tax bears down more severely on the low-paid than on the high-paid. In order to offset this, there are two methods by which goods and services, especially those heavily consumed by the relatively poor, can be tax-relieved. The first method is where a taxable person does not charge any VAT to a customer and also reclaims any VAT paid to his supplier. In this case total VAT is zero. **Zero rating** applies, *inter alia*, to most food; reading matter; construction of new buildings; exports; public transport fares; young children's clothing and footwear; prescription medicines; and caravans, encompassing in aggregate nearly one quarter of total consumer spending.

The second method is where a taxable person does not charge any output tax to a customer, but is not entitled to deduct or to reclaim the input tax. In this case total VAT is not zero and the final good or service is said to be **VAT-exempt**. Exemption applies, *inter alia*, to land (including rents); insurance; postal services; betting; finance; education; health; and burial and cremation, encompassing in aggregate roughly 4 per cent of total consumer spending.

In the Spring 1993 Budget the Chancellor moved to boost tax receipts by introducing VAT for the first time on domestic fuel and power, at 8 per cent in fiscal 1994–95 and at 17.5 per cent in 1995–96.

□ 7.5.10 Taxing Savings

In the UK savings have not generally been encouraged by the tax system. First, income is taxed, and then the savings set aside out of net-of-tax income are frequently taxed as well. This is not universally the case because, for example, pension contributions are deducted from gross income without incurring a tax liability, but it is sufficiently common to be a matter of considerable contention in tax-reforming circles.

It has often been argued that only **spending** should be taxed, which would provide an incentive to save more. However, most of the recent discussion has been concerned with tax **neutrality** – that is, the desire to treat all savings in the same way by taxing **all of them** either once or twice (see Robinson, 1990). In the 1990 Budget the then Chancellor, John Major, moved several steps towards single taxation by extending tax exemptions on savings. This was in the form of TESSAs (Tax Exempt Special Saving Accounts) which could be added to the PEPs (Personal Equity Plans) introduced by Nigel Lawson. It is important to bear in mind, however, that Lawson was concerned primarily with the abolition of tax breaks for savers such as tax relief on insurance premiums, and that both PEPs and TESSAs were expected to divert savings out of one channel and into another, more tax efficient one rather then to increase substantially the total level of saving.

In April 1996, the tax on savings income, such as bank and building society interest, was reduced to 20 per cent for basic rate taxpayers.

Personal Equity Plans

PEPs were first announced in the 1986 Budget and brought into operation in January 1987 as a simple way to invest in shares, especially for small savers and first-time investors unfamiliar with the stock market. The amount which could be invested in a single plan in any one year was originally £2400. In 1987, 270 000 PEPs were taken out and £480 million invested. 1988 was a poor year for PEPs, but in 1989, 300 000 PEPs were taken out and PEPs became firmly established as a savings vehicle.

In the 1990 Budget the requirement that investors had to keep their investments in their PEPs for at least a complete calendar year to qualify for tax benefits was abolished. Currently, up to £9000 in total can be invested in any one year in two separate PEPs with returns free from income and capital gains tax, of which £6000 can be placed in a general plan and £3000 in a single company plan. Up to £6000 of this total can be invested in investment and unit trusts, corporate bonds and convertibles of UK non-financial companies and preference shares in UK and EU companies.

Tax Exempt Special Savings Accounts

TESSAs were introduction in the 1990 Budget to become operational as from 1 January 1991. A taxpayer is permitted one TESSA which confers the right to receive interest on building society and bank deposits tax-free. A maximum of £9000 can be deposited over a five-year period, either in lump sums or in irregular amounts, up to £3000 in the first year and then up to £1800 a year for the subsequent years subject to the overall limit. If capital is withdrawn early all tax relief is lost, but interest earned can be withdrawn at any time at the net-of-tax rate. At the end of five years the TESSA is wound up, although a new TESSA can be started with up to £9000 transferred into it from the previous one within six months of its maturing. Beyond that data the reinvestment limit is £3000.

7.5.11 Hybrid Taxes: The Council Tax

The UK tax system has long been dependent upon taxes raised within the confines of a local authority rather than of the UK as a whole. These taxes were traditionally based upon property, both domestic and commercial (but excluding farms). The calculation of tax liability required that each property be given an imputed rental value, called a **rateable value**, in accordance with a complex formula devised by the responsible local authority to take into account location, size, amenities, provision of public services and so on. The local authority then levied a uniform rate per pound of rateable value, with a small rebate for domestic as against commercial property. A supplementary rate was then added to cover water, sewerage and environmental services.

The **rates**, as they were known, were a hybrid tax in the sense that whilst they were wholly divorced from a property occupier's income and clearly therefore not an income tax, they were not based directly upon the market value of a property and hence not exactly a wealth tax either. Obviously, house prices varied considerably over time, thereby making it necessary to revalue per-

iodically in order to preserve equity between different properties. The sheer cost of the exercise militated against intervals of less than 10 years, but this in turn meant that some people would find their rateable values sharply increased, to their immense annoyance, whereas those who had seen their bills reduced thought this no more than their just desserts. The political ill-will engendered by the revaluation of 1973, coming as it did at the end of a period of sharply rising house prices, discouraged a repeat of the exercise in both 1978 and 1984. The Scottish revaluation of 1985 was blamed for the severe loss of Conservative electoral support in the subsequent General Election.

The failure to alter rateable values did not imply an inability to raise the yield form the rates. The ruling political party in a local authority could impose any rate poundage that it thought fit, although it would have to be subject itself to periodic re-election. However, a number of local councils, especially in the larger towns and cities, had such large majorities that they could do virtually anything they liked and make their ratepayers, including local businesses (with no right to vote independent of the rights of their employees to vote as individual ratepayers if eligible), and also the government (which supplied over one half of all local authority revenue via a **rate support grant**) foot the bill. The ability to charge high taxes, yet remain politically popular, reflected the high proportion of the total bill laid at the door of government and businesses (over 75 per cent by 1970 and higher still by 1980), and also the fact that domestic rates took no account of the number of individuals living in a property. Large, under-occupied properties in expensive areas could be made to pay very high rates, whereas small, over-occupied, properties were frequently exempted from rates altogether because their main occupier was entitled to a rate rebate by virtue of his or her income.

Not surprisingly, those who paid heavy rates wanted services to be cut and rates to be reduced, whereas those who paid little or no rates demanded more and more services regardless of expense. In the bigger towns, the latter were often in a clear majority, and elected councils committed to ever-higher expenditure. When the Conservatives were elected in 1979 on a platform of reductions in public spending, their attention was inevitably drawn to the alleged profligacy of the local authorities. Since the highest-spending local councils were all Labour-controlled, the issue inevitably became political as well as economic. The power of such councils, democratically elected though they were, had, in the government's view, to be subjugated to the constitutionally superior power of the democratically elected central government.

But how was this to be achieved? For several years the government sought desperately for a foolproof method of keeping local authority spending in check. However, the fatal flaws in most schemes were either that the local authorities could raise the rate poundage to substitute for reductions in revenue supplied by central government, or that, if prevented from so doing by **rate capping**, they could introduce increasingly innovative methods of raising finance such as swaps and sale-and-lease-back deals on local authority-owned assets. The government's position was that all local voters had to be made to pay personally for increases in spending if that was what they wanted and voted for. The chosen solution was (a) to take the **non-domestic (business) rate** away from the local authorities and transfer it to central government which set it nationally at a uniform level (to be known as the **Uniform Business Rate**). The revenue was then distributed to local authorities as a **per capita** grant; and (b) to introduce a **Community Charge** (often referred to as the **poll tax** because it required everyone above the minimum voting age of 18 to register with their local authority) to be paid by all voters either in full or in part (if eligible for a rebate) at a **flat-rate**. The changes were introduced in Scotland in April 1989 and in England and Wales in April 1990.

This solution was not without its drawbacks. It clearly implied a major redistribution of the burden of taxation, both from the single-adult household to the multiple-adult household, and from the well-off to those previously considered too poor to pay any rates at all. It was also costly to administer because it was problematic to get all those who should be paying the Charge to register

for that purpose, and to track them down if they refused to do so. This did not necessarily imply that spending on the rump of services left in the hands of local authorities would fall, because voters could opt for as many such services as they were willing to pay for, but the underlying assumption was that spending would indeed fall in order to keep the Charge as low as possible. However, it would still be the case that most spending by local authorities would be covered by central government grants and the apportioned non-domestic rates.

The way the poll tax system worked was (1) for each local authority to be given a spending target according to its needs; (2) the central government set a 'community charge for standard spending' or 'headline' charge; (3) non-domestic rate income was distributed; and (4) the difference between (1) and (2 + 3) was supplied as a grant. Although any authority could exceed its Total Standard Spending, the extra spending fell **entirely** on local charge-payers. This could raise the local tax sharply, but then so could a miscalculation by civil servants of local needs.

As part of the 1991 Budget, the Conservative government sought to reduce the political fall-out of the poll tax by reducing the headline Community Charge by £140 per charge-payer (down from £385 to £245), to be financed by a 2.5 per cent increase in VAT from 15 to 17.5 per cent. Net of rebates and reliefs, the average charge was expected to be roughly £175. This left only 11 per cent of local authority spending to be raised locally, inducing many commentators to wonder why the central government did not simple scrap local taxes and be done with it. But on 23 April 1991 the Environment Secretary, Michael Heseltine came up instead with a new **Council Tax**, introduced in April 1993, the main features of which are as follows:

1. It reflects the capital value of a property occupied by two adults and gives a 25 per cent discount to a single person.
2. Properties are assigned to eight bands based upon value.
3. Payment in the top band is limited to three times that levied in the bottom band.

4. There is a single bill for each household.
5. The poor are protected by discounts.
6. There is no minimum contribution.
7. Second homes receive a 50 per cent discount.
8. Transitional relief in the form of a £340 million Transitional Reduction Scheme (TRS) prevented an individual from incurring too large an increase in his or her tax bill.

The poll tax proved to be a costly blunder, both politically and economically. As early as April 1989 the government was obliged to produce a £500 million package of adjustment to income-related social security benefits. To this must be added the £1.7 billion poll tax reduction package of January 1991, transitional relief, extra collection costs and at least £1 billion of extra non-payment each year. If the shift to the higher rate of VAT is added on, the extra annual cost compared to the rates for the final two years of the Community Charge amounted to roughly £7 billion.

In the end, the poll tax had to go because if set at realistic levels in relation to local authority spending it would impose a crippling burden on millions of households, whereas at realistic levels in relation to household incomes it would contribute an unacceptably small proportion of local authority finance. The Council Tax is an improvement in that, although it remains somewhat regressive because properties of below average value pay proportionately more tax, the tax does rise with property values. It is also relatively cheap to administer because it is based upon the household rather than the individual. Outstanding debts for the first year of the tax amounted to £200 million compared with £1.5 billion still outstanding at the time in unpaid Community Charge.

A summary of local authority finance is shown in Table 7.5.

7.5.12 The EU and Tax Harmonisation

The UK is obliged, as a member of the EU, to contribute tax revenue to cover EU expenditure in

Table 7.5 *Local Authority Finance (£ billion)*

	1994–95 Outturn	1995–96 Estimate	1996–97 Forecast
Total Aggregate External Finance[1]	42.1	42.5	43.6
Other current grants	13.7	14.1	13.5
Total current	55.8	56.6	57.1
Capital grants	1.4	1.9	1.8
Credit approvals	4.0	3.6	3.1
Total capital	5.4	5.5	4.9
Total central government support to LAs	61.2	62.1	62.0
LASFE[2]	11.8	12.3	12.5
Total LA expenditure	73.0	74.4	74.5

Notes:
[1] Includes Revenue Support Grant, distribution of Non-domestic Rate revenue and a number of specific grants which fund part of the expenditure on a specific service or activity.
[2] Local authority self-financed expenditure.

Source: FSBR 1996–97, Table 6.7.

the areas of agriculture, social policy and regional policy. The EU Budget is financed by its 'own resources', comprising the proceeds of the common external tariff (**less** 10 per cent); a share in national VAT proceeds and a share of GNP (see **pp. 273–4**). EU members have compiled a collection of goods and services known as the **common assessment base**. The UK calculates the total value of sales of the base every year, applies VAT, and remits the EU's share to Brussels. This share is currently 1.4 per cent. In practice, the UK has always argued that its contribution is excessive compared with that made by other EU members, and has had part of it returned each year (see **p. 274**). It is also obviously the case that some of the money is returned in the form of EU expenditure in the areas set out above.

Under the terms of the Single European Act 1985, there is supposed to be **fiscal harmonisation** in the EU. Initially, progress towards this objective achieved very little since, whereas VAT is levied in every country, each member state wished to impose its own preferred rates upon the others. The only progress of any note arose in that, since taxes within the EU are not supposed to favour domestic as against imported goods, the European Court of Justice felt obliged periodically to implement this principle in a piecemeal way by, for example, obliging the UK to reduce excise duties on wine (largely imported) relative to beer (largely domestic).

However, the debate about tax harmonisation became considerably more heated with the onset of the Single European Market. The original blueprint was proposed by the then European Commissioner, Lord Cockfield, on behalf of the EU in late 1987. In the Single European Act 1985 the internal market is defined as 'an area without internal frontiers'. What the Cockfield plan proposed was that all border controls within the EU should be abolished by 1992, and it concluded that this could not be achieved without first harmonising rates of VAT and excise duties within the EU. It thus proposed that the wide array of VAT rates should be grouped into two 'bands', comprising a **standard rate band** at 14–20 per cent and a **reduced rate band** at 4–9 per covering goods which member states wished to keep cheap for social reasons.

The Cockfield plan also recommended a single EU-wide excise duty for alcohol, petrol and tobacco. This arose because VAT is levied on the price of goods **inclusive of** excise duty, and were excise duties to vary the proposed VAT bands would be distorted. This is an important consideration because, like VAT, excise duties historically varied enormously within the EU, being very low in the south – where, for example, most wine is produced – and high in the north for health and environmental reasons.

It is hardly surprising that the Cockfield proposals were contentious. On the one hand, if existing VAT rates were retained, but frontier controls abolished, the citizens of high-VAT-rate countries would be expected to pour across their frontiers with countries where VAT rates were lower in order to shop there, which would be unacceptable to the former countries. On the other hand, harmonising tax rates would force prices up in those countries where rates were below the designated minima while at the same time causing tax revenue to fall in those countries where rates were above the designated maxima.

EU member states, with the exception of the UK, always favoured a minimum rate of VAT in order to protect their tax revenue (and hence their ability to spend). Reflecting this majority view, the European Commission came up with a proposal to set a legally binding 15 per cent minimum standard rate of VAT, together with a number of special lower rates where their abolition would be politically damaging. Ironically, given that the UK would be less affected by these rates than almost any other country, the UK initially used its veto on tax matters (which require unanimity) to stop the proposal, which was somewhat difficult to justify given that the UK had accepted the principle of a minimum for excise duties on alcohol and tobacco. Clearly, an (unspoken) consideration was that a minimum rate of VAT would make it impossible to rebalance the tax system from indirect to direct tax on a future occasion should it be politically expedient.

In June 1991, the Council of Ministers declared that they would all apply a minimum standard rate of VAT of 15 per cent from 1 January, 1993, and a directive to that effect was finally sanctioned in October 1992. The Council also agreed that there should be one or two optional reduced VAT rates of not less than 5 per cent. For member states with existing VAT rates below the reduced rate minimum, a super-reduced rate (as well as a zero rate) may be retained during a transitional period which is expected to last until 1 January 1997, at which point changes may be introduced by unanimous agreement in the Council.

After that date, VAT is in principle to be levied in the country of origin with goods despatched on a tax-paid basis. An origin system favours countries which export which would see a rise in VAT revenues which would be collected for all goods originating in their territory, but be damaging to importing countries which are better off under the traditional country of destination system. Compensating via a 'clearing house' for switches in revenue following a switch in the system is severely complicated by the existence of different VAT rates in importing and exporting countries.

Since 1993 a transitional system has applied whereby individuals follow the origin system but businesses retain the destination system. The likelihood that the origin system will be installed on 1 January 1997 are considered to be effectively zero in the absence of an agreed structure for the 'clearing house'.

The VAT regime ruling in 1996 is still highly variable between member states. The UK rate is a little below average, with the standard rate varying between 15 per cent for Luxembourg to 25 per cent for Denmark and Ireland. France recently raised its rate to 20.5 per cent. Reduced rates remain common, so the UK system is actually one of the simplest. Attempts to harmonise VAT are only a relatively modest step along the path towards tax harmonisation because, by virtue of the fact that VAT is payable only in the country of sale, there can be no biasing effect on the location of firms. This is not, however, the case if one considers, for example, taxes on companies. The UK currently has almost the lowest EU rate of mainstream corporation tax at 33 per cent, and other countries have been obliged to bring their rates into rough conformity in order to avoid excessive tax competition. For the foreseeable future, 'approximation' rather than 'harmonisation' is likely to remain the order of the day in this respect. The issue of harmonisation is, ultimately, bedeviled by the fact that firms in countries with special concessions are most reluctant to give them up in the cause of greater European harmony. As for harmonisation of income tax, that is too far off even to worry about.

Bibliography

CSO (1995) 'Taxes and Social Security Contributions: An International Comparison 1983–1993', *Economic Trends* (November).

Giles, C. and P. Johnson (1994) 'Tax Reform in the UK and Changes in the Progressivity of the Tax System, 1985–95', *Fiscal Studies*, 15 (3).

Hills, J. and H. Sutherland (1991) 'The Proposed Council Tax', *Fiscal Studies*, 12 (4).

House of Commons (1995) *Financial Statement and Budget Report 1996–97*. HC 30 (London: HMSO).

Kay, J. and M. King (1990) *The British Tax System* (Oxford: OUP) 5th edn.

Keen, M. (1991) 'Tax Reform', *Oxford Review of Economic Policy*, 7 (3).

Local Government Act 1988.

Local Government Finance Act 1988.

Local Government and Housing Act 1989.

Local Government Finance Act 1992.

Macleay, I. (1993) 'A Technical Note on the Treatment of the Council Tax in the National Accounts', *Economic Trends* (January).

OECD (1991) 'The Public Sector: Issues for the 1990s', *OECD Working Paper No. 90* (Paris: OECD).

Robinson, W. (1990) 'How Should Savings Be Taxed?', *National Westminster Quarterly Review* (November).

Robson, M. (1995) 'Taxation and Household Saving: Reflections on the OECD Report', *Fiscal Studies*, 16 (1).

Skinner, D. and M. Robson (1992) 'National Insurance Contributions: Anomalies and Reforms', *Fiscal Studies*, 13 (3).

Chapter 8

Spending, Borrowing and Debt

Peter Curwen

■ 8.1 Introduction

Whereas the government has shown some ambivalence about the presentation of its policy objectives since 1979, its public spending plans have always been an important element of its strategy. The government's stated objective has long been to hold the rate of growth of public spending (excluding privatisation proceeds) below the growth rate of the economy as a whole, and thus to reduce public spending as a proportion of national income. This should then make it possible to ease the burden of taxation without any accompanying increase in the overall burden of the National Debt, and from this should flow the enterprise and efficiency which leads to growing output and employment. Once our discussion of public spending is complete, we will move on to examine in sequence the Budget, the government's borrowing requirements and their impact upon the National Debt.

■ 8.2 Public Expenditure Growth

As shown in **Figure 8.1**, public expenditure (GGE – general government expenditure) has grown enormously during the twentieth century, a phenomenon common to all advanced industrial economies, albeit to varying degrees. The lesson of history is that it is very difficult to reduce public expenditure once it has taken root, so it is of considerable interest briefly to review the origins of the growth of public expenditure in the UK.

At the microeconomic level, it is possible to argue that governments are constantly intervening in order to offset the undesirable side-effects of free markets. In the case of what are known as **public goods** such as national defence and street lighting which, even if consumed by one person can still be consumed by others, there is unlikely to be adequate provision in a private market since the provider will be unable to obtain payment from the beneficiaries of his provision. Equally, in the case of **merit goods** which it is generally accepted ought to be consumed by everyone, the provision in a private market of such things as health and education will be limited to those with the ability to pay.

At the macroeconomic level, the basic premise is that goods and services provided by the public sector have **high income elasticities** – that is, demand for them grows faster than the rate of growth of incomes. This sharp rise in demand manifests itself not only in the case of merit goods, including public housing, but also in the case of income support, including pensions, sickness pay and unemployment benefits. The 'displacement theory' put forward by Peacock and Wiseman suggested that the growth in public spending was not a broadly smooth and continuous process as previously thought, but rather

was periodically ratcheted upwards onto a permanently higher level by events such as wars, which caused a radical reappraisal of the status quo. Recent evidence from New Zealand suggests that much public spending is driven by prior increases in tax revenue (see letter by O. McShane in *The Economist*, 11 May 1996, p. 8).

It is difficult, however, to decide whether such upwards displacements in public expenditure are permanent or transitory, especially since they are divorced from the more general political influences that were referred to in Chapter 1. What is evident is that if public expenditure is maintained in a recession – which is both standard Keynesian practice and a necessary consequence of needing to pay out much larger sums to the unemployed – the proportion of public spending in total national income is bound to rise, albeit temporarily. It follows logically, as discussed

Figure 8.1 *General Government Expenditure (GGE) as % of GDP, 1890–1999[1]*

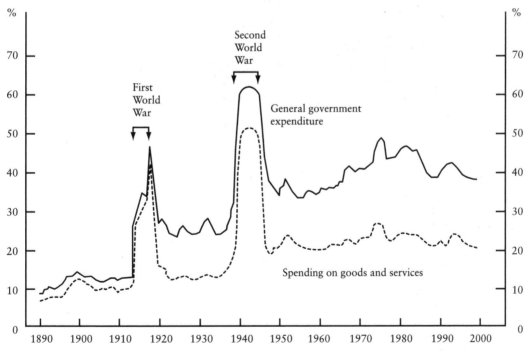

Note:
[1] Excluding privatisation proceeds and adjustments to remove the distortion caused by the abolition of domestic rates. Figures for 1995–96 onwards are projections.

Source: Economic Trends (October 1987); *Statistical Supplement to the 1996–97 Financial Statement and Budget Report.*

later, that the opposite argument holds during periods of rapid growth.

■ 8.3 Public Expenditure Breakdown

There are different ways of defining 'public spending', and different aggregates are relevant for different purposes. The measure which is used for the formulation of macroeconomic policy and the Medium Term Financial Strategy (MTFS) is **general government expenditure** (GGE), consisting of the combined capital and current spending of central and local government including debt interest. This represents the amount which needs to be raised by taxation and borrowing. However,

for the purposes of planning and control of programmes, the public expenditure new **control total** is the relevant figure, since it is built up from the control totals for departmental programmes including public corporations.

Table 8.1 illustrates GGE and the control total over a five-year period. 1994–95 is retrospective and is known as an outturn. 1995–96 is an estimated outturn, and the other years represent plans and projections. The figures are published in November in the Financial Statement and Budget Report (FSBR), known as the 'Red Book'. The plans and projections will be subject to extensive revision over time, and should be treated as indicative rather than as gospel. The 1996 Red Book was published when this edition was at proof stage. The expenditure data proved to be very

Table 8.1 *Public Expenditure Totals (£ billion)*

	1994–5 Outturn	1995–96 Estimated Outturn	1996–97 Plans and Projections	1997–98 Plans and Projections	1998–99 Plans and Projections
Central government[1,2]	174.5	181.1	184.0	188.0	191.9
LA expenditure[3]	73.0	74.4	74.5	75.0	76.5
Nationalised industries' financial requirements	0.7	–	−0.8	0.1	−0.3
Reserve	–	–	2.5	5.0	7.5
Control Total	248.2	255.5	260.2	268.2	275.6
Cyclical social security[3]	14.3	14.0	13.9	14.2	14.7
Central government net debt interest	17.6	20.5	22.3	24.0	24.0
Accounting adjustments	9.0	9.6	9.7	9.1	9.6
GGE (X)	289.2	299.6	306.1	315.5	324.0
Privatisation proceeds	−6.4	−3.0	−4.0	−2.5	−1.5
Other adjustments[4]	5.0	5.5	6.2	6.5	6.3
GGE	287.8	302.1	308.3	319.5	328.7

Notes:
[1] Excluding cyclical social security.
[2] Projections assume constant unemployment.
[3] Comprises total central government support for local authorities and local authorities self-financed expenditure.
[4] Lottery-financed spending and interest and dividend receipts.
Source: FSBR 1996–97, p. 18.

similar to those published in 1995 and reported in what follows. For example, the forecasts for 1997—98 for the control total, GGE (X) and GGE were respectively £266.5, £314.7 and £319.0 billion.

As can be seen, the major difference between the control total and GGE is interest on debt instruments issued by the central government. This amount depends both upon the total debt outstanding and upon interest rates, so it is very difficult to forecast accurately. Its size is related to the historic and current borrowing needs of government which are discussed towards the end of this chapter. In practice, it was stable in nominal terms during the late 1980s, implying that it was falling in both inflation-adjusted terms and as a percentage of GDP, but this is no longer the case as can be seen in the table. The other major difference between the two halves of **Table 8.1** relates to cyclical social security, and represents an innovatory element in the presentation of public expenditure. It should also be observed that it is customary to insert a rolling reserve in the control total. It is not unusual for this to be consumed by unforseen demands upon the public purse almost as soon as the financial year begins, especially at a time of recession.

■ *8.4* Local Government Financing

The approach to the calculation of public spending contained in this discussion dates back to the original surveys of public spending which were set up in accordance with the recommendations of the Plowden Committee (Cmd 1432, 1961).

However, in a White Paper entitled **A New Public Expenditure Planning Total** (Cm 441, 1988), the government proposed a change in the coverage of the planning total, to take place when the new arrangements for local government financing came into operation in England and Wales in 1990. Under this proposal the planning total included (**1**) spending on the government's own programmes; (**2**) grants, current and capital, paid to local authorities; (**3**) credit approvals issued by government for local authority borrowing for capital expenditure; (**4**) payments to the local authorities from the proceeds of the national non-domestic rate; (**5**) the external financing limits of public corporations; (**6**) privatisation proceeds; (**7**) a Reserve. Data collection in the appropriate form could not be integrated into the 1988 Public Expenditure Survey because it was already in progress, but commenced with the 1989 Survey.

The underlying purpose of this change was to distinguish that part of local authority spending which was the responsibility of central government from that part which local authorities determined and financed for themselves. Public spending control was thereby enhanced in a number of ways – for example, by the inclusion of grants in the planning total for the first time. Furthermore, since this required the grants to be planned for three years ahead, it helped the local authorities to plan their own expenditure more effectively.

It should be noted that this change had no effect upon the total for general government expenditure. The effect, in accounting terms, was to remove local authority self-financed expenditure from the planning total and to place it, in terms of **Table 8.1**, together with interest and other adjustments.

The control total was introduced in the 1992 Public Expenditure Survey. It differs from the planning total in three ways:

1. Cyclical social security does not score in the control total but did score in the planning total.
2. Local authority self-financed expenditure (LASFE) scores in the control total but did not score in the planning total.
3. Privatisation proceeds are excluded from the control total but they did score in the planning total.

The justification for these changes is that the government wishes to include as much public spending as possible in the control total, given the fundamental objective of controlling GGE over time, but nevertheless wishes to insulate programme spending so far as is possible from the effects of the cycle. For this reason LASFE has been included in the control total, given that it is a significant component of GGE and is not primarily cyclical. Equally, the main unemployment-related elements of social security (unemployment benefit and income support for non-pensioners) have been excluded from the control total whereas non-cyclical elements have been included (Heald, 1995).

It is important to note that the control total implies a change in the approach to bargaining between spending ministers and the Treasury (*Ibid.*, p. 229). Previously, spending ministers would submit bids, and after they had been totted up the Treasury would decide how many of them it was willing to sanction, so spending was partly driven by the size of bids. By comparison, the new 'top-down' system begins with the Chancellor and Prime Minister fixing the total in advance. As a result (at least in theory), any additional resources for one department can only be generated by reducing those available to other departments by an equivalent amount. In the event of dispute, a Cabinet committee chaired by the Chancellor will adjudicate.

■ 8.5 Public Expenditure Trends

Table 8.2 provides an overview of public expenditure spanning the period 1971–72 to 1998–99. Various aspects of the overall picture are picked up in the subsequent discussion. For the moment, it is necessary merely to remark upon the missing data for the control total. This arises because it has not proved to be possible to recalculate the local authority element in the control total on the current definition for the years pre-1984–85.

Table 8.2 indicates the path of general government expenditure (excluding privatisation proceeds) in real terms and as a percentage of GDP. Care must be taken insofar that the decision was taken in 1995 not merely to subtract privatisation proceeds from GGE in order to determine GGE (X), but also to subtract spending financed out of National Lottery proceeds and to net off interest and dividend receipts from gross payments. The growth of real GGE (X) was exceptionally rapid from 1963–64 to 1967–68, and then again

from 1969–70 to 1974–75. After a setback during the first OPEC crisis, it moved upwards again until 1984–85, albeit not quite as fast as during the previous two upturns. Subsequently, it barely grew at all until the end of the decade, but it took off again in 1991–92. This surge lasted only until 1994–95, since when it has remained static. Almost no movement is forecast for the rest of the decade, although that may well prove to be over-optimistic in practice, especially given the impending election.

The early 1960s surge in real spending was much faster than GDP growth. The second surge, commencing in 1968–69, resulted in a 8 per cent rise in the real GGE/GDP ratio, with an overall effect, allowing for a brief fall at the end of the 1960s, of 12.5 per cent. The OPEC crisis subsequently forced real spending down at a time when GDP continued to rise, thereby hauling back the ratio by 6 points within only two years.

Although much of this improvement proved to be transitory once the crisis was over, no government post-1976 has ever showed as much enthusiasm for public spending as was manifested in the mid-1970s. Nevertheless, it is notable that the 1980–81 recession prevented the first Thatcher government from getting to grips with spending. Only after 1985–86 did the ratio of real spending to GDP start to fall rapidly, yet even at its lowest level in 1988–89 the ratio was back only to the level of 1966–67, and it is currently back to the levels customary in the late 1970s.

Whether recent experience should be seen as an achievement is a matter to which we will return. What is clear, as shown in **Figure 8.1**, is that even the best performance in recent years was no great achievement when viewed over the long term. Furthermore, for reasons discussed below, there is no foreseeable likelihood that the ratio of GGE to GDP will unwind to levels customary pre-1970. It is interesting to note, however, the difference between the two lines shown in **Figure 8.1**. GGE includes transfers, and shows the extent to which the government has to raise taxation and to borrow on the financial markets in order to finance its activities. The narrower measure, which covers goods and services only, shows the extent to which the nation's resources are being directly absorbed by the government. It is very evident

Table 8.2   *Public Expenditure, 1971–72 to 1998–99*

| | Control Total[1] | | GGE(X) | | | Privatisation Proceeds | GGE |
	£ bn	Real terms[3] £ bn	£ bn	Real terms[3] £ bn	Per cent of GDP[2]	£ bn	£ bn
1971–72			23.3	168.8	40		24.4
1972–73			26.4	177.0	$39\frac{3}{4}$		27.6
1973–74			30.5	191.4	$41\frac{1}{2}$		32.0
1974–75			41.0	215.2	$46\frac{3}{4}$		42.9
1975–76			51.6	215.8	$47\frac{1}{4}$		53.8
1976–77			57.0	210.1	$44\frac{3}{4}$		59.6
1977–78			61.7	199.9	$41\frac{1}{2}$	−0.5	63.9
1978–79			72.0	210.1	$42\frac{1}{4}$		75.0
1979–80			87.0	217.3	$42\frac{1}{2}$	−0.4	90.0
1980–81			104.8	221.3	$44\frac{3}{4}$	−0.2	108.6
1981–82			116.3	224.0	$45\frac{1}{2}$	−0.5	120.5
1982–83			127.8	229.8	$45\frac{1}{2}$	−0.5	132.7
1983–84			136.6	234.7	$44\frac{3}{4}$	−1.1	140.4
1984–85	126.0	206.2	147.7	241.6	$45\frac{1}{4}$	−2.0	150.8
1985–86	129.6	200.9	154.9	240.2	$43\frac{3}{4}$	−2.7	158.5
1986–87	136.0	204.8	163.3	245.8	$42\frac{1}{4}$	−4.5	164.6
1987–88	148.6	212.4	172.9	247.1	$40\frac{1}{2}$	−5.1	173.5
1988–89	156.1	209.1	180.7	242.1	38	−7.1	179.8
1989–90	175.1	219.3	198.0	248.0	$38\frac{1}{4}$	−4.2	200.9
1990–91	193.5	224.4	217.3	251.9	39	−5.3	218.2
1991–92	213.2	232.6	238.6	260.4	41	−7.9	236.2
1992–93	231.7	242.8	263.6	276.4	$43\frac{1}{2}$	−8.2	260.6
1993–94	240.7	245.3	277.9	283.1	$43\frac{1}{2}$	−5.4	277.3
1994–95	247.9	248.2	289.2	289.2	$42\frac{3}{4}$	−6.4	287.8
1995–96	255.2	248.7	299.6	291.6	42	−3.0	302.1
1996–97	260.6	246.4	306.1	289.9	$40\frac{1}{2}$	−4.0	308.3
1997–98	266.5	247.8	315.5	291.5	$39\frac{3}{4}$	−2.5	319.5
1998–99	273.7	249.1	324.0	292.8	$38\frac{3}{4}$	−1.5	328.7

Notes:

[1] Figures for the Control Total are only available on a consistent basis for the years shown. Figures are estimated outturn for 1995–96 and plans for 1996–97 onwards.

[2] An adjusted series for money GDP is used in the calculation of the ratio for the years up to 1989–90. This has been constructed to remove the distortion caused by the abolition of domestic rates.

[3] Cash figures adjusted to price levels of 1994–95.

Source: Financial Statement and Budget Report, 1996–97.

that the latter has changed remarkably little over the past four decades. In other words, it is **transfer payments of all kinds which have largely accounted for the much enlarged role of central government in people's lives.**

Given that the government does not itself consume transfer payments, there are those who prefer to discuss the role of government in terms of the lower rather than the upper line. On the other hand, taxes and social security levies must be raised to cover the entire sum spent by government, and the upper line is accordingly more appropriate in terms of the coverage of this chapter.

■ *8.6 Public Expenditure Targets*

In the course of the Autumn Statement for 1990, the government restated its position in relation to both expenditure and taxation as follows:

> The Government's medium term objective for public spending is that, over time, it should take a declining share of national income, while value for money is constantly improved. This is consistent with the policy of maintaining a balanced budget over the medium term and reducing taxation when it is prudent to do so. The public spending objective is expressed in terms of the ratio of general government expenditure (GGE), excluding privatisation proceeds, to gross domestic product (GDP). GGE is the main spending aggregate used in the Medium Term Financial Strategy (MTFS).

The Financial Statement and Budget Report 1996–97 subsequently stated the objectives as being to:

- keep the PSBR on a downward track;
- reduce public spending as a percentage of national income while protecting priority services, developing new partnerships with the private sector, and improving the efficiency of the public sector;
- allow people to keep more of the money they earn and save; help ensure their needs will be met in old age; and encourage enterprise and business.

Throughout the 1980s it was the custom for the government to produce figures for its expenditure which showed a clear downward trend over time as a percentage of GDP. Initially, the planned percentages were consistently over-optimistic by a wide margin. By the mid-1980s the outturns were proving to be only modestly worse than the plans, and by the end of the decade the outturns were an improvement on the plans.

During the recent recession, public spending inevitably rose as a percentage of GDP, but the government remains proud of its record, claiming that unlike its predecessors it has got to grips with public spending. But has it? In the first place, it must be remembered that we are dealing here with a **ratio**, which can fall in value for a variety of different combinations of changes in numerator and denominator. Originally, in the 1980 White Paper, the government expressed its spending objective as a progressive reduction of its expenditure in real terms over the subsequent four years. When this failed to transpire in practice, its objective became to hold expenditure constant in real terms, but this was not achieved either, despite the best efforts of the 'Star Chamber', a small committee of senior politicians set up specifically to bring into conformity the desire on the part of ministers to spend and the desire on the part of the Treasury not to spend.

Clearly, therefore, the government expressly never wanted its spending to rise in real terms, yet that, as we have seen in **Table 8.2**, is precisely what did happen taking the 1980s as a whole (although the second half was better than the first and there was a modest reduction in 1988–89). Not surprisingly, the government also failed to bring spending down as a percentage of GDP on an ongoing basis until 1985–86, after which point it fell rapidly for three successive years despite the fact that real spending remained almost constant. In other words, real spending as a percentage of GDP essentially fell **not because real spending was itself falling but because GDP was rising rapidly.**

Our conclusions from the above discussion are that: (**1**) in terms of its **original** public spending targets, the government has been a failure; (**2**) by moving the goalposts the government did manage, during the late 1980s, to hit its targets; but (**3**) this could be ascribed much less to successful curbs on real spending than to the effects of rapid economic growth; and hence (4) the government will be unable to hit its targets again without the greatest of difficulty.

According to its most recent projections, the government is apparently anticipating little upwards movement in real GGE (X) before the end of the century, even though inflation is low by the standards of the 1980s. This translates into the projection of a constantly declining ratio of real GGE (X) to GDP, remarkably similar to that achieved during the late 1980s, although it naturally assumes fairly buoyant rates of economic growth. It is evident, therefore, that the government puts a favourable gloss on its spending performance. However, it is particularly revealing that when reference is made these days to public expenditure **cuts**, this actually means a **reduction in the forecast rate of growth of spending**.

Whilst it is evident that the government has missed its spending targets more often than not, it is nevertheless necessary to ask **just how much of a failure it has been**. It must be recognised, first of all, that the government took office at the end of the era of profligate public spending which not merely rose sharply in real terms but as a percentage of GDP – up from 36 per cent in 1964–65 to over 47 per cent in 1975–76, although the Labour government stemmed the tide in the late 1970s. Some of the blame for that rise could be laid at the door of the Plowden Committee. In the first place, planning subsequently came to be done on a volume basis which meant that spending Departments could expect their real spending to be maintained. Secondly, the volumes were adjusted upwards on the basis of forecast economic growth which never fully transpired in practice, with the result that spending rose faster than GDP.

In setting out to cut real spending the first Thatcher government was, therefore, trying like King Canute to turn back the tide, and although it failed **so did almost everyone else**. On average, public spending as a percentage of GDP rose sharply in OECD countries during the 1970s (and in absolute terms also). **Table 8.3** covers the European Community/Union plus the USA and Japan over the period 1970–97. For many

countries, including the UK (at 45.3 per cent), the position in 1985 represented a markedly higher ratio than the average for the previous decade. The ratios typically fell back after 1985, Scandinavia excepted, as public spending became, temporarily, less fashionable and GDP was on an upwards trend. During the 1980s as a whole, however, only the UK and West Germany among the larger economies managed to rein back their ratios at all significantly. Elsewhere in Europe, high spenders such as Sweden and Holland made negligible progress overall, although in many cases quite sharp reductions towards the end of the decade more than offset rising ratios at the beginning. Compared to the long-term trend, the position in Spain and Italy had deteriorated seriously by 1990, and even the USA had moved up towards European levels of spending, Reagan notwithstanding.

Since 1990, only the Netherlands has achieved a significant reduction in its ratio although, after peaking in 1993, the EU average has fallen back to the position in 1991. On the face of it, the average looks to be set to fluctuate around the 50 per cent mark during the 1990s, several percentiles higher than during the previous decade. The UK has remained some 7 or 8 percentiles below the EU average for over a decade, and the 1997 forecast suggests that only Ireland will achieve a noticeably lower ratio. It is important to note that comparable countries such as France and Italy are currently more than a decile higher, and that even the Japanese ratio is creeping inexorably upwards.

Given the difficulties faced elsewhere in controlling public spending, it was arguably fortunate for Britain that its difficulties in the mid-1970s brought the desirability of spiralling public spending into question at a relatively early point in history. Gradually, expenditure was transformed onto a cash basis, a process completed in 1981, and this was accompanied by a more determined pursuit of value for money in public spending during the Thatcher years. The government's **efforts** could not be denied, but such progress as was made has to be set against a decade of Thatcherite determination. A recession combined with a 'wetter' government has served to unwind the gains made in the late 1980s.

Table 8.3   *General Government Total Expenditure (as % of GDP) 1970–97*

Country	1970–73	1974–85	1986–90	1991–93	1994–97	1992	1993	1994	1995	1996	1997*
B	43.6	56.9	57.0	55.8	54.1	55.7	56.3	55.6	54.3	53.4	53.0
DK	42.1	53.0	56.8	60.1	59.1	60.1	62.3	62.1	59.0	58.4	56.8
D	40.1	47.6	46.0	49.0	49.1	48.8	50.0	49.4	49.8	48.8	48.2
GR	–	–	47.1	45.2	47.3	44.8	46.9	48.0	47.4	47.3	46.7
E	23.0	32.6	41.9	46.8	46.3	46.1	49.3	47.9	46.5	45.8	44.9
F	38.2	47.2	51.0	53.1	54.5	52.8	55.5	55.4	54.6	54.2	53.6
IRL	35.9	47.4	45.3	41.1	39.4	41.3	41.3	41.5	40.1	38.5	37.3
I	34.4	42.7	51.2	54.7	52.4	53.6	56.9	54.1	53.1	52.0	50.6
L	33.1	47.6	–	–	41.2	–	43.7	42.3	41.4	41.0	40.0
NL	44.2	55.7	57.0	56.0	51.6	56.1	56.3	54.1	51.9	50.7	49.8
A	40.0	48.6	51.0	51.5	52.3	51.1	53.3	52.4	52.8	52.3	51.8
P	24.9	–	39.4	43.0	42.3	42.3	43.4	42.3	42.9	42.3	41.8
FIN	31.5	40.5	45.5	59.4	56.6	60.7	61.9	60.7	58.2	54.8	52.6
S	45.4	59.7	60.5	68.5	66.9	68.6	74.1	70.5	68.0	65.5	63.5
UK	37.7	43.7	40.3	42.6	42.1	43.3	43.8	43.1	42.8	41.8	40.8
EUR	37.1[1]	45.7[2]	47.7	50.5	50.4	50.7	52.5	51.4	50.9	50.0	49.1
USA	31.3	34.1	36.4	37.9	35.9	38.5	37.7	36.1	36.2	36.0	35.4
JAP	21.2	30.8	32.3	33.2	35.4	32.8	34.7	34.9	35.6	35.7	35.3

Notes:
[2] EUR without Greece.
[1] EUR without Greece and Portugal.
* Forecast
Source: European Economy, Supplement A, January 1996.

This does not bode particularly well for the future, yet there is one saving grace of a kind. In the UK, almost uniquely amongst advanced economies, the old-age dependency ratio (the number of people aged over 65 as a percentage of the working population) is set to fall up to the year 2010. As the dependency ratio rises so does the bill for health care and pensions, so whereas the Japanese government, for example, currently spends a much lower proportion of GDP than that of the UK (yet provides excellent services), its dependency ratio is set to rise from 17 per cent in 1990 to 28 per cent in 2010.

Looking further ahead to 2030, the UK's dependency ratio is set to rise, and the effect of health and pensions expenditure alone will possibly be to raise the spending/GDP ratio by 3 per cent. However, this is less than half the projected rise in other major economies, so in the longer term the UK will be well down the league table of big spenders even if the ratio of public spending to GDP is higher than currently.

8.7 Functional Analysis of Expenditure

In seeking to analyse why even a decade of Thatcherism failed to make any inroads into the absolute level of real public spending we need to dis-aggregate public spending into its main functions, as in **Figure 8.2**. The key lesson of **Figure 8.2** is that roughly 70 per cent of public spending is accounted for by only four functions, namely health, social security, education and science and defence. Over the period 1980–81 to 1995–

96 these four functions absorbed an increased share of total spending, as shown by the dotted line, although it has remained stable at just over 70 per cent for the past decade aside from a temporary dip in 1990–91.

It is important to remember that real spending rose between 1979–80 and 1995–95 from £191 billion to £262 billion at 1994–95 prices (by 37 per cent), so this was an **increasing share of an increasing real total**. In other words, any increase in the share necessarily means that additional **real** (not simply nominal, but inflation-adjusted) resources are being pumped into the function in question, and this may still be true even if the share declines slightly. Given the current controversy over health care, it has been put at the foot of each column in order to bring out the essential reality that the government has **pumped significant additional real resources into health care** over the past decade and a half. The biggest share has long been taken by social security, reflecting in particular long-term growth in pension liabilities and, up until the late 1980s and also recently, substantially higher unemployment benefits. As unemployment eased after 1986, so social security began to absorb a smaller share of the total, but the cost of the welfare state has once again begun to escalate sharply in recent years.

Education and science has had a patchier time, partly because of the adjustment necessitated first by falling then by rising school rolls, but currently has much the same share as during the late 1980s. By contrast, after peaking in the middle of the 1980s, defence is on a downward trend in terms of its share of total spending, and this is set to continue, the Gulf War notwithstanding. Housing is also included in **Figure 8.2** because it took a significant share of total spending in 1980–81, but

Figure 8.2 *General Government Expenditure on Services by Function, % Share of Total, 1980/81 to 1995/96*

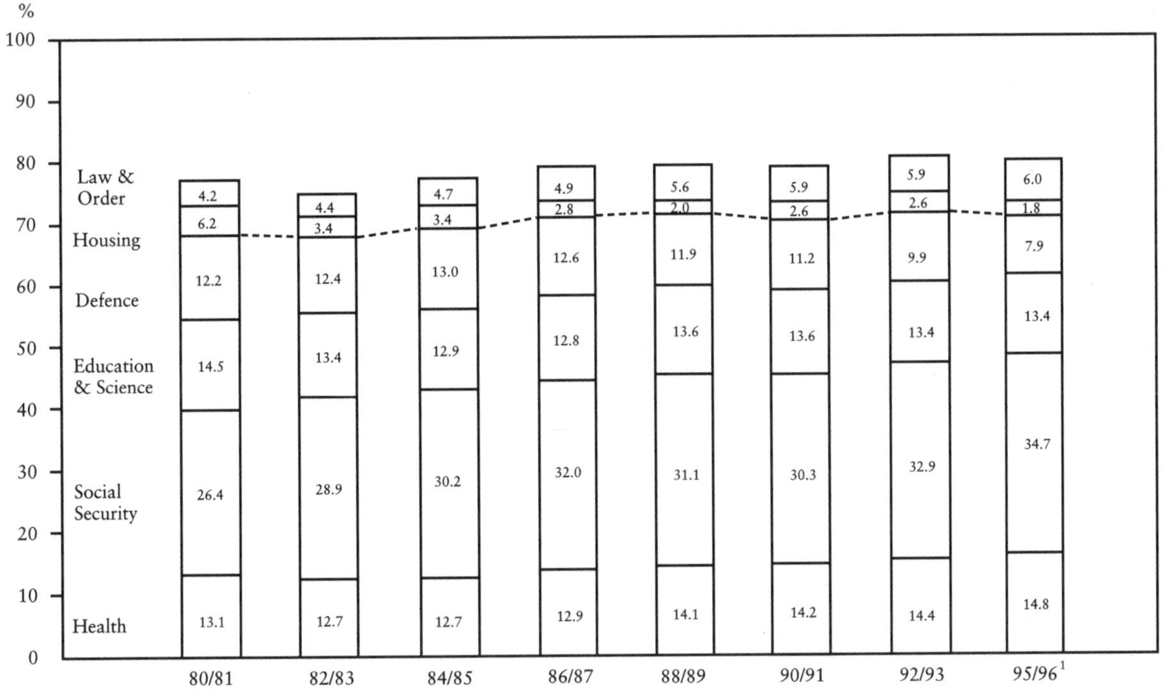

Note:
[1] Estimated outturn.
Source: Statistical Supplement to the 1996–97 Financial Statement and Budget Report, Table 1.3.

the sale of council houses and the upgrading of rents towards market levels halved housing's share of total spending by 1985–86 and it is currently at an all-time low. However, whereas law and order started off in 1980–81 with a much smaller share than housing, it ended the decade with more than twice the share and currently has in excess of three times. It would therefore appear to be the case that in simple spending terms (but not necessarily in terms of results) the present government is indeed the party of law and order.

These changes are brought out more clearly in **Table 8.4** which shows the percentage change in real spending between 1979–80 and 1995–96, and also between 1980–81 and 1995–96 (in order to avoid disputes about whether the government should be held responsible for spending during its election year). In either case, the biggest increase was in spending on law and order, with both social security and health showing very substantial increases. With real spending on health up by 67 per cent, it is, frankly, rather unrealistic to accuse the government of undermining the national health service.

On the other hand, education and science did much less well, and real spending on transport was only slightly larger overall. A clear reduction took place in real defence spending, but the really significant reduction, as can be seen, was in real spending on housing, down by over one half.

These developments can also usefully be re-expressed in terms of capital (investment) versus current spending. In 1973, investment constituted 12 per cent of general government expenditure whereas by 1986 it constituted only 4.5 per cent. The reduction in the real level of fixed investment by roughly one half during the decade beginning in 1975 was particularly pronounced in housing. Public corporations were also squeezed, as were investment grants to private sector organisations. It was also noticeable that subsidies were cut sharply, but although this tendency to make investment obey the rules of the market place sat comfortably within the philosophy of the Conservative government, the reduction in investment was ironically much sharper under the Labour government in the late 1970s than under its Conservative successor. By the late 1980s, the government was obliged to increase real investment in, for example, roads and prisons (because it was increasing the jail population), but it is trying to involve private capital in these and other areas in order to keep its own capital investment under control.

One reason for the erratic approach to capital spending arises from the accounting system which writes off investment in the year the money is spent, exactly as though it was current spending, thereby ignoring the stream of future benefits that it generates. This is at odds with private sector practice, and makes it only too easy, for example, to cut spending on replacing sewers.

One obvious conclusion to be drawn from the above discussion is that the government's efforts to control real spending during the 1980s **were successful only in areas which did not absorb a big share of its spending** – trade and industry was another in this category. Now these functions have been cut back to the bone, there is no more fat to trim. Hence, **further reductions can occur only in major heads of spending** – yet as we have seen those are precisely the areas where even the Conservative government had little or no success. The number of pensioners cannot be reduced; unemployment remains high by 1970s' standards; the number of school children and college students has risen; and the health service is impervious to cuts.

Table 8.4 *Increase in Real Expenditure by Function (%)*

	$\dfrac{1995–96}{1979–80}$	$\dfrac{1995–96}{1980–81}$
Law and order	93.0	87.0
Social security	80.9	77.3
Health	66.8	53.6
Agriculture & fisheries	40.0	26.4
Education & science	34.1	30.1
Transport	2.3	3.4
Defence	−9.6	−11.9
Housing	−64.4	−58.0

Source: Statistical Supplement to the 1996–97 FSBR, Table 1.3.

■ 8.8 The Spending Conundrum

It is surely one of the greatest ironies of Mrs Thatcher's decade in power that, having claimed for many years that a major objective was to **cut** public spending (but having failed in real terms to do so), it eventually became politically expedient to claim to the **contrary**, for example in the case of the health service. But by that time the propaganda machine had been so successful that no one would believe the government, even though what it claimed was true.

We already know that real spending on the health service rose significantly during the 1980s, yet the medical establishment has complained endlessly that the health service is under-resourced and (prospective) patients certainly believe that the service they receive (or cannot obtain) is deteriorating. How can this be?

Many categories of public expenditure, such as health and education, are currently labour-intensive. This means that the public expenditure debate has been directed primarily towards **inputs** rather than **outputs**. The GDP deflator, which is used to express spending in real terms is, however, output-based and is therefore inappropriate for evaluating the **volume** of provision of **labour-intensive services**. This suggests that an own-cost deflator should be used in such circumstances, namely one based upon the **costs of inputs used** in each category. A study by Levitt and Joyce (1987) has demonstrated what a difference this can make. In the case of health, real GDP-deflated spending rose by 25 per cent between 1979 and 1986, whilst own-cost deflated spending rose by only 9 per cent. Since population growth absorbed over half of this latter increase, and technological advances absorbed the rest, the actual volume of health care delivered **per capita** was **effectively identical** throughout the entire period. Thus, when the government claims to have increased real spending on the NHS, and the medical profession categorically denies that the resource base has improved, they are **both in their respective ways telling the truth.**

The obvious difficulty this creates is that, if real spending has to be constantly increased simply in order to deliver an unchanged volume of provision in crucial labour-intensive areas such as health, the only painless way to cut public spending as a percentage of GDP is to make GDP grow rapidly. One could, of course, alternatively move public spending into the private sector, so it is hardly surprising that educational loans rather than grants, and the tendering out of NHS services, are being actively promoted. However, these changes are very difficult to deliver politically even for a government with a clear majority.

The demand for more resources in, for example, the NHS is inevitably couched in terms of **inputs** – too few nurses, hospital beds and so on. However, this tells us nothing about how **efficiently** these resources are going to be used, so the government has understandably tried to switch the emphasis of the public expenditure debate onto **outputs and productivity**. It introduced the programme of scrutinies of efficiency by the Cabinet Office under Lord Rayner in 1979; the Financial Management Initiative (FMI) in 1982; and the publication of performance indicators in the then Autumn Statement. The drawback here is that one can, for example, show an increase in the number of in-patients treated per available bed by discharging patients more quickly than before. If, as a consequence, this means that many of them need to be readmitted, then they count as new patients and productivity remains high. There is also an inevitable tendency to use readily accessible measures of performance such as the size of GP's lists, the pupil-teacher ratio in schools or the crime clean-up rate per police officer. However, there is no guarantee that reducing either of the first two will improve the quality of output, which would need to be measured by the ratio of cured patients per doctor or examination passes per teacher.

And, finally, what if the Labour Party get elected? As *The Economist* (1996c) neatly puts it, Labour has set itself three goals: to spend no money; to help the poor; and to avoid scaring the voters. Under the circumstances, it has decided that whatever it says will be at least partly incompatible with one or more of these objectives, so it has sensibly decided to say as little as possible.

■ *8.9* The Budget

The Budget is an annual event, held up to and including 1993 in either March or April, but switching to November in 1993 (requiring a second Budget in that year) for reasons discussed below (Dilnot and Robson, 1993). It exists both to set out the government's proposals for changes in taxation and to provide an occasion for the annual review of economic policy. Normal procedure was for the proposals to be announced to the House of Commons by the Chancellor of the Exchequer in the Budget Statement, and to be published in the Financial Statement and Budget Report (FSBR).

The Budget statement is followed by the moving of a set of Ways and Means resolutions embodying the Budget proposals, and these form the foundations for the Finance Bill which goes forward for debate in Parliament. The Ways and Means resolutions exist so that taxes can be levied at the new levels set out in the Finance Bill pending its enactment. The Finance Bill, subject to any amendments volunteered by, or forced upon, the Chancellor during debate, is then passed as the Finance Act.

Tax proposals are concerned primarily with changes in the rate or coverage of taxes, the introduction of new taxes and the abolition of existing ones, or changes in methods of administration. Most taxes are permanent, but in the case

Figure 8.3 *Sources of Revenue, 1996–97*

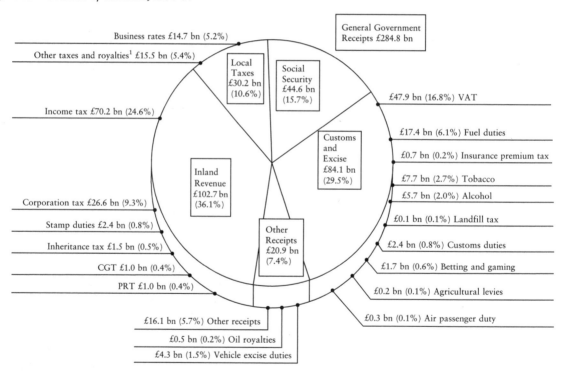

Notes:

[1] Includes council tax.

[2] Includes interest and dividends, gross trading surpluses, rent, other financial transactions and payments to the National Lottery Distribution Fund.

Source: FSBR 1996–97, Table 1.7.

of income tax and corporation tax the Finance Act is needed every year to keep them in existence. It is, however, perfectly proper either to have a mini-Budget at any time of year, which necessitates amendments to the Finance Act, or simply to operate the Regulator which permits VAT to be varied by up to 25 per cent, and the main excise duties by up to 10 per cent between Budgets.

Figure 8.3 represents the breakdown of total government revenue forecast for 1996–97. As can be seen, 36.8 per cent of all revenue comes under the control of the Inland Revenue, while a further 30.2 per cent is handled by Customs and Excise. **It is not generally appreciated how dependent tax revenue is upon a narrow range of** taxes. NICs account for slightly less than VAT, which is itself exceeded only by income tax. Between them, these three account for 58.4 per cent of total revenue. A decade ago, in 1985, duties on fuel plus petroleum revenue tax (PRT) were the next most important, followed by corporation tax, but the effects of the fall in the price of oil and of fiscal drag resulted in corporation tax yielding almost twice as much (8.6 per cent) as the other two combined in 1991–92. After dipping in 1993–94, corporation tax is once again much larger than the other two combined, and corporation tax and fuel duties each generate a much higher proportion than for any other individual tax levied by central government.

The Budget contains an array of changes to the tax system. It is clear, however, from the above discussion, that very few of these have other than marginal effects upon total revenue, whereas changes in income tax of an apparently modest kind (for example, a 1p reduction in the marginal rate) have quite dramatic effects (altering revenue by more that £1 billion). **Table 8.5** gives an indication of the sorts of changes that have a reasonably significant effect upon tax receipts, in the context of the Budget in November 1995.

The purpose of raising revenue is primarily to fund expenditure, so it was a little curious that the Budget was traditionally divorced from the two main discussions of public expenditure set out in the Autumn Statement and Public Expenditure White Paper. The Treasury did not like making statements about revenue in the Autumn because tax receipts could alter sharply between November and April (perhaps due to fiscal drag). On the other hand, public expenditure needed to be planned well in advance and did not have to be financed solely through tax receipts. The drawback to the separation in time was that any increases in spending in the Autumn had been largely forgotten by April, so any buoyancy in tax receipts immediately led to demands for yet further spending.

In 1993 the Chancellor finally decided to bite the bullet and announced that henceforth there would be a unified tax and spending Budget, of which the first would take place in November 1993. This necessitated a second Budget in 1993, although the first was set up so as to eliminate the need to take much action in the Autumn. The Finance Bill is thereby set back to January, which has the advantage of giving taxpayers a clear idea of most tax changes well before the date that they take effect, as compared to the previous situation where legislation was not enacted until well after the start of the tax year. Nevertheless, excise duties still need to be raised on the day of the Budget. The FSBR is published at the time of the Budget containing spending plans covering the three years commencing the following April.

8.10 The Public Sector Borrowing Requirement and Public Sector Debt Repayment

The difference between the total receipts and total expenditure of the public sector is known as the public sector borrowing requirement (PSBR) or debt repayment (PSDR). The public sector consists of central government, local government and the public corporations. The global figure for the PSBR does not, therefore, show flows between the three sectors, normally from central government to the other two and on a very large scale, but does include public corporations' borrowing from the money markets and overseas. The PSBR can be distinguished from the slightly larger Central Government Borrowing Requirement (CGBR) which excludes borrowing for on-lending to local

Table 8.5   *Direct Effects of Budget Measures, November 1995 (£ million)*

	£ million	yield (+)/cost (−) of measure		
	Changes from a non-indexed base 1996–97	Changes from an indexed base 1996–97	1997–98	1998–99
INLAND REVENUE (26 changes) of which:[1]				
Basic rate – reduced to 24 per cent	−1 600	−1 600	−2 000	−2 100
Married couple's allowance – indexed	−90	–	–	–
Lower rate band – increased by £700	−520	−370	−530	−510
Basic rate limit – up by £1200	−270	–	−80	−80
Age related allowances – up by £280	−120	–	–	–
Tax on savings income cut to 20 per cent	−800	−800	−400	−450
Inheritance tax threshold up to £200 000	−155	−130	−250	−295
Small companies corporation tax rate cut to 24 per cent	–	–	−95	−130
Insurance equalisation reserves – tax relief	–	–	−100	−100
Relief for Class 4 NICs – withdrawn	–	–	240	190
CUSTOMS AND EXCISE (20 changes) of which:[1]				
VAT payments on account – changes	600	600	–	–
Excise duties on beer/wine unchanged	–	−150	−150	−155
Landfill tax introduced	110	110	450	460
VEHICLE EXCISE DUTY (5 changes) of which:[1]				
Duty on cars, etc. up to £140	115	–	–	–
BUSINESS RATES (1 change) Business rates – transitional scheme amended	−135	−135	−95	–
NATIONAL INSURANCE CONTRIBUTIONS (5 changes) of which:[1]				
Employer NICs – main rate reduced by 0.2 per cent	–	–	−495	−580
Class 4 NICs – rate reduced to 6 per cent	–	–	−270	−205
Earnings thresholds raised	−120	–	–	–
TOTAL RECEIPTS	−4 145	−3 140	−4 590	−4 790

Note:
[1] Separate listing where effect is at least ± £75 million in the financial year.
Source: FSBR 1996–97.

Table 8.6 *Borrowing Requirements of Central Government (CGBR) and Public Sector (PSBR) (£ bn, cash)[1,2]*

	1994–95	*1995–96*	*1996–97*	*1997–98*	*1999–2000*	*2000–01*
GGE	287.8	302.1	308.3	319	329	338
General government receipts	250.0	271.9	284.8	304	323	340
CGBR	37.8	30.2	23.5	16	6	−2
Public corporations' market and overseas debt repayment	−1.9	−1.2	−1.1	−1	–	–
PSBR	35.9	29.0	22.4	15	5	−2
Money GDP at market prices	678	712	754	795	836	876
PSBR as % of GDP	$5\frac{1}{4}$	4	3	2	$\frac{3}{4}$	$-\frac{1}{4}$

Notes:
[1] Rounded to the nearest £1 billion from 1997–98 onwards.
[2] 1994–95 is an outturn; 1995–96 and 1996–97 are forecasts; 1997–8 onwards are projections.
Source: FSBR 1996–97.

authorities and public corporations (FSBR, 1996–97, p. 81). This, in turn, is somewhat smaller than the General Government Financial Deficit (GGFD – see FSBR 1996–97, p. 69) which is used to measure budget deficits as part of the move to Economic and Monetary Union.

The PSBR figures for the past two years, and projections for the next four, are to be found in **Table 8.6**. These are in cash terms, and the PSBR is also expressed as a percentage of GDP.

The longer-term trend of the PSBR can be seen in **Figure 8.4**, again expressed as a percentage of GDP. It is helpful to note at this point the accounting convention used for privatisation proceeds when they first appeared. In the 1980s, they were recorded as **negative spending**. The government argued that, since the purchase price appeared as public expenditure when assets were taken into public ownership, it was only logical to treat any monies arising when they were sold back to the private sector as negative spending. Sceptics argued that the purpose of this exercise was to reduce the declared amount of public spending in order to reduce the PSBR. Since it is undeniable that the government does spend the actual amount indicated before privatisation proceeds are subtracted, it therefore seems to be more sensible to treat the PSBR as the excess of gross public expenditure over total tax revenue, and to treat privatisation proceeds as a **means of financing the shortfall**. The government did subsequently move to an emphasis upon GGE (X), as shown in **Table 8.2**, although with privatisation proceeds on the decline, their impact upon expenditure is no longer particularly significant.

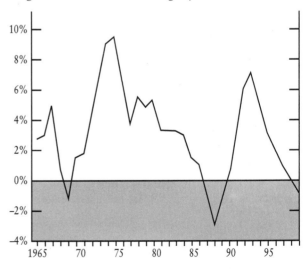

Figure 8.4 *PSBR as Percentage of GDP*

Source: FSBR, various years.

During the oil crisis in the mid-1970s the ratio came close to reaching double figures and, despite some subsequent improvement, rose back to 5 per cent when the present government was first elected. Indeed, throughout the initial part of the present government's period in office, the PSBR remained stubbornly higher than forecast. Tax overshoots were generally more modest than those for spending, and the PSBR consequently did no better than hit its target value for the six consecutive years beginning in 1981–82.

The dramatic turnaround came in 1987–88 when tax revenue overshot the forecast by an astonishing £7.5 billion, with the result that, despite a serious £4 billion overshoot in spending, the PSBR became negative for the first time since 1971 as shown in **Figure 8.4**. It became the custom to refer to the PSDR – public sector debt repayment. Strictly speaking, a PSDR did not arise **excluding** privatisation proceeds until 1988–89. The then Chancellor, Nigel Lawson, never did, however, advocate the desirability of a PSDR as such. Indeed, he formally advocated the desirability of a **balanced budget** only in the FSBR of 1988, and did so then only on the grounds that 'it provides a clear and simple rule, with a good historical pedigree'. In the event, his avowed strategy fell foul of the buoyancy of tax revenue, and on either definition there was a PSDR in 1988–89 and 1989–90 – quite substantial ones if privatisation proceeds are included. As the economy sank into recession during 1990, the original forecast of a further substantial PSDR gradually gave way to less-optimistic views about the eventual outturn.

The FSBR in 1992–93 forecast that the PSBR would peak in 1993–94 at roughly 8 per cent of GDP, and fall rapidly thereafter back to zero. However, this proved to be over-optimistic, and the 1996–97 FSBR effectively re-utilised the previous year's forecast, thereby pretending that 1995–96 never really took place. In its Summer forecast of 1996 the Treasury neatly restated its objective as being to 'bring the PSBR back *towards* balance over the medium term', claiming that this had anyway been the case in 1993 and 1995 with the 'towards' disappearing only in 1994. On that basis, the PSBR is now officially expected to decline steadily from 4 per cent of GDP in 1995–96 to balance at the end of 1999–2000 (see the figure in Wolf (1996) which depicts the ever-changing forecasts of the PSBR). It should be borne in mind that the redefinition of GGE (X) in 1995 helped to curb forecast expenditure; that capital expenditure during financial years 1995–99 was reduced in the 1995 Budget from £55.6 billion to £47.1 billion, on the grounds that it would largely be replaced by the Private Finance Initiative; and that the National Lottery contributed £1.2 billion in receipts in 1995–96. Despite this, the latest forecasts for the PSBR may yet again prove to be over-optimistic since tax revenues may fall below expectations (and, indeed, the Treasury is currently trying to fathom out why VAT receipts are so far below forecast – see *Financial Times*, 15 April 1996) unless economic growth picks up significantly, so unofficial forecasts for 1996–97 are already creeping up towards £30 billion.

There can be no doubt that the turnaround from massive and apparently uncontrollable PSBRs in the 1970s to PSDRs in the late 1980s was an achievement worthy of note. Indeed, merely in achieving a PSDR the UK could be compared only with Japan among the major industrialised nations. Unfortunately, the PSDR has proved to be a transitory phenomenon in the UK, as shown in **Table 8.7**, and indeed for those smaller EU economies such as Denmark which also achieved a PSDR in the late 1980s. In 1990–91 the UK fiscal books were in balance, but only if privatisation proceeds were included. However, with the onset of recession the situation deteriorated alarmingly, with a PSBR of approximately 7 per cent of GDP in 1993–94. The deterioration in the fiscal outlook between 1988–89 and 1993–94 was equivalent to the better part of 10 per cent of GDP, and as such was the worst by far of any EU country. However, the situation also deteriorated badly in Spain, France and Portugal after 1989, and in Austria, Luxembourg and Finland after 1990, and the PSBR remains much higher in Italy, Greece and Sweden. The UK is still set to do better than the EU average even in 1997. Although the USA has been heavily criticised for the size of its PSBR, it has to be said that it has invariably out-performed the EU average. Indeed, it is cur-

Table 8.7   *General Government Lending (+) or Borrowing (−) as a % of GDP, 1974–97*

	1970–73	1974–84	1986–90	1991–93	1994–97	1992	1993	1994	1995	1996	1997
B	−3.8	−8.2	−7.2	−6.8	−4.1	−7.1	−6.7[3]	−5.3[3]	−4.5	−3.1	−3.5
DK	4.3	−2.8	0.9	−3.2	−1.9	−2.9	−4.5	−3.8	−2.0	−1.3	−0.5
D	0.2	−2.8	−1.5	−3.2	−2.7	−2.8	−3.5	−2.6	−2.9[4]	−2.8	−2.4
GR	−	−	−13.0	−11.7	−9.1	−11.7	−12.1	−11.4	−9.3	−8.3	−7.3
E	0.4	−2.8	−3.8	−5.5	−5.2	−4.2	−7.5	−6.6	−5.9	−4.7	−3.6
F	0.7	−1.7	−1.8	−4.1	−4.5	−4.0	−6.1	−6.0	−5.0	−3.9	−2.9
IRL	−4.1	−10.5	−5.5	−2.3	−2.0	−2.4	−2.4	−2.1	−2.7	−2.0	−1.3
I	−5.4	−9.6	−10.8	−9.8	−6.9	−9.5	−9.6	−9.0	−7.4	−6.0	−5.2
L	2.7	1.9	−	1.5	1.0	0.8	1.8	2.2	0.4	0.6	0.7
NL	−0.5	−3.9	−5.1	−3.3	−2.8	−3.9	−3.2	−3.2	−3.1	−2.7	−2.2
A	1.5	−2.4	−3.2	−2.9	−4.9	−2.0	−4.1	−4.4	−5.5	−5.0	−4.6
P	1.9	−	−4.7	−5.7	−5.0	−3.3	−7.1	−5.8	−5.4	−4.7	−4.1
FIN	4.6	3.7	4.0	−5.1	−3.2	−5.9	−8.0	−5.8	−5.4	−1.5	0.0
S	4.5	−1.7	3.2	−7.4	−6.3	−7.8	−13.4	−10.4	−7.0	−4.5	−3.2
UK	−0.4	−3.7	−1.1	−5.5	−4.6	−6.1	−7.8	−6.8	−5.1	−3.7	−2.8
EUR	−0.7[1]	−4.0[2]	−3.7	−5.3	−4.3	−5.1	−6.3	−5.5	−4.7	−3.8	−3.1
USA	−0.7	−1.9	−2.4	−3.7	−1.8	−4.3	−3.4	−2.0	−1.6	−1.9	−1.8
JAP	0.8	−3.2	1.3	1.0	−2.7	1.5	−1.4	−2.4	−2.7	−3.1	−2.6

Notes:
[1] EUR without Greece.
[2] EUR without Greece and Portugal.
[3] The figures for 1993 and 1994 include the proceeds from the sale of participations, indirectly owned by the public sector. The amounts involved are BFR 32.2 bn in 1993 and 12.7 bn in 1994.
[4] Not including unification-related debt assumptions by the federal government in 1995 (Treuhand and eastern housing companies) equal to 236 bn DM.

Source: European Economy, Supplement A (January 1996).

rently Japan that is fast sliding into the kind of fiscal morass well known to many EU countries, especially if the funds that are channelled into public investment through the Fiscal Investment and Loan Programme are taken into account.

A further comment concerns the so-called 'golden rule', which states that public-sector deficits should not exceed capital formation. Despite the difficulties inherent in valuing the latter concept, it appears this rule was satisfied during the late 1980s, but not during the early 1980s and early 1990s. It should be satisfied again in 1996–97, all being well, and in subsequent years. This suggests that public sector finances have operated in a sensibly counter-cyclical manner and that this is set to continue, although a change of govern-

ment might affect that forecast. In the longer term, all those unfunded pension liabilities need to be taken into account, and permanent budget surpluses may become necessary, but for the time being the situation appears to be reasonably under control.

Finally, what if the Labour Party is elected in 1997? Understandably, Labour has so far avoided saying anything specific at all, restricting itself to imprecise generalities such as that it will introduce a higher rate for high income earners (see, for example, the discussion in *The Times*, 27 April 1996, p. 27) and then denying it. At the end of the day, either there is more economic growth or there is not. If there is, the PSBR will shrink, and if not, it won't. If there was a magic ingredient for growth, every government would be using it, so it is safe to assume that Labour do not have one. Do not, therefore, expect the PSBR to be much different irrespective of who is elected in 1997.

■ *8.11* The National Debt

It is of some importance to remember that the first claim on tax revenue is **interest on the national debt**. Were there to be no such debt, public spending on real goods and services could be increased by £20 billion each year without any need to raise further taxes. While this may currently appear to be a pipe-dream, there was much discussion of such an outcome as a result of the succession of debt repayments at the end of the 1980s.

The ability to repay debt exists provided there is an excess of taxation over expenditure adjusted

for privatisation proceeds. This, as we have seen, occurred during the financial years 1987–88 to 1990–91 inclusive, and although the government was not obliged to use the surplus to repay the debt, it chose to do so, thereby expunging well over £20 billion of debt in 1988–89 and 1989–90 alone. At the beginning of the fiscal year 1991–92, the outstanding **net** debt was accordingly worth a 'mere' £150 billion. It is also possible to treat total debt in its **gross** form, in which case the equivalent figure was £190 billion. The transformation from gross to net debt requires the deduction of liquid assets held by the public sector, of which well over one half is currently in the form of gold and foreign exchange reserves.

It has been claimed that the national debt is in reality nearly twice as large as is officially admitted. This arises because certain public sector pension schemes are notionally rather than actually funded. The government borrows the excess of pension contributions over expenditure and

Figure 8.5   *Public Sector Debt as % Money GDP[1]*

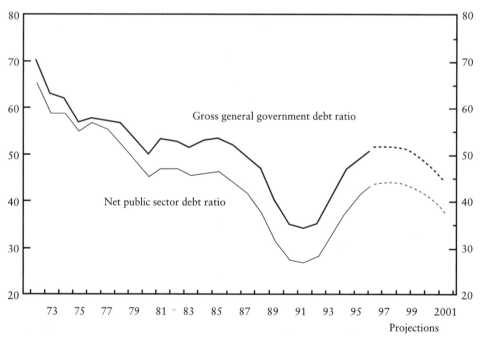

Notes:
[1] At end-March as a per cent of money GDP in four quarters centred on end-March.
FSBR 1996–97, Chart 4.2.

dummy gilt-edged securities are created (but not actually issued). This, it is alleged, is the national accounts equivalent of off-balance-sheet borrowing by corporations.

With this proviso in mind, we will continue the analysis using the official figures. The gross government debt, expressed as a percentage of GDP, is set out in **Figure 8.5** over the period from 1971 to 1999. During the 1970s, the high rate of inflation meant that the inflation-adjusted value of the outstanding debt fell rapidly. In 1985–86, prior to the first PSDR, the ratio was 54.5 per cent, roughly the same it had been at the turn of the 1980s. By the beginning of the 1990s, debt repayments plus inflation had changed the situation dramatically, with the result that the ratio had fallen by almost a further 20 per cent. The recession, which reduced GDP, taken in conjunction with the return of substantial PSBRs, has caused the ratio to rise back to 50 per cent. Provided the PSBR does not

exceed 2 per cent in future years, the ratio will stabilise at roughly this level, and if the PSBR is eliminated, the ratio will fall back somewhat.

It is enlightening to compare the UK's experience during this period with that of other EU countries on the basis of the figures for gross public debt as a percentage of GDP as shown in **Table 8.8**. Over the 20-year period beginning in 1970, only two EU countries managed to reduce this ratio, namely the UK and Luxembourg. In the latter case it started out relatively low, whereas the ratio for the UK was the highest in the EU in 1970. By 1990, the UK ratio had halved, whereas the EU average had risen by one half and that for West Germany had more than doubled. At this point only Luxembourg in the then EU had a lower ratio than the UK, while by 1993 the ratios for Belgium, Italy and Greece had all risen well above 100 per cent as a consequence of the string of massive borrowing requirements shown in

Table 8.8   *Government Gross Debt as a percentage of GDP, 1980–97*[1]

	1980	1985	1989	1990	1991	1992	1993	1994	1995	1996	1997
B	78.8	123.1	130.9	130.9	130.3	131.1	137.5	135.0	134.4	132.3	130.0
DK[2]	–	72.0	59.5	59.6	64.6	69.0	80.3	75.6	73.6	72.7	70.5
D	–	–	–	43.8	41.5	44.1	48.2	50.2	58.8	59.5	59.3
GR	–	–	–	82.6	85.4	91.6	114.5	113.0	114.4	114.0	113.1
E	17.5	43.7	43.2	45.1	45.8	48.4	60.4	63.0	64.8	65.8	65.4
F	20.1	31.0	34.4	35.4	35.8	39.6	45.3	48.4	51.5	53.4	54.2
IRL	–	–	–	96.5	96.7	94.3	97.4	91.1	85.9	81.3	76.9
I	57.8	82.3	95.6	97.9	101.3	108.4	119.4	125.4	124.9	123.9	122.3
L	–	–	–	4.6	4.1	5.1	6.3	5.9	6.3	6.7	6.8
NL	47.6	71.5	79.1	78.8	78.8	79.6	81.3	78.0	78.4	78.2	77.8
A	37.3	50.5	58.9	58.3	58.6	58.3	63.0	65.2	68.0	69.9	71.5
P	–	–	–	68.6	70.2	62.4	67.2	69.4	70.5	71.0	70.9
FIN	11.8	16.5	15.0	14.5	23.0	41.5	57.3	59.8	63.2	64.6	64.5
S	41.0	63.8	45.5	43.5	53.0	67.1	76.2	79.7	81.4	80.8	79.8
UK	–	–	–	–	35.7	41.9	48.6	50.1	52.5	53.3	53.2
EUR[3]	37.3	58.2	62.2	58.7	56.0	60.3	66.2	68.1	71.0	71.6	71.3

Notes:
[1] As defined by the Council Regulation n° 3605/93 on the excessive deficit procedure.
[2] Government deposits with the central bank, government holdings of non-government bonds and public enterprise related debt amounted to some 23% of GDP in 1994.
[3] Aggregated with the available country data which are incomplete until 1991.

Source: European Economy, Supplement A (January 1996).

Table 8.7. The debt/GDP ratio in the UK turned up sharply in 1992, but the current level of 53 per cent still means that it remains the lowest in the EU (bar Luxembourg) at almost twenty per cent below the EU average.

The precise implications of the trend in the absolute size of the debt for **debt interest payments** is complicated by such matters as interest rate volatility and the effects of inflation on index-linked debt. The enormous improvement over the 1980s, high interest rates notwithstanding, was especially notable, but the upturn in the early 1990s, shown in **Table 8.7**, has given some cause for concern, although it will hopefully stabilise in coming years.

In that respect, it is fortunate that interest rates are somewhat lower than they were, since the problem can rapidly spiral out of control. This is due to the fact that the gross debt and its associated interest charge need to be rolled over from year to year. Each year's interest charge gets added to the gross debt of that year, and in the following year interest would have to be paid on the previous year's interest unless the gross debt has itself been reduced in the meantime by running a budget surplus. In the case of Belgium, Italy and Greece, where a string of deficits has added greatly to the gross debt for many years past, this has caused annual debt interest payments to escalate to 8.5, 10.8 and 13.5 per cent of GDP respectively. This can be compared with the 2.5 per cent for the UK in 1996, the same as when the Conservatives were first elected and the 5.0 per cent figure for Europe as a whole.

A further issue concerns the financing of the National Debt, particularly if the financial markets have lost faith in the government's determination to control the PSBR. For example, the total additional amount to be financed in 1993–94 was £50 billion, to which needed to be added the refinancing of all the debt that matured during the year as well as any underlying increase in the foreign exchange reserves. As a consequence of the growing deficit, the government was obliged to announce a change in its policy of **fully funding** this aggregate (that is, the sale of debt instruments equal in value to this) as part of the 1992 Autumn Statement.

The rationale for fully funding government borrowing is to ensure that it is financed in a non-inflationary way, and this was long interpreted to require sales of securities exclusively to the non-bank private sector (that is, the transfer of existing privately-held cash deposits to the Treasury in return). Under the new regime sales of securities (but excluding Treasury bills) to banks and building societies count as funding, although full funding is to remain the order of the day (that is, there is still to be no printing of new money by the authorities to pay its bills).

In principle, an enormous increase in the scale of funding should result in a sharp upturn in interest rates in order to attract buyers, but this has not occurred in the UK (nor has it in the USA where the absolute amounts borrowed are much larger). Indeed, interest rates are currently low by the standards of the 1980s, at least in nominal terms although they are positive in inflation-adjusted terms. Concern was expressed about the ease with which buyers could be found for UK government securities under these circumstances. The initial auctions in 1993 were successful, although the ratio of the amount bid to the amount on offer was extremely low by historical standards. Since then, the situation has eased somewhat. What is clear is that the need to finance the PSBR is seen as placing a floor below which interest rates cannot readily be driven, especially if they are rising in other EU countries.

Bibliography

Alesina, A. and R. Perotti (1995) 'The Political Economy of Budget Deficits', *IMF Staff Papers*, 42 (1).

Chote, R. (1996) 'Costs of Social Transfers', *Financial Times* (15 January).

Cmnd 1432 (1961) *Control of Public Spending* (London: HMSO).

Cmnd 9714 (1986) *Paying for Local Government* (London: HMSO).

Cm 441 (1988) *A New Public Expenditure Planning Total* (London: HMSO).

Cm 1867 (1992) *Budgetary Reform* (London: HMSO).

Denby, S. (1995) 'The Net Debt of the Public Sector: End-March 1995', *Bank of England Quarterly Bulletin*.

Dilnot, A. and M. Robson (1993) 'The UK Moves from March to December Budgets', *Fiscal Studies*, 14 (1).

HC 30 (1995) *Financial Statement and Budget Report 1996–97* (London: HMSO).

Jackson, P. (1990) 'Reflections on the Growth of Public Expenditure', *British Review of Economic Issues* (June).

Levitt, M. and M. Joyce (1987) *The Growth and Efficiency of Public Spending* (London: NIESR).

Ritchie, A. and D. Lawton (1993) 'The Definition of the PSBR', *Economic Trends*, 479 (September).

Skidelsky, A. (1996) 'Public Spending is a Matter for the Public to Decide', *The Times* (8 February)

The Economist (1996a) 'It's Not What You Do' (20 January) p. 94.

The Economist (1996b) 'The Burdensome National Debt' (10 February).

The Economist (1996c) 'Into the Clouds Again' (11 May) pp. 25–26.

Wolf, M. (1996) 'The Fiscal Trap for Labour', *Financial Times* (9 July) p. 14.

Chapter 9

The Balance of Payments

Peter Curwen

■ *9.1* Introduction

There are enormous differences in the extent to which individual nations are dependent upon transactions with the outside world. The UK has always been an 'open' economy, both importing and exporting on a massive scale. Superficially, this may simply be seen to reflect the difficulties which any nation the size of the UK must inevitably face in trying to be self-sufficient across the whole range of goods and services. However, it is important to note both that the UK's degree of openness has been increasing steadily over the past several decades (as has also been true elsewhere in the EU), and that external transactions increasingly involve one-way flows of capital which are unrelated to the immediate consumption requirements of UK residents.

In recent years the value of both imports and exports has grown to exceed 30 per cent of the UK's GDP, and it is obvious that these trade flows impact significantly upon the UK's industrial structure, the level of employment, the standard of living of UK nationals and so on. In other words, the **internal and external sectors are inex**tricably linked, and it is impossible to control internal macroeconomic objectives such as the level of employment and the rate of inflation without taking into account their links with the external sector. Indeed, as we shall see, much of the postwar history of UK macroeconomic policy can be viewed in terms of a struggle **to find acceptable trade-offs between the internal and external objectives of policy.**

Economic policy is frequently focused upon the **balance of payments**, and our first task is, therefore, to set out the accounting system used to measure it, and to explain how policy objectives are expressed in relation to these accounts. The other central task is to examine the primary instrument used to achieve this objective, namely the **exchange rate**. However, as we will discover, these apparently straightforward tasks are in practice greatly complicated by the need to take account of other related policy objectives and instruments, of the behaviour of other countries insofar as it impinges upon the UK, of international institutions and of the whole plethora of arrangements which govern the conduct of the world economy.

9.2 The System of Balance of Payments Accounts

9.2.1 Recording Transactions

The Balance of Payments (BoP) may be defined as a **systematic record, over a given period of time, of all transactions between residents and non-residents of the UK**. The term 'resident' covers both individuals living permanently in the UK and corporate bodies located therein, but not their overseas branches and subsidiaries. It also includes government agencies and military forces located abroad. 'Permanent' residence is determined by the intention to remain in the UK for at least one full year.

The object of the accounting system is to record these transactions in a format that is suitable for analysing the economic relations between the UK economy and the rest of the world. The transactions may represent **resources** provided by or to UK residents (imports and exports of goods and services, and the use of investments); **changes** in the UK's **foreign assets or liabilities**; or **transfer payments**.

In principle, transactions are recorded when the ownership of goods or assets changes and when services are rendered. In practice, however, trade flows are recorded on a **shipments basis**, and the payments which match these shipments are not only almost invariably delayed, but the length of this delay is quite erratic from one period to another. In the longer term all the shipments and monetary flows can be matched up, but the short-term picture is almost inevitably quite heavily distorted. This is important because, first, both foreign exchange markets – and indeed sometimes the government – respond in a volatile way to monthly or quarterly BoP statistics and, secondly, because the annual accounts are constantly being adjusted retrospectively to a degree that can turn surpluses into deficits or vice versa. In other words, the short-term picture can conflict with the longer-term perspective, yet by the time the latter is visible it is too late to take appropriate action.

A further element of ambiguity is introduced by the need to **convert currencies**. The general rule in international trade is that the exporter dictates the form in which payment is made – which, in the case of a developed nation like the UK, is mostly in its own currency. A much smaller proportion of UK imports will also be paid for in sterling. All non-sterling payments must then be converted into sterling at the ruling exchange rates, but these may fluctuate enormously during the course of a financial year, with the result that the valuation of imports and exports can be influenced by the **precise timing of currency conversion**.

9.2.2 Double-entry Accounting

The BoP accounts are, like any accounting system, constructed according to the **double-entry principle**. Every transaction involves equal credit and debit entries but, instead of arranging these in separate columns, all BoP entries are arranged in a single column, and given different signs so that they sum to zero. It is therefore the case that the BoP accounts **must balance by definition**. This should not, however, be confused with the concept of **equilibrium**, which is discussed below. This method accommodates account items which are generally recorded only on a **net** basis.

Under the conventions of the accounts, all credit items are entered with a **plus (+) sign**. The credit relates to the **flow of currency** and not to the flow of resources. If resources are provided in the form of exports of goods or services, then the corresponding payment in currency **flows into the UK** and is recorded with a plus sign in the accounts. Where resources are provided to UK residents – for example, as imports of goods or services – payment **flows out of the UK** and is recorded with a **minus (−) sign** in the accounts.

Every positive entry must, as indicated, have its matching negative entry, but this may appear in a variety of forms. For example, an export of goods can be matched by either (**a**) an increase in the foreign assets owned by UK residents (where the export receipts are, for example, deposited in a bank outside the UK); (**b**) a reduction in non-residents' holdings of sterling in the UK (which are transferred to the exporter's bank account); or (**c**) a direct exchange for imports of equal value (barter trade). It is undoubtedly rather confusing, at first, to regard an **increase in foreign assets** as a **negative** item in the accounts, but it makes sense in terms of identifying **where the currency goes**. The above example works exactly in reverse where one starts with a negative entry for an import of goods.

In order to make things somewhat easier to follow, the BoP accounts are currently divided into two halves. The accounts have been recalculated in this format going back as far as is necessary for the purpose of this book, but it should be recognised that variants of the accounts published before 1987 are in the original format which is difficult to match up with the new and should, therefore, no longer be used. This division was introduced in order to bring the UK BoP accounts broadly into line with the fourth edition of the International Monetary Fund's Balance of Payments Manual (BPM). A fifth edition was published in 1993, and this was linked to the revised version of the United Nations System of National Accounts (SNA), published in February 1994, which is very similar to the structure of the European System of Accounts (ESA) on which the UK national accounts are themselves broadly based.

The explicit link between the BPM and SNA is designed to emphasise the fact that the BoP is part of a wider system of national accounts (see Lakin, 1994). The main changes in presentation required by the revised BPM include:

- Redefinition of the current account to exclude items of a capital nature and the introduction of a capital and financial account.
- The new capital account will contain some elements previously included in the current account such as capital transfers.
- The creation of the financial account nevertheless will remain broadly similar to the previous capital account.
- A clearer distinction between economic categories, especially between services and income and a much extended analysis of services.
- An extended and restructured analysis of financial flows.
- Introduction of a reconciliation account to show how changes in stocks (balance sheets)

are related to financial transactions by identifying valuation and other changes.

The EU is planning to make legal provision requiring data in the form of the new ESA (including the effect of the new BPM) in 1998, in respect of periods from 1995, the final full year covered in what follows. These changes will be incorporated into the next edition, but in the meantime the format remains unchanged from the previous edition.

In this format, the upper half of the accounts is called the **current account**. In this are to be found transactions covering exports and imports of goods and services, investment income, and transfers. The lower half of the accounts is called **transactions in UK external assets and liabilities**. In this are to be found inward and outward investment; external transactions by banks in the UK; borrowing and lending overseas by other UK residents; drawings on and additions to the official reserves; and other capital transactions. For simplicity this will be referred to as the **capital account**.

Where there is a positive entry in the current account – arising, for example from the export of goods – the corresponding negative entry is, as indicated above, normally to be found in the capital account as in (a) or (b) above. However, it must also be noted that corresponding plus and minus entries may both appear in the capital account, as would be the case if a UK resident borrowed from a bank in France in order to buy shares in a French company. An interesting illustration of this phenomenon is Japan in the 1980s where, despite a substantial current account surplus, large sums were borrowed from abroad in order to finance overseas investment.

It is also necessary to remind ourselves about the difficulties of estimation with respect to items in the BoP accounts because, as previously noted, the accounts must balance as a matter of definition. The two entries made in respect of each transaction are generally derived from separate sources, and the methods of estimation are neither complete nor precisely accurate. As a consequence, the two entries either may not match precisely, and/or may fall within different recording periods. It is also possible that two entries, both in the same foreign currency, have been converted at different exchange rates. Hence, when all the entries in the accounts are added together, they never actually do sum to zero, and in order to make them do so the **balancing item** has to be added at the foot of the accounts.

9.3 The Structure of the UK Visible Trade Accounts

□ 9.3.1 The Current Account

The full set of accounts is set out for the period of 1987 to 1995 in **Table 9.1**, omitting certain intermediate years. The first part of the accounts covers exports and imports of goods, and the **net** figure was traditionally called the **visible balance** or, more commonly, the **balance of trade**. As of June 1996, the term 'visibles' has been replaced by **goods** (see *Financial Times*, 27 June 1996). Note that both exports and imports are entered as positive amounts, but the net figure is plus or minus as appropriate. The data for trade in goods within the EU are compiled according to the Intrastat system (see Williamson and Porter, 1994).

The next entry relates to credits and debits generated by trade in services, which are again entered as positive amounts with the net figure, traditionally called the **invisibles balance** (but henceforth apparently a term to be avoided as it downplays the individual sectors by emphasising their 'invisibility'), signed as appropriate. This net balance would then be broken down into its three component parts – services (primarily sea transport, civil aviation, tourism and financial); investment income (formerly interest, profits and dividends); and transfers (primarily central government grants to overseas countries and contributions to the EU Budget and to international organisations, and private transfers of assets by migrants). It should be noted that only the services part of the invisibles balance arises from trading, while the larger part arises as a result of movements of money.

The change in terminology is an irritation which is allegedly designed to improve presentation rather than to lead to a massaging of the data, and as with the capital account, the old terminology will probably persevere in practice and will continue to be used in the text which follows.

The sum of the visible and invisibles balances, signed as appropriate, is called the **current balance**. Adjustments to the current balance usually occur as a result of changes in national income both at home and abroad, the proportion of it which is spent, and the proportion of that spending which goes on domestic as against overseas goods and services. A sharp deterioration in the current balance is usually taken to indicate an upturn in consumption (either private or public) which has spilled over into imports, but an alternative, and more beneficial, interpretation is that it indicates the importation of capital goods for investment by UK companies to improve their productive capacity. Unfortunately, it is very difficult for analytical purposes to distinguish in the short term between these interpretations.

□ 9.3.2 The Capital Account

The rest of the accounts can be distinguished by virtue of the fact that **no goods and services flow in the opposite direction to the flows of currency**. What are being acquired are foreign assets such as shares and securities. When such flows of currency are recorded, they can be attributed to a number of basic influences. The first, of critical importance in recent years, is the **structure of interest rates** in the UK compared to that overseas. If interest rates are higher in the UK than elsewhere, after adjusting for any risk of default, currency will tend to flow into the UK in very large amounts. For the most part, such currency flows will be **short-term** (colloquially called **hot money**). The second influence is the **rate of return on investment**. If a UK company takes over a foreign company, it does so in the belief that the investment will yield a higher rate of return than would result from the takeover of another UK

Table 9.1   *UK BoP Accounts, Selected Years 1987–95 (£ m)*

	1987	1989	1991	1993	1994	1995
CURRENT ACCOUNT						
Visible trade						
Exports (fob)	79 153	92 154	103 413	121 398	134 666	152 346
Imports (fob)	90 735	116 837	113 697	134 858	145 497	163 974
Visible balance	−11 582	−24 683	−10 284	−13 460	−10 831	−11 628
Invisibles						
Credits	79 194	107 203	114 692	118 278	124 936	146 528
Debits	72 425	104 918	112 311	115 572	116 525	135 792
Invisibles balance	6 769	2 285	2 331	2 706	8 411	8 736
of which:						
Services balance	6 242	3 361	3 564	5 516	4 747	6 142
Investment income balance	3 927	3 502	150	2 197	8 691	9 572
Transfers balance	−3 400	−4 578	−1 383	−5 007	−5 027	−6 978
Current balance	−4 813	−22 398	−7 953	−10 754	−2 420	−2 892
TRANSACTIONS IN EXTERNAL ASSETS AND LIABILITIES						
Investment overseas by UK residents						
Direct	−19 147	−21 503	−9 056	−17 026	−18 363	−25 546
Portfolio	5 324	−36 524	−29 157	−84 828	17 968	−40 327
Total UK investment overseas	−13 823	−58 027	−38 213	−101 854	−395	−65 873
Investment in the UK by overseas residents						
Direct	9 449	18 567	9 058	10 298	6 823	20 480
Portfolio	22 233	14 647	17 024	45 466	32 609	16 859
Total overseas investment in the UK	31 682	33 214	26 082	55 764	39 432	37 339
Foreign currency lending abroad by UK banks	−45 909	−26 217	27 729	12 939	−49 967	−24 145
Foreign currency borrowing abroad by UK banks	43 668	33 369	−13 590	22 842	41 237	28 797
Net foreign currency transactions of UK banks	−2 241	7 152	14 139	35 781	−8 370	4 652
Sterling lending abroad by UK banks	−4 613	−2 909	4 840	−8 263	308	−2 733
Sterling borrowing and deposit liabilities abroad of UK banks	8 784	12 152	−9 412	390	6 342	7 542
Net sterling transactions of UK banks	4 171	9 243	−4 572	−7 873	6 650	4 809
Deposits with and lending to banks abroad by UK non-bank private sector	−5 291	−9 466	−4 661	−8 812	−10 902	−11 096
Borrowing from banks abroad by:						
UK non-bank private sector	2 613	7 931	13 750	12 286	−1 389	18 932
Public corporations	−166	−1 726	−53	−24	−118	−151
General government	105	529	−65	−2 944	−133	−97
Official reserves (additions to −, drawings on +)	−12 012	5 440	−2 679	−698	−1 045	200
Other external assets of:						
UK non-bank private sector and public corporations	−278	1 384	−4 805	−48 314	27 473	−19 761
General government	−796	−873	−894	−609	−619	−637
Other external liabilities of:						
UK non-bank private sector and public corporations	1 627	21 178	11 707	80 296	−53 507	30 316
General government	1 818	2 198	−2 292	80	633	1 812
Net transactions in assets and liabilities	7 410	18 176	7 445	13 080	−2 650	446
Balancing item	−2 597	4 222	508	−2 326	5 070	2 446

Source: UK Balance of Payments 1996, Tables 1.3 and 1.7.

company. Equally, private investors in the UK will buy shares in foreign companies if they believe that the dividend yield and/or the prospect of capital gains is better than that to be achieved in the UK. These currency flows are mostly **long-term**. If interest rates are relatively low in the UK, or rates of return in the UK are relatively low, the flows will operate in the reverse direction.

It should be noted that the distinction between short-term and long-term capital flows is much easier to establish in principle than it is in practice. The capital account is not divided up specifically to illustrate this distinction, and we will accordingly be using the term 'hot money' to refer to highly mobile international capital.

The third influence is the **exchange rate**. All capital flows must take place in a particular currency, the value of which can vary quite considerably over time. While long-term investment is not much affected by this influence, given that exchange rate movements in the longer term are impossible to predict and that the investor can anyway hedge against changes in currency value, speculative flows are a different matter. Even where the interest rate on offer is higher than in other financial centres, a financial asset, denominated in a currency the value of which is expected to rise sharply, will prove popular even if its yield is very poor, as this will be more than compensated by the prospect of a capital gain in the asset. This proposition is developed in more detail on **p. 250**.

Direct investment primarily comprises net investment by overseas companies in their UK affiliates including the reinvestment of retained profits, and by UK companies in their overseas branches, subsidiaries and associates.

Portfolio investment by UK residents comprises net purchases and sales of overseas government, municipal and company securities, while portfolio investment in the UK primarily comprises net purchases and sales of UK company securities and government stocks. These flows clearly affect the **net asset/liability position** of the UK relative to the rest of the world. In principle, one simply adds or subtracts the net annual change to the existing cumulative net value of assets, but in addition there may be capital gains and losses arising from, for example, changes in share prices which cannot show up in the BoP accounts until such time as an asset is sold.

Net foreign currency transactions of UK banks consist of changes in deposits of foreign currencies made with UK resident banks by non-residents, and loans by the banks in those currencies to non-residents. **Net sterling transactions** of UK banks consist of sterling advances and overdrafts (net of repayments) provided to overseas residents (including banks abroad) by UK banks, sterling commercial bills discounted, acceptances, and sterling borrowing and deposit liabilities abroad.

Deposits with, and lending to, banks abroad by the UK non-bank private sector consist of UK residents' deposits with banks in the Bank for International Settlements (BIS) reporting area together with assets held in the custody of banks in the USA. **Borrowing from banks abroad** predominantly covers borrowing from commercial banks in the BIS reporting area, the European Investment Bank and the United States Export-Import Bank.

We come next to changes in the **official reserves**, which are analysed in more detail below. Other external assets include identified trade credit between unrelated companies, inter- governmental loans by the UK and subscriptions to international lending bodies, while other external liabilities include broadly the same items. The balancing item has already been discussed above.

■ 9.4 The Accounts in Retrospect

In taking a retrospective view of the BoP accounts it is clearly not practicable to operate at the detailed disaggregated level presented in **Table 9.1**, except insofar as it is needed to shed light on the peculiarities of recent policy in relation to the external sector. **Table 9.4**, which covers the period commencing soon after the Conservative government's election and its full period in office, accordingly treats transactions on external assets and liabilities only in the aggregate. This accords with the customary presentation of the accounts in the media.

9.4.1 The Meaning of Equilibrium

Before proceeding we need firstly to consider the meaning of the term 'equilibrium' in the context of the accounts. As we have explained, the accounts as a whole must balance by definition, but to achieve that it is not necessary for any individual component of the accounts, for example the current balance, to have a zero value. The main issue accordingly is how best to express the objective of policy concerning the balance of payments. The messages sent out about the state of the economy by the current and capital accounts are rather different, and the focus of concern about the accounts has always been upon the **current balance**. It is, therefore, often argued that this should be in equilibrium in the sense that it should have a value of zero.

However, given that the UK has historically been predominantly a manufacturing nation, it is sometimes argued that attention should be focused more narrowly upon the **visible balance**, more commonly referred to as the **balance of trade**, and that this should be kept in equilibrium with the value of zero.

Occasionally, reference is made to the **basic balance**, which is the sum of the current balance plus the balance of long-term capital flows (that is, it excludes hot money). It can be argued that hot money merely 'accommodates' the basic balance, which thus gives a true insight into the current and longer-term prosperity of the trading sector. However, as we have noted, the basic balance cannot be estimated accurately because of the difficulty of separating out the short-term from the long-term capital flows.

The first important lesson from the above is that when the word 'equilibrium' is encountered, it requires one to look carefully to see to which part of the accounts it is being applied. In the second place, there is clearly a time dimension to the issue. The current balance might sum to zero over a period of years, and hence yield an equilibrium, albeit possibly more by chance than by design. This may be preferable to the requirement that it be in equilibrium over a period of months,

or in any given year, since it will allow for cyclical adjustments and the problems of data collection discussed above. But unless a government is prepared to state in advance that it is pursuing a set of policies intended to achieve equilibrium within a specified period, the fact that it can retrospectively identify such an equilibrium cannot be said to prove anything one way or another about its policies.

In any event, the whole issue is clouded by the choice of a particular exchange rate regime. Without discussing this in detail here as it is covered below, the essential point is that it is possible to choose a regime which will, other than in the very short term, keep the visible balance in equilibrium. However, it will not keep the other components of the accounts in equilibrium, and there are also likely to be conflicts with other objectives of policy which rule out this approach to the achievement of equilibrium.

9.4.2 The Balancing Item

The balancing item is a very volatile item in the accounts. Some part of it will be permanent insofar as, for example, the data collection system consistently fails to record certain transactions. Other parts will be erratic and arise because, for example, the data collection system either becomes able to record transactions in the capital account which could not previously be attributed to any of its headings, and therefore had to be lumped into the balancing item, or cease to be able to do so, with the reverse effect. Large balancing items (whether plus or minus) have been a feature of the 1980s in the accounts. This is partly because, since 1982, a substantial proportion of trade credit between unrelated companies, required to bridge the gap between the time goods are shipped and the settlement of the invoice, has been switched from the capital account to the balancing item. Furthermore, in 1986, the high level of capital flows during the period leading up to and following 'Big Bang', created difficulties of attribution to appropriate headings in the capital account.

Hopes that the balancing item would settle down, as it did in 1987, have unfortunately been confounded. This is more important that it seems because, if the balancing item is large, and if it is not known whether it is created by under- or over-recording in the current account, it is difficult to know how seriously to take the recorded data.

Since 1975 the balancing item has been positive in every year except 1982, 1987 and, possibly temporarily, 1993. A positive balancing item implies either unrecorded net credits in the current account or unrecorded net inflows in the capital account or both. In practice, the balancing item is highly volatile on a quarterly basis (see Bank of England, 1990, p. 497), and individual quarters have been as large as +£10 billion and -£5 billion in recent years. Nevertheless, the Bank of England considers that of late the under-recording of inflows has become a structural problem. Transfers from the balancing item to portfolio inflows in the accounts have ameliorated the situation somewhat (the cumulative balancing item was, at the time, shown as £35 billion for 1986–88), but it remains unclear exactly where the problem lies.

The Bank believes that the recording of visible trade should be highly accurate, although anyone who has cause to examine trade data at a disaggregated level is fairly sure to believe to the contrary. It believes that there are problems with data on services, but does not see how these errors could account for more than a small part of the overall balancing item. Hence, 'it seems likely that the explanation for the majority of the balancing item lies in the capital account' (Bank of England, 1990, p. 498). In particular, the Bank considers that 'the bulk of omission may be in portfolio inflows'. It is particularly notable that the £7.3 billion balancing item which appeared in the previous edition for 1990 was reduced to £1.2 billion with an offsetting addition of £7.2 billion to net transactions, although it has doubled again since then.

There is an additional factor to consider. Taking the world as a whole, while as a matter of simple definition total world exports must equal total world imports, they fall short in practice by a wide margin. It therefore follows that in many parts of the world exports are significantly under-recorded. The situation is fluid because the discrepancy for a given year tends to decline over time as the data are improved, but imbalances remain large.

The International Monetary Fund indicate where they believe the problem arises, and in recent years their preference has been to attribute it to under-recorded investment flows in industrial countries. The official version of events thus has it that the balancing item consists of under-recorded capital account **inflows** and, taking the IMF line, that missing world exports are predominantly not of goods but of services and anyway do not originate at all from the UK. If they are right then this has serious implications for the value of the UK's net overseas assets. The sceptics' view, on the other hand, is that a significant part of the balancing item is unrecorded exports of goods and services, and that these also exist for the UK as part of the black hole in the world's trading accounts. If the sceptics are right then the trading account is healthier than it appears to be.

In many ways, the most surprising aspect of the above debate is that both politicians and currency dealers set so much store by the monthly data on the balance of payments which should clearly carry a government warning concerning their use (and abuse). This does not arise solely because of the constant process of re-attribution from the balancing item to other items in the accounts, but also because of the acknowledged misrecording of both current account and capital account flows.

9.4.3 Index Numbers of UK Visible Trade

It must be recognised that when one has become used to regarding a current account deficit of £10 billion as giving cause for concern, there is a tendency to be dismissive of historic deficits of a 'mere' £1 billion, let alone those of £100 million. Yet these figures, in their historic context, were regarded with equal dismay because of their size in relation to the then value of GDP. The escalation in the numbers partly reflects the effects of economic growth, but primarily those of continuous – and in many individual years very rapid – inflation. It is possible to give a general impression of the relative effects of growth and inflation by the use of index numbers, as in **Table 9.2**.

The **volume** index for visible exports rose by roughly 60 per cent between 1970 and 1980, a markedly better performance than for the volume of imports. However, from 1982 to 1989 as shown in **Table 9.2**, growth in the volume of imports was twice that of exports (although 1985 was the one year which went against the trend). Nevertheless, the growth differential was shrinking from 1987 onwards and became positive in 1990. In 1991 the volume of imports actually fell for the first time since 1981 whereas, unlike in 1981, the volume of exports continued to rise.

Table 9.2   *Index Numbers, UK Visible Trade (1985 = 100)*

	Volume indices[1]						Unit value index[2]		Terms of trade ((a)/(b))
	Exports			Total	Imports		(a) Exports	(b) Imports	
	Manufactures		Share of world exports of manufactures		Total	Manufactures as % Total Final Expenditure			
	Semi	Finished							
1972				55.9	64.1		20.3	18.6	109.2
1973				63.4	73.0		22.8	23.7	96.3
1974				68.0	73.3		29.0	34.6	83.7
1975				65.2	66.9		35.6	39.5	90.2
1976				71.7	71.3		42.6	48.4	88.1
1977				77.6	72.8		50.5	55.9	90.3
1978	97	91	117	79.6	76.1	11.4	55.5	58.0	95.5
1979	99	98	110	83.1	83.5	11.8	61.4	61.8	99.4
1980	93	89	105	84.1	79.0	10.8	69.9	67.8	103.1
1981	85	86	96	82.6	75.8	10.1	76.2	73.7	103.4
1982	86	87	102	85.3	80.3	10.7	81.4	79.9	101.9
1983	91	84	99	87.2	87.2	11.7	88.0	87.6	100.5
1984	97	93	98	94.5	96.5	12.7	95.0	95.3	99.6
1985	100	100	100	100.0	100.0	12.8	100.0	100.0	100.0
1986	106	102	102	104.0	107.2	12.9	90.1	95.4	94.4
1987	113	112	105	109.8	114.8	13.3	93.5	98.0	95.4
1988	120	120	103	112.5	130.5	14.0	93.4	96.9	96.4
1989	123	136	105	117.3	140.8	14.6	100.8	104.1	96.8
1990	131	147	107	125.1	142.7	14.0	106.2	108.0	98.3
1991	135	151	107	126.7	135.1	12.9	107.7	109.3	98.5
1992	142	152	107	129.7	144.0	13.2	109.9	110.3	99.6
1993	n/a	n/a	107	134.4	149.5	n/a	123.3	121.3	101.6
1994	n/a	n/a	107	148.0	155.4	n/a	126.2	125.7	100.4
1995	n/a	n/a	107	157.4	160.8	n/a	136.4	139.3	97.9

Notes:
[1] Seasonally adjusted.
[2] Unadjusted.
Source: UK National Accounts Pink Book (CSO, 1996); *National Institute Review; Economic Trends; Monthly Digest of Statistics*, Table 15.8.

Over the period 1970 to 1980 the **value** of both visible exports and imports roughly quadrupled, so prices of both exports and imports were clearly rising rapidly, albeit faster for imports than for exports. The unit value indices continued to out-run the volume indices until 1985, although prices of imports and exports were rising in unison during this period. However, from 1986 to 1992 the situation reversed itself, with volumes outrunning unit values by a substantial margin. During this period the unit value indices moved more or less in unison, but with that for imports always remaining slightly above that for exports.

If the unit value of visible exports is divided by the unit value of visible imports we get a measure of the **terms of trade**. As can be seen, these worsened sharply between 1972 and 1974, but subsequently improved more steadily until 1981. They worsened sharply again in 1986, but after climbing back steadily they have almost regained the level of 1985.

The terms of trade must be treated with care. On the face of it, an improvement, resulting perhaps from relatively high inflation in the UK, enables the same volume of imports to be bought in exchange for a lesser volume of exports than before. However, much depends upon the price elasticity of demand for exports and imports. If demand for UK visible exports is elastic, as is generally the case, an increase in price results in a reduction in revenue. Equally, if demand for visible imports its inelastic, as is generally the case, a reduction in price results in an increase in payments. Thus, overall, the balance of trade (visible exports **less** visible imports) will worsen rather that the reverse. In other words, a dose of domestic inflation in the UK is likely to cause serious damage to the visible trade balance, and is also likely to damage invisibles trade in an increasingly competitive world. The, albeit modest, improvement in recent years has not, therefore, been beneficial to the UK.

It is of particular interest to examine the other columns in **Table 9.2** in the light of the alleged collapse of manufacturing capability in the UK. What the first two columns show is that at the end of the 1970s, and through the 1980–81 recession, the volume of exports of semi-manufactures and

finished manufactures suffered a setback, particularly as the exchange rate was driven up by North Sea oil coming on stream. There was a sharp recovery in 1982 and 1983 respectively, with both categories back to their 1978 volumes in 1984. From that point on to the end of the decade export volumes rose rapidly, demonstrating that the manufacturing capability which survived the 1980–81 recession was fully capable of selling competitively in international markets.

This has continued to be the case, albeit to a lesser degree, during the 1990s. As a result, the volume of finished manufactures was more than half as great again in 1992 as in 1985, and is now roughly twice the level of 1983. The consequences for the UK's share of world exports of manufactures are important because so many attacks on government policy include a claim that it is continuously falling – but **this is untrue**. It did indeed fall rapidly at the end of the 1970s. Commencing at 9 per cent in volume terms in 1972, it fell from 8 per cent in 1978 to 6.5 per cent in 1981. However, once the 1980–81 recession was over it rapidly stabilised around the 5.5 per cent level and has shown no subsequent inclination to fall any further (see, for example, *Autumn Statement 1990 and 1992*). Bearing in mind the export success of, for example, the Asian 'tigers', this has been a creditable performance, and it would surely be unreasonable to expect a mature economy like the UK to gain much market share in the intensely competitive environment of international trade in manufactures (nor have most others, as shown in **Figure 9.1**).

On the imports side, the picture is less rosy, with manufactured imports rising as a proportion of TFE from 1981 to 1989 at which point UK domestic demand fell away, taking the demand for exports with it. The fact that import and export volumes of manufactures rise together is a commonplace of advanced countries which, for example, trade different makes of car and electronic goods. The purchase of cheap, high quality, imports is not to be deplored as such – provided, of course, one believes more or less in free trade. The key issue is whether or not a country can compensate by maintaining exports of goods and

Figure 9.1 *Share of World Exports of Manufactures (%)*

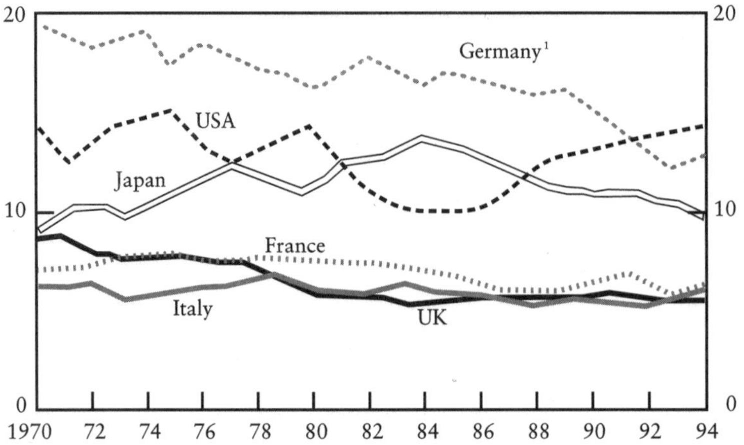

Note:
[1] Unified Germany from 1992.
Source: DTI estimates from OECD data.

services in order to keep the current account balance in rough equilibrium.

☐ 9.4.4 Visible Trade in Retrospect

Prior to 1967, the UK managed to keep the current balance in surplus but, with the exception of 1956 and 1958 when the visible balance was positive, the pattern of a negative visible balance more than compensated by a positive invisibles balance was already well-established. There was considerable volatility with respect to short-term capital flows, but long-term capital flows were mostly outflows, and hence negative in the accounts. In looking at the current situation, one might be tempted to believe that nothing much had changed since the 1960s. However, as we shall see, this is not the case because of differences in the exchange rate regime in operation, in the UK's reserve position and in the contribution of North Sea oil.

The steady deterioration in the UK's share of world trade in manufactures, exacerbated by an uncompetitive fixed exchange rate and combined with a tendency for hot money to pour out of the UK whenever a crisis loomed, thereby draining the inadequate reserves, was an unsustainable

situation. The BoP accounts gave every appearance of being in 'fundamental disequilibrium', and only a reduction in the value of the pound could remedy the situation. This duly took place in November 1967, and a programme of domestic deflation was set in hand. The combination proved successful, albeit not immediately and not soon enough to prevent a change of government. Starting from a balance of −£286 million in 1968, the current account moved to +£460 million in 1971. While long-term capital continued to flood out of the UK, an even larger amount began to flood in after 1969, and this was paralleled by net inflows of hot money sustained by the belief that the UK was making a determined attempt to restore sound finance. It was true that the domestic deflation was taking its toll in terms, for example, of rising unemployment, but this was of less concern at the time than the symbolic value of the deflationary measures.

From this point on fundamental disequilibrium never reappeared in the same guise as before. One major factor was the abandonment of the fixed exchange rate regime in 1972, which subsequently permitted the exchange rate to be used more positively to regulate the current balance. A second factor, which was initially of much less help, was the sharp increase in the price of North Sea oil. From 1975 to 1979, the visible balance remained heavily in deficit. The invisibles largely offset the damage, although the negative transfer component (including contributions to the Community) grew too rapidly to allow for a substantial current account surplus other than in 1978, at the end of a long period of oil price stability. The exceptionally high rate of inflation, partly triggered by the first oil price rise, was ultimately the key problem, because although long-term capital was flowing in to finance the development of the North Sea oilfields, international confidence in the UK's ability to deal with its domestic problems caused a massive outflow of hot money. This forced the then Labour government both to deplete the reserves and to borrow from the IMF

(agreeing in return to deflate the economy along 'monetarist' lines), as shown in **Table 9.3**.

With confidence restored by the IMF intervention, the reserve position took a dramatic turn for the better, and although the reserves remained fairly volatile they never again fell to a level which suggested further recourse to the IMF would be needed.

□ 9.4.5 Visible Trade in the 1980s

With North Sea oil coming on stream, the visible balance actually returned to surplus from 1980 to 1982, and the oil surplus itself grew steadily from £0.3 billion in 1980 to £8.1 billion in 1985. Under the circumstances, it seems extraordinary that the

Table 9.3   *UK Official Reserves, 1975–95, End-Year Values[1] ($ m)*

	Gold	*SDRs*	*Reserve position at IMF*	*Convertible currencies*	*TOTAL*
1975	888	840	366	3 335	5 429
1976	888	728	–	2 513	4 129
1977	938	604	–	19 015	20 557
1978	938	500	–	14 230	15 694
1979	3 259	1 245	–	18 034	22 538
1980	6 987	560	1 308	18 621	27 476
1981	7 334	1 048	1 513	13 457	23 352
1982	4 562	1 233	1 568	9 634	16 997
1983	5 914	695	2 168	9 040	17 817
1984	5 476	531	2 110	7 577	15 694
1985	4 310	996	1 751	8 486	15 543
1986	4 897	1 425	1 820	13 781	21 923
1987	5 792	1 229	1 579	35 726	44 326
1988	6 466	1 341	1 694	42 184	51 685
1989	5 457	1 125	1 610	20 453	38 645
1990	5 235	1 142	1 534	30 553	38 464
1991	5 039	1 232	1 733	36 122	44 126
1992	4 770	539	2 007	34 338	41 654
1993	4 558	289	1 869	36 210	42 926
1994	5 314	465	1 896	36 223	43 898
1995	5 242	417	2 518	38 809	46 986

Notes:
[1] The level of the reserves is affected by changes in the dollar valuation of gold, Special Drawing Rights (SDRs) and convertible currencies as well as by transactions.
Source: Bank of England Quarterly Bulletin; Table 8.1.

visible balance should have returned to deficit so rapidly, as shown in **Table 9.4**, but whereas non-oil visibles were £1 billion in surplus in 1980, they had collapsed to show a deficit of £11 billion by 1984. The huge reduction in the size of the UK manufacturing sector when the Conservative government first took office, resulting from a combination of a deliberate policy of domestic deflation, the UK's relatively high rate of inflation and the high value of the effective exchange rate was largely to blame, since the damage done at the time has never been fully rectified. Whereas the effective exchange rate fell to an historic low by 1986, and the rump of the manufacturing sector performed very creditably in export markets, the growth in the UK economy sucked in vast amounts of foreign manufactures, many of which could no longer be produced at all in the UK. Individual events such as the coal-miners' strike in 1984–85 added to the difficulties, and it is possible to argue that although many UK products were highly competitive on price alone, they fell down with respect to non-price factors such as quality and speed of delivery.

It is also necessary, in looking at the visible balance, to appreciate a peculiarity of the way in which exchange rates work. In practice many products, and especially raw materials including oil, are priced in dollars. Thus, if the pound rises in value against the dollar these become cheaper in sterling and vice versa. However, exports to the EU are affected by the rate at which the pound is exchanged for EU currencies. If the pound rises against these currencies, then UK exports become expensive and vice versa. The worst combination for the UK is, therefore, for the pound to fall against the dollar, making raw material imports expensive, and to rise simultaneously against EU currencies, making exports expensive. From 1979 to 1985 this combination broadly held true, and the visible balance was only salvaged by North Sea oil coming on stream.

From 1980 to 1988 the invisibles balance remained very healthy. The balance on private services was the major contributory factor. Equally, while interest payments needed to be made on outstanding government borrowings from abroad, the long-term capital outflows in the 1970s mentioned above resulted in a sharp upturn in private sector investment income (appearing, note, in the **current** rather than the capital account).

Because of its diversity, the capital account is much more difficult to interpret. Account must be taken of the lifting of exchange controls in October 1979, which resulted in a sharp upturn in investment overseas by UK residents from £12.6 billion in 1983 to £34.4 billion in 1986. These were offset by large amounts of foreign currency borrowing by UK banks and, as already mentioned, short-term inflows were heavily influenced by sterling's new status as a petro-currency and by the government's determined attack upon inflation, initially via its 'monetarist' policies and subsequently via high interest rates. UK companies continued to perform creditably in export markets, but **Table 9.4** indicates the scale of the problem. From 1985 to 1987 the volume of visible exports rose by roughly 10 per cent, but the volume of imports rose by 15 per cent, and the gap continued to widen during 1988. If the comparison is linked only to manufactured goods, then the margin of difference was considerably wider. The consequences, taken in conjunction with the collapse in the price of North Sea oil, show up clearly in the visible balance which worsened sharply in 1986 to record a deficit of £9.6 billion. This would have been worse had sterling not risen against the dollar, thereby cheapening raw material imports, and fallen against EU currencies, thereby cheapening UK exports. The invisibles balance, on the other hand, improved sharply in 1986, and almost matched the visible deficit.

□ *9.4.6 The Past Decade*

In 1987, the visible balance deteriorated further to show a deficit of £11.6 billion. The invisibles balance registered a surplus of £6.8 billion, resulting in a current account deficit of £4.8 billion for the year, the first major deficit of the 1980s. 1987 seemed at first to be exceptional in relation to earlier years in the decade in that net transactions were recorded in the 1988 'Pink Book' as being

Table 9.4 *BoP of the UK, 1982–95 (£ m)*

	1982	1983	1984	1985	1986	1987	1988	1989	1990	1991	1992	1993	1994	1995
CURRENT ACCOUNT														
Visible Balance	1911	−1537	−5336	−3345	−9559	−11582	−21480	−24683	−18809	−10284	−13104	−13460	−10831	−11628
Invisibles:														
Services	3022	3829	4205	6398	6223	6242	3957	3361	3689	3564	4950	5516	4747	6142
Investment income	1460	2830	4344	2296	4629	3927	4566	3502	1269	150	3124	2197	8691	9572
Transfers	−1741	−1593	−1732	−3111	−2157	−3400	−3518	−4578	−4896	−1383	−5102	−5007	−5027	−6978
Invisibles Balance	2741	5066	6817	5583	8695	6769	5005	2285	62	2331	2972	2706	8411	8736
CURRENT BALANCE	4649	3529	1482	2238	−864	−4813	−16475	−22398	−18747	−7953	−10132	−10754	−2420	−2892
TRANSACTIONS IN EXTERNAL ASSETS AND LIABILITIES[1]														
Net Transactions	−2519	−4562	−8534	−3720	−3820	7410	14917	18176	16543	7445	4965	13080	−2650	446
Allocation of SDRs	0	0	0	0	0	0	0	0	0	0	0	0	0	0
Balancing Item	−2130	1033	7052	1482	4684	−2597	1558	4222	2204	508	5167	−2326	5070	2446

Notes:
[1] Assets: increase −/decrease +. Liabilities: increase +/decrease −. Not seasonally adjusted.

Source: UK Balance of Payments 1996, Table 1.1.

only marginally negative, a turnaround of £13 billion in one year. This was widely thought to be due to the appreciation of sterling which lowered the sterling value of assets priced in other currencies, and also because UK residents ran down their overseas investments, mainly after the stock market crash in October. The attraction of the UK as a haven for hot money grew even stronger because of the combination of fiscal rectitude and high nominal interest rates. The year was also unusual in that the balancing item appeared to fall sharply. However, the revisions published in subsequent Pink Books swung from a £7 billion outflow on net transactions to the latest £7.4 billion inflow, and from a +£11 billion balancing item to the latest estimate of a negative balancing item of £2.6 billion. No wonder the government set in hand a major overhaul of the statistical service!

During 1987–88, the current account deteriorated rapidly, as shown in **Figure 9.2** where the

data are presented as a percentage of GDP. The visible balance recorded an unprecedented deficit of £21.5 billion in 1988, which was only partially compensated by an invisibles surplus that was itself falling sharply from its 1986 peak. Hence, the current account deficit was an alarming £16.5 billion which even the large positive balancing item could not explain.

One factor, apart from the general surge in imports of all kinds, was a sharp decline in the oil surplus as domestic industry increased its oil consumption and the Piper Alpha platform disaster affected supplies. This appeared to herald the end of an era for North Sea oil and gas insofar as it affects the balance of payments, an issue addressed in the next section.

The visible trade deficit worsened in 1989, and with the invisibles surplus shrinking further, so did the current account deficit. It goes without saying that in many quarters these figures were taken as evidence that the obsolete ship SS Great

Figure 9.2   *Current Account, % of GDP*

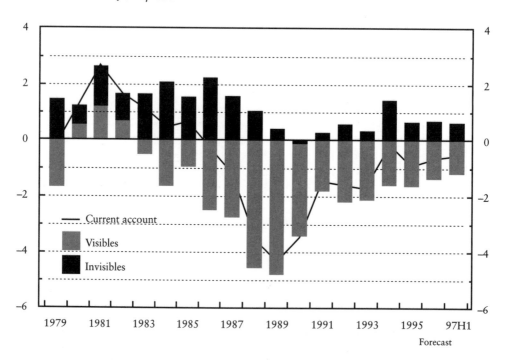

Source: FSBR 1995–96, Chart 3.21.

Britain was sinking without trace. As a result the government was forced to scratch around with increasing desperation to explain why they were merely a 'blip' rather than a trend.

The situation began to improve noticeably in 1990 as the recession began to take hold in the UK at a time when export markets remained fairly buoyant, and in the second quarter of 1991 the current account appeared at the time to be once again in balance. Unfortunately, this proved to be a false dawn, with the deficit on visibles promptly building up again at the same time as the surplus on invisibles began to erode. The current account deficit for the year, at £8.0 billion, was indeed a big improvement on 1990, but there was a further modest deterioration, after allowing for inflation, in 1992 and again in 1993 after which things improved considerably.

As can be seen in **Table 9.4**, not merely were invisibles much lower than previously between 1989 and 1993, especially in relation to GDP, but for the first time ever they actually recorded a roughly zero balance in 1990. This resulted from an unfortunate combination of circumstances, bringing together a collapse in investment income and a sharp increase in payments to the EU. Once again, this set off much scaremongering about ongoing and permanent structural changes but, as is commonplace where the BoP is concerned, the following year saw a reversal of fortune even in the context of negative investment income, and 1994's invisibles balance was exceptionally large on the back of a massive surge in investment income which continued through 1995.

One recent structural feature does seem to be a noticeably higher level of payments to the EU. The level of income from services is relatively stable, so the volatility is now almost entirely introduced by flows of investment income. Given the substantial swing between 1991 and 1994, forecasting the invisibles balance has become a precarious pastime, and as shown in **Figure 9.2**, the Conservative government's response was to assume 'no change' overall in relation to GDP. Indeed, that was also its attitude towards the visible balance and hence the current account, and the visible balance has certainly been unusually stable in nominal terms since 1991 although

the situation in early 1996 has worsened as EU economies have slowed while domestic activity has remained relatively strong.

Given the role played by manufactures in explaining the size of the current account deficit, it is worthwhile at this stage to examine a number of sub-sectors of the accounts in order to gain some insight into the UK's future prospects.

Trade in Cars

The general tone of commentators is so pessimistic that it seems almost sacrilegious to suggest that there are rays of sunshine amid the gloom, yet that is truly the case where trade in cars is concerned. It is not so long ago that the traditional British car industry more or less disappeared without trace. Car production in 1982 was only 800 000 units, roughly half its current level. Although the American/British car industry had in part replaced it, this was not on a scale such that a massive trade deficit in cars could be prevented, especially since many Fords and Vauxhalls were actually imports.

Nevertheless, the most notable improvement in the balance of trade during 1990 resulted from an end-year surge in exports of cars and commercial vehicles (motors). In the whole of 1990, 414 000 cars were exported, with the final quarter figures up 60 per cent on 1989. Overall, the motor trade account remained in deficit to the tune of £4.6 billion, but this was much better than the 1989 deficit of £6.6 billion. Ford and Vauxhall resumed large-scale exports to the Continent for the first time in over a decade, and the Nissan factory in Sunderland became the first Japanese plant to produce 'UK' exports of cars.

In the final quarter of 1991, the motor industry achieved its first trade surplus for almost a decade, and the deficit for the year fell to £1 billion. The situation deteriorated in 1992 with a deficit of £2.4 billion which reached £4 billion in 1994 (although it is now on a declining trend), essentially because companies like Ford and Vauxhall continue to import finished vehicles in order to complete their product ranges and also because luxury cars for the company market are largely imported. However, the longer-term perspective is rosier than is generally admitted. By 2000, Nissan, Toyota and Honda will between them be building 800 000 cars a year in Britain. A significant proportion of all manufacturers' output (reaching roughly one half in 1995) is destined for export markets. Furthermore, these companies' cars will displace existing imports. The ultimate impact of these developments is dependent upon the UK home market and the proportion of UK content in both exports and imports of cars (Rhys, 1990). In principle, all EU member states are obliged to remove barriers against the importation of Japanese/UK cars by the end of the decade, although the current recession in mainland Europe is causing some rebellion about concessions in the short term.

It is not altogether clear whether, or when, the motor trade deficit will ever completely disappear, although the indications are that it will eventually (Rhys predicts by 2000). The 1992 fall in the value of the pound has led some to argue that it will be sooner rather than later. Either way, as the motor trade constituted roughly one quarter of the total visible trade deficit in 1990 (and slightly more in 1989), this does offer some support for the expectation that the visible trade deficit will shrink permanently to a more manageable size.

Trade in Electronics

The process described above is by no means confined to cars. Even though, for example, there are no longer any UK-owned TV manufacturers, colour TV exports began to exceed imports in 1989. Ferguson, the last substantially UK-owned manufacturer of TV sets was bought by Thomson of France in 1987, but once again it is primarily the Japanese who have spear-headed the attack on overseas markets. Sony, the largest UK-based manufacturer, has won three Queen's Awards for Export Achievement since it established its factory in South Wales in 1974. The UK is currently the possessor of the fourth largest electronics industry in the world after the USA, Japan and Germany. In 1992 electronics exports were 15 per cent smaller than imports, but a decade pre-

viously the gap was twice as large. Currently, the UK is running a trade surplus in computers and television sets.

Foreign-owned companies account for an even bigger share of exports of office machinery than for cars. Needless to say, the invasion by foreign companies has generated an intense debate about whether ownership as such is important, but in simple balance of payments terms the consequences for the visible balance are undoubtedly positive. We will return to this issue in our subsequent analysis of the commodity composition of visible trade.

In examining the reasons for the UK's poor performance in manufacturing trade such as poor education and training, bad design and quality and too little research and development, it is salutary to remember that the sectors in which the UK trades successfully such as chemicals, pharmaceuticals and aerospace, operate in exactly the same domestic environment as the sectors in which the UK trades unsuccessfully. It is possible to hypothesise that sectors which are currently successful are successful precisely because they always had to operate in international markets, whereas those such as white goods and motor cycles which relied almost entirely upon the home market proved easy pickings for internationally competitive overseas producers.

The situation may, therefore, become more stable than in the recent past, especially if continued inward investment serves to replace uncompetitive UK-owned business with Japanese-owned subsidiaries as in the case of cars. It is not the case that the UK's problems are particularly in high-technology sectors since the aerospace industry trades successfully. Indeed, it is in areas such as white goods, which are essentially low-tech, that the worst problems have typically arisen.

However, the pessimists can still make out a fairly convincing case in the short term since it was widely expected that import penetration would fall back sharply in the recent recession, much as it did in the early 1980s, and this did not happen. Simple extrapolation of the trend in **Figure 9.3** certainly gives cause for concern, although it should be noted that virtually all advanced countries have suffered increased import penetra-

Figure 9.3 *Import Penetration*[1]

Notes:
[1] Imports as a percentage of total final expenditure, in constant prices.
Source: Bank of England Quarterly Bulletin (May 1995) p. 141.

tion over the past decade. It is slightly ironic that part of the 'problem' lies in the exceptionally efficient UK retail sector. The inefficient system of retail distribution in Japan is undoubtedly one of the subtle protectionist devices used to keep out imported manufactures, whereas the ease with which such products find their way into British stores, and the ease of 'comparison shopping' in such outlets, has ruthlessly exposed price and quality shortfalls in domestic products.

☐ *9.4.7 Balance of Payments Effects of North Sea Oil*

The BoP effects of the North Sea show up in four ways. The first two are current account items, appearing mainly in the visible balance. First, there is the balance of trade in oil and gas. This,

as discussed above, was heavily in deficit during the 1970s, but showed a healthy surplus during the 1980s until the more than halving of the price of oil in early 1986. This surplus is no longer of sufficient size to warrant the level of attention accorded to the oil balance over the period to 1987. The second item relates to the net purchase of goods and services required to discover and extract the oil and gas. This was a significant deficit item in the early 1970s, but is no longer of any consequence. One of the other two effects appears in the capital account, namely capital inflows to finance the discovery and extraction activities. These basically can be set against the cost of purchasing goods and services, and like them have been inconsequential for a good many years. However, in the usual way, these inflows of capital generate the final effect, namely a requirement to pay interest, profits and dividends at a later date, which have accordingly been a negative item in the invisibles during the 1980s.

If this is set against the worsening in the balance of trade in oil and gas, it is clear that net revenue from the North Sea is unlikely to be able to offset any further deterioration which may occur in trade in manufactures. It is possible to speculate that this offset will continue because the price of oil will rise over time, but this is less than probable. It is equally possible to argue that the output of oil and gas will rise rapidly, subject to a supportive tax regime, since there is no shortage of reserves, but there are no immediate signs of this and it is anyway dependent upon trends in prices.

If the BoP benefits of North Sea oil and gas have now largely come to an end, but the non-oil variables generally remain in deficit, it is certainly possible to argue that the existence of North Sea resources has simply been used as an excuse for not tackling some of the most deep-rooted problems of the economy. On the other hand, it has to be asked whether the huge increase in the net overseas assets of the UK in the 1980s had anything to do with the use of the money generated by the production of North Sea oil. If so, then it is unreasonable to regard the money as 'wasted' even if it has not been put to the purpose preferred by all parties.

It is also possible to argue that the UK's net trading position with respect to manufactures has been permanently damaged by the effects of North Sea oil on the exchange rate. As noted elsewhere, the willingness of the government to let the exchange rate appreciate rapidly at the beginning of the 1980s, in response both to the current account benefits of oil and to the boost to foreign confidence in the UK which accompanied it, made it very difficult for many firms to sell in export markets. The subsequent decline in the oil balance was not, however, accompanied by a parallel resurgence in manufactured exports.

☐ *9.4.8 The Invisibles Balance*

In aggregate, as shown in **Table 9.1**, UK exports of invisibles are normally worth much the same as visible exports. The only country that exports

significantly more invisibles than the UK is the USA. Tradeable services account for roughly 20 per cent of UK GDP, whereas the comparable figure is smaller for all other major industrial countries (it is nearer 5 per cent for both the USA and Japan).

Despite this, the invisibles balance has for some time been a cause for concern, as noted previously, although the last quarterly deficit was in 1991 so that concern is becoming more muted. The UK, at £20 billion per year, remains the world's largest exporter of financial services (the Cayman Islands, interestingly, is the main rival), so it is tempting to see the problem as an excess of foreign transfers – primarily to EU institutions. Given the political unanimity concerning the UK's membership of the EU, and given the fact that the UK has wrung whatever concessions it is likely to get from other EU members, the long-term negative impact of such transfers upon the invisible balance is best treated as a simple fact of life. The issue is thus whether the other elements in the balance can rise to compensate for this difficulty.

It is hard to be altogether optimistic on this matter. The raising of virtually all barriers to the free flow of international capital cannot help but put the City of London under increasingly competitive pressure, and although it looks certain to hold its own, it cannot be expected to make much headway. Equally, the British have become rather fond of their holidays abroad (the travel account will be over £5 billion in deficit in 1996), and there seems little prospect of them staying at home for the sake of the invisibles balance.

The major saving grace is the 'other business services' account which has for several years been running an annual surplus of £6–7 billion (for all of these figures see, for example, *UK National Accounts*, Table B5).

Investment income (*Ibid.*, Table B6) is a fairly critical factor. The massive holdings of overseas assets should be generating a substantial inflow of capital, but there is no need for such capital to be repatriated. If, for example, it is reinvested abroad then the short-term effect is a deterioration in investment income although the longer-term outlook is clearly improved. It is also significant that the large deficits of 1988 and 1989 necessitated an inflow of hot money which caused UK banks to become net borrowers from overseas rather than the reverse. Furthermore, interest rates were considerably higher in the UK than in most other advanced economies, so these borrowings were expensive to service.

Investment income has improved since the deficit of 1991, especially in 1994, partly as a reflection of lower absolute and relative interest rates in the UK, but the best thing that could happen would undoubtedly be an agreement under GATT auspices to lift barriers to trade in services in which the UK has a comparative advantage. Failing that, fewer natural disasters would be a boon to the insurance sector which has taken a hammering at a time of softening premiums.

9.4.9 Prognosis for the Late 1990s

The recession has become history in the UK, although some export markets such as Germany are teetering on the edge of recession. At the end of 1990, the growth of import volumes was negative after a period of two years during which it had once again shot ahead of export growth (see **Table 9.2**). Meanwhile the buoyancy of exports, resulting from continued growth overseas, especially elsewhere in the EU which lagged the UK in the economic cycle, opened up a large positive gap between export and import volume growth. Commencing in mid-1991, the import volume growth line rose sharply once again and caught up with the more slowly rising export growth line. The fact that most of the EU collapsed into recession was a negative factor in relation to exports, while the tendency for rising domestic demand to suck in imports remained a fact of life.

The latest figures reflecting the period since the 1992 devaluation are mildly encouraging, with import volumes growing overall much more slowly than export volumes, although the unit value index has moved much less favourably, particularly over the most recent period. Current account deficits will accordingly remain the order of the day. Just how big these deficits will ultimately prove to be in value terms is difficult to forecast

(especially in the short term because of data collection problems). We have already commented on the improvement in certain parts of the trading accounts, but much will ultimately depend upon the growth path of other EU member states, and to a lesser degree of the USA. The trade deficit is unlikely to return to pre-1990 levels, and it is possible to anticipate a much improved situation towards the end of the decade. Meanwhile, the government should continue to attract inward investment, since manufacturing salvation is most unlikely to arrive on the back of purely domestic companies. The significant depreciation in the value of the pound since the UK left the Exchange Rate Mechanism in October 1992 (see **pp. 290–2**) cannot help but improve the current account, although the Conservative government currently appears to be happy with boosting the exchange rate (possibly in order to restore its tarnished image). Much therefore depends upon the eventual equilibrium value for the pound, and upon the demand elasticity for British exports.

A final caveat relates back to the exercise in national income accounting discussed on **p. 27**. There we concluded that investment in the UK economy must be financed either by domestic savings, a budget surplus or by running a current account deficit. Domestic savings have indeed risen in recent years, as noted earlier, but the budget deficit has escalated rapidly, thereby effectively neutralising domestic savings as a source of investment funds. It therefore follows that economic growth will have to be financed by drawing in overseas capital. As we have shown, a surplus on the BoP capital account has its mirror image in a deficit on the current account, and this kind of deficit is not amenable to improvement via devaluation. It follows, therefore, that the current account will not return into surplus until the budget deficit is itself brought under control.

9.5 International Perspectives

9.5.1 The Current Deficit

The ongoing current account deficit needs to be seen in a wider international context, as in **Table**

9.5. This indicates that the UK deficit is typically relatively large by EU standards expressed as a percentage of GDP, but the EU does tend to be almost exactly in balance as a whole. The difference between the UK situation and the EU average was quite marked at the end of the 1980s, but the 1992 devaluation has largely taken care of that differential. What the table does reveal is that it is indeed possible to produce a significant swing into surplus, as was achieved over the past decade in the case most notably of Ireland and also of Denmark (in surplus in the 1990s unlike the previous three decades). The only example of a member state swinging into deficit in recent years is in respect of Germany post-unification. The UK is not entirely alone in having remained in deficit throughout most of the period under consideration, but it is worth reminding ourselves once again that, with EU states mostly trading with one another as discussed below, there have to be some deficit countries if others are to remain in surplus.

☐ *9.5.2 Trade with Japan*

From the beginning of 1987, until the third quarter of 1990, Japan's plans to reduce its trade surplus were widely acknowledged to be succeeding. Imports grew, on average, by 17.7 per cent whilst export growth slowed down to average 2.9 per cent. Furthermore, Japan exported capital on a much increased scale, thereby easing the adjustment problems of countries with which it was running big current account surpluses.

The overall current account surplus for 1990 was the lowest for five years at £18.3 billion, in particular because of a big rise in the deficit on invisibles. As a proportion of GNP this represented 12 per cent compared to 4.4 per cent in

Table 9.5   *Balance on Current Account as a percentage of GDP, 1961–96*

	1961–73	1974–86	1987	1988	1989	1990	1991	1992	1993	1994	1995	1996[1]
B	1.1	−1.2	1.3	1.8	1.7	0.9	1.8	2.2	4.6	5.1	5.8	5.7
DK	−2.0	−3.7	−2.9	−1.3	−1.5	0.5	1.1	2.5	2.9	1.9	1.4	1.9
D	–	–	–	–	–	–	−1.1	−1.2	−1.4	−1.8	−1.8	−1.8
WD	0.7	1.1	4.1	4.3	4.8	3.5	–	–	–	–	–	–
GR	−2.4	−2.6	−2.6	−3.2	−6.7	−7.2	−6.1	−4.0	−3.2	−2.4	−2.3	−2.6
E	−0.7	−1.2	0.1	−1.1	−3.2	−3.7	−3.6	−3.6	−1.3	−1.8	−1.9	−1.8
F	0.4	−0.2	−0.2	−0.3	−0.5	−1.0	−0.5	0.1	0.1	1.0	0.9	0.8
IRL	−2.4	−7.4	−0.2	0.0	−1.7	−0.7	2.0	3.3	6.5	7.0	6.9	6.8
I	1.4	−0.6	−0.2	−0.7	−1.3	−1.4	−1.8	−2.2	1.1	1.5	2.7	3.4
L	6.9	28.0	30.3	30.8	34.0	34.2	27.9	30.0	28.8	27.4	26.1	24.7
NL	0.5	2.0	1.9	2.8	3.5	3.8	3.5	3.1	3.7	4.6	4.7	4.9
A	0.1	−0.9	−0.2	−0.2	0.1	0.7	0.0	−0.1	−0.5	−1.0	−1.4	−1.2
P	0.4	−5.2	0.6	−3.4	−0.9	−2.4	−1.9	−1.3	−1.5	−1.9	−0.2	−0.4
FIN	−1.4	−1.9	−2.0	−2.6	−5.1	−5.1	−5.4	−4.6	−1.0	1.1	2.4	1.4
S	0.2	−1.5	−0.6	−1.1	−2.7	−3.6	−2.1	−3.1	−1.1	−0.8	0.7	2.0
UK	−0.1	−0.2	−2.2	−5.0	−5.7	−4.9	−2.7	−2.6	−2.3	−0.0	−0.2	0.4
EUR	0.3	−0.2	0.6	−0.0	−0.5	−0.7	−1.3	−1.2	−0.1	0.2	0.3	0.5
USA	0.5	−0.6	−3.4	−2.4	−1.7	−1.4	0.1	−1.0	−1.5	−2.3	−2.6	−2.4
JAP	0.6	1.1	3.6	2.8	2.0	1.3	2.5	3.3	3.2	2.9	2.5	2.1

Note: [1] Forecast.

Source: European Economy. Supplement A. January 1996.

1986, and Japan was loudly proclaimed to be behaving like a model world citizen.

However, throughout the latter half of the 1980s, Japan's trading relationship with the USA continued to deteriorate, and the USA made it increasingly clear that it would use the provisions of the 1988 Omnibus Trading Act to resist further Japanese incursions into the US market. As a consequence, Japan began to search for alternative markets, and found them in Asia and Europe. Had the Japanese current account deficit continued to shrink this would not have mattered, but in the fourth quarter of 1990, despite the recession in the USA and Canada, Japan exported $81 billion of goods, the largest ever quarterly amount by value. Importantly, the surplus with the EU exceeded that with the USA beginning in the Spring of 1991.

In 1992 Japan's trade surplus rose by 37.6 per cent to a record $107 billion on a customs basis, and included a 14 per cent rise in relation to the EU. The equivalent surplus on a BoP basis was $135 billion. Hence, there was once again the distinct probability of a massive Japanese current account surplus for the entire decade. Furthermore, this surplus was expected to increase in relation to the EU. In practice, the EU member state with the worst trading imbalance with Japan is the UK, which ran a trade deficit of $7.5 billion in 1992, whereas not all members are even in deficit. Understandably, therefore, the UK government voiced its concern about its trade with Japan.

The current account surplus in Japan is the inverse of the capital outflow which is the result of domestic savings exceeding domestic investment. Until the UK ceases to need to attract Japanese capital, the imbalance in trade is set to continue. Nevertheless, in aggregate, the situation has changed radically in recent months with the Japanese current account even recording a small deficit for the first time in five years in January 1996 (though not when seasonally adjusted), and the surplus falling by 22 per cent during 1995. Furthermore, in April, the balance of trade surplus fell for the 17th consecutive month to the lowest monthly level for 13 years. This reflected the effects of the overvalued yen which had caused nearly 10 per cent of Japanese output to move abroad (including to the UK) from where it was largely exported back to Japan.

■ 9.6 Direct Investment

For centuries past an unfailing characteristic of the UK has been the willingness of its inhabitants to engage in foreign direct investment. That this enthusiasm has continued in recent years is not, therefore, altogether surprising. What is surprising is that it reached unprecedented levels during the latter half of the 1980s, as shown in **Table 9.1**. As a consequence, the gross stock of UK-owned foreign assets grew very rapidly.

The second surprise is that, after dipping below zero in 1984, **inward** investment first rose sharply to £9.4 billion in 1987 and then shot up to £18.6 billion in 1989 with the consequence that it constituted a much higher proportion of GDP (over 4 per cent) than for any other equivalent economy.

The Japanese have located more than one-third of their investment in the EU in the UK, and the UK's Invest in Britain Bureau (IBB) estimate that the UK attracts 40 per cent of the EU's overall inward investment. Inward investors are encouraged by, for example, relatively cheap but acceptably skilled labour, relatively low corporate taxes, good telecommunications and golf. As the UK tends to offer less by way of grants than most international rivals, that does not seem to explain the UK's success although it does make a difference as to which particular part of the UK is chosen. Foreign companies are, interestingly, generally able to generate much higher levels of productivity than their domestic counterparts. However, it should be remembered that most inward investment goes into the services sector, and especially into banks and finance.

During the ensuing three years, there was nothing like the amount invested as in 1989, with France if anything becoming a more popular destination, partly because of the apparent lack of enthusiasm in the UK for the Maastricht Treaty and partly because the era of massive green-field investments was temporarily over. However, there was a very sharp increase recorded for

1995, which bears out the IBB's claim that there has been a sharp upturn since 1993 (see *Financial Times*, 12 June 1996, p. iv), reaching record levels for three successive financial years with 477 new projects announced in the year to April 1996 (see *Financial Times*, 10 July 1996, p. 7). KPMG Corporate Finance valued inward investment in 1995 at £23.3 billion (*The Times*, 29 January 1996), and there have certainly been a spate of large investments reported in the press during 1995 and 1996 (for example the £1.7 billion investment in Wales by LG Group of Korea – see *Financial Times*, 11 July 1996). Until the issue of the UK's attitude towards the EU is resolved, there must remain some uncertainty over the scale of future investment although, as noted elsewhere, it is widely accepted that it is important for the revitalisation of the UK's manufacturing sector that Japanese, Korean and other overseas companies are induced to set up in the UK.

9.6.1 Foreign-owned Multinationals

The existence of foreign-owned multinationals in the UK is not a new phenomenon. Indeed, many US companies such as Ford and General Motors have been around for so long that their cars are widely regarded as British rather than foreign.

The more recent influx of investment has been particularly associated with Japan and increasingly Korea, for example the takeover of ICL by Fujitsu and the car plants set up by Nissan, Honda and Toyota. During 1988–90 some 80 Japanese manufacturers set up in the UK, but their role should not be exaggerated since the USA accounts for roughly 40 per cent of all foreign-owned assets in Britain (worth around £30 billion), Holland for another 18 per cent and Japan for only 5 per cent.

It is unsurprising that the arrival of the Single European Market has triggered an influx of foreign direct investment into the EU. Nevertheless, the fact that much the largest slice of US investment in the EU is in the UK, as well as over 30 per cent of Japanese EU investment, indicates that the importance of inward investment cannot be ex-

aggerated. The Invest in Britain Bureau recently calculated that although overseas companies investing in the UK represent only 1 per cent of businesses, they account for nearly 20 per cent of UK manufacturing jobs, 25 per cent of net output, 33 per cent of net capital expenditure and 40 per cent of manufactured exports. Curiously, the continuation of this development is not welcomed in all quarters. It is often argued that the balance of payments will deteriorate as a consequence, since the Japanese will use the UK as a glorified assembly plant while manufacturing high value-added products in Japan and exporting them to the UK and, furthermore, that profits made in the UK will subsequently be repatriated. However, this argument is less than convincing for several reasons. In the first place, it is evident that if the Japanese do not, for example, set up car plants in the UK and use them as a base for exporting to other EU countries, then there will be no substitute exports for UK-originated products that no longer sell well overseas. The same applies for any products no longer manufactured at all by UK firms. Secondly, as a result of infighting between the EU and Japan, the Japanese have conceded the need to create much more value-added in the EU then they had originally intended. Finally, their imposition of much higher quality standards compared to UK manufacturers has caused some UK suppliers to improve their products to the point at which they are attractive in export markets.

9.6.2 The External Balance Sheet of the UK

We have previously referred to the external balance sheet of the UK which has been analysed in great detail in, most recently, the *Bank of England Quarterly Bulletin* of November 1995. This claimed that the UK had net external assets of £17.7 billion at the end of 1995 compared with a revised estimate of £33.9 billion at the end of 1994. It is particularly notable that the 1995 figure was the net difference between gross assets of £1,617 billion and gross liabilities of £1,567 billion. In other words, UK residents are roughly as enthusiastic about buying up overseas assets as overseas residents are about buying up UK assets. Why this should be so is something of a puzzle, although the predilection for UK residents to invest overseas dates back over a century (at which time the UK invested 5 per cent of its GDP overseas), and the various factors underpinning inward investment in recent years are discussed elsewhere in the text.

The first point to note is that, because it is customarily denominated in dollars for comparative purposes, the equivalent sterling value can be highly variable. This can be seen in **Figure 9.4**

where the net capital flows (above the line is an outflow and below the line is an inflow) are rather small (generally below £10 billion) whereas the effects of revaluation due to exchange rate changes, the movement of security prices, write-offs and revaluations of direct investments are much larger.

In 1987, 1989 and the first half of 1990 the revaluation was primarily due to the exchange rate effect – when the pound rises against the dollar the value of external assets falls in dollar terms and vice versa – whereas in 1988 it was almost entirely due to revaluations of share and bond prices. The collapse of the dollar in the

Figure 9.4 *Contributions to the Change in the UK Net External Assets (£bn)*

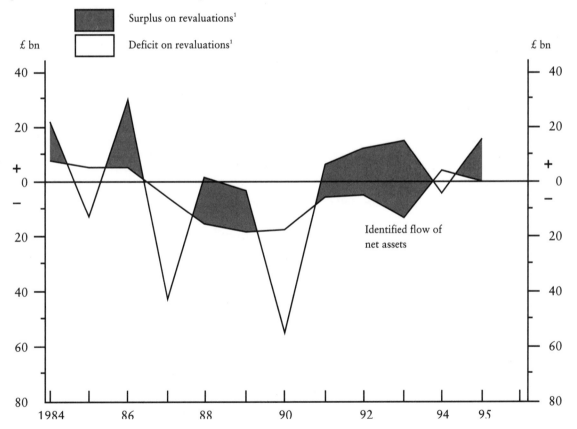

Notes:
[1] Residual component = difference between change in recorded net stock and net identified outflows.
Source: Bank of England Quarterly Bulletins November 1990, p. 488; November 1993, p. 509; November 1995, p. 356; November 1996, p. 419.

second half of 1989, followed by its equal and opposite rise during the first half of 1991, caused the external balance sheet to fluctuate widely in value even though net capital flows remained modest.

The biggest shifts between 1988 and 1989 took place firstly in inflows of direct investment (up from £12 billion to £18.6 billion), and secondly in UK residents' purchases of overseas portfolio investments (up from £11.2 billion to £36.5 billion). Direct investment overseas remained at its previously high level. This latter item collapsed back by more than half in 1990 as did portfolio investment overseas, while portfolio investment into the UK fell back by 65 per cent although the absolute difference was much smaller. Direct investment overseas has yet to recover fully from its 1990 level, although it is approaching its 1989 level in nominal terms (see **Table 9.1**). Portfolio investment, in contrast, has vacillated enormously, ranging from an extraordinary outflow of £84.5 billion in 1993 (see **Table 9.1**) to an inflow of £18.1 the following year. Meanwhile, direct investment into the UK remains well below what it was in 1989, although portfolio investment is running at three times the level of that year.

The acquisition of £200 billion of overseas assets in the course of the five years 1988–92 inclusive seemed rather extraordinary for a country running large current account deficits and allegedly brought to its knees by a decade of Thatcherism. However, even this was dwarfed by the £101.6 billion invested overseas in 1993 although this was unsurprisingly followed by a year in which the outflow was zero. A consequence of this capital outflow at a time of current account deficits was the need to borrow to cover the gap at high interest rates (see Davies, 1990, pp. 34–9).

Given that the dividend yield on overseas investments was lower than the interest costs of financing those investments, this appeared to be irrational behaviour on the part of UK investors. It has to be borne in mind, however, as argued by Cliff Pratten (*Financial Times*, 18 July 1990, p. 15 and Pratten (1992)) that no account was taken of **capital gains** in this respect. It was the case in almost every year during the 1980s that part of the return on investments took the form of capital

gains which **did not appear in the current account** of the BoP. In 1990, Pratten estimated the total capital gains during the 1980s as £95 billion and during 1990 as £12 billion (adjusted for inflation). In Pratten (1992) a figure of £82.3 billion is estimated for the 1980s. The methodology is complicated, and the estimates are precisely that, but there is considerable justification for his conclusion that 'during the 1980s capital gains more than offset deficits on the current account of the balance of payments'. This would suggest that concern over the state of the current account is overdone, although it should be noted that since the gains were mostly unrealised, there was, and there remains, a **liquidity** problem resulting from short-term borrowings to cover the capital outflows.

This view is not universally shared. Coutts and Godley (1990), for example, conducted their own analysis of the accounts and concluded that, first, only £3 billion of the (then) £20 billion current account deficit in 1989 could be compensated by adjustments for capital gains and inflation and, secondly, that if the balancing item represented under-recorded net exports, then the net stock of overseas assets was much smaller than official estimates suggested and hence that Britain would become a debtor nation if the balance of trade was not rapidly restored to a surplus. According to a calculation by Keith Skeoch, the chief economist at James Capel, adjusting for capital gains of foreign assets in Britain which he assumed to have accumulated as a result of, first, officially identified investments and, secondly, under-recorded capital inflows, meant that Britain already was a net debtor.

All of this may, understandably, leave the reader wondering just what is the real truth of the matter. If so, he or she is not alone, since by the same reasoning it has been alleged that the USA is not really a net debtor at all, as shown in **Table 9.6**, but a net creditor. The US government actually refuses to publish the official (horrendously large) figure for the net debt, claiming that it is erroneous and misleading. Nevertheless, respected US analysts claim that a proper revaluation of both assets and liabilities leaves the official net position almost unchanged.

Table 9.6 *International Comparisons of External Net Asset Positions*

End-years	1981	1985	1991	1992	1993	1994
United States						
$ billions	374.3	139.1	−355.1	−515.7	−545.3	−680.8
Percentage of GNP	12.3	3.4	−6.2	−8.6	−8.6	−10.1
Japan						
$ billions	10.9	129.8	383.1	513.6	610.8	689.0
Percentage of GNP	1.0	10.0	10.6	13.7	14.5	14.5
Germany						
$ billions	29.2	52.8	325.2	289.7	240.9	212.0
Percentage of GNP	4.0	9.0	18.5	16.6	14.6	11.2
France						
$ billions	56.4	6.1	−74.4	−95.0	−66.8	−38.3
Percentage of GNP	8.6	1.0	−5.7	−7.5	−5.6	−2.8
United Kingdom						
$ billions	62.2	102.6	−3.7	11.0	19.6	27.7
Percentage of GNP	11.9	22.4	−0.4	1.2	2.1	2.6

Note:
[1] The data underlying this table are taken from national sources, the IMF *International Financial Statistics Publication* (GNP figures) and OECD *Financial Statistics Part 2*. National sources may use differing methodologies.

Source: Amos (1995) p. 357.

☐ *9.6.3 Rejigging the Accounts*

Measured in constant 1980 dollars, the value of world-wide foreign direct investment was roughly ten times as large at the end of the 1980s as it had been at the beginning of the 1970s. UN estimates suggest that global flows increased by 30 per cent annually between 1983 and 1990 (Amos, 1995, p. 358). The peak figure of $230 billion was attained in 1990, and although FDI was temporarily reduced by the ensuing recession, that peak figure was reached again during 1994. We have noted the very large outflows of FDI from the UK during the late 1980s when it was, in fact, the world's largest investor concentrating upon the USA. As yet, the 1989 peak has not been exceeded.

The effect of these enormous overseas investments has been to change the ownership structure of business in many countries, and at the same time to cast doubt upon the conventional way of calculating trade balances. For example, an increasing amount of trade takes the form of transfers between the domestic operations of a multinational business and its overseas subsidiaries. On an 'ownership-based' accounting system these would not be counted as international trade. In addition, some sales in a domestic market are to the subsidiaries of foreign businesses which it may be argued are analogous to exports, as are the sales of overseas subsidiaries in overseas markets. On the other hand, it may be argued that domestic purchases from the subsidiaries of foreign-owned businesses are analogous to imports, as are purchases by overseas subsidiaries in overseas markets.

Until the 1980s, rejigging trade flows onto an ownership basis would not have made much overall difference, and it currently makes relatively little difference in the case of, for example, Japan. In the case of the USA, however, it totally transforms the trade balance, converting a very large deficit into a modest surplus (see also discussion in *Financial Times*, 14 November 1994). The effects upon the UK accounts are not known, but given the surge in outward investment during the 1980s, an ownership-based system of trade accounts would presumably look much more favourable today than it did a decade ago and thus help to allay fears about the overall trading position.

9.6.4 Is There a Current Account Crisis?

It is now possible to draw some tentative conclusions about allegations that 'crisis' is a word that can be applied to the UK current account. These allegations partly relate to the fact that at the trough of the 1980–81 recession the UK ran a surplus equal to 2.7 per cent of GDP, whereas at the trough of the 1990–92 recession it ran a deficit of 1.7 per cent of GDP. At the end of the 1980s, the so-called 'Burn's Doctrine' held that such a crisis was an illusion because (1) it was temporary; (2) invisibles were replacing visibles; (3) the external asset base was growing; (4) the deficit could be financed without difficulty. It is our considered view in relation to (1) that the imbalance will be with us for the foreseeable future, but that it should not be assumed to be permanent, at least not on a scale such as to cause real concern. Point (2) is no longer taking place on any significant scale, but manufacturing exports are anyway

Figure 9.5   *Investment Goods as a Share of Imported Finished Manufactures[1]*

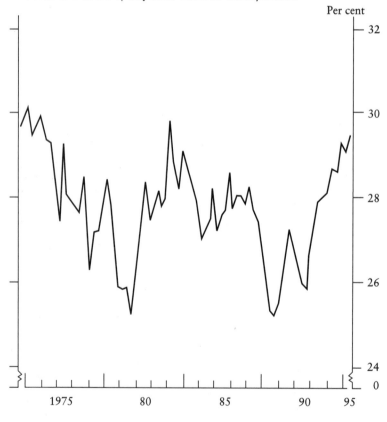

Note:
[1] Excluding the erratic items.
Source: Bank of England Inflation Report (February 1996) p. 25.

holding up quite well. Point (3) both appears to be true currently and is likely to remain so (although foreign ownership of UK assets is approximately of equal value). Point (4) has been true for a long time and should remain so.

One further point relates to investment goods, since it is argued that if manufactured imports are in this form then, unlike finished manufactures for consumption, they should not be regarded as a problem. As shown in **Figure 9.5**, the importation of investment goods collapsed during the latter part of the 1970s, but revived substantially as the economy came out of recession in the early 1980s. This pattern repeated itself, but from a lower base, at the end of the decade, and we are once again seeing a revival of some magnitude. This pattern is not particularly beneficial – it would clearly be much better were the share to remain consistently at or above the 30 per cent mark throughout the cycle – but at least some attempt is currently being made to ensure that the capacity of the UK to produce finished manufactures is not being eroded any further.

Overall, therefore, we are inclined in the light of the above to see a 'modest problem' where others see a 'crisis', but it nevertheless remains true that the government has the capacity to convert it into the other category, particularly if it ceases to pursue fairly conservative fiscal policies.

■ 9.7 Competitiveness

□ 9.7.1 Measuring Competitiveness

It is appropriate to refer, at this point in our discussion of trade performance, to the **competitiveness** of the UK. Competitiveness is impossible to measure in any absolute sense, so it must be judged by compiling indices of **relative performance** compared to other relevant countries. Even this is fraught with data collection difficulties, because we need to take some relevant characteristic of the UK economy, measure it over time as an index, and compare that index with the corresponding indices for other countries. Since no single index can be expected to tell the whole story, we need to provide as wide a variety as

possible. However, while some of these should incorporate non-price characteristics, they cannot realistically be measured, so indices must concentrate upon **cost and price competitiveness**, on the assumption that price and non-price factors are interdependent.

Many goods are in practice sold almost entirely on the home market, so the indices need to incorporate only those goods that are internationally traded on a major scale. As manufactured goods comprise the largest element in both UK imports and exports, they are used exclusively for the indices. Additionally, because competitiveness is affected by the exchange rate, all the costs and prices need to be converted into a common currency, in this case dollars, at the ruling spot rate. With every country's index valued in a common currency, the ratio expressing one relative to another can then be measured as an absolute number.

Figure 9.6 illustrates the most important measures of competitiveness on a quarterly basis for the past 10 years. These measures represent changes in the degree of competitiveness over time. The ratios are compiled as follows:

Import price competitiveness: UK wholesale price index for home market sales of manufactures (other than food, drink and tobacco) divided by the unit value index of imports of finished manufactures (SITC sections 7–8, Revision 2)

Relative normal unit labour costs: index of normal labour costs per unit of output in the UK divided by a weighted geometric average of competitors' normal unit labour costs adjusted for exchange rate changes.

Relative producer prices: UK wholesale price index for home sales of manufactures (including food, drink and tobacco) divided by weighted average of the indices of competitors' wholesale prices.

Relative profitability of exports: ratio of the UK export unit value index for manufactured goods (SITC sections 5–8, Revision 2) to the UK wholesale price index for home market sales of the

Figure 9.6 *Measures of UK Trade Competitiveness (1990 = 100)*

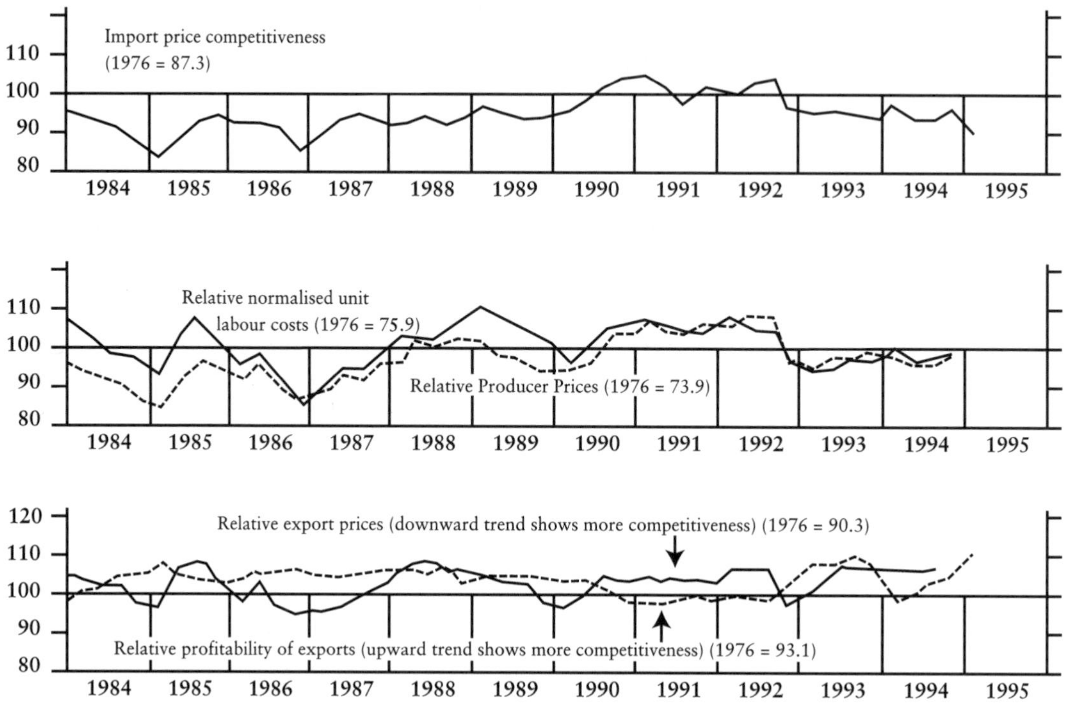

Source: Economic Trends, Table 2.15.

products of manufacturing industries (other than food, drink and tobacco).

Relative export prices: unit value index of UK exports of manufactured goods divided by a weighted average of competitors' export price indices for manufactures.

All of these indices are subject to data measurement problems. However, the various measures of competitiveness do appear to follow the same pattern, so the overall picture can be taken as acceptably accurate.

☐ 9.7.2 The Historical Pattern

During the 1970s, sterling's effective exchange rate (EER) fell steadily, thereby cheapening ex-

ports and making imports more expensive. Unfortunately, this did not, as we have seen, prevent the trade balance from remaining firmly in deficit. The reason can partly be seen in the data for relative normal unit labour costs, where the index (based on 1990 = 100), standing at 74.6 in 1977, rose sharply to 114.5 in 1980, and actually peaked at over 129.3 in the first quarter of 1981. Irrespective of non-price factors, which in any event were unfavourable for the UK, it is understandable that the UK's high costs caused relative export prices to move unfavourably despite the advantage of a falling exchange rate. Equally, even though this caused import prices to rise, domestic prices also rose steadily, albeit less dramatically relative to import prices. The only positive feature was that the steady rise in relative export prices, which also rose from 69.6 in 1976Q4 to a peak of 123.1 in 1981Q1, maintained the relative profitability of exports on an even keel.

A generally similar picture is shown in **Table 9.2.** The UK's share of world exports of manufactures had been falling throughout the postwar period. This, of itself, was only to be expected since the initially very high share held by the UK reflected the early date of industrialisation, and progressive entry into her markets by newly industrialising countries, using more modern technology, was bound to have a profound impact. The disturbing aspect was, however, that the total volume of world trade in manufactures was itself rising very rapidly, commonly at over 10 per cent per annum, so there was plenty of room for new entrants without the need to eat heavily into the market share of existing producers, and indeed the UK was unique amongst the established industrial nations in suffering more than a marginal loss in market share.

The increased share of imports in Total Final Expenditure (TFE) was also to be expected as industrialised nations increasingly traded manufactured goods with one another, and indeed was characteristic of all such nations. Again, however, the disturbing aspect was the relatively rapid pace at which this occurred in the UK, reflecting in part the UK's relatively high income elasticity of demand for imports.

However, the overall picture during the period from 1981 to 1984 was a generally much happier one. As shown in **Table 9.2**, the UK's share of world exports of manufactures appeared to have reached an equilibrium situation. **Figure 9.6** shows that relative normal unit labour costs declined steadily to 1985Q1, and with the effective exchange rate moving sharply downwards, relative export prices became significantly more competitive, and the relative profitability of exports rose slowly but steadily. Despite the rise in import prices, the competitiveness of imports also improved, albeit understandably more slowly, and the visible balance showed several years of surplus. The major problem was, however, the fact that imports as a share of TFE had bottomed out in 1981, and by 1984 was up 2.6 percentage points. The visible balance in 1984 was accordingly back in substantial deficit.

During 1985, competitiveness suddenly deteriorated, in particular because of a sharp rise in relative normal unit labour costs and in the EER, and although the following year witnessed a recovery, it was clear that the first quarter of 1985 was going to prove difficult to emulate, let alone outperform. The situation from 1985 to the end of 1988 was very gloomy. Relative normal unit labour costs resumed their upward climb, and both relative export prices and import competitiveness followed suit. Imports as a percentage of TFE rose yet further, but the one modest saving grace was an increase in the UK's share of world exports of manufactures and the resilience of relative export profitability. With the EER being prevented from falling much as a matter of policy, and wage demands showing signs of escalating, it was reasonable to suppose that competitiveness would continue to deteriorate for the foreseeable future.

In practice, relative normal unit labour costs did dip again in 1989 only to concede all the ground gained during 1990. Relative export prices followed suit and relative export profitability dipped below the 100 index at the end of 1990 for the first time since 1983. With inflation rising relative to its trading partners, the UK inevitably suffered a loss of competitiveness in 1990 and 1991.

As ever, it is important not to get too fixated with domestic problems taken in isolation. Compared to most OECD advanced countries, Britain managed to remain relatively competitive during the latter part of the 1980s. The likes of Taiwan and Hong Kong were the real exporting successes of the decade, but Britain held on to its markets better than Japan and most of the EU.

Since 1990, there have been two distinct periods divided by the devaluation of 1992. Whilst the effects were largely positive on the export side, it can be seen that relative export prices subsequently rose as did the relative profitability of exports – in other words, exporters chose to improve their profit margins quite considerably (see FSBR 1995–96, Chart 3.17) while the going was good. With import prices on the rise, the other indicators also moved favourably, and these factors have helped to keep a cap on the visible deficit although they have clearly been insufficient, in the face of recession in some of the UK's main export markets, to do any more than that.

One final factor is worthy of mention. If the current balance as a percentage of GDP is plotted against the rate of unemployment (a sort of 'Phillips Curve' for the external sector) an interesting pattern is visible. What this reveals is that from 1968 to 1974 the current balance ratio fluctuated considerably while the unemployment rate remained fairly constant. As unemployment began to rise rapidly post-1974, the current balance ratio improved steadily from −4 per cent of GDP in 1974 to +3.1 per cent in 1981. Between 1981 and 1988, the current balance ratio deteriorated steadily back to −4 per cent without unemployment falling below its rate in 1981 until well into 1988. In other words, the current balance ratio was no longer responding significantly to high unemployment. Since 1988 the current balance ratio has remained negative despite unemployment fluctuating between 6.5 and 10.5 per cent.

As in the case of the Phillips Curve, this suggests firstly that there is no imminent likelihood of a return to the 'golden days' of the 1960s, although the exchange rate system in operation at the time (see following chapter) made it much harder than currently to shrug off current account deficits. Secondly, because major economies are no longer in synchronisation with respect to the business cycle, domestic deflation with higher unemployment has too little effect upon the current balance ratio to be worth the sacrifice in terms of lost jobs. The last time the current balance ratio stood at roughly 0 per cent, in 1986, the unemployment rate was intolerably high, and in 1994, at least, the combination was much more favourable overall.

9.8 Area Composition of UK Visible Trade

During the nineteenth century, circumstances conspired to create a pattern of trade in the UK consisting essentially of the importation of raw materials and the exportation of finished goods. This arose in the first place because the UK was the earliest country to industrialise, and secondly because most of the trade was conducted with former or existing colonies. The latter was to a considerable extent a consequence of the former, since other newly-industrialising countries erected barriers against imports from the UK in order to protect their infant industries, but in any event the existence of a common language facilitated trade even with ex-colonies such as the USA.

Trading links with Europe developed gradually during the twentieth century, but as **Tables 9.7 and 9.8** indicate, Europe accounted for only one quarter of UK imports and a slightly higher proportion of exports even in 1955. At that time, the LDCs accounted for roughly 40 per cent of both UK imports and exports, of which very little was contributed by the Eastern bloc countries. Over the past three decades, the UK has come to trade increasingly with other developed countries. In the case of exports, the share has risen to roughly 80 per cent, although there was a marked temporary dip in the mid-1970s due to the oil-price effect discussed below. In the case of imports, the growth in the share taken by the developed countries has been much steadier, with no comparable mid-1970s effect, and the current developed country share is, as a consequence, even higher than that for exports. It is clear that this growth cannot continue if the UK is to maintain any meaningful trade links with the LDCs, and **Tables 9.7 and 9.8** give some reason to believe that the ultimate equilibrium between developed and less developed countries has possibly been reached of late.

The increased share of both imports and exports taken by developed countries has not, however, been evenly distributed. The UK joined the Community in 1972 at a time when trade links with Western Europe were already significantly outweighing those with developed countries outside Europe. Exports to America were still fairly buoyant, whereas imports had only very recently begun to decline, but a marked reduction in trade with other English-speaking ex-colonies had by then become evident.

Prior to 1972, the switch from non-Community to Community countries was already quite marked, but the sharp increase in the share of UK imports from the Community between 1970 and 1975, and the even bigger increase in the share of UK exports taken by Community countries between 1975 and 1980, can reasonably be attrib-

Table 9.7 *Area Composition of UK Exports, 1955–95, % Total Value*

	1955	*1965*	*1970*	*1975*	*1980*	*1985[1]*	*1990*	*1993*	*1994*	*1995*
EU	15.0	26.3	28.9	32.3	45.4	48.6	57.6	56.8	57.0	58.2
Other Western Europe	13.9	15.5	17.1	15.9	12.1	9.7	4.6	4.3	4.2	4.1
North America[2]	12.0	14.8	15.0	11.8	11.2	17.0	15.0	14.5	14.3	13.4
Other OECD[3]	20.5	14.8	12.0	9.5	5.6	4.9	4.6	3.8	4.0	4.2
Oil exporting	5.1	5.6	5.8	11.6	10.2	7.6	5.3	5.3	4.2	4.1
Rest of world	33.5	23.0	20.8	19.0	15.5	12.2	12.9	15.3	16.3	16.0

Notes:
[1] Old definitions up to 1985. Figures for all years post-1985 relate to 1994 composition of EU.
[2] Including Mexico.
[3] Japan, Australia, New Zealand. Previously included South Africa. 1985 equivalent on new definition = 3.6%.
Source: UK Balance of Payments 1996, Table 2.2.

Table 9.8 *Area Composition of UK Imports, 1955–95, % Total Value*

	1955	*1965*	*1970*	*1975*	*1980*	*1985[1]*	*1990*	*1993*	*1994*	*1995*
EU	12.6	23.6	28.3	36.5	45.1	50.0	58.4	55.1	56.6	56.7
Other Western Europe	13.1	12.2	14.9	14.9	13.0	14.3	7.6	6.9	6.3	6.2
North America[2]	19.5	19.6	20.9	13.3	14.9	13.5	13.6	13.2	13.2	13.5
Other OECD[3]	14.2	11.9	10.1	7.7	6.2	7.3	6.4	7.0	6.9	6.7
Oil exporting	9.2	9.8	7.2	13.5	8.4	3.2	2.1	2.6	2.0	1.8
Rest of world	31.4	22.9	18.6	14.1	12.4	11.7	11.9	15.2	15.0	15.1

Notes:
[1] Old definitions up to 1985. Figures for all years post-1985 relate to 1994 composition of EU.
[2] Including Mexico.
[3] Japan, Australia, New Zealand. Previously included South Africa.
Source: UK Balance of Payments 1996, Table 2.2.

uted to UK membership. The share of UK exports taken by Community countries continued to rise until the early 1990s, but this in part reflected the exchange rate effects which favoured the Community as a market compared to the USA. The quadrupling of the share of UK imports originating from the Community has undoubtedly been the most dramatic adjustment of UK trade patterns over the past three decades, and it is hardly surprising that the UK economy has been reorien-tated geographically, swinging around from north-west (feeding trade with America) to south-east (feeding trade with Europe). Within the EU, the dependence upon imports from Germany (15 per cent of total UK imports), France (9.5 per cent) and the Netherlands (7.5 per cent) is quite marked. Japan provides less than these three despite the impression sometimes given in the media. Furthermore, it is relatively even less important as a destination for UK exports of which in excess of 30 per cent are accounted for by the these three EU countries.

As previously mentioned, the oil price has affected the pattern of UK trade with the LDCs. The effect of the sharp increase in the oil price in 1974 was to transfer huge sums to OPEC countries, and as **Table 9.7** shows this resulted in a doubling of the share of UK exports to oil exporting countries in 1975. Imports did not follow suit on the same scale because only one product was involved, but in the short term the low price elasticity of UK demand for oil did result in a marked increase in the value of oil imports. The oil price rose sharply again in 1980, but by then the UK was becoming self-sufficient. Subsequently, imports from OPEC have virtually disappeared, although exports remain more signifi-

cant because the OPEC countries have much greater spending power.

The reasons behind some of the changes described above are fairly obvious, but the heavy dependence upon imports from other developed countries is less so, given that they must consist primarily of finished manufactures which traditionally formed the bulk of UK exports. However, it is increasingly a phenomenon of advanced industrial countries that they simultaneously import and export the same types of product such as cars and electronic apparatus, and there has also been a marked reduction in the dependence of the UK economy upon the exportation of finished manufactures.

One further point is of interest. Analysis of the area composition of trade in relation to the cur-

Figure 9.7   *Current Account Balances (£bn)*

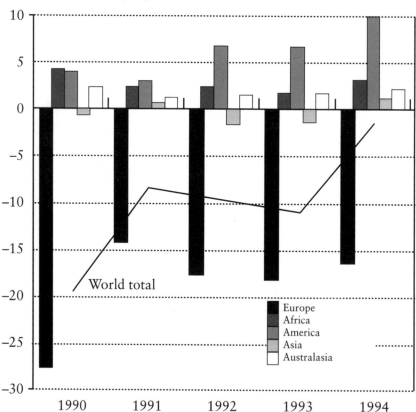

Source: CSO (1995) p. 14.

rent account has traditionally concentrated upon manufactures which are relatively easy to trace. For this reason, much media attention has been focused on issues such as the inroads being made by 'Asian tigers' upon markets for UK manufactures. However, a recent analysis by the CSO (CSO, 1995) puts this into perspective, as shown in **Figure 9.7**.

In 1994, the UK ran a current account deficit of £7 billion with the then 12 members of the EU, and a further £9 billion with EFTA. This indicates, among other things, that the 1992 sterling devaluation failed radically to tip the playing field in favour of the UK despite frequent claims to the contrary. In contrast, although large visible trade deficits also existed in respect of Japan and the rest of Asia, these were more than offset, for the first time in respect of the four 'tigers', by a surplus on invisibles boosted by investment income. Furthermore, the surpluses with Africa, American countries and Australasia all increased in 1994 compared to 1993, and transactions with Core Newly Industrializing Countries recorded its first surplus after several years of deficits. The individual countries yielding the biggest surpluses were the USA, Canada, South Africa and Australia.

9.9 Commodity Composition of UK Visible Trade

As indicated above, the UK was traditionally an importer of raw materials and an exporter of manufactured goods. Even in 1955, as shown in **Tables 9.9 and 9.10**, raw materials constituted some 75 per cent of UK imports, whereas over 80 per cent of UK exports consisted of semi-manufactured or finished manufactured goods. However, the switch towards European markets documented above went hand-in-hand with a sharp change in the nature of imports during the 1970s, such that raw materials currently constitute less than one-fifth of the total value of imports.

As can be seen in **Table 9.10**, the steady decline in this share disguised some volatile behaviour among the sub-aggregates. In particular, fuel im-

ports move up as a result of OPEC during the mid-1970s, only to decline sharply and continuously thereafter as the UK became self-sufficient in oil.

The share of semi-manufactured imports has also oscillated, while that of finished manufactured imports has risen fairly continuously, although it fell back slightly during the recent recession. As a result, the two main parts of **Table 9.10** currently stand in approximately the inverse ratio to that of 1955. It is difficult to assess whether the current position is near to its ultimate equilibrium, but it is hard to see how much further the rebalancing between the two totals can rationally go. One factor is that whereas it may be argued that the UK is no longer much dependent upon imports of food, beverages and tobacco, this sector nevertheless currently presents major trading problems, as noted below, once exports are taken into account.

The situation with respect to exports has generally been more stable overall. However, from 1975 to 1985 the share of exports taken by manufactured goods of all kinds declined whilst there was a sharp increase in the share taken by fuels. Fuel exports collapsed after 1985, and their share of total exports was entirely taken up by manufactures of all kinds on the back of rising productivity and a sustainable exchange rate in relation to other Community countries. Since 1990, there have been signs that equilibrium has been restored, and it is interesting that the situation bears a remarkable resemblance to the position between 1965 and 1975.

Nevertheless, the aggregates disguise some significant switches between industrial sectors. Amongst the semi-manufactured exports the share taken by chemicals rose steadily throughout the period from 1955, whereas that of metals fell by almost one half and that of textiles by three quarters. The chemicals industry has been a major success story for UK exports, although its 13 per cent share of total exports has risen only slightly since 1985.

Engineering products constituted roughly one-third of all exports in both 1955 and 1985. However, its share peaked some 10 per cent higher in 1970, and there has been a steady decline since

Table 9.9 *Commodity Analysis of Exports, % Total Value*

	1955	1965	1970	1975	1980	1985	1990	1994	1995
Food, beverages and tobacco	6.0	6.6	6.2	7.1	6.8	6.3	6.9	7.4	7.3
Basic materials	3.9	4.0	3.2	2.7	3.1	2.7	2.2	1.9	1.9
Fuels[1]	4.9	2.7	2.2	4.2	13.6	21.5	7.7	6.7	6.1
Total	14.8	13.3	11.6	14.0	23.5	30.5	16.8	16.0	15.3
Semi-manufactured	36.9	34.6	34.4	31.2	29.6	25.6	28.3	28.6	28.5
Finished manufactured	43.5	49.0	50.2	51.0	44.0	41.2	52.7	54.3	55.0
Total	80.4	83.6	84.6	82.2	73.6	66.8	81.0	82.9	83.5
Unclassified	4.8	3.1	3.8	3.8	2.9	2.7	2.2	1.1	1.2

Note:
[1] Roughly 95% oil.

Source: UK Balance of Payments 1996, Table 21.

Table 9.10 *Commodity Analysis of Imports, % Total Value*

	1955	1965	1970	1975	1980	1985	1990	1994	1995
Food, beverages and tobacco	36.9	29.7	22.6	18.0	12.2	10.6	9.6	9.5	9.3
Basic materials	29.0	19.3	13.7	8.4	7.4	6.0	4.6	3.8	3.9
Fuels	10.6	10.6	8.3	17.5	14.2	12.8	6.2	4.1	3.4
Total	76.5	59.6	44.6	43.9	33.8	29.4	20.4	17.4	16.6
Semi-manufactured	17.9	23.8	29.2	23.9	27.3	24.8	26.2	26.1	27.5
Finished manufactured	5.3	15.4	24.6	29.9	36.6	44.0	51.8	55.7	55.0
Total	23.2	39.2	53.8	53.8	63.9	68.8	78.0	81.8	82.5
Unclassified	0.3	1.2	1.6	2.3	2.3	1.8	1.6	0.8	0.9

Source: UK Balance of Payments 1996, Table 21.

that time. A good part of this was in the road motor vehicles classification. This accounted for only 1.5 per cent of total exports in 1984, but its share has subsequently more than doubled.

It is also of interest to look at the visible balance for each of the aggregates as depicted in **Figure 9.8**, although it should be borne in mind that this is based upon a different accounting system to that used in **Table 9.1**, and sums to a larger total trade deficit than in **Table 9.1**. Throughout the period 1970–96, imports of food, beverages and tobacco have consistently exceeded exports, and this has also been the case for basic materials. However, whereas the oil aggregate fell to a record deficit of £4 billion in 1976, it had moved into surplus by 1980 where it has remained. The record surplus of £8 billion in 1985 therefore represented a turnaround of £12 billion over a 10–year period (although less marked after adjusting for inflation), but the surplus remained at half that value for the next two years and fell sharply again in 1988 and 1989 after which it stabilised. It is fortunately now once again on an upwards trend given that it is the only aggregate substantially in surplus.

Semi-manufactured goods remained in surplus until 1983, but recorded deficits through until the end of the decade, with the problem deteriorating rapidly from 1985 to 1989. Since then it has improved, even returning to surplus in 1993 and 1994.

However, this swing is insignificant compared to the situation with respect to finished manufac-

Figure 9.8 *Visable Trade Balance, Current Prices*

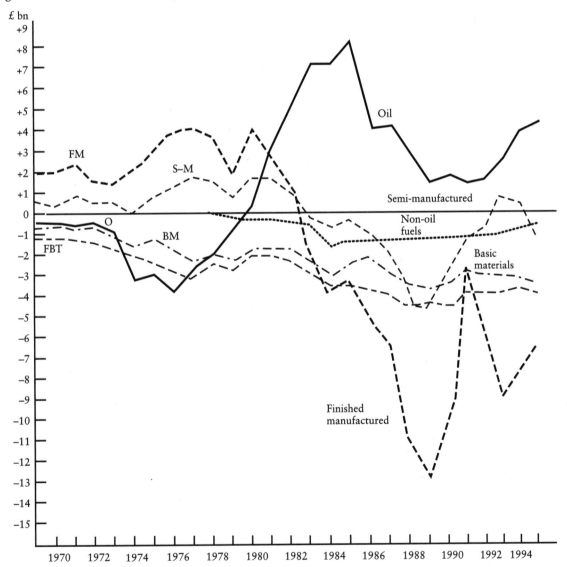

Source: UK Balance of Payments 1996, Table 2.1.

tured goods, which also remained in surplus until 1983 before moving sharply into deficit thereafter. The surplus of £4 billion in 1980 was transformed into a £6 billion deficit in 1987, a somewhat smaller turnaround than for oil but accomplished in half the time. In 1988, the deficit soared to £11 billion followed by £13 billion in 1989. Not surprisingly, much of the policy debate at the time focused on this phenomenon although the situation did improve dramatically in 1990 and 1991 with the onset of recession. This gave cause for hope that the deficit would disappear in its entirety, but that is evidently not to be, and it remains the largest single problem area.

During the greater part of the 1980s, the sector which contributed most to the deficit in manufactures was motor vehicles. As we have noted, this sector is on the mend, and is unlikely ever to play that undesirable role again. What is rather alarming is that food, beverages and tobacco has been performing so badly even though it is non-manufacturing and even though one half of the deficit is accounted for by products that can be grown in the UK. It would appear that British farmers' ability to market their products is put into the shade by their continental rivals.

Davies (1990) has calculated that well over two-thirds of the worsening in the trade balance between 1986 and 1989 was derived from those items which relate to goods that are used in the process of production – raw materials, semi-manufactures and intermediate finished manufactures. As a consequence, it would appear that the government was correct in claiming that it was a deterioration in these inputs rather than any direct increase in the deficit on consumer goods which 'explained' most of the deterioration in the trade deficit, but also that the Opposition was correct in claiming that it had not been caused by an inflow of capital machinery which would have enhanced the UK's capacity to produce in the future. As Davies notes, a key issue is whether the industrial inputs have been used, after being subjected to further processing, for investment or consumption. His conclusion is that these were almost equally responsible for the deterioration in the current account during 1986–89. However, taking the period 1979–89 as a whole, private consumption appeared to be the villain of the piece.

Consumption was severely depressed post-1990 and this combined with a lower exchange rate effected the improvement which is clearly visible in **Figure 9.8**. The fact that there is now a larger element on the positive side of the line is a cause for some optimism about the future, but the persistence of the deficits for basic materials, food, beverages and tobacco, and finished manufactures, particularly in the context of what is now looking increasing like an ongoing upturn in consumption, is reason enough to expect the visible trade deficit to persist for some time to come.

Bibliography

Amos, W. (1995) 'The External Balance Sheet of the United Kingdom: Recent Developments', *Bank of England Quarterly Bulletin* (November).

Ayres, R. (1992) 'Britain's Trade in Invisibles', *British Review of Economic Issues* (February).

Bank of England (1990) 'The External Balance Sheet of the United Kingdom: Recent Developments and Measurement Problems', *Bank of England Quarterly Bulletin* (November).

Bank of England (1992) 'The External Balance Sheet of the United Kingdom: Recent Developments', *Bank of England Quarterly Bulletin* (November).

Financial Times (1996) 'Survey: Inward Investment into the UK' (18 July).

Central Statistical Office (1995) 'Geographical Analysis of the Current Account of the Balance of Payments', *Economic Trends* (October).

Clayton, A. (1996) 'The External Balance Sheet of the United Kingdom: Recent Developments', *Bank of England Quarterly Bulletin* (November).

Coutts, K. and W. Godley (1990) 'Prosperity and Foreign Trade in the 1990s: Britain's Strategic Problems', *Oxford Review of Economic Policy*, 6 (3).

Davies, G. (1990) 'The Capital Account and the Sustainability of the UK Trade Deficit', *Oxford Review of Economic Policy*, 6 (3).

Dumble, A. (1994) 'UK Trade – Long-term Trends and Recent Developments', *Bank of England Quarterly Bulletin* (August).

Holtham, G. (1990) 'World Current Account Balances', *Oxford Review of Economic Policy*, 6 (3).

Lakin, C. (1994) 'Presenting the Balance of Payments Accounts', *Economic Trends* (May).

Muellbauer, J. and A. Murphy (1990) 'Is the UK Balance of Payments Sustainable?', *Economic Policy* (October).

Office for National Statistics (1996) 'Geographical Analysis of the Current Account of the Balance of Payments', *Economic Trends* (April).

Pain, N. and P. Westaway (1990) 'Why the Capital Account Matters', *National Institute Economic Review* (February).

Pratten, C. (1992) 'Overseas Investments, Capital Gains and the Balance of Payments', *Research Monograph 48*, Institute of Economic Affairs.

Rhys, D. (1990) 'The Motor Industry and the Balance of Payments', *Bank of Scotland*

The Economist (1995) 'In Defence of Deficits', *Review* (December).

The Economist (1996) 'The Miracle of Trade', 27 January 1996, pp. 70–1.

Thirlwall, T. (1992) 'The Balance of Payments and Economic Performance', *National Westminster Quarterly Bank Review* (May).

Williamson, K. and Porter, F. (1994) 'UK Visible Trade Statistics – the Intrastat System', *Economic Trends* (August).

Chapter 10

External Transactions

Peter Curwen

■ *10.1* Exchange Rates

□ *10.1.1 Introduction*

An exchange rate is the **price of one currency**, for our purposes the £ sterling, **in terms of another currency or set of currencies**. As such, it is in principle determined in the market place for currencies, and moves up or down in accordance with the relative forces of demand and supply. In this case the market place is no longer physical, since currency transactions are these days conducted on electronic screens, and this in turn means that anyone can deal in currencies at any time of the day or night anywhere in the world. Not surprisingly, exchange rates are as a consequence constantly on the move as dealers try to make money by taking advantage of very small movements in rates. Most transactions are for immediate delivery at the current price on the **spot** market, but it is possible to transact in the **forward** market where a price is agreed today for delivery **at some future date**. Buying or selling forward is valuable for firms engaging in trade, since it guarantees for them the amount of pounds sterling which they will have to pay for imports or receive for exports.

However, although currency transactions are open to all, there are huge discrepancies between the market power of different participants. In particular, governments, especially of industrial nations, have powers derived from being the ultimate suppliers of currencies which are widely traded, and they are therefore in a position to influence strongly the way the currency markets behave. At the one extreme, they may be happy to allow the markets to trade freely, neither deliberately adding to, nor subtracting from, the amount of their own currencies in circulation that arise from imbalances in their balance of payments accounts. At the other extreme, they may set out to prevent the exchange rate from varying at all, by buying and selling their own currencies on whatever scale is necessary to neutralise exactly any buying or selling in the market place. Between these extremes there are a host of variants which reflect gradations in the extent to which governments seek to prevent the market working freely. Nevertheless, it must be borne in mind that non-governmental traders are **in aggregate** also very powerful, and it is not altogether clear in principle whether they, or governments, will be the dominant influence on exchange rates. The average **daily** turnover in the London foreign exchange market (the world's largest and fastest-growing with a 30 per cent share) is roughly $500 billion (Thomas, 1995), and in total world forex markets turn over in excess of $1300 billion a day (with the substantial recent growth primarily accounted for by forward currency business, largely swaps between banks). A reasonable view might accordingly be that, whereas traders in aggregate can dominate **individual** governments, they cannot dominate the major industrial nations **acting in concert** over extended periods of time. Since in practice, as we will discover below, this latter eventuality is uncommon (it occurs typically twice a year), it is fair to say that in the long term, exchange rates are broadly determined by market forces irrespective of which exchange rate system is nominally in operation.

The very appearance of the authorities in the foreign exchange markets is potentially an encouragement to speculation. In the absence of intervention, a speculator can make gains only at the expense of other speculators and hence tends to tread a little carefully for fear of being outwitted. However, once the authorities enter the markets to buy a particular currency it becomes obvious to all speculators that this currency cannot otherwise be held at its desired level, and they realise that they can all become sellers and impose losses upon the authorities rather than upon others of their kind. Furthermore, if they can create sufficient selling pressure then the authorities may have to withdraw from the markets in order to avoid using up scarce foreign currency and/or suffering too great a trading loss, whereupon the currency will drop sharply in value and produce huge speculative gains for sellers when they repurchase at much lower prices than those at which they sold.

It follows that half-hearted inventions by the authorities are largely counter-productive. Intervention is only successful **insofar as it imposes losses on speculators**. If the authorities in several major economies, acting in concert, suddenly enter the markets with large-scale buy orders for a particular currency which speculators are selling on a modest scale, or vice versa, speculators will get their fingers burned and act more circumspectly on future occasions. However, it may

strictly be necessary only to **threaten** such behaviour to discourage a good deal of speculation, since if one group of speculators is selling heavily another group may move to buy in anticipation of similar behaviour by the authorities should the rate fall too far (which, naturally, does not then happen).

When the forces of the market are dominant, and the exchange rate is constantly on the move in response either to excess demand or supply, an upwards movement is called an **appreciation** and a downwards movement is called a **depreciation**. Where, however, the government engineers a **unilateral change** in the rate from one value to another, an upwards adjustment is called a **revaluation** and a downwards adjustment is called a **devaluation**. The action of the UK government may not be intended to alter the rate, but rather to halt its upward or downward movement. When it intervenes in the foreign exchange markets in order to prevent sterling from rising, it is obliged, via the Bank of England, to sell sterling and to buy foreign currency in exchange. This is then mostly deposited in the official reserves. When, however, the government wishes to prevent sterling from falling, it is obliged to buy sterling and in exchange to sell foreign currency which is withdrawn from the official reserves.

As suggested above, the government may, or may not, be successful in its endeavours. To some extent this is conditioned by whether or not the government has openly declared the value at which it wishes the pound to be stabilised, since this is bound to affect market expectations. Even if there is no official upper or lower limit to the value of the pound, the currency markets can work out the unofficial policy by retrospective inspection of changes in the reserves. Clearly, if there has been, for example, a rise of $1 billion in the monthly reserves figure, it follows that the Bank of England must have been intervening heavily in order to prevent the value of the pound from rising against the dollar (by selling pounds and buying dollars).

It is reasonable to suppose that, officially or unofficially, the government will usually have a clear view about the appropriate level for the exchange rate because of its effects upon the balance of payments. However, it must be recognised that the currency markets are not interested in the official position other than as a source of guidance to whether to buy or sell a currency at a particular point in time. They do not necessarily agree with the government about the consequences of its economic policy, and having formulated their own view about the probable direction of change of the pound, will be looking for signals from the Bank of England in order to determine whether they will be allowed to push the rate to what they believe it should be, or whether – and to what extent – they are likely to be thwarted by intervention.

The view about the exchange rate, whether governmental or market, will be influenced by a whole host of factors, of which the following are the most important: the rate of inflation compared with that of major competitors, the structure of interest rates compared with that of major competitors and the balance of payments on current account. In addition the market view will, as indicated, be influenced by its forecast of how the government will respond to these factors. Clearly, in order to form an opinion about these matters their underlying causes will themselves have to be studied with care – including, for example, the rate of growth in the economy, capacity constraints, unit labour costs, the fiscal and monetary aggregates and so on. Under the circumstances, it is hardly surprising that there should be disagreement about the 'proper' value for the exchange rate.

☐ 10.1.2 The Theory of Purchasing Power Parity (PPP)

This theory, which dates back to the 1920s, has traditionally been used to explain long-term trends in the exchange rate. PPP states that the exchange rate between two currencies depends upon the **purchasing power of each currency in its country of origin**. If both the UK and USA can produce a set of identical products, in the former case for £100 and in the latter for $100, PPP dictates an exchange rate of £1 = $1.

The change in the exchange rate comes about through adjustments to trade flows. In the above example, at the original exchange rate, it would pay UK residents to buy US exports for £100 in preference to identical domestic products at any higher price, and that would continue to be the case until the £/$ exchange rate had fallen in value (by one half if UK prices had doubled – thereby restoring the original **real** exchange rate). Unfortunately, this is an oversimplified view of the real world in which sets of identical products are difficult to identify, and are certainly less than comprehensive. In addition, allowance must be made for **trading costs**, including transportation costs, when comparing prices in domestic and foreign markets. In any event, these matters relate only to **visible trade flows**, and the exchange rate is likely to be affected by capital flows which fall outside the confines of the theory.

A looser – and hence by implication a more accurate but at the same time less analytically helpful – definition of PPP is that the currency of a country which has a **higher inflation rate** than its main trading partners will **depreciate**, and vice versa. Such testing of the theory as has been undertaken (and even that has to be treated with care because of problems with respect both to the measurement of the price level and of the exchange rate, and to the choice of countries) indicates that, starting at any particular year, the exchange rate eventually reaches an equilibrium level compatible with PPP, but that in the intervening period it may deviate significantly from it in either direction. For example, IMF calculations over the period 1973–95 indicate that changes in the dollar exchange rates of the main industrial countries have been almost entirely offset by those countries' inflation differentials with the USA (see *The Economist*, 1996, p. 82).

The interesting implication of such a tendency, should it prove to be more generally valid, is that there is no point in trying to use devaluation as a long-term solution to a problem of lack of competitiveness (unfortunately for the UK). In the short term, however, the issue is rather cloudier. For example, there is little point in devaluing if there is insufficient slack in the economy to meet any surge in export orders (one of the reasons why many decry the UK's loss of manufacturing capacity). Equally, there is little point in devaluing if workers respond to the erosion of their living standards via higher import prices by quickly obtaining compensatory wage increases. In effect, devaluation must hurt somewhat to be effective.

Looking at the UK during the period after the sharp drop in the exchange rate in 1992 (or for that matter at Italy or Sweden where exchange rates also plunged), it is evident that the drop did achieve a distinct improvement in competitiveness since there was spare capacity due to recession, high unemployment and fiscal tightening to make room for exports. However, it must also be borne in mind that the drop was very large, driving the nominal exchange rate well below PPP, thereby obviating any need to keep interest rates high to deter further speculation.

It may finally be observed that macroeconomic policy is primarily dealing with short-term issues, and in the short term, as any holiday maker knows, some countries are a good deal cheaper to visit than others.

☐ *10.1.3 Interest Rates*

We have already remarked upon the fact that hot money is attracted to countries which, after allowing for risk, offer the highest short-term rates of interest. This is also true, but on a much lesser scale, where non-residents wish to hold longer-term interest-bearing securities. If UK interest rates exceed those in the USA, West Germany and Japan there is going to be great demand for pounds to invest in the UK, and hence upwards pressure upon the exchange rate. The sums involved can best be thought of in terms of billions rather than millions, but there is fortunately a limiting device in operation.

This arises because, when a non-resident buys sterling at the current or 'spot' exchange rate in order to acquire an interest-bearing asset, he or she may wish to protect against a capital loss, should interest rates rise further, by arranging to sell the asset 'forward' at an agreed price. Buying in the present pushes the spot rate up, while selling in the future pushes the forward rate down. The greater the volume of sterling being bought and sold, the greater the difference between purchase and sale prices. Hence, beyond a certain point, the extra interest earned by investing in the UK is in principle entirely offset by the loss resulting from the need to sell at an exchange rate lower than at the time of purchase. The **interest rate parity theory** argues that the difference between spot and forward rates will automatically adjust to neutralise differences in short-term interest rates between countries, thereby greatly limiting flows of hot money. However, this argument may be defeated by the sheer volume of hot money, since it follows that a flood of hot money will drive up the exchange rate even higher, and hence even though forward rates are below the matching spot rates at any point in time, they will be rising above the spot rates which ruled in the preceding period. If sterling becomes a 'one-way bet' to continue rising, there is thus no necessity to accept a forward rate until it has risen above the spot rate at the time of purchase, or even perhaps to trade forward at all, since the spot rate at the time of sale will almost certainly be higher than any forward rate contracted previously.

In practice, the above effect is frequently stronger than any influence which the current account surplus or deficit may have upon the exchange rate. This is not to argue that the latter cannot be significant, but it follows logically that if the exchange rate is driven by the current account, then the current balance should be perpetually close to, or at, equilibrium. Since this has rarely been the case for the UK it follows that, particularly in the short term, **the exchange rate is more responsive to capital flows**. The obvious exception is where the current account deficit becomes so large that, even after adjusting for offsetting capital inflows, the reserves will run out unless the exchange rate is devalued. Where this is not an issue, it is quite possible that even a massive current account deficit will have less influence upon the exchange rate than hot money responding to rising interest rates, and hence that the **exchange rate will itself continue to rise**.

10.1.4 Interest Rates and Exchange Rate Risk

Let us assume that:

A US investor has $100 to invest.
The interest rate is 5% in the USA and 10% in the UK.
The exchange rate is initially $1 = £1 and does not vary.

Hence:

If $100 is converted into £ sterling it becomes £100 (ignoring transaction costs).
After earning interest in the UK at 10% it becomes £110.
And when converted back into $s it becomes $110.

This then compares **favourably** with the $105 which would have arisen in the USA.

However:

Suppose the value of sterling can vary, and it **falls** by 10% (that is, £110 = $100).
Then the £110 earned in the UK will convert back to $100.

This then compares **unfavourably** with the $105 which would have arisen in the USA.
On the other hand:

Suppose the value of sterling can vary, and it **rises** by 10% (that is £100 = $110).
Then the £110 earned in the UK will convert back to $121.

This represents a return of 21 per cent compared to only 5 per cent if the money is left in the USA.

It follows, therefore, that whether a higher nominal interest rate in one country compared to another is sufficient to attract an inflow of capital depends upon **expectations** of changes in exchange rates. If a country is expected to have a strengthening exchange rate then it will not need to have a high nominal interest rate. This was traditionally the situation for Japan and Germany, but circumstances have changed considerably since 1990.

For example, at the end of 1990 the US government was determined to reduce interest rates in order to offset the recession. The Germans, on the other hand, were anxious to raise interest rates in order to offset the inflationary impact of reunification. Ordinarily, this would have caused the DM to surge against the dollar, whereas precisely the opposite happened because the post-Gulf War euphoria and hopes of recovery made investors buy the dollar, whereas fears about the cost of reunification made investors sell the DM. Once it was clear that this was going to continue well into 1991, it became possible for the US government to cut interest rates even further without triggering a run on the dollar. Meanwhile, in the UK, the government refused to follow suit, only reducing interest rates slowly and by small increments, for which it was quite properly much criticised.

Where a country's exchange rate is expected to weaken, it will normally need to have a much higher nominal interest rate than elsewhere. The only way to eliminate exchange rate risk is to lock exchange rates together, a factor which underlay the decision to enter the Exchange Rate Mechanism (ERM), but even the wide band was clearly sufficient to create expectations of exchange rate variability in the UK, and to create worries in the minds of the government that interest rate reductions would trigger a sharp fall in the value of the pound.

Once the above is understood, it is possible to unravel the mystery as to why the correlation between saving and investment in any given country is stronger than one would expect in a world of freely mobile capital. At the end of the day, no matter how high the nominal interest rate on offer in, say, the UK, the fear of capital losses on the exchange rate will be enough to deter the more timid investor who will keep his or her money firmly at home. This is borne out by the astonishing size of capital flows during the era of the gold standard when exchange rate risk did not exist. When the topic of capital flows is under discussion, few remember that prior to 1915 the UK ran an average current account surplus of 5 per cent of GDP over a period of three decades, and that the money was exported all over the world to finance development in, for example, North and South America. It would appear, therefore, that talk of a global capital market is a touch premature, and is anyway not a new concept.

10.1.5 Measuring the Exchange Rate

It is such a commonplace to read about movements in 'the' exchange rate that few non-economists ever bother to question whether it is always the **same** exchange rate which is moving. In fact it isn't, so we must consider below the appropriate ways to measure exchange rate movements.

It is clear, to begin with, that there is an exchange rate linking sterling to every other currency belonging to a country with which the UK conducts trade. Naturally, some of these are much more important than others, either in terms of the pattern of UK trade or because of their significance for world affairs. For both these reasons it is customary to place most attention, in terms of individual exchange rates, upon the dollar, and it is indeed the £/$ rate which is most often quoted in the media. However, as shown in the section on the area composition of trade in the previous chapter, the UK now trades increasingly with the EU, and within the EU the German currency, the Deutsche Mark (DM), plays a central role, so there are often good reasons to concentrate upon the £/DM rate. While Japan is also very important from the point of view of its share of total world trade, the yen has less significance that the $ or DM specifically in terms of UK trade patterns. Nevertheless, it must be recognised that if the $/yen rate alters sharply, then this is bound to have some repercussions for the £/$ rate as well.

Measuring exchange rates in terms of individual currencies does, however, have drawbacks. In the first place, such rates can be very volatile, as the discussion of recent history below will demonstrate. Moreover, this volatility is much greater in certain cases, such as the dollar, compared to others such as the DM, and individual rates may not simply move in the same direction but at **different speeds** and in **opposite directions**. Clearly, to concentrate exclusively on the dollar when it is rising against the pound, at a time when the DM is simultaneously falling against the pound, may prove highly misleading in terms of consequences for the UK economy.

In order to adjust for this, the sensible procedure is to measure the exchange rate in terms of a **basket of currencies** which includes all those of any significance in terms of the UK and, by implication, of world trade. One could simply take the arithmetic average of all the rates included in such a basket, but it also seems sensible to make adjustments for the **relative importance of different countries in terms of UK trade** through a system of **weights**. Such a weighted average is in use, and is called the **effective** exchange rate (EER), where the weights used represent the share of total UK world trade conducted with each country whose currency is included in the basket. It follows that, if a volatile currency is highly weighted, as is true of the dollar, then the EER will itself show a tendency to be volatile, albeit on a much reduced scale. However, a low-weighted currency will have little effect upon the EER, no matter how volatile it is. The basket was revised in February 1995 in order to increase the total weight of European currencies from 55.6 per cent to 70 per cent, with the largest increase for Germany and Spain. In contrast, the dollar fell from 20.4 per cent to 16.5 per cent. The number of countries covered was increased from 17 to 21.

Unfortunately, because the EER measures the pound in relation to other **currencies**, it may be a poor guide to changes in the **competitiveness** of UK goods and services. For this reason, it is preferable for certain purposes to use a **real** exchange rate (RER), which measures the price of UK goods (and hence of UK exports) relative to the average price of foreign goods (and hence of UK imports). Since the latter need to be converted into sterling, the average price of foreign goods is multiplied by the EER for this purpose, and the RER is given by: UK price index divided by overseas average price index multiplied by EER. If the RER **falls** then UK competitiveness **improves** because, converted to sterling, imports have become more expensive

Table 10.1   *Selected Sterling Exchange Rates and Effective Rate Index (ERI), 1975–95, Annual Averages*

	Exchange value of sterling in US$	DM	Yen	ECU	Sterling effective ERI[1], (1990 = 100)
1975	2.220	5.447	658.1		136.7
1976	1.805	4.552	535.4		117.2
1977	1.746	4.050	467.7		110.8
1978	1.920	3.851	402.6		110.6
1979	2.123	3.888	465.6		117.2
1980	2.328	4.227	525.6	1.674	128.9
1981	2.025	4.556	444.6	1.811	130.3
1982	1.749	4.243	435.2	1.785	124.5
1983	1.516	3.870	359.9	1.704	115.3
1984	1.336	3.791	316.8	1.694	110.2
1985	1.298	3.784	307.1	1.700	109.5
1986	1.467	3.183	246.8	1.495	100.2
1987	1.639	2.941	236.5	1.420	98.7
1988	1.780	3.124	228.0	1.506	105.3
1989	1.638	3.080	225.7	1.489	102.3
1990	1.786	2.876	257.4	1.400	100.0
1991	1.768	2.925	237.6	1.428	100.7
1992	1.767	2.751	223.7	1.362	96.9
1993	1.501	2.483	166.7	1.284	88.9
1994	1.533	2.481	156.4	1.292	89.2
1995	1.578	2.260	148.4	1.221	84.8

Note:
[1] The weights used for the ERI used to be calculated by the IMF using its Multilateral Exchange Rate Model. However, as from January 1989, the index is that published in the IMF's *International Financial Statistics*, where the weights reflect the relative importance of other countries as competitors to the UK in both domestic and overseas markets. The base year is 1985. The weight of the $US in the new ERI has fallen compared to the old ERI, whilst that of the DM has risen.

Source: Bank of England Quarterly Bulletin; Economic Trends.

relative to exports. One obvious drawback to the RER is that not all UK and foreign goods are traded, so the formula is something of an approximation as a measure of competitiveness in the traded goods sector, but it provides a useful supplement to other exchange rate measures.

Table 10.1 sets out the data for the three most important bilateral exchange rates, for the EER and the ECU. During the period 1975–88 the DM and the yen were the world's strongest currencies, and as can clearly be seen, the pound depreciated steadily against both currencies other than during the period 1979 to 1981 and, more recently,

against the DM in 1988 and 1991 and the yen in 1990. However, the £/$ rate was much more volatile, with peaks in 1972, 1980, 1988 and 1990, and troughs in 1977, 1985, 1989 and 1993. As these are annual averages, they obviously understate the daily high and low values for each year, some of which are also referred to in the following sections. Again, it is important to remember in the wider context that, even if the pound is falling against the DM while simultaneously rising against the dollar, the DM is not necessarily also rising against the dollar, and so forth.

The EER is also plotted graphically, on a quarterly basis, in **Figure 10.1** since the annual averages are a little misleading. From early 1977 to early 1981, the EER appreciated steadily to stand once again at a value almost exactly equal to that of mid-1975, only to collapse back to a value of just over 100 at the end of 1984. On an annualised basis, the EER continued to fall until the end of 1987, but as **Figure 10.1** shows, the quarterly pattern was actually quite volatile, and showed a rising tendency from 1986 to 1988 before falling sharply again in 1989. During the latter half of 1990 the EER rose sharply (gaining 15 per cent against the dollar alone), but the sudden recovery of the dollar against the pound at the beginning of 1991 promptly reversed the sequence. The obvious collapse of the EER in October 1992, falling from 99.4 in 1992Q2 to 87.7 in 1992Q3, is set aside for discussion in the chapter which follows. As can be seen, the EER has been reasonably stable since then, aside from a fairly sharp drop from 87.2 in 1995Q1 to 84.3 in 1995Q2, and a very sharp rise at the end of 1996.

It is worth noting that the UK's EER has **in general** shown less volatility than that of other major countries, and especially Japan as can be seen in **Figure 10.2** which includes events post-October 1992. Hence, a quite different perspective is gained in the longer term when comparing volatility in the EER with volatility in, say the £/$ rate. In the short term the EER normally shows little volatility because it is a composite measure, even though bilateral rates may be highly volatile, which might be taken as a lesson for financial markets that what you see depends upon where you look.

The RER is rarely mentioned in the media, so detailed figures are not given here. By and large the RER is affected mostly by the EER in the short term, and mostly by relative inflation rates in the longer term, much as one would expect. Since the UK has almost continuously suffered more inflation than her main competitors since 1975, this has exerted constant upward pressure upon the RER and led to a corresponding loss of competitiveness. During those periods in which the EER

Figure 10.1 *Sterling ERI, 1980–96, Quarterly Averages (1990 = 100)*

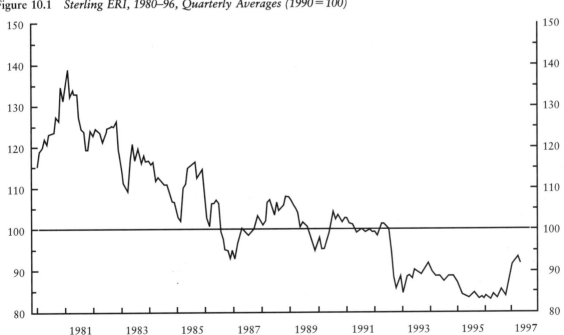

Source: Bank of England Quarterly Bulletin.

has risen sharply, for example in 1979–80, this has combined with the relative price effect to produce a disastrous loss of competitiveness. The same combination, albeit on a lesser scale, was evident in 1988 and 1990. At other times, however, the decline in the EER has more than outweighed the relative price effect, and the RER has fallen (as in 1986–87). It is finally worth noting that a country which is undergoing a strong currency appreciation need not necessarily become uncompetitive. As the Japanese have frequently demonstrated, the RER can still be induced to fall provided domestic prices can be kept down relative to world prices.

□ *10.1.6 Exchange Rate Regimes*

Gold Standard

Although there is no realistic prospect of an equivalent exchange rate regime being restored, it is of some importance to explain briefly the workings of the old **gold standard** which involved strict rules, but which did not require any international co-operation since each country could apply the rules independently of the others. The gold standard operated in the UK from 1821 to 1914, and from 1925 to 1931. During these periods, the UK money supply was determined by the gold reserves, and gold was the medium used to settle international indebtedness. Each country's currency was absolutely fixed in value in terms of gold, which in turn meant that the value of each currency was absolutely fixed in terms of all other currencies. If a country ran a BoP deficit, it would have to transfer gold to the country in surplus. This in turn would lower the money supply in the former and raise it in the latter, with prices subsequently following suit. This movement in relative prices would then boost the exports of the deficit country, and reduce those of the surplus country, until equilibrium was restored.

At the time, the fact that the gold standard left no leeway for discretionary behaviour on the part of individual governments, while restoring BoP equilibrium and bringing prices into line, was seen as a great virtue. In practice, the adjustment me-

Figure 10.2 *EERs (1985 = 100)*

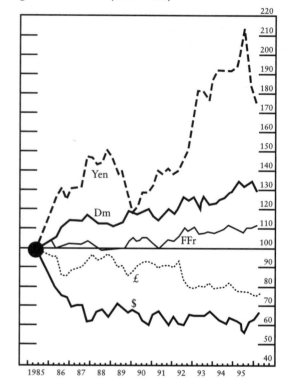

Source: Bank of England Quarterly Bulletin.

chanism was far from smooth since, for example, prices tended to be insufficiently flexible. The attempt to go back to the gold standard in the UK in 1925 was fairly disastrous because the conversion rate of sterling into gold was set at too high a level, and after the 1929 Crash the worldwide rush to convert currencies into gold forced the UK, whose gold reserves were limited, to suspend convertibility and to float the pound in 1931.

From a more modern perspective, a gold standard type of mechanism is sometimes advocated because it provides a strong brake upon inflation. However, against this has to be set the fact that an individual country cannot **choose** its rate of inflation, it cannot use money supply control as an instrument of demand management, and it cannot vary the exchange rate to deal with BoP problems arising either because of differences in national inflation rates, or because of unforeseen external shocks. The fact that it might no longer be possible to use gold to underpin the mechanism because it is unavailable in sufficient quantities does not rule out the use of the mechanism as such. Something else which is available can quite easily be used instead. This could either be an existing currency such as the dollar, or an artificial currency linked to a basket of existing currencies.

Bretton Woods 1944–71

At the end of the Second World War a new set of rules was introduced for controlling the world's monetary system. These included a fixed exchange rate mechanism harking back in many respects, but in a less rigid manner, to the gold standard. All members of the IMF had to peg their currencies to the dollar, which was in turn pegged to gold at a rate of $35 per ounce. However, this peg was not immovable, but 'adjustable'. Any individual currency could freely move up or down by up to 1 per cent in relation to its $ par value, but beyond that point the relevant central bank would have to intervene, and to use its reserves in order to keep within the permitted variance about the par value. In addition, any country could, without seeking the permission of the IMF, unilaterally lower (devalue) or raise (revalue) its currency by up to 10 per cent. If a larger alteration was thought to be necessary, then the permission of the IMF had to be sought, but this was certain to be forthcoming provided the country could demonstrate that its BoP was in 'fundamental disequilibrium'. Since no specific definition of this term existed, it was hard to see how the IMF could refuse a country which claimed that such a condition was indeed in existence.

For the most part, the adjustable peg worked quite well until the later 1960s. It was a period of generally sustained growth, and the gold reserves of the USA were sufficient to settle trade imbalances in the few cases where dollars, effectively as good as gold, were unacceptable. Compared to the gold standard, inflation control was weakened because currencies could be realigned, but the widespread adoption of fiscal policy as an instrument of demand management overcame a serious

deficiency of the gold standard in that it had no instruments for demand management.

However, the Bretton Woods system came under increasing pressure, primarily because (1) countries arguably in fundamental disequilibrium, such as the UK in the 1960s, were afraid to admit they had to devalue, since their governments feared the political consequences of being seen as unable to manage their economies. While devaluations did occur, as in the UK in 1967, these were always by too little and too late; (2) since such countries preferred instead to deflate their economies by fiscal means, their growth was held back; (3) countries in surplus generally refused to revalue, arguing that this would stimulate spending on cheap imports and impart an inflationary bias to their economies; (4) which meant consequently that speculators could be fairly certain that a fundamental disequilibrium would be resolved by a devaluation, effectively yielding a one-way bet which in turn put further pressure on deficit countries' reserves; (5) the dollars needed to maintain international liquidity, and to allow for BoP deficits to be paid for, had to come as a result of the USA running a BoP deficit and paying its debts in its own currency (which no other country could do). Eventually, these dollar holdings outside the USA grew larger than the value of the gold reserves held in the USA to which they were fixed, and the whole system became over-dependent upon US macroeconomic policy. Confidence in this policy could not be restored and, as a result, attempts were made to convert dollars into gold at the fixed parity, and the USA was forced to suspend convertibility in August 1971. This signalled the end of the era during which gold played an important role in international trade.

In an attempt to salvage the adjustable peg, agreement was reached at the Smithsonian Conference in December 1971 to increase the permitted fluctuation around par values from ±1 per cent to ±2.25 per cent, to revalue certain strong currencies, and to raise the $ price of gold (which was worth far more in the free market than when held in reserves). However, the situation could not be salvaged, and in the particular case of the UK the BoP problems of the early

1970s forced the government to float the pound in June 1972. One year later, floating exchange rates were the norm rather than the exception.

Managed Floating

The floating exchange rate system adopted after 1973 was 'dirty' (managed) rather than 'clean'. Even so, it was considered that a number of advantages would follow compared with the adjustable peg, many of which were compatible with the newly popular monetarist doctrines. In this latter respect it was argued that the adjustable peg had necessitated the use of monetary instruments to manage demand, with a view to keeping the BoP in equilibrium. Once the exchange rate was floating, equilibrium would automatically be restored by appreciation or depreciation of the currency, and as a result monetary instruments could be transferred to their proper use, namely control of inflation. Strictly speaking, this required the float to be clean if it was to work properly, but even a dirty float would free up the hands of the authorities to some extent.

In principle, any country experiencing relatively rapid inflation should not suffer a permanent competitive disadvantage. As prices rise faster than in competing countries, so the exchange rate should depreciate to offset this. The nominal exchange rate thus adjusts to keep the real exchange rate constant. However, this should not create unemployment in uncompetitive countries. As their currencies depreciate, the price of imports – and hence retail prices in general – will begin to rise. Provided nominal wages stay more or less unchanged, real wages will accordingly fall and bear the brunt of the adjustment rather than the number of jobs on offer. Furthermore, there should be much reduced scope for destabilising speculation compared with the adjustable peg. By buying cheap and selling dear, speculators actually move the currency towards its equilibrium value, and hence reduce the opportunities for further speculation.

Unhappily, the era of managed floating was not an unqualified success, and a number of serious drawbacks manifested themselves in practice.

Most importantly: (1) certain currencies remained over-valued in relation to the current account, which accordingly remained heavily in deficit with the deficit financed by capital inflows; (2) monetary policy often did not succeed in controlling domestic inflation because, for example, of the problems of defining the monetary aggregates for this purpose, and so the exchange rate needed to be depreciated further, once again driving up import prices. Where domestic wage rises were demanded by way of compensation, further damaging effects upon inflation and employment ensued; (3) exchange rates were much more volatile than could be accounted for by differences in inflation rates, leading to large fluctuations in real exchange rates which had damaging effects upon world trade flows; (4) speculation at times was very heavy. Whereas it is clear that if one party gains £1 another party must have lost £1, it does not necessarily follow that winners and losers come from the same group. Professional speculators may gain continuously at the expense of the ill-informed.

In essence, acknowledgement of these difficulties led to two distinct developments. Firstly, the Community introduced the European Monetary System (EMS – discussed in detail in Chapter 11), which harks back to the adjustable peg in that it requires much the same degree of co-operation between participants, but in the context of a somewhat less rigid set of rules. Secondly, the USA under President Reagan attempted to move away from unco-ordinated floating towards a system centred essentially on the dollar, the yen and the deutsche mark (and hence linking in to the EMS), requiring progressively more co-operation and the adherence to progressively more specific rules. Before discussing this, it is worth noting that the UK was party to both these developments, either as a member of the Community or as a member of the Group of 5 (G5) or 7 (G7) major industrial countries, but until 1990 remained on the side-lines pursuing a policy of an essentially ad hoc nature.

There have been a large number of minor milestones along the road which may, perhaps, best be labelled 'informal' management of the world's major three currencies. Among them the more notable ones were the **Plaza Agreement** of September 1985, the **Louvre Accord** of February 1987 and the Group of Seven Statement of December 1987 (issued in the absence of a formal meeting).

In March 1985 the $ stood at Y260 and DM3.4, a rise of roughly one-half in its RER since 1980. This was viewed in the USA as a virtue insofar as it reflected the strength of the US economy, and simultaneously as a vice insofar as it produced huge BoP deficits and stirred up strong protectionist sentiments. The dollar then began to fall of its own accord, but only temporarily. The Plaza Agreement (between the members of G5 including the UK) was designed to talk it down a further 10 per cent or so, essentially by stating that it was too high. The sum of $18 billion was made available for supportive intervention. By October the dollar had fallen to its desired level, but it continued to fall sharply, thereby raising fears in Japan and Germany that it was not going to achieve a 'soft landing'. Eventually this led to the Louvre Accord which agreed 'reference rates' for the dollar of Y153.50 and DM1.825.

Intervention to maintain these reference rates was initially successful, but the G7 summit in Venice in June 1987 failed to instil confidence in the financial markets that the USA was determined to deal with its twin budget and BoP deficits, and this provided the trigger for the stock market crash of October 1987, subsequent to which the dollar fell sharply. Initially, this did not please the Japanese, but they soon came to realise that their exporters could learn to live with a highly valued yen, and thereafter they lost interest in active intervention. The West Germans saw little reason to support the dollar until the USA got to grips with their domestic problems. Meanwhile the UK allowed the pound to float around for a while, before adopting a policy of shadowing the DM prior to officially joining the ERM.

■ 10.2 Exchange Rate Issues

It is helpful at this stage to summarise some of the threads which run through the preceding discussion. We may note, for example, that each exchange rate system can be designated according, first, to the rigidity of its rules, and secondly to the degree of co-operation required of participants.

The postwar years have witnessed a considerable diversity of systems, all quite distinct from the pre-war gold standard. This, as explained above, required currencies to be fixed in terms of gold, with no discretion to alter the rate and with each country able to fix its rate wholly independently of other countries. Subsequently, countries have periodically reimposed either fairly rigid rules or adopted an independent stance, but never both together. The Bretton Woods 'adjustable peg' allowed for some variation around par values, and also for periodic realignment of currencies, so it was less rigid than the gold standard, but it differed from the latter primarily insofar as it could only operate successfully through co-operative behaviour. However, the willingness to set supranational interests above national interests was distinctly limited, and indeed the system ultimately faltered because of a general unwillingness to adopt co-operative solutions.

The EMS is essentially a more flexible version of the adjustable peg, but like that system it allows participants to behave in somewhat different ways. The country at the centre of the system, Germany, has more room for manoeuvre than any of the others. Those participants which peg themselves to the DM, such as Holland, are relatively rule-bound compared with those that are willing to realign their currencies.

The UK, from 1979 to 1990, largely did its own thing. It avoided becoming rule-bound by not pegging sterling to any other currency, although it latterly shadowed the DM prior to entry into the ERM. This once again holds true now that the UK has once again left the ERM. For most of the earlier period the dollar was also managed very independently, although it subsequently showed a clear preference for international co-operation, albeit of a flexible kind.

Countries which are eager to grow at above-average rates tend to prefer an undervalued exchange rate, since this keeps down export prices. Equally, if control of inflation is the primary concern, an overvalued exchange rate becomes more desirable because it keeps down import prices. It is difficult to prove that exchange rates are deliberately managed in order to pursue national interests (at the expense of other countries) since governments are overtly dedicated to better co-operation. But insofar as it does occur, it prevents rather than enhances the move towards equilibrium in international trade.

10.3 The International Monetary System

☐ 10.3.1 International Liquidity

As has become clear from our previous discussion, it is impossible to isolate an individual country such as the UK from the economic forces which affect the rest of the world. The UK is not merely linked into these forces via the institutions which try to control them, but also through the flows of international liquidity that are the physical manifestation of these forces.

International liquidity is the stock of assets that is held by the appropriate body in each country on behalf of its government, in order to settle BoP deficits and to defend the exchange rate. The assets in question must obviously be acceptable throughout the non-Eastern bloc world, and at any point in time the great bulk of them are to be found in the official reserves of the major industrialised countries. However, since few individual countries are either able – or indeed wish – to hold sufficient reserves to cover every eventuality, existing reserves need to be supplemented by a variety of sources, whether money markets or international institutions, from which additional liquidity can be obtained as required.

International liquidity is no different from domestic money in terms of its functions, such as acting as a medium of exchange or a unit of account, but it is much more restrictive in its physical forms. A greatly expanded volume of world trade has caused a dramatic escalation in the need for such liquidity since the 1970s. This was to be expected, since it is obviously a precondition for international liquidity that it is acceptable not merely within an individual country, but well beyond its borders.

International liquidity takes three basic forms – namely gold, the domestic currencies of individual countries which are acceptable as 'reserve' currencies, and non-domestic currencies artificially created by international bodies such as the IMF. The holdings of gold and reserve currencies are largely to be found in the reserves of individual countries, but substantial quantities are also held by the IMF independently of its own 'artificial' currency.

Until fairly recently, gold was the most favoured form of international liquidity, since it has always been universally desired for its intrinsic qualities. Given that its value has always greatly exceeded its production costs, those countries which mine it – mainly the ex-USSR and South Africa – have profited enormously from its supply, but the main economic issue is that this supply is inflexible even in the face of a rapid increase in its price. Hence the enormous increase in the demand for international liquidity after 1945 could not be met via an increase in the supply of gold at its existing price. Whereas it would have been possible to raise the value of the existing stocks to the required level, this would have seriously affected the world economy because of the very unequal distribution of gold stocks between countries. Thus, so long as gold was fixed in terms of dollars, as was the case until 1972, the increasing demand for international liquidity had to be met in other ways, although gold still constitutes a significant proportion of the value of reserves held by industrialised nations.

The use of domestic currencies as reserve currencies has many advantages. Paper money is cheap to produce and to store, it can be supplied on any scale that can conceivably be required, and there is widespread familiarity with its use. It is also worth noting that reserves do not have to be held in the form of currency as such. Rather, the currency can be placed on deposit and hence earn interest, or be converted into financial instruments denominated in the relevant currency.

Most international liquidity has been held in the form of reserve currencies since 1945. The obvious drawback is that no-one wishes to hold reserves in the form of a currency that is subject to capital losses. Until 1972 the dollar was pegged to gold, and hence was a universally popular reserve currency – unlike the pound which devalued in 1949 and 1967. Since 1972 the volatile behaviour of the dollar has considerably undermined its desirability, and the yen and the DM have tended to replace the dollar. However, the vast dollar reserves built up over the years (issued in settlement of US balance of payments deficits) mean that international liquidity will remain dominated by the dollar for the rest of the decade and well beyond.

There are clear advantages accruing to a country whose currency is used for reserve purposes, not least of which is its ability to settle its debts in its own currency which it can print endlessly at very little cost to itself. The main drawback is that if there is a severe loss of confidence in the currency, attempts by outsiders to convert into other, stronger, currencies may have severe implications for the domestic economy. When there is a run on a currency, it is unlikely that the country whose currency it is will by itself have the reserves in other currencies to stem the tide. Hence international co-operation is a prerequisite for stability in the international monetary system.

10.3.2 Special Drawing Rights (SDRs)

The shortage of gold, and the increasing over-dependence upon the dollar, stimulated moves towards the creation of an 'artificial' form of currency (that is, one controlled not by the monetary authorities of an individual country but by an international body). As part of the Bretton Woods agreement discussed above, the IMF had been set up to oversee the adjustable peg mechanism and to help countries in BoP difficulties to set their houses in order. To facilitate this it received funds from member countries, varying according to their ability to pay. Originally, these funds were paid as a quota, of which 75 per cent constituted the domestic currency of the contributor and 25 per cent constituted gold. The funds were then lent in the same form by way of temporary loans to countries in difficulties, in the expectation that they would be repaid within three to

five years once the difficulties had been resolved (in accordance with guidelines laid down by the IMF).

In 1969 the IMF managed to obtain international agreement for the introduction of an international currency called **Special Drawing Rights** (SDRs), and these first began to circulate in 1970 following an amendment to the IMF's Articles of Agreement. The SDRs are not put into circulation in the form of banknotes, but rather exist as **credits in ledgers to be drawn on as required in relation to members' quotas**, as explained below.

The creation of SDRs was certainly a major improvement on preceding arrangements because it offered a permanent solution to the shortage of international liquidity that existed at the time, rather than the kind of ad hoc arrangement adopted previously. In particular, the General Agreements to Borrow (GAB) had been brought into being in 1962 whereby members of the Group of Ten (major industrial countries) agreed to increase allocations of their domestic currencies to the IMF if other members of the group needed to withdraw larger amounts than the IMF had in stock. The UK was itself able to utilise GAB during its periodic BoP crises in the 1970s, and especially in 1976. Over the years, the sums allocated to GAB have been periodically revised, with Switzerland joining the other ten members in 1984, and the possibility of access to GAB being extended beyond its immediate membership.

Like GAB, SDRs are available only temporarily (the World Bank being the appropriate body to approach for more permanent financing). Each country paying over its quota to the IMF is guaranteed a borrowing facility related to the size of the quota, which is measured in terms of SDRs. Furthermore, this facility rises in value over time as the size of the quotas is periodically raised.

A country seeking to borrow from the IMF obviously desires reserve currencies and/or gold. It purchases these with its SDRs, acquired either in return for its quota payments or as a loan from the IMF, thereby transferring the SDRs to the country supplying the currency which is being borrowed.

The IMF expects to influence a borrowing country's macroeconomic policy in order to ensure that the borrower creates the capacity to repay. However, no conditions are imposed where the borrower seeks a loan no greater than 25 per cent of its quota. This is called its **reserve tranche**, and is contained in the figure for the borrower's official reserves (denoted 'reserve position at IMF' in the BoP accounts). Conditions begin to be imposed when a loan exceeds this figure, and are made increasingly stringent as the size of the loan increases. Loans in excess of the reserve tranche are available in four equal instalments, each amounting to 25 per cent of a country's quota. These **credit tranches** can thus bring total borrowings up to a maximum of 125 per cent of a country's quota, but unlike the reserve tranche they are recorded, where relevant, in the BoP accounts as 'allocation of Special Drawing Rights'.

The conditions placed upon credit tranches are understandably somewhat unpopular in the borrowing country. When the UK was forced to borrow in 1976, the IMF demanded that public spending be sharply reduced and that the growth of the money supply be curtailed, neither policy being likely to appeal to the Labour government of that time. Inevitably, borrowers are wont to place the blame for austerity measures at the IMF's door, since this avoids explaining why the problems arose in the first place, so the IMF has something of an image problem. It also has something of a credibility problem because it is dealing in an artificial currency on a scale which is deliberately restricted by the major industrial countries wielding large blocks of votes on its governing board.

The size of quotas is subject to five-yearly reviews, but the initial intention steadily to replace reserves held in other forms by SDRs has never found favour with the major industrial countries, which are understandably wary of handing over control over monetary matters to a supranational body. Certainly, some attempts were made over the years to bring the SDR into increasing prominence, including the partial or full payment of increases in quotas in the form of SDRs rather than gold, and the payment of attractive rates of interest to countries receiving SDRs in exchange for their currencies, but a major consideration has been the ready availability of dollars as noted previously (for a discussion of the future role of the SDR see *Financial Times*, 18 March 1996).

■ 10.4 The International Debt Crisis

☐ *10.4.1 Origins of the Crisis*

During the period prior to the early 1970s, the volume of world trade was growing rapidly, to the mutual benefit of developed and less-developed countries (LDCs). Lending to the LDCs, whether via the banks or institutions such as the IMF, was not considered to be at widespread risk of default since these countries were, with occasional exceptions, generating sufficient national income to service the interest payments on their debts. However, the sudden sharp rise in the price of oil engineered by OPEC in 1974–75 severely affected not merely the non-oil LDCs but some of the more developed countries as well, and so reduced their national income as to prevent full payment of outstanding debt interest. The second oil price rise in 1979 worsened their situation still further – partly via increased costs of production, and partly via the resultant recession amongst their industrialised customers.

It is not altogether easy to attribute responsibility for the debt crisis. On the one hand, high oil prices and interest rates, deterioration in the terms of trade, poor external advice, an over-willingness on the part of western bankers to lend money and the fall-out from the colonial era can all be regarded as factors which were largely beyond the control of debtor countries. On the other hand, poor investment strategies, mismanagement and, in certain cases, blatant corruption, have also made a contribution.

During the 1970s, the IMF provided very limited assistance. The largest sum lent in any one year was $3 billion, and that included loans to developed countries in difficulties. The burden of lending accordingly fell upon the commercial banks in industrialised countries which, rather foolishly in retrospect, were happy to offer short-term loans tied to floating interest rates.

At the time, such behaviour did not appear to be quite so foolish. In the first place, the borrowers were sovereign states which, unlike industrial concerns, were not thought to be in any danger of bankruptcy. Secondly, the OPEC surpluses were swilling around the banking system looking for a profitable home, and with industrial profitability falling sharply in domestic markets, the number of clients wishing to borrow expensive money was on the decline.

With interest rates floating upwards rather than down, it gradually became clear that sooner or later a major default on interest payments was going to occur, and that this could have a disastrous impact if such a default threatened to bankrupt commercial banks, which would then call in other loans to LDCs, and so on. In 1982, the three largest debtors, Mexico, Brazil and Argentina, between them owed $220 billion in debt, with an annual interest bill of $13 billion. Since it was clear that countries such as these literally lacked the capacity to repay, some kind of debt rescheduling operation was clearly required.

Between them, the IMF and banks devised a way to proceed. The IMF stood ready to make further loans available, albeit on a relatively modest scale, through a variety of programmes such as the extended fund facility, the supplementary financing facility, the compensatory financing facility and the enlarged access policy. Most of the loans were not merely made 'conditional' upon changes in the macroeconomic policies of the debtor nations, but also conditional upon the creditor banks accepting a restructuring of those debts and, if necessary, further increases in their lending. In other words, the banks needed the reassurance of an IMF-imposed austerity programme, while the IMF needed the banks' co-operation in order to induce the debtor countries to accept such a programme.

During 1983 and 1984 the IMF lent some $20 billion to 70 countries, although the effect was multiplied many times by the debt rescheduling which accompanied this lending, and the feared collapse among the banks, whose balance sheets contained what, on any definition, were bad debts in excess of their issued capital, was headed off. However, the problem did not go away. The drop in the oil price did provide some relief for the non-oil LDCs, but it simultaneously created problems for oil-producers such as Mexico and Nigeria.

Between 1982 and mid-1987 the 'Paris Club' creditor governments rescheduled $48 billion of debt for 39 countries, as shown in **Figure 10.3**. Meanwhile the banks set out to strengthen their balance sheets and began to make provisions for the probability that some debts would never be repaid, a reasonable assumption given that the ratio of debt to export earnings was continuing to rise in most debtor countries. In spite of this, the IMF was obliged to acknowledge at the end of 1988 that instead of it financing debtor nations, the debtor nations were financing the IMF as a result of loan repayments.

Figure 10.3 *LDC Debt Rescheduling*

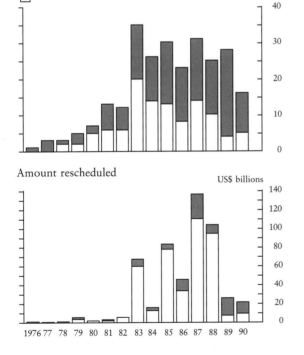

Source: Bank of England Quarterly Bulletin (November 1991).

☐ *10.4.2 Recent Developments*

In early 1989, the debt problem was suddenly pushed back into prominence by rioting in Venezuela, triggered by price rises introduced to qualify for new IMF loans. The US Treasury Secretary, Nicholas Brady, hastily cobbled together a plan which proposed that commercial banks voluntarily exchange loans for bonds with either lower face values or lower interest rates, thereby reducing the cash burden on debtors. The problem was to get something concrete in return. Debtor nations wanted the resolution of their problems to be divorced from internal reform, but this provoked a protest which centred around the argument that debtor countries should privatise their inefficient state enterprises, crack down on corruption and introduce market forces.

The refusal by debtor nations to implement structural reforms had previously caused the demise of the Baker Plan of 1985, but the softer line contained in the **Brady Plan** induced a more positive reaction by debtor nations. By the end of 1990, three 'Brady-style' deals were accordingly completed with Mexico, the Philippines and Costa Rica, and countries such as Venezuela and Uruguay were negotiating further deals. However, the overall problem was not improving because arrears of interest payments had built up rapidly after 1988, and the banks were losing their patience, especially as they had come to believe that the IMF was giving the impression to debtor countries that failure to pay off arrears would not disqualify them for further official assistance.

Faced with insufficient progress under the Baker Plan, attempts had been made to enhance the existing secondary market in LDC debt with additional financial innovations. By selling all of its outstanding debt, a bank could clean up its balance sheet – but only by taking an actual rather than a theoretical loss. For the most part, the debt was bought by other banks which raised loans to pay for it. Brazil and Argentina introduced 'exit bonds' which if taken up relieved a bank of the obligation to supply new money. Some debtors such as Chile permitted debt to be converted into equity, whereas others ran auctions at which banks bid to swap their customers' foreign debt

for local currency which they needed for projects in those countries.

Some of these schemes were successful. Chile, for example, raised its debt's value to 80 per cent of its face value in 1991 through a debt-to-equity scheme, but the schemes made few inroads given the enormity of the problem, and in almost every case the secondary market value of debt fell after 1986 as shown in **Figure 10.4**. Since this was something of a deterrent to prospective purchasers, action on the official debt seemed to be essential, and in June 1990 President Bush followed up the Brady Plan with an 'Enterprise for the Americas' initiative involving partial forgiveness, on a case-by-case basis, of official bilateral debts for South American countries pursuing IMF/World Bank adjustment programmes.

There were also proposals for **debt-for-nature** deals whereby LDCs would be forgiven their debts provided they refrained from environmentally damaging activities such as chopping down rain forests. However, it simultaneously became evident that debt problems in Eastern Europe, which had previously attracted little attention, would also need to be addressed as a matter of some urgency, particularly in view of the overthrow of communist regimes in 1990. Eastern European debt rose from $70 billion in 1985 to

Figure 10.4 *Secondary Market Bank Debt Prices*

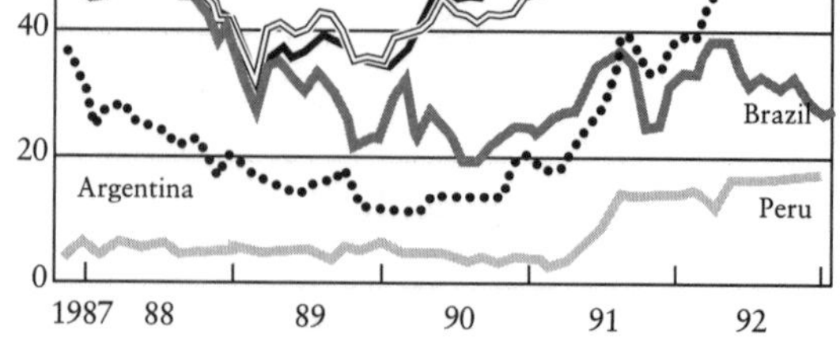

Source: Salomon Brothers.

$99 billion in 1987, and by 1989 Poland's debts alone amounted to $40 billion.

A major difference in the Polish case was that most of the debt was official, and it initiated economic reforms subsequent to the overthrow of communism. These considerations made it much easier to forgive the debt than in the case of other LDCs, and early in 1991 it was accordingly agreed by the Paris Club that one half of the official debt would immediately be forgiven (subject to the negotiation of an equivalent reduction with creditor banks which was not signed until March 1994, after which the second part of the Paris Club agreement was initiated), which did not go down well in South America. The same facility was extended to Egypt in gratitude for its role in the Gulf War.

Subsequently, a dramatic turnaround was evident in respect of many South American debtors, as shown by the rise in debt prices in **Figure 10.5**. Where governments welcomed international capital, opened their economies to outside influence through a lowering of trade barriers, set their fiscal books in order and curtailed their public sectors, their own citizens have repatriated their capital with foreign investors following hard on their heels. With lower interest rates and inflation, and a more benign attitude towards debt rescheduling, the short-term position improved immeasurably.

However, the capital inflows included a good deal of 'hot money' which could flow out again if interest rates rose again in the USA and EU. Equally, countries beset by corruption and political instability such as Brazil fared less well, and some commentators (for example, Bird (1992)) were less than sanguine about the longer-term prognosis. The adjustment process was certainly painful, and social unrest remained a worry. This was even truer of the former members of the Soviet bloc. In April 1993, western creditor nations came to the rescue of Boris Yeltsin by agreeing to reschedule the bulk of the estimated $20 billion of debt service obligations for the year, but this provided a breathing space rather than a solution and a further Paris Club restructuring was needed in June 1994 with no agreement forthcoming on a rescheduling of commercial bank

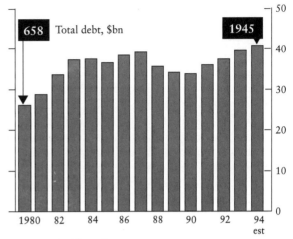

Figure 10.5 *Developing Countries' External Debt as % of GDP*

Source: World Bank.

debt. In May 1996, the Paris Club signed Russia's largest- ever rescheduling agreement, giving Russia 25 years to repay $38.7 billion to other governments with a six-year period during which it need pay only interest. Technically, of course, these debts are covered by what Russia is owed by its former client states.

The situation also remained dire in Africa, where formerly oil-rich Nigeria had a foreign debt of $30 billion at the end of 1993 with arrears in excess of $5 billion. Total African external debt amounted to $150 billion which cost a quarter of export earnings to service. Sub-Saharan nations received official support via concessionary lending, debt restructuring and forgiveness, but their per capita incomes fell by twenty per cent between 1984 and 1994, and little short of a total debt write-off appeared to offer a resolution of the problem. What was initially forthcoming in practice was, for example, an agreement with the Ivory Coast in March 1994 which cut its debt by $2.5 billion.

In April 1994, Brazil became the last of the four big Latin American debtors to secure a Brady restructuring (following on Mexico, Venezuela and Argentina). This deal was innovatory in that interest arrears of $17 billion were negotiated separately, and prior to the restructuring of $31 billion of principal debt, and also because there was no accord in place with the IMF due to the latter's concern with the stability of the country's economic reforms.

The Brady bond index rose by 44 per cent in 1993 on a much increased volume of trading, but fell back sharply in 1994. The index improved considerably when, in December 1994, the Paris Club agreed to write off 67 per cent of the maturing debt of 27 of the poorest countries, which would also for the first time get softer terms on the rest of their debt. However, by this point in time developing countries as a group were more indebted, as shown in **Figure 10.5**, at 39.7 per cent of their combined GDP, that at any time during the 1980s debt crisis. In January 1995, for example, a devaluation caused Mexican Brady bonds fell to their lowest level in four years and prices in the $135 billion (currently $150 billion) market subsequently slumped to an historic low. In effect, sovereign insolvency had become an epidemic, with 68 governments engaged in multilateral restructuring of their official or commercial debts. By April 1995, the Brady bond index was back at its level of late 1992.

At the end of the day, the Catch-22 for bankrupt states had become only too clear. The more such states attempt to extract resources from their citizens and the fewer the services they supply, the more discredited they become and as a result they become even less able to extract further resources. Hence, the only certain solution is debt forgiveness in the short term and in the longer term to speed up the rate of growth in debtor nations so that they acquire the capacity to repay debts without eroding the standard of living of their inhabitants. The World Bank appeared to accept this prognosis in September 1995 when it published a plan reversing its long-standing opposition to writing off multilateral debt via the medium of a Multilateral Debt Facility (see, for example, *The Economist*, 16 September 1995, p. 130). Unfortunately, this was opposed in many quarters, notably the IMF, not least because it introduces a major problem of moral hazard – what incentive is there to avoid over-borrowing if debts will ultimately be forgiven? (*Financial Times*, 14 March 1996).

Since May 1995 the Brady bond index has soared by 50 per cent (see *The Economist*, 24 February 1996, p. 112; *Financial Times*, 8 July 1996, p. 23). Nevertheless, it would be foolish to assume that this amounts to a vote of confidence in the resolution of what appears to be a never-ending problem.

Bibliography

Bank of England (1991) 'The LDC Debt Crisis', *Bank of England Quarterly Bulletin* (November).

Bird, G. (1992) 'Ten Years Older and Deeper in Debt? The Developing Country Debt Problem in Retrospect and Prospect', *Economics* (Spring).

Bordo, M. (1993) 'The Gold Standard, Bretton Woods and Other Monetary Regimes: A Historical Appraisal', *Federal Reserve Bank of St Louis Quarterly Review* (March/April).

Coutts, K. and W. Godley (1990) 'Prosperity and Foreign Trade in the 1990s: Britain's Strategic Problems', *Oxford Review of Economic Policy*, 6 (3).

The Economist (1994) 'Bretton Woods Revisited' (9 July) pp. 89–91.

The Economist (1996) 'A Much Devalued Theory' (20 January) pp. 82–3.

Thomas, D. 'The Foreign Exchange Market in London', *Bank of England Quarterly Bulletin* (November) pp. 361–74.

Zurlinden, M. (1993) 'The Vulnerability of Pegged Exchange Rates: The British Pound in the ERM', *Federal Reserve Bank of St Louis Quarterly Review* (September/October).

Chapter 11

The European Union

Peter Curwen

■ 11.1 Introduction

The distinction between external transactions and external relations is necessarily a rather fine one, and there are doubtless other ways to manage the division of material. Essentially, however, there seemed to be advantages in assembling together most of the material that impinges upon the role of the UK as a member of the EU (see box below) and this chapter is broadly given over to this topic. This means that the issues pertaining to exchange rate relationships within the EU are also contained within this chapter, even though the more general discussion of exchange rates appears in Chapter 10.

Readers may understandably find it difficult to distinguish between the ERM, EMS, EMU and the SEM (Exchange Rate Mechanism, European Monetary System, Economic and Monetary Union and the Single European Market respectively), and these are accordingly dealt with in sequence at the beginning of this chapter. The chapter which follows then goes on to concentrate upon relationships between the EU and the rest of the world, treating the UK in its capacity of EU member state, and concludes with a detailed examination of the Common Agricultural Policy, which is simultaneously an issue in terms of the UK's relationship with the EU and also in terms of the EU's relationship with other agricultural trading blocs.

■ 11.2 The Single European Market

☐ 11.2.1 The Single European Act 1985

The Single European Market (SEM), which came into being on 1 January 1993, has its origins in the Single European Act (SEA) of 1985. This was one

---

Membership of the Community

1958 (6): Belgium, France, Italy, Luxembourg, Netherlands, West Germany (now reunified with East Germany and known as 'Germany')

1974 (9): Denmark, Ireland (Eire), United Kingdom

1981 (10): Greece

1986 (12): Portugal, Spain

1995 (15): Austria, Finland, Sweden

---

in a line of Acts that had the underlying purpose of amending the original Treaty of Rome which brought the Community into being in 1958 (see box above). The institutions that existed in 1985, and still do, are set out in **Table 11.1**.

When he was first appointed in 1984, the then President of the Commission M. Delors considered carefully the areas in which to concentrate his attention. His first priority was to create an economic and monetary union within the Community, but neither the UK nor West Germany showed sufficient enthusiasm for that idea. He accordingly turned next to matters of foreign policy, but again found no takers for a policy of increased co-ordination. His third choice proved more inspired. Noting the movement towards deregulation and liberalisation in economic affairs, he advocated **freedom of movement for goods and services, people and financial flows** throughout the Community, now enshrined in Article 8A of the Single European Act.

At the present time, there are still a number of developments working their way through the complicated and time-consuming process of ratification by all Community members, as shown in **Figures 11.1** and **11.2**. The co-operation procedure was introduced in the light of the SEA, but was limited to ten Treaty articles with the European Parliament relatively powerless in other respects. The negotiations over the Maastricht Treaty involved seven different legislative modes, and this led to pressure for a simplified system which emerged as the so-called co-decision procedure. This has replaced the co-operation procedure in respect of such issues as completion of the Single Market. The European Parliament has gradually become a more powerful body. It now has the right to veto the admission of new applicants to the Union, and its assent by a majority of MEPs is needed, for example, on issues concerning citizenship, structural funds and cohesion funds.

Most decisions under the SEA are subject to **qualified** (weighted by size of member states' economies) **majority voting**, although some important and sensitive issues, such as those concerned with **taxation**, require **unanimous** approval. The qualified majority for Commission proposals is **62** votes out of a total of **87**, of which the UK has **10** (in other cases 10 member states also have to be in favour). In the case of a vote requiring unanimity, abstention does not count as an opposing vote (contrary to the arrangement in the case of qualified majority voting) and hence does not prevent decision-making.

Table 11.1 *Institutions of the European Union*

1.	European Commission	20 members of whom 1 (Jacques Santer) is president. Commissioners are allocated by country. The UK has 2: Sir Leon Brittan and Neil Kinnock. The Commission is the EU's civil service and has no direct political power. Its main role is to instigate proposals such as directives and see them through to acceptance or rejection.
2.	Council of the European Union	Consists of 15 representatives, one from each member state. The make up of the Council varies according to the subject under discussion (15 agricultural ministers if the subject is agriculture, and so forth). Voting is either **unanimous** or by **qualified majority**. Only the Council has the power to ratify a proposal. Grand strategy is left to the meeting of the 15 heads of state: the **European Council**.
3.	European Parliament	626 Euro MEPs who sit according to their position on the political spectrum rather than by country. The main groups are the Party of European Socialists (221) and the European People's Party (Christian Democrats + Conservatives – 173). The Parliament's powers have been enhanced under the new *co-decision procedure*, but are not comparable with those of the Council.
4.	European Court of Justice	Consists of 13 judges and 6 advocates-general who make preliminary rulings in the Court of First Instance. Rulings are supranational and take precedence over legal rulings on the same issues in national courts.

Figure 11.1 *Community Legislative Process: Cooperation Procedure*

```
                        ┌─────────────────────┐
                        │     COMMISSION      │
                        │      Proposal       │
                        └─────────────────────┘

        ┌─────────────────────┐   ┌─────────────────────┐
        │      COUNCIL        │   │    PARLIAMENT       │
        │  begins deliberating│   │      Opinion        │
        └─────────────────────┘   └─────────────────────┘

                    ┌─────────────────────────┐
                    │       COMMISSION        │
                    │   takes a view on the   │
                    │   Parliament's opinion  │
                    └─────────────────────────┘

    (Traditional Procedure)        (New Cooperation Procedure)

     ┌─────────────────────┐      ┌─────────────────────────┐
     │      COUNCIL        │      │        COUNCIL          │
     │ takes final decision│      │ adopts a common position│
     └─────────────────────┘      │   by qualified majority │
                                  └─────────────────────────┘
```

within 3 months the	PARLIAMENT		
approves or *takes no* Council *position* position *or*	*amends* Council common position by absolute majority of members	*or*	*rejects* Council common position by an absolute majority

COUNCIL	within one month COMMISSION	COUNCIL
adopts act	reviews EP amendments and may revise its proposal	may act only by authority

within 3 months the	COUNCIL				
may adopt the Commission proposal on the table by qualified majority	*or*	may adopt EP amendments not approved by the Commission by unanimity	*or*	otherwise amend the Commission proposal by unanimity	*or* may fail to act

```
                                      ┌─────────────────────────────┐
                                      │ Possible one-month extension│
                                      │  if agreed by the Parliament│
                                      └─────────────────────────────┘

              ┌──────────────────────────────┐
              │ Commission proposal lapses    │
              │ if Council does not act       │
              └──────────────────────────────┘
```

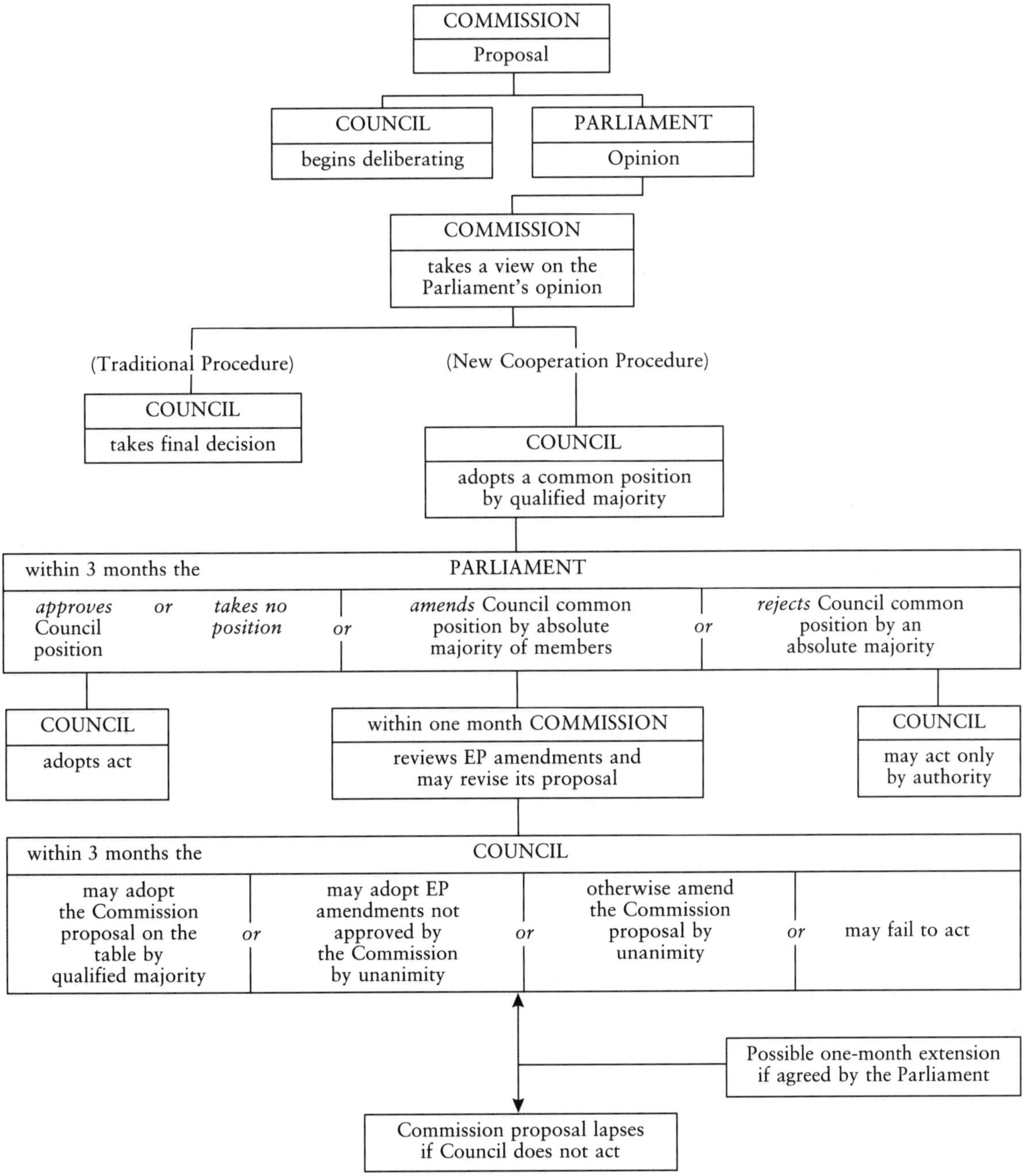

Note:
EP=European Parliament.

Source: The Single Market – the Facts (London: DTI, 1990).

Figure 11.2 *Co-decision Procedure*

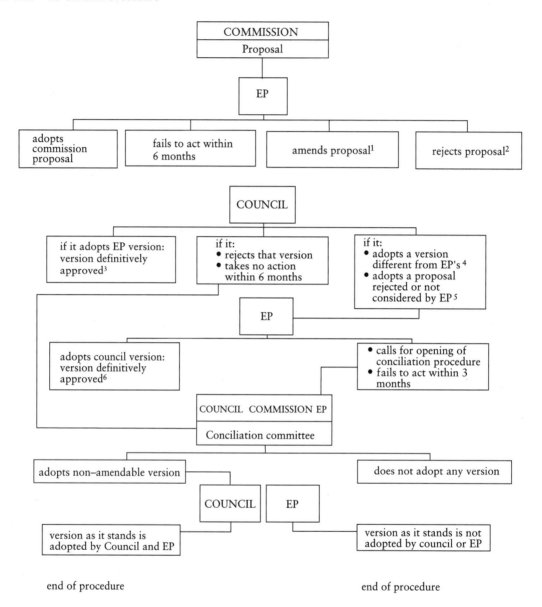

Notes:
1 Amendments opposed by Commission must be adopted by majority of MEPs.
2 By a majority of its Members.
3 Qualified majority.
4 Qualified majority – unanimously if Commission opposes amendments tabled.
5 Unanimously.
6 Simple majority.
7 Parliament: simple majority: Council qualified majority.

Qualified Majority Voting

10 votes: France, Germany, Italy, UK
8 votes: Spain
5 votes: Belgium, Greece, Netherlands, Portugal
4 votes: Austria, Sweden
3 votes: Denmark, Ireland, Finland
2 votes: Luxembourg

87 votes in total: qualified majority = 62 votes

The great majority of these measures have been adopted by the Council of Ministers. In principle, the SEM is accordingly close to completion. However, member states have varying difficulties in passing the necessary national laws, sometimes intentionally (see, for example, Andrews, 1994), so that in practice it will be some time before the SEM is completed at a national level. Problematic areas identified by the Commission (CEC, 1996a, p. 11) include insurance, public procurement, new technologies and services, and intellectual and industrial property. The UK, somewhat surprisingly given its reputation as an unenthusiastic member, has a generally good record in implementation, as shown in **Figure 11.3** (it publicly refused to implement an EU law for the first time in March 1996 in respect of a ban on the use of Emtryl for game birds!), although the Danes have long been the clear leaders. The Belgians and the

Should other countries be permitted to join the EU, these proportions will obviously have to be altered. Voting power is incompatible with what is strictly warranted in relation to economic strength. Whereas the big four members represent almost 75 per cent of Community GDP, they control less than 50 per cent of the votes.

The SEM consists essentially of a set of measures, primarily in the form of directives (see box below), which are initially tabled by the European Commission. There are technically 282 such measures although for various reasons (see CEC, 1996a, p. 9) the end-1995 total was 276, and when they have passed through the procedure illustrated in **Figures 11.1** and **11.2**, and have thereby become EU law, 222 must subsequently be placed upon the statute book of individual member states by a specified date unless there is a derogation exempting a member state from the measure for a stated period.

Figure 11.3 *Single-Market Laws Enacted by National Governments by 31 December 1995*

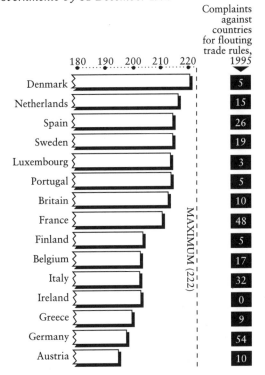

Source: Commission of the European Communities, 1996a.

A **directive** states the result that must be achieved within a stated period. It is left up to each member state to introduce or amend laws to bring about the desired effect. Failure to implement a directive may result in the Commission referring the matter to the European Court of Justice. This can be compared with a **regulation** which automatically applies to member states and hence does not need to be ratified by national parliaments. Regulations take precedence over national laws.

Italians have less to be proud of, and this shows up in the number of times they have been dragged before the European Court of Justice to be admonished for their dilatory behaviour. Whereas Denmark had only been rebuked once by the end of 1991, and the UK three times, the Belgian score was seventeen and the Italian was thirty five. The biggest surprise is nevertheless the position of Germany, which has deteriorated relative to other members over the past few years, and of Austria which lags well behind another recent member, Sweden. Whether foot-dragging will continue on this scale is a moot point, but it must be recognised that the countries most complained about are generally also those least willing to allow anything to be done about it (see, for example, *Financial Times* 16 June 1994).

The legislative programme of the Commission has been winding down since the turn of the decade, as shown in **Table 11.2** below. There are doubtless those who will see this as a good thing, although it has to be said that the Commission's work programme does not consist primarily of directives and other legislation (see CEC, 1995a).

☐ *11.2.2 Enlarging the Community*

The issue of enlargement has become increasingly contentious as the queue of applicants to join has grown, as shown in **Table 11.3**. There are several reasons why the pressure to enlarge has recently increased. For example, the collapse of the Soviet empire has led most of the countries at its western extremity to see the EU as their natural home if they are to prosper as independent states; some EU countries such as the UK have preferred to emphasise widening as an alternative to deepening; and the growth of trade blocs elsewhere in the world has promoted the view that the EU itself needs to become bigger to compete (see Lintner, 1994).

Table 11.3 *Enlarging the Community*

Members	Population	Council votes
Germany	80.6	10
UK	58.0	10
France	57.6	10
Italy	57.0	10
Spain	39.2	8
Netherlands	15.3	5
Greece	10.4	5
Belgium	10.1	5
Portugal	9.9	5
Sweden	8.7	4
Austria	8.0	4
Denmark	5.3	3
Finland	5.1	3
Ireland	3.6	3
Luxembourg	0.4	2

Applied		Potential votes[1]
Turkey	57.8	10
Poland	38.4	8
Romania	23.3	6
Czech Republic	10.5	5
Hungary	10.4	5
Bulgaria	8.7	5
Slovakia	5.3	3
Lithuania	3.8	3
Latvia	2.8	3
Slovenia	2.1	3
Estonia	1.7	3
Cyprus	0.7	2
Malta	0.5	2

Declined to join	
Norway	(November 1994)
Switzerland	(December 1992)

Note:
[1] Estimated, under extension of existing rules.

Table 11.2 *Legislative Proposals Adopted by the Commission*

1990	1991	1992	1993	1994	1995	1996
61	52	51	48	38	25[1]	19[2]

Notes
[1] As of 19 October 1995.
[2] Forecast.

When the previous discussions were held over the entry terms for the Scandinavian countries and Austria, the wealthy applicants were 'bought off' by trading their objections for cash. They were offered £2.7 billion in 1995–96 to offset the instant alignment of their higher farm prices with EU levels, and beyond that date they were asked to contribute ECU 1.7 billion net to the EU Budget, representing only half the original figure.

Such largesse clearly cannot be extended to the much poorer queue of applicants listed in **Table 11.3**, and member states, preoccupied with renegotiating the Maastricht Treaty, are keen to avoid making any financial commitments at all for now. Malta and Cyprus are relatively advanced, and therefore expect to be in the first wave which the EU Commission recently pencilled in as being delayed until 2002 (see *Financial Times*, 17 June 1996). The Czech Republic, Poland and Hungary are also in contention for this date. Several among the applicants have negotiated 'Europe Agreements' which offer limited and selected access to EU markets and some limited financial co-operation, and there is currently some advocacy of partial or 'semi-permanent' membership. Delay may well prove, however, to be the order of the day (see, for example, Andrews, 1994, p. 14).

Although Norway declined to join the EU it is a member, together with Iceland and all EU members, of the European Economic Area, created on 1 January 1994.

☐ *11.2.3 Supra-nationality*

At this juncture we need to take a general look at the Single European Market, concentrating in particular upon those aspects which affect trade flows between member states. It has to be borne in mind that every step towards a single market implies a loss of national sovereignty on the part of member states. The original impetus towards a Europe of independent nation- states came from de Gaulle in France. However, when the French attempted to expand their way into prosperity in the early 1980s, their failure caused them to reverse direction and become the arch advocates of the single market. The fact that M. Delors maintained close

links with the French Socialist Party created a suspicion in other countries that he is pressing for a predominantly French version of the single market. This has never gone down well in the UK. When M. Delors was ill-advised enough to boast that 80 per cent of economic legislation, and perhaps tax and social legislation, would be decided in Brussels by the end of the millennium, he was abruptly brought back to earth by Mrs Thatcher who pointed out that she did not expect the loss of national sovereignty on such a scale to take place during her lifetime. The UK's attitude has mellowed somewhat since her replacement as Prime Minister, but the backbench rebellion over the Maastricht Treaty and the continued strength of 'Euroscepticism' have demonstrated more recently that a referendum on the issue might result in a vote to depart from the Community.

☐ *11.2.4 Harmonisation and Mutual Recognition*

One of the primary reasons underlying the failure, prior to the 1980s, of the Community to develop much beyond the running of the Common Agricultural Policy, was the issue of **harmonisation**. By insisting, for example, that imports of beer would have to match the purity of the domestic product, the West Germans were able to create an effective non-tariff barrier against imports. Attempts by the European Commission to introduce rules which, if adhered to, would make products universally accepted throughout the Community, foundered constantly because member states with the highest standards tried to harmonise the proposed Community-wide standards with their own.

The pointer to a way out of this dilemma came in the form of the **Cassis de Dijon Judgement** of the European Court of Justice. This ruled that if a product satisfied the laws governing its production and sale in one member state, then it could also be sold in an identical form in any other member state even if the laws of those states prohibited its domestic production in that form. Importation of the product would not affect domestic laws, so it would remain illegal to make the product domestically. In this respect 'domestic' was taken to mean production by a national company, its subsidiaries and branches and subsidiaries of foreign companies operating within the boundaries of that nation.

Up to that time, products which were exported had to be compatible with the laws of the **importing** country. It was accordingly proposed by the Commission that they had to be compatible only with the laws of the **exporting** country. This is known as **mutual recognition**, and it obviously simplified enormously the problems facing a company wishing to engage in intra-Community trade. If an exporter was already making products in conformity with the laws of the importing country, he could either continue to do so or he could opt to produce in conformity with his domestic laws. One situation where the exporter would wish to continue to adhere to the laws of the importing country would be where the product exported was illegal on the home market. Although it appeared to be reasonable, this ruling was not without its own problems. In the first place, once frontier controls are dismantled it becomes relatively easy to move a product from a country where it is legal to one where it is not. Secondly, the ruling favours imports from outside the EU altogether. Once imported legally into any one EU country these can, in accordance with Article 9 of the Treaty of Rome, be sold in every EU country without restriction. Hence, an importer has only to get his product accepted in an EU country of his choosing to gain access to countries where the product cannot legally be produced for domestic consumption.

Under certain circumstances set out either in the Treaty of Rome or in judgements of the European Court of Justice (for example, concerning health and safety), a member state can prohibit imports from any source. However, these circumstances are much less pervasive than might be imagined. In the example cited above, the West Germans were unable to prohibit imports of beer on the grounds that they were adulterated and hence harmful to health, and the same principle was applied when the Italians tried to prohibit imports of pasta. In both cases the Court of Justice ruled that the health of consumers was not seriously threatened and that their interests

could be adequately protected by labelling clearly the contents of the products.

It is interesting to speculate whether mutual recognition will bring about a condition akin to total harmonisation. It is evident that a country which prohibits the domestic manufacture of a product cannot exclude the importation of that product in a form which is compatible with the laws of any other member state. Hence it follows that the domestic prohibition serves only to deny opportunities to domestic producers. Equally, if higher standards are required of a domestic producer than of producers who export from other states, the domestic producer must suffer some competitive disadvantages. It may accordingly make sense for prohibitions to be lifted and for exceptionally onerous domestic rules to be eased, not merely in order to permit domestic producers to reclaim the domestic market, but also to permit them to export successfully. Market forces may in this manner harmonise national standards, albeit not in accordance with the pre-existing highest standards of any individual country but in accordance with those set at a less onerous level.

Unsurprisingly, this scenario holds little appeal for countries such as Germany which can foresee their high-quality domestic products driven out of both domestic and export markets by lower-quality foreign products. Furthermore, in order to discover whether the foreign products should be sold in the domestic market, they must be checked not against the domestic standards, which are well-known, but against the standards set in each country of origin, which are unfamiliar. In order to avoid excessive bureaucracy an importer will generally have to trust the exporting country's own inspectorate, but it is understandable that, for example, Germans are suspicious of quality controls in Greece.

■ *11.3* The European Union Budget and the UK

□ *11.3.1 The EU Budget*

The EU Budget is agreed annually between the Council of Ministers and the European Parliament on the basis of a draft by the European Commission. It is formally adopted by the Parliament which has the final say on 'non-compulsory expenditure' whereas the Council has the final say on 'compulsory' expenditure. Spending which is **compulsory** is that which arises directly from the provisions of the Treaty of Rome or from other Acts adopted in accordance with the Treaty. In practice, it is almost all related to agricultural support and overseas aid. Spending which is **non-compulsory** includes that on regional development and social policies. Agricultural spending, together with the Regional Development Fund, the Social Fund and grants to farmers for modernisation or environmentally beneficial projects are known as the **structural Funds**. These Funds require **additionality**, that is they must supplement, and not replace, existing local and central government commitments to the projects selected.

The EU Budget relies, apart from periodic intergovernmental agreements (IGAs), upon its **own resources**. These comprise: (**1**) the Common Customs Tariff – duties and levies on goods imported from non-EU countries (net of a 10 per cent contribution to cover collection and administration costs); (**2**) agricultural levies on imported produce; (**3**) the amount which would be raised if VAT up to a specified rate were levied on the same basket of spending on goods and services in each member state (itself worth a maximum of 55 per cent of GNP at market prices); (**4**) payments related to each member state's GNP at market prices, set at a level sufficient to bridge the gap between total expenditure and the yield of the other three own resources.

There is a legally-binding ceiling, called a **guideline**, on the total own resources available to finance the Budget, which is expressed as a proportion of EU GNP. The Budget is set initially to provide some leeway below the guideline, but if there are problems with, for example, agricultural spending, that leeway can be rapidly eroded. The various contributions made by the UK are itemised as UK debits in **Table 11.4**. In return for these the UK receives credits, primarily from the European Agricultural Guarantee and Guidance Fund (EAGGF), the European Social Fund and the European Regional Development Fund. The differ-

ence between debits and credits represents the UK's net contribution to the EU Budget.

Gross of any abatements, the UK's share of total EU own resources is roughly 14 per cent. The UK receives back a much smaller share of total EU expenditure, so it is hardly surprising, therefore, that the UK is a major net contributor to the EU Budget. This arises because agricultural and other levies and duties are boosted by the UK's relatively heavy dependence on non-EU imports, because UK citizens' high propensity to consume generates large amounts of VAT and because the UK's relatively efficient agricultural sector attracts only modest levels of support.

In 1979, debits were 2.5 times as large as credits, and the net contribution amounted to almost £1 billion. As a consequence the UK government sought, and obtained, agreement for a series of annual refunds based upon the UK's excess net contributions to EU Budgets in earlier years. In addition, certain modest **adjustments** were made with respect to previous years' gross contributions. In 1984, at the Fontainebleau Summit, an **abatement** mechanism was negotiated which is now formally part of EU law. Under this agreement, the UK's **gross** contribution to the Budget in any given year is currently abated by an amount which is broadly equivalent to two thirds of the UK's **net** contribution in the previous year.

As can be seen in **Table 11.4**, the UK's contribution is rather erratic. This arises because of the need to make adjustments for inaccurate forecasts in previous years. It should be noted that, between 1979 and 1991, the EU Budget rose on average by 4.3 per cent annually whereas the UK's contribution rose on average by 0.5 per cent. If nothing else, Mrs Thatcher knew how to tough it out at the bargaining table. Germany bears the brunt of making contributions, but it has understandably lost some enthusiasm for that role now that it carries the burden of paying for the integration of former Eastern Germany.

In order to understand recent events, it is helpful to begin by looking back to the key Budget negotiations which took place in 1988. These negotiations were, as usual, conducted in an atmosphere of impending crisis. On this occasion, however, there was clear evidence that previous

Table 11.4   General Government Transactions with the Institutions of the EU (£ m)[1]

	1984	1985	1986	1987	1988	1989	1990	1991	1992	1993	1994	1995
EU BUDGET												
UK CREDITS												
Transfers												
Services	186	157	157	126	85	5	5	8	5	3	3	7
EAGGF	1353	1151	1385	1345	1379	1315	1496	1761	1813	2257	2297	2441
Social Fund	283	256	335	429	277	406	225	618	437	588	320	755
Regional Development Fund	184	274	298	404	370	347	441	370	551	425	608	437
Negotiated refunds[2]	528	61	—	—	—	—	—	—	—	—	—	—
Other	11	15	41	42	71	43	17	9	17	18	26	25
TOTAL	2545	1914	2216	2345	2182	2116	2184	2766	2823	3291	3254	3665
UK DEBITS												
Transfers												
Agriculture and sugar levies	260	189	244	355	226	192	135	205	206	199	201	203
Customs protective duties	1276	1291	1244	1417	1522	1638	1555	1529	1558	1754	1795	2016
GNP 4th Resource	—	—	—	—	—	303	1	813	934	1608	2340	1639
Adjustments[3]	—	—	—	—	—	—	—	—	-20	-50	-269	187
VAT (gross before abatement and adjustments)	1720	1930	2742	3347	2886	3143	4148	3796	4356	4964	4189	4635
Abatement[2]	—	-166	-1701	-1153	-1595	-1156	-1697	-2497	-1881	-2540	-1726	-1208
Adjustments[3]	-55	145	263	84	-127	311	516	-538	-297	-493	-1068	210
IGAs	—	370	—	—	613	—	—	—	—	—	—	—
TOTAL	3201	3759	2792	4050	3525	4431	4658	3308	4856	5442	5462	7682
BALANCE	-656	-1845	-576	-1705	-1343	-2315	-2474	-542	-2033	-2151	-2208	-4017

Notes:
[1] For all years sterling figures reflect actual payments made during the year, not payments in respect of particular Budgets.
[2] Refunds and abatements received in respect of the UK's excess net contributions to EU Budgets in earlier years.
[3] Adjustments reflecting reassessments of the gross contributions required for the EU Budgets for the previous years.
Source: UK Balance of Payments 1996, Table 1.5.

measures to reduce both the degree of price support and also surplus production had failed to rein back expenditure on the CAP. In 1975, the EU Budget amounted to ECU 6.2 billion, of which ECU 4.6 billion went to the EAGGF. By 1980 the respective figures were ECU 16.1 billion and ECU 11.6 billion, subsequently rising to ECU 28.2 billion and ECU 20.5 billion respectively in 1985. In each year, the percentage allocated to the EAGGF was over 70 per cent. However, although in 1987 the EAGGF allocation had risen to ECU 23.9 billion, this represented only 67.0 per cent of the total Budget of ECU 35.5 billion, with a much enlarged share allocated to the Regional Fund and Social Fund.

It was widely accepted that the Budget should continue to be readjusted towards regional and social spending, and within the EAGGF towards structural support. However, there were problems of implementation given that allocations to the CAP were the only obligatory element in the EU Budget, and that the Council of Agricultural Ministers, backed by the business interests dependent upon agriculture, had a strong vested interest in maintaining the status quo. Nevertheless, the package put forward by M. Delors, known as **Delors I**, included a proposal to double the Regional Fund and Social Fund by 1992.

A Summit was called in February 1988 to discuss the proposed package, and for once Mrs Thatcher was obliged to make significant concessions. It was agreed, with retrospective effect as from 1 January 1988, that the EAGGF growth rate would be limited to 74 per cent of the annual growth of EU GNP in volume terms; that the Budgets should absorb no more than 1.2 per cent of EU GNP; that the VAT base of each member state would be capped at 55 per cent of its GNP, with the continuation of the ceiling of 1.4 per cent of VAT proceeds to be given over; that a **fourth source** of revenue should be introduced based on shares in GNP, the rate levied to be that which is required, given all other revenue, to balance the Budget; that a production levy of 3 per cent would be placed on cereal production, at the beginning of each year up to 1992, which would be reimbursed only if total output fell below a ceiling of 160 million tonnes (with small farmers exempted),

and that if this figure was exceeded the price in the following year would be reduced by 3 per cent (a policy known as a budget **stabiliser**); that a similar scheme would be applied to oilseeds; and that farmers agreeing to take land out of production for five years would receive **set-aside payments** of between ECU 100 and 600 per hectare by way of compensation, provided at least 20 per cent of arable land was set aside and also not reutilised as grazing.

ECU 600 million was allocated for set-aside payments up to 1992, enough to fund 2 million hectares. The EAGGF was also to be rebalanced, with 50 per cent of the funds being used for structural purposes by 1992, and with a greater proportion directed towards the less developed member states. These various changes served to raise the Budget ceiling by roughly 40 per cent compared to what it would have been had the financial system which prevailed until 1985 not been changed. Whereas part of the intention was to provide funds other than for the CAP, it was ultimately the ongoing costs of the CAP which largely accounted for this substantial increase in budgetary resources.

The 1989 and 1990 negotiations were as usual acrimonious, but CAP spending was reasonably under control. However, with mountains and lakes reappearing in 1991, and an adjustment needed to allow for the incorporation of former East Germany into the CAP, it looked like the guideline would sooner or later be breached unless remedial action was taken. By the time of the Budget for 1992, the share of spending taken by the CAP had fallen to below 60 per cent of the total, with the structural Funds correspondingly much enlarged.

The structural Funds were an increasingly thorny issue. When the Commission drew up its first five-year spending plan in 1988, covering the period 1988–92 inclusive, the key to harmony lay in the doubling of structural Funds and the associated ceiling on CAP costs. However, in return for their signatures on the Maastricht Treaty, the poorest four EU members demanded an additional transfer of resources from richer northern members on the grounds that the latter would be the main beneficiaries of the treaty. This transfer, in the form of a **Cohesion Fund**, was to be incorporated in the new five-year plan commencing in 1993, known as **Delors II** as summarised in **Table 11.5** (and see Shackleton, 1993 and Scott, 1993).

Under Delors II, it was proposed that the structural Funds would be increased by roughly 60 per cent. In addition, the funds allocated to external action were to be doubled. Unfortunately, these proposals would cause the Budget, in real terms at 1992 prices, to rise to ECU 87.5 billion, an annual growth rate of 5 per cent. It was accordingly proposed that the own resources ceiling be raised from 1.20 to 1.37 per cent of EU GNP. This in turn meant that a fifth own resource might need to be tapped.

In June 1992, the European Council agreed to set up the Cohesion Fund, which was to benefit any member state with a GNP per capita of less than 90 per cent of the Community average and which had drawn up a programme for meeting the convergence criteria laid down in the Maastricht Treaty on budget deficits. Later that year, at the Edinburgh Summit, a number of compromises were reached (see Scott, 1993, pp. 80–1), including:

Table 11.5 *Community Budget Plans (spending commitments in billion ecus, 1992 prices) – Delors II*

	1987	1992	1997
Agriculture	32.7	36.3	40.1
Structural funds	9.1	18.6	29.3
Internal policies	1.9	4.0	6.9
External action	1.4	3.6	7.2
Administration and repayments to members	5.9	4.0	4.0
Total	51.0	66.5	87.5
Total as % of GNP	1.05	1.15	1.34
Ceiling as % of GNP	none	1.20	1.37

Note: annual average GNP growth 1987–92 3.1% (actual).
    1992–97 2.5% (projected).
Source: European Commission.

- the planning period was extended to cover 1993–99 inclusive;
- the own resources ceiling would rise gradually to 1.27 per cent in 1999;
- despite falling below the Delors II figure, this still implied a rise in appropriations to ECU 84.1 billion in 1999;
- the ceiling on the uniform rate of VAT would be reduced to 1 per cent during 1995–99;
- the arrangements for calculating the UK abatement would remain unaltered;
- the 1988 guidelines concerning the rate of growth of CAP spending would continue.

With own resources equivalent to 4p on the basic rate of income tax in the UK, it is understandable that the UK government was, as a net contributor, less happy than most with Delors II, which not merely included a new Cohesion Fund but continued with huge subsidies to farmers and significant, albeit smaller, subsidies to inefficient EU industries.

In April 1993, the Commission approved the first draft of the 1994 Budget, pencilling in a 7 per cent rise in spending to ECU 70.1 billion (see *Bulletin of the European Union*, No. 4, 1993, p. 82). The calculation of the initial allocation of the Cohesion Fund indicated, to general embarrassment, that the UK was eligible even though it was a net contributor to the Budget – not that the UK wished to stake a claim! However, by taking a longer timespan for the calculation, the UK could be shifted out of the net. At the same time, Germany let it be known that it had reached the limit of its contributions, and called for future Budget payments to be linked more closely to per capita incomes which were no longer higher there than everywhere else in the EU. The Budget was finally agreed at a figure of ECU 73.4 billion (see *Bulletin of the European Union*, No. 4, 1994, p. 87).

Needless to say, the Delors II calculations were much affected by the enlargement of the Community to 15 members, so the draft 1995 Budget comprised ECU 76.5 billion in payments and ECU 80.9 billion in appropriations while respecting the own resources ceiling still in force of 1.20 per cent of EU GNP. On this occasion, the European Parliament decided to flex its muscles, declaring the Budget finally adopted in December 1994 at a level unacceptable to the Council. This led to an appeal to the European Court of Justice which annulled what the Parliament had done (see *Bulletin of the European Union*, No. 1/2, 1996, pp. 120, 128).

In the meantime, the draft 1996 Budget was approved by the Council comprising ECU 81.6 billion in payments and ECU 86.3 billion in appropriations, an increase of roughly 8 per cent in relation to the 1995 Budget. Payments included an increase in CAP payments by 10.5 per cent to ECU 40.8 billion (almost exactly 50 per cent of the total – see **Figure 11.4**), caused by a fall in the dollar, completion of CAP reform and enlargement (see *Bulletin of the European Union*, No. 4, 1995, p. 76; No. 11, 1995, p. 101). The structural Funds rose to ECU 29.1 billion including a 10.6 per cent increase in the Cohesion Fund to ECU 2.4 billion.

The total gross payments made by the UK stood at £7 billion in 1992, but had risen to £10 billion by 1996 (equivalent to roughly £400 per taxpayer). In return, the UK expects to receive roughly £4.5 billion in 1996, and adding in abatements and adjustments reduces the expected net

contribution to £3.5 billion, up from £2.0 billion in 1992. Most of this increase is, however, accounted for by a combination of economic growth and inflation, although the UK continues to pay considerably more than is justified by its relative income per head.

□ *11.3.2 In Or Out?*

Understandably, in the light of the above, there is some dispute as to whether remaining in the EU is cost efficient for the UK (see, for example, Wolf, 1996). This dispute will never be settled in practice, not least because that would require agreement on forecasts based on highly speculative assumptions about what would happen if the UK decided to depart the EU.

On the evidence of the Asian 'tigers', prosperity is not dependent upon membership of a trading bloc, and indeed Norway believes that to be true in respect of the EU. However, Norway never joined in the first place, and the EU might well respond to the UK's departure by denying it preferential treatment. Departure would undoubtedly save the UK a considerable sum in relation

Figure 11.4   *1996 Budget Commitments and Resources*[1]

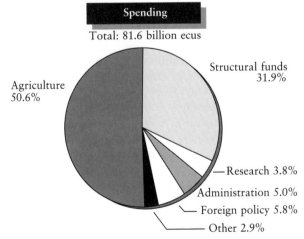

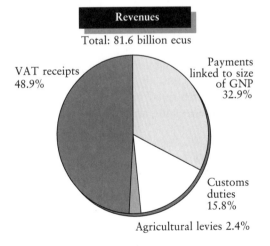

Note:
[1] The EU cannot run a budget deficit
Source: The European Commission.

to the no-longer-applying CAP plus cessation of net contributions to the EU. On the other hand, the UK is the most favoured country for inward investment looking for a launch pad into the rest of the EU, and that would cease. Whether it will be much reduced anyway is, of course, a moot point given the EU's determination to load non-wage costs onto the UK (or alternatively to cut them elsewhere), so there many ambiguities about the costs of departure. On balance, the UK will almost certainly make few additional gains in the near future by staying in unless it can persuade other members to liberalise services and public procurement. However, the costs of departure could be unacceptably high, so the optimal policy appears on balance to be to stay in and try to retain the UK's competitive advantage, particularly by 'opting out' of policies designed to erode it.

▌ 11.4 The European Monetary System (EMS)

In the Treaty of Rome, which originally set up the EEC in 1957, a target of 12 years was set by which all time all tariffs and quotas were to be removed between EEC members. This proved to be more than a little unrealistic, since it became clear that individual countries were in no rush to give up their national sovereignty. However, an attempt was made to take a major step forward with the publication of the Werner Report in 1970, which proposed the setting up of a European Monetary Union (EMU). Initially, this took the form of a narrowly constrained adjustable peg mechanism linked to the existing adjustable peg based on the dollar.

The widening of the dollar-based peg in 1971 resulted in the EMU taking the form of the '**snake in the tunnel**', whereby each EMU member's currency was allowed to fluctuate only narrowly around its own par value, thereby restricting the gap between the strongest and weakest currency to no more than 2.25 per cent, while the EMU currencies **taken as a whole** were permitted to fluctuate against the dollar within a 4.5 per cent band.

The EMU, operated by the original six EEC members from the beginning of 1972, and also by the UK for one month in May 1972, quickly fell apart at the seams. In part this reflected the continuing precedence of national interests over monetary union, but the EMU also, by chance, coincided historically with the demise of the adjustable peg system (the UK dropping out of both when it floated in June 1972). Other EMU members either withdrew permanently or moved in and out of the system, and by the mid-1970s it was regarded as terminated in practice even if not in principle.

The idea of monetary union was resurrected at the Bremen Summit in July 1978, which resulted in the setting up of the European Monetary System in March 1979. The idea behind the EMS, apart from the longer-term objective of an economic and monetary union within the Community was firstly to promote economic convergence in the Community by inducing member governments to adopt the sorts of policies being implemented by its most successful member, West Germany, and in particular to bring inflation down to the West German level, and secondly to create a 'zone of monetary stability' which would facilitate trade between EU members while providing insulation against the erratic behaviour of the dollar.

▐ 11.4.1 The European Currency Unit

The major innovation of the EMS was the introduction in 1979 of a new European currency, the **European Currency Unit** (ECU). This is a weighted average of the EMS currencies (and therefore has to be recalculated when new members join), where the weights are calculated according to the relative importance of the individual currencies in terms of key indicators such as national output and the volume of trade with other members. Belgium and Luxembourg are treated as a single entity. The deutsche mark dominates the ECU, with the franc also a significant contributor, whereas the Portuguese, Greek and Irish currencies are insignificant. The 'official' ECU performs the function of unit of account to the exchange rate mechanism described below, and also provides a currency which can circulate between central banks throughout the EU. In recent years, a separate private market for securities denominated in ECU has come into being, but, as noted previously, this has yet to form more than a marginal part of the total Eurocurrency markets.

A five-yearly recomposition of the ECU took place in September 1989. The European Commission decided in June 1989 that the currencies of members admitted since 1984, namely Spain and Portugal, should be included in the constitution of the ECU, the weight which was to be assigned to them and from which other currencies to transfer it. Clearly, this was as much a matter of political infighting as straightforward assessment of relative economic strength. The 1984 recomposition had given rather too much weight to the deutsche mark and guilder, and rather too little to the lira, in relation to their relative economic strength at the time, and the weight of the DM should in principle have been reduced to roughly 24 per cent in order to make way for the new currencies and also to adjust for slow growth in the West German economy. This proved objectionable to the West Germans, so the adjustment was in practice rather more modest. It is also the case that since bonds issued in each ECU contributor's own currency yield different interest rates, altering the balance of the ECU necessarily also affects the yield of bonds denominated in ECU. Considerable instability in the ECU bond market will therefore result from a major restructuring of the ECU, and this is always likely to operate to keep any restructuring within modest bounds.

Subsequent upon the signing of the Maastricht treaty, the pre-existing composition of the ECU was reconfirmed (see *Official Journal of the European Communities L350/27* of 31 December 1994) to hold until such time as stage 3 of EMU was attained.

11.4.2 The Exchange Rate Mechanism

The second element of the EMS is the **exchange rate mechanism** (ERM). Sterling joined the ERM on **8 October 1990** and departed from it on **16 September 1992**. Members of the EMS can contribute to the ECU without being members of the ERM, as is the case for the UK, Italy, Portugal and Greece. The ERM is a dual mechanism similar to, but more complex than, the old-style adjustable peg. In the first place, the member countries are slotted into a **parity grid** which summarises the bilateral central and intervention rates. Each currency was originally permitted to move bilaterally against any other currency in the grid by up to 2.25 per cent in either direction (the narrow band), although certain currencies could be given a dispensation to widen this movement to 6 per cent in either direction (the wide band). Currently, all ERM currencies are permitted a 15 per cent movement in either direction with the exception of the DM/Guilder link. It is important to note, however, that a currency must stay within its permitted band against **all other currencies simultaneously**. In other words, the strongest currency can never be more than 15 per cent above the weakest currency. The **effective limits** in relation to all other currencies are accordingly less than 15 per cent.

When any two currencies reach their compulsory intervention rates against each other the two central banks concerned are obliged to meet all bids/offers made to them at the relevant limit rate. In principle, currencies should not reach their effective limits because of the existence of the **divergence indicators**. Whenever a currency 'diverges' by more than 75 per cent from its central rate against the **ECU** (the divergence threshold) it is supposed to act as an early warning device which sets in motion a change in the way in which the country in question is conducting its economic policy. Where the divergence is below the central rate a suitable response might be a tightening of interest rates, and where it is above the central rate it might be a relaxation of fiscal policy. It should be noted that the permitted divergences are all different. This is because, when a currency's central rate moves, it also alters the value of the ECU.

If the early warning system is effective it should prevent the currency running up against its upper or lower limit on the parity grid, although the speed of response to signs of excessive divergence has in practice been too slow to achieve much in this respect. Hence, there have been a number of occasions when currencies have run up against the limits of the parity grid without either adjustment of domestic policies or intervention by central banks proving sufficient to prevent these limits being breached. As a consequence, both devaluations and revaluations have occurred, as set out in **Table 11.6** which covers the period to September 1992.

Given that remedial action was expected to be taken at two prior stages, a currency realignment was intended to be a last-resort operation, and a total of eleven realignments over as many years may, therefore, appear superficially to represent a rather excessive use of this ultimate remedy. However, as **Table 11.6** shows clearly, prior to 1992 realignments mostly took place in the early days of the EMS when it was moving towards a longer-term equilibrium, and the system was much more settled (perhaps excessively so) between 1983 and 1992. As explained above, it was a characteristic of the adjustable peg that currencies were almost always devalued rather than revalued, whereas there were more revaluations than devaluations under the EMS between 1979 and 1992. This reflected, in particular, a general tendency for the deutsche mark to rise, mirrored by the guilder, and for the French franc and the lira to decline.

It has nevertheless been argued that the weaker members of the ERM have borne most of the burden of adjustment because bilateral parties with the DM rather than the ECU have been crucial, and in order to dampen pressure for realignment weaker currency countries have had to adjust their interest rates relative to the German rate.

11.4.3 European Monetary Co-operation Fund

The other major component of the EMS is the European Monetary Co-operation Fund (EMCF), the purpose of which is to provide funds to assist with the stabilisation of exchange rates. At the inception of the EMS, members were required to deposit 20 per cent of their gold and dollar reserves with the EMCF (which the UK does also), in return for which they received a credit in ECUs which they could then use to settle indebtedness with other members or for intervention purposes. It was originally anticipated that this would evolve into a fully fledged European Monetary Fund as a major step on the path to monetary union, but this never developed as intended. The EMCF uses funds deposited with it to offer a range of credit facilities, responding to requests by individual countries rather than to policy adjustments jointly agreed by all members. Virtually unlimited funds are available on a very-short-term basis. The very-short-term financing (VSTF) facility has been available since the advent of the Basle-Nybord Accord in November 1987. However, only modest amounts, measured in ECUs, can be provided on either a short-term (up to nine months) or medium-term (two to four years) basis. In the case of the UK these latter credit facilities are virtually an irrelevance, in the first place because the UK has not borrowed from an international institution since 1977, and in the second place because it already has much larger credit facilities lying untouched at the IMF.

11.4.4 The EMS in Operation

It is possible to interpret the pattern shown in **Table 11.6** as indicating that in the early stages of the EMS there was a hard currency option offered by the West German Bundesbank and a soft currency option offered by the Banque de France (Weber, 1991). The guilder stayed with the DM, whereas the other currencies first devalued against the DM then interspersed devaluations with periods of stability from 1983 onwards (except the lira which fell continuously relative to the DM until 1990). What this suggests is that the latter countries, by effectively adopting an adjustable peg against the DM, chose to forgo the tough anti-inflationary stance of West Germany in favour of the less rigorous approach espoused by France. For this reason, although there was a tendency for inflation to fall in all EMS countries

Table 11.6 *Central Parity Realignments[1] within the EMS, 1979–90 (%)*

	September 1979	November 1979	March 1981	October 1981	February 1982	June 1982	March 1983	July 1985	April 1986	August 1986	January 1987	January 1990
Deutsche Mark	+2.0			+5.5		+4.25	+5.5	+2.0	+3.0		+3.0	
French franc				-3.0		-5.75	-2.5	+2.0	-3.0			
Guilder				+5.5		+4.25	+3.5	+2.0	+3.0		+3.0	
Lira			-6.0	-3.0		-2.75	-2.5	-6.0				-3.7[2]
Belgian/ Lux. franc					-8.5		+1.5	+2.0	+1.0		+2.0	
Krone	-3.0	-5.0			-3.0		+2.5	+2.0	+1.0			
Irish £							-3.5	+2.0		-8.0		

Notes:
[1] + indicates a revaluation, – indicates a devaluation.
[2] When Italy moved from the wide band to the narrow band in January 1990, it moved the central parity down towards the existing lower limit, thereby subtracting 3.75% (6% –2.25%) from its value. Technically, this does not count as a realignment.
Source: European Commission.

during the early 1980s, convergence on the German rate was quite slow and unsteady until 1985.

It is interesting to compare the abrupt and rapid fall in inflation in the UK and USA after 1980 with the much slower fall in other EMS countries. However, after 1985, the hard currency option offered by the Bundesbank became the dominant influence, and disinflation in the EMS continued with noticeable convergence upon the German inflation rate. This was by no means a costless experience for all participants. In France, for example, unemployment remained at a very high level throughout the 1980s whereas it fell steadily in the UK from 1986 to 1990. Indeed, it should be clearly understood that if an EMS participant has an above-average inflation rate and is thereby becoming uncompetitive, the burden of adjustment must fall upon real wages and employment precisely and insofar that it cannot be borne by the exchange rate.

The general tendency for inflation rates among ERM countries to converge was constantly reiterated as a major potential benefit of UK membership of the ERM once inflation in the UK began to rise again in the late 1980s. Nevertheless, it has never been proved satisfactorily whether this convergence was specific to ERM **arrangements** or whether it was a general feature of the **period** during which both ERM and non-ERM countries such as the UK and USA committed themselves in their macroeconomic strategies to conquering inflation (see Haldane, 1991 and Weber, 1991). It is also notable that the anti-inflationary anchor provided by Germany has slipped in recent years, especially in the period since July 1990 when monetary union between East and West Germany took place.

As noted in Haldane (1991) and Artis (1991), there is evidence to support the argument that the ERM helped to stabilise both nominal and real intra-ERM bilateral exchange rates, but it had much less effect upon the stability of members' global Effective Exchange Rates. The recent sharp fluctuations of the dollar is an obvious case in point since the dollar has not moved consistently against all ERM currencies.

A related issue is whether lower intra-ERM exchange rate volatility was achieved at the cost of greater short-term interest rate variability. It would appear to be the case (Weber, 1991, p. 82) that during the early EMS period (1979–83) highly volatile movements at relatively high levels of interest rates corresponded to speculative attacks upon the currencies which were devalued. Disinflation, capital controls and policy adjustments in the following period (1983–87) reduced this volatility markedly while also exerting downwards pressure on interest rates generally. The period from 1987 to 1991 saw rates move or less in line, but mostly in an upwards direction. Here again, the influence of Germany appeared to be crucial.

The decision to remove all capital controls is often held to have heralded the coming of the 'new EMS' (Haldane, 1991). Because speculative capital flows had been such a destabilising force under the adjustable peg, steps were taken under the Basle–Nyborg Agreement in September 1987 to offset these through, for example, the introduction of the VSTF. Furthermore, realignments of ERM currencies were put into effective abeyance as the message was sent out to the financial markets that the ERM countries would act in concert to maintain exchange rate stability and to base their macroeconomic policy upon that in Germany.

So successful was this policy that the paradox of **excess credibility** became apparent. High inflation countries such as Spain and Italy needed to maintain high interest rates to keep inflation under control. As noted previously, inflows of hot money, attracted by these interest rates, would normally be discouraged by the exchange rate risk involved (see **p. 250**), but this risk was no longer serious for ERM currencies, especially those in the narrow band. Hence, hot money flooded into Spain and Italy, driving the lira and peseta perversely to the top of the grid.

☐ 11.4.5 Sterling and the ERM

In the course of the first edition we discussed at length whether the UK should join the ERM. That discussion could be said to have once again become relevant in that the UK is currently outside the ERM, but the circumstances surrounding the question of re-entry warrant a different approach in the discussion which follows. However, one issue which will inevitably resurface concerns the appropriate entry value for the pound.

There was considerable controversy in 1988 concerning whether the pound was overvalued at entry relative to the deutsche mark. It is necessary to adjust for inflation when seeking to address such a question, which can be done using different deflators. If unit labour costs are used as the deflator, then on that basis it would appear that the rate at entry was sustainable (and that indeed was the prevailing opinion both in the UK and elsewhere in the Community), as indeed it would have been had it been either slightly higher or slightly lower. However, it was subsequently counter-argued that the EER should be used rather than the DM, and that it should be deflated by export unit values. On that basis the real EER was well above its long-term average on entry, and this allegedly speeded up the descent into recession. We can expect to see this debate resurface at such time as re-entry is contemplated no matter what central rate is chosen.

It is helpful at this stage to set out the developing situation in graphical form. **Figure 11.5** illustrates the nominal relationship between the DM and sterling over the 10–year period prior to ERM entry. As can be seen, the period 1987–90 when

sterling was effectively shadowing the DM was far less volatile than the preceding period, although there was a tendency for the rate to stay above DM3 to the £ until the latter half of 1989.

The technical arguments about the 'correct' rate of entry, which in any event fell somewhat short of proof, played little part in influencing opinion outside the Treasury. The central parity chosen, namely DM2.95 to the £, did not appear to be particularly high taking a superficial longer-term perspective as in **Figure 11.5**. Nevertheless, the rate had been somewhat lower during the first half of 1990, and there were many who felt that the UK should have entered at a lower rate simply in order to give industry a competitive advantage. The period commencing with the Autumn of 1990 is covered in **Figure 11.6**. An added feature of **Figure 11.6** is the sequential reduction in the banks' base rate which occurred post-ERM entry. The pattern is significant because, as can be seen, the sharp rise in the £/DM rate at the time of entry drove sterling to the upper limit of its parity grid and thus permitted base rates to be cut by 1 per cent without seriously undermining its value. Nevertheless, sterling rapidly turned down, and remained below its central rate against the DM until April 1991. On 1 February 1991, sterling became the weakest currency in the ERM. The authorities understandably felt unable to make any further dramatic cuts

Figure 11.5 *DM per £, 1980–90*

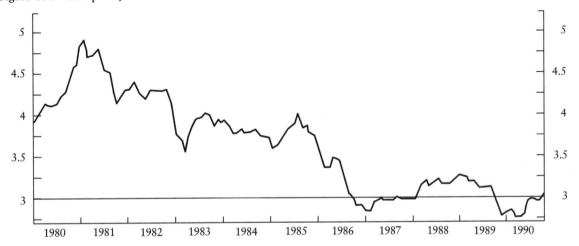

Source: CSO.

Figure 11.6   *DM per £, 1990–91*

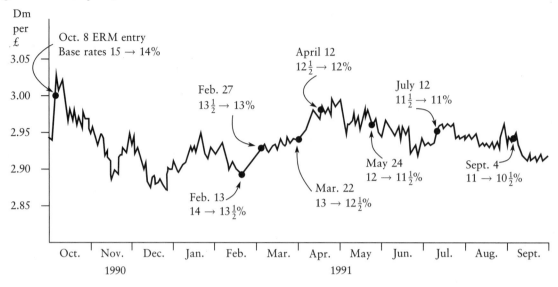

Source: Daily rates posted in *The Times*.

in interest rates, but rather chose to engage in a succession of half-point reductions as sterling rose steadily from mid-February to May. Given the strength of the recession this may be viewed as ultra-cautious, especially as, in practice, sterling was not adversely affected by each sequential reduction. In order to understand what happened after the end of 1991, it is first necessary to discuss EMU and EPU.

■ *11.5* EMU and EPU

☐ *11.5.1 Economic and Monetary Union*

The EMS is seen in many quarters as simply a necessary step on the road to a 'United States of Europe', incorporating a single European currency in an EMU structure. The Single European Act refers to EMU as '**co-operation** in economic and monetary policy' and talks about 'EMU's progressive realisation'. These are sentiments with which even Mrs Thatcher was happy to comply.

Economic and monetary union involves two rather different concepts. **Economic** union is es-

sentially concerned with the Single European Market – that is, a common market with an element of economic policy co-ordination between member states. **Monetary** union is essentially concerned with a single currency area with a common monetary policy.

The Delors Committee was set up in 1985 to recommend how best to proceed towards eventual EMU. It proposed a three-stage process leading to irreversible fixity of EU currencies and at some point a single currency, possibly the ECU, to replace national currencies. At the Madrid Summit, in June 1989, an attempt was made to set a rigid timetable for the full implementation of EMU. However, Mrs Thatcher managed to delay matters, which led in part to her loss of office and replacement by Mr Major who espoused a more pro-European stance.

☐ *11.5.2 The Maastricht IGCs*

In December 1991, there was a double intergovernmental conference (IGC) held at Maastricht under the auspices of the Dutch presidency of the EU. These IGCs were instigated at the Rome

Summit in December 1990. The French were very keen to introduce EMU in order to offset what they saw as the dominant role of the deutsche mark and the Bundesbank. In return, the Germans persuaded the French that this would work better if there was also closer political integration and more democratic control over EU decision-making. Afraid that combining the two sets of issues together would delay his pet project of EMU, Delors insisted that they be discussed separately, although for convenience the two IGCs, one on EMU and the other on political union (EPU) took place simultaneously.

□ *11.5.3 Federalism*

In a draft preamble to a rewritten Treaty of Rome drawn up by the Luxembourg presidency, the phrase 'a union with a federal goal' appeared for the first time as a description of the Community. The UK Foreign Secretary, Douglas Hurd, promptly rejected this on the grounds that while the world 'federal' might mean different things to different nationalities, 'it has come to mean something tight and integrated in English'. Curiously, the term 'federal' means **decentralisation** in some countries even though it means **centralisation** in English. Denmark and Portugal were also less than keen on the term, so it needed to be written out of the new treaty.

Given the unfortunate recent history of such federations as the USSR, Yugoslavia and India, the UK's objection was not altogether surprising. However, the Treaty of Rome already commits the UK to 'an ever closer union', which in theory at least commits the UK to forge more and more links with other EU members, so a federal structure in which the UK's sovereign rights are more or less permanently defined might even seem to be the lesser of two evils.

□ *11.5.4 The Maastricht Treaty*

The EMU sections began by stating that:

The activities of the member states and the Community shall . . . include:

- the irrevocable fixing of exchange rates leading to the introduction of a single currency, the ECU;
- the definition and conduct of a single monetary policy and exchange rate policy the primary objective of both of which shall be to maintain price stability; and,
- without prejudice to this objective, to support the general economic policies in the Community in accordance with the principle of an open market economy with free competition.

It then went on to state that:

A European System of Central Banks (ESCB) and the European Central Bank (ECB) shall be established in accordance with the procedures laid down in this Treaty . . . The basic tasks to be carried out through the ESCB shall be:

- to define and implement the monetary policy of the Community;
- to conduct foreign exchange operations consistent with the provisions of Article 109; and
- to hold and manage the official foreign reserves of the member states.

The ESCB shall be composed of the ECB and of the central banks of the member states.

The ECB was to be established before the end of 1992. Neither it nor the ESCB, nor individual central banks were to seek or take instructions from Community institutions or bodies, or from any government of a member state, thereby guaranteeing independence.

The core of the treaty concerned the path of EMU. This was expressed in terms of 'a high degree of sustainable convergence' which itself required the following criteria to be satisfied:

- that a currency should have kept within the normal fluctuation margins of the ERM for at least two years without severe tensions;
- that the consumer price index should not exceed by more than 1.5 per cent that of at most the three best performing member states in terms of price stability over the past year;

- that the planned or actual general government financial deficit should not exceed 3 per cent of GDP at market prices, unless either the ratio has declined substantially and continuously and reached a level that comes close to 3 per cent or the excess is only exceptional and temporary;
- that the ratio of general government gross debt to GDP at market prices should not exceed 60 per cent unless the ratio is sufficiently diminishing and approaching 60 per cent at a satisfactory pace;
- that over the past year the average nominal long-term government bond rate should not exceed by more than 2 per cent that of at most the three best performing member states in terms of price stability.

It should be noted that the first stage of EMU relates to membership of the ERM in the narrow band, so the UK is temporarily not even at stage one. Prior to the second stage of EMU, which commencing on 1 January 1994, all EU members were obliged to abolish all restrictions on the movement of capital and set their economic houses in order. Once stage 2 had begun, a European Monetary Institute (EMI) was set up to:

- strengthen co-operation between central banks;
- strengthen co-ordination of monetary policies;
- replace the European Monetary Co-operation Fund;
- monitor the functioning of the EMS;
- facilitate the use of the ECU.

At the end of 1996, the EMI was obliged to specify the regulatory, organisational and logistical framework for the ESCB.

During stage 2, the European Commission has been monitoring the progress towards convergence of each country. The Council of Ministers having so recommended on the basis of a qualified majority, the European Council (composed of Heads of State or of Government) is now obliged to consider:

- whether a majority of the member states fulfils the necessary conditions for the adoption of a single currency;

- whether it is appropriate for the Community to enter the third stage of EMU, and if so, when.

If the date for the commencement of stage 3 cannot be agreed before the end of 1997 then it will automatically begin on 1 January 1999. The Council's decision will be by qualified majority, as will be the decision concerning which countries will be permitted to proceed to full EMU, and which are to be given a derogation. At least once every two years, or at the request of a member state with a derogation, the Commission and the ECB will recommend to the European Council whether other countries have met the convergence criteria.

At the beginning of stage 3, all member states which qualify for full EMU will adopt the conversion rates at which their currencies will be irrevocably fixed in terms of the ECU which will then become a currency in its own right.

It is worthy of note that it is not essential that a country meets all of the five convergence criteria simultaneously since it would appear to be possible for the European Council to bend the rules somewhat in practice when deciding which countries qualify. This is probably just as well in view of the fact that only Germany, France and Luxembourg might meet all five criteria in 1997, as shown in **Table 11.7**, and even that is doubtful as noted below (p. 295).

It is a touch ironic that, on a **strict** reading of the Maastricht criteria, Germany is not currently (end-1996) ready for full EMU. It is frankly doubtful whether Italy, Greece or Portugal ever will be. As for the UK, it insisted on an 'opt-out clause' to the effect that '*The UK shall not be obliged or committed to move to the third stage of economic and monetary union without a separate decision to do so by its government and Parliament*'. If the UK does opt-out then it will not count when calculating the majority needed to proceed to full EMU. It is probable, however, that if the UK were to move back into the ERM, and to keep itself there for two years, it would be eligible for full EMU.

The EPU sections began by stating that: 'By this Treaty, the High Contracting Parties establish among themselves a European Union . . . This

Table 11.7 *EMU Convergence Criteria: 1997 forecast*

	Exchange rate[1]	Price index	Budget	Public debt	Bond rate[2]	Score
B	Yes	Yes	No	No	Yes	3
DK	Yes	Yes	Yes	No	Yes	4
D	Yes	Yes	Yes	Yes	Yes	5
GR	No	No	No	No	No	0
E	Yes	No	No	No	No	1
F	Yes	Yes	Yes	Yes	Yes	5
IRL	Yes	Yes	Yes	No	Yes	4
I	Yes[3]	No	No	No	No	1
L	Yes	Yes	Yes	Yes	Yes	5
NL	Yes	Yes	Yes	No	Yes	4
A	Yes	Yes	No	No	Yes	3
P	Yes	No	No	No	No	1
FIN	Yes[4]	Yes	Yes	No	Yes	4
S	No	Yes	No	No	Yes	2
UK	No	Yes	Yes	Yes	Yes	4

Notes:
[1] The widening of the 'narrow' band to ±15% casts some doubt upon the interpretation of this criterion.
[2] It remains unclear exactly how this is to be measured, so the ratings are somewhat speculative (see European Commission, 1996, p. 18).
[3] Italy rejoined the ERM in November 1996. However, there is some doubt as to whether it will be able to sustain a link of ±2.25% to the DM for two years.
[4] Finland joined the ERM in October 1996.

Treaty marks a new stage in the process creating an ever closer Union among the peoples of Europe, where decisions are taken as closely as possible to the citizens'.

The preamble then goes on to refer to the issue of **subsidiarity** which is defined for the first time in article 3b as follows:

the Community shall take action . . . only if and insofar as the objectives of the proposed action cannot be sufficiently achieved by the member states and can therefore, by reason of the scale or effects of the proposed action, be better achieved by the Community . . . Any action by the Community shall not go beyond what is necessary to achieve the objectives of this treaty.

The concept of subsidiarity is causing considerable difficulties of interpretation. It may be asked, firstly, whether it is more **effective** to take a decision at the centre, and secondly whether it is **necessary** for that decision to be taken centrally. These are independent issues insofar as it is possible to argue that whereas a decision can be taken more effectively at the centre, it is unnecessary to do so because it can be taken perfectly satisfactorily at a national level. The UK's preference has always been to interpret subsidiarity such as to minimise the powers of the Commission. Initially, this approach was poorly supported, but in recent months, as public opinion has swung against ratification, the Commission has become a convert to the virtues of national decision-making – at least for the time being.

The new treaty nevertheless both amends and extends the list of activities as set out in the Treaty of Rome and the SEA which fall within the competence of the Commission. This encompasses:

- the strengthening of economic and social cohesion;
- measures concerning the entry and movement of persons in the internal market;
- a policy in the sphere of the environment;
- the promotion of research and technological development;
- measures in the spheres of energy, consumer protection, civil protection and tourism;
- contribution to the attainment of a high level of health protection;
- contribution to education and training of high quality, and to the flowering of the cultures of the member states.

As noted above, cohesion essentially means a transfer of resources from north to south, which will be costly for the UK as a net contributor to the EU Budget. It is also worth observing that this extension of powers will make it harder for aspiring members to reach EU standards.

Readers will, perhaps, be pleased to learn that they have become 'citizens of the Union', a title awarded in the treaty to all EU nationals who 'shall have the right to move and reside freely within the territory of the Member States'. In principle, the EU is to be known officially as the European Union, but there is likely to be plentiful use of the 'Community', especially by the British (anyway helpful when looking backwards over the EEC/EC/EU as in this book), and some may even remain loyal to the 'Common Market'.

The treaty enhances the powers of the European Parliament. Whereas, as shown in **Figure 11.1**, the Parliament previously needed the Commission's backing to get its amendments through the Council, it now has the right (as from 1 January 1995) to negotiate directly with the relevant ministers the changes that it wants to make, and to reject any proposed legislation that does not contain them. This was originally to be called the 'co-decision' process (and indeed generally still is in the literature), but this was technically vetoed by the UK on the grounds that it smacked of loss of sovereignty and is known officially as 'the procedure laid down in Article 189b'! It covers laws on the internal market; consumer protec-

tion; the free circulation of labour; the right of individuals and companies to establish themselves in other member states; the treatment of foreigners; vocational training; public health; and trans-European infrastructure.

In respect of foreign policy, the Parliament also has to give its assent to such matters as the objectives of the structural Funds and the rights of citizenship created by the treaty.

11.5.5 Events Immediately Post-Maastricht

The period following upon the Maastricht IGCs was so volatile that it is helpful to begin by providing a chronology of major events.

1992

5 Jan.	Norman Lamont, the then Chancellor of the Exchequer states: **Realignment is another word for devaluation. We are not going to devalue the pound.**
7 Feb.	Treaty is signed.
6 April	Portuguese escudo joins ERM in wide band.
3 June	Danish referendum on treaty. Treaty is rejected 50.7% to 49.3%, but Danes vote to remain in EU.
11 June	UK government postpones parliamentary debate on treaty until the Autumn.
12 June	German government and federal states deadlocked over latters' wish to retain the deutsche mark and have a veto over transfers of sovereignty to EU.
18 June	Irish referendum on treaty. Vote is two-to-one in favour.
9 July	UK government admits there is no prospect of ratification in 1992.
10 July	Lamont states: **Leave the ERM, cut interest rates and let the pound find its own value . . . it's the cut-and-run option. The credibility of our anti-inflationary strategy would be in tatters. And quite soon interest rates would have to go back up again.**
20 Aug.	Sterling breaches ERM divergence indicator for first time since entry to ERM.

28 Aug. DM rises to top of EMS grid for first time since 1989.

1 Sept. Sterling rises above $2, but is at lowest level against the DM since May 1990.

3 Sept. Lamont states: **Devaluation . . . would lead to a collapse in market confidence and a damaging rise in interest rates. Withdrawal from the ERM . . . would see a huge fall in the pound and an explosion in inflation.**

8 Sept. Finland abandons ECU–markka peg.

10 Sept. Major states: [**ERM**] **membership was no soft option. The soft option, the devaluer's option, the inflationary option would be a betrayal of our future.**

12 Sept. Decision taken to devalue the lira by 7% against all other ERM currencies.

14 Sept. Bundesbank announces smaller than expected interest rate reduction.

16 Sept. Lamont states: [**Britain**] **will take whatever measures are necessary to maintain sterling's ERM parity.**
Minimum lending rate (MLR) raised from 10% to 12%. MLR later raised to 15%. Lamont states: **Britain's best interests would be best secured by suspending our membership of the ERM.**
Sterling suspended from ERM.
MLR reduced to 12%.

17 Sept. Lira suspended from ERM.
Peseta devalued by 5%.
MLR reduced to 10%.
Sterling falls to DM2.64.

18 Sept. Lamont states: **We are floating and we will set monetary policy in this country . . . It will be a British economic policy and a British monetary policy.**

20 Sept. French referendum vote 51.05% in favour of treaty.

22 Sept. MLR reduced to 9%, bringing rate below that in Germany for first time in 11 years.

23 Sept. Spain reimposes exchange controls.
Chancellor Kohl launches attack on Brussels bureaucracy, calling it 'too powerful, constantly expanding and exterminating national identities'.

30 Sept. Kohl rejects the idea of 'two-speed' Europe.
The Bundesbank reveals that it had spent DM44 billion (£17.3 bn) defending the £ and lira.

5 Oct. Lira depreciates by 5%.

6 Oct. Lira depreciates by 6% then appreciates by 8%.
Sterling rises from DM2.37 to DM2.45.

10 Oct. European Commission admits existence of secret draft of second Maastricht treaty to be used if first is not ratified.

2 Nov. Sterling falls to $1.53 and the EER to 77.7.

5 Nov. Major reveals that Parliament will not complete ratification of treaty until after Danes hold a second referendum. Denmark pencils in May 1993 and demands opt-outs to the effect that it should be free not to participate in European defence policy; not to implement stage 3; not to implement co-operation on police and legal matters on a supranational basis; and not to be committed to introduce union citizenship.

19 Nov. Sweden abandons ECU-krona peg.

22 Nov. Peseta devalued by 6% but Spain lifts controls of 23 Sept.
Portugal devalues escudo by 6%.

11 Dec. Norway abandons ECU-krone peg.

16 Dec. Portugal lifts exchange controls.

1993

1 Jan. Ireland lifts exchange controls.

30 Jan. Ireland devalues pound by 10%.

12 Feb. EER falls to 75.7.

24 Feb. Sterling falls to DM2.31

13 May Spain devalues peseta by 8%.
Portugal devalues escudo by 6.5%.

18 May Second Danish referendum produces 56.8% yes vote.

1 June European Commission says UK right to withdraw from ERM.

22 July Government suffers defeat in vote on Protocol on Social Policy (see below) when 23 backbenchers rebel.

23 July   Government tables vote of confidence to retain the Protocol, and has a majority of 40 in favour of ratification of the treaty as negotiated.

29 July   Bundesbank leaves discount rate unchanged. Massive intervention is needed to keep the franc and other ERM currencies within their trading limits.

1 Aug.   Announcement that ERM currencies to trade within +/- 15% of central rates (although the guilder/DM link stays unchanged).

2 Aug.   The UK officially ratifies the treaty.

12 Oct.   German federal constitutional court approves treaty.

1 Nov.   The treaty becomes law.

□ 11.5.6 Black or White?

16 September 1992 is a date most frequently referred to as 'Black' Wednesday but known in some circles as 'White' Wednesday. The distinction is straightforward. Those who believe that participation in the ERM, and eventually in stage 3 of EMU, is essential for the long-term health of the economy regard the events of 16 September as a disaster. The government was initially to be counted among these. However, those who believe that the ERM was a straight-jacket resulting in the imposition of inappropriate Germanic policies upon the UK are happy to see the exchange rate trading at well below DM2.95, and hope that the UK is now participating a period of export-led growth. The Conservative government is currently to be numbered among these, a U-turn of truly noble proportions.

Indeed, Black or White, Wednesday 16 September tells us a great deal about the ineptness of those who govern us, although constraints on space prevent too deep an examination of this issue! Suffice it to say that the Conservative government appeared to believe that it made no errors of judgement – and not just the government since the then governor of the Bank of England, Robin Leigh-Pemberton, stated that 'Having joined [the ERM], we were right to endeavour

to stick with it; and, in the circumstances which evolved, we were also right to withdraw.'

True or false? It is reasonably clear that the ERM collapsed under a combination of pressures. Arguably the most important was the decision at the time of German (re)unification to exchange one Ostmark for one D-Mark and to promise West German wage levels to much less productive East German workers, combined with a promise not to raise West German taxes. The response of the Bundesbank to the inflationary pressure this stoked up was to raise interest rates at precisely the point in time when the rest of the EU, and especially the UK, needed to lower theirs.

Secondly, although the Basle–Nyborg agreement specified to the contrary, the French in particular treated stage 1 as though it required fixity of exchange rates, and they were unwilling to countenance any realignments prior to the French referendum, which had itself created tensions within the ERM given the possibility of a no vote.

However, as sterling fell to its floor against the DM, the UK government was unwilling, and felt unable for political reasons for fear of providing ammunition to Euro-sceptics, to raise interest rates in order to bolster the pound. Slightly oddly, perhaps, the Bank of England took the view that this failure to act in good time was beneficial, since speculators could not expect to make money selling a currency which was already at its floor value, given the oft-repeated determination of the UK government to defend sterling at all costs.

Unfortunately, the markets realised that it would be the Bundesbank rather than the Bank of England that would have to buy sterling in exchange for DM, and that it would be dismayed by the fact that this would pump up the German money supply as the D-Marks were put into circulation. Furthermore, the constant bickering between finance ministers and central bankers at meetings earlier in 1992 had created the impression that, for example, the Bundesbank would not feel all that enthusiastic about requests to defend sterling. In this respect much was made of comments by Helmut Schlesinger, in the course of an interview on 15 September, to the effect that he believed sterling to be vulnerable. It must also be borne in mind that the devaluation of the lira during the previous weekend, while compatible with Basle–Nyborg, was a further indication to the markets that a concerted attack upon a currency rendered vulnerable as a result of an unremedied lack of competitiveness in the relevant economy would drive it below its floor in the ERM.

Finally, it should be remembered that virtually all exchange controls within the EU had been lifted by September 1992. The stability of the ERM in previous years had tended to obscure the fact that this had removed a potential final line of defence in the face of a concerted attack upon a currency (for a fuller analysis of some of the above arguments, see Sandholtz, 1996).

□ 11.5.7 Consequences

There can be no doubt that in the Autumn of 1992 something had to give. The US economy, despite very low interest rates, was not growing at all strongly. Meanwhile, most of the EU was subsiding rapidly into recession. With unemployment high and growing, a balance of trade deficit in a recession and a rapidly expanding fiscal deficit, the UK desperately needed to find a way out of its difficulties and it was plain that its trading partners were not going to put themselves out to be of assistance.

There is little point in agonising over precisely how much help the Germans, for example, could or should have provided. At the end of the day, the UK government made its own decision about the entry rate when joining the ERM, despite German disapproval, and its own incompetence contributed to the scale of the recession post-1989.

Insofar as the UK's suspension of ERM membership appeared to provide the logical escape hatch to possible prosperity, it is possible to argue that the extent of Euro-scepticism was a contributory factor since the markets were aware that failure to remain in the ERM would allow the UK to 'opt-out' of stages 2 and 3 by the back door. The Conservative government reiterated its intention to stay out of the ERM until the EU as a

whole had regained its stability. In this context, it is instructive to remember that from 1979 to 1987 the franc fell by 31 per cent against the DM whereas the pound, outside the ERM, fell only by 20 per cent. Between 1987 and 1990, sterling rose against both the DM and franc, and only weakened perceptibly after it joined the ERM. As recent experience has shown, the pound may regain a good deal of the ground lost since its ERM suspension irrespective of any official commitment to rejoin, and there are those who argue strongly (see, for example, Minford, 1992) that the optimum solution is to move towards an EU-wide float combined with coordination of monetary policies.

In conclusion, although it is difficult to pin down the precise commencement of economic recovery, it is evident that life post-ERM is generally quite pleasant and, from an economic perspective, disaster-free. The exchange rate has recovered a significant part of the initial losses, and it is even alleged that it is becoming undesirably strong (see **Figure 11.7**).

The oft-expressed fear that interest rates would have to rise on account of increased uncertainty in a post-ERM world has been demonstrated to be untrue (although real rates have generally remained quite high), just as it has become clear that floating has been beneficial for growth. On balance, therefore, there seem to be good reasons for preferring the 'White' to the 'Black' version of Wednesday 16 September 1992.

□ 11.5.8 The Ratification Muddle

The document which had to be ratified in the UK was the **European Communities (Amendment) Bill**. This amended the **European Communities Act 1972** effectively by adding to it the relevant parts of the Maastricht Treaty. It also required, as noted previously, that stage 3 of EMU could not be embarked upon without passing an Act through Parliament to that effect.

The Bill contained a mere three clauses, of which one gave the title of the Bill. Clause 1 incorporated the Protocols (appendixes), including the Protocol on Social Policy which itself

Figure 11.7   *Sterling against the DM (DM per £)*

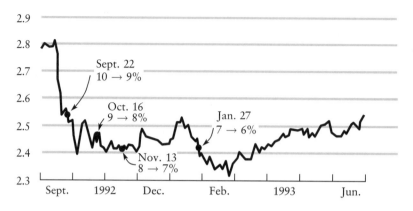

Source: Daily rates posted in *The Times*.

incorporated the Agreement on Social Policy (Social Chapter).

The UK, having opted-out, was specifically exempted from the terms of the Protocol on Social Policy. However, in February 1993, Amendment 27 to the Bill (there were 450 altogether) was proposed to the effect that the words 'with the exception of the Protocol on Social Policy' be added to the Bill. The rationale for this Amendment (which was odd in that it was proposed by anti-treaty groups even though it sought to exclude rather than include the Protocol) was that the removal of the Protocol would simultaneously remove the opt-out clause, thereby theoretically forcing the UK to renegotiate the treaty.

Just exactly what all this **really** meant became irrelevant when early in March the deputy speaker ruled the Amendment out of order. However, the government was defeated for the first time in three years only a few days later on a Labour amendment which forced the Bill to go to the 'report stage', thereby delaying ratification. Subsequently, Amendment 75 was tabled which would have the effect of preventing powers being transferred to European institutions under the legislation until the Commons had decided whether the Protocol on Social Policy should apply to the UK. The purpose here was to try to force the government at the last minute (post-royal assent) to choose between a treaty containing the Social Chapter and no treaty at all, although this did not appeal to the Tory rebels who had absolutely no desire to force the former choice on the government.

Early in May, faced with another likely defeat in the Commons, the government was forced to accept Amendment 2 which called for the Protocol on Social Policy (opt-out included) to be deleted from the version of the treaty to be enshrined in UK law. This did not, however, remove the opt-out from the version of the treaty to be ratified by the UK.

On 22 July, as noted above, the government was defeated in a vote on Amendment 75, and the following day invoked a vote of confidence in respect of the treaty, including the opt-out, which it duly won. On 2 August the ratification process was completed ahead of schedule.

11.5.9 The 1996–97 Inter-governmental Conference

The 1996 IGC is not going to be a momentous occasion. The IGCs which preceded Maastricht, as we have noted above, were concerned with major structural changes in the operation of the EU. However, EMU is now on its way, the Single Market is largely complete and the Commission is well aware that any attempt to take on board further supranational powers will conflict with the accepted principle of additional subsidiarity.

Thus, the emphasis will be upon fine-tuning the three pillars of the EU, much of which is of no direct relevance to the issues addressed above. What is arguably relevant is that:

- there will be pressure to extend majority voting, partly in response to enlargement of the EU, which the Conservatives oppose;
- there will be an attempt to simplify decision-making procedures and to improve their transparency;
- there will be pressure on countries such as the UK to forgo their 'opt-outs';
- there will be pressure to reduce 'hostage taking' whereby countries use veto threats to extract concessions on unrelated matters.

In the latter regard, the worst recent examples have arguably been Italy blocking a Budget agreement until its fine for exceeding milk quotas was heavily reduced and Spain refusing to ratify enlargement until it received concessions on fish quotas.

Enlargement is a key issue, but will be fudged because, firstly, the extension of an unreformed CAP to Eastern Europe would break the Budget and, secondly, because unless the structural Funds are hugely increased, new members would be taking money away from other relatively poor members. The IGC is accordingly likely to drag on without resolving much at all. Of course, this might even result in a new UK government becoming a participant.

□ *11.5.10 Forward to EMU?*

Most EU countries do not need to be persuaded of the joys of EMU even if they are not currently in a position to participate. Scepticism is more rife in Scandinavia, and when the new treaty is put to an obligatory referendum the result may be a close call in one or more cases. So far, the talk of a referendum in the UK has been precisely that, but just in case a brief summary of the pros and cons

in to be found in **Table 11.8** (an alternative list is to be found, for example, in the *Sunday Times* of 21 July 1996).

As usual, there is a Catch-22. The idea is that if countries sign up to EMU, then the lower fiscal deficits this necessitates will lead to lower interest rates and thence to more investment, employment and tax revenue, thereby paying off accumulated debt. The catch is that the initial lower deficit will first require either more taxation, less spending or both, and hence initially more unemployment (and taking to the streets).

The EU knows this perfectly well, and partly as a consequence has recently given up on any prospect of an early start to the third stage of EMU (see CEC, 1995b) which is now pencilled in for 1 January 1999. Realistically, since a year is almost

Table 11.8 *Pros and Cons of EMU*

PROS

- EMU will eliminate transactions costs arising from currency exchange and hedging
- Without EMU, there will be competitive devaluations
- Countries not joining will become isolated and lose influence
- EMU will impose anti-inflationary discipline which will keep down interest rates
- Financial centres in non-participants will lose a lot of business
- Inward investment to non-participants will dry up

CONS

- EMU will lead to a loss of control over national destinies
- Flexibility will be greater without EMU
- Non-participants will not be obliged to bail out the fiscally imprudent
- EMU will involve ever bigger internal transfers to relatively poor participants
- National currencies will disappear
- National control over interest rates will be lost
- Devaluation is too useful a weapon to forgo
- Which means even more unemployment

certainly needed to complete the changeover, the decision about which countries are to proceed should be taken at the beginning of 1998, but will in practice be delayed until such time as reliable data for 1997 become available. The central currency against which national currencies will be irrevocably locked (via a 'legally enforceable equivalence') is to be known as the **EURO** (converted on a one-for-one from the ECU). The official ECU basket will cease to exist on 1 January 1999, and the national currencies of EMU members will cease to be legal tender on 1 January 2002.

The Germans insisted that the Maastricht criteria should be applied strictly to prospective EMU members through the medium of a 'growth and stability pact'. This pact was supposed to result in automatic fines on EMU members which run budget deficits in excess of 3 per cent of GDP, with exceptions allowed only for severe reasons in which the economy contracted by over 2 per cent. This was fascinating because the Commission calculated that only Germany, France, Luxembourg (which cannot anyway be counted separately because it does not have its own currency and has a monetary union with Belgium) . . . and the UK will qualify on 1 January 1999 in respect of both fiscal criteria, although Ireland may slip through on the grounds of a much improved performance for its debt/GDP ratio. The Danes are also moving in the right direction, albeit more slowly (see **Figure 11.8**), so they might also be allowed to join. This is regarded by the Commission as distinct progress given that Luxembourg was recently the only country comfortably meeting both fiscal criteria. However, both the UK and Denmark have a provision for an 'opt-out', and it is hard to see how Ireland could join if the UK did not. Furthermore, as the deficit ratio for France is forecast at 2.9 per cent, and showing signs of failing to improve as much as forecast, and as the debt/GDP ratio for Germany is forecast (unreliably) at 59.3 per cent, absolutely nobody could prove to be eligible, which is why siren voices such as those of the EMI and national bank governors are already being heard advocating the delay of EMU to 1 January 2002. It should be remembered that the Maastricht Treaty only

reverts to an automatic start date for EMU of 1 January 1999 if no other date has been agreed before the end of 1997. On the other hand, the official Commission view is that if there is any delay beyond 1999 there will be a 'credibility crisis' in the EU.

In order to avoid this, the alternative approach is to loosen the fiscal criteria. This might be done via a 'flexible' interpretation of the precise wording of the treaty (see Pollard, 1995, p. 12). In 1996, the French Budget was backed by a one-off, anomalous £4.6 billion payment form the partial privatisation of France Télécom even though this was not strictly permissible under the rule for deficit reduction – but the European Commissioner still sanctioned it. The Belgians have also resorted to 'creative accounting' (see *Financial Times*, 9 October 1996 and 21 October 1996). More justifiably, flexibility can be supported on the not unreasonable grounds that budgetary policy should behave counter-cyclically. The deficits in countries in recession should therefore not be expected to meet the criteria otherwise, inter alia, even more unemployment will be generated than is already the case. As France is currently a case in point, it is unsurprising that this view largely originates there.

France therefore insisted that the stability pact should permit countries to plead 'exceptional circumstances' if their economies shrink at all, and that fines must be approved by the Council of Ministers. The new draft of the pact is full of 'as a rule' terminology, which means in effect that the Germans have lost the battle (see *The Economist* (21 December 1996) pp. 41–2).

It has been pointed out, on the basis of the UK's experience in the ERM, that if fiscal tightening is accompanied by monetary loosening in order to avoid unemployment, then the exchange rate is likely to come under huge pressure to devalue, which is incompatible with full EMU. This suggests that the Maastricht criteria should have taken more account of growth and employment, and should, perhaps, now be amended, especially as other criteria, though less problematic to meet for most countries, have also attracted criticism (see, for example, Pollard, 1995 and *The Economist*, 1995b).

Figure 11.8 *Meeting Fiscal Criteria*

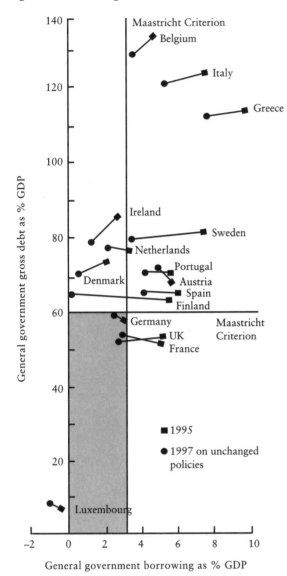

Source: European Commission.

reflect the view in Germany that as long as the improvident Mediterranean countries are initially kept out, EMU can be fiddled to include even the likes of Belgium. The risk is that those left out might respond by resorting to competitive deva-luations, so the general idea is that they will be promised the opportunity to join later on easy terms so long as they do not rock the boat during the interim period. The Conservatives in the UK will naturally have none of this, whilst Labour remains unable to make up its mind on the issue.

□ *11.5.11 Whither Sterling?*

Assuming that sterling remains outside the ERM, how is it likely to perform? In order to answer such a question, we need to consider its relation-ship predominantly to the DM and $, but also to other EU currencies in general. The first issue is obviously how it performed from 1992 until very recently. Relative to the DM, sterling performed similarly to the lira and the peseta – that is, although it held up rather better from the initial drop in 1992, which eventually bottomed out at DM2.31 in February 1993, through to the end of 1993, like them it subsequently moved predomi-nantly downwards until March 1995, whereupon it fell sharply again. Starting at DM2.62 in Jan-uary 1994, it had fallen below DM2.40 by August, and from the same value in January 1995, it succumbed sharply to DM2.19 by 17 March.

Several points can be made about this. Firstly, even the latter trough was not all that much below the trough two years previously. Secondly, it was universally agreed that sterling was trading sig-nificantly below its PPP, although by how much was a matter of dispute. Thirdly, economic fun-damentals were not too bad. The problem seemed to stem internationally from the fall-out from the Mexican crisis, which precipitated a flight to-wards safe-haven currencies, and domestically from squabbling among Conservatives over Eur-ope, indicating the possibility of an early election.

On 9 May an even lower value was recorded at DM2.177 as a result of inflation and interest rate jitters, but the crisis quickly passed with un-

For what it is worth, it has to be said that the financial markets have decided that EMU will begin in 1999, as evidenced by the rise of the French franc back into its narrow band relation-ship with the DM and the disappearance of the customary interest rate differential between French and German bond yields. This seems to

changed interest rates and by 12 May sterling was worth DM2.26 again. The lira and peseta also fared badly, and more significantly the French franc, given that it was DM strength rather than weakness elsewhere which was the driving force behind changing currencies. In June, sterling plunged again below DM2.20, and after a further recovery, it dropped to its lowest ever value of DM2.173 on 17 November. This time the domestic trigger was the fear that the government would indulge in a bout of pre-election fiscal loosening together with lower interest rates. Once again, this was patently an excessive response, and early 1996 saw a sustained rise which eventually took sterling to DM2.37 in early June in the face of DM weakness. However, the strengthening of the DM during July saw the rate fall back sharply to DM2.30. This was not to last. With the oil price showing signs of continuing buoyancy, the economy continuing to grow rapidly and order books filling out leading to expectations of higher interest rates, sterling began to move upwards very rapidly, crossing the DM2.50 mark in November.

Such pronounced oscillation, considerably divorced at times from economic fundamentals, is what transpires when there is no explicit exchange rate target and a determination to stay outside the ERM. The real fear is obviously that too low a rate will cause a resurgence of inflation, which would in turn necessitate raising interest rates, but as that does not seem to be much of a concern in reality, a low exchange can be seen in an advantageous light as offering huge potential to exporters. The current rate of over DM250 is regarded as undesirably high in that context, but the 'proper' rate is anyone's guess and continued oscillation is to be expected. However, it may well not drop so far again since whatever the rate might be if a new government were to opt back in to the ERM, it will definitely be above DM2.25 and probably around DM2.50.

Of course, the story in terms of the dollar is rather different, though it may be said to be less important given the current trading pattern of the UK. The severe drops in relation to the DM, enumerated above, would in earlier times have had the critics screaming 'crisis', only on this occasion sterling was simultaneously holding its own against the dollar. At the time of the ERM crisis in 1992, sterling was trading at almost $2, but by early 1993 it had fallen precipitously to just over $1.40. Since then, it has rarely traded outside the $1.47 to $1.63 range. Indeed, it has mirrored the dollar's trend to an unprecedented extent, especially during 1995. At this time, the dollar was falling heavily against the yen and DM, but whether by luck or judgement this trend was reversed so successfully that by mid-1996 the dollar had risen 35 per cent against the yen and 13 per cent against the DM. Not only did sterling rise in tandem, but so did the lira and other weak currencies. In the somewhat topsy-turvy modern world of currencies, Italy promptly started to discuss rejoining the ERM in order to stop the lira rising any further. As in the case of sterling, however, such a recourse may well prove to be unnecessary for that objective to be achieved.

Bibliography

Adams, J. (1990) 'The Exchange Rate Mechanism of the European Monetary System', *Bank of England Quarterly Bulletin* (November).

Andrews, J. (1994) 'The European Union', *The Economist* (22 October).

Arrowsmith, J. (1995) 'Economic and Monetary Union in a Multi-Tier Europe', *National Institute Economic Review* (May).

Artis, M. (1991) 'The European Monetary System', *Economics* (Spring).

Bank of England (1994) 'The Role of the European Monetary Institute', *Bank of England Quarterly Bulletin* (February).

Barrell, R. (1990) 'Has the EMS Changed Wage and Price Behaviour in Europe?', *National Institute Economic Review* (November).

Cm 419 (1988) *Decision of the Council of the European Communities on the System of the Communities' Own Resources* (London: HMSO, 24 June).

Commission of the European Communities (1992) *Seventh Report of the Commission to the Council and the European Parliament Concerning the Implementation of the White Paper on* the Completion of the Internal Market. COM (92) 383 (Brussels: CEC, 2 September).

Commission of the European Communities (1995a) *Report on Implementation of the Commission's Work Programme in 1995*. COM (95) 513 final (Brussels: CEC, 13 October).

Commission of the European Communities (1995b) 'The Scenario for the Changeover to the Single Currency', *Bulletin of the European Union*, 12 (section 1.49).

Commission of the European Communities (1995c) *The Single Market in 1994*. COM(95) 238 final (Brussels: CEC).

Commission of the European Communities (1996a) *The Single Market in 1995*. COM(96) 51 final (Brussels: CEC).

Commission of the European Communities (1996b) 'Final Adoption of the General Budget of the European Union for the Financial Year 1996', *Official Journal of the European Communities*, L22/1 of 29/1/96.

Connock, M., A. Gully and H. Hillier (1995) 'Macroeconomic Convergence in Europe: A Review of the Maastricht Conditions', *The Review of Policy Issues*, 1 (4).

European Commission (1995) 'The Community Economic Outlook: 1995–1997', *European Economy*, Supplement A (December).

European Commission (1996) 'Report on Convergence in the European Union in 1995', *European Economy*, Supplement A (January).

Franklin, D. (1993) 'The European Community: Back to the Drawing Board', *The Economist* (3 July).

Giles, M. (1991) 'Business in Europe', *The Economist* (8 June).

Haldane, A. (1991) 'The Exchange Rate Mechanism of the European Monetary System: a Review of the Literature', *Bank of England Quarterly Bulletin* (February).

Harrison, B. (1992) 'EMU: Progress, Problems and Prospects', *Economics* (Winter).

Johnson, C. (1996) *In With the Euro Out With the Pound* (Harmondsworth: Penguin).

Lintner, V. (1994) 'The Economics of EU Enlargement', *Economics and Business Education*, 2 (1).

Main, D. (1991) 'Regional Policy Initiatives from Brussels', *The Royal Bank of Scotland Review* (March).

Mayes, D. (1992) 'The Realities Behind the European Single Market', *Business Economist*, 23 (2).

Minford, P. (1992) 'What Price European Monetary Union?', *Economics* (Autumn).

Pollard, P. (1995) 'EMU: Will It Fly?', *Federal Reserve Bank of St Louis Quarterly Review* (July/August).

Sandholtz, W. (1996) 'Money troubles: Europe's Rough Road to Monetary Union', *Journal of European Economic Policy*, 3 (1).

Scott, A. (1993) 'Financing the Community: The Delors II Package', Chapter 4 in J. Lodge (ed.) *The European Community and the Challenge of the Future* (2nd edn) (London: Pinter Publishers).

Shackleton, M. (1993) 'The Budget of the EC: Structure and Process', Chapter 5 in J. Lodge (ed.) The European Community and the Challenge of the Future (2nd edn) (London: Pinter Publishers).

The Economist (1995a) 'From Here to EMU' (5 August).

The Economist (1995b) 'The Challenge to EMU' (9 December).

Townend, J. (1996) 'Changeover to the Single Currency', *Bank of England Quarterly Bulletin* (February).

Weber, A. (1991) 'Reputation and Credibility in the European Monetary System', *Economic Policy* (April).

Wolf, M. (1996) 'Thinking the Unthinkable', *Financial Times* (18 June) p. 15.

Zis, G. (1990) 'European Monetary Union: Policy and Institutional Implications', *Economics* (Autumn).

Zis, G. (1995) 'Will the EMS Suffer the Same Fate as the Bretton Woods International Monetary System?', *British Review of Policy Issues*, 17 (June).

Chapter 12

Trading Relations

Peter Curwen

■ *12.1* The Demise of Free Trade?

Government policies in all the OECD countries have been moving in a market-oriented direction in recent years. There is, however, one rather notable exception to this general trend, namely international trade. The trade regimes of most OECD countries are currently less liberal than they were 15 years ago. In a survey carried out by the *Harvard Business Review*, some 11 700 managers in 25 countries proved themselves generally to be as two-faced about free trade as politicians (cause and effect?). 83 per cent of British managers, for example, supported the idea of free trade along with minimal protection for domestic firms – but 80 per cent went on to support the idea that governments should actively assist domestic firms in international markets (see *The Economist*, 11 May 1991, p. 96). South Koreans, however, were all in favour of protection whereas the Japanese claimed to be much more in favour of free trade then managers in the USA and the EU!

Free trade is easy to justify – even if one's trading partners do not consider it to be to their advantage. Suppose, for example, the Japanese refuse to buy UK products but have themselves developed a life-saving drug. Should the UK refuse to purchase it on a tit-for-tat basis? Clearly, welfare in the UK will be enhanced if the drug is bought **no matter what the Japanese choose to do**. Bilateral free trade is better than unilateral free trade, but unilateral free trade is much better than no trade at all (for a discussion of such matters as the cost to Japan of protection see *The Economist*, 7 January 1995, p. 66).

Once upon a time, there was an enormously strong trading nation called Great Britain which considered that its best interests were served by free trade, and thrived mightily on account of it. But when the Germans and Americans began to take over its markets, it began to wonder whether it was such a good idea after all. After the recession of the 1930s, when the collapse of trade was instrumental in prolonging and worsening the recession, another great trading nation, the USA, considered that its best interests were served by free trade. Because of its economic strength, it was able to impose its will upon other, less enthusiastic, nations, but all came to appreciate that removal of trade barriers would be in their **mutual** best interests.

Even the oil shocks of the 1970s failed to push the USA off course, but its confidence was steadily being damaged by the rapid progress of Japanese trading. In this respect, democracy can be flawed. Free trade provides benefits to all of society, but these benefits are hard to quantify. If import barriers are erected, they bring large benefits to small groups who accordingly lobby endlessly for their introduction. If introduced, they affect individual consumers so little that they rarely complain. The die is accordingly cast in favour of protection, and governments must show determination to set their faces against the lobbying.

Two issues about free trade need to be understood. In the first place, few businessmen and politicians appreciate that the classical case for free trade emphasised the merits of **unilateral** free trade. During the postwar period, the USA promoted free trade primarily by promoting the idea of an **exchange of concessions** through the General Agreement on Tariffs and Trade (GATT). In the modern world, countries **expect to be compensated** for removing barriers to trade.

Secondly, it is evident that free trade is not universally the best solution, and even the classical economists admitted as much. For example, the need to protect 'infant industries' is an idea dating back to Adam Smith which is probably familiar to most readers (see Crook, 1990; Bhagwati, 1994). A brief summary of the pros and cons of protection is set out in **Table 12.1**. The important point to bear in mind, however, is that while new theories of trade which emphasise imperfect competition and externalities do provide some justification for export subsidies and tariffs, they do so in **only a limited number of cases**, and not as a general rule.

Managed trade should not, therefore, be dismissed out of hand. It must also be borne in mind, however, that if it is to be managed then its management must be **in the interests of society as a whole**. Needless to say, this is not what happens in practice, and it was the usurping of the intellectual defence for managed trade by lobbyists in the USA, as it progressively lost its markets to Japanese and other products, which lies at the roots of the current malaise in trade affairs.

Unfortunately, as anyone who has read about the 1930s will know, this is no laughing matter. In

Table 12.1 *Pros and Cons of Protection*

PROS

- If cheap foreign imports are destroying domestic industries, they must be kept out to preserve domestic jobs and acceptable levels of domestic wages
- If goods are being 'dumped' in the domestic market, they must be kept out to preserve output and jobs in what may be efficient domestic businesses
- If other countries are introducing protectionist devices, retaliation is necessary to level the playing field
- Protection is needed for 'infant industries' until such time as they are of a sufficient size to compete in international markets
- Protection is a legitimate device to prevent the sudden collapse of an industry and to enable an orderly transfer to other activities to take place
- Protection is justified if a country has a permanent balance of payments problem which it has been unable to resolve in more acceptable ways

CONS

- Since protection inevitably inspires retaliation, it causes a reduction in the volume of international trade, thereby causing damage to the economies of all nations dependent upon such trade for improvements in their economic welfare
- Because of retaliation, protection is not anyway going to be successful.
- Arguments over protection create political ill-will between nations which may have adverse effects beyond the trade sector

most years, recessions excepted, the increase in the volume of merchandise trade provides a major driving force promoting the growth of world output, as shown in **Figure 12.1**. In recent years, the USA and (West) Germany have vied for the title of the world's greatest exporting nation, while Great Britain sits a comfortable fifth in the list and consequently has much to lose through a decline in world trade.

Figure 12.1 *World merchandise by Volume, Annual Percentage Change*

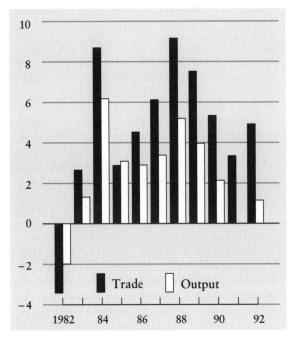

Source: *Financial Times*, 29 March 1993.

■ *12.2* Protection

□ *12.2.1 Forms of Protection*

Protection has become a matter of controversy primarily because of the difficulties which the US government has had in reducing its enormous current account deficit by more acceptable means. All countries operate some protectionist policies, but it is fair to say that the UK was one of the less protectionist minded of the industrial countries throughout the 1980s. Protection is generally a negative-sum game, in that once the process is set in motion in one country its main trading partners usually respond with offsetting measures of their own, thereby causing all of them to lose out. It is therefore possible that the UK will be drawn into protection if it is instigated elsewhere on a sufficiently large scale.

Until fairly recently, the commonest form of protection was the **tariff**, which is a tax imposed on imports either as a lump sum or as a percentage of their value. This drives up domestic prices, which is not particularly desirable, but the government obtains an additional source of revenue to fund its expenditure and the illusion is given that the foreign exporter is suffering most because he is virtually forced to pay the tax.

Tariffs have been restricted because major industrial countries have agreed to abide by the GATT rules (see below) which greatly limit their use, but in any event their inflationary consequences are undesirable and can apparently be avoided by resort to other non-tariff barriers. Of these the commonest are **quotas**, which serve to limit the access of overseas producers to the domestic market. Quotas are generally fixed in terms of the **number** or **value** of imports to be permitted. Inflationary consequences might still arise if the importer takes advantage of the artificial shortage of the product to put up its price, in which case it is the private sector, rather than the government, which gets the extra revenue, but the government could obtain extra revenue by auctioning import licences. In recent years many countries have preferred to avoid overt confrontation by 'requesting' foreign governments to limit their exports of particular products. In the case of cars, for example, both the EU and USA agreed import quotas with Japan during the 1980s.

Underlying such **voluntary export restraints** (VERs) is an unspoken threat of 'official' quotas if compliance if not adhered to. It is alleged that the Japanese impose unofficial quotas by requiring foreign products such as cars to meet specifications, for safety or other reasons, which they cannot meet without expensive modifications. The Japanese counter-argument is, naturally, that products of 'inferior' quality simply do not sell on their domestic market.

Occasionally certain imports and/or exports are embargoed (given **a zero quota**). This is usually to 'punish' a country which is pursuing domestic polices unacceptable to the wider political community. The present UK government has never favoured such methods of dealing with errant regimes, but irrespective of the moral issues it has to be said that embargoes are constantly being broken.

A rather more subtle procedure is to **subsidise exports**. This obviously costs the government a good deal of money, but it protects jobs and hence, indirectly, the **tax base of the domestic economy**. An industry which is subsidised almost everywhere is the shipbuilding industry, which has long suffered from chronic world overcapacity. These subsidies are more subtle in the sense that they can be disguised as regional development grants or 'infant industry' support. The UK also operates **export credit guarantees** which insure exports against default by overseas buyers.

Finally, there is the possibility of introducing various forms of **exchange control**. Exchange controls operated in the UK until 1979. Such controls were philosophically incompatible with the free market beliefs of the incoming Conservative government, and their abolition was the first major step along the path to widespread deregulation. However, there was also an underlying economic rationale to abolition. At the time, the balance of payments on current account was about to improve markedly as a result of North Sea oil coming on stream. This was bound to exert strong upward pressure on the exchange rate, and while the government did not wish to intervene to keep the rate down, it was realised that the abolition of exchange controls would result in a huge outflow of capital, mostly for long-term investment, and that this would help to limit the appreciation of sterling. Furthermore, there would be a net inflow of interest and dividends in later years.

Other major countries have followed the UK example, but there is still pressure in certain circles to reinstate exchange controls on the grounds that the capital being exported could be better used within the UK. Such controls could be reimposed in a variety of forms. In the past there have been controls both on capital inflows, for example by suspending the convertibility of foreign currency into sterling, and upon capital outflows, for example by sending requests to obtain foreign currency via the central bank which has the right to refuse authorization, or by refusing permission for private individuals to export capital other than in small amounts.

It is worth observing, by way of conclusion, that most of the forms of protection discussed above were developed during the era of fixed exchange rates. Obviously, if exports are uncompetitive, the simplest ways to deal with the problem where the exchange rate can float are to allow the currency to depreciate or to devalue. This is much less likely to invite retaliation, although competitive depreciation is by no means unknown, but it has to be said that this policy can help only those industries which were close to being competitive at the higher exchange rate. Where an industry, such as shipbuilding, is regularly being undercut by up to 50 per cent, selective assistance, whatever its merits, is the only solution if it is to survive.

☐ *12.2.2 Effects of Protection*

In a major review, the OECD (1985) concluded that non-inflationary growth was being impeded by protection. The simple Keynesian model indicates that if one country refuses to buy the exports of another country, then the latter will suffer a reduction in its national income and hence reduce its own imports. The original country thus protects jobs in its industries previously losing out to import substitution, but suffers job losses in industries dependent upon exporting. One might have thought that this lesson was learned in the 1930s following the US Smoot-Hawley Tariff of 1930, but regrettably this is not the case. In the first place, the jobs saved by protection are more immediate and more visible than the jobs lost as exports subsequently suffer. Secondly, as noted previously, it is easy to organise a combined lobby of politicians, businessmen and trade unions to support an endangered local industry.

The GATT regulations on trade barriers are based upon 'reciprocity'. **First-difference reciprocity** aims to reduce trade barriers through the requirement that a country provides a tariff reduction **comparable in value** to that introduced by a trading partner. In the USA, however, there has recently been a movement towards the principle of **full reciprocity**. This requires **equal access**, which is measured by the balance of trade overall and/or in specific sectors. A trade deficit is taken to be evidence of unequal access and to justify retaliation. The worst offender is, as usual, claimed to be Japan. It is, perhaps, naive to point out that bilateral trade balances are rarely in equilibrium in the normal course of events, because even if the UK is in overall equilibrium it will almost certainly be in surplus with, for example, the USA while simultaneously in deficit with, for example, Japan. Indeed, the principle of comparative advantage should bring about precisely such an outcome.

■ *12.3* 1992 and EU Trade

In principle, all border restrictions on trade between member countries of the EU were discarded at the end of 1992. In principle, goods and services, labour and capital flow freely across national borders. However, this is not exactly the case in practice. There are, inter alia, a host of protectionist agreements involving individual EU members and non-EU countries. There is, for example, a quota regulating the importation of Japanese cars into the UK.

From the viewpoint of consumers there is a clear gain where the common external tariff (CET) is lower than that ruling prior to 1992, since prices on the domestic market will be lower. On the other hand, the reverse will be true where the new common external tariff provides a higher degree of protection than before. The issue of subsidies is especially critical in this respect, since countries which have been unhappy with lower trade barriers have tended to respond by introducing a substitute protection in the form of subsidies.

■ *12.4* Subsidies

According to the European Commission the average level of subsidies fell slightly during the 1980s. The EU 10 averaged roughly ECU 89 billion during 1981–86, and the EU 12 roughly ECU 82 billion during 1986–88. Of this sum, ECU 11 billion was accounted for by agriculture, ECU 13 billion by coal, ECU 26 billion by railways and the rest by industry.

These figures appear to be very high when compared to OECD data which, while it is consistently defined and illustrates a similar pattern during the 1980s, covers only direct grant aid. If other forms of aid are included the pattern changes considerably for industrial countries. It is very unlikely that, despite years of research, the Commission has managed to unearth the most opaque forms of assistance. Were it to do so, the position of the UK would look even more favourable since its subsidy policy is relatively transparent. During the 1980s, the Thatcherite approach was to reduce aid to 'lame ducks' and to cut back severely on regional policy. Independent estimates by the Kiel Institute and others suggest that 4 per cent of GNP in pre-unification West Germany was devoted to subsidies (financed by commensurately high levels of taxation). The situation has deteriorated now that the former, hopelessly inefficient, industrial sectors of East Germany have been drawn into the fold, and even Italy will have to look to its laurels as the EU's subsidiser-in-chief, as shown in **Table 12.2** which compares 1988–90 with 1990–92, the latest-available period.

Under the circumstances, the key issue is whether or not the EU competition commissioner can stem the tide, based on the premise that an illegal subsidy is one which involves any action whereby the state, as owner, acts differently from a private investor. The awkward problem this raises is that state ownership becomes pointless if the state must run its firms as though they were private. It is probable that problems with balancing budgets will stem the subsidy tide rather than any overt desire to bend to the will of the Commission in this respect.

■ *12.5* The General Agreement on Tariffs and Trade (GATT)

The GATT was originally signed on a 'provisional' basis in 1947 by 23 countries (currently some 123 with 20 more standing in line) determined to avoid a repetition of the worst consequences of protection evidenced during the 1930s. Its aims were to reduce existing barriers to free

Table 12.2 *State Aid to the Manufacturing Sector: Annual Averages, 1990–92 and 1988–90 (in brackets)*

	In per cent of value added		In ECU per person employed		In mio ECU[1]	
	(1988–1990)	1990–1992	(1988–1990)	1990–1992	(1988–1990)	1990–1992
Belgium	(5.0)	4.3	(1 744)	1 527	(1 280	1 119
Denmark	(2.3)	2.2	(685)	638	(365)	336
Germany[2]	(2.6)	2.1	(1 099)	979	(8 488)	7 134
new Länder	–	n/a	–	4 385	–	4 848
Greece	(16.9)	12.3	(2 420)	1 579	(1 764)	1 032
Spain	(3.7)	1.7	(1 080)	493	(2 902)	349
France	(3.7)	3.0	(1 449)	1 138	(6 424)	5 044
Ireland	(3.9)	2.9	(1 821)	1 411	(389)	307
Italy	(7.8)	8.9	(2 426)	2 611	(12 162)	12 526
Luxembourg	(3.4)	4.1	(1 369)	1 573	(51)	58
Netherlands	(3.2)	2.6	(1 266)	978	(1 177)	929
Portugal	(1.3)	5.2	(911)	625	(736)	479
United Kingdom	(1.9)	1.5	(756)	525	(4 067)	2 661
EUR 12	(3.8)	3.7	(1 372)	1 293	(40 704)	37 822

Notes:
[1] *1988–90 averages in 1991 prices.*
[2] In its borders before October 1990.

Source: Commission of the European Communities (1992a) *Third Survey of State Aids in the European Community in the Manufacturing and Certain Other Sectors* (Brussels: CEC), Table 3.

trade (but excluding agriculture and services, which are not covered), to eliminate trade discrimination and to curb the reintroduction of protectionist measures by requiring member countries to consult together prior to such action. A critical principle was the **'most-favoured-nation' clause**, whereby any member country offering a tariff reduction to another country was obliged to offer the same reduction to all other member countries.

It may be argued that the oddest thing about the GATT was the need for anyone to join. Given that members already accepted the principle that more trade was better than less trade, it had to be in their mutual self-interest to lower tariff barriers. The necessity to treat a tariff reduction as a concession requiring reciprocity would seem to be redundant when self-interest dictates that tariff reductions should anyway be pursued, since bilateral tariff reductions should be taking place in the absence of reciprocity conditions. However, as discussed above, the economic virtues of free trade are not always self-evident to interest groups when domestic industries are being 'destroyed' by imports, so governments needed to counteract this by reference to their obligations to maintain GATT rules. In any event, governments have always been afraid of appearing to be weak when allowing competitors free access to their markets in the absence of publicly-stated reciprocity. In this respect the attitude of the present UK Government is interesting, since it continues to play the reciprocity game even though, according to its economic philosophy, reciprocity cannot be a precondition for trade.

The GATT (and currently the new World Trade Organisation – see below) therefore existed as a precaution against the facile adoption of the 'imports are bad, exports are good' creed, a creed which is intuitively appealing to the proverbial man-in-the-street. A virtue of the most-favoured-nation clause in this respect is that if a tariff is raised against one competitor it has to be raised against them all, thereby greatly increasing the risk of retaliation – an argument which the government can fall back on when pressed to protect a specific bilateral trade. This is bolstered by the principle of reciprocity, since it becomes possible to counter the argument that tariff reductions will damage domestic industries with the claim that benefits of equal value will accrue to exporting industries.

☐ 12.5.1 The Tokyo Round

The seventh, Tokyo Round began in 1973 (see **Table 12.3**). New or reinforced agreements called **codes** were established in respect of subsidies and countervailing duties; government procurement; technical standards; import licensing procedures; customs valuation; and anti-dumping.

Table 12.3   *GATT Rounds*

Geneva	1947
Annecy	1948
Torquay	1950
Geneva	1956
Dillon	1960–61
Kennedy	1964–67
Tokyo	1973–79
Uruguay	1986–94

The code on subsidies and countervailing duties prohibited direct export subsidies other than in agriculture. Given the widespread use of subsidies, a distinction was made between domestic and export subsidies. A domestic subsidy that treated domestic and export sales in a neutral way was normally permissible under GATT rules. However, a tariff designed to offset an export subsidy given to a foreign supplier – known as a **countervailing duty** (CVD) – was prohibited unless domestic producers could be shown to have suffered (or were expected to suffer) 'material' injury as a consequence. In addition, a country could seek redress against another when the latter's subsidised exports had replaced the former's sales in a third country.

The code on government procurement stated that, in respect to qualifying non-military purchases, governments and organisations under their control were obliged to treat domestic and foreign producers in the same way (for a discussion as to whether CVDs are primarily protectionist or, alternatively, devices to reduce trade distortions, see Marvel and Ray (1996)).

The anti-dumping code set out rules for anti-dumping investigations, the imposition of anti-dumping duties and the settlement of disputes. A method for assessing the degree of injury sustained was set out. Developing countries were expected to be given preferential treatment by developed countries.

☐ 12.5.2 The Uruguay Round 1986–94

The oil price shocks and inflationary conditions of the 1970s, followed by the 1980–81 recession, made trading conditions problematic for many countries. Understandably, no country, least of all the USA which had been instrumental in using the GATT as the vehicle for liberalising world trade, wished to flout GATT rules in an open manner. Thus the favoured tactic was to 'bend' the rules in such a way as to offer some degree of protection to domestic industries threatened by imports, particularly those originating from Japan. In place of the **multilateral** agreements previously negotiated in the GATT, the USA and the EU began increasingly to negotiate **bilateral** arrangements, many of which took the form of VERs. By and large, the Japanese were happy to go along with this arrangement since it enabled them to concentrate on selling top-of-the-range, high-value-added products which could be sold very profitably in competition with high-priced, uncompetitive domestic products.

Governments also resorted increasingly to **subsidies** which they alleged did not infringe the rules of the GATT, and the tactic grew up during the 1980s of imposing **anti-dumping duties** on manufactured products, especially those originating in Japan and the Far East, on the alleged grounds that they were being sold for less than was being

Figure 12.2 *Industrialised Countries, Average Tariffs (%)*

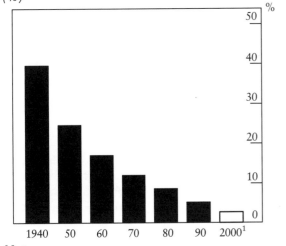

Notes:
[1] Forecast.
Source: Centre for International Economics.

charged on the exporter's home market (Messerlin and Reed, 1995).

In some ways, this behaviour was not altogether unexpected given that tariffs on the importation of manufactured goods had fallen to an average of less than 5 per cent (**Figure 12.2**) thereby offering inefficient domestic producers very little protection against imports. The proliferation of restraints on trade, which could be said to be compatible with the rules of the GATT only by exercising a good deal of imagination, nevertheless posed a severe threat to its continued role as the instrument for trade liberalisation.

Furthermore, the Japanese and West German onslaught had served in part to reduce the dependence of other countries, and especially of the USA, upon domestically produced manufactured goods. The service sectors which grew up in their place did not fall under the rules of the GATT since they were traditionally regarded as domestic rather than suitable for international trade. However, they were increasingly becoming the driving force underlying economic growth in countries such as the USA, and these countries wished to exploit their comparative advantage in the service sectors in international trade in return

for making further concessions with respect to manufactures.

Other deficiencies in the GATT also became increasingly evident. There was, for example, the issue of the sectors which, for various reasons, had been given special dispensations from the rules of the GATT. Of these the **Multi-Fibre Arrangement** (MFA) covering textiles and clothing was a particular irritant to developing countries whose access to the markets of advanced countries was limited by quotas. More importantly, there was the **agricultural sector** which was not covered at all by the rules of the GATT. Up until the end of the 1970s, this had posed few problems since the EU had been a net importer of agricultural products, thereby allowing the USA to export its surpluses to everyone's mutual advantage. However, once the EU became a major net exporter in its own right, the agricultural sector became the battleground between the three dominant trading blocs – the EU, NAFTA and Japan – without there being a set of GATT rules to determine fair conduct in the field.

Given the proliferation of disputes, especially those relating to dumping, the inability of the GATT disputes settlement mechanism to act swiftly and to impose penalties with sufficient deterrent value to discourage deliberate abuse of the rules also became of key importance. Equally, the expansion of the role of GATT not merely to cover trade in **services** but also **intellectual property rights** (IPRs) came to the forefront of debate about the role of the GATT, because it was too much to expect any country or trading bloc to make unilateral concessions.

The advanced nations were anxious that developing countries should open their markets to imports of services, and that they should honour intellectual property rights rather than turn a blind eye to outright piracy of patents and copyrights. In their turn, the LDCs want the advanced nations to open their markets to imports of textiles, clothing and agricultural commodities. Japan was unwilling to do anything much about its so-called 'structural impediments' to trade (for example, by allowing foreign firms to bid for public procurement contracts) unless the USA and the EU agreed to curtail the stream of anti-dumping actions aimed at Japanese products. Almost everyone wanted to stop the USA using the **super-301 provisions** of the 1988 Trade Act to take punitive action against them without recourse to the GATT, and so forth. Because no country was prepared to make concessions without first securing the desired **reciprocity** from other countries, the Uruguay Round dragged on for over six years.

☐ 12.5.3 The GATT and Protection

The move towards increased protection discussed above obviously threatened the foundations on which the GATT was built. Many countries busied themselves negotiating bilateral agreements to the detriment of excluded countries, but the Uruguay Round did little to stem the tide. One obvious difficulty was that the GATT secretariat had no resources to dispose in order to support its powers of persuasion, nor indeed any real sanctions other than adverse publicity, so it was obliged to fall back upon its stature as a body which existed to foster free trade without favour to any individual country. The trouble then, however, was that too-overt criticism of countries which were abusing the rules was likely to send their representatives scuttling home claiming unfair discrimination.

The thorniest question concerned bilateral agreements which as noted were advocated on the grounds that they promoted free trade between the signatories. The outcome of NAFTA, for example, was that the USA bought certain products from Canada which were previously acquired from more expensive domestic sources. However, there was no most-favoured-nation clause which required the treatment accorded to the most favoured trading partner to be made available to others, and it therefore followed that other products would be bought from Canada rather than, say, the UK, since they would now be cheaper from the former source on a tariff-free basis. This simply served to **divert** trade rather than to **create** it, and indeed resulted in the purchase of tariff-free products from an inefficient source being substituted for tariff-bearing products from a more effi-

cient source. NAFTA was, fortunately, not dissimilar in its effects to the EU which served more to create trade than to divert it (see *The Economist*, 16 September 1995), and it kept to most of the GATT rules insofar as it covered 'substantially all trade' and did not result in the raising of tariff barriers against other countries.

☐ 12.5.4 Anti-dumping Suits

Faced with breaking GATT rules if they were overtly protectionist, both the EU and the USA resorted increasingly to a subtle, but no less effective, method of curbing Japanese and South Korean imports (see Messerlin and Reed, 1995, p. 1572 for consequences). This method was to threaten to take the exporters to court in an **anti-dumping suit**. Under the GATT's anti-dumping code, **dumping** was held to occur when a good was sold abroad at less than its 'normal value', that is at a price lower than that charged by the exporter for the same good in his home market, and it was permissible to impose penalties where deliberate underpricing was causing, or threatening to cause, **material injury** to producers in the importing countries.

By writing rules to regulate anti-dumping duties into the GATT during the Tokyo Round (Grimwade, 1996, p. 100) these duties were effectively legitimised, and they proliferated in a manner that was never the GATT's intention. In particular, anti-dumping suits were brought against specific countries in a deliberately discriminatory manner, and were often instigated with the intention of eliciting a voluntary restraint from the defendant.

The common rationale for an anti-dumping suit was that the exporter was engaged in predatory pricing designed to drive the domestic supplier out of the business (Messerlin and Reed, 1995, p. 1568). Nevertheless, for some unaccountable reason, most EU anti-dumping suits were actually brought against exporters with a small share of the EU market! All the complainant had to demonstrate was that the exporter was either making a loss or selling at below the price in the exporter's home market, and that this was not helpful to the complainant.

Once a complaint had succeeded, it became necessary to calculate the **dumping margin** – the difference between the price of a good in the exporter's home market and its price when exported. Both the EU and the USA were past masters at calculating preposterously high margins (Grimwade, 1996, p. 99). Adding insult to injury, the USA proposed that the GATT code be amended to include products which might exist if dumping were not taking place, while the EU proposed that if a rise in imports coincided with a fall in domestic production this should be taken as 'proof' of successful dumping.

In August 1988, the European Commission imposed duties on imported video-cassette recorders on the grounds that unless the EU could remain conversant with the technology it would lose the ability to develop new high-tech products. Whereas this could be construed as a legitimate aim of industrial policy, it was hardly surprising that the Japanese, who traditionally dislike airing trade disputes in public, felt compelled to complain to GATT's anti-dumping committee that it could be regarded as evidence of dumping only by stretching GATT rules well beyond breaking point (see *ibid.*, p. 99 for a discussion of how the victims at this time later began to take the offensive).

Much the same could be said about duties levied in April 1988 on typewriters and scales actually assembled in the EU by Japanese companies, which the European Commission claimed was simply a device to dodge the duties (*ibid.*, p. 101). The EU was particularly fond of the **screwdriver plant** ploy at this point in time, especially in respect of cars. The idea was that any imported components of Japanese products made in the EU could be saddled with anti-dumping duties unless more than a certain proportion of the total value of the end-product was added in the EU. Not surprisingly, most Japanese manufacturers adopted the line of least resistance and increased value added in the EU. Nevertheless, a complaint to the GATT resulted in this rule being outlawed in 1990.

Undeterred, the Commission applied anti-dumping duties to Japanese audio-cassettes even though a substantial proportion were made in the EU and the share taken by the imports from Japan

was falling. Furthermore, the Japanese products were actually more expensive than those made by EU companies. Indeed so, argued the Commission, but that was because the Japanese had 'forced the Community industry to undersell to hold its market share'.

The 'offending' Japanese producers typically responded to these duties by holding prices constant and reducing profit margins. As what the Commission really wanted was for import prices to rise, they decided to introduce additional penalties where the duties were not added to the price. The reader may by now be beginning to wonder just how all of this benefits the consumer, but there really is no need to wonder – it doesn't! However, lest 'Fortress Europe' be taken too readily to be a fact of life, it is worth noting that, as shown in **Table 12.4**, the situation did not become materially worse after the introduction of the 1992 programme, with 1992–93 proving to be a peak year.

Table 12.4 indicates the scale of anti-dumping and countervailing duty cases lodged with the GATT after 1980. According to the World Bank, average tariffs in the entire US manufacturing sector would have been 23 per cent in 1993 as compared to the official 6 per cent if they had been adjusted to take account of the cost of dumping duties on imported steel, textiles and cars. In other words, many of the apparent gains from the GATT were illusory.

Australia at the time was currently the worst offender in respect of anti-dumping actions, although the USA remained busy and was a notable upsurge in actions taken by the developing countries after 1990. It has been observed that anti-dumping actions have served primarily as a means to delay restructuring of uncompetitive industries, and hence that the original problem has rarely disappeared over time.

□ 12.5.5 GATT into WTO

Officially, time ran out on the Uruguay Round at the end of 1990, but it did not expire altogether. In the USA, the **fast track** authority, which requires that legislation implementing trade pacts be voted

Table 12.4 *Anti-dumping and Countervailing Duty Cases*

	Jan. 80 to Jun 80	80–81	81–82	82–83	83–84	84–85	85–86	86–87	87–88	88–89	89–90	90–91	91–92	92–93
		July to June												
Australia	36	61	54	71	70	63	54	40	20	19	23	46	76	61
Canada	26	48	64	34	26	35	27	24	20	14	15	12	16	36
EU	17	37	39	26	33	34	23	17	30	29	15	15	23	33
US	37	24	51	19	46	61	63	41	31	25	24	52	62	78
Other developed countries	1	3	2	0	1	0	2	5	9	12	5	9	21	8
Developing countries	0	0	0	0	0	0	3	4	13	14	14	41	39	38
Total	117	173	210	150	176	193	172	131	123	113	96	175	237	254

Source: Financial Times, 15 December 1992 and 26 November 1993.

on by Congress as a package without amendment, was introduced at the beginning of the Tokyo Round. Its original expiry date for the Uruguay Round was March 1991, at which point there was supposed to be a vote on the entire GATT package. In practice, there was no package because of the ongoing disputes about matters agricultural (for details see Ingersent, Rayner and Hine, 1994).

In principle, agriculture, which accounted for only some 13 per cent of world trade, did not seem of sufficient importance to destroy the entire Round, but in practice many of the concessions which were proposed in other areas were a quid pro quo for agricultural reform. The reasons for the agricultural disputes are discussed subsequently, but even though they remained unresolved, the US Congress chose to extend the fast track authority to 15 December 1993 in the hope of seeing the Round through to a successful conclusion.

US trade negotiators were much better placed than those representing the EU. The EU's position in each area inevitably reflected a series of compromises among its members, and hence its negotiators felt unable to budge from the agreed positions lest individual members withdrew their support. To other countries, this smacked of intransigence and a 'Fortress Europe' mentality.

Nevertheless, as final final deadline followed final deadline, an agreement was eventually cobbled together which, though by no means meeting all of the objectives of the Uruguay Round, could be signed by all participants at Marrakech in April 1994, to come into effect on 1 January 1995. The key features of the new agreement were:

- a set of rules to cover services for the first time;
- protection for all kinds of intellectual property;
- the phasing out of the Multi-Fibre Agreement over ten years;
- a commitment to reach agreement on farm trade;
- a commitment to cut tariffs by at least one-third, and in respect of certain tariffs imposed by the biggest economies, to eliminate them altogether;
- a commitment to reform the rules on subsidies;
- a commitment to curb the misuse of rules on dumping;
- a commitment to prevent the use of VERs;
- the phasing out of trade-related investment measures;
- a commitment to extend earlier agreements on government procurement and civil aircraft;
- the speeding up of disputes arbitration and restrictions on opportunities to go to appeal;
- clarification of existing rules.

A key feature was that the GATT would be replaced by a new World Trade Organisation (WTO), which would be permanent, with formal legal powers which would be binding on all signatories (no opt-outs).

It may be noted that there are a lot of 'commitments' in the above list. However, there was never any realistic prospect of reaching agreement on such matters as agriculture despite seven years of negotiation, so the best alternative was to agree to carry on negotiating. In the case of agriculture, a 'peace clause' was added to prevent signatories from challenging each other's agricultural systems for nine years commencing 1 January 1995.

It was also agreed that every attempt would be made to set flesh upon the framework General Agreement on Trade in Services (GATS), but this task should not be under-estimated. In the case of telecommunications, for example, the final deadline of July 1996 for agreeing to open up markets was notable only for the agreement to set a final final deadline of February 1997.

In many ways, the last two items on the list were the most critical because by 1993 there was almost wholesale refusal by GATT members to accept its rulings, and even where they were accepted, members generally 'forgot' to implement the required remedy. In respect of disputes, an independent appeals body was therefore to be set up in conjunction with a tougher, speedier procedure which prohibited signatories from blocking adverse rulings and which allowed for sanctions and compensation. It was widely accepted that if signatories still continued to refuse to abide by WTO rulings, then it would rapidly collapse. However, this new system was clearly popular in principle since over 20 disputes were laid before the WTO during 1995, the highest number ever in a single year (see *Financial Times*, 29 November 1995), and with 26 filed during the first half of 1996, the WTO is getting busier by the day. The USA, EU, Japan and Canada are involved individually or together in 43 disputes so far either as complainant or defendant, but developing countries have also launched 21 complaints.

Finally, it may be noted that the new Safeguards Agreement provided for the phasing out of all VERs and other measures deemed to be inconsistent with the WTO over a four-year period commencing 1 January 1995, or their conversion into other compatible forms. This led Grimwade (1994, p. 104) to conclude that in their absence there would be even more recourse than

before to anti-dumping actions, and this view was echoed in the WTO's first annual report (*Financial Times*, 14 December 1995) which noted that in June 1995, 128 anti-subsidy measures were in force of which 80 per cent were in the USA. However, the EU led the field with 37 anti-dumping actions. Altogether, 805 measures were in force, of which 60 per cent were maintained by the USA and EU, with the favoured targets being China, the EU and South Korea.

Somewhat embarrassingly, a draft OECD report (see *Financial Times*, 21 September 1995) concluded that dumping had actually posed no threat to competition in 90 per cent of cases initiated during the 1980s by the USA and EU. The report did not receive the latters' endorsement! The most interesting ironies were Japanese companies established in the EU complaining about dumping by South Korea, and EU companies complaining about their domestic competitors importing cheaply from their screwdriver plants overseas.

■ *12.6* Agriculture

Although agriculture is a domestic industry, and could therefore be discussed in other contexts, most of the issues which it raises are concerned with relationships both within the EU and between the EU and other trading blocs. It raises issues of protection and involves the GATT, and this section has, therefore, been placed in its entirety alongside the sections which deal with the latter topics.

The markets for agricultural products operate poorly in the absence of intervention. Demand tends to grow slowly over time, both because population growth in developed countries is very low and because as incomes rise the extra money does not get spent on agricultural produce. Supply, on the other hand, grows rapidly as a consequence of mechanisation, improved crop strains and the intensive use of fertilisers. In a free market these forces would anyway tend to drive down prices (CEC, 1994, Graph 1) – and hence also farmers' incomes – but the situation is further compounded by the unpredictable effects of climatic conditions and the small size of individual farms in relation to total supply, which conspire to leave farmers with very little control over the prices of their products.

□ 12.6.1 Rationale for Intervention

In practice, the governments of developed countries have, with few exceptions, been unwilling to let agricultural prices be determined by the forces of the free market during the postwar period. The rationale for intervention has taken a variety of forms, including the contribution of the sector to employment and to the balance of payments, the need for security of food supply in the event of external aggression, the need to protect the rural way of life and the need to ensure delivery of the rural vote. Although many of these justifications currently have an archaic ring about them, it must be recognised that, once a pressure group has been built up to keep them in the public eye, it becomes very difficult to persuade the public that they are no longer relevant.

Broadly speaking, farmers in any single domestic market, such as the UK, can be protected against the forces of the free market either by paying them subsidies or by erecting a wall around the domestic market through which imports cannot pass at prices which undercut domestic suppliers. Given that the UK had traditional obligations towards the Commonwealth, which included the freedom for Commonwealth countries to export to the UK, the widespread use of tariff barriers or quotas was considered to be inappropriate, and those UK farmers who could not match import prices were therefore paid a subsidy known as a **deficiency payment**. The burden of financing such a payment fell upon the taxpayer, and not upon the consumer who paid a shop price based upon the costs of the cheapest world suppliers. As agricultural productivity rose, and agricultural prices accordingly fell, the deficiency payments scheme became increasingly burdensome, and the government began to toy with the use of tariffs and quotas.

The supremacy of the latter form of protection came with the devising of the Common Agricul-

tural Policy (CAP) in 1958 by the original six members of the EEC. At the time, UK agriculture was considerably more efficient than its continental counterparts, in good part because the system of inheritance whereby land had been handed down to the eldest son, rather than dispersed among all male children as was the custom in, for example, France, had kept land holdings intact. Furthermore, UK farmers were used to competing in the open market unprotected by tariffs. As a consequence, a much smaller proportion of the UK population was employed in agriculture in 1960 than in continental Europe.

The objectives set out for the CAP under Article 39 of the Treaty of Rome were not, of themselves, incompatible with the objectives of UK agricultural policy. They were: (1) to increase agricultural productivity by promoting technical progress, and by ensuring the rational development of agricultural production and the optimum utilisation of the factors of production, in particular labour; (2) To ensure a fair standard of living for the agricultural community, in particular by increasing the individual earnings of persons engaged in agriculture; (3) To stabilise markets; (4) To guarantee the availability of supplies; (5) To ensure reasonable consumer prices. However, their implementation over the ensuing decade did create certain incompatibilities with UK practice, in particular the much greater emphasis upon import controls and, as a consequence, the payment by the consumer in the shop of a price sufficient to cover the full costs of operating the CAP.

It should be borne in mind that, at the time of its inception, the CAP was not expected to generate huge surpluses with their attendant difficulties. The reason for the rather dreadful mess in which it currently finds itself is that the Community sought to respond to the developing crisis of overproduction in a piecemeal way. No one ever sat down and tried to rethink the CAP from first principles in the light of the changes which had occurred in agricultural markets during the 1970s and 1980s. Hence reform has typically been too little, too late.

Since 1958, the Community has acquired a further nine members, amongst them the UK. Not surprisingly, the history of agriculture in the UK has created major disparities between the UK and other members, especially the most recent who have not as yet implemented the attempts at restructuring directed at their predecessors.

12.6.2 Overview of EU Agriculture

The Utilised Agricultural Area (UAA) is slowly but steadily decreasing as a proportion of total land use in the EU. It dropped below 60 per cent during the late 1980s, and may well drop as far as 50 per cent during the 1990s. The proportion is unusually high in Ireland and the UK. Approximately one half of the UAA is arable land which is tilled and cultivated annually, some 40 per cent is grassland and the other 10 per cent consists of permanent crops (orchards, vineyards and olive groves which are prominent in southern Europe and almost non-existent in the north).

It is obvious from the above that there is considerable diversity in the patterns of agricultural output between different EU members. Employment in agriculture provides 5.4 per cent of all jobs in the enlarged EU, but these workers contribute less than 2 per cent of GDP (defined as gross value added as a percentage of GDP). In the UK, the proportions are both very low, whereas in southern countries the proportions both tend to be higher.

The number of farms in the EU has fallen sharply over the past two decades to stand currently at a total of roughly 7.8 million. In Italy, Greece and Portugal there are almost as many farms as there were in 1970 and, predictably, as shown in **Table 12.5**, these countries currently have average farm sizes significantly smaller than other EU members. By comparison, fewer than 60 per cent of farms in Belgium and Luxembourg have survived since 1970, and fewer than two-thirds in Denmark, France and West Germany.

The typical EU farm has a UAA of 16.4 hectares (roughly 40 acres). On average, those in Denmark, Luxembourg, France and Sweden are at least twice this size, but they in turn are half the size of the typical farm in the UK where in excess of 30 per cent of all farms have a UAA of at least

50 ha. Farms of this size are almost non-existent in Italy, Portugal and Greece where, as in Spain, farms of less than 5 ha predominate. It does not take much imagination to realise that this great diversity in farm sizes, combined with very different patterns of land use, represents a major difficulty in drawing up a common agricultural policy.

Between 1970 and 1987, the agricultural population in the EU fell by roughly one-quarter, with individual member variances ranging from a few per cent in the Netherlands to nearly 40 per cent in Luxembourg. There are currently roughly 7.9 million agricultural workers in the EU, of whom perhaps one-quarter work full-time.

In part this reflects the age structure of the agricultural population. Nearly one-half of all agricultural workers are age 55 or over, which in turn reflects a clearly expressed preference by younger generations to head for the towns and cities. It follows that in the course of time the retirement of large numbers of farm workers will create a much more efficient farming structure in many EU countries.

12.6.3 Price Support

The system of price support has two distinct strands, one applicable to EU products and the other to imports as illustrated in **Figure 12.3**. At the apex of the price pyramid for EU products sits the **target price**, which is the notional market price negotiated annually by the Council of Agricultural Ministers for the place where a product is in shortest supply. For certain products the terms 'guide', 'norm' or 'basic' price are also used. In practice, a product's price will rise to its target level only at a time of great shortage, so target prices have little operational meaning. Of greater importance is the **intervention price**, which is the lowest level to which product prices are permitted to fall before the relevant intervention agency is obliged to buy in all surplus supply. This price is fixed annually as a percentage of the target price by the Council of Ministers on an individual product basis. Payments are delayed to discourage selling into intervention. Should producers be willing to export, they are paid a subsidy, equal

Table 12.5   *EU Agricultural Statistics*

					Employment in agriculture		
		Utilised agricultural area (000 ha)	*Number of holdings (000 holdings)*	*UAA per holding (ha)*	*Number (000 persons)*	*Share in employed civilian working population (%)*	*Final production of agriculture (ECU mn)*	*Share of agriculture in the GDP[6] (%)*
		1994	1993	1993	1994	1994	1994	1994
	EUR 15	140 553	7 815	16.4	7 878	5.4	206 496	1.8
Belgium		1 380	76	17.7	95[4]	2.5[4]	6 864	1.6
Denmark		2 739	74	37.0	146	5.7	6 392	2.5
Germany		17 162	606	28.1	1 035	3.0	31 396	0.8
Greece		5 741[1]	819	4.3	790	20.8	8 722	7.5
Spain		29 756	1 384	17.9	1 151	9.8	22 174	2.7
France		30 217	801	35.1	1 048	4.8	43 917	2.0
Ireland		4 444[3]	159	26.9	140	12.0	4 307	5.4
Italy		17 215[2]	2 488	5.9	1 572	7.9	32 332	2.6
Luxembourg		127	3	42.3	6	2.8	186	0.9
Netherlands		1 977	120	16.8	264	4.0	16 808	3.2
Austria		3 962	267	12.9	476[4]	13.3[4]	5 412	2.2
Portugal		3 983	489	8.1	514[4]	11.6[4]	3 217	2.0
Finland		2 605	192	14.0	168	8.3	3 581	1.8
Sweden		3 367	92	36.5	135	3.4	3 357	1.0
United Kingdom		15 878	244	67.1	565	2.2	17 831	0.9
	EUR 12	130 619	7 264	16.4	7 098	5.5	194 145	1.8
USA		426 948	2 065	206.7	2 040[4]	1.7[4]	160 575[4]	1.7[5]
Japan		5 204[3]	3 724[4]	1.4	3 633[3]	6.4[5]	76 236[5]	1.6[5]

Notes:
[1] 1988.
[2] 1989.
[3] 1991.
[4] 1993.
[5] 1992.
[6] Gross value added ÷ GDP

Source: Commission of the Economic Communities (1996).

to the difference between the world price and the EU market price, in the form of an **export restitution.**

The position for imports is that, almost without exception, they must be sold in the EU at a **threshold price** which is equivalent to the target price adjusted for transport and storage costs. The minimum price at which non-EU products can be imported into the EU is known as the **reference** (or sluice-gate) **price,** and to this is added a **variable levy** in order to bring the actual import price (which may exceed the reference price) up to the threshold price (see **Figure 12.3**). All proceeds from the variable levy are paid into the EAGGF, often identified by its equivalent French initials as FEOGA, which uses roughly

Figure 12.3 *Prices in the CAP*

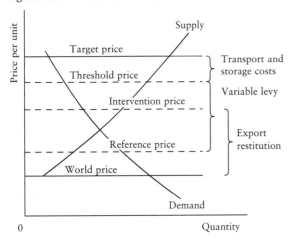

the vast majority of the proceeds in order to fund intervention buying and export restitution payments (**guarantees**). The residual is spent on **guidance**, largely to finance structural improvements. Guidance spending is discretionary, and EU funds usually have to be matched by recipient countries.

Since the inception of the CAP, the proportion of agricultural produce which has attracted some degree of price support has risen inexorably, and currently stands at roughly 90 per cent. However, it is significant that two thirds of all price support expenditure goes upon milk, arable crops and beef (CEC, 1996, p. 144). This arises because all of these products are automatically bought into intervention. The others attract much less support spending and certain products, such as potatoes and flowers, are assisted only by the existence of the variable levy. Intervention buying applies predominantly to products originating in northern Europe, and although guidance expenditure is directed largely to the more southerly members, the disparity between the guarantee and guidance funds represents a strong bias in favour of northern members.

□ 12.6.4 Agri-money

At the inception of the CAP, it was intended that agricultural produce should have a common price throughout the Community. In a world of fixed exchange rates and zero inflation, it is clearly possible to fix the price of, for example, wheat in several currencies, and to keep those prices constant for evermore. However, where exchange rates are subject to adjustment, and where different countries suffer different rates of inflation, common prices can be maintained only through the introduction of a complicated adjustment mechanism.

Agricultural products in the EU are priced in ECUs. These are converted into a number of units of a national currency at the prevailing exchange rate between that currency and the ECU, and the farmer then receives as payment the appropriate amount of his domestic currency. But if that currency is devalued against the ECU, then the farmer ends up with more of his domestic currency than before (less in the case of a revaluation) even though the price in ECUs has not altered. It was in order to avoid this outcome that 'green' currency was introduced.

Green currency was introduced in 1969 when the French franc was devalued and the deutsche mark was revalued. The French were unhappy that this would cause the price of food to consumers to rise and the Germans were unhappy that this would cause the incomes of farmers to fall. It was accordingly agreed that currency changes should be introduced only gradually for agricultural products, and that during the adjustment period artificial exchange rates would apply, to be known as representative or **green** rates.

This practice of using artificial exchange rates for agricultural products subsequently became institutionalised under the CAP. When a currency rose against the ECU it was the custom to leave the green rate unchanged in order to protect the incomes of farmers. Hence the adjustment which involved MCAs (monetary compensatory amounts) in order to prevent consequent distortions of intra-country trade operated such that: green rate = market rate **less** MCA. The MCA was thus **positive** and took the form of a subsidy to that country's exports and a levy on imports from other countries.

On the other hand, if a currency fell against the ECU, but the green rate either stayed unchanged or was devalued by less, the adjustment which involved MCAs in order to prevent distortions of intra-country trade operated such that: green rate = market rate **plus** MCA. The MCA was thus **negative** and took the form of a levy on that country's exports and a subsidy to imports from other countries.

In 1984, the 'switchover' mechanism was introduced with a view to eliminating positive MCAs. This meant that any ERM reshuffle that would lead to the creation of positive MCAs would instead lead to a redefinition of the ECU (thus leading to payments to all other countries).

It was recognised that a system which had been introduced originally in order to permit an orderly movement towards market exchange rates had ended up, inevitably, as a permanent system of dual exchange rates, and the EU decided to bring the process of fixing an annual green rate for each currency to an end at the end of 1992. This partly reflected the fact that there was a good deal of cross-border smuggling in order to avoid MCA levies, but primarily it was a response to the fact that the concept of the Single European Market was incompatible with a system of dual exchange rates. Although it was frequently alleged that the CAP was the only element of the EU which could truly be called a common market, this was demonstrably untrue in reality since the common currency, the ECU, had two values, one market and one green, in respect of each currency.

The new system introduced on 1 January 1993 (see *Bank of England Inflation Report*, May 1995, p. 46) did not, however, abolish either green rates or the switchover mechanism as such, but set out to bring green rates more into line with market rates. To this end, new rules required that exchange rates be monitored over a series of 10–day reference periods and, if the gap between a green rate and its equivalent market rate exceeded a predetermined trigger level, the green rate would automatically be either devalued or revalued.

In practice, devaluations predominated between 1 January 1992 and April 1995, occurring 124 times compared to only 17 revaluations, with the same countries involved in both sets of cases. Since the devaluations served to drive up domestic support prices in the UK and elsewhere without compensatory reductions in strong currency countries, there was therefore an inbuilt upwards bias in levels of support.

Naturally, the emphasis upon devaluations reflected the fact that revaluations were politically unappealing in countries such as Germany because they depressed prices in national currencies, although ironically it was Germany which actually lost out in the end because, as the largest net contributor to the Budget, it continuously paid out more than its own farmers received in compensation.

At the end of 1994, the Commission proposed that the switchover mechanism be abolished as currency markets had undergone a period of stability, with green and market rates moving closely together within narrow bounds. Whilst most countries supported this move, Germany insisted that a mini-switchover be retained from 1 February 1995 which would compensate all farmers if real exchange rates moved two percentage points below or five percentage points above the green currency rate. Subsequent upon further currency turmoil, the rules were relaxed such that they required that, in the case of a positive gap between the green and market rate exceeding 5 per cent, the green rate would be frozen for a further five reference periods (although price changes caused by devaluations would still be triggered after ten days – thereby promoting a preference for devaluations rather than revaluations).

Unhappily, this still meant that by mid-1995 certain continuously appreciating currencies should have triggered a number of compensatory payments to farmers. It was agreed that compensatory payments for income losses due to support price cuts in national currencies would be made as a consequence of a green rate revaluation, with the green rate frozen until 1 January 1999 at the rate immediately preceding revaluation for the purposes of calculating direct payments to farmers (see CEC, 1996, p. 28). This made the CAP somewhat cheaper to run, although the UK still registered its displeasure on the grounds that support levels would henceforth differ as between member states leading to less than level playing fields for competition.

France then argued that the depreciations in the UK, Italian and Spanish currencies had adversely affected its farmers' competitiveness, and managed to get agreement in October for national aid to farmers to compensate for real income losses over a period of no more than three years arising from currency movements in other member states (*ibid.*). Subsequently, in response to UK and other objections, this was amended such that aid could be reduced or cancelled if the income losses used to justify them were reversed.

□ 12.6.5 Mountains and Lakes

In the UK, between 1975 and 1985, disposable incomes, prices in general and processed product prices in particular rose at an almost identical rate. However, starting in 1978, farm-gate prices began to lag behind. This meant that the only way for farmers to maintain their incomes was to raise their output, which in turn meant more intensive use of fertilisers. However, the latter rose in price much faster than end-products, partly because of their oil-based content, and the ratio of producer prices to input prices fell sharply, both in the UK and in the EU as a whole.

This had a number of consequences. In the first place, **farmers' incomes**, as officially recorded, failed to keep pace with incomes in other sectors. However, it is important to note in this respect that very few studies have ever been done on agricultural incomes, so there is great uncertainty about the validity of income comparisons. Those studies that exist indicate that farmers' incomes (though not those of their labourers) were on average well above the average for the whole economy before 1980 (although a large part of these incomes was a return on the ownership of land rather than on the farming of the land), and that the cost-price squeeze served merely to reduce this differential somewhat; that the indiscriminate nature of price support means that large-scale farmers never have been, nor are likely to be, near the breadline – on average, the wealthiest 25 per cent of farmers receive nearly ten times as much in subsidies as their poorer counterparts; and that while small-scale farmers may earn only modest incomes from their farms, they generally have other sources of income, and in many cases

farming is a secondary rather than a primary occupation. Although some farmers clearly have little to show for their labours, it is also the case that no one really knows how to identify which farmers genuinely need help and which could survive quite happily with a reduced level of price support, or even with none at all.

In the second place, there was the problem of **vast overproduction**, which is illustrated in **Table 12.6** for both the UK and EU. This in turn created a major problem of storage. In practice, these stocks could be disposed of, but only at prices well below those paid to buy them into intervention, and this difference was an immense strain upon the Community Budget.

□ 12.6.6 Direct Income Aid

Partly as a response to pressure exerted by the USA during the Uruguay Round to switch agricultural support onto a production-neutral basis, the EU farm ministers agreed in January 1989 to the use of **direct income aids** to farmers based on livestock numbers, crop acreage etc (as distinct from market intervention to support prices discussed above), although it was clear from the start it would have to be introduced on a purely voluntary national basis.

A number of objections were raised, in particular by the UK. It was argued, first, that adequate and universally applicable social security systems already existed throughout the Community, so there was no need for a special scheme for farmers, especially one which would have to be paid for out of national taxation receipts. In any event, farmers themselves would prefer not to be singled out for special payments for fear of attracting further adverse publicity. It was also felt that the scheme could turn out to be yet another open-ended commitment, although this point was dealt with in practice by ring-fencing the scheme. The key elements of the scheme which became operational in 1991 were:

- It was voluntary. If offered, any national scheme had to be approved by the European

Table 12.6 *UK and EU Intervention Stocks*

Date[1]	1988	1989	1990	1991	1992	1993 provisional	1994 forecast	1995 forecast	1996 forecast
Cereals									
UK stocks ('000 tonnes)[2]	1737	706	562	653	679	1730	1283	633	233
Value (£ million)	124	44	17	22	28	73	94	46	17
Equivalent supply (days)[3]	104	44	34	39	42	96	76	40	14
EU stocks ('000 tonnes)[2,4]	10952	8963	12030	17550	24316	26158	n/a	n/a[6]	n/a
Equivalent supply (days)	32	31	67	167	231	248	n/a	n/a	n/a
Beef									
UK stocks ('000 tonnes)	32	8	42	122	153	141	133	120	107
Value (£ million)	49	9	32	107	143	87	146	132	119
Equivalent supply (days)[3]	15	4	15	52	66	62	58	53	47
EU stocks ('000 tonnes)[4]	670	151	305	741	641	680	n/a	n/a[8]	n/a
Equivalent supply (days)	42	7	23	43	38	43	n/a	n/a	n/a
Butter									
UK stocks ('000 tonnes)	49	9	20	33	10	9	8	5	2
Value (£ million)	76	12	11	21	6	5	6	4	1
Equivalent supply (days)[3]	76	12	36	61	17	16	14	9	4
EU stocks ('000 tonnes)[4]	221	32	188	390	353	161	n/a	n/a[7]	n/a
Equivalent supply (days)	50	7	47	100	80	37	n/a	n/a	n/a
Skimmed milk powder									
UK stocks ('000 tonnes)		–	7	10	2	2	3	3	3
Value (£ million)	–	–	4	5	1	1	2	2	2
Equivalent supply (days)[3]	–	–	12	18	3	4	6	6	6
EU stocks ('000 tonnes)[4]	14	5	340	491	93	38	n/a	n/a	n/a
Equivalent supply (days)	4	1	86	126	21	9	n/a	n/a	n/a

Notes:
[1] The years indicated refer to EAGGF accounting years for intervention activity (30 September).
[2] UK stocks mainly barley and wheat – EU stocks include other cereals such as durum.
[3] Calculated using EU Commission figures for consumption.
[4] Figures derived from the Financial Reports on the EAGGF Guarantee Section published by the Commission.
[5] UK holding only 40 tonnes.
[6] Roughly 6,000 in mid-1995.
[7] Roughly 28 in mid-1995.
[8] Roughly 15 in mid-1995.
n/a = not available.

Source: Ministry of Agriculture and Fisheries (1994) Table 12.

Commission and had to meet rules concerning eligibility and the level of funding.

• Eligibility required that a 'significant' (ill-defined) part of household income was derived from agriculture and that the total income was low relative to national **per capita** GNP.

- Payments could be made for no more than five years to any individual, commencing no later than four years after the scheme's inception.
- Payments could not exceed ECU 2500 per individual per year.
- The EU contribution to the total paid was limited to 70 per cent of the total for the least developed member states and to no more than 25 per cent for the remaining member states.
- Recipients were to receive decreasing amounts of aid each year, with the EU's contribution to be reduced by 15 per cent during each successive year of payment.
- The scheme was to be capped at ECU 16.8 million in 1994.

12.6.7 Producer and Consumer Subsidy Equivalents

The purpose of farm support is to transfer income from consumers to producers. The particular instruments chosen to effect that outcome are, however, inefficient and create a huge waste of resources. Hence, the policy-induced increase in the cost of food and taxation is much greater than the corresponding increase in farm incomes. There is a further distributional inefficiency insofar as a disproportionate share of payments to farmers go to the largest farm units.

The OECD calculates the effect of agricultural programmes on producers and consumers by recourse to **Producer Subsidy Equivalents** (PSEs) and **Consumer Subsidy Equivalents** (CSEs). A PSE is defined as 'the payment that would be required to compensate farmers for the loss of income resulting from the removal of a given policy measure. Expressed as a percentage, it represents that part of the value of output accounted for by assistance of various kinds'. A PSE cannot, however, incorporate intervention in the form of, for example, quotas which have no budgetary cost. A CSE corresponds to the implicit tax on (or subsidy to) consumption food prices and of taxes required to maintain farm incomes.

If we start by looking back at the position a decade ago (OECD, 1987) then the evidence shows clearly that Japan was much the worst offender in PSE terms, especially in respect of cereals. The EU also came out badly, its highest PSE being for dairy products. The USA came out well for all non-dairy products, although the PSE for sugar was surprisingly high.

CSEs for dairy products were almost identical in every case, indicating that consumers everywhere were paying one-quarter more than they would have done in a free market. The fact that the Japanese paid 45 per cent extra for their rice and 30 per cent extra for their beef was especially noteworthy. In the case of the EU, the burden on consumers was fairly well spread out over different products, but was especially high for sugar (expensive domestically produced beet rather than cheap imported cane) and for coarse grains.

During the 1980s, the situation worsened considerably. The OECD's calculation of PSEs for 1984–86 indicated a Japanese PSE of close to 70 per cent and a PSE for the USA up sharply to 28 per cent. The only exception was the EU where the PSE rose only by a few percentage points. A study by Tyers and Anderson (1988) concentrated upon the ratio of producer (domestic) prices to border (international) prices, as shown in **Table 12.7**. The ratio rises in line with policy-induced distortions to trade, and as can be seen the ratio for all industrial economies changed from a situation where domestic prices were on average 40 per cent higher than international prices in 1980–82 to a situation where they were twice as high in 1988.

The figures largely speak for themselves, but the marked deterioration in respect of wheat, rice and sugar is especially interesting. The study confirms the OECD's own conclusions which are summarised in **Table 12.8** and **Figure 12.4**. According to the OECD, between 1973 and 1986 PSEs provided a 'mere' 34 per cent of farmers' incomes, whereas the 1993 equivalent was 42 per cent.

Looking at net PSEs in terms of the value of production, **Figure 12.4** shows that the EU percentage has risen slowly but steadily from a moderately high base, a fact not helped by the above-average PSE ratio in new entrants. The USA, in

Table 12.7 *Effect of Agricultural Programmes on Domestic Farm Prices, 1980–82 Average and 1988 (Ratio of Producer to Border Prices)*

	United States		EC		Japan		All industrial economies	
	1980–82	1988	1980–82	1988	1980–82	1988	1980–82	1988
Wheat	1.15	2.20	1.40	3.40	3.90	8.00	1.25	2.45
Coarse grains	1.00	1.60	1.40	2.40	4.30	11.65	1.15	1.75
Rice	1.30	1.85	1.35	2.40	3.35	8.20	2.50	5.65
Beef and Veal	1.10	1.30	1.95	2.75	2.80	5.40	1.50	2.05
Pork and poultry	1.00	1.00	1.25	1.60	1.50	1.90	1.20	1.40
Dairy	2.00	2.20	1.75	2.50	2.90	5.55	1.90	2.55
Sugar	1.40	2.05	1.50	2.80	3.00	7.10	1.50	2.60
Weighted average, all commodities	1.20	1.50	1.55	2.25	2.35	3.80	1.40	2.00

Source: R. Tyers and Anderson K. (1988) 'Liberalizing OECD Agricultural Policies in the Uruguay Round: Effects on Trade and Welfare', *Journal of Agricultural Economics* (May). Table 1.

Figure 12.4   *PSEs as % of Value of Production*

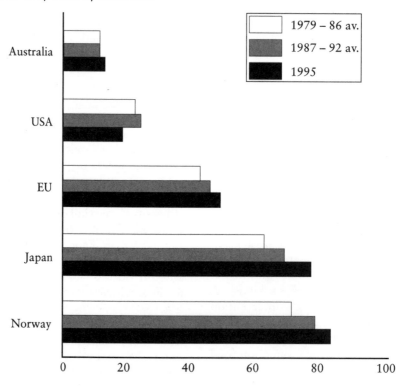

Source: OECD.

contrast, has consistently performed better and has also reduced its ratio in recent years. Both, however, are dwarfed by the ratios in Japan which have crept up overall from a base of roughly 60 per cent in 1979 to nearly 80 per cent today (although it is interesting that Norway and Switzerland, which declined to join the EU, both have higher ratios). All of these can be compared unfavourably with the position in Australia and New Zealand (which currently has a 4 per cent ratio, the only one lower than in 1979) which have demonstrated that, despite short-term pain, PSEs *can* largely be eliminated.

Table 12.8 indicates the actual sums involved. Between 1979 and 1986, the average for the OECD as a whole was $98 billion. Even allowing for inflation, the 1995 equivalent of $182 billion shows considerable growth. Much the largest sum goes to Japanese farmers (their gross inefficiency provides an interesting comparison with their performance in manufacturing). The EU as a whole exceeds this comfortably whereas the USA, in contrast, is paying out less than $20 billion. The Uruguay Round was intended to put paid not only to part of these PSEs but also to the CSEs which had increasingly replaced them. It is, perhaps, premature to express an opinion on this matter, but the omens are as yet far from favourable.

Total payments to farmers in the EU (and elsewhere) do not stop with PSEs, but encompass payments made by individual member states and import duties. The amount of overall support in the EU currently exceeds £10 000 per full-time farmer and £650 per hectare of farmland.

Table 12.8 *Net Producer Subsidy Equivalents ($ bn)*

	1987	1990	1993	1995
Australia	1.1	1.3	1.0	1.2
Japan	35.1	30.9	35.0	49.3
USA	45.1	35.9	28.4	18.9
EU	73.0	81.6	79.6	79.3
OECD	176.8	175.5	163.2	182.0

Source: OECD.

12.6.8 Refining the CAP: 1968–87

The CAP has been in a constant state of flux since its inception. Various reforms have been set in motion, but these have been wholly insufficient to prevent recurrent crises. The Mansholt Plan of 1968 was an early attempt to reform the CAP which recommended a reduction in land use for farming with the remaining land reorganised into fewer farms, thereby reaping economies of scale. The resultant unemployment would be resolved by finding new jobs for ex-farmers.

Disagreements among member states, combined with a poor economic climate, put paid to the Mansholt Plan, and it was not until 1981 that major reforms returned to the Community agenda with the publication of *Guidelines for European Agriculture* (EC, 1981). This proposed that prices should eventually be brought down to world market levels, and pointed out that 'it is neither economically sensible nor financially possible to give producers a full guarantee for products in structural surplus'. Subsequently, price support was limited to pre-determined levels of production which, if exceeded, would cause a response in the form of, for example, a quota for sugar; a co-responsibility levy for milk, which taxed production in excess of quotas in order to help pay for its disposal; or a reduction in the intervention price for cereals.

Unfortunately, these restrictions were nothing like tough enough to prevent the piling up of surpluses, and the cost of financing these grew to the point at which, despite some creative accounting, the CAP had effectively bankrupted the EU. At a summit meeting at Fontainebleau in 1985, remedial action was taken to deal with this crisis. This included action on the agricultural front to the effect that agricultural prices would not be allowed to rise as fast as inflation, MCAs would be phased out and milk production would be limited by quotas (which became tradable the following year).

Quotas on milk production exemplified the problems of the CAP. With output rising faster than consumption during the early 1980s, the proportion of EAGGF guarantee spending devoted to dairy products stabilised at roughly 30 per cent. What was really needed was a price reduction of at least 10 per cent to discourage output, whereas the solution adopted in the form of quotas and co-responsibility levies failed utterly to resolve the problem because the quotas were set well above the level of self-sufficiency.

Quotas work inefficiently because, for example, farmers with expensive machinery cannot afford to leave it lying idle, and therefore seek to buy quotas from other farmers. While this helps to unfreeze arbitrary market shares, which ironically are largest for these farmers who started with the largest supplies, it often results in a farmer's milk quotas becoming more valuable than the land which he farms. Furthermore, cows no longer wanted for their milk will be slaughtered for beef, thereby adding to the beef mountain.

Although the initial quotas achieved very little, a tougher set, introduced in December 1986, combined with harsher penalties on overproduction, effected a noticeable improvement. In the UK, farmers offered to pay up to 50 pence per litre for unused quotas in order to avoid the penalties. Nevertheless, the cost of supporting dairy and other surpluses remained excessive, and the political unwillingness by member states to allow their domestic farmers to suffer (while simultaneously extolling the virtues of austerity) once again left the CAP in a state of crisis in 1987.

The accession to the Community of Spain and Portugal in 1986 was a contributory factor in this respect, given that they had inefficient agricultural sectors by Community standards and produced a range of products somewhat different to those grown in northern European which, since its inception, had attracted most CAP support. The CAP had thus to cope with a huge increase in the output of citrus fruits and olive oil, and to a lesser extent of wine and fresh vegetables.

■ *12.7* Negotiations at the GATT

At the mid-term review of the multilateral trade negotiations (MTN) on agriculture at Montreal in December 1988, negotiations effectively broke down. When discussions were renewed in Geneva in April 1989 the participants agreed that the long-term objective of the MTN was to achieve a 'fair and market oriented agricultural trading system' through the 'substantial progressive reduction in agricultural support and protection resulting in correcting and preventing restrictions and distortions in world agricultural markets'.

This wording was intended to permit short-term problems to be resolved while working towards long-term goals. The USA had previously insisted that it was unprepared to deal with immediate market imbalances until there was general agreement to abolish all trade-distorting policies. This latter objective was total anathema to the Community, which wanted to make some immediate progress by instituting a freeze on subsidies of all kinds. By agreeing 'substantial progressive reduction' it was possible for all parties to maintain that their own positions were still fully operative.

The USA submitted the first detailed proposal for agricultural reform in October 1989, which it refined progressively during 1990. In effect, the amended proposal required the phasing out of all trade-distorting government interventions whether domestic or foreign. The key element in the proposal was **tariffication**. This meant that all non-tariff barriers to imports would be converted into tariffs and cut over 10 years to zero or very low rates. Tariffs would be 'bound', meaning that once introduced they could not be raised again. However, 'minimally trade distorting policies' would be permitted, as would direct supports not linked to production or marketing.

Tariffication was most obviously directed both at the variable import levies used under the CAP and voluntary export restraints. A special **safeguard mechanism** would protect countries against import surges during the 10–year transition period. Governments would be permitted to revert to a higher level of tariff protection for the remainder of a year if imports exceeded specified proportions of the previous year's domestic consumption.

The USA proposed secondly that all **export subsidies** should be subjected to cut-backs. Policies such as government-administered pricing policies, income supports linked to production or marketing, transport subsidies and any investment subsidy provided to producers and processors other than on an equal basis would be **prohibited** at the end of the 10–year adjustment period. By way of contrast, income supports not linked to production or marketing, environmental and conservation programmes, bona fide disaster assistance and other minor items would be **fully permitted**. Finally, anything not covered by these two categories would be **subjected to GATT rules** designed to prevent them being used in ways that would cause prejudice or material injury to another country.

A key aspect of the US proposal was that its scope would encompass the USA's own non-tariff barriers in the sugar and dairy sectors, its export enhancement programme and possibly its deficiency payments scheme for grain farmers, although the latter were seen essentially as internal supports which did not distort trade. By and large, the US proposal was unacceptable to the EU. The EU did not waver from its position that agriculture was a special case where the utopian level playing field, which would exist were all trade-distorting policies to be abolished, would do more damage than good. It much preferred to take an overall view of these policies, as reflected in an **Aggregate Measure of Support** (AMS) covering the first three elements of the US proposal – to be called a Support Measurement Unit (SMU) – which all parties would agree to reduce gradually over time. This would not rule out tariffication *per se*. Partial tariffication would be acceptable provided it encompassed UK-style deficiency payments, but only one element of such a tariff would be fixed, which would be the part reflecting the difference between domestic and market prices. There would also need to be a flexible element (known as a 'corrective factor') which would take into account such factors as currency fluctuations and serious market disturbances. In return for its agreement to partial tariffication, the EU insisted that '**rebalancing**' be allowed. This meant that provided the overall trend was downwards, some subsidies could be increased at the same time as others were reduced.

The view in Brussels was that the US proposal was designed primarily as an attack upon EU export subsidies. The EU, however, was concerned about inroads being made into the animal foodstuffs market by cereal substitutes such as manioc and corn gluten feed, and hence wanted to **balance concessions** on lowering export subsidies on gains against increased protection for cereal substitutes.

With the divide between the EU and US proposals apparently unbridgeable, and with the Japanese continuing to insist that food security was of paramount importance, hopes faded of any resolution of the agricultural sector's problems by end-1990 when the Uruguay Round was due to come to a close. Suddenly, and without any prior discussion with, let alone the approval of, EU farm ministers, the then EU Farm Commissioner, Raymond MacSharry, announced on 31 July 1990 that he would cut EU support to farmers.

In effect a three-stage process was required: (1) keeping within the 1991 Budget's 'guideline' for CAP spending; (2) getting agreement by EU farm ministers to a reform package; (3) getting this package agreed in the GATT. Attempts to avoid (1) by raising the guideline were frustrated by the UK and Dutch farm ministers, but by going to the limit of the guideline, combined with a little fiddling of the accounts, the immediate crisis was resolved. Mr MacSharry's proposal for the longer-term was, first, that cereal prices would be cut by 35 per cent over a three-year period, with compensatory income support paid on a sliding scale. This compensation would be geared to a **set-aside** programme such that arable farmers with less than 20 hectare would be exempt from set-aside; those with 20–50 hectare would have to set-aside 15 per cent of their land to qualify for compensation but would also be compensated for the set-aside; those with in excess of 50 hectare would be compensated only for a 15 per cent set-aside which did not attract further compensation. This was opposed by the UK on the grounds that it discriminated against relatively large UK farms, that the effect over the period to 1995 would be to bump up the cost of running the CAP (although savings might eventually emerge) and that the proposal was biased against northern farmers.

The proposed price reduction for beef was 15 per cent, and it was further proposed that the emergency safety net be abolished. In principle, this could lead to the cessation of intervention buying of beef. Dairy farmers would face 4 per cent reductions in milk quotas, but the smallest producers would be exempt. Prices would also be cut for other products such as sugar and tobacco.

Throughout 1991 and early 1992, EU farm ministers fought over the MacSharry plan. In May 1992, it was agreed that the proposed price cut for cereals should be reduced from 35 to 30 per cent over three years, but with less compensation. A ceiling on stockpiles of beef was agreed at 800 000 tonnes in 1993, descending gradually to 300 000 in 1997. The beef safety net would have its price trigger lowered from 72 to 55 per cent of the intervention price, itself set 15 per cent lower. The price of butter would also be reduced by 5 per cent over two years, and milk quotas cut by 1 per cent in 1993 and 1994. The minimum threshold for set-aside was fixed at 92 tonnes, which penalised UK farms given their relatively large size. 54 per cent of UK farmers were expected to apply for set-aside of £88 per acre compared to a 11 per cent average for the entire EU, in the process taking 16.5 per cent of cereal land out of production. However, given the need to rotate set-aside land, it was difficult to see how the fallow land could be used for long-term environmentally-friendly activities.

Although farm ministers felt these developments to be worthy of self-congratulation, it was observed that they would only serve to reduce food prices overall by 2 per cent over three years, even assuming supermarkets passed on the benefits. In either event, the cost of the CAP would rise initially because of the additional compensation.

Unimpressed, the USA decided to force the EU back to the Uruguay Round bargaining table by threatening to dump 29 million tonnes of heavily subsidised wheat on world markets. Meanwhile Greek farmers took more than half their peach crop straight from the orchard to the dump, and the EU Court of Auditors published a 1100 page report on mismanagement and fraud in the CAP thought to total up to £4 billion.

In mid-November 1992, the USA and EU signed the so-called Blair House Accord, which firstly sought to resolve the five-year dispute over the EU's subsidised production of oilseeds. The EU agreed to limit production to a maximum of 9.5 million tonnes and to binding arbitration if it exceeded that figure. This forestalled the imminent trade sanctions against EU white wine exports to the USA. The EU also agreed to:

- cut import tariffs by an average of 36 per cent;
- the conversion of protectionist devices such as variable import levies into tariff equivalents, with the latter to be cut by 36 per cent on average. The EU nevertheless reserved the right to reintroduce a form of variable levy if prices fell below certain predetermined levels;
- reduce total support for agriculture, as measured by the AMS, by 20 per cent, with exemptions for non-production-distorting payments and those linked to specific production limitation programmes;
- reduce expenditure on export subsidies, 'product by product', by 36 per cent;
- reduce the volume of subsidised exports, 'product by product', but excluding processed products, by 21 per cent;
- guarantee minimum access quotas starting at 3 per cent of consumption and rising to 5 per cent where exports are very low in relation to domestic consumption.

All of the above reductions were to take place over a six-year period commencing mid-1995, and were to be calculated in relation to the average for 1986–90, which was subsequently changed to 1991–92 in order to allow the EU to export more of its intervention stocks of cereals.

As the Uruguay Round drew to a close, some further minor concessions were made, but the Uruguay Round Final Act, which formally brought agriculture within the scope of international trade negotiations for the first time, substantially reflected Blair House terms. The Act hopefully stated its objective as the establishment of 'a fair and market-oriented agricultural trading system . . . to provide for substantial progressive reductions in agricultural support and protection'. From a UK perspective, this should not be unduly taxing given its overall efficiency, although produce from the Antipodes remains substantially cheaper. Obviously, some marginal farmers will be (perhaps terminally) threatened, but recent turmoil in, for example, the UK milk market as a result of the introduction of competition is likely to be of more immediate significance.

A key issue is nevertheless whether the CAP and the Blair House Agreement on Agriculture can be kept fully compatible. The required reduction is unlikely to prove problematic given the base year chosen, and the clause 'safeguarding' the variable import levy should prevent too many difficulties in meeting the new arrangements for imports. On the whole, therefore, it is the commitment to reduce subsidised exports which may prove to be the most difficult to maintain.

☐ 12.7.1 Recent Developments

EU farmers have reason to feel happy as their incomes reached a 20–year high in January 1996, having risen on average by 2.6 per cent in real terms during 1995 (and by 16.6 per cent in the UK mainly due to the ongoing depreciation of sterling amounting to 30 per cent during 1992–95). In the UK, arable land values were badly depressed at the beginning of the 1990s, but between 1992 and 1995 prime land rose in value from £1300 to £2000 per acre.

True, farming costs also rose sharply but, especially in recent years, less rapidly than output prices. A particular element in this is the volatile pattern in the market for wheat. During the 1980s, the emphasis was, as noted, upon reducing the size of the wheat mountain, but set-aside was so successful that, combined with weather patterns resulting in supply shortfalls, wheat stocks fell to the lowest level (at 48 days of world consumption) since World War II at a time of rising demand, especially in Asia (CEC 1996, p. 61: *Financial Times*, 5 January 1996). Wheat prices accordingly rose to record highs. Whilst supply is set to recover somewhat, prices are set to remain relatively high.

Export subsidies came to a halt in July 1995 for only the second time in 30 years. In December 1995, the EU imposed a £21 per tonne tax on wheat exports in order to damp down prices with a view to benefitting EU livestock producers, actually reducing prices below world levels. Beef mountains may also be a thing of the past, with increases in the productivity of dairy cows leading to the need for fewer cows and hence fewer beef calves, restrictions on imports from Eastern Europe and the absorption of surplus beef from former East Germany. However, the longer-term effects of the current BSE scare are difficult to predict, and since it will obviously lead to the destruction of large numbers of animals the beef mountain may support.

These developments followed a decision in September 1995 to cut set-aside to a new single rate of 10 per cent of a farmer's arable acreage. One effect was to lead to a prediction that the EU would underspend its agricultural budget. This is expected to continue for some time as direct aid payments agreed as part of the 1992 CAP reform peak in 1996, and subsidised exports are reduced under the terms of the Agreement on Agriculture.

In July 1996, the Council of Ministers agreed to cut set-aside further to 5 per cent in order to boost production of cereals; to reform the fruit and vegetable sector through production subsidies not exceeding 4 per cent of the value of output, rising to 4.5 per cent in 1999; and to take (as yet unspecified) action to rebalance the beef market in the wake of the BSE crisis via additional intervention buying (see *Financial Times*, 25 July 1996).

On the face of it, therefore, progress has been made since the CAP reform of 1992 in that mountains are lower and lakes drier, and costs are under control. Nevertheless, the CAP remains a problem for the EU and, indeed, for the rest of the world. It is transferring vast sums from taxpayers and consumers to farmers, yet has a regressive effect upon the incomes of both consumers and farmers; it distorts trade and damages the interests of the EU's trading partners; it stimulates fraud; it is incompatible with the Single European Market; and it is environmentally damaging.

The 'peace clause' in the Uruguay Round Final Act prevents signatories from challenging one another's policies except in special circumstances, yet it is idle to suppose that further reform is unnecessary, as indeed the EU Commisioner for agriculture recently admitted (*Financial Times*, 24

November 1995) when taking the first steps to the creation of a new agenda for the renewal of trade talks in the year 2000. The new US Farm Act will increase pressure for reform since it abolishes planting restrictions on arable crops and will inevitably lead to much increased grain exports in competition with the EU (see *The Economist*, 9 March 1996, pp. 53–4).

Bibliography

Ackrill, R. (1992) 'The Common Agricultural Policy – Its Operation and Its Future', *Economics* (Spring).

Anderson, K. (1994) 'Multilateral Trade Negotiations, European Integration, and Farm Policy Reform', *Economic Policy*, 18.

Bhagwati, J. (1990) 'Multilateralism at Risk. The GATT Is Dead. Long Live the GATT.', *The World Economy* (June).

Bhagwati, J. (1994) 'Free Trade: Old and New Challenges', *The Economic Journal* (March).

Canberra Centre for International Economics (1988) *Macroeconomic Consequences of Farm Support Policies* (Canberra: CIE).

Carr, E. (1992) 'The New Corn Laws', *The Economist* (12 December).

Commission of the European Communities (1992) *Third Survey of State Aids in the European Community in the Manufacturing and Certain Other Sectors* (Brussels: CEC).

Commission of the European Communities (1994) 'EC Agricultural Policy for the 21st Century', *European Economy*, 4.

Commission of the European Communities (1995) *Fourth Survey on State Aid in the European Union in the Manufacturing and Certain Other Sectors* (Brussels: CEC).

Commission of the European Communities (1996a) *The Agricultural Situation in the European Union – 1995 Report* (Brussels: CEC).

Commission of the European Communities (1996b) *Cohesion Fund, First Review (1993–94)*. Cohesion Fund Information Sheet 15 February 1996.

Crook, C. (1990) 'A Survey of World Trade', *The Economist* (22 September).

Curzon, G. and V. Curzon (1989) 'Non-Discrimination and the Rise of 'Material Reciprocity'', *The World Economy* (December).

Ford, R. (1990) 'The Cost of Subsidising Industry', *OECD Observer* (October/November).

Giles, M. (1991) 'Business in Europe', *The Economist* (8 June).

Grant, W. (1995) 'Is Agricultural Policy Still Exceptional?', *The Political Quarterly*, 66 (3).

Grimwade, N. (1996) 'Anti-Dumping Policy After the Uruguay Round – An Appraisal', *National Institute Economic Review* (February).

Ingersent, K., A. Rayner and R. Hine (1994) *Agriculture in the Uruguay Round* (London: Macmillan).

Main, D. (1991) 'Regional Policy Initiatives from Brussels', *The Royal Bank of Scotland Review* (March).

Marvel, H. and E. Ray (1995) 'Countervailing Duties', *Economic Journal*, 105 (November).

Messerlin, P. and G. Reed (1995) 'Antidumping Policies in the United States and the European Community', *Economic Journal*, 105 (November).

Ministry of Agriculture, Fisheries and Food (1994) *The Government's Expenditure Plans 1994–95 to 1996–97*. Cm2503 (London: HMSO).

Ministry of Agriculture, Fisheries and Food (1996) *The Government's Expenditure Plans 1996–97 to 1998–99*. Cm3204 (London: HMSO).

OECD (1985) *Costs and Benefits of Protection* (Paris: OECD).

OECD (1987) *National Policies and Agricultural Trade* (Paris: OECD).

OECD (1991) *Agricultural Policies, Markets and Trade. Monitoring Outlook, 1991* (Paris: OECD).

The Economist (1993) 'The Eleventh Hour' (4 December 1993).

The Economist (1995) 'The Right Direction?' (16 September 1995).

Tyers, R. and K. Anderson (1988) 'Liberalizing OECD Agricultural Policies in the Uruguay Round: Effects on Trade and Welfare', *Journal of Agricultural Economics* (May).

Wolf, M. (1989) 'Why Voluntary Export Restraints? An Historical Analysis', *The World Economy* (September).

Chapter 13

Employment and Unemployment

Peter Curwen

■ *13.1* Introduction

The purpose of this chapter and of Chapter 14 which follows is to examine the workings of the labour market in the UK. This divides into three main issues. First, there is the need to discuss **employment and unemployment** and the changes which have taken place in both, primarily during the period since 1979. Secondly, there is the need to examine the role played by the **trade unions** and to assess how they have fared since 1979. Thirdly, there is the need to assess the record with respect to **education and training**, the latter of which has been a central policy issue only since the early 1980s. Inevitably, all of these issues have something to do with the rewards to labour, and so we will need to say something about that also. However, wider issues concerning the distribution of income are left until Chapter 15.

The Thatcher era was undoubtedly one which has been closely associated in people's minds with attempts to improve the workings of the labour market although, as we will discover, not all such attempts were successful and hence we need to examine why this was so. Certainly, the 1980s witnessed many changes in the laws controlling the labour market, and these are set out below. Nevertheless, the first Thatcher government had largely to live with the labour market as it found it in 1979, and a few remarks about the market prior to 1979 are therefore in order.

In the first place, there is the obvious contrast between the period of Keynesian 'full' employment which lasted for over two decades after the end of the Second World War, and the period of protracted unemployment, even in years of buoyant demand, which began in the late 1970s and which looks to be a permanent feature of the UK economic life for the foreseeable future. These days, few economists believe that governments can maintain full employment using predominantly fiscal instruments in the textbook Keynesian manner. Instead, they view the government's role as one of **creating the appropriate climate for sustained investment by the private sector**. The traditional method for achieving this was to declare that the government would do everything in its power to maintain full employment. In response to this, firms were willing to invest to make goods and to provide services since they were assured that there would be no shortage of customers with incomes from employment to be spent. But the investment itself created jobs and incomes which could be spent on consumer goods, and so the expectation of buoyant demand became a self-fulfilling prophecy.

The housing market was also important in this respect since most people who buy a house take on a very long-term commitment in the form of a mortgage, and hence need to be fairly certain of remaining in constant employment while paying it off. Equally, the mortgage provider needs to believe that this will be so before making the loan, in order to avoid defaults. The expectation of full employment hence leads to buoyant demand for housing and creates demand, and hence jobs and incomes, in the construction sector, which again helps to ensure that full employment comes about.

The main drawback to this virtuous circle was that the trade unions ceased to fear the spectre of unemployment which had haunted them during the 1930s, the more so as the old-time union leaders faded away and were replaced by individuals who had never experienced anything other than an era of full employment. Wage demands accordingly began to escalate, accompanied by the threat of strike action, and employers generally gave in quickly, hoping to be able to pass on higher wages into higher prices. Full employment thus became a pre-condition for inflation, and also led to a deterioration in manufacturing standards because of the belief that there would always be ready buyers, even for poor quality products. The Japanese and West Germans were happy to disprove this hypothesis, in the process creating unpleasant problems for the UK's balance of payments.

Although there were various ways in which this combination of problems could have been tackled, Mrs Thatcher's chosen solution after being elected in 1979 was to discard any commitment to full employment and to engineer a recession which demonstrated that this was not mere bluff. The consequences of this changed approach form a unifying trend in the discussion which follows.

There was also the matter of **workers' rights**. By and large, the tradition in the UK up to the 1970s was to limit workers' rights to those who held specified types of jobs and who worked full-time. Compared to those available in other advanced countries, these rights were patchy at best. During the 1970s the situation was to a considerable extent remedied. A series of Acts of Parlia-

ment extended to workers the rights to a contract of employment; to notice before termination of contract; to appeal against unfair dismissal; to redundancy payments; to maternity leave; to protection against discrimination; and to participate in union activities.

Whenever possible, employers responded by taking on workers who fell outside the limits fixed for access to these rights, resulting in an upsurge in female part-time labour. But for the purposes of our discussion below the key factor was that the Thatcher government set about limiting some of these rights. To some extent, as detailed below, this has come up against supranational EU laws in recent years, but there can be no doubt that the balance of power has shifted from workers to employers during the past decade.

■ 13.2 Employment

□ *13.2.1 The Working Population*

The total population of the **UK** grew steadily from 50.3 million in 1951 to 52.8 million in 1961 and 55.9 million in 1971 where **Table 13.1** picks up the story, but has since grown much more slowly. The 1990s are expected to exhibit a modest quickening of population growth, but this is expected to fall off again early in the next century and the population is actually forecast to fall beyond the year 2030 back to its level in the year 2000.

The number of children under 16 increased in the UK by over 1 million between 1961 and 1971, but this was followed by a decline of just under 3 million, to 11.5 million, in 1991 (*Social Trends*, 1995, Chart 1.1). The average age at which mothers give birth in the UK now exceeds 28, and the fertility rate has fallen from 2.4 in 1971 to 1.8 in 1991 (*ibid.*, Table 2.21). However, during the period 1971–91, the younger adult (16 to 39) and pensioner (65 and over) age groups grew by 3 million and 1.6 million respectively. Between 1991 and 2011, the number of children is projected to rise once again to a peak of 12.6 million, whereas the number of younger adults is projected to fall back by 2 million. By way of contrast, the number

Table 13.1 *Population by Age and Gender, UK*

	Percentages					All ages (=100%) (millions)
	Under 16	16–39	40–64	65–79	80 and over	
Mid-year estimates						
1971	25.5	31.3	29.9	10.9	2.3	55.9
1981	22.3	34.9	27.8	12.2	2.8	56.4
1991	20.3	35.3	28.6	12.0	3.7	57.8
1993	20.6	34.9	28.8	11.9	3.9	58.2
Males	21.6	36.3	29.2	10.6	2.4	28.5
Females	19.6	33.5	28.4	13.1	5.4	29.7
Mid-year projections[1]						
2001	20.7	32.9	30.6	11.4	4.3	59.8
2011	19.2	30.0	34.1	11.9	4.7	61.3
2021	18.3	29.7	32.7	14.3	5.1	62.1
2031	18.2	28.4	30.5	16.3	6.6	62.2
2041	17.6	27.8	30.1	16.8	7.8	61.2
2051	17.6	28.0	30.3	14.9	9.2	59.6
Males	18.2	28.9	30.9	14.5	7.5	30.9
Females	17.0	27.2	29.7	15.2	10.9	30.1

Notes:
[1] 1992-based projections.

Source: Social Trends, 25 (1995 edn) Table 1.4.

of pensioners is expected to rise by a further 40 per cent to 14.6 million by the year 2031 (*Social Trends*, 1993, Chart 1.5).

From the total population can be extracted a summary statistic known as the **population of working age**, which by convention encompasses all those who might work and excludes those at school or in retirement. However, parts of the population of working age are economically inactive. Some are engaged in further and higher education, some in raising children and some are physically unable to work. On the other hand, by no means all who retire officially are economically inactive. By adjusting for those factors a further summary statistic is arrived at called the **labour force** (or the **civilian labour force** if those in the armed forces are excluded) which comprises those willing and able to work.

The civilian labour force in **Great Britain** was 24.9 million in 1971 and 26.2 million in 1981.

However, it fell back to 25.9 million by 1983, before rising once again to 28.2 million in 1990. It has subsequently fallen slightly and did not rise back to 28.2 million until 1995 with 29.0 million forecast only in 2002. The population of working age is driven primarily by variations in the birth rate, which surged immediately after 1945 and hence created a cyclical effect approximately every two decades. However, it is also driven by retirements, which are dependent upon the birth rate six to seven decades previously. In its turn, the civilian labour force reflects changes in the population of working age.

However, this relationship has been fairly weak. Between 1951 and 1989 the civilian labour force grew by 3.1 million, considerably faster than the population of working age. Furthermore, whereas the latter grew at much the same rate for males and females, almost 90 per cent of the growth in the civilian labour force comprised of females.

This trend is projected to continue. During the current decade, the number of males in the civilian labour force is expected to remain static at around 16 million, while the number of females is projected to increase by 0.7 million to reach 13 million by the year 2000, at which point women will constitute 45 per cent of the civilian labour force.

Considerable additional detail is forthcoming from the Labour Force Survey (LFS) which is a survey of roughly 65 000 private households throughout the UK, conducted annually in Spring (but only biannually between 1973 and 1983). In the early 1980s, a fairly large number of workers dropped out of the labour force, and the LFS estimated that 340 000 workers in total had become **discouraged** because they did not expect to get a job even if they tried hard to do so. International Labour Office (ILO) estimates indicate 220 000 a year were discouraged during 1984–86 and 110 000 a year during 1988–90.

The notion of 'discouragement' is somewhat ambiguous since some discouraged workers will have jobs in the unofficial, black economy. They may not, however, be as numerous as is often made out in the media since, on the whole, those who are unemployed and who have lost their jobs either because the economy is in recession, or because their particular skills are no longer needed, are unlikely to be much in demand in the black economy either. On the other hand, those with skills in the official economy such as TV repairers will also find their skills in demand in the black economy.

The desire to work in the black economy is obviously influenced by taxation, and the reduction in tax rates during the 1980s may have induced a transfer of activity from the unofficial to the official economy. What is certain is that in 1995–96 there were more than twice as many people (1.27 million) in Great Britain, compared to 1980–81, who declared themselves to have a second job (see *Labour Market Trends*, July 1996, Table 5). From 1981 to 1985 more men had second jobs than women, but by 1987 this had reversed itself quite sharply (see *Social Trends,* 1991, Chart 4.15). Of those with second jobs in 1995–96, 70 per cent of those jobs were as employees and 30 per cent were self-employed.

□ *13.2.2 Self-employment*

In 1971, there were 2 million self-employed in Britain. By 1979 this figure had fallen to 1.9 million. However, numbers surged during the 1980s, to 2.2 million in 1981, 2.7 million in 1986, 3.0 million in 1987, 3.4 million in 1989 and 3.5 million in 1990 (see *Employment Gazette,* June 1992, pp. 269–92 and *Social Trends,* 1993, Chart 4.10). At the end of 1995, there were 3.2 million, numbers having picked up again after a setback during the recession as a consequence of the recession. Between 1981 and 1990, the net increase was 59 per cent overall (52 per cent for men as against 87 per cent for women although there were well under one million self-employed women even in 1990 and 800 000 currently). The net increase was the difference between very large numbers entering and leaving self-employment each year. Two-thirds of the self-employed worked by themselves.

This increase in Britain was very much greater than in other EU countries, the USA and Japan, although Britain had proportionately fewer self-employed outside agriculture in 1979 than any of the other countries. As a result, the UK self-employed rate is currently close to the EU average. More than 60 per cent of the self-employed are in services. The largest number work in distribution, catering and repairs, followed by construction, other services and banking, finance and insurance. In many sectors such as other services there was roughly 100 per cent growth in numbers between 1981 and 1990, but the overall average growth was only roughly 50 per cent because numbers were static in agriculture and forestry and grew only very modestly in distribution, the largest sector (where they fell after 1986). Whereas many self-employed persons struggle to make a decent living, it is equally the case that many highly-skilled individuals have prospered as a result of setting themselves up as suppliers of business and financial services.

The rapid growth in self-employment is partly accounted for by the 1980–81 recession, which created a large pool of unemployment from which large numbers of individuals chose to emerge as self-employed. Previously, self-employment was much higher in countries with extensive job protection and high social security charges, where employers preferred not to offer full-time jobs. In addition, the Conservative government fostered self-employment both through changes in the fiscal system and by its promotion of the joys of self-reliance. Start-up capital has also become more readily available. Needless to say, the failure rate among the self-employed is high, so the significant overall growth in numbers does indicate that the switch to self-employment is more than just a flash-in-the-pan consequence of the 1980–81 recession. However, now that the UK has caught up with the EU average, the situation is likely to remain far less changeable than during the 1980s.

□ 13.2.3 Activity Rates

The proportion of the resident population who are in the civilian labour force is usually referred to as the economic **activity rate**. Activity rates have always been very different for males and females, but have been converging steadily during the postwar years. In the case of men, the activity rate has been falling since the 1930s. In part, this has been due to an increase in the numbers staying on in further and higher education, although that factor was probably most important in the 1960s. More recently, the decline has been due to earlier retirements, stemming from improved pensions, and to the 'discouraged workers' effect.

In 1971, the activity rate in Britain for males of 16 and over was 80.5 per cent. Subsequently it fell to 74.2 per cent in 1983 before rising back to 74.5 per cent in 1984, at which point there was a definitional changeover to the ILO/OECD system. On the latter basis, as shown in **Table 13.2**, the male activity rate stood at 74.2 per cent in 1990 and is projected to fall back to 71.5 per cent by the year 2001.

The female activity rate in 1971 was only 43.9 per cent, but in spite of a setback during 1981–83 it had risen to 52.8 per cent by 1990, and is projected to rise further to 55.5 per cent by the year 2001. This increase in female activity rates has largely been due to the switch over to service sector employment, to an increase in the availability of part-time jobs and to other economic and social changes encouraging women into the labour force.

Data for the UK as a whole are also available in a somewhat different format that excludes those over the age of retirement. These reveal a notable difference in the pattern between the activity rates of married and unmarried women. Activity rates for unmarried females have been reasonably constant since 1971, although there was a dip during the 1990–92 recession. Among the younger age group, there has been an increased tendency for females to stay on in further and higher education, and a sharp upturn in the number of single-parent families living off state benefits. Married women, on the other hand, have become increasingly active in the labour market, even through the recession. Clearly this has much to do with the modern tendency to delay having a family and to have fewer children, together with the economic necessity to supplement family earnings, especially when the husband is out of work, and the widespread social acceptance of women working outside the home. In addition, the widespread introduction of labour-saving devices in the home has eased the burden of housework.

The most significant change in recent years has been in the proportion of women with a dependent child under 5 years of age who work either full-time or part-time. In 1984 this stood at 27 per cent whereas by 1994 it had risen to 46 per cent (see *Social Trends*, 25, Table 4.5; *Labour Market Trends*, April 1996, p. 192). This is the cause of some unease about the structure of modern society, but this goes beyond the scope of our present discussion. A summary of the role of women in the labour market is contained in **Table 13.3**. It is worth adding briefly (see below for further details) that with unemployment remaining relatively high for men, the proportion of employees who are currently women has risen to 48 per cent (for an analysis by occupation and industry see *Labour Market Trends* (July 1996) p. LFS36). However, this figure is deceptive because, for example, the great majority of the self-employed are male and unless women give up child care wholesale they will never form half the workforce as occasionally predicted.

Table 13.2 *UK Labour Force Economic Activity:[1] By Gender and Age (%)*

Estimates	16–24	25–44	45–59	60–64	65 and over	All aged 16 and over
Males						
Estimates						
1984	81.8	96.1	90.0	57.5	8.7	75.9
1986	82.6	95.9	88.8	53.8	7.9	75.2
1991	81.2	95.7	88.1	54.2	8.6	74.9
1992	77.5	95.1	87.5	52.8	8.9	73.9
1993	76.1	94.5	86.3	52.2	7.4	72.9
1994	75.1	94.1	86.1	51.0	7.6	72.6
Projections						
1996	72.4	94.2	86.4	50.4	7.5	72.2
2001	70.3	94.4	85.3	49.7	7.0	71.5
2006	69.3	94.2	83.7	49.1	6.8	70.0
Females						
Estimates						
1984	69.1	65.6	63.3	21.8	3.1	49.2
1986	70.6	67.4	64.0	19.1	2.7	50.0
1991	71.3	73.0	66.9	23.9	3.1	53.1
1992	67.5	72.8	68.4	23.4	3.6	52.8
1993	66.0	73.6	68.5	24.7	3.5	53.0
1994	64.6	73.5	69.3	25.3	3.2	53.0
Projections						
1996	63.6	74.8	70.4	26.6	3.0	53.7
2001	63.3	77.8	71.9	29.0	2.8	55.5
2006	63.2	81.3	72.6	31.9	2.9	56.7

Notes:
[1] The percentage of the population that is in the labour force.
Source: Social Trends, 26 (1996 edn) Table 4.4.

Among the countries of the EU in 1994, as shown in **Table 13.4,** the UK had the second-highest economic activity rate behind Denmark, and this applied both for males and for females. In the now enlarged EU, Sweden also has a higher rate than the UK. The difference between the sexes in Denmark was only 12 per cent, much smaller than the 21 per cent for the UK, so there is some reason to expect the gap to narrow further in the UK over the coming decade. It would appear from this evidence that UK residents are relatively keen to work. Unfortunately, that does not necessarily mean that their time is used productively.

13.2.4 Population and Activity Rate Effects

Population effects represent the changes in the labour force which would occur if activity rates stayed the same and only the size and age distribution of the population changed, whereas the 'activity rate effects' represent the changes in the proportion of the population which is in the labour force.

In every year since 1971, and up to the year 2006 according to projections (Ellison, Melville and Gutman, 1996, p. 203), the overall changes in

Table 13.3 *The Role of Women in the Labour Market*

According to analysis of the 1991 LFS for Great Britain

- Over 70 per cent of women of working age were active in the labour market in Spring 1991.
- Between 1979 and 1991 the number of women in employment grew by just under 20 per cent.
- In Spring 1991, 43 per cent of employed people of working age were women; of these, just over 40 per cent worked part-time and a third had dependent children.
- There were 740 000 self-employed women in Spring 1991, more than double the number in 1979.
- In Spring 1991 the unemployment rate (on the ILO definition) among women of working age was 7 per cent, compared to 9 per cent for men.
- 0.68 million women returned to the labour market between Spring 1990 and Spring 1991.
- 82 per cent of working women had jobs in the service industries in Spring 1991 compared with 54 per cent of men.

Source: Employment Gazette (September 1992), pp. 33–59.

the labour force are more positive (or less negative) for women than for men. The population effects are always positive for both women and (particularly) men. They rose during the 1970s to

Table 13.4 *Economic Activity Rates[1]: By Sex, EU Comparison, 1992 (%)*

	Males	Females	All
Denmark	74.5	62.7	68.5
United Kingdom	74.0	52.8	63.0
Portugal	71.9	50.2	60.3
Germany[2]	71.5	48.4	59.4
Netherlands	71.1	46.5	58.6
Belgium	62.0	37.1	49.1
France	65.7	48.0	56.4
Irish Republic	70.6	37.7	53.9
Luxembourg	69.7	39.5	54.2
Italy	65.4	34.9	49.5
Spain	65.6	34.1	49.2
Greece	65.5	34.8	49.4
EU average	68.9	44.6	56.2

Notes:

[1] The civilian labour force aged 16 years and over as a percentage of the population aged 16 and over.

[2] As constituted since 3 October 1990.

Source: Social Trends, 25 (1995 edn), Table 4.7.

reach a peak around 1983, but despite declining subsequently they are projected to remain positive from now until the year 2006.

Activity rate effects are typically larger, and much more variable, from year to year. It is these, rather than population effects, which explain both the fall in the labour force which occurred (even for women) between 1981 and 1983, and the large rises in 1983–84 and 1988–89. In most years, they are positive for women but negative for men – on occasion to such an extent as to outweigh the population effect and result in falls in the male labour force.

☐ *13.2.5 Working Hours*

Data on working hours are produced on a national basis and also on an internationally comparative basis by the EU and OECD. As a result of differences in definitions the data are not fully compatible, although the trends revealed are clear-cut. Since the mid-1980s there has been a steady downwards trend in the number of hours worked in the UK, superimposed upon which has been a pro-cyclical pattern. The trend line is readily explained by the substitution effect – that is, the tendency for increasing numbers of workers to substitute leisure for working hours as their real incomes rise over time.

The tendency for hours worked to rise during booms and to fall during recessions essentially reflects the volume of work on offer, and is much more marked in the manufacturing sector as compared to services, and among males as compared to females.

It is estimated from the Labour Force Survey that four out of five male employees have basic weekly hours (that is **excluding** meal breaks and overtime) of between 35 and 45. Those at the lower end are mostly in manual jobs in manufacturing, energy and transport. Half of all female employees work for less than 35 hours per week and over two thirds for between 35 and 40 hours. For both sexes the self-employed work longer hours than employees.

The official dividing line for part-time work is set at 30 hours per week. Women who work fewer hours invariably describe themselves as part-timers, but surveys reveal that 20 per cent of men who work fewer hours nevertheless describe themselves as full-time employees.

In 1979, the engineering working week was cut from 40 to 39 hours, and within three years a further 6 million workers had won a similar reduction. In 1989, more than 600 000 manual workers in the engineering and water industries won the promise of a 37.5–hour week, and by the end of 1992 this applied to the majority of manual workers. There has been considerable reluctance in other industries to follow suit, but in February 1992, for example, British Nuclear Fuels negotiated a 35–hour week subject to improved working practices which made the deal self-financing.

International comparisons must be treated with care. Average weekly hours worked fell during the 1980s in most OECD countries, although Americans worked slightly longer and the Japanese exactly the same. Given the general tendency for the statutory working week to be shortened, and for official holidays to be extended, this is not particularly surprising. What is surprising is the enormous disparity between the Dutch working

Table 13.5   *Average Hours Usually Worked[1] per Week, by Gender, EU Comparison, 1994*

	Males			Females		
	Full time	Part time	43.5	Full time	Part time	33.9
United Kingdom	45.4	16.0	43.5	40.4	17.9	30.6
Portugal	42.7	26.3	42.4	39.3	20.2	37.9
Greece	41.4	25.6	41.0	39.0	21.5	38.0
Irish Republic	41.6	21.2	40.6	37.8	18.0	33.9
Spain	41.0	19.6	40.6	39.5	17.5	36.3
Luxembourg	40.6	26.7	40.5	37.9	19.7	34.3
France	40.6	22.5	39.8	38.8	22.4	34.2
Italy	39.7	30.1	39.5	36.3	23.0	34.7
Germany	39.9	18.9	39.3	39.2	20.2	33.0
Belgium	38.8	21.1	38.3	36.9	20.9	31.9
Denmark	39.8	14.2	37.1	38.0	21.2	32.0
Netherlands	39.6	18.6	36.3	39.1	17.9	25.2
EU average	41.1	19.5	40.2	38.9	19.7	32.8

Notes:
[1] Employees only. Excludes meal breaks but includes paid and unpaid overtime.
Source: Social Trends, 26 (1996 edn), Table 4.14.

week and the Japanese working week which is ten hours longer. This is, however, something of an illusion because the incidence of part-time relative to full-time work biases the data and the Netherlands, for example, has proportionately twice as many part-timers (at 25 per cent of the workforce) as Japan. Equally, the Japanese holiday entitlement (typically at 2 weeks) is very low compared to that in Europe. Combining annual leave with public holidays yields 40 days' holiday for Germans, 36.5 days for the French, 33.5 days for Italians but only 31 days for UK citizens (only the Irish get fewer at 28).

The latest year for which hours worked data are available for the 12-member EU is 1994 (**Table 13.5**), and it should be noted that these data **include overtime**. On average, men in the UK worked longer hours than their EU counterparts, whereas women worked fewer hours than elsewhere in the EU apart from the Netherlands. A slightly different version is obtained by a comparison of Labour Force Surveys (see *Labour Market Trends*, June 1996, p. LFS30). If hours worked are combined with holiday entitlement, it becomes evident that Danes work far fewer hours per year than the Portuguese, and that UK citizens work many more hours than the French. While this does not make much difference in any one year, it makes a huge difference over a 45–year working life. The combination of extended overtime working and a heavy reliance upon part-time workers distinguishes the UK from most comparable countries.

In theory, at least, it suggests that the UK has a flexible labour market. Furthermore, there has been a noticeable tendency for firms to cease to do many jobs in-house and to sub-contract them to outside bodies as and when they are needed. **This is a significant factor in explaining the switch from manufacturing to services in the national accounts, since a service provided in-house by a manufacturing concern is listed as a manufacturing activity, whereas the instant it is sub-contracted-out it becomes listed as a service activity, even if it involves the identical group of workers.**

From an economic perspective, these developments obviously make sense for large companies, which thereby need to incur relatively low over-heads and which can flex in line with the economic cycle. On the other hand, sub-contractors are increasingly vulnerable to economic downturns, and this helps to account for the exceptionally high number of bankruptcies during the 1990–92 recession.

The government has attempted through its own policies to foster **increased flexibility** in the workplace, in particular via the attack upon restrictive practices contained in the series of Employment Acts during the 1980s. The Employment Act of 1989 was also notable for removing restrictions on the hours of work of young people and for abolishing most of the remaining legislation concerned with sex discrimination.

New contractual agreements introduced by Japanese companies are also of interest given their relative success in manufacturing. At the Nissan car plant in Sunderland the collective agreement specifies that 'there will be complete flexibility and mobility of employees', and also that 'to ensure flexibility and change, employees will . . . undertake training for all work as required'. Despite union resistance elsewhere, these kinds of agreements are likely to become commonplace. Nevertheless, as demonstrated in Chapter 14, the Conservative government (and its predecessors) have something to answer for in terms of their failure to create a system of education and training appropriate to the needs of the rapidly evolving labour market.

☐ *13.2.6 The Demand for Labour*

Changes in the size of the labour force and in activity rates are aspects of the supply of labour. Once the analysis turns to **employment** and **unemployment**, the demand side comes more into its own.

Measuring employment is not as easy as it looks, if only because they are a whole variety of terms in use as indicated in the box. Furthermore, some data are available for Great Britain and some for the UK. In the UK, until Spring 1992, quarterly estimates of employment were available only from the Workforce in Employment

Employees (LFS measure) (22 648 000 in March 1996)	A count, obtained from household surveys, of persons aged 16 and over who regard themselves as paid employees. People with two or more jobs are counted only once.
Employees in employment (21 985 000 in March 1996)	A count, obtained from surveys of employers, of jobs held by civilians who are paid by an employer who runs a PAYE tax scheme. People with more than one job are counted more than once.
The labour force in employment (26 333 000 at end of 1995)	A count, obtained from household surveys and censuses, of employees, self-employed persons, participants in government employment and training programmes and persons doing unpaid family work.
The civilian labour force (28 482 000 in March 1996)	The labour force in employment plus the ILO unemployed less HM forces.
The workforce in employment (25 731 000 in March 1996)	A count of employees in employment (from employer survey based measures), self-employed persons, all HM forces and participants in government employment and training programmes.
The workforce (27 917 000 in March 1996)	The workforce in employment plus the claimant unemployed.

(WiE) series, which showed the number of occupied jobs by industry sector. Information about persons in employment, based on the Labour Force Survey (LFS) of households was only available annually. However, commencing in Spring 1992, quarterly LFS results have become available only six weeks after the survey period.

The two series are conceptually different and are largely independent as regards data sources (see Perry, 1996, for details). However, between 1984 and the beginning of 1992, they were broadly equivalent. Subsequently, the WiE dropped twice as fast and then rose much more slowly (*ibid.*, Figure 1), opening up a gap of 0.6 million by mid-1995. This led to a revision of the WiE methodology with revisions back to September 1991 which has eliminated some, though by no means all, of the deviation between the series.

A particular issue to which we will be referring below is the switch away from manufacturing and into services during the past two decades. This transfer has been common to all advanced economies, and indeed has proceeded much more rapidly in the USA than in the UK. It was inevitably going to accelerate in the UK in the face of rising energy prices after 1975 and the exploitation of North Sea oil and gas which subsequently followed. The former produced a move away from energy-intensive manufacturing and towards services which were economical on energy use. In the latter respect, it is often held that the benefits of North Sea oil were traded off (unwisely) in exchange for manufactured imports and an expansion of the internationally uncompetitive protected sectors of the economy.

The transfer of demand caused large numbers of jobs to be lost in manufacturing. Prior to 1979, the transfer from manufacturing to service sectors was proceeding fairly smoothly, but the 1980–81 recession bit deeply into the manufacturing sectors without making any real dent in service employment. By 1988, the total number of jobs stood once again at precisely the level of 1971 (and hence still well short of the 1979 aggregate). However, taking the UK as a whole, and allowing for some inaccuracy in the count, the manufacturing sectors employed roughly 3 million less than in 1971 and the service sectors roughly 3.5 million more as shown in **Table 13.6**. The reduction in all manufacturing sectors was almost identical at 30 per cent, but the changes in the four service sectors were quite different, varying from a reduction of 12 per cent for transport to an increase of 85 per cent for banking and finance. The missing 0.5 million were lost in agriculture, energy and construction. Although this reduction was absolutely small, it represented a reduction of over 40 per cent in the energy sector.

More recently, there has been a change to the industrial classification system in use. Historically, figures were classified according to the Standard Industrial Classification 1980 (SIC80). However, the 1993 Census of Employment results were classified according to SIC92, a more up-to-date international system made obligatory for EU member states in 1990, and a back-series to 1978 calculated (see Naylor (1995) for details).

This re-classification was better at identifying the split between manufacturing and services, resulting in up to half a million employees per year in **Great Britain** being switched from the former to the latter from 1978 onwards (*ibid.*, Table 4). These new data now appear as Table 1.2 in *Labour Market Trends*. The July 1996 issue, for example, covers June 1982 to April 1996, and shows manufacturing employment declining from 5.36 million in June 1982 to 4.95

Table 13.6 *Employees in Employment, by Industry, UK (000)[1]*

	1971	1979	1981	1986	1990[2]	1991	1992
Manufacturing							
Extraction of minerals and ores other than fuels, manufacture of metal, mineral products, and chemicals	1 282	1 147	939	729	721	657	635
Metal goods, engineering, and vehicle industries	3 709	3 374	2 923	2 372	2 310	2 139	2 030
Other	3 074	2 732	2 360	2 126	2 106	1 997	1 924
Total manufacturing	8 065	7 253	6 222	5 227	5 137	4 793	4 589
Services							
Distribution, hotels, catering, and repairs	3 686	4 257	4 172	4 298	4 822	4 686	4 605
Transport and communication	1 556	1 479	1 425	1 298	1 382	1 349	1 324
Banking, finance, insurance, business services, and leasing	1 336	1 647	1 739	2 166	2 744	2 687	2 639
Other	5 049	6 197	6 132	6 536	6 996	7 022	7 076
Total services	11 627	13 580	13 468	14 298	15 944	15 744	15 644
Agriculture, forestry, and fishing	450	380	363	329	298	291	283
Energy and water supply industries	798	722	710	545	449	439	403
Construction	1 198	1 239	1 130	989	1 070	962	839
All industries and services	22 139	23 173	21 892	21 387	22 899	22 229	21 758

Notes:
[1] As at June each year.
[2] The effect of revisions undertaken in 1991 impacted primarily on the 1989 and 1990 data.

Source: Social Trends, 23 (1993 edn), Table 4.9; *Employment Gazette*.

million in 1984, after which it stayed fairly constant until June 1990. Although the subsequent recession understandably took its toll, there has been little change since June 1992, with the total standing in April 1996 at 3.82 million. In contrast, employment in services grew steadily from 13.48 million in June 1982 to 15.93 million in June 1990, remained fairly constant until June 1994 and subsequently grew again to 16.24 million in April 1996.

An alternative approach is to conduct the analysis by splitting the workforce between **private** and **public** sectors (see *Economic Trends*, February 1996, pp. 14–20). The peak employment in the UK public sector (general government plus public corporations) occurred in 1979, since when it has declined every year without fail to stand at roughly 5 million in mid-1995. However, employment in general government remained roughly constant from 1976 to 1989 and was untouched by the 1980–81 recession. The entire reduction of well over 1 million during 1979–89 accordingly took place in the public corporations, initially as a consequence of recession and subsequently as a consequence of the privatisation programme. Employment in the UK private sector peaked in 1979, fell sharply, recovered back to the 1979 level by 1986 and subsequently grew strongly. As a consequence, the public sector accounted for roughly 30 per cent of the workforce in 1981, but had fallen back to just over 20 per cent by 1995. Since 1990, jobs lost in the public sector have predominantly been in central government with the restructuring of the civil service, and losses due to privatisation have effectively come to a halt in 1996. The UK is almost unique among advanced economies in having reduced public sector employment since 1979.

Finally, it is possible to split employment down by **occupation** (see *Employment Gazette*, July 1995, p. LFS36). In Winter 1994–95, men dominated manual occupations and women non-manual occupations. Of the 10.3 million women employees, only 0.3 million worked in craft and related occupations (15 per cent of all those employed) compared to 2.7 million in clerical and secretarial (73 per cent) and 1 million as professionals (43 per cent).

13.2.7 The 'Flexible' Labour Market

We have already referred to the prevalence of part-time work by females, and this can be seen more clearly by reference to **Figure 13.1**. The recent recession has understandably induced more males to take up part-time jobs, although these represented only roughly 5 per cent of all male jobs in more normal years in the 1980s. By contrast, they have not represented less than 40 per cent of all female jobs for over a decade. It is reasonable to conclude from this that there are forces involved which will continue into the longer term, such as the switch from manufacturing into services, and furthermore that these forces will significantly affect full-time job opportunities for males. Nevertheless, full-time employment in Great Britain is no longer on the decline, and during the three years following the trough in Winter 1992–93 full-time employment rose by 275 000 jobs, of which 208 000 were filled by men (compared to an increase of 453 000 in the number of part-time jobs, of which 283 000 were filled by women).

There has been a protracted debate about the reasons for the switch to 'non-standard' or 'flexible' labour, which in the UK primarily refers to part-time jobs although it also encompasses aspects of self-employment, temporary working, variations in working arrangements (see Beatson, 1995; *Social Trends*, 26, Table 4.15), double-jobbing (see Bassett in *The Times*, 13 June 1995) and home working (*Social Trends*, 26, Table 4.16). The evidence from the Employers Labour Use survey indicates very strongly that firms employ part-time workers for tasks that require a limited time for their completion and to a lesser degree to match staffing levels to patterns of demand. Other factors such as cost savings, avoidance of unionisation and less employment protection are ultimately much less important.

The switch from full-time to part-time jobs and associated gender effects have resulted in a number of English counties and Scottish Regions having more female than male employees. Ironically, recent figures from the Equal Opportunities Com-

Figure 13.1   *Full-time and Part-time Employment by Sex, GB, 1984–96*

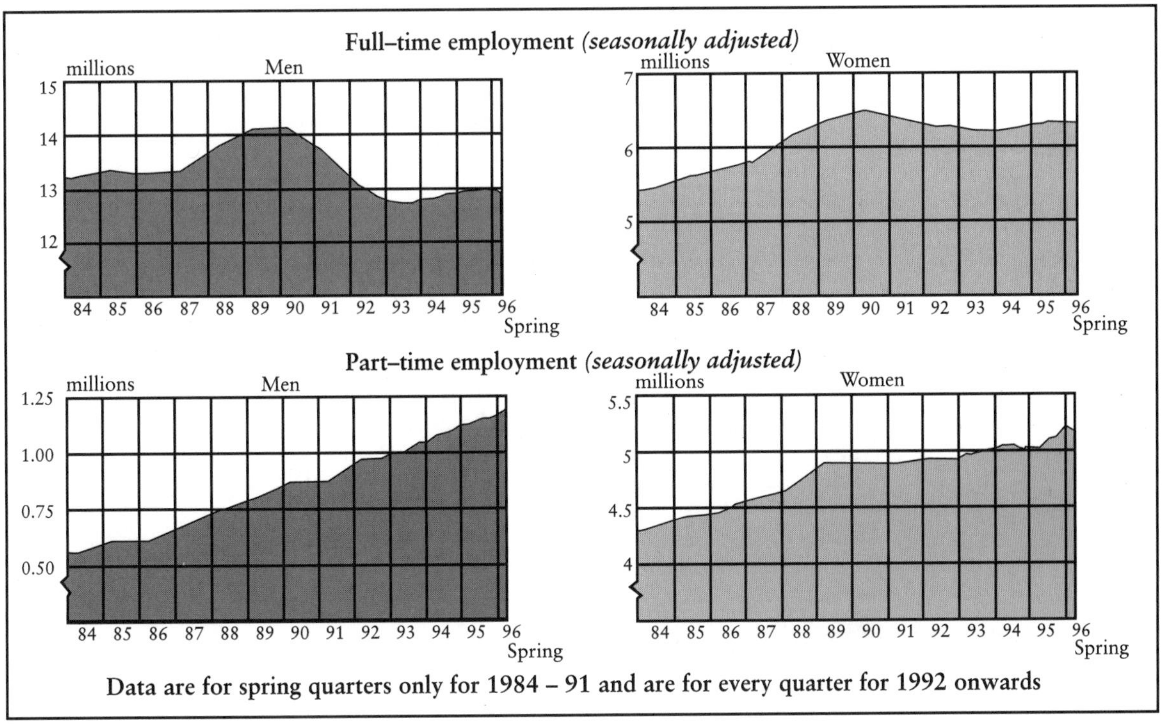

Full–time employment (*seasonally adjusted*)

Part–time employment (*seasonally adjusted*)

Data are for spring quarters only for 1984 – 91 and are for every quarter for 1992 onwards

Source: LFS Quarterly Bulletin (September 1996) p. 9.

mission revealed that 40 per cent of complaints now come from men fighting employer assumptions about the female nature of certain jobs. There can be no question but that UK employment laws and welfare regulations remain geared to a standard full-time working week even though that is becoming increasingly uncommon. This raises important issues about rights for part-timers, but it also indicates that something needs to be done urgently to make it more worthwhile for men to take up part-time work without excessive loss of benefits.

There is nevertheless an important distinction to be made between part-time and temporary work in the context of the EU at the present time. The prevalence of part-time work for women in the UK is, at least according to most of the evidence (see, in particular, *Employment Gazette*, May 1993; *Labour Market Trends*, July 1996, p. LFS38) largely a voluntary phenomenon which is mutually agreeable to both employer and employee.

Figure 13.2 reveals that there are relatively few temporary workers in the UK. Temporary workers are, however, becoming more prevalent and, in Great Britain, there were in total 1.6 million in Winter 1995–96 (7.1 per cent of all employees) of whom 890 000 were men (see also *Financial Times*, 1 February 1996 and 10 July 1996 for higher recent estimates). Of these, 40 per cent sought, but could not find, a permanent job (see *Labour Market Trends*, July 1996, p. LFS38). At present, most EU countries have minimum wage laws which discourage full-time employment. Social security costs are also often much higher than in the UK. The most important factor is, however, the cost of firing rather than of hiring. It is relatively easy to fire full-time workers in the UK but extremely difficult in Spain where, unsurprisingly, employers have responded by putting one-third of the labour force onto temporary contracts.

It is helpful to bring together the data on the various types of non-standard work as shown in

Figure 13.2   *Temporary Employment in the EU, Spring 1994 (%)*

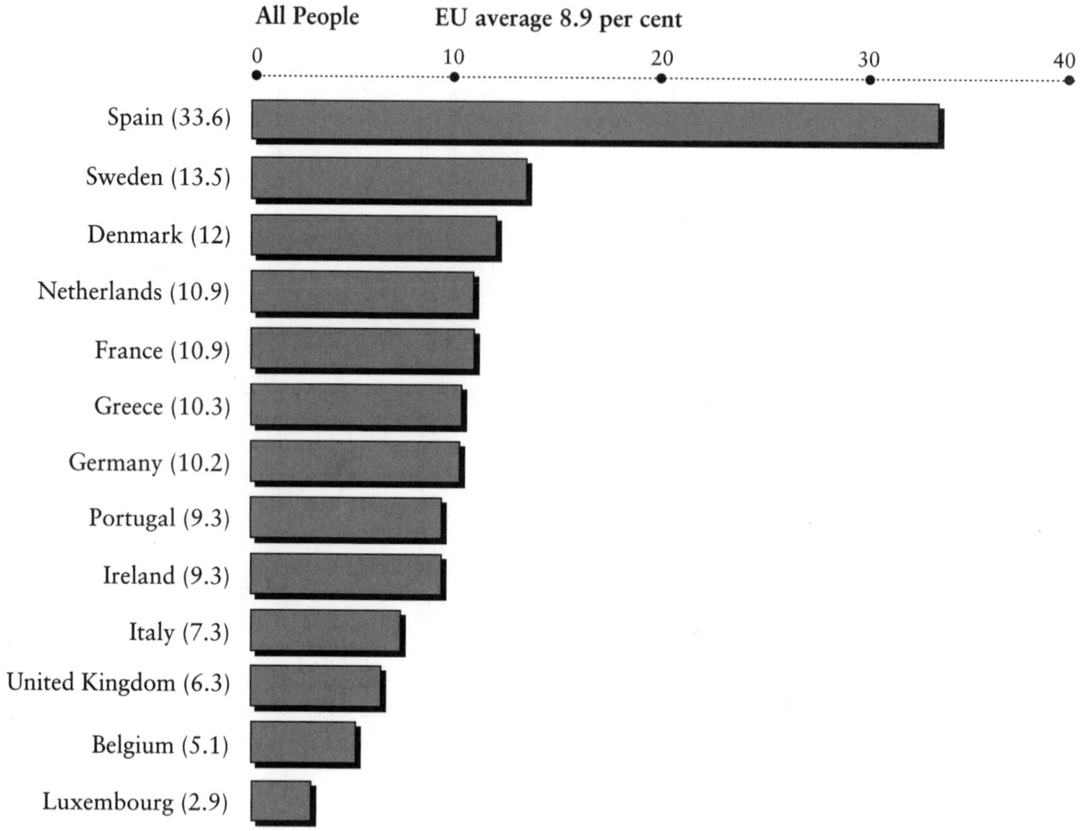

| All People | EU average 8.9 per cent |

| 0 | 10 | 20 | 30 | 40 |

- Spain (33.6)
- Sweden (13.5)
- Denmark (12)
- Netherlands (10.9)
- France (10.9)
- Greece (10.3)
- Germany (10.2)
- Portugal (9.3)
- Ireland (9.3)
- Italy (7.3)
- United Kingdom (6.3)
- Belgium (5.1)
- Luxembourg (2.9)

Source: Employment Gazette (September 1995) p. LFS48

Figure 13.3. Whilst each component does not rise steadily every year, the overall pattern is clear-cut.

The evidence for the UK, taking into account other relevant factors both microeconomic and macroeconomic, points fairly conclusively towards increasing flexibility (see Beatson, 1995, Table 1), although it must always be borne in mind that if part-time work is to be viewed as 'flexible', it is by no means a phenomenon associated with the past decade since there were 4 million part-time workers in 1971. Furthermore, many part-time jobs are every bit as permanent in practice as their full-time equivalents, and most self-employed persons would regard themselves as in permanent employment (see Gregg and Wadsworth, 1995).

Flexibility is desirable in that it permits firms to work closer to full capacity and hence to meet increased demand without running into capacity constraints. It also helps suppress upwards pressure on wages. The downside is that it introduces greater insecurity into employee contracts, to the point at which some employees find themselves working as 'portfolio workers', hopping from job to job and in and out of education, or on a 'just-in-time' basis, with payment per actual hour worked. On the other hand, most successful companies in the past have been extremely protective towards their workforces, which is not altogether surprising since these will have accumulated company-specific skills (see, for example, *The Economist*, 8 July 1995, p. 77). It is not yet clear what

Figure 13.3 *Part-time, Temporary and Self-employed Workers as a Percentage of All Employees/Workforce; Great Britain 1971–1994*

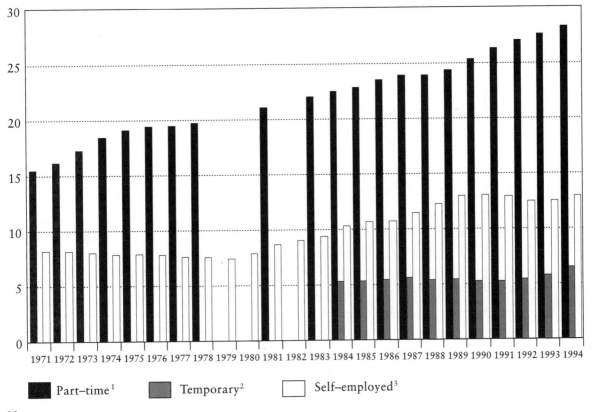

Percentage of employees/workforce

Part–time[1]   Temporary[2]   Self–employed[3]

Notes:
[1] Part-time employees as a percentage of all employees, June, seasonally adjusted.
[2] Temporary employees (self-defined) as a percentage of all employees, spring.
[3] Self-employed as a percentage of the workforce in employment, June, seasonally adjusted.
Source: Beatson (1995), Figure 1.

the effects of these trends will be, and caution is advised because there is inevitably a lot of scare-mongering in the media. Basically, it all boils down to who you are, where you are and what you do (see, for example, Bassett in *The Times*, 11 June 1996). In the UK, for example, the average duration of male jobs has fallen, whereas that for women has risen, compared to 1979, so it is possible to conclude that 'lifetime jobs' are still commonplace (see, for example, Taylor in *Financial Times*, 7 April 1995, 31 May 1995 and 8 March 1996; Burgess and Rees in *Financial Times*,

9 December 1994). Those in their middle years with skills have barely been touched by insecurity, whereas the relatively young and the relatively old, and especially the low-skilled among them, have indeed become much more insecure. An added factor is that although it is often fairly easy to obtain a new job, it is now less likely to be either full-time or permanent (for an analysis of job growth, see Bassett in *The Times*, 17 May 1995). Hence, people are afraid of losing their jobs only partly because it is becoming more likely, but also partly because the penalty for doing so is

becoming greater. An alternative view would be that job duration has fallen less than might have been expected because workers are much less willing to leave voluntarily than they were twenty years ago. Ultimately, insecurity is partly a fact of the labour market and partly a state of mind (contributing to the 'feel-bad' factor).

At a macroeconomic level, flexibility should enable the economy to respond to demand relatively early in the economic cycle, and there is evidence for this in that output began to rise only four quarters after the 1992 trough in GDP whereas it took eight quarters after the 1981 trough.

Employment growth has become a 'hot' issue in the EU, and is clearly linked to the issue of flexibility (for recent survey evidence see CEC (1995) which shows in Table 3 that flexible working practices are overall much the most common in the UK). During the decade to 1995, job growth in

the USA was 16.8 per cent or 1.6 per cent a year. Japan did almost as well, whereas France, Germany (and indeed, the UK) barely showed any improvement, particularly after 1990, and Italy actually lost jobs over the whole period (see *The Economist*, 29 June 1996, p.128 – the situation is much worse if men alone are considered). This provoked much agonizing within the European Commission (for example, see CEC, 1993), but with Continental Europe firmly setting its face (at least officially) against any extension of 'Anglo-Saxon' flexibility, it produced little of practical value to deal with the problem (Curwen, 1995).

■ 13.3 Unemployment

The most important measure of the demand for labour is unemployment. This represents the difference between the **workforce in employment**

Figure 13.4   *Workforce and Workforce in Employment,*[1] *UK, Seasonally Adjusted (million)*

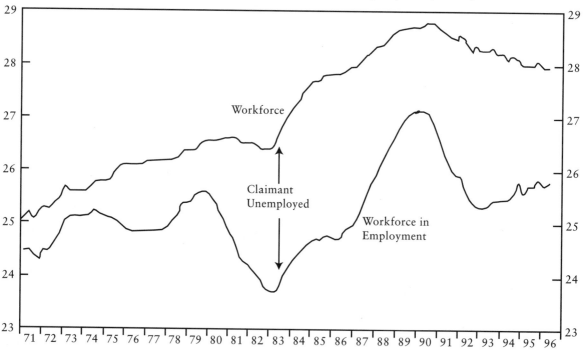

Note:
[1] As revised (see *Employment Gazette*, April 1991).
Source: *Economic Trends Annual Supplement* (1996 edn); *Labour Market Trends* (November 1996).

and the **workforce** (see box on **p. 334** above). This is illustrated in **Figure 13.4**, where the data have been adjusted to take account of the revisions referred to earlier with respect to calculating employment.

The trend in the number of unemployed can be seen more clearly in the form of **Figure 13.5** which also includes the number of vacancies notified to Job Centres. Unemployment is here measured according to the monthly claimant count (as reported in the newspapers: see section on measuring unemployment below). The total number of unemployed on this definition reached 1 million in December 1975, 2 million in March 1981 and 3 million in February 1985. The peak figure was 3.12 million recorded in July 1986. Subsequently, the number unemployed fell for 44 successive

months, reaching a low point of 1.60 million in March 1990, after which it grew rapidly to reach almost exactly 3 million in January 1993. It has subsequently fallen steadily to a figure of 2 million at the end of 1996. The pattern of the 1990s can be clearly distinguished from that of the 1980s in that the build-up to the peak was much faster.

Particular attention should be paid to the fact that the low point of each successive cycle lay above the preceding one. If that pattern is repeated, as is looking increasingly likely, unemployment can be expected to remain not much below two million even at the end of the current period of relatively strong growth of output.

An alternative way to express unemployment figures is as a **rate**, where the numbers in **Figure 13.5** are divided by the total workforce. This appears on an annual average basis in **Figure 13.6**, which also contains the unemployment rate for males and females separately. The most notable features of Figure 13.6 are, first, the very sharp upturn for males in 1980–81 (the rate for females rose to a much lesser degree) and in 1990–91, and

Figure 13.5 *Unemployment[1] and Vacancies,[2,3] UK, 1971–96 (million)*

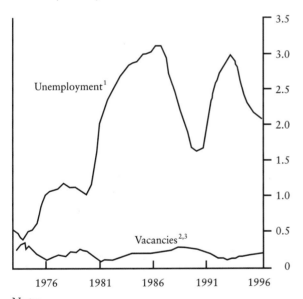

Notes:
[1] Seasonally adjusted unemployment (claimants aged 18 and over).
[2] About one-third of all vacancies are notified to Job Centres.
[3] Vacancy data prior to 1980 are not consistent with current coverage.

Source: Economic Trends Annual Supplement (1996 edn); Labour Market Trends, Table 2.1.

Figure 13.6 *Unemployment Rate,[1] Annual Averages, UK (%)*

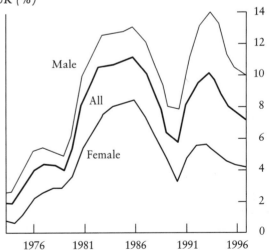

Note:
[1] The estimates use the seasonally adjusted series and are consistent with the current coverage of the claimant count. 1996 is a forecast.

Source: Labour Market Trends, Table 2.1.

secondly, the sharp downturn from the 1986 peak for both males and females. The rate for females may well be understated in practice since many among them do not accumulate the necessary National Insurance Contributions to qualify for unemployment benefit. Furthermore, unemployed women are less likely than men to say they are immediately available for work both because they often have to make arrangements for child-care and also because they may not perceive themselves to be unemployed when actively doing housework.

☐ 13.3.1 Stocks and Flows

The total number of persons who are unemployed is counted at a point in time, and thus represents a stock which we can call the **unemployment pool** (**Figure 13.7**). It is, however, important to remember that even if the unemployment pool remains unchanged in size from one point in time to another (conventionally one month later), this does not mean that the **same people** are continuously unemployed. In the course of a year, a very large

Figure 13.7   *The Unemployment Pool*

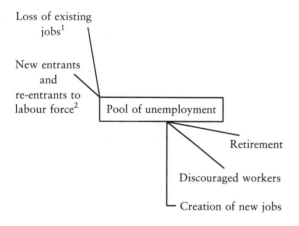

Notes:
[1] Loss of existing jobs can be voluntary or involuntary.
[2] New entrants and re-entrants consist of school leavers and college graduates; housewives; immigrants; the long-term sick and disabled; and those who do not wish to work.

number of people move in and out of employment, yet the unemployment pool will remain constant provided the inflow exactly matches the outflow.

In general, such exact matching does not occur either on a monthly or longer-term basis, as indicated in **Figure 13.8** which plots the inflow and outflow of both males and females combined during the period commencing February 1995. This was a period during which the total number of unemployed people fell in the majority of months on a seasonally adjusted basis. It can be seen that the numbers involved in these flows are very large in relation to the total unemployment pool of between 2.0 and 2.5 million. Outflows typically lag inflows by by just over a year, which is roughly equal to the average duration of unemployment (see *Employment Gazette*, September 1995, p. 355).

What **Figure 13.8** does not reveal is any information about the **characteristics** of those who entered and exited from the pool, nor the **reasons** why they did so. Nor does it tell us anything specific about the **duration of unemployment**, since it might be the case either that the outflow during the period comprised almost entirely those flowing in, in which case most of those unemployed at the beginning of the period would still be unemployed at the end, or that the outflow comprised almost entirely those unemployed at the beginning of the period, in which case the average duration of unemployment would be dropping rapidly.

There are two categories of people who enter the unemployment pool. First, there are those people who have lost a job previously held, either voluntarily by giving notice or involuntarily by being made redundant. This constitutes 55–65 per cent of the total. Secondly, there are those people who are either entering the labour force for the first time or re-entering after a gap and who have no job to go to directly. This latter category has a number of distinct elements, namely school leavers and college graduates (normally about 15 per cent of the total); those, most commonly housewives, who have been engaged in economic activity not recognised in official statistics as 'employment' (normally about 20 per cent of the total, but

Figure 13.8 *UK Unemployment Flows, February 1992–July 1993 (thousand)[1]*

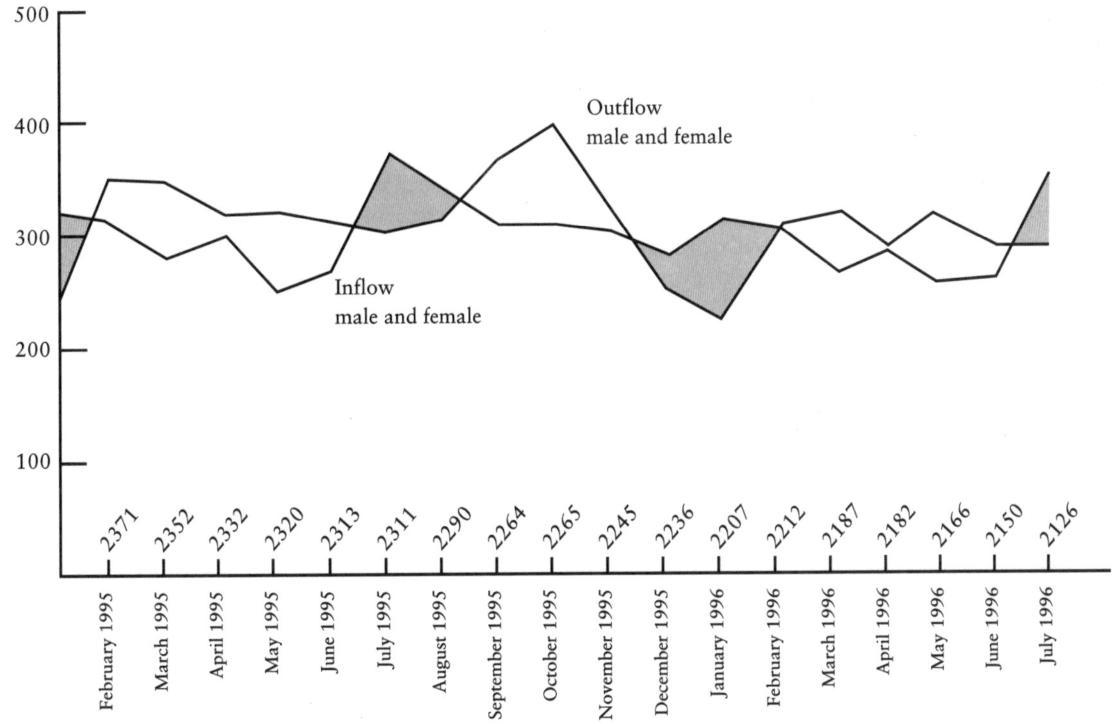

Notes:
[1] Not seasonally adjusted, standardised to $4\frac{1}{3}$-week months.
[2] Number of unemployed, seasonally adjusted (thousand).
Source: :Labour Market Trends, Tables 2.1 and 2.19.

nearly half of all females); immigrants; the long-term sick and disabled; and those not wishing to work.

It is immediately evident that the unemployment pool cannot be held constant simply by creating a new job for each person who loses one. In order to achieve that objective, the total outflow must equal the total inflow including those who have never previously been employed. In effect, jobs must be created much faster than they are being lost if the unemployment pool is not to grow. There are, admittedly, devices open to a government to mitigate this problem such as the obligation that a school leaver enter a training scheme, but the general proposition remains valid. It is, therefore, understandable that a recession causes the number of unemployed to rise

sharply, since the unemployment pool is filling up both with those who have lost their jobs and with those who wish to enter the labour force for the first time. Equally, the pool will tend to empty fairly slowly since many of the jobs created as business picks up will be filled by new entrants to the labour force rather than by those already in the pool, especially where there is a mismatch in terms of skills, location, flexibility and so forth between the new jobs on offer and the workers in the unemployment pool.

The flow through the pool can also be affected by retirement of part of the existing workforce, either at the official retirement age or earlier. When a worker reaches retirement he or she may be replaced by another person, in which case the post will either be filled by employing someone who is not registered as unemployed (which will not affect the unemployment pool although the unemployment **rate** will fall) or by someone who is registered as unemployed (which will reduce both the unemployment pool and the unemployment rate). Where a retired person is not replaced the labour force will shrink, and since this will not affect the unemployment pool the unemployment rate will rise.

A further issue is concerned with the tendency of certain workers who end up in the unemployment pool, or prospective workers who go straight into the pool without ever having had a job, to become **discouraged** by this experience. Under such circumstances they might decide not to continue to search for work, and thereby to cease to be qualified according to the rules as an unemployed person. While this would cause the unemployment pool to shrink, it would do so in a way which disguised the full extent of the unemployment problem.

We would expect the unemployment pool to empty fairly slowly were employers to decide, as a consequence of a recession, to alter their hiring practices. During the period of 'full' employment, essentially the 1950s and 1960s, labour was in short supply and hence employers were reluctant to shed labour in the face of a downturn in demand. In effect, they expected downturns to be short-lived because of governments' commitment to the principles of Keynesian demand management, and although some savings would be possible were workers to be laid off, these would be offset by any additional costs of training replacement workers were the laid-off workers to have found alternative employment in the interim. In that sense **underemployment**, rather than unemployment, was a characteristic of periods of depressed demand.

However, once the commitment to 'full' employment has gone by the board, and a prolonged recession becomes a realistic scenario, it becomes more cost-effective to lay off workers than to hold them on the books. The election of the Thatcher government in 1979 and the severe recession which followed understandably, therefore, caused a sharp upturn in official unemployment which reflected in part a decline in the hoarding of labour. Equally, when demand picked up again after 1981, most firms did not rush out to take on additional permanent full-time staff who might not be needed in the longer term, but rather preferred either to increase the hours worked by existing workers, to take on part-time workers or to sub-contract certain activities. As a result, the unemployment pool was much slower to empty than in previous periods.

The experience of the early 1990s was in part a consequence of the experience of the 1980s. There is good reason to believe that firms responded much faster to the 1990–92 recession than the previous time around, but in so doing they almost certainly over-reacted, laying-off so many employees that they could not cope with improved order books when demand began to pick up again. Consequently, they were obliged to rehire some of those who had been made redundant, in the process bringing the rise in the numbers unemployed to a halt much earlier than could have been predicted on the basis of prior experience.

There is one other factor of particular interest when comparing the recession of 1990–92 to its predecessors. Manufacturing once again lost the great majority of jobs, but whereas previously the same 10 to 15 per cent of the workforce moved in and out of employment, unemployment in 1990–92 extended much further both occupationally and regionally. As a result, roughly 25 per cent of the workforce became unemployed at least once during the latter period which in turn affected confidence much more severely than had previously been customary.

13.3.2 Measuring Unemployment

Unemployment can be measured in different ways, but there are two basic approaches to collecting the information. The first uses surveys of individuals asking about whether they have a job or would like work, and the steps they have taken to find work, and the second counts people recorded as unemployed at government offices (for a full history of unemployment statistics since 1881, see Denman and McDonald, 1996).

In Great Britain, the main survey is the **Labour Force Survey** (LFS), the results of which were published only every second year from 1973 to 1983, annually from 1984 to 1991 and quarterly from 1992. Since 1984, the definition of unemployment used has been made compatible with that of the International Labour Office (ILO), and comprises people who:

- are without a paid job.
- are available to start in the next fortnight.
- have either looked for work at some time in the previous four weeks or are waiting to start a job already obtained.

The ILO definition is used both by the OECD and the US Bureau of Labor Statistics, and hence provides a standardised basis for international comparisons of unemployment. The ILO's unemployment rate is expressed as a proportion of the corresponding estimate of economically active people (employed **plus** unemployed).

Since, however, surveys are expensive and take time to process, the UK, in common with most EU countries, uses as its main monthly indicator of unemployment the count of those registered as unemployed. Since October 1982, the monthly figures have been based directly on the number of people claiming benefits at unemployment benefit offices, known as the **claimant count**. It is the frequency with which results are available that makes the monthly count the most widely-quoted measure of unemployment.

'Claimants' include those people who claim Unemployment Benefit, Income Support and National Insurance Credits and who are out of work, available for, capable of and actively seeking employment. They are counted in mid-month. Unemployment rates based on the claimant count are expressed as a percentage of the corresponding

Figure 13.9 *Comparison of Alternative Measures of Unemployment*

United Kingdom

Millions

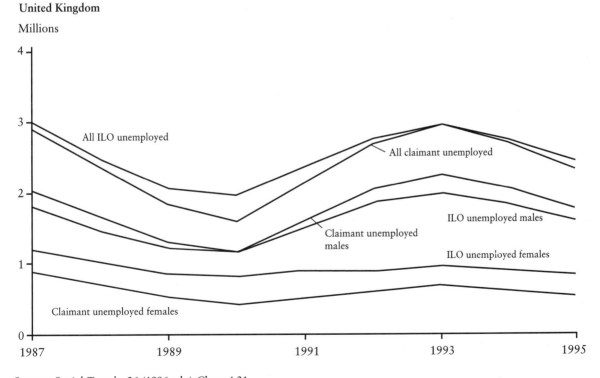

Source: Social Trends, 26 (1996 edn) Chart 4.21.

mid-month estimate of the workforce. These rates are available on a seasonally-adjusted basis going back to 1971 in a series which is consistent with the current coverage of the count.

The latest LFS which has been fully analyzed at the time of writing is that for Winter 1995–96. In order to reconcile this number with the claimant count, unemployment must be confined to those aged 18 and over because in September 1988 a guaranteed place on a Youth Training Scheme was offered to all 16- and 17-year-olds, which effectively removed them all from the claimant count. The LFS/ILO figure accordingly needs to be adjusted down. The residual link between the two series is more complicated than might be expected, given the proximity of the figures at certain points in time as illustrated in **Figure 13.9**. The key point is that only some 60 per cent of the LFS/ILO unemployed are claimants and only some 60 per cent of claimants are LFS/ILO unemployed. Nevertheless, in practice, the two series could still tell the same story.

In practice, the claimant count had been rising to Spring 1986, whereas during the same period the ILO measure had fallen from its Spring 1984 peak. During the period Spring 1986 to Spring 1989 the claimant count fell rapidly, by 1.23 million in total, whereas the ILO measure fell by only 0.99 million during the same period. During 1987 and 1989, the numbers ceasing to search for work according to the ILO definition were heavily outweighed by the numbers ceasing to claim benefit. During 1988 and 1989, there was a surge in the number of people taking up new full-time jobs. When a claimant takes up employment, he or she necessarily forgoes benefits. There is accordingly little financial advantage in taking up a part-time job. A drop in the number of claimants is therefore likely to be associated with growth in full-time rather than part-time jobs, and the number of claimants did indeed fall sharply in 1988 and 1989. The more modest reduction in the ILO data is unsurprising given that most of those searching but not eligible to claim will be women looking for part-time jobs, and these grew more slowly than in previous years from 1988 to 1990.

As can be seen, significant discrepancies between the different measures largely disappeared as they were progressively put onto a standardised basis, but the gap apparently opened up again during 1990 before disappearing completely during 1992. It has subsequently opened up again, although it is possible to argue that minor discrepancies of a quarter million or less are inevitable and should be disregarded for policy-making purposes.

However, given that it is doubtful whether the definitional issue can ever be fully laid to rest, the measurement of unemployment provides an excellent subject for a game of political football. Critics on the far right of the political spectrum argue, for example, that the unemployed should exclude all those who could be in education and training; all those who could have retired early; all women, or at least all who are married; and all those who have been unemployed for less than six months. On their reckoning, therefore, unemployment is largely an illusion. Critics on the far left argue to the contrary, claiming that unemployment is not merely real but understated. This is because many people do not choose to register as available to work, and also because the Conservative government has deliberately distorted the official figures.

There can be no doubt that the Conservative government changed the methods of recording unemployment statistics after it was first elected in 1979. According to the version of events proposed by the Unemployment Unit, there were 31 alleged 'changes' to the claimant count between 1 October 1979 and 31 February 1994 (see Fenwick and Denman, 1995). In every case except one the changes caused the numbers of unemployed to fall, so it is fair to say that the government was in effect being accused of 'fiddling' the statistics.

It has to be borne in mind, however, that many of the changes resulted from a genuine desire to improve accuracy and from an obligation to bring the statistics into line with international practice. Furthermore, it should not be forgotten that even if the official figures are indeed understated, no account is taken of those who, despite being officially unemployed, are economically active in the black economy.

There are accordingly grounds in principle for expecting the official figures to be simultaneously both overstated and understated, and these effects

Table 13.7 *Changes in the Official Method of Recording Unemployment Statistics, 1979–94*

Date	Change	Effect on numbers
Oct. 1979	Fortnightly payment of benefits	+20 000
Nov. 1981	Men 60 and over offered higher supplementary benefit to leave the working population	−37 000
Oct. 1982	Registration at Job Centres made voluntary; Computer count of benefit claimants substituted for clerical count of registrants	−190 000
Apr. 1983	Men 60 and over, not entitled to benefits, no longer required to sign on to receive National Insurance Credits	−108 000
June 1983	Men 60 and over, entitled to long-term supplementary benefit, no longer required to sign on	−54 000
July 1985	Discrepancies in Northern Ireland count corrected	−5 000
Mar. 1986	Two-week delay in compilation of figures to reduce over-recording	−50 000
Sep. 1988	Removal of all under-18s who have left school and not found a job but guaranteed a YTS place	−40 000
July 1989	Changes in conditions of the Redundant Mineworkers Payment Scheme	−15 500
Feb. 1994	System for administering benefits in Northern Ireland fully integrated into UK system	−1 500

Source: Labour Market Trends (November 1995).

inevitably cancel out to a considerable extent. However, this still leaves open the question as to how much of any reduction in unemployment is the result of justifiable government policy and how much is due to statistical chicanery.

According to the government statistical service, there are two methods of maintaining the statistical integrity of the claimant count. The first method is to recalculate a series backwards in order to keep the historical coverage consistent with the current criteria for claiming benefits. This recasting approach is perceived to be conceptually superior and more accurate than the alternative method which is to maintain a consistent series using a measure based on previous benefit rules. On that basis, Employment Department statisticians claim that during the period there were only 9 discontinuities relevant to the coverage of the claimant count and where the numerical effect was significant enough to be included. Of the remaining 22, 10 were held to be discontinuities of negligible effect and the rest to be irrelevant for various reasons (set out in *Labour Market Trends*, November 1995, pp. 398–400).

Of the 9 official changes, the first of only two official redefinitions took place in October 1982 for two connected reasons. At this time, the old system of registering at an unemployment centre for both benefits and another job was abolished. Under the old system, an unemployed worker would receive benefits and might be offered a choice of three jobs from which to pick one. If s/he refused the job offers and could not find alternative work, s/he might forfeit benefits. The system thus contained an incentive to find work and not to stay unemployed unnecessarily. What the new system did was to split the payment of benefits (which was handed over the DHSS) from the problem of finding a job. The argument for the changes was that it would improve efficiency by enabling the staff at Job Centres to concentrate on trying to fit workers to suitable jobs. However, the split meant that there was no compulsion to register at the Centres and the effect was to decrease measured unemployment.

The second official redefinition took place in March 1986 when the production of the monthly figures was deferred by two weeks to take place three weeks instead of one week after the specified count date. The change was necessary to take account of those who had already ceased to be unemployed on the count day but had not yet been removed from the register.

Officially, there have been a further 7 significant changes to the **rules** concerned with benefit entitlement. These are listed briefly in **Table 13.7**. These 7, plus the other two definitional changes, are accommodated in the consistent (seasonally adjusted) claimant count which goes back to 1971, and which it is claimed offers a distortion-free comparison over time. There have also been two changes to the way in which unemployment **rates** have been calculated. In July 1986, the denominator of the equation was expanded, in particular to take account of the much enlarged number of self-employed. This, given an unchanged numerator, inevitably caused the rate to fall. The denominator was expanded further in July 1988 with the inclusion of those on work-related government training schemes. However, this followed their inclusion in the statistics of the employed workforce and had very little effect on the rate of unemployment. These changes in the way unemployment rates have been calculated have not, however, affected the **numbers** included in the unemployment count.

Insofar as the accusation of fiddling the numbers can be made to stick it relates, firstly, to the introduction of the 'Restart' programme and the introduction of tighter 'availability-for-work' tests in 1986 and, secondly, to the 'actively seeking work' clause in the Social Security Act 1989. These changes can be justified insofar as they weeded out people who should not have been on the unemployment register in the first place. They are excluded from **Table 13.7** because, effectively, they involved neither a change in rules nor a change in the coverage of the count. Nevertheless, they accounted for a reduction in the official count of the unemployed, and therefore created the reasonable suspicion that the government was trying simultaneously to claim credit both for generating a huge fall in unemployment and for cleaning up the statistics.

The most recent episodes concerned the replacement of Sickness Benefit and Invalidity Benefit by Incapacity Benefit in April 1995, and the introduction of the Jobseeker's Allowance in October 1996 (see Fenwick and Denman, 1995). The first was deemed to be irrelevant, but the latter may prove significant enough to require a recasting of the unemployment series (see also House of Commons, 1996, p. xvii).

The House of Commons Employment Committee recently gave the issue of measuring unemployment a good airing. They concluded (*ibid.*, p. xxvii) that:

> We have no reason to believe that there has been any attempt deliberately to manipulate the statistics, in order to claim a reduction in unemployment.

13.3.3 Unemployment by Age, Duration and Sex

The overall position in the UK as of April 1996, when there were 2.2 million unemployed according to the claimant count, is shown in **Figure 13.10**. In each case the unemployed are broken down into three age groups, namely 18–24, 25–49 and over 50 respectively, and also according to the duration of unemployment, namely up to 25 weeks, 26–52 weeks and over 52 weeks respectively. Each sub-section thus represents a combination of a specific age group and duration. The proportion of all those who fell into each sub-section who were male is also specified (and hence by subtraction from 100 per cent the proportion who were female can be deduced).

If one compares the situation in April 1987 when total unemployment stood at 3.1 million, with that in April 1993 when there were 3 million unemployed, it is interesting to note that the relationship between age and unemployment was very similar despite the sharp drop in unemployment during the interim period. In 1987, there was a little less unemployment in the 25–49 age group and a little more in the others. Of greater importance was the change in duration. Whereas 38 per cent of the unemployed were unemployed for up to 26 weeks in April 1987, this had risen to 42 per cent in April 1989 and to 57 per cent in July

Figure 13.10   *UK Claimant Unemployment by Age, Duration and Sex, April 1996 (000)*

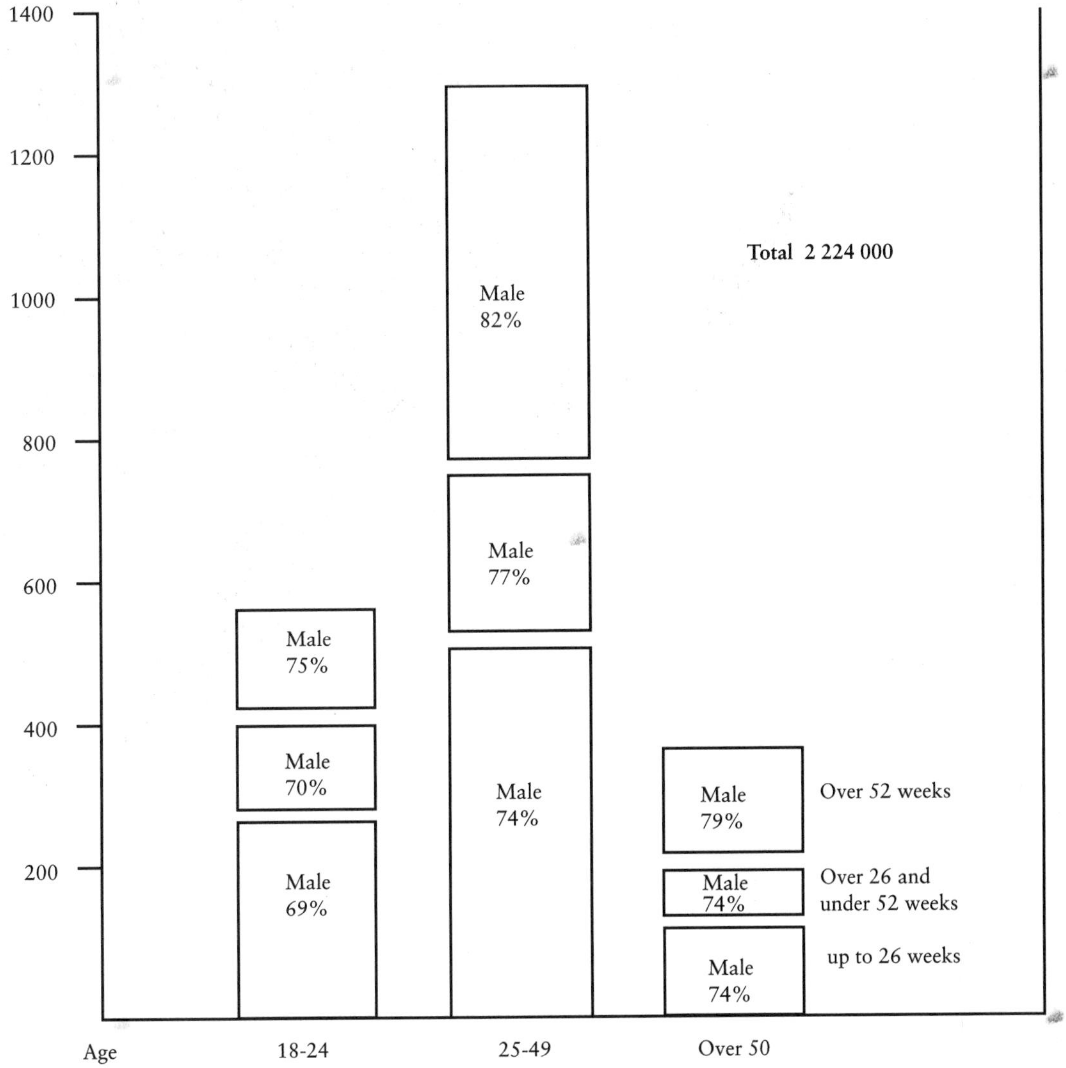

Source: Labour Market Trends (June 1996), Table 2.5.

1990. However, by 1993 it was only back to the 1989 figure rather than to that of 1987. The most significant fall occurred among those unemployed for over one year, where the percentage fell from 42 per cent in April 1987 to 40 per cent in April 1989 and then to 31.5 per cent in July 1990. By 1993 the percentage had risen back only to 34 per cent.

This clearly demonstrated that **unemployment becomes increasingly transient** during a period of economic growth. Unfortunately, it also demonstrated that long-term unemployment was both far more pervasive than it was during the period of 'full' employment after 1945 and also that it was likely to stay that way in spite of the improvement during the late 1980s. Nevertheless, compared to other advanced economies the UK's record, as shown below, was by no means one of the worst.

By April 1996, overall unemployment had fallen by one quarter and was still on a downward trend, albeit very slowly. It had fallen most in the youngest age group, and least in the middle age group, but this still left the former group with the highest rate and the latter group with the lowest rate. 44 per cent of the unemployed, much the same as in 1993, were unemployed for up to 26 weeks, and the long-term unemployment proportion was slightly higher at 36 per cent.

Figure 13.10 also contains information on the relative incidence of unemployment on males and females. Most of the percentages fall within the 70/30–80/20 range, but it is notable that, first, females are disproportionately likely to be unemployed in the 18–24 age bracket and disproportionately unlikely to be unemployed in the 25–49 age bracket for periods in excess of one year (both factors have now held good for a decade). The fact that, as a general rule of thumb, males are three times as likely to be unemployed as females, irrespective of age or duration of unemployment, is clearly less to do with aggregate numbers (see the earlier discussion on activity rates) than with the particular sectors in which redundancies have occurred and with the willingness of females to take up part-time jobs which may be plentiful but nevertheless shunned by most unemployed males.

It should be noted that the LFS/ILO data produce rather different results to the above (see *Social Trends, 26,* Tables 4.23 and 4.24) although the age divisions are also slightly different.

☐ *13.3.4 Non-Employment*

The relatively low number of those who are officially unemployed at age 50 or over is almost certainly deceptive. According to the OECD, and to Incomes Data Services in the UK (and, indeed, everyday experience), formal employment for men and women aged 55 or over is going out of fashion in the industrialised world. A recent figure for males in the USA is 37 per cent, compared to 33 per cent in the UK, 28 per cent in

France and 11 per cent in Italy. The figures for females are at roughly half these levels. Two decades ago, the figures were typically 60–70 per cent higher.

The sum of those of working age who are either unemployed or economically inactive is referred to as **non-employment**, which is estimated to apply to 25 per cent of men and 50 per cent of women over 50 throughout the OECD. The OECD blame these high figures on social security rules, occupational pension schemes and a large increase in the number of people covered by sickness and invalidity schemes. In the UK roughly the same number of people were claiming sickness and invalidity benefit in 1986 as in 1980, whereas by 1990 the number of male claimants had risen by 25 per cent and of women claimants had more than doubled.

Non-employment can usefully be expressed as a rate by dividing the population of working age without employment by the population of working age. The non-employment rate not unnaturally broadly replicates the pattern of unemployment if they are superimposed (see *Bank of England Inflation Report,* August 1996, Chart 4.4). It was only a little below the LFS/ILO unemployment rate line during the mid-1980s boom, and only a little below it during 1989–91. Unusually, however, after 1993 the non-employment rate fell very little at a time when unemployment fell sharply, opening up a substantial gap between the trend lines. This indicated either that more people were becoming discouraged or that more people were entering further/higher education. Using a 8-year moving average demonstrates that non-employment has been on a gradual downwards trend since 1988 (*ibid.,* Chart 4.5).

Normally, lower unemployment would also be associated with lower inactivity as a specific element of non-employment. However, the inactivity rate has not fallen more than fractionally since 1990 (see *Bank of England Inflation Report,* May 1996, Chart 4.5), and here it is evident that since the early 1990s the sharp increase in student numbers has been reflected in sustained inactivity rates.

Discouraged workers, defined as those who would like to work but have not looked for it in the past four weeks because they do not believe it is available, are numerically small at roughly 125 000 in early 1996.

These distinctions are helpful but are generally rather broad-brush (possibly lumping together students, housewives and the retired). Nevertheless, it can be argued that unemployment should be defined to include not merely discouraged workers but also 'involuntary part-timers' (see *The Economist*, 1995b). The evidence supporting this contention is in reality somewhat tenuous, but it is worth noting apropos the discussion below that certain countries such as Japan would be heavily affected by a change in definition of this kind (see *The Economist*, 1 July 1995, p. 58) which would make little difference in the case of the UK

13.3.5 Long-term Unemployment

Just as employment becomes more transient for individuals in booms, so it becomes increasingly drawn-out in recessions. Depending upon whether one is using the claimant count (*Employment Gazette*, September 1995, pp. 352–6) or the LFS (*LFS Quarterly Bulletin*; *Social Trends*, 26, Table 4.24) the scale of the problem represented by those unemployed for one year or more differs somewhat, but remains severe. Nevertheless, a number of EU countries normally have a far worse record if the long-term unemployed are represented as a proportion of the total unemployed, especially Ireland, Spain, Italy and Belgium. These can be compared with the far lower proportions in the USA and Japan, and also with Norway which devotes considerable resources to the prevention of long-term unemployment.

It is notable that far more Americans lose their job every month (roughly 2 per cent) than workers in the EU (roughly 0.3 per cent in France and Germany), yet they remain unemployed for an average of only 2.5 months, much less than is typical in the EU. This reflects the very fluid labour market in the USA where workers move rapidly from one relatively low-paid service sector job to another and where, for example, there is a

tradition of working one's through college. This has helped to keep the US unemployment rate below that in the EU, where the immovable block of the long-term unemployed creates a base level of 3 to 4 per cent unemployment even at times of growth.

In most EU countries, the problem of long-term unemployment got worse during the 1980s, in some cases (such as Ireland and Greece) markedly so. Only in Britain, where the 1987 rate as a proportion of total unemployment was relatively high at 44 per cent (it had fluctuated between 10 and 20 per cent during most of the 1960s and 1970s), did the problem improve noticeably after the mid-1980s as the government began to address itself more seriously to remedying the problem by focusing labour market policies on the long-term unemployed. A key issue is that these must have an incentive to maintain active job status. In the early 1980s no such incentive existed, and numbers grew rapidly. The introduction of Restart interviews and tougher availability for work testing were crucial in accounting for the speed of the subsequent fall as well as the fact that the 1994 peak was 'only' 39 per cent of total unemployment. However, toughness alone is clearly insufficient, and high quality training and job search programmes are also needed.

As a corollary, the relatively high incidence of short-term unemployment in the UK in recent years is often cited as a key factor in explaining why unemployment has had an unusually depressive effect upon wages.

13.3.6 Unemployment and Qualifications

Over the past decade the unemployment rate has been higher for people with lower levels of qualification than for well-qualified people. For example, 12.6 per cent of economically active people with no formal qualifications were unemployed in Spring 1992, whereas among graduates and others with qualifications above GCE 'A'-level or equivalent the unemployment rate was only 4.3 per cent (see *Employment Gazette*, June 1993, p. 288).

Figure 13.11 *Regional Unemployment*

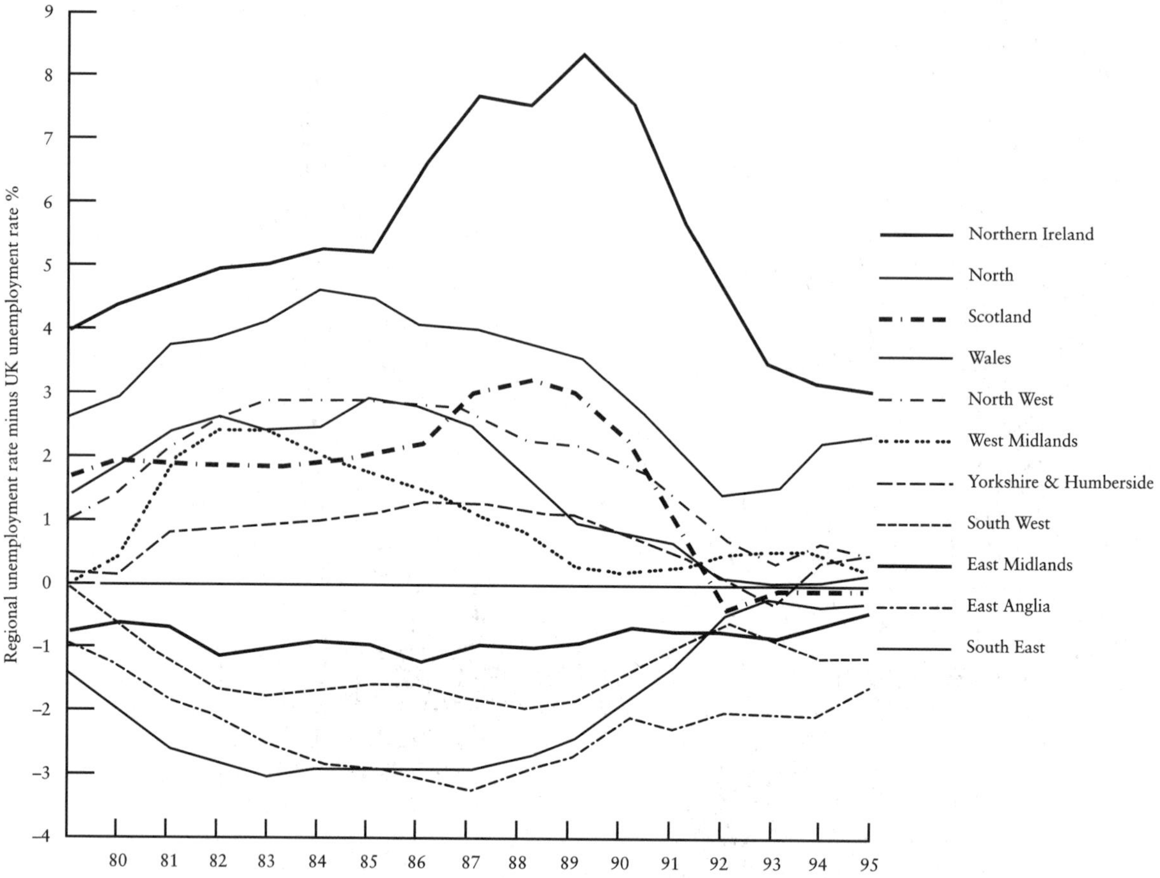

Source: *Employment Gazette*; *Labour Market Trends*, Table 2.3.

Qualification levels are closely related to age, with younger people tending to have higher levels of qualification. Those with higher levels of qualification tend to have been out of a job and looking for work for shorter periods than those with lesser or no qualifications.

13.3.7 Regional Dispersion of Unemployment

Figure 13.11 illustrates the changing pattern of the regional dispersion of unemployment since 1979, measured as the difference between the rate in each of the eleven regions of the UK and the UK average. By the standards of many other EU countries such as Italy, the regional disparities in the UK have never been particularly severe, and it is reasonable to treat Northern Ireland as something of a special case, permanently marooned at the top of the unemployment pile. As an approximation, excluding Northern Ireland, the region with the highest rate of unemployment suffered twice as much unemployment as the region with the lowest rate from 1979 to 1991, irrespective of the stage in the trade cycle.

Prior to 1979, the gap between lowest and highest had closed somewhat due to regional policy, but this was largely allowed to wither away after 1979. Despite this, the gap closed again at the end of the 1980s, and did so very rapidly after 1989, in which year the rate was 10.2 per cent in the North and 3.6 per cent in East Anglia. In 1992 the rate was 11.3 per cent in the North but 7.8 per cent in East Anglia, indicating clearly that the gap had largely closed from below.

The same regions have, with the exception of the South East, appeared consistently at the top and bottom of the distribution. From 1979 to 1991, the same regions also appeared consistently above and below the UK average. The experience of two regions since 1979 are nevertheless of particular note. In 1979, the West Midlands was still very prosperous, but the 1980–82 recession caused it to suffer a disproportionate rise in unemployment (up from 5 per cent in 1979 to 12.5 per cent in 1984). However, it improved markedly after 1986, is currently once again very close to the UK average. Secondly, Scotland, which enjoyed relatively little of the late-1980s prosperity, did best of all as the economy sank into recession and is now close to the UK average. This can be contrasted with the experience of the North, which appeared to be converging on the UK average only to move away again after 1992. Interestingly, East Anglia (with its small working population) has for the past decade had less unemployment even than the South East, partly as a result of improved communications.

Northern Ireland excepted, it would appear that the improvement in the employment situation to mid-1990 was fairly evenly dispersed. In contrast, whereas unemployment rose everywhere after the first half of 1991, the rate of increase was less severe in regions which were manufacturing for export than in the South East and South West which were far more dependent upon non-exportable services.

The evidence from the data is that unemployment fans out along a north-south axis. For the UK as a whole, unemployment first began to fall during the third quarter of 1986, whereas this occurred one quarter later in the case of Scotland. The UK average turned up again during the second quarter of 1990. In the South East and East Anglia, unemployment bottomed out during the fourth quarter of 1989 and one quarter later in the South West. By way of contrast it had not bottomed out until the third quarter of 1990 in the North West and it was still falling in Scotland and

Northern Ireland at the end of that year. The only real puzzle is that the first region to exhibit a reduction in unemployment was the North, a whole year earlier than in Scotland.

The consistency of the pecking order in terms of regional unemployment is a feature common to EU countries and Japan (with the UK exhibiting the most consistent order of all) but not to the USA. This suggests that it has its roots in labour immobility, and hence that it remained a feature of the UK economy in the absence of local wage bargaining and in the presence of wide regional house price differentials. The latter, at least, have been eroded significantly over the past five years and, as shown in **Figure 13.11**, seven of the eleven regions currently have remarkably similar rates of unemployment and there is no evidence at all for the kind of dispersion which was such a notable characteristic of the 1980s. Such circumstances do not indicate any urgent need for regional policy measures, but rather a need to focus upon specific unemployment blackspots, such as towns where the main industry has gone into terminal decline and the inner areas of large cities, irrespective of where they are located.

13.3.8 International Comparisons of Unemployment

It is possible to make international comparisons of unemployment using either national (but mostly incompatible) data or standardised data published by the OECD (see *Employment Gazette*, September 1992, pp. 421–31). **Table 13.8** presents the latest comparative standardised data for a selection of (mostly EU) developed countries. Whereas the UK rate is on the high side historically, it nevertheless looks more than acceptable by current standards compared to that in Spain and Ireland, not to mention the EU as a whole. The data at one point in time can, however, be deceptive since it does not indicate the direction of the trend line. **Figure 13.12** accordingly plots the OECD data over the past two decades for five major industrialised countries and for 8 members of the EU taken as an average.

Table 13.8 *Standardised Unemployment Rates*[1]

	% rate	Latest month
Spain	22.2	Feb. 1996
Finland	16.4	Aug. 1996
France	12.6	Aug. 1996
Ireland	12.5	Aug. 1996
Italy	12.1	Jul. 1995
EU average	11.2	Jul. 1996
Sweden	9.9	Jun. 1996
Canada	9.8	Jul. 1996
Belgium	9.2	Aug. 1996
Germany (West)	8.9	Jun. 1996
Australia	8.4	Jul. 1996
United Kingdom	8.0	Aug. 1996
Portugal	7.3	Dec. 1995
Netherlands	6.1	Jul. 1996
United States	5.1	Aug. 1996
Norway	5.0	May. 1996
Japan	3.4	Jul. 1996

Note:
[1] Seasonally adjusted OECD standardised rates.
Source: Labour Market Trends, Table 2.18.

There are, as ever, certain reservations that need to be borne in mind when interpreting the data. Relatively high unemployment, as in Spain, can be attributed in part to slow growth. Relatively low unemployment, as in Portugal, does not, however, necessarily have anything to do with rapid growth. In fact, it results from very low productivity. Activity rates are highly divergent as are rates of youth and female unemployment and rates of self-employment – matters which have been addressed above. Hence, it is important to compare like with like in assessing the performance of the UK in respect of unemployment. On that basis, the UK's record was undoubtedly satisfactory until 1974 and, in relation to countries other than West Germany and Japan, no worse than average until 1980 when the recession began to bite in earnest. Between 1979 and 1983, the UK's rate more than doubled, but this was less out of line with experience elsewhere in the EU than is generally believed to be the case. The rate in Spain, for example, also doubled from 8.5 to 17.2 per cent,

and indeed continued to rise to a peak of 21.4 per cent in 1985. Partly as a consequence (the rates in Ireland and the Netherlands were also very high by 1983), the rapid fall in the rate in the UK after 1986 (the turning point measured using national data) brought it down below the EU average and indeed very close to the rate being experienced in West Germany. In France, after rising continuously from 1974 to 1987 (a fourfold rise overall), the rate remained stubbornly high, registering 9 per cent in July 1990. At that time the rate in Ireland was 14.7 per cent and in Spain 16 per cent, compared to 6.2 per cent in the UK.

It would appear, therefore, that countries in the EU which chose not to engineer such a severe recession as was suffered by the UK during 1980–81 had initially made the wiser choice. However, the UK appeared to be reaping benefits in the longer term once unemployment began to fall after 1986. Countries elsewhere in the EU which preferred to protect jobs rather than restructure their economies during the early 1980s, discovered that their problems did not go away, and that the need, as in the case of France, to bring inflation down to West German levels in order to stave off devaluation in the EMS meant maintaining tight control on demand and hence high rates of unemployment.

When the UK also found itself under a similar constraint through joining the ERM, the UK rate rose briefly back through the EU average. However, once the UK departed the ERM the UK rate turned down sharply again even though it was either rising or falling more slowly elsewhere in the EU. Furthermore, it is now comfortably below that in West Germany and France, and considerably below that in Germany as a whole. The gender consequences of these divergent trends should prove interesting since over the past decade the UK has consistently been the only member state where the unemployment rate for women has been lower than that for men (Commission of the European Communities, 1992, Chart 6).

The data indicate clearly that unusually high rates of unemployment by historical standards are not a peculiarly British affliction. What is particularly interesting is why they do not affect Japan. Part of the answer is, as usual, a matter of statist-

Figure 13.12 *Unemployment Rates, International Comparisons, 1975–96 (%)*

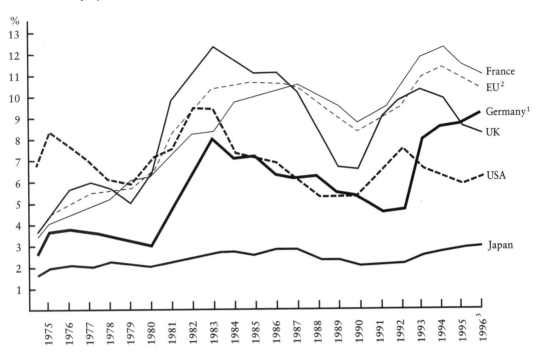

Notes:
[1] Germany unification took place at the end of 1990. These figures are cited in *Labour Market Trends* for West Germany.
[2] Germany, France, UK, Italy, Belgium, Netherlands, Portugal and Spain.
[3] Forecast.

Source: Social Trends, 23 (1993 edn), Chart 4.2.3; *Labour Market Trends*.

ical definition since it is far less common for part-time workers who lose their jobs in Japan to be recorded as actively seeking a new job than it is in the EU. More importantly, in terms of potential lessons for the UK, is the degree of **wage flexibility** in the Japanese labour market.

In Japan a significant element in the total wage bill consists of bonuses which are cut sharply during times of recession. This reduction in wages makes it possible for Japanese employers to keep their employees in work, and indeed in many cases to offer a virtual guarantee of life-long employment. In effect, rising wages are traded off against job security. Unfortunately, such an idea has been alien to the culture of the UK labour market, although the 1990–92 recession witnessed the introduction of Japanese-style agreements. So

long as workers in the UK regard an annual pay rise as their unalienable right, and furthermore a rise as large as that awarded to 'comparable' groups of workers, the UK's rate of unemployment will remain stubbornly high by Japanese standards even if it continues to improve relative to the EU.

13.3.9 Labour Market Flexibility Revisited

We have previously noted that the UK labour market appears to have become more flexible during the 1980s given the evidence of increased overtime working, part-time working and self-employment, and this can usefully be put forward as an explanatory factor for the relative improvement in the UK's unemployment performance. As usual, however, there is a downside. For example, it can be argued that temporary work may indeed be precisely that, and may lead subsequently to a (further) period of unemployment rather than to a permanent job. Further, part-time jobs, mostly undertaken by females, neither utilise properly such skills as the workforce possess nor offer many opportunities for skill acquisition and advancement. Finally, self-employment is partly a response to unemployment and utilises such skills as already exist without offering many opportunities for skill enhancement. In view of these factors it may be argued that the UK's labour market does not provide a model that others should try to emulate despite currently higher unemployment.

Clearly, a flexible labour market requires skills to be acquired **in advance of** their being needed, so that skill shortages do not automatically appear as soon as demand picks up. Furthermore, skills that are acquired must be **transferable**, rather than occupation or firm specific. During the 1980–81 recession, when training was predominantly privately funded, it mostly went by the board. This situation should not recur to the same degree given the public funding of training programmes, but there is a good way to go before there is a smooth transition between such programmes and full-time employment.

It may anyway be argued that the key issue for the UK is that what is needed is more flexibility with respect to pay rather than to jobs. During the 1980–81 recession wages remained too high and the recession manifested itself via a sharp upturn in unemployment. As noted elsewhere, this is not what happens in Japan where bonuses are cut rather than jobs when demand falls back.

Much of the problem lies with the fact that, in the UK, higher productivity is typically passed on as higher wages rather than as lower prices combined with job security. Whilst this can be justified for the individual firm, it is an undesirable outcome for the economy as a whole. This is firstly because higher wages inevitably leak into sectors where productivity is not rising, and therefore cause rising prices in these sectors. Secondly,

it is preferable that the real wage of workers should be increased by combining modest wage rises with constant or falling prices rather than by combining much higher wages with somewhat more slowly rising prices. Such a conclusion does not need to be spelled out in competing countries, but even a decade of Thatcherism largely failed to get the message through in the UK. The longer-term effects of the 1990–92 recession have so far proven to be more positive in this respect, but as noted in the discussion on inflation, the jury must remain out for now on the question as to whether or not wage inflation is set to flare up again, especially in the context of the forthcoming election.

☐ *13.3.10 Types of Unemployment*

It has become customary to divide unemployment up into four main types:

- **Frictional unemployment:** consists mainly of people temporarily out of work as they move from one job to another.
- **Structural unemployment:** arises when there is a mismatch of skills and job opportunities when the pattern of demand and output changes.
- **Demand-deficient unemployment:** otherwise known as Keynesian unemployment, it arises when demand falls and wages and prices have not yet adjusted to restore full employment.
- **Classical unemployment:** arises when the wage level stays above that at which the labour market will clear, possibly as a result of the exercise of union power or the existence of minimum wages legislation.

Unemployment can also be seasonal, but the unemployment data is normally 'seasonally-adjusted' to prevent this from showing up independently.

However, the current debate about unemployment is usually conducted in terms of whether it is **voluntary** or **involuntary**, although the distinction is not as clear-cut as it might seem at first sight. Unemployment is 'voluntary' if a worker is offered a job but is unwilling to accept it at the real wage on offer. Clearly, frictional unemployment is voluntary because the workers concerned have chosen to be temporarily unemployed while moving from one job to another (and it is anyway evident that such unemployment does not merit a policy response by the government to eliminate it – indeed, if it did not exist the economy could not evolve to meet changing patterns of demand). Structural unemployment can also be regarded as voluntary insofar as any worker who has become unemployed in one industry or occupation refuses to accept a job which is on offer in another occupation. The fact that the worker may find the job unappealing, or may consider the wage on offer to be lower than is acceptable, does not detract from the fact that such behaviour is voluntary.

Classical unemployment is also voluntary insofar as it occurs when a worker – or more likely a group of workers organised in a trade union – refuse to accept the wage on offer for existing or potential jobs. However, this is strictly true only if the trade union has been mandated by the workforce to seek a wage higher than the firm is willing to pay while keeping them all in employment. If an individual worker who is willing to work for a lower wage rather than become redundant is prevented from so doing through the behaviour of a union which he does not support, then he can be said to be 'involuntary' unemployed. Nevertheless, **involuntary** unemployment is **predominantly caused by a deficiency of demand** such as occurs during the downswing of the economic cycle.

Given the above distinction, it is possible to envisage the labour market when unemployment is purely **voluntary**. In other words, the level of demand is sufficiently high to provide a job for everyone who is willing to work at whatever real wage results from the equilibrium between the demand for, and supply of, labour in the labour market. In such circumstances it is reasonable to consider employment to be 'full'. However, this does not mean that, as was true during the 1950s when voluntary unemployment was predominantly frictional, fewer than half a million workers would currently be unemployed if demand was not deficient because, for various reasons, the numbers of those unwilling to work at the market-clearing real wage may have increased substantially.

The gap between the rate of unemployment which would exist were the labour market to be in equilibrium and the rate which actually exists at any point in time is known as the **natural rate of unemployment**. The natural rate cannot, by implication, be eliminated through a policy of generating additional demand. It is a problem which is created on the supply side of the economy and hence can be tackled only using **supply-side** measures.

13.3.11 Why is Unemployment so High?

At the beginning of the 1980s, unemployment was approximately ten times as high as it had been two decades earlier, and it has remained very high by postwar standards for the past decade. In many ways, it is easier to explain what did **not** cause this long-term adjustment to happen than to explain what did.

For example, it had little to do with the **growth in the labour force**. In the short term, an increase in activity rates or in the number of school leavers can create an excess supply of labour, but past experience in the UK, as well as experience overseas, demonstrates that demand adjusts to supply changes within a few years. Nor was **insufficient investment** to blame. It is evident that a given stock of capital can be combined with a variable number of workers by working it for longer hours. In any event, when capacity becomes scarce there is typically a surge in investment to enhance the capital stock, as in 1988.

It is also very difficult to demonstrate that **machines replace labour**, although new technology does cause temporary structural employment. If, for example, the typewriter was supposed to destroy the jobs of all those clerks inefficiently wielding quill pens, where did all the clerical jobs come from which the advent of the computer was subsequently supposed to destroy? As information processing speeds up, so more information gets processed!

Nevertheless, it has been argued that it is different this time around with computers because (1) they do not affect single industries but are all-pervasive; (2) the switch to computers has occurred so quickly that there has been insufficient time for the labour market to adapt; (3) work has become increasingly independent of its location (see *The Economist*, 1995a). Nevertheless, this tends to ignore the fact that improved technology makes societies richer and generates a demand for new goods and (particularly) services, and that computers themselves generate immense demands for labour intensive software to be developed, and so forth. The ultimate effects are frankly unpredictable (*The Economist*, for example, argues for rough neutrality) but it is clear that there will more likely be structural shifts within a given workforce rather than a change in the size of the workforce itself.

On a more positive note, Layard and Nickell (1986), examining male unemployment from 1956 to 1983, concluded that there were seven major contributory reasons for the upturn in unemployment, as shown in **Table 13.9**.

There was considerable variation in the contribution made by each factor cited, and during sub-periods several appeared to have had the effect of reducing unemployment. During the period up to the early 1970s, the second-strongest influence was exerted by unemployment benefit. In other words, as the **replacement rate** – the ratio of unemployment benefit to wages – rises, so workers become more selective about the jobs they are prepared to accept. However, it is notable that from the mid-1970s onwards this ceased to be a factor in rising unemployment because benefits ceased to rise relative to wages. Until 1974, only trade union power exerted a stronger influence, and one that remained constant up to the end of the decade, although by then it was making a proportionately smaller contribution to the higher level of unemployment. During the early 1980s, however, it became much less significant, which was to be expected given the effects of the recession and

Table 13.9 *The Causes of Male Unemployment in the UK*

	Effect on Unemployment Rate (%)		
Changes In	*1956–66 to 1967–74*	*1967–74 to 1975–79*	*1975–79 to 1980–83*
Employers' labour taxes	0.25	0.38	0.44
Unemployment benefit	0.54	−0.09	−0.10
Trade union power	1.18	1.17	0.80
Real import prices	−0.58	1.47	−0.93
Mismatch of skills	0.16	0.20	0.49
Incomes policy	–	−0.36	0.49
Demand factors	0.12	0.54	6.56

	1956–66	*1967–74*	*1975–79*	*1980–83*
Estimated 'natural' rate of unemployment	2.0	4.2	7.6	9.1
Actual rate of unemployment	2.0	3.8	6.8	13.8

Source: Layard and Nickell (1986).

the attack on union powers and privileges by the Thatcher government.

Throughout the period, employers' labour taxes remained a positive factor contributing to unemployment. This was only to be expected given that labour taxes have the effect of raising the marginal cost of employing additional workers. The mismatch of skills also continued to exert a positive influence which grew modestly throughout the period, but which in aggregate accounted for well under 10 per cent of male unemployment. Incomes policies made little contribution in any sub-period and were neutral taking the period as a whole.

During the middle sub-period, the biggest contribution was made by rising real import prices. In the face of the quadrupling in the price of oil and sharp increases in other commodity prices, many firms responded to the consequent costs by laying-off workers. However, real import prices also tend to fall significantly at times, and as can be seen reductions in real import prices were a factor – much the most significant factor – contributing to the maintenance of employment during the other sub-periods. Hence, in the long term, it is not to be expected that real import prices will exert a strong uni-directional force upon unemployment.

Prior to the latter part of the 1970s, demand management was used primarily to sustain employment, although to increasingly less effect as inflation came progressively to be regarded as a more important policy objective. By the end of the decade it had effectively been discarded as a means to maintain employment, and it was viciously reined back by the incoming Thatcher government. As **Table 13.9** shows, this swamped out all other factors contributing to the rise in unemployment at that time.

As can be seen in the lower part of **Table 13.9**, there was little difference between measured unemployment and estimates of the natural rate until the end of the 1970s. In other words, the slow but almost continuous rise in measured unemployment had little to do with a deficiency of demand and could largely be explained by supply-side factors. These factors also served to maintain the rise in unemployment during the early 1980s,

but were temporarily swamped by a massive dose of deflation, so it is hardly surprising that unemployment followed the pattern illustrated previously.

The natural rate is by its very nature a difficult concept to measure accurately, and there is no unanimity about Layard and Nickell's calculations (see Dawson, 1990). Nevertheless, the natural rate almost certainly began to fall after 1983, and there was subsequently, as we have seen, a four-year period during which measured unemployment fell continuously. The gap between the natural rate and actual unemployment is important because if actual unemployment exceeds the natural rate than the gap can be bridged by expanding demand without setting off an inflationary spiral, whereas if there is no gap an expansion of supply must precede any increase in demand if an inflationary spiral is to be avoided.

The relationship between inflation and unemployment can be used as an alternative means to identify the natural rate. When actual unemployment is less than the natural rate and there is excess demand in the labour market, inflation will tend to **accelerate** – in other words, it will be higher in any one time period than in the preceding period irrespective of what the rate was in the earlier period. Equally, when actual unemployment is greater than the natural rate, and there is excess supply in the labour market, inflation will tend to **decelerate**. When the two rates are identical, and the labour market is in equilibrium, inflation will consequently **remain steady at whatever rate exists at the time**. This is known as the NAIRU – **the non-accelerating inflation rate of unemployment**. Thus, in principle, the natural rate can be identified by the fact that the rate of inflation is neither rising nor falling.

In practice, this may not be easy to pin down. What is certain is that the natural rate shifted considerably during the 1980s as the supply conditions of the economy evolved under a variety of pressures, as shown in **Table 13.10**. A number of these are discussed in Chapter 14, such as the concerted attack upon trade union power and the insider-outsider distinction. Others were referred to in the earlier section on supply-side economics (see also *The Economist*, 1994b).

Table 13.10   *NAIRU Estimates for the UK (claimant definition)*

	Period within which the estimates fall:			
	1969–73	*1974–80*	*1981–87*	*1988–90*
NAIRU range	1.6%–5.6%	4.5%–7.3%	5.2%–9.9%	3.5%–8.1%
Actual U rate	2.5%	3.8%	10.1%	6.8%
Number of estimates	·11	13	15	5

Source: Bank of England Quarterly Bulletin (May 1993), Table 4.A.

If the supply-side measures have been successful, then the natural rate should be permanently lower in the 1990s compared to the 1980s. The Bank of England is hopeful, albeit cautious, in this regard (see *Bank of England Inflation Report*, August 1996, p. 37 – see also *The Economist*, 16 December 1995, p. 108 for a discussion in relation to the USA). Nevertheless, one problem which has, if anything, become harder to resolve is the mismatch between job-seekers and vacancies. While this could have something to do with increasing choosiness about jobs by those out of work, this is unlikely given the increasingly tight rules to qualify for unemployment benefit. It is much more likely to be due to imperfections in the housing market where there are big differences in house prices in different regions, and where jobs are normally most plentiful in areas where house prices are relatively high. The reduction in private sector rentals and the difficulties of exchanging council houses only make the problem worse.

13.3.12 Unemployment and Real Wages

During the 1980s, real wages rose exceptionally fast in the UK although they fell in the USA. However, this may simply have reflected relative productivity. Rising real wages which are wholly offset by rising productivity do not eat into profits, in which case there should be no need for firms to shed labour.

We have previously examined the trend in productivity, but what exactly is the link to real wages and jobs? Poret (1990) seeks to answer this question by setting real wages against productivity. Real wages are defined as nominal wages deflated by the private consumption deflator, while labour efficiency is defined as output per employee adjusted for the replacement of workers by increased capital investment. Poret divides the former by the latter and expresses this ratio as an index with the average value of the ratio for 1960–89 set at 100.

The ratio fell during the 1980s in virtually every OECD country. In 1989, the ratio was below its 1960–89 average with very few exceptions, among which the most prominent was Britain. From 1983–87 the ratio remained steady in Britain at around 95, but in 1989 it rose back up to 100 where it had previously been in 1981. So why was Britain so different?

The OECD study discovered that the biggest single factor in explaining the slower growth in real wages during the 1980s was basically the higher unemployment sustained during that decade. The study measured this using the gap between actual unemployment and the NAIRU (defined as the level at which unemployment exerts neither upwards nor downwards pressure on real wages relative to labour efficiency). As a proxy measure for this gap the study used a measure based on a moving average of actual unemployment.

After 1982, the gap opened up throughout the OECD. In 1989, it still existed in France (where, as we have noted, unemployment grew steadily during the 1980s), whereas in Britain, by 1989, the gap had become negative (actual unemployment less than the NAIRU, which was calculated at the time as 8 per cent) by two percentage points. This was the largest negative gap anywhere in the OECD. What this indicates is that unless unemployment is allowed to rise to at least the NAIRU then real wages in Britain are likely to exceed what is warranted by productivity. Supply-side reforms do not appear, on this evidence, to have made any difference to what has been a long-standing relationship (see also *Bank of England Inflation Report*, August 1996, p. 37).

13.3.13 The Reduction of Unemployment

Unemployment is colossally expensive for society; benefits for the unemployed currently cost the Exchequer roughly £14 billion a year, but the figure would be much higher were lost revenue from tax and NICs to be included, not to mention the cost of reduced output, lost trade, bad debts and social consequences. Clearly, therefore, unemployment should be reduced if humanly possible. Naturally, the problem is ultimately more complex than many commentators would like the public to believe, because the aim is simultaneously to create jobs, reduce unemployment and promote equality in incomes, and incompatibilities between these objectives mean that there cannot accordingly be any simple nostrum to make the problem disappear (for a more theoretical review of the reasons why people do not find work see Snower, 1993).

What we have established so far is that sharp, short-term changes in unemployment are normally demand-driven, whereas the medium to long-term adjustment takes place on the supply side. The use of demand management, when demand is deficient in the short term, is appropriate where the initial unemployment rate exceeds the NAIRU. For obvious reasons, it is undesirable to use it if there is subsequently going to be an inflationary spiral. Hence, insofar as additional demand is to be created, it must be targeted towards those parts of the economy where there is the greatest excess supply. Clearly, however, whenever the actual unemployment rate remains below

the NAIRU, the appropriate response must be to improve supply conditions in the labour market.

Taking a longer-term view, there is evidence that both demand and investment have been substantially the same in the EU and the USA. However, capital per worker in the EU has risen sharply whereas in the USA it has not. Hence, there has been a tendency in the EU to produce higher productivity from the existing workforce whereas in the USA more jobs have been forthcoming (see *The Economist*, 20 May 1995, p. 102). People with jobs have prospered as a result in the EU, whereas many have gained little, if anything, in the USA. However, it follows that if investment in the EU continues to be capital-intensive, it will prove difficult to create jobs.

The range of other possibilities is too great to warrant detailed coverage in this section. It includes, for example, macroeconomic stability; promoting entrepreneurial behaviour; increasing flexibility; reforming provisions governing job security; introducing pro-active labour market policies; and reforming tax/benefit systems. Some other solutions, like incomes policy, are popular in certain quarters, although only in a more flexible form than has been customary in the past. It is unlikely, however, that they will currently find favour in Labour let alone Conservative circles.

It should be remembered that if the problem is that there is insufficient incentive to take a job, then the answer is to reduce the burden of taxation and transfers on those at work. However, if the problem is primarily that regulations governing pay and working conditions make it uneconomic to hire workers, then it is these regulations which must be addressed. In practice, both aspects play a part, albeit one that varies from country to country, with the latter being more important in continental Europe than in the UK.

An alternative is to reduce taxation – or perhaps more appropriately, given the need to reduce labour costs, to reduce NICs, either for all workers in regions suffering severe unemployment or for all very low-paid workers. The payment of a working wage combined with minimal NICs is to be preferred to a policy of low wages combined with income support measures, although both may need to be used in practice.

Jobs can be increased by providing subsidies (see *The Economist*, 20 August 1994, p. 63) However, awkward problems arise in practice. For example, it is necessary to ensure that subsidies are not offered to an employer to provide jobs which he intended to fill in any case, and to ensure that workers are not subsidised who are going to find a job without a subsidy; Equally, subsidies should be directed only towards the provision of the kinds of high-skill jobs which are comparatively rare in the UK compared to its main competitors. Furthermore, subsidies should not be provided simply to deal with short-term problems, but should be associated with the provision of jobs which will be needed over the longer term.

On the whole, previous attempts to employ subsidies have met with very limited success. Clearly, therefore, these problems indicate the need for better targeting, and it has been proposed that a key element is to increase the subsidy in line with the length of unemployment, and in line with the amount of training provided. Giving a voucher to an unemployed worker may be inefficient since it may make him or her feel stigmatised, so a refundable tax credit may be a better way to provide the subsidy. The lack of targeting is, incidentally, a major problem with minimum wages since a large proportion of those who will be helped will be students working at the likes of Burger King.

Given that the low skills ethos in much of British industry has something to do with the influx into the labour market of ill-prepared 18-year-olds and part-time women workers, it is evident that something needs to be done to improve the long-term career aspirations of these groups. One of the key issues here is to ensure that the basic education, whether academic or vocational, provided both for school children and for those who re-enter the education system as mature entrants is comparable to that provided by successful competitors such as Germany. Nevertheless, this is inevitably a longer-term policy and better education and training do not create jobs *per se* but rather improve the productivity of those in work.

All of this may appear rather grandiose in relation to the apparent inability of governments to reform UK institutions in the past. For this reason, there are those who believe that the best solution which can be effected very quickly is to introduce a harsher regime for those who are out of work. In fact, as we have noted, the rules relating to eligibility for benefit were tightened up considerably during the 1980s, and the replacement rate, which stood at nearly 70 per cent in 1970 and remained well above 60 per cent until 1978, fell sharply to 59 per cent in 1979 and to only 41 per cent in 1982. It is currently even lower, and it seems unlikely that 'living off the dole' is any longer a comfortable prospect. Whether the unemployed should be 'forced' to do some kind of 'work' if they are to be entitled to any help from the state at all remains even more controversial (for a discussion of 'workfare' see **p. 381**).

It is also of crucial importance that information about the availability of jobs is circulated as efficiently as possible. During the 1970s, as disclosed previously, the provision of information about jobs was divorced from the payment of benefits. Job information came to be provided by the Job Centres which at that time were responsible to the Manpower Services Commission, and the payment of benefits was handed over to the DHSS. On the face of it, the Job Centres were very efficient: 40 per cent of vacancies were filled within one day and 68 per cent were filled within two weeks. However, employers notified only those vacancies to Job Centres which they thought they could deal with efficiently and, as previously noted, only about one third of all vacancies are notified to Job Centres.

Information is available on the job search methods of the unemployed from the Labour Force Survey (see *LFS Help-Line* in *Labour Market Trends*). Visiting a Job Centre or government employment office is a method of job search especially favoured by males and non-married females, whereas married females rely primarily upon studying situations vacant columns in newspapers. Answering advertisements and personal contacts and direct approaches to firms and employers are less popular. Private agencies are used by only a small minority.

Job Centres are favoured particularly by younger job seekers, whereas the use of situations vacant columns increases with age. Job Centres are used most frequently by the unskilled. As workers grow older and acquire some skills they turn increasingly to the newspapers. In effect, the state appears to provide a subsidised information service for low-income groups.

During the 1970s and well into the 1980s, Job Centres were ill-equipped to deal with the unemployed. One reason for their failure was the divorce of information transmission from both the provision of training and unemployment benefits. In an ideal system, these three functions would be brought together in an effort to assist the unemployed because the three functions address four issues – namely, the matching of an unemployed person with a vacancy; the length of time that a job is likely to last; the savings to the community of a person being permanently employed or placed on a training programme; and the costs to the community of a person being permanently unemployed. Unfortunately, the issues became separated in the 1970s, when the payment of unemployment benefit was handed over to the DHSS and there was no compulsion on the unemployed to use Job Centres. Moreover, when attempts were made to improve the efficiency of Job Centres by cutting costs, the Centres reacted by reducing the amount of assistance to the long-term unemployed, and as a result many of the costs of unemployment were transferred to the DHSS. In 1987, an attempt was made to improve the efficiency of Job Centres by linking advice and assistance through the Job Restart Scheme which was introduced to do something for the long-term unemployed. Nevertheless, there is room for further improvement in methods of information dissemination in the labour market.

One way of assessing the efficiency of job search is via an unemployment-vacancies (Beveridge) curve (see *Bank of England Inflation Report*, August 1996, Chart 4.12). During the 1960s and early 1970s, the relationship between unemployment and vacancies was fairly stable, but over the following decade the curve appeared to shift outwards. Since 1993, the curve has moved sharply inwards, indicating improved job search, so in this respect the necessary action appears to have been set in hand.

Finally, it is worthy of note that reducing the level of unemployment can be made more difficult by legislation introduced for other purposes. For example, the incentive to work has been affected adversely by the Social Security Act 1988. In the housing market the philosophy has been to allow rents to be set at market-clearing levels, both in the private and public rental sectors, and to target subsidies more narrowly upon those **families** unable to afford these rents, rather than to offer subsidies on all rented **houses** via, for example, rent controls. Under the 1988 Act, rent is determined by family income and circumstances, and hence when it rises so does housing benefit paid to eligible families. As a consequence, recipients of benefit have no incentive to quibble over rent increases. More importantly, the loss of benefits as income rises obviously creates a severe poverty trap even where incomes are reasonably high if, as in London, rents are also very high.

Another factor reflects rigidities in product markets rather than labour markets (see *The Economist*, 19 November 1994, p. 100). In the UK, as in the USA, factors such as reduced restrictions on opening hours and highly competitive retail markets have generated a lot of service sector jobs, especially in comparison to a country such as Germany.

In conclusion, certain basic facts need to be faced. In the UK since 1979 there have been dramatic changes in the labour market, some of which are discussed more fully in the chapter which follows. The labour market has been extensively deregulated, making it easier to hire and fire workers and encouraging the switch from male to female employment. The power of trade unions has been eroded with a consequent reduction in strike activity. The desirability of living off state benefits has been eroded. In addition, newly industrialised countries have increasingly taken over markets for manufactured products.

All of these factors have combined to diminish the job prospects of the low-skilled, poorly-educated male who wants a decently-paid, full-time job in manufacturing in the old industrial heartlands of the UK. So much for the problem. The UK believes that it has an answer of sorts, although there is inevitably a price to be paid in terms of increasing inequality, shifts in economic power between the sexes, growing insecurity and so forth. This price is seen as excessively high in many quarters, which is fair enough since 'excessive' is a subjective matter. Unfortunately, most of the allegedly objective alternatives are at best futile. For example, some EU countries favour an employment chapter in the treaty arising from the current inter-governmental conference (which will simply be ignored); some favour job targets (central planning lives again); some favour raising minimum standards (but why would this create as against destroy jobs?); some keeping out immigrants; some even sending women back to the kitchen (or leaving them there in the case of southern Europe).

Looking to the immediate future, there is a case to be made for taking a somewhat more relaxed view about the possible resurgence of inflation in order to stimulate an above-trend rate of growth. This entails risks, but ultimately without growth employment generation will probably stultify, so the risks seem acceptable. Equally, although it may do little directly to mitigate inequality in the short term, it should be remembered that, as in the USA, the increasingly well-off may be induced to give up DIY and employ tradesmen instead. Meanwhile, experiments with more sophisticated job subsidies, fine-tuning the tax/benefit system to avoid unemployment and poverty traps, and correcting the defects in the educational and training fields should pay dividends in the longer term.

Bibliography

Barrell, R. (ed.) (1994) *The UK Labour Market* (Cambridge: Cambridge University Press).

Bean, C. (1994) 'European Unemployment: A Retrospective', *European Economic Review, 38*, pp. 523–34.

Beatson, M. (1995) 'Progress Towards a Flexible Labour Market', *Employment Gazette* (February) pp. 55–66.

Blanchflower, D. (1984) 'Union Relative Wage Effects', *British Journal of Industrial Relations*, pp. 311–22.

Blanchflower, D., M. Stevens and A. Yates (1991) 'Unionisation and Employment Behaviour', *CLE Discussion Paper 339*.

Brown, W. and S. Wadhani (1990) 'The Economic Effects of Industrial Relations Legislation Since 1979', *National Institute Economic Review* (February).

Butcher, S. and Hart, D. (1995) 'An Analysis of Working Time 1979–1994', *Employment Gazette* (May) pp. 211–222.

Campbell, M. and M. Daly (1992) 'Self-Employment into the 1990s', *Employment Gazette* (June).

Commission of the European Communities (1992) *Employment in Europe – 1992*, COM(92) 354.

Commission of the European Communities (1993) *Green Paper: European Social Policy*, COM(93) 551.

Commission of the European Communities (1995) 'Employment and Labour Market Flexibility', *European Economy, Supplement A*, 10.

Curwen, P. (1995) 'Social Protection Versus Unemployment in the European Union', *European Business Journal*, 7 (2) pp. 43–8.

Dawson, G. (1990) 'Interpretation of the Natural Rate of Unemployment', *Economics* (Summer).

Denman, J. and P. McDonald (1996) 'Unemployment Statistics From 1881 to the Present Day', *Labour Market Trends* (January) pp. 5–18.

Department for Education and Employment (1995) 'New Developments in the Pattern of Claimant Unemployment in the United Kingdom', *Employment Gazette* (September) pp. 351–8.

Ellison, R., D. Melville and R. Gutman (1996) 'British Labour Force Projections: 1996–2006', *Labour Market Trends* (May) pp. 197–205.

Felstead, A. and N. Jewson (1995) 'Working at Home: Estimates From the 1991 Census', *Employment Gazette* (March) pp. 95–9.

Fenwick, D. and Denman, J. (1995) 'The Monthly Claimant Unemployment Count: Change and Consistency', *Labour Market Trends* (November) p. 397.

Freeman, R. (19950 'The Limits of Wage Flexibility to Curing Unemployment', *Oxford Review of Economic Policy*, 11 (1) pp. 63–72.

Glyn, A. (1995) 'The Assessment: Unemployment and Inequality', *Oxford Review of Economic Policy*, 11 (1) pp. 1–25.

Gregg, P. (1992) 'Out for the Count Again? A Social Scientist's Analysis of Unemployment Statistics in the UK', *National Institute Discussion Paper No.25* (October).

Gregg, P. and J. Wadsworth (1995) 'A Short History of Labour Turnover, Job Tenure, and Job Security, 1975–93', *Oxford Review of Economic Policy*, 11 (1) pp. 73–89.

House of Commons Employment Committee (1996) *Third Report: Unemployment and Employment Statistics*. HC 228, 27 February (London: HMSO).

Hughes, A. (1996) 'Employment in the Public and Private Sectors', *Labour Market Trends* (August) pp. 373–9.

Lawlor, J. and C. Kennedy (1992) 'Measures of Unemployment: the Claimant Count and the Labour Force Survey', *Employment Gazette* (July).

Layard, R., S. Nickell and R. Jackman (1991) *Unemployment: Macroeconomic Performance and the Labour Market* (Oxford: Oxford University Press).

McGregor, A. and A. Sproull (1992) 'Employers and the Flexible Workforce', *Employment Gazette* (May).

Michie, J. and Grieve Smith, J. (eds) (1994) *Unemployment in Europe* (London: Academic Press).

Morgan, J. (1996) 'Structural Change in European Labour Markets', *National Institute Economic Review* (February) pp. 83–6.

Naylor, K. (19950 'Revised Employment Estimates and a New Classification System June 1978 to March 1995', *Employment Gazette* (October) pp. 379–84.

Nickell, S. and B. Bell (1995) 'The Collapse in Demand for the Unskilled and Unemployment Across the OECD', *Oxford Review of Economic Policy*, 11 (1) pp. 40–62.

Nickell, S. and S. Wadhani (1989) 'Insider Forces and Wage Determination', *Economic Journal* (June).

Osborne, K. (1996) 'Earnings of Part-Time Workers: Data From the 1995 New Earnings Survey', *Labour Market Trends* (May) pp. 227–31.

Perry, K. (1996) 'Measuring Employment: Comparison of Official Sources', *Labour Market Trends* (January) pp. 19–27.

Poret, P. (1990) 'The "Puzzle" of wage moderation in the 1980s', *OECD Working Paper*, 87 (Paris: OECD).

Shonfield, D. (1995) 'The Jobs Mythology', *IDS Focus*, 74.

Snower, D. (1993) 'Why People Do Not Find Work', *CEPR Discussion Paper No. 883* (December).

Snower, D. (1995) 'Evaluating Unemployment Policies: What Do the Underlying Theories Tell Us?', *Oxford Review of Economic Policy*, 11 (1) pp. 110–35.

Taylor, A. and C. Lewis (1993) '1991 Census of Employment Results', *Employment Gazette* (April).

The Economist (1994a) 'Labour Pains' (12 February) pp. 80–1.

The Economist (1994b) 'A Bad Case of Arthritis' (26 February) pp. 92–3.

The Economist (1994c) 'The Manufacturing Myth' (19 March) pp. 91–2.

The Economist (1994d) 'Workers of the World Compete' (2 April) pp. 69–70.

The Economist (1995a) 'A World Without Jobs?' (11 February) pp. 23–5.

The Economist (1995b) 'Counting the Jobless' (22 July) p. 92.

Thomas, P. and K. Smith (1995) 'Results of the 1993 Census of Employment', *Employment Gazette* (October) pp. 369–77.

Tonks, E. (1995) 'Revisions to the Quarterly Labour Force Survey: Re-Weighting and Seasonal Adjustment Review', *Employment Gazette* (May) pp. 223–32.

White, A. and J. Leyland (1993) 'How Unemployment is Measured in Different Countries', *Employment Gazette* (September).

Chapter 14

The Labour Market

Peter Curwen

■ 14.1 Introduction

In the UK there is continuous public debate about how to improve the quality of education and training, and about how to transform it into something suitable for the future. However, interest in the topic tends to ebb and flow, with surges in interest usually triggered by the unearthing of some piece of evidence to the effect that the UK is either falling further behind, or failing to catch up with, its competitors (see, for, example, 'uproar over test failures by 11-year-olds', *Financial Times*, 26 January 1996). Technological change has the awkward habit of speeding up rather than slowing down, and as a consequence no industrialised country can afford to go without a well-educated, well-trained workforce. Unfortunately, although it is generally possible to demonstrate that deficiencies exist, it is by no means easy to identify the precise reasons why this is the case, and hence what should be done to resolve it.

■ 14.2 Education

Up until the age of 16, education is **compulsory**. The school leaving age is currently at its highest-ever level, partly in order to keep down the num-bers of the unemployed. Education is primarily provided by public sector institutions which, for older children, conform with few exceptions to a common pattern known as the comprehensive school. The growth of the independent, private sector and pressure to restore the grammar school attest to widespread dissatisfaction with the quality of primary and secondary education. At the beginning of 1991, Her Majesty's Inspectors of Education reported that the teaching of reading was 'less than satisfactory' in a fifth of the institutions of lower learning which they had visited. In June 1993, the Adult Literacy and Basic Skills Unit published research indicating that one in five of the UK's 21-year-olds were innumerate while one in seven were illiterate.

Clearly, something has gone wrong with the state of educational provision, but what exactly, and what should be done to remedy it? It may be argued that parents do a good deal of the damage by ignoring their children's pre-school education. Furthermore, although the school leaving age is quite late by international standards, it is only very recently that the majority of children have **volunteered** to continue their education beyond the age of 16. The improvement from 1980–81 to 1993–94, according to what is now the Department of Education and Employment's annual

Table 14.1 *Young People in Full-time and Part-time Education: by Gender and Age[1], UK (%)*

	Full time			Part time		
	1980/81	*1991/92*	*1993/94*	*1980/81*	*1991/92*	*1993/94*
Males						
16	–	64	71	–	18	15
17	–	46	54	–	20	13
18	–	28	36	–	19	14
19–20	14	21	27	18	14	12
21–24	5	7	10	11	12	10
All males aged 16–24	15	21	26	19	14	11
Females						
16	–	72	77	–	17	15
17	–	54	62	–	14	10
18	–	30	38	–	13	11
19–20	11	20	28	12	14	13
21–24	3	6	9	16	19	17
All females aged 16–24	15	22	27	16	16	15

Note:
[1] As at 31 August.

Source: Social Trends, 26 (1996 edn) Chart 3.19.

Education Statistics for the United Kingdom, is shown in **Table 14.1**. However, there are significant regional variations within these totals, with the proportions in Barnet in London at twice the level of Knowsley on Merseyside.

Although fully-disaggregated data are unavailable for 1980–81, the overall percentage for full-time males and females had risen by over a decile by 1993–94. The figures also include part-time participation, in which respect the UK has an unusually high rate. In respect of full-time attendance only, the UK participation rate in 1993–94 was, however, less than many other countries in the developed world for 16 and 17-year-olds (compare the near 100 per cent rate for 16-year-olds in Canada and Germany). The fall-off in the participation rate post-16 is also relatively high in the UK, although there has been considerable improvement during the 1990s (see also Cm 3210, 1996, Figure 1.5).

The recent increase in participation is clearly related to the downturn in opportunities for employment. Furthermore, it represents no more than a catching up process in relation to Japan and even the USA, although the latter faces severe quality problems which the former appears able to avoid. Nevertheless, irrespective of the triggers, and some such as the switch to GCSEs noted below have been positive, this fondness for knowledge must be regarded as a desirable development.

Until very recently, it was customary to sit either Ordinary (O)-level or Certificate of Secondary Education (CSE) examinations at the age of 15 or 16. 'O'-levels were 'academic' and seen as the test of suitability for further years spent in school whereas CSE candidates were mostly expected to move straight out into the labour market. On the whole, it was generally accepted that the latter were insufficiently educated for the needs of an advanced society.

Secondary school children now sit a common General Certificate in Secondary Education (GCSE), but problems remain. For example, despite the great scientific and engineering traditions of nineteenth century Britain, there has developed a strong bias towards arts subjects since the War.

Compared to countries such as Germany, engineers are held in relatively low esteem and are relatively badly paid in the UK. A weakness in mathematics also goes hand in hand with a weakness in English. One often gets the impression that the inhabitants of countries, especially in Northern Europe, where English is a compulsory second language, speak better English than the British.

Stung by these kinds of criticisms the government passed the Education Reform Act in 1988 which, although highly controversial, may ultimately be seen as a lasting achievement. The underlying premise behind the Act was that control over teaching should not be left entirely in the hands of teachers who, in the course of applying 'fashionable' theories about education, were allegedly failing to deliver the well-educated workforce which was so desperately needed. During its first two terms in office, the Conservative government had held off from reform. Now it began the process by introducing a basic core curriculum designed to give all children skills in reading, writing and arithmetic and a passing acquaintance with science. The 10–subject core would be 'assessed' at ages 7, 11, 14 and 16.

An administrative apparatus was constructed, but this proved too unwieldy because of the excessive burden of assessment. In February 1990, the government accordingly began to beat a retreat, starting with a decree that at the ages of 7 and 11 the national assessments would apply only to 'key aspects' of mathematics, science and English, and that the other seven subjects would be assessed by teachers without the control of a national standard test.

In June 1990, the government promised simpler tests for 7-year-olds, and in January 1991 it was announced that the full national curriculum would be taught only to children aged up to 14, with music and art as optional subjects. Later in 1991, the first national tests for 7-year-olds took place, but proved to be excessively time-consuming, triggering a process of simplification of testing at all ages which nevertheless failed to mollify the teaching profession.

The first league tables of secondary schools' GCSE results were published in November 1992. These stirred up a good deal of controversy, mainly on the grounds that they failed to take proper account of the uneven quality of pupil 'inputs', and the teachers' unions voted for a programme of resistance, to include boycotts of compulsory testing. In response, the government commissioned a report by Sir Ron Dearing which was published in August 1993. This noted that the central problem was confusion over the purpose of testing. Whereas only simple tests were needed to assess pupil achievement in order to compare nationwide school performance, they had become overly complex, and required a complex curriculum to support them, because they were simultaneously seen as a means to diagnose individual pupil's needs. The report accordingly recommended that the two purposes should be divorced, with the latter left to teachers outside the scope of national tests. Furthermore, the tests should concentrate upon English, mathematics and science. The government accepted the report without qualification, and the national curriculum was accordingly slimmed down to occupy less than 90 per cent of the timetable in primary schools and 75 per cent in secondary schools. This did not, however, provide a recipe for peace in schools, with teachers boycotting the tests for 11-year-olds until 1995 at which time (under the old national curriculum) 56 per cent failed to reach the required level in maths and 52 per cent in English. In contrast, roughly 70 per cent of 7-year-olds reached the expected standard across all subjects (*Financial Times*, 26 January 1996) despite the fact that Ofsted, the school inspection agency, found the quality of teaching to be unsatisfactory in 30 per cent of junior school lessons in 1995, with one school in ten in respect of reading and one in four in respect of writing not making satisfactory progress. The Chief Inspector of Schools accordingly advocated greater use of streaming according to ability, more use of 'whole class' teaching and the retraining or sacking of incompetent teachers.

In future, testing at age 11 will become more stringent, and secondary schools will be permitted to select a larger share of their intake on the basis of academic ability (*Financial Times*, 26 June 1996). As schools already have the facility to 'opt-out' of local authority control (although only 5 per cent have done so), this could lead to the recreation of 'grammar school' sector (but not if Labour gets elected). In addition, the Conservatives plan an 'education market' whereby all schools, obliged to become 'self-governing', purchase back-up services from whichever local authority they choose (*Financial Times*, 24 December 1995).

Since its introduction in 1987–88, the proportion of 15-year-olds gaining 5 or more GCSE at grades C or above has risen sharply, as has the proportion of 17-year-olds gaining 2 or more Advanced ('A') levels (*Social Trends*, Tables 3.5 and 3.6). Given that the UK spends relatively little per head on primary and secondary education (*ibid.*, Table 3.28), this would appear to paint a more positive picture, but the proportion of 16-year-olds leaving school without any qualifications is also rising (*Financial Times,* 19 November 1995) and there are allegations of 'grade inflation', possibly resulting from competition between examination boards to attract 'customers'.

There are other controversial matters which remain unresolved, such as the link between class size and the quality of education (*Financial Times,* 13 November 1995). Another concerns how to give parity of esteem to technical and vocational subjects so that even those school children intent upon further and higher education come to perceive them as more worthy of consideration. In February 1991, the government proposed that 16-year-olds could leave school with vocational qualifications instead of GCSEs. Up to 70 per cent of class time beyond the age of 14 could be spent on vocational study, but this would be of equal rigour to academic study. This General National Vocational Qualification (GNVQ – see Cm 3210, 1996, Chapter 4) is currently preferred by roughly one-fifth of that age group, and it is being supplemented by a 'general diploma' to be awarded to 16-year-olds gaining GCSEs at grades A to C in English, maths, science and two other subjects, or vocational equivalents. The vocational element, chosen from such subjects as manufacturing and leisure/tourism, initially results in GNVQs equivalent to GCSEs. The Advanced GNVQs have ostensible parity with 'A' levels, and may be renamed 'applied 'A'-levels', subject to more rigorous assessment, to reinforce this claim. This was part of a new structure set out in a recent (March 1996) report by Sir Ron Dearing, the government's chief curriculum adviser (*Review of Qualifications for 16 to 19-year-Olds*), advocating a new National Advanced Diploma to be taken at 18 (see also Cm 3210, 1996, Figure 1.7 for an analysis of the contribution of vocational and academic courses to the growth of participation in full-time education of 16 to 18-year-olds in England). At one end of the educational spectrum, the government has introduced nursery vouchers for 4-year-olds in a pilot scheme at four local authorities, with the rest obliged to participate in 1997 (*Financial Times*, 10 January 1996). At the other end, the decision to stay on in education beyond 18 is much affected by parental ambitions – graduate parents expect their children to get a degree – and by the relative pay of those who go to work at 16 and those who enter the workforce with qualifications at a later age. The amount of state and parental financial support for those who stay on is also a major factor. Unlike in the USA, there is no tradition of 'working one's way through college'; 'A'-levels and degrees are generally done on a full-time attendance basis. The 1980–81 and 1990–92 recessions also served to drive home the realisation that unemployment typically affects the unskilled and unqualified more harshly than the skilled and those with educational qualifications.

The highly specialised nature of 'A'-level courses is peculiar to Britain (it is broader based in Scotland than England) and has been a major deterrent to those wishing to stay on at school. This combined with the fact that the proportion of the age cohort able to enrol on degree programmes at universities was, until very recently, exceptionally low by international standards. The virtue of this system was that those who took British degrees were on average academically superior to their counterparts almost everywhere else in Europe since excess demand was used to ration by academic quality rather than by price. In addition, the system was very efficient, with a low cost per graduate, since it had a very low drop-out rate by international standards. Thus, ironically, the annual output of graduates in the UK was actually higher than elsewhere in Europe (see Cm 3210, 1996, p. 47).

The drawbacks were that the system was physically constrained, over-specialised and inflexible, with the consequence that unless a school child did sufficiently well at GCSE to stand a reasonable chance of a place on a course in further or higher education, he or she tended to drop out of education as soon as the rules allowed. Further and higher education also remained very much a middle-class preserve, despite the abolition of grammar schools and attempts to improve opportunities for children from working-class backgrounds.

The government was particularly concerned to expand the numbers of those who stayed on in mathematics and the sciences. Unfortunately, most of those who stay in education are concerned about their job prospects and future incomes, and hence prefer courses in business studies and the professions. Presumably, if there really was a severe shortage of science graduates then relative pay would rise to clear the market, but there is little sign of this happening so far. On the other hand, there is undoubtedly a need for more qualified technicians, and it may be argued that insufficient resources have been invested in further education to meet this objective.

In line with its general philosophy, the government set out to make further and higher education more responsive to the market place. It released the Polytechnics from the shackles of local education authority control and allowed them to rename themselves as universities, and went on to release further education and sixth-form colleges from local authority control in April 1993. These changes were associated with an enormous expansion of provision. The universities increased the overall number of graduates by 130 per cent between 1985 and 1995 (although further expansion is no longer anticipated – see Cm 3210, 1996, Figure 1.8), and 31 per cent of 18-year-olds currently go to university (*ibid.*, p. 47). However, physical facilities have not expanded anything like as rapidly, nor staff numbers, leading to further controversy about 'grade inflation' and the longer-term effects upon quality.

In response to the spiralling cost of funding this expansion, the Conservative government adopted a policy of forcing higher education institutions to

earn an increasing proportion of their income in the market place via research, consultancy and full-cost courses. It reduced the value of mandatory grant aid to students (see Cm 3210, 1996, Table 1.11), and introduced a system of student loans on generous terms with repayment over the five years post-graduation subject to means-tested deferral. Given the cost, any new government is unlikely to alter this new system. Even fees paid from tax revenues are no longer sacrosanct, with individual universities determined to introduce 'top-up' charges. All in all, the UK education system has been undergoing a seemingly endless round of reform, and it is to be hoped that the end-results will justify the pain.

■ 14.3 Labour Market Measures

□ *14.3.1 Introduction*

Public sector labour-market measures encompass unemployment pay and 'active employment measures' such as training. The latter have been primarily a phenomenon of the past decade and their incidence is patchy in relation to GDP, as indeed it is outside the EU. The UK's spending on training is widely criticised domestically, but it is not unfavourable **in relation to the rate of unemployment** compared to most of the EU.

In inflation-adjusted terms spending on training roughly tripled during the decade post-1979, as shown in **Table 14.2**, which is a little surprising given the government's preference for market solutions to problems such as a shortfall in skills. However, if companies are reluctant to instigate

Table 14.2   *Training Expenditure (£ m)*

	Cash Prices	Constant (1990–91) Prices
1975–76	171.7	620.2
1978–79	377.3	954.3
1989–90	2658.8	2871.5

Source: Employment Gazette (January 1991), p. 39.

training programmes on a voluntary basis, and if the government is unwilling to compel them to do so, then either training is largely publicly funded or it is largely non-existent.

Traditionally, training in the UK took place 'on the job'. In the case of craftsmen this involved an apprenticeship supplemented by City and Guilds examinations. The first significant state intervention came with the Industrial Training Act 1964. This Act created **training boards** which were to be financed mainly by levies on firms with a supplement from the State. The boards consisted of representatives of employers, trade unions and civil servants.

14.3.2 Justification for Government Intervention

The justification for the levies was that instead of training their own workers, many firms preferred to poach workers from other firms that did. The levies could be returned only to those firms that incurred training costs by way of compensation for the benefits transferred to the poachers. However, the levies were generally unpopular with employers who argued that investment in training would be worthwhile only if the skills acquired by their workers were specific to their particular businesses, since such skills could not, by definition, be poached. Where skills were general, and hence could be used in a variety of firms and industries, it would not be sensible for an individual firm to invest heavily in training since trained workers would subsequently be able to sell their skills to the highest bidder. In effect, the investment would yield much greater benefits to the individual than to the firm.

But even if poaching could be prevented, it might not pay a firm to invest in training. If workers are performing well in their present jobs they will often want to move on to more challenging tasks. Yet if they are trained to do them, they may simply become even more anxious to move on to even more demanding jobs, which are unavailable unless the workers move to other firms. The lack of transferable skills may be the only thing which keeps workers from leaving many firms.

It may be argued that any workers who realise that the acquisition of skills will result in a much higher wage will finance skills acquisition themselves. However, this will often be successful only if their firms allow them time off to train, if the unions lend their support and if there are readily available funds for this purpose. Government help to overcome these potential hurdles may thus be more sensible than trying to browbeat reluctant employers into policies which they do not perceive as self-serving.

It may also be added that since support for public investment in training comes from employers, unions, educationalists and parents (see *The Economist*, 1996), it is hardly surprising that so much is invested irrespective of whether it is truly justifiable in economic terms.

14.3.3 Measures in Retrospect

Given the attitude of many employers, it is hardly surprising that the shortage of trained workers proved to be persistent, and the decision was taken in the early 1970s to create a national training programme under the umbrella of the Manpower Services Commission (MSC), a semi-autonomous body set up separately from the Department of Employment in 1973 (for a discussion of this period see King, 1993). The MSC operated a corporatist strategy in that it tried to obtain a consensus view about what the problems were and what should be done about them, rather than attempting to force its own strategy upon reluctant employers and unions. The system it created was inherited by the Thatcher government in 1979.

The history of labour-market measures from 1975 to 1992 is summarised in **Table 14.3**, and for subsequent years in **Table 14.4**. Most of these measures have been terminated, and space does not permit a detailed discussion of their contents (but see Gregg, 1990, pp. 49–52).

From 1974 to 1979 the Labour government concentrated upon the traditional approach of creating more demand for labour, especially for specific groups of workers and in specific locations. Subsidies such as the Temporary Employ-

Table 14.3 Employment and Training Schemes, Great Britain, 1975/76 to 1992/93[1]

Scheme	Incentives for employers to maintain current employment	Incentives for employers to raise employment	Direct employment by government or its agencies	Work sharing or reducing labour supply	Training-based schemes	Other	Initials	Introduced in	Phased out in	Replaced by
Restart Interviews						✓	RI	86/87	Live	X
Employment Action						✓	EA	91/92	93/94	TFW
Employment Training Scheme					✓		ET	88/89	93/94	TFW
Job Training Scheme					✓		JTS	85/86	88/89	ET
Youth Training Scheme					✓		YTS	83/84	Live	X
Youth Credits					✓		YC	91/92	Live	X
Jobshare				✓			JS	87/88	Live	X
Job Release Scheme				✓			JRS	76/77	Live	X
Community Programme			✓				CP	82/83	88/89	ET
Community Enterprise Programme			✓				CEP	81/82	82/83	CP
Special Temporary Employment Programme			✓				STEP	78/79	81/82	CEP
Job Creation Programme			✓				JCP	75/76	78/79	STEP
Jobstart Allowance		✓					JA	n/a	Live	X
Enterprise Allowance Scheme		✓					EAS	82/83	Live	X
New Workers Scheme		✓					NWS	86/87	88/89	X
Young Workers Scheme		✓					YWS	81/82	86/87	NWS
Small Firms Employment Subsidy		✓					SFES	77/78	80/81	X
Youth Opportunities Programme		✓					YOP	78/79	82/83	YTS
Youth Employment Subsidy		✓					YES	77/78	78/79	YOP
Recruitment Subsidy for School Leavers		✓					RSSL	75/76	76/77	YES
Temporary Short-Time Working Compensation Scheme	✓						TSTWC	78/79	84/85	X
Temporary Employment Scheme	✓						TES	75/76	78/79	TSTWC

Note:
[1] This is not by any means a complete version; see, for example, *Training Statistics 1990* (London: HMSO), p. 35.
Source: Department of Employment; P. Gregg (1990).

Table 14.4 *Employment and Training Schemes, Great Britain, 1991–1997*

Scheme	Incentives for employers to maintain current employment	Incentives for employers to raise employment	Direct employment by government or its agencies	Work sharing or reducing labour supply	Training-based schemes	Other	Initials	Introduced in	Phased out in	Replaced by
Workstart Pilot		✓					WP	93/94	Live	X
Work Trials		✓					WT	93/94	Live	X
Training for Work					✓		TFW	93/94	Live	X
Community Action					✓		CA	93/94	96/97	X
Learning for Work					✓		LFW	93/94	93/94	X
Project Work					✓		PW	96/97	Live	X
Modern Apprenticeships					✓		MA	94/95	Live	X
Job Review Workshops						✓	JRW	91/92	96/97	JP
Open Learning Credits						✓	OLC	92/93	n/a	X
Skill Choice						✓	SC	93/94	n/a	X
Jobplan Workshops						✓	JW	93/94	Live	X
Jobseeker's Allowance						✓	JSA	96/97	Live	X
Jobfinder's Grant						✓	JG	94/95	Live	X
Jobmatch						✓	JM	95/96	Live	X
Jobsearch Plus						✓	JP	96/97	Live	X

ment Scheme (TES), Youth Employment Subsidy (YES) and Small Firms Employment Subsidy (SFES) were the primary instrument to achieve this, with a little help from the Job Release Scheme (JRS) on the supply side. The use of training-based schemes was very modest until the **Youth Training Scheme** (YTS) was initiated in 1983.

The Thatcher government largely forsook the traditional approach, which raised the demand for labour at the existing wage, in favour of wage flexibility designed to match supply and demand at an acceptable level of employment. This initially involved the Young Workers' Scheme (YWS) followed by the New Workers' Scheme (NWS). From 1983 onwards, it placed considerable emphasis upon training-based schemes, primarily the YTS, but also for adults after the inception of the Job Training Scheme (JTS) in 1986.

Coupled with Restart and benefit regulations that require active job search, as noted by Gregg (1990) 'it produces a consistent policy response if the problem of unemployment persistence is too high reservation wages and too little job search by the unemployed, coupled with growing problems with skill acquisition by the young, skill maintenance when unemployed and a skills mismatch.'

The **Restart Programme** was introduced in 1986, and was aimed at the long-term unemployed. Initially, anyone unemployed for one year or longer was invited to an interview at a Job Centre and offered opportunities designed to help him or her back to employment. In 1987, coverage was extended to anyone unemployed for six months or longer. By 1993, the opportunities on offer included an interview for a job; a place on Training for Work; a place on a Restart Course; a Jobstart Allowance (JA); a place on an Enterprise Allowance Scheme (EAS); or a place in a Jobclub. **Jobclubs** aim to help people who have been unemployed for six months or more by providing help in finding jobs and free facilities such as telephones and stationery.

Throughout 1989–91, an evaluation of Restart was carried out in the form of the **Restart Cohort Study** (see *Labour Market Quarterly Review*, November 1992). This indicated that Restart helped individuals to leave unemployment more quickly

than they would otherwise have done, and made a significant difference to the amount of time during the study period for which they were claiming benefit. It also significantly increased the average amount of time spent by participants on Employment Training and other government programmes, and reduced the average time taken to enter such programmes.

The particular problems of **youth unemployment**, which arose in the late 1970s, led initially to the Youth Opportunity Programme (YOP). In 1983, this was replaced by the YTS and was expanded to cover almost all 16-year-olds not in education. The YTS placed greater emphasis upon training at employers' premises. In 1986, the YTS was itself expanded to provide a two-year structured period of training and work experience for 16-year-old school leavers. Subsequently, benefit entitlement was withdrawn for those who did not participate, effectively compelling all those eligible to join. All trainees who are not employed receive a minimum weekly allowance, currently £29.50 for 16-year-olds and £35 for those aged 17 or over. In every year since 1990–91 the YTS has cost roughly £850 million to administer.

In 1990, the YTS comprised the largest of the three main strands of government policy in the labour market. The second was the **Enterprise Allowance Scheme** (EAS), first introduced on a national scale in 1983 to help those setting up their own business. It provides a weekly subsidy for up to a year for a claimant who must invest modestly in his or her own business. About one half of EAS ventures last six months beyond the termination of the subsidy.

The dominant adult scheme in usage until 1993 was **Employment Training** (ET), introduced in September 1988 with the slogan 'Training the workers without jobs to do the jobs without workers'. ET replaced 34 pre-existing schemes, but only two were nationally significant, namely the Community Programme (CP) and the Job Training Scheme (JTS). Its objectives were, firstly, to give the long-term unemployed the skills which they needed to get and keep jobs and, secondly, to guarantee a training opportunity for all those aged 18 to 24 who had been unemployed for between six and twelve months and for all those aged 18 to 50 who had been unemployed for more than two years. The scheme normally ran for six months, and occasionally for twelve, so the 300 000 places were expected to handle roughly 550 000 people a year.

The unemployed were allocated to training agents (who could be employees' or employers' organisations) and while on ET continued to receive benefits as though they were unemployed together with training allowances and, if eligible, Income Support and travelling expenses. In addition, training managers were allowed to make discretionary payments without affecting benefits or liabilities for tax. As noted previously, ET was closely tied up with the Restart Programme. Of the 890 000 interviewed in January 1991, the largest proportion of those (roughly 75 per cent) who took up an offer of some kind ended up in ET.

The MSC subsequently evolved into the **Training Commission**. In 1987, the government proposed a New Training Initiative which the unions objected to on the grounds of under-funding. As a result, the government decided in September 1988 to absorb the former MSC within the Department of Employment under the umbrella of a new **Training Agency**. This Agency would operate in tandem with the **Employment Service**, formed in 1987 to bring together unemployment benefit, Job Centre and other services centred on the unemployed.

In the White Paper on training (*Employment for the 1990s*, Cmnd 540, 1988) the government went a stage further by setting in motion a restructuring of training through the establishment of 82 locally-based, employer-led **Training and Enterprise Councils** (TECs) in England and Wales, together with 22 Local Enterprise Companies (LECs) in Scotland. The Department of Employment then invited local groups of employers to submit proposals for setting up the TECs which were given responsibility for drawing up local training programmes, arranging for their delivery by signing up providers including voluntary organisations, stimulating enterprise and building better industry/education links. TECs started off by signing a contract with the Training Agency. All 82 TECs were contracted up by October 1990, with 31 fully operational and 51 in the development phase, some two years ahead of schedule. At least two thirds of a TEC Board of Directors must be top private sector business leaders with the balance drawn from local authorities, trade unions, the voluntary sector, education and others.

TEC directors were unenthusiastic about using up their funds, at a time of rising unemployment, solely on managing anti-unemployment schemes such as ET and YTS. On the other hand, few felt themselves to be in a strong position to raise private finance for innovatory programmes. Given that one quarter of TEC income was to be related to the gaining of qualifications, fears were expressed that TECs would concentrate upon the provision of intensive courses for people who were easy to train, and largely ignore the needs of the handicapped and ex-prisoners who needed basic, expensive education if they are to become employable.

On 1 April 1991, the Department of Employment handed over control of its training budget to the TECs. It simultaneously (27 March 1991) launched a £120 million scheme to give 10 per cent of school leavers training vouchers called **Youth Credits** (YC), worth from £500 to £5000, to spend on an approved training scheme of their choice. YC is now national.

In May, a White Paper was published entitled *Education and Training for the 21st Century*. A key proposal was to extend the provision of Training Credits to every 16 and 17-year-old by 1996. It also proposed the extension of the use of the National Record of Achievement for school leavers.

In July, the Employment Secretary announced a new package of measures to help the unemployed. A new programme called **Employment Action** (EA) was created, commencing in October 1991, to offer up to 60 000 long-term unemployed people in a full year the chance to keep their skills up to date by work experience on local projects. It paid state benefits plus £10 a week, and was administered by the TECs. Taken in conjunction with ET, the annual cost was approximately £1 billion in 1990–91, falling to roughly £900 million in subsequent years. In December 1991, a new

Employment Service scheme called **Job Review Workshops** was initiated to help up to 50 000 unemployed executives and managers back into work or further training. The workshops consist of 12 people who have been unemployed for roughly 13 weeks working together with a leader.

A White Paper, *People, Jobs and Opportunity* (Cm 1810, February 1992) announced TEC-delivered pilots to trial **Open Learning Credits** for unemployed people to purchase open learning materials and support. It also announced the **Skill Choice** initiative (commencing April 1993) whereby individuals are offered credits to buy the guidance and assessment services of their choice.

However, these initiatives were dwarfed by that announced in the Autumn Statement of 1992, the main elements of which were:

- A new programme, **Training for Work** (TFW), would replace Employment Training and Employment Action from April 1993. Delivered through TECs, TFW would provide 320 000 adults with an opportunity to improve, update and learn new skills or do work of benefit to the local community. Those eligible would include people unemployed for 6 months or longer, people with disabilities and returners to the labour market who had been out of the labour market for two years.
- All people who had been unemployed for a year, and who did not take up other offers of help, would be required to attend a one week **Jobplan Workshop**.
- The Jobclub and Job Interview Guarantee Schemes would be expanded, together with a major expansion of work trials with employers for the unemployed.
- Additional places would be provided in **Job Review Workshops**.
- Additional **Career Development Loans** (first introduced in July 1988) would be provided to help both employed and unemployed people to take the training course of their choice.

Further measures were introduced in the 1993 Budget, which, though modest in scale, showed a more innovatory approach. In particular, there was an acceptance of the principle of job subsidies to employers who take on the unemployed, an idea previously resisted by the Treasury. The initial tests in four **Workstart Pilot** (WP) areas, two run by TECs and two by the Employment Service and involving 1000 people at a cost of £2.6 million, would be based on the Benefit Transfer Programme concept proposed by Dennis Snower. The government's version would be open to those unemployed for more than two years, and would provide a one-year subsidy to the employer of £60 per week taken from benefits which would have been paid. The unemployed person would get a normal wage, and the subsidy would taper off as the period of employment progressed. Employers would be prevented from using the subsidy to displace existing staff.

A **Community Action** (CA) programme was also introduced which would provide benefit plus £10 a week for 60 000 people who were willing to work part-time on projects run by voluntary organisations while receiving help with job hunting during the rest of the week. While this would be similar to TFW, it would be run by the Employment Department rather than the TECs (thereby, in principle, permitting it to be treated as a form of 'Workfare').

Some £67 million was also made available to provide up to 300 000 places on vocationally-related, full-time courses for people unemployed for over 12 months under a **Learning for Work** (LFW) scheme, and an additional £21 million to supplement the TEC-run Business Start-Up scheme. Finally, TECs would be invited to bid for £25 million in a TEC Challenge scheme to develop and run innovatory ways to tackle unemployment.

The **Work Trials** (WT) programme was initiated in 1994 to encourage employers to consider long-term unemployed people for their vacancies. Those unemployed for over six months get to try out a job for up to three weeks while continuing to receive benefit plus expenses.

☐ *14.3.4 Recent Developments*

A full review of programmes designed to help unemployed people into work is set out each year in the Departmental Report of what is now the

Department of Education and Employment, of which the most recent is Cm 3210 of March 1996.

One major recent change, introduced in the Jobseekers Act of June 1995 and implemented in October 1996, was the introduction of a **Jobseeker's Allowance** (JSA) designed to replace Unemployment Benefit and Income Support for unemployed people. Its main objectives are (*ibid.*, p. 100):

- to improve the operation of the labour market by helping people in their search for work, while ensuring that they understand and fulfil the conditions for receipt of benefit;
- to secure better value for money for the taxpayer through closer targeting;
- to improve the service to unemployed people through a clearer single benefit with one set of rules and through one main point of delivery, usually the Jobcentre.

JSA will include drawing up individual Jobseekers' Agreements which will set out the steps to be taken to get back to work; interviewing jobseekers to assess their availability and efforts to seek work; and applying labour market sanctions where necessary. JSA halves from 12 months to six months the period for which non-means-tested benefit is payable.

A new emphasis is being placed on the period of 13 weeks of unemployment since half the people who make a claim leave unemployment within three months. To help those who remain unemployed, the **Job Search Seminar** and Job Review Workshops were replaced in August 1996 by **Jobsearch Plus** (JP) (see *Financial Times*, 20 August 1996). In addition, eligibility for the **Travel to Work Scheme** (TWS) subsidies were changed in 1996–97 to include those unemployed for 13 weeks as against the current four weeks.

In addition to Jobplan Workshops for those over 24-years-old, older people unemployed for over one year are assisted through **Workwise**, a four week job search programme combining workshop attendance with jobsearch activity, and 1–2–1 interviews with an adviser.

The **Jobfinder's Grant** (JG) was piloted during 1994 and became nationally available in April 1995. It is a one-off payment that can be made to those who have been unemployed for two years or more when they start work.

Jobmatch (JM) was piloted in April 1995. Its purpose is to encourage people who have been unemployed for two years or more to take part-time work as a stepping stone to full-time employment. Participants receive an allowance of £50 per week for six months when they take a part-time job. Training vouchers worth £300 are offered, and bonuses are paid to participants who remain in employment after the allowance finishes. Its expansion onto a national basis was announced as part of the 1996 budget.

Project Work (PW) pilots of mandatory work experience for people out of work for two years or more who have failed to benefit from other help provided were introduced in April 1996 to run for 15 months in two Travel to Work areas. All those in the pilot areas aged 18–50 and unemployed for two or more years are included. While on the programme, participants receive benefit plus £10 per week, with failure to take up a place subject to a loss of benefit sanction. In the light of the above changes, Community Action was terminated in 1996.

A particularly interesting development was the national introduction of **Modern Apprenticeships** (MA) in September 1995, delivered by the TECS, following prototypes operating in 17 industry sectors during 1994–95. Industry Training Organisations (ITOs) and TECs have, together with employers, developed the apprenticeship training frameworks, which lead to National Vocational Qualifications (NVQs) at level 3 or above. MAs are aimed primarily at 16 or 17-year-olds. YT provides vocational training to NVQ level 2, and young people with the potential to reach level 3 can transfer to MAs. YT and MA provide a minimum of £29.50 per week at age 16 and £35 per week at age 17 or above, but most Modern Apprentices are expected to be paid a proper wage.

Finally it was announced in the 1996 Budget that pilot projects would be set up in three or four cities for a **Contract for Work** scheme. These will involve the use of private contracting companies in helping initially up to 6000 long-term unemployed into jobs. The companies will only be paid when they find jobs.

☐ *14.3.1 Assessment*

It is clear from the above not merely that the government is concerned about training but also that it has devoted an enormous amount of money and energy into devising programmes. As a consequence, as shown in **Figure 14.1**, roughly 14 per cent of all employees in Britain are being trained at any point in time, slightly down from the 1990 peak. Unfortunately, however, this does not necessarily imply that the training achieves anything worthwhile either for the trainee or for the long-term health of the economy.

In the first place, it may be argued that expenditure on training is, if anything, excessive (see Shackleton (1992) for a detailed analysis of this proposition and *The Economist*, 1994b and 1996). The figures for expenditure in **Table 14.1** above are deceptive in that they do not include individuals' loss of earnings while learning on the job nor expenditure by firms. Adding these in produces total expenditure on training roughly equal to ten per cent of GDP. This would be justifiable if there was a clear proven link between the amount of expenditure and economic growth, but as yet this does not exist. What this highlights is the danger of concentrating training upon non-transferable skills, and, less directly, the danger inherent in creating vested interests in the provision of training. It should be emphasised that even those most sceptical about the virtues of training are not arguing against training as such, but rather against its scale and its particular formats. We have previously commented briefly, and favourably, about Restart, but it has been argued that this success has been based in part upon the diversion of people to the kinds of benefit support, such as disability benefit, that take them off the unemployment register.

Figure 14.1   *Employees Receiving Training*[1]

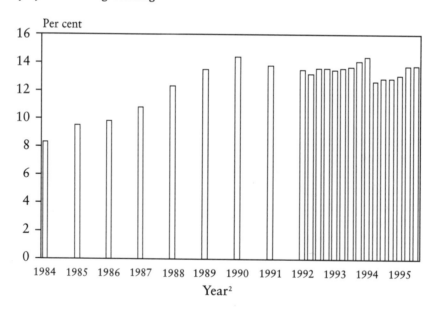

Notes:
[1] Employees of working age receiving job-related training (on or off-the-job) in the last four weeks (seasonally adjusted). Working age is defined as men aged 16–64 and women aged 16–59.
[2] 1984–1991 Spring data only. 1992 onwards Spring, Summer, Autumn and Winter of each year.
Source: Labour Market Quarterly Review, May 1996, p. 5.

Table 14.5 *Training for Work: Expenditure and Performance, England*

	1991–92[1] outturn	1992–93[1] outturn	1993–94[2] estimated outturn	1994–95 plans	1995–96 plans	1996–97 plans
Expenditure (£ million)	710	753	762	705	724	718
Number of starts (000s)	252	291	240	273	273	262
Average number of participants (000s)	117	124	121	115	114	109
Cost per participant (£)	6 050	6 069	6 296	–[3]	–[3]	–[3]
Average length of stay (weeks)	24	22[4]	22[4]	22	22	22
Percentage of leavers gaining positive outcomes (jobs, further education or training)	34[5,6]	38[5,6]	30	35	40	41
Cost per positive outcome (£)	7 640	6 757	8 880	7 326	6 638	6 611
Percentage of leavers gaining qualifications (including a credit towards a qualification)	32[5,6]	36[5,6]	35	40	45	46
Cost per qualification (£)	8 120	7 132	7 611	6 410	5 900	5 892
Percentage of leavers gaining NVQs levels 1 to 4	N/A	19[5]	25	30	35	36

Notes:
[1] Includes Employment Action, which began in October 1991.
[2] Training for Work, which began in April 1993.
[3] Figures are only available for past years. Planned figures will depend on the numbers and targets agreed in annual TEC business plans prior to the start of the operating year.
[4] Cannot give outturns until every participant has left programme.
[5] Applies to ET only, as Employment Action is not measured by positive outcomes and not intended to lead to a qualifications.
[6] Estimate derived from GB figures.

Source: Department of Education and Employment (1996), Table 5.

The key programmes are Training for Work and Youth Training (including Youth Credits). A review of TFW is contained in **Table 14.5**. Between September 1988 and March 1993, its predecessor Employment Training dealt with roughly 1.4 million joiners. Of those who left the programme between July 1991 and June 1992, 31 per cent obtained employment within three months and 33 per cent gained qualifications (see *Labour Market Quarterly Review*, May 1993).

An analysis of the effectiveness of ET, based upon a sample taken in 1989 and reported in the same journal, indicated that participation in ET had the effects of reducing time as a claimant and increasing time spent in employment. However, the study was too limited to be generalisable to all ET/EFW participants. It was also argued that the Employment Service counselling service has a higher success rate even though it cost only £275 per job placement compared to £10 000 for ET. The results of a further study are reported in *Labour Market Quarterly Review* (1996), which concluded that ET leavers' chances of getting a job were significantly greater than those of non-participants; the advantage conferred by ET persisted and grew over time; and programmes had the greatest effect on prospects of securing full-time jobs.

Information on TFW for Great Britain as well as England is published in *Labour Market Trends*, Tables 8.1 to 8.3. This shows that the 1996–97 estimate of roughly 40 per cent of TFW leavers gaining jobs and so forth is much the same as in 1990 (for ET) with a considerable fall-off during the intervening recession. As shown in **Table 14.5,** the cost per positive outcome is, however, somewhat lower, albeit still substantial, but a positive feature is that the percentage of leavers gaining NVQs at levels 1 to 4 is rising steadily.

During 1993 (and fairly consistently since then), there were roughly 275 000 young people on YT (including Youth Credits) in Britain. Of these, one half took up employment, but this represented a significant deterioration compared to the 68 per cent peak recorded in 1989 (*Labour Market Quarterly Review*, Table 8.4). It was argued that, because of the recession, increasing numbers of young people had never had a job, and had lost any sense of discipline, thereby rendering them virtually unemployable in the longer term even when the labour market picked up. The number of YT leavers in jobs has picked up again, reaching 58 per cent in 1995, which is somewhat disappointing but not necessarily demonstrating the truth or otherwise of the preceding argument. Meanwhile, the number of YT leavers gaining a qualification, or a credit towards one, has hovered between 45 and 50 per cent since 1991. This is the positive aspect. Unfortunately, it does not take account of the high drop-out rate which is currently roughly 50 per cent, nor of the fact that at least 20 per cent of participants who completed their training are normally unemployed (*ibid.*), hardly any different from the age group as a whole. The introduction of Modern Apprenticeships may be seen as an acknowledgement of this failing (for information on apprenticeships see *Labour Market Quarterly Review*, August 1995 and for an analysis of the virtues of, particularly German, apprenticeships see *The Economist*, 1994a, p. 22), although these may well pander to those who are already the most employable.

The main criticisms that were initially directed specifically at TECs claimed firstly that they over-concentrated on short-term concerns and secondly that they over-concentrated upon industry-specific needs (Mawson, 1992). Subsequent evidence indicated that, albeit with widely differing performances, TECs were getting better at placing young people in training schemes and where they were gaining improved qualifications, and were equipping more unemployed adults with vocational qualifications. However, the TECs claimed that it was the government that prevented them from doing more to promote enterprise through, for example, attracting inward investment and setting up loans for firms. In September 1995, the TEC National Council went so far as to accuse the government of a 'serious failure to meet its contractual obligations to TECs and its commitment to unemployed people' (*Financial Times*, 18 September 1995).

Where exactly blame lies is, naturally, a moot point. In February 1996, the House of Commons Select Committee on Employment reported that only 27 per cent of adults on TEC courses obtained jobs, with almost none reaching a 50 per cent success rate. This led the Committee to conclude that the TECs merely performed in line with economic conditions generally rather than making inroads into the problems they were set up to address. There is always the problem of isolating those who would have got jobs anyway and those who took jobs at the expense of others. Adjust for these groups and the only really worthwhile programmes appear to be those that provide basic job search advice. Otherwise, it is claimed (see *The Economist*, 1996, p. 22), training programmes largely serve only to convert the long-term unemployed into the short-term unemployed.

It can be argued fairly convincingly that what are needed most of all, aside from job-search skills, are elementary skills such as basic literacy which are essentially the proper preserve of the educational system. Beyond that, training should be on-the-job providing firms with the job-specific skills that they are themselves willing to finance.

Further, it may be noted that is much controversy over the system of NVQs and GNVQs (see, for, example, *Financial Times*, 27 March 1996). NVQs are particularly criticised on the grounds that assessment is conducted in the workplace, the same approach is used for training all age groups and recognising competence in the workplace is little use to those without jobs. Although they are widely supported by industry they are being used much less than the government expected. Meanwhile, GNVQs are held to be turning into simply another university entry qualification with insufficient relevance to the world of work.

Finally, the Labour Party has evidently turned its face against the reintroduction of compulsory training levies, advocating instead tax incentives; 'individual learning accounts' for training funded jointly by companies and employees; and privileged savings accounts for individuals who put aside money for general training.

☐ 14.3.2 Workfare

The Conservative government increasingly began to toy with the introduction of increased compul-

sion in unemployment schemes. Whereas Restart questioned people after two years of being unemployed, and Jobplan Workshops after one year, a pilot scheme announced in April 1993, called North Norfolk Action, questioned participants each week about their progress in looking for work. The scheme offered temporary part-time work on community projects for 100 people who have been unemployed for more than six months. However, this type of scheme was widely criticised on the grounds that it was inferior to temporary work with a regular employer at standard rates of pay. It was also alleged that it would push increasing numbers of young people into the black economy and crime (as in the USA).

For these reasons, there has been much advocacy of recruitment subsidies, but the government's Workstart scheme referred to above was itself criticised on the grounds that there were no plans to monitor employers' assurances that they will not use the subsidy to displace existing employees nor any sanctions to apply where they did (see Snower in *Financial Times*, 23 February 1993 and 19 May 1993). Although it has come increasingly to accept the need for selective subsidies, the government has also decided to persevere with an element of compulsion, as is evident from the recently introduced Project Work pilots.

☐ 14.3.3 Skill Shortages and Their Consequences

The only long-standing and consistent indicator of skill shortages comes from the CBI Quarterly Industrial Trends Survey which covers Great Britain. What this shows, as in **Figure 14.2**, is that as unemployment rose rapidly during the first half of the 1980s so, perversely, did shortages of skills. In 1982, roughly 2.5 per cent of manufacturing companies cited skill shortages as a constraint on output. By October 1988, this figure had risen to 28 per cent. By this time unemployment was falling progressively, yet in January 1991 the figure had fallen back to 6 per cent and remained at or below that level until the latter part of 1994, at which point the renewed growth in the economy was beginning to show up again as skill shortages.

Figure 14.2   *Expectations of Skill Shortages, Great Britain, 1975–96*

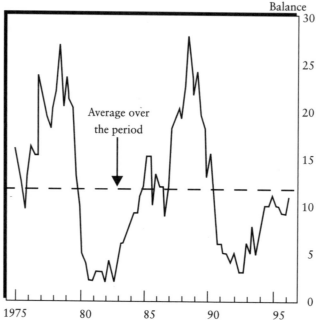

Q: What factors are likely to limit your output over the next four months?
A: Skilled labour.

Source: Bank of England Inflation Report (August 1996) Chart 4.7.

The Department of Employment has also published three surveys on skill needs in Britain (see *Labour Market Quarterly Review*, November 1992) covering 1990–92. These confirm that recruitment difficulties remained at a low level during this period, partly because recruitment had fallen off during the recession.

Skill shortages are location-specific, and are understandably most acute in newly-established high-technology companies. In the face of an inflexible supply of qualified personnel, companies respond either by bidding workers away from one another, which is something of a zero-sum game the main consequence of which is to escalate wage inflation, or by resorting to extensive overtime. If the response of the government to such upwards pressures on wages is to curb demand to the point of generating widespread unemployment, then skill shortages can be viewed as a primary cause

of the deterioration in the unemployment/inflation trade-off previously discussed.

What is evident is that, first, the disappearance of skill shortages during the period 1988–93 did not result in any downwards pressure on earnings growth. Secondly, the high of 28 per cent in 1988 was nevertheless well below the peaks recorded in the 1960s and early 1970s, while the 1991 and 1992 lows were comparable to that recorded in July 1980. Given that July 1980 and January 1991 represented almost identical points in successive economic cycles, it is evident that the pattern of skill shortages is consistent over time and cannot, accordingly, have had more than a marginal impact upon the unemployment/inflation trade-off. It would therefore appear to be the case that this trade-off will not be improved other than marginally through improved training.

It is alleged that the UK's relatively poor long-term productivity performance can be blamed, in good part, upon the shortage of skills. This is a highly contentious matter since there must inevitably be considerable uncertainty over the boost to productivity to be expected from a given programme of education and/or training. This is not to downplay the virtues of education and training, rather it is to remind ourselves that they cannot provide a miracle cure for the economy's ills in isolation. If they are combined with a German system of collective bargaining then the effects are going to be rather better than where they are combined with the system existing in the UK.

■ 14.4 Trade Unions

In their manifesto of 1979, the Conservatives stated that 'a fair balance between the rights and objectives of unions, management and the community in which they work is essential to economic recovery'. By this, they meant that the balance needed to be tilted away from the unions and towards management and the community. As the manifesto went on to say: 'We cannot go on, year after year, tearing ourselves apart in increasingly bitter and calamitous industrial disputes. In bringing about economic recovery, we should all be on the same side'.

It is not difficult to discern why the manifesto inferred that everyone was not on the same side in 1979. Trade unionism is essentially a twentieth century phenomenon. Illegal prior to 1824, unions spent the first 50 years of their legal existence primarily as organisations of craft workers. Hence, membership grew slowly despite the widespread onset of industrialisation. At the turn of the century, where we pick up the data on union membership in **Figure 14.3**, membership was still modest, but the unions were beginning to make their voices heard in the face of the adverse trading conditions faced by the UK economy at the time. The erosion of the UK's pre-eminent position as a producer and exporter of manufactures, combined with the massive transfer of workers out of agriculture, depressed wages and caused unemployment.

During the period 1906–13, the government granted immunities to unions from damages incurred in contemplation or furtherance of trade disputes and introduced minimum wage legislation. After 1914, unionism spread rapidly into the transport, energy and iron and steel industries, and unions secured a political power base by putting their voting power behind the newly-formed Labour party. During the 1920s, unions flexed their muscles, as in the General Strike of 1926 which, while it was a failure, established the political power of organised labour.

During the decades after 1945, the trade union movement grew enormously in both economic and political strength such that, by the 1970s, it effectively held the Labour party in thrall and demanded a say in the governing of the country. The attempt by the Labour party to meet the conditions imposed by the International Monetary Fund in 1976 eventually led to the 'Winter of Discontent' which ushered in the first Thatcher government.

□ 14.4.1 Conservative Legislation

The Conservative government had no intention of allowing the unions any say in the political process. On the other hand, it could do little immediately to strip the unions of their accumulated privileges and immunities. A more immediate weapon was the 1980–81 recession which cost large numbers of union members their jobs, causing union membership to fall away progressively from its 1979 peak (see **Figure 14.3**).

During the 1980s, the succesive Thatcher governments put in place a new legislative framework which redefined, in a cumulative fashion, the role of unions in the economy. There were six main pieces of legislation (for a detailed analysis see Marsh (1991)).

The Employment Act 1980

- Employers were given the power to take legal action where strikers sought to disrupt business at a workplace other than their own – known as **secondary picketing**.

- They were also empowered to take legal action if their employees disrupted their business in order to assist the employees of a separate organisation in the pursuit of a dispute which did not concern them directly.
- Employees could opt out of union membership, even where a closed shop existed at their place of work.
- Industrial action could no longer be taken on the basis of a show of hands, but required the backing of a postal ballot for which the government would provide funds.
- There was no longer to be a statutory obligation upon employers to recognise the rights of unions at their workplaces.

The Employment Act 1982

- Whereas previously an employer could cite only individual union organisers when taking legal action in respect of disruptions to his business, he could now take action against the union itself.
- Where a strike was **political** – that is, it involved neither employment matters nor a dispute between an employer and his own employees – an employer could seek redress from his striking employees.
- Any contract which sought to enforce the exclusive use of union members would be deemed to be illegal.
- Where a closed shop had not been approved by an overwhelming majority of the workforce, its provisions could not be legally enforced upon either an employer or dissenting employees.

The Trade Union Act 1984

- All elections for senior union posts would have to be by secret (generally postal) ballot.
- Unless a strike ballot was held by means of a secret vote, an employer could sue the organising union for damages.
- A union would be required to ballot its members every 10 years if it wished to maintain a fund for political purposes.

The Employment Act 1988

- Industrial action to enforce closed shops became illegal.
- If a union member refused to participate in an industrial dispute, and his union subsequently sought to discipline him, he could take legal action against the union.
- A union member could take out an injunction to prevent his union engaging in industrial action without a prior ballot, or engaging in such action before the ballot showed a clear majority in favour.
- All union presidents and general secretaries could be elected only where the ballot was fully postal and supervised by an independent body.
- The use of union funds was to be limited to certain purposes, and members were to have access to their union's accounts.
- A Commission for Union Affairs was to be established in order to finance union members wishing to take legal action against their union.

The Employment Act 1989

The 1978 Employment Protection (Consolidation) Act was amended to limit the duties in respect of which an employer was required to allow officials of a recognised trade union time off with pay. The Act was also amended to ease other burdens on employers.

The Employment Act 1990

- It became unlawful to refuse to employ a person because he or she is, or is not, a trade union member, or because he or she will not agree to become or cease to be a member, and that any person refused employment for such a reason may complain to an industrial tribunal.
- It removed the immunities under section 13 of the Trade Union and Labour Relations Act 1974

for acts in contemplation or furtherance of trade disputes involving calling for, or otherwise organising, 'secondary' action unless made in the course of peaceful picketing as the law allows.

- It extended section 15 of the Employment Act 1982, which prescribed circumstances in which a union is legally responsible for organising industrial action. In particular, if any union shop steward calls for industrial action, his union will be liable unless and until it effectively repudiates what he has done as soon as reasonably practicable.
- It gave employers greater freedom to dismiss employees taking part in unofficial action.

So far, the 1990s have seen one further major piece of legislation in addition to **The Trade Union and Labour Relations (Consolidation) Act 1992** which brought together much of the legislation set out above.

The Trade Union Reform and Employment Rights Act 1993

This Act, which largely came into force on 30 August 1993, departed from earlier legislation in two respects. First, it contained detailed regulation of the daily running of unions, and secondly, it reversed the long-standing assumption that collective bargaining is to be encouraged. Specifically (for details see *Employment Gazette*, August 1993):

- It gave employees the right, when pregnant, to a minimum entitlement of 14 weeks' maternity leave, and enhanced protection against dismissal on maternity related grounds.
- It gave employees the right to receive explicit written details of hours, pay and holiday entitlement.
- It gave employees the right to protection against being dismissed for exercising statutory employment rights.
- It gave individuals greater freedom to belong to the union of their choice.
- It gave trade union members the right not to have union subscriptions deducted from their

pay except with their written consent, which is to be subject to periodic renewal.
- It required union industrial action ballots to be conducted fully-postal voting only, and to be independently scrutinised.
- It required unions to provide employers with at least seven days' notice of official industrial action.
- It created a new 'Citizen's Right' to restrain unlawfully organised industrial action.
- It abolished the remaining Wages Councils and their statutory minimum pay rates.

□ 14.4.2 Trade Union Membership

A list of trade unions is maintained by the Certification Office of Trade Unions and Employers' Associations in accordance with section 8 of the Trade Union and Labour Relations Act 1974. Section 28 contains the definition of a union, primarily in terms of a requirement that it is an organisation of workers which has the regulation of relations between workers and employers as one of its principal purposes. All listed and unlisted unions are required under section 11 to submit annual returns, which include membership figures, to the Certification Officer.

The number of unions recorded by the Certification Office is somewhat different from that recorded by the Employment Department (which are used below) because the latter counts only 'parent' unions such as the National Union of Mineworkers, and includes unions with their head office in Northern Ireland.

Figures for union membership are those provided by the Employment Department which are compatible with those of the Certification Office for the UK as a whole. However, membership figures which are also now available, as a result of a question included for the first time on the 1989 Labour Force Survey, are calculated in a manner which results in a lower membership figure compared to the Employment Department (see Sweeney, 1996; Cully and Woodland, 1996). The discrepancy arises because the LFS count excludes those who were unemployed, wholly retired or overseas at the time of counting. In addition, the LFS counts individuals in membership rather than individual memberships, whereas the Certification Office counts the number of memberships even if individuals belong to more than one union.

Figure 14.3 illustrates the long-term membership trend. As can be seen, although membership slumped during the 1920s for reasons indicated in Chapter 1, it rose steadily from the early 1930s to a peak of 13.3 million in 1979. Subsequently, it has been downhill all the way, with the end-1995 figure standing at an estimated 8 million (the LFS equivalent was 7.3 million), a reduction of 40 per cent from the peak figure.

Figure 14.3 provides data for both union membership and the number of unions. The sharp downturn in membership during 1981 and 1982 comes as no surprise given the severity of the recession at the beginning of the decade, but it is surprising to observe that the previously noted upturn in employment from 1986 onwards failed to reverse the downwards trend. This can be seen more clearly in **Figure 14.4**, which also matches up membership changes to changes in employees

in employment. Membership has fallen in every year since 1979 and appears to have been wholly unresponsive to the pick up in employment since 1992. Indeed, the proportionate falls in 1992, 1993 and 1994 were the largest on record bar that in 1981 (Sweeney, 1996, p. 51).

In part, this can be attributed to inefficient practices among the unions themselves. Workplaces where unions are recognised encompass roughly 60 per cent of the workforce, yet one-third of these workers are not union members. Under such circumstances, it is easy to give up union membership without the expectation of disapproval by fellow workers. It is also the case that entrepreneurial (and, often, medium-sized) firms are neglected by union officials who prefer to service existing agreements with larger companies. The old-style bargaining methods utilised by male officials are also unlikely to strike a sympathetic chord in a modern factory full of female part-time workers.

It is reasonable to argue that the growth of female part-time workers and of small companies would have caused some erosion of union mem-

Figure 14.3   *Trade Unions: 1900–94*

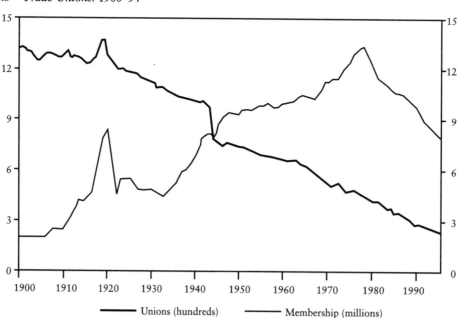

Unions (hundreds)   Membership (millions)

Source: Employment Gazette, May 1993; Labour Market Trends, February 1996.

Figure 14.4 *Year on Year Changes in Employees in Employment and Trade Union Membership*

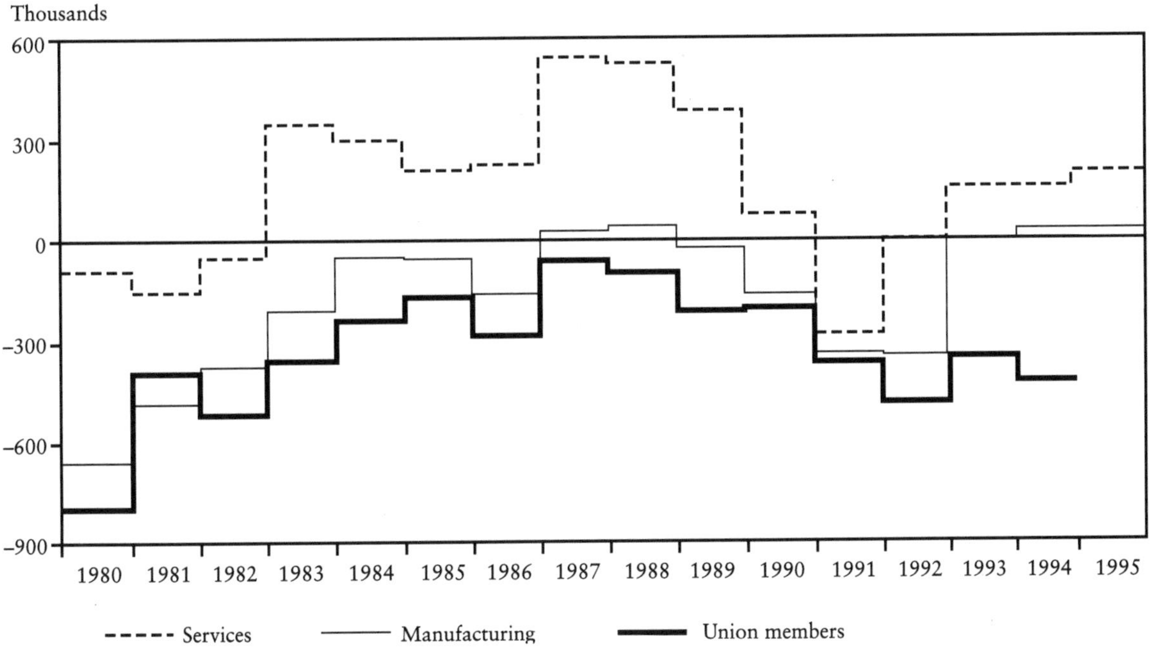

Source: *Employment Gazette, Labour Market Trends.*

bership even if officials had tried harder to recruit in non-traditional ways. Nevertheless, there is evidence to suggest that the attitude towards unions in different types of workplace is a more critical factor. In general, managers in large companies with full-time workforces are happy to foster union membership in order to simplify bargaining arrangements. Where the employers in small companies also seek to encourage unions there is typically an equally high membership ratio. Where, however, such companies – almost all of which operate in the private sector whereas many of the largest employers operate in the public sector – discourage membership it is typically only one third as high.

It is often believed that workers are much more likely to join unions in the traditional manufacturing regions as compared to the south-east. However, the significant switch of employment to the south-east does not, of itself, seem to have had much effect upon union membership. Rather, the explanation is to be found in the points outlined above, namely that the type of company shedding labour in the north is much more likely to encourage membership than the newer companies taking on labour in the south-east.

Furthermore, there is no reason to attribute the decline in membership to the switch from unskilled to relatively skilled and managerial occupations. If anything, the latter group appear to have a more favourable image of unions than their unskilled counterparts. On the other hand, as suggested above, the unions themselves may show less enthusiasm for recruiting among their ranks.

An important longer-term factor is that the most significant decline in membership during the 1990s has been among those aged under 25. This reflects the rise in the number of young people in higher education, high unemployment among the under-25s and the loss of apprenticeships.

A number of highly-publicised confrontations have given the impression that attempts by employers to derecognise unions have accounted for a major decline in membership. Such incidents, however, have been relatively rare and the effects of derecognition correspondingly insignificant. Indeed, recent surveys such as those by Industrial Relations Services (for example, *IRS Employment Trends* 553, 1994) have indicated that falling union membership and a desire to link pay more closely to performance are among the most common reasons employers have for derecognition. According to the LFS (see Cully and Woodland, 1996, p. 222), roughly 10.2 million employees worked in workplaces where unions were recognised, a reduction of less than 2 per cent over the three-year period 1993–95.

It would appear, therefore, that the switch from public sector to private sector employment, from manufacturing to services and from male to female employment have been instrumental in loosening the grip of unions on the workforce, and that the unions themselves have done little to counteract these trends. It should also be noted that the unions are not perceived by their members as delivering a satisfactory service. Only about one in ten workers, whether unionised or not, believes that unions are successful in defending the rights of workers. Nevertheless, this does not appear to make workers feel hostile towards unions, nor does it appear to explain why more than a modest proportion – roughly 15 per cent according to a 1989 Nuffield College study – give up their membership.

In conclusion, it would appear to be the case that, as the industrial structure has evolved, employees have become increasingly disenchanted with traditional trade unionism and that the unions have failed to respond to the challenge. At the same time, the stream of industrial relations legislation has created an increasingly hostile environment for the union movement, and the relatively high levels of unemployment together with, until recently, rapidly rising wage levels for full-time male employees, have also had a depressive effect upon membership. Interestingly, whereas the clause in the 1993 Act whereby union dues cannot be deducted from an employee's pay packet without his or her consent seemed particularly likely to affect membership adversely, commencing in 1994, this does not appear to have happened.

□ 14.4.3 Trade Union Numbers

As shown in **Figure 14.3**, the number of unions has fallen from 500 in 1975 to 243 in 1994. The number peaked at 1384 in 1920, and numbers fell steadily thereafter with the exception of 1973 and 1977 when small increases were recorded. In fact, new unions are constantly being formed – there were 10 even in 1988 – but mergers and transfers of membership have been the dominant factor throughout the period.

Even today most unions are small. In 1994, 42 per cent of all unions had fewer than 1000 members, accounting for 0.4 per cent of total membership. By way of contrast, the 17 largest unions, each with more than 100 000 members, accounted for 79 per cent of total membership and the 7 largest unions, each with more than 250 000 members, accounted for 60 per cent of total membership. The most recently available data are presented in **Figure 14.5**.

□ 14.4.4 Trade Union Finances

Falling memberships, coupled with a failure to raise subscriptions as a proportion of members' earnings, have resulted in a steady decline in the primary source of income for virtually all unions. Whether this creates severe financial problems depends, however, upon their expenditure. Where unions take on large numbers of full-time officials and push for expansion, as in the 1970s, spending tends to outrun revenue and causes a reduction in real net worth (which almost halved for registered unions between 1965 and 1980). Although real net worth rose by over one quarter during the 1980s, this reflected in part, as noted previously, the failure by the unions to engage in an aggressive membership drive in smaller workplaces where, due to lack of co-operation by management, recruitment was costly.

Unions have sought to save costs by merging together, in several recent cases thereby creating 'super-unions' such as the Amalgamated Engineering and Electrical Union (AEU/EEPTU) in April 1992 and Unison (Nalgo/Nupe/Cohse) in July 1993, but this has often been a financial

Figure 14.5   *Membership and Number of Unions, by Size, 1994*

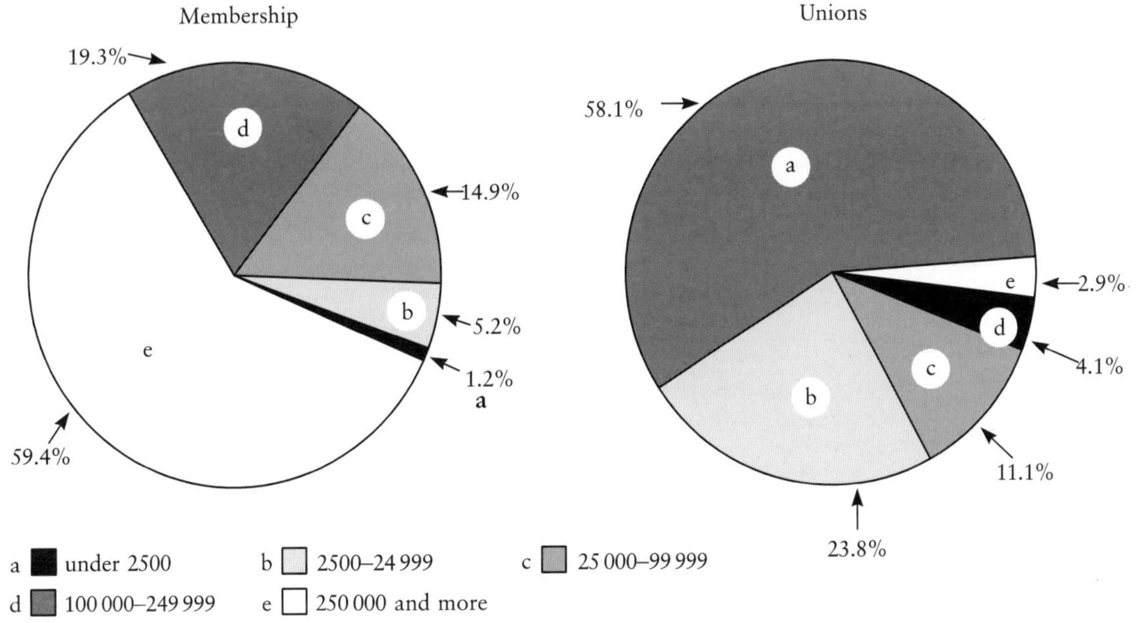

Membership

Unions

a ■ under 2500	b ☐ 2500–24 999
c ▨ 25 000–99 999	
d ▨ 100 000–249 999	e ☐ 250 000 and more

Source: Labour Market Trends, February 1996, p. 51.

disaster due to inaccuracies in the accounts of smaller unions and their tendency to exaggerate their memberships and hence their subscription income. The salaries of officials also tend to be boosted as a consequence of mergers. During the 1980s, the careful investment of accumulated reserves helped to offset these costs, but many unions, even such giants as the Transport and General Workers' Union, found it hard to avoid operating at a loss and hence eating into those reserves. As a consequence, the unions have been obliged to pull in their horns during the 1990s, and this has restricted their ability to enlarge their membership, although there are exceptions, typically in the public sector such as Unison, which are still prosperous.

☐ *14.4.5 Union Density*

'Union density' is simply the number of individuals in each category who are members of either a trade union, staff association or both, expressed as a percentage of all individuals in that category. It is possible to obtain data using this 'tight' definition through the Labour Force Survey (LFS), although alternative measures are also available using somewhat different definitions (see *Employment Gazette*, August 1990, p. 413).

Table 14.6 summarises the data on union density in 1995 for Great Britain. The overall density for employees was 32 per cent, down from 37 per cent in 1991. Density was higher among males than among females, but the gap in 1991 was twice as large at 10 per cent, and it was notable that the proportional fall in male membership in 1994 was the largest ever. As a result, men represented only 57.5 per cent of membership in 1994, with women outnumbering men in five of the ten largest unions. In addition, areas that traditionally were a stronghold of unionism suffered the largest declines, almost eradicating in the process the historic differential compared to areas where unions were weakest.

Table 14.6   *Union Density in Great Britain 1995 (%)*

All employees	32
Men	35
Women	30
Married/Cohabit	35
Unmarried	22
Manual	33
Non-manual	32
Full-time[1]	36
Part-time	21
Production	34
Services	33
Professional	52
Manager/Admin	21
Craft & related	37
Sales	12
Annual contract	50
Mainly at home	6

Note:
[1] The definition of full-time and part-time is based on the respondent's own assessment, not on the number of hours usually worked.

Source: Cully and Woodland (1996).

The differential between manual and non-manual workers shrunk from 9 per cent in 1989 to 1 per cent in 1995, an almost identical reduction to that between production and service industry employees. However, sharp differences in density still exist according to the number of employees per workplace. Roughly 38 per cent of all workers in workplaces employing 25 or more employees were union members in 1995, compared to 16 per cent found in workplaces employing no more than 24 workers.

Full-time workers were twice as likely to be union members as part-time workers in 1990, but the proportions had fallen respectively to 36 per cent and 21 per cent in 1995 (the latter having changed very little over this period). Previous LFS estimates have revealed (*Employment Gazette,* January 1993) that female part-time employees are roughly twice as likely as their male counterparts to be union members. This appears to arise because these females are predominantly middle-aged married women who stay with the same employers for long periods of time, whereas part-time males tend to be either relatively young or relatively old and treat their jobs in a much more transient manner.

A significantly greater proportion of those aged 30 years of age or older in 1995 were union members as compared to the proportion in employment, whereas the opposite held true for those aged under 20 who no longer seem much interested in the concept of 'solidarity'. Density also increased with length of service.

Looked at from an occupational perspective, union densities varied enormously, for example registering 52 per cent among professionals but only 12 per cent among those engaged in sales. Nevertheless, the union movement still consists predominantly of workers in occupations such as clerical and catering where union densities are relatively low. A final factor is region of residence. In 1995 union density was highest in Wales (44 per cent) and lowest in the South East excluding Greater London (23 per cent).

It is possible to take a more sanguine view of the decline in density when account is taken of the somewhat lower densities in many other EU member countries (only 6 per cent in France despite much taking to the streets, but over 70 per cent in much of Scandinavia), and of the overall density of 16 per cent in the USA. The unions in the UK clearly need to recruit amongst workers in the private sector, where density is 23 per cent, yet that is harder than in the public sector (62 per cent unionised in 1995). On the whole, the evidence indicates that in the private sector non-union plants are more productive and more profitable than their unionised counterparts. Hence non-union workers tend to be better rewarded and to enjoy better relations with management. Their employers understandably often refuse to recognise unions, and derecognition may occur. Unless statutory recognition is introduced, the union movement is likely to concede further ground. Certainly, it is notable that there are currently virtually no disputes about union recognition.

The prevailing view is now that, to be successful, unions must maintain the allegiance of employees as they move between employers and through different cycles of their careers.

□ *14.4.6 Industrial Disputes*

Table 14.7 contains data on industrial disputes in the UK covering a period of two decades. As can be seen, there are various ways of measuring the incidence of disputes and the various series tell a somewhat different story. For the purpose of making international comparisons it is customary to use the number of working days lost per 1000 employees, although there are definitional ambiguities (for example, only the UK and USA exclude data on political stoppages – see *Employment Gazette*, December 1990, p. 610).

Table 14.7 *Stoppages[1] in Progress, UK, 1970–95*

Year	No. of Recorded Stoppages in Progress	Workers involved in Period (000)	Working Days Lost (000)	Working Days Lost per 1000 Employees[2]
1970	3 943	1 801	10 980	489
1971	2 263	1 178	13 551	612
1972	2 530	1 734	23 909	1 080
1973	2 902	1 528	7 197	317
1974	2 946	1 626	14 750	647
1975	2 332	809	6 012	265
1976	2 034	668	3 284	146
1977	2 737	1 166	10 142	448
1978	2 498	1 041	9 405	413
1979	2 125	4 608	29 474	1 273
1980	1 348	834	11 964	521
1981	1 344	1 513	4 266	195
1982	1 538	2 103	5 313	248
1983	1 364	574	3 754	178
1984	1 221	1 464	27 135	1 278
1985	903	791	6 402	299
1986	1 074	720	1 920	90
1987	1 016	887	3 546	164
1988	781	790	3 702	166
1989	701	727	4 128	182
1990	630	298	1 903	81
1991	369	176	761	34
1992	253	148	528	24
1993	211	385	649	30
1994	205	107	278	13
1995	235	174	415	19

Notes:
[1] The statistics relate to stoppages of work in the UK due to industrial disputes between employers and workers, or between workers and other workers, connected with terms and conditions of employment. Work to rules and go-slows are not included; neither are stoppages involving fewer than ten workers or lasting less than one day unless the total number of workers' days lost in the dispute exceeds 100. The statistics include lock-outs and unlawful strikes (see *Employment Gazette*, July 1989, p. 359).
[2] Based on the latest available mid-year (June) estimate of employees in employment.
Source: Employment Gazette; Labour Market Trends.

What the data show fairly unambiguously is that the number of stoppages has fallen noticeably since 1979, and especially since 1988. Excluding the Winter of Discontent in 1979–80, which effectively preceded the first Thatcher government, the number of working days lost per 1000 employees also tended to be lower during the 1980s, with the exception of 1984 due to the miners' strike discussed below and, less obviously, 1986 where the printers' strike does not show up in the data, but the really dramatic decline began in 1990.

14.4.7 Key Disputes and Data Distortion

In interpreting the data, care has to be exercised in respect of the two key disputes during the 1980s. The first of these, the miners' strike of 1984–85, caused an enormous increase in the number of days lost through strikes in 1984 even though the number of stoppages was relatively modest. By way of contrast, the print union strike of 1986–87, which was almost comparable in its intensity, does not show up at all in the data for days lost because the workers involved had lost their jobs although the company, News International, carried on production.

It is interesting to relate these disputes to the union law then in existence. In the case of the miners, their defeat can most obviously be ascribed to a determined government, astute planning by the Coal Board and an unsympathetic public, rather than to the use of new laws which were largely ignored. On the other hand, it is possible that the failure of the National Union of Mineworkers to involve other unions in the dispute may have had something to do with the law on secondary picketing and fear of having funds sequestered.

In the case of the dispute between News International and the National Geographical Association and SOGAT 82, the dismissal of the strikers took place under the terms of pre-1979 legislation, but injunctions were also taken out to prevent secondary picketing and secondary action by other union members to disrupt the company's business. Perhaps the crucial matter arising out of these disputes is that certain unions, whether newly-formed in the case of the Union of Democratic Mineworkers or long-standing in the case of the EEPTU, have now decided to act wholly in accordance with the new laws and to use this as a lever to gain recognition in place of other unions, such as the NUM and SOGAT, which are wholly opposed to them. The new Acts have, therefore, served to weaken the union movement primarily by dividing it from within.

14.4.8 Are Strikes a Thing of the Past?

In 1994, the number of stoppages in progress was the lowest for more than 50 years, as it had been in the previous five years, although the exclusion of some of the smallest stoppages from the recorded data during this period casts some doubt over this conclusion. The number of working days lost showed a broadly similar pattern, although it rose slightly for four successive years from 1985 before falling back sharply in 1990. This phenomenon was also manifested in other advanced economies, but the UK's relative position in terms of working days lost per 1000 employees has improved substantially taking 1990–94 compared to 1985–89 (see *The Economist*, 20 April 1996, p. 120).

Throughout the 1980s, four sectors of industry were especially prone to disputes – namely mining and quarrying, manufacturing, construction and transport and communication, both in the UK and elsewhere (although the UK in particular suffered relatively due to the 1984–85 miners' strike – see *Employment Gazette*, December 1990, p. 611). In other sectors, strikes are therefore of little economic significance, and even in the more troublesome sectors the period post-1985 was a huge improvement compared both to 1980–84 and to 1970–79.

On the whole, bearing in mind that the 1980s were a decade during which there was a good deal of disruptive restructuring, there is reason for a cautiously optimistic response to the above question in the sense that, whereas industrial disputes will always remain with us, their incidence and economic effects do seem to have reached an equilibrium at an acceptable level (see Sweeney and Davies, 1996 for an analysis of 1995 when, for the first time ever, there was no strike in coal mining).

It is worth observing, however, that the absence of strikes may reflect a cowed workforce as well as a contented one. A strike has two basic elements, namely an unsatisfied grievance and an ability to strike. Hence, a reduction in strike activity must reflect a decline in unsatisfied employee grievances and/or a decline in the ability to strike. It is notable that there does not appear to be a shortage of grievances, and it is at least possible that the election of a Labour government will lead to enhanced strike activity as employees' expectations of redistribution in their favour are at least partially frustrated.

The one-day strike has become the weapon of choice, with one and two-day strikes accounting for 25 per cent of working days lost since 1990 compared to 6 per cent in the 1980s. The data on overtime also indicate that, at least in the private sector, overtime bans were twice as likely to occur as strikes during the 1980s. Interestingly, techniques such as just-in-time deliveries have made the overtime ban an increasingly effective weapon, and fear of unemployment is more likely to discourage strikes than overtime bans. In any event, it is worth noting that absenteeism causes the loss of several hundred times more working days than strikes, so it may no longer be appropriate to devote so much effort to the latter problem.

14.4.9 Effects of Legislation Upon Union Behaviour

It is generally believed that the huge improvement in corporate performance after the end of the 1980–81 recession can be ascribed, at least in part, to the stream of anti-union legislation emanating from the various Thatcher governments. It is difficult to 'prove' the precise form of the relationship between the two (as Marsh (1991) observes, in the private sector at least the government can do no more than influence the legislative and ideological context), but such evidence as exists (in particular the work of the Centre for Labour Economics at the London School of Economics) lends little support to the popular view that unions deter investment and hold back productivity growth, thereby creating unemployment (their effects upon wage differentials are discussed separately below).

What the studies show is that the 1980–81 recession would have created a positive climate for change even in the absence of supporting legislation, since it threatened union members with unemployment and companies with bankruptcy unless they rapidly improved their performance. What it is certainly fair to say is that there was a great deal of potential for such an improvement at the turn of the decade, and that the conservative attitudes of unions during the 1970s in resisting change had a great deal to do with this fact.

The British tradition was that, in a bargaining situation, the union was concerned only with pay and job security whereas management was concerned with efficiency and productivity. One obvious consequence was the debilitating miners' strike of 1984–85 which was fought in order to preserve jobs in arguably the least-pleasant occupation on offer, rather than to ensure that miners' sons could be found something else to do of a less-arduous kind.

Irrespective of cause, however, the studies showed that unionised companies seemed to have more organisational change, higher investment and higher productivity growth after 1981 without the unions seeking to oppose these developments. The comparison of productivity growth between highly-unionised companies, with more than half the workforce in a union, and companies with little or no union representation is especially interesting. Throughout the 1970s neither group held the ascendency for other than short periods, and each held it for roughly half the period. From 1981 to 1985, however, the highly-unionised group performed much better, especially from 1983 to 1985. Unfortunately, it is as yet unclear whether this trend, which came to an end during 1985, was simply a one-off response to the recession or is a more permanent feature of the industrial landscape.

Insofar as the government chose to believe that their anti-union legislation was responsible for this improved performance, it is understandable that they chose to introduce several more Acts, set out above, during the latter part of the decade. The interesting question is, therefore, whether this legislation was mere overkill, although it was certainly electorally popular which may ultimately prove to be its main justification.

□ 14.4.10 The Closed Shop

Closed shops come in two varieties – namely **pre-entry** whereby a worker cannot be hired unless he or she is already a member of a union with negotiating rights at the workplace where employment is sought, and **post-entry** whereby it becomes a condition for being hired that a worker joins an appropriate union as soon as possible after being given a job. It is argued that closed shops are only fair because otherwise non-members will be able to 'free-ride' on the backs of members and secure the same improvements in terms and conditions which the members pay for via their subscriptions to the union.

It is also the case that closed shops typically come into existence only when union density has reached a high level, and that many employers look upon them with favour, particularly in the public sector, because they find it much easier to enter into collective agreements with a specific union. During the 1960s and 1970s, closed shops became increasingly popular, and at their peak in 1978 they covered in excess of 5 million workers. Subsequently, however, partly as a result of the Thatcher government's labour legislation and the effects of the 1980–81 recession, numbers employed in closed shops fell away sharply to a total roughly 3.5 million in 1985, of whom roughly 0.5 million were covered by a pre-entry shop according to the Workplace Industrial Relations Survey (WIRS).

Further research by the government undertaken as a prelude to the Employment Act 1990 indicated that there were only 2.6 million workers in closed shops in 1989, although rather more than had been thought appeared to be in pre-entry shops. The closed shop, therefore, appeared to be fading away without any further assistance, but the 1990 Act, as we have seen, nevertheless made it illegal to refuse to employ a worker who neither was, nor wished to become, a union member. This arose largely because, prior to the Act, a worker who believed that he had been refused a job simply because he was not a union member could obtain no redress against the company in question. The European Court of Justice has also ruled that it is unfair to dismiss workers who refuse to join a union.

□ 14.4.11 The Union Mark-up

In an ideal world, the success or otherwise of a union can be judged by its ability to raise the pay of its members above levels ruling for non-union members while simultaneously maintaining full employment for its members. In certain industries, and during certain periods, this happy combination (from the union's perspective since it is unlikely to be conducive to improved profitability) was achieved.

In general, the 1970s were a good decade for the unions, with incomes rising at the expense of profits and with the incomes of union members rising faster than those of non-union members. A comparison of unionised sectors with non-unionised sectors during the period 1964–79 by Minford indicated an enormous differential in favour of union members. However, it is more customary to treat the mark-up as the difference in pay for two workers doing exactly the same kind or work, but where one belongs to a union and the other does not. Defined in this way, the mark-up appears to have risen, on average, only from roughly 5 per cent to 10 per cent during this period, but also to have shown considerable variability as between different occupations and industries. One study (Blanchflower, 1984) reached the somewhat surprising conclusion that whereas the mark-up was only approximately 1 per cent for skilled workers in 1980, it was roughly 10 per cent for semi-skilled manual workers (for a summary of other studies see Brown and Wadhwani, 1990, pp. 65–8).

Intra-industry variability is to be expected because of significant differences which exist in product markets. By and large, unions cannot establish much of a differential where there is intense product market competition, especially from foreign companies, whereas a protected home market combined with a closed shop necessarily greatly strengthens the union's hand. For our purposes, the most interesting questions are whether the 1980–81 recession eroded differentials and whether these were restrained further by anti-union legislation.

The initial impact of the recession was undoubtedly minor. Faced by the choice between taking a reduction in pay or accepting the loss of jobs which could no longer be justified at existing wage levels, unions almost invariably preferred the latter to the former. Eventually, the sheer scale of job losses, wholesale plant closures and the onset of legislation ate significantly into differentials, but the buoyant employment situation during the latter part of the decade served to restore part of what had been lost except in circumstances where either closed shop arrangements had been removed or unions had been derecognised (Gregg and Machin, 1992). When compared to the effect exerted by changing market forces, the effect of anti-union legislation appears to have been minor (Brown and Wadhwani, 1990 and Gregg and Machin, 1992).

☐ *14.4.12 Insiders and Outsiders*

The sluggish response of differentials to the rapid rise in unemployment during the early 1980s – and, indeed, their continued existence, albeit at somewhat reduced levels, at a time when between 2 million and 3 million people were unemployed – is something of a puzzle. Clearly, the labour market is imperfect in its operation, and an explanation for why that is so can be found by reference to the distinction between **insiders** and **outsiders**.

'Insiders' comprise those people who are either in work or who have recently lost their jobs but who retain valuable skills. A significant proportion among them will belong to unions. 'Outsiders', by way of contrast, comprise those people who have lost their jobs recently but whose skills are largely non-transferable, those who lost their

jobs more than a year ago (the long-term unemployed) and those who have never held a job at all (school leavers and housewives).

Outsiders may become very numerous, but they may nevertheless have little effect upon the labour market. In the first place, unions may be more concerned with protecting the position of their members who are still employed than with the interests of the unemployed (who will tend to let their membership lapse). Secondly, employers will not be interested in taking on workers with either redundant skills or none at all, unless absolutely necessary. Thirdly, some outsiders will be content to live off social security, at least for a time. Under these circumstances, an upturn in demand is likely to lead to overtime working and the re-employment of skilled workers only recently laid off. As a consequence, wages will continue to rise despite the existence of a large pool of unemployed workers. This becomes even more probable where there is a geographic imbalance between the places where the unemployed reside and the places where demand is growing.

In general, it is fair to say that any convincing analysis of how the labour market works must contain some elements of the insider–outsider dichotomy. Nevertheless, it is also fair to say that it explains persistently high unemployment more easily than changes in unemployment.

☐ *14.4.13 Political Levies*

It is hardly surprising that the Thatcher governments heartily disliked union political funds since they provided the main source of revenue for the Labour party. What rankled above all else was the fact that large numbers of union members were voting for the Conservative party whereas the unions' political funds were being passed in their entirety to the Opposition. Allowing members to 'contract out' of making payments into a political fund was an step in rectifying this anomaly, but inertia combined with a preference not to be at logger-heads with fellow workers meant that relatively few took up this option.

The government accordingly made it obligatory under the Trade Union Act 1984 for unions to hold a ballot on the question of whether or not to have a political fund. However, much to the government's annoyance, the answer in almost every case was in the affirmative.

■ 14.5 Equal Pay and Pensions

□ 14.5.1 Equal Pay

The Equal Pay Act 1975 required that women who performed similar tasks to men should be treated equally. The Sex Discrimination Act 1975 further required that men and women should be guaranteed equality of opportunity. In 1970, women's hourly earnings relative to those of men, as calculated from data in the annual New Earnings Survey, stood at 63.1 per cent. In 1975, the comparable figure was 72.1 per cent and in 1976 it was 75.1 per cent. It is reasonable to attribute most of the increase to the existence to these Acts. All alternative explanations, such as the existence of flat-rate incomes policies, an upturn in the demand for female labour or a reduction in the supply of female labour lack explanatory power, either because they did not happen (the reduction in supply); because they were not permanent yet there was no reversal of the relative earnings ratio when they ceased to apply (incomes policies); or because they were permanent (the increased demand for female labour) yet the earnings differential ceased to narrow after 1977.

Other actions to improve things were taken supranationally. In 1983, for example, the European Court of Justice ruled that the UK was in contravention of Community legislation which defined equal pay in terms of equal value. The Equal Pay (Amendment) Regulations were speedily enacted to bring the UK into line with this ruling. Unfortunately, this did not resolve the precise meaning of the term 'equal value', and a body of case law has had to be accumulated for this purpose.

In the case of *Hayward v. Cammell Laird Shipbuilders* (1980), for example, the House of Lords eventually ruled that equal pay literally meant equal money wages, and chose to disregard differences in perks. In June 1989, a woman records

assistant employed by Northern Ireland Electricity was awarded equal pay with a male manual worker by a Belfast tribunal in the first case in which parity was established between white collar and blue collar jobs. An important current case revolves around a claim first lodged in 1985 by a district speech therapist against Frenchay District Health Authority claiming parity with hospital pharmacists. The initial ruling that the speech therapist had no case was upheld by an appeals tribunal in January 1991.

This judgement meant that separate collective bargaining arrangements which result in unequal pay between men and women cannot be challenged under equal pay laws unless it can be shown that the arrangements are **directly** discriminatory, whereas cases are typically based on claims of **indirect** discrimination. However, an appeal to the European Court of Justice resulted in a ruling (see Fredman, 1994) to the effect that employers must justify objectively any differences in pay between groups of men and women doing jobs of equal value even if the differences result from collective agreements which do not appear to be discriminatory.

Recent evidence from the DES (Research Paper 71, 1996) indicates that differentials have reduced significantly since 1980, partly because women are better educated, but that they continue to remain fairly large because men and women work in different industrial sectors, because women are more likely to work part-time and because of time taken off for child rearing.

□ 14.5.2 Job Equality

Community law allows leeway from the strict principle of equality where governments are seeking 'to promote equal opportunities for men and women, in particular by removing existing inequalities which affect women's opportunities'. However, the ECJ ruled in October 1995 that the German State of Bremen had been breaking Community law by giving jobs to women ahead of equally qualified men. In future, job quotas may still be permissable, but will clearly have to be made far less overt.

☐ *14.5.3 Pension Equality*

The key case involved a gentleman called Mr Barber who was made redundant by the Guardian Royal Exchange Assurance at the age of 52. Under the GRE severance scheme, men and women made redundant 10 years before the scheme's normal retirement ages would be treated as taking early retirement, thus qualifying for an immediate pension. Mr Barber received a deferred pension and redundancy compensation whereas a woman of the same age would have received an immediate pension. Mr Barber made a claim on the grounds of sex discrimination to an industrial tribunal and the Employment Appeal Tribunal, but both dismissed his claim.

On appeal, the Court of Appeal referred the case to the European Court of Justice to give a ruling as to whether the benefits received in connection with compulsory redundancy in the circumstances of the case constituted 'pay' within Article 119 of the Treaty of Rome, and accordingly whether they had to be equal for men and women.

The UK government argued that the benefits paid from a pension scheme fell with Articles 117 and 118, not Article 119. The Court of Justice gave a judgement on 17 May 1990, ruling that: (i) the benefits paid by an employer to a worker in connection with redundancy fall within Article 119; (ii) pensions paid under occupational pension schemes, including contracted out schemes, fall within Article 119; (iii) equal treatment must apply to each component part of remuneration including components of a pension; (iv) Article 119 has direct effect and does not apply to state social security benefits.

The situation was further complicated by a case involving former employees of Coloroll, a home furnishing company which had gone into liquidation. At the end of April 1993 the Court of Justice delivered a preliminary opinion to the effect that equal treatment applied to periods prior to May 1990 only where the claimant had initiated proceedings before that date. This forestalled enormous additional claims on pension schemes, but simultaneously induced the great majority of UK employers to respond by equalising the age of eligibility for all members of their occupational schemes in order to be able to finance claims for the period beyond 1990.

A second issue on which the Court ruled simultaneously concerned lump-sum retirement benefits, in respect of which it was held that employers must not take into account that women live longer than men and hence require a larger lump-sum on retirement to provide them with monthly income for the rest of their lives.

Although Community law allows member states to keep different pension ages for men and women, men in the UK were required to pay contributions for at least 44 years to qualify for a full state pension compared to 39 years for women. Even if a man had paid contributions for 44 years, he still had to continue making contributions until he retired or reached 65, whereas women stopped paying at 60. The Court of Justice ruled against these provisions, which obliged the UK government to equalise the age of eligibility for state pensions. For it to lower the male retirement age to 60 would have been hugely costly. Raising the retirement age to 65 for women would have saved money but been damaging politically. A common age of 63 would have provided a potential compromise with the adjustment phased in over a period of years. The government understandably opted for a common 65 with gradual phasing-in arrangements to ensure that no woman aged 44 or over in 1993 was affected (see Secretary of State for Social Security, 1993, p. 10).

■ *14.6* The European Dimension

It would go beyond our immediate purpose to examine in detail the implications of the SEM for the UK labour market. Nevertheless, a number of comments are in order.

In the first place, the SEM is likely to have consequences for union structures. The idea of pan-European unions in specific sectors must inevitably hold some appeal for unions which are facing an adverse climate in the UK. However, this may prove difficult to realise in practice because, for example, most other EU countries are less-highly unionised; the industries in decline in the UK are generally also in decline elsewhere; there are political and cultural differences to overcome; and there is the small matter of linguistic difficulties, at least for UK union leaders.

Secondly, there are implications for the structure of wage bargaining. Those EU countries, including the UK, where unions are big enough to influence wages but too small to care about their effect on the whole economy, have generally performed worse than countries where either bargaining is centrally organised, and hence unions have to take into account the effects of their actions on the economy as a whole, or bargaining is highly decentralised and unions are too weak to affect wage levels. Insofar as the SEM will open up EU markets to greater internal competition it will weaken the power of unions, especially those in previously sheltered industries. By implication this should yield benefits for the performance of the UK economy.

Thirdly, there is the matter of the European Community Charter of Workers' Fundamental Social Rights, better known as the **Social Charter**, which was first approved by the European Commission in May 1989. Its purpose is to guarantee the basic rights of workers in the EU and it covers, *inter alia*, employment and remuneration, living and working conditions and information, consultation and participation. It is proceeding primarily via the issuing of directives, known as the **Social Action Programme**, which must eventually be translated into national law once they are adopted by the Council of Ministers.

The Programme got fully into its stride in June 1990 with a draft directive giving the same rights, such as training and holidays, to **part-time and temporary workers** as to full-time workers. Initially vetoed by the UK government in December 1994, this was subsequently accepted in principle, even if not in law, after the House of Lords ruled in favour of equality of rights (Curwen, 1995, p. 45).

In July 1990, a draft directive appeared on **working hours**. Among the then 12 EU members only Denmark and the UK did not regulate the maximum daily working period, but this was of little relevance since actual working hours for full-time employees were in most cases well below the

maximum set. The UK was also unusual insofar as it was one of only two countries which did not regulate overtime. This was because the ideal UK working week was seen as one where official working hours were short – the lowest in the EU in many industries – but there was plenty of overtime available at higher rates of pay.

Aside from fixing a maximum compulsory working week of 48 hours, this directive accordingly concentrated upon shift and night work. On average, 20 per cent of EU employees do shift work, with the highest rates in the UK and Spain (29 per cent). The directive sets out that every worker will be entitled to mandatory rest breaks after six continuous hours work; at least 11 hours of consecutive rest in 24 hours; an average of one rest day a week; and four weeks annual paid holiday. Night work will be limited to eight hours a day, averaged over two weeks. The directive was finally adopted in June 1993, but there will be exemptions and the UK has a grace period until at least November 2003 before the directive needs to be fully implemented.

In October 1994, a further directive on **maternity leave** became operational. This sets out that women will get at least 14 weeks' maternity leave. Jobs will also be protected during this period. Women will qualify after six months with their employer. In aggregate, the measures in the directive are more generous than those previously ruling in the UK.

Under the terms of a directive adopted in September 1994, any EU company with more than 1000 employees and where at least 150 of them work in each of two EU countries, is required to set up a **European works council**, effectively a consultative council at group level where strategic decisions will be discussed which touch on plant closures and employment contracts. However, this does not apply to the UK which vetoed it originally, only to see it resubmitted successfully under the **Agreement on Social Policy**, annexed to the **Protocol on Social Policy** (generally known as the **Social Chapter** and itself attached to the Maastricht Treaty), from which the UK negotiated an 'opt-out'. In September 1994, the government also vetoed a draft directive which would have given fathers of newborn or adopted children the right to three months' unpaid **paternity leave** (*ibid.*, p. 45), only to see that take the same route. The part-time directive may follow.

The latest battlefield comprised the **posted workers directive** which required companies carrying out contracts in member states other than their own to pay employees at the same rates as the host country. The UK government claimed this was inconsistent with the principles of the SEM, but failed to halt its adoption (see *Financial Times*, 30 March 1996).

In its anxiety to turn many of the directives into European law, the European Commission has put them forward as health and safety directives which can be adopted by a qualified majority vote. This was necessary because the UK government was opposed to a good many, arguing that such matters are best dealt with at a purely national level, and that the directives will impose costs running into billions upon UK industry, with consequent serious damage to its competitiveness. The Conservative government not only felt that the Agreement on Social Policy route was in breach of an 'understanding' reached at Maastricht, but went so far as to appeal to the European Court of Justice in respect of the working time directive on the grounds that unanimity was required. Predictably, it lost the case (see *Financial Times*, 13 March 1996).

The Social Charter will nevertheless proceed and, if the UK refuses to participate in future social legislation (the Labour Party has stated that it will discontinue the 'opt-out if elected), the other member states intend to press ahead anyway, if necessary via the Agreement on Social Policy, leaving the UK to catch up later when it comes to appreciate the error of its ways.

Pending the next election, the UK government intends to obstruct this course of action at every turn, confident that, in the face of persistently high unemployment throughout the EU, the illogic of imposing additional costs upon businesses will cause other members to reconsider their positions.

Bibliography

Bean, R. (ed.) (1989) *International Labour Statistics* (London: Routledge).

Beatson, M. and S. Butcher (1993) 'Union Density Across the Employed Workforce', *Employment Gazette* (January).

Bilsborough, M. and N. Ross (1993) 'The National Education and Training Targets – Progress Made in 1992', *Employment Gazette* (August).

Blanchflower, D.(1984) 'Union Relative Wage Effects', *British Journal of Industrial Relations* pp. 311–22.

Bosworth, D. and P. Simpson (1995) 'Skills, Training and Economic Performance', *Economics and Business Education*, 3 (3) pp. 103–9.

Brown, W. and S. Wadhani (1990) 'The Economic Effects of Industrial Relations Legislation Since 1979', *National Institute Economic Review* (February).

Cully, M. and S. Woodland (1996) 'Trade Union Membership and Recognition: An Analysis of Data From the 1995 Labour Force Survey', *Labour Market Trends* (May).

Curwen, P. (1995) 'Social Protection Versus Unemployment in the European Union: Can the Circle Be Squared? *European Business Journal*, 7 (2) pp. 43–8.

Daly, M. *et al.* (1992) 'Job Creation 1987–89: Preliminary Analysis By Sector', *Employment Gazette* (August).

Department of Employment (1994) *The Government's Expenditure Plans 1994–95 to 1996–97.* Cm 2505 (London: HMSO, March).

Department for Education and Employment (1996) *The Government's Expenditure Plans 1996–97 to 1998–99.* Cm 3210 (London: HMSO, March).

Department of Employment (1990) 'Provisions of the Employment Act 1990', *Employment Gazette* (November).

Department of Employment (1993a) *The Government's Expenditure Plans 1993–4 to 1995–6,* Cm 2205 (London: HMSO, February).

Department of Employment (1993b) 'Evaluating Training and Employment Measures For the

Unemployed', *Labour Market Quarterly Review* (May).

Department of Employment (1993c) 'Membership of Trade Unions', *Employment Gazette* (May).

Department of Employment (1993d) 'The Trade Union Reform and Employment Rights Act 1993', *Employment Gazette* (August).

Eltis, W. and D. Higham (1995) 'Closing the UK Competitiveness Gap', *National Institute Economic Review*, 4, pp. 71–84.

Everett, M. *et. al.* (1996) 'Modern Apprenticeships: Further Lessons from the Prototypes', *Labour Market Trends* (February) pp. 55–9.

Fredman, S. (1994) 'Equal Pay and Justification', *Industrial Law Journal*, 23 (1) pp. 37–40.

Gregg, P. (1990) 'The Evolution of Special Employment Measures', *Royal Bank of Scotland Review* (September).

Gregg, P. and S. Machin (1992) 'Unions, the Demise of the Closed Shop and Wage Growth in the 1980s', *Oxford Bulletin of Economics and Statistics* (February).

King, D. (1993) 'The Conservatives and Training Policy 1979–1992: From a Tripartite to a Neoliberal Regime', *Political Studies*, XLI (2) pp. 214–35.

Labour Market Quarterly Review (1996) 'Measuring the Impact of Programmes for the Long-Term Unemployed', *LMQR*, (May) pp. 13–16.

Marsh, D. (1991) 'British Industrial Relations Policy Transformed: the Thatcher Legacy', *Journal of Public Policy*, 11 (3) pp. 291–313.

Mawson, J. (1992) 'Training and Enterprise Councils – an Initial Assessment', *Regional Studies*, 25 (2).

Nolan, P. (1992) 'Trade Unions and Productivity: Issues, Evidence and Prospects', *Employee Relations*, 14 (6).

Poret, P. (1990) 'The "Puzzle" of Wage Moderation in the 1980s', *OECD Working Paper 87* (Paris: OECD).

Secretary of State for Social Security (1993) *Equality in State Pension Age*, Cm 2420 (London: HMSO, December).

Shackelton, J. (1992) *Training Too Much?* (London: IEA, Hobart Paper 118).

Shackleton, J. (1995) *Training and Employment in Western Europe and the United States* (Aldershot: Edward Elgar).

Sweeney, K. (1996) 'Membership of Trade Unions in 1994: An Analysis Based on Information From the Certification Officer', *Labour Market trends* (February).

Sweeney, K. and J. Davies (1996) 'Labour Disputes in 1995', *Labour Market Trends* (June).

The Economist (1994a) 'Training for Jobs' (12 March) pp. 19–22.

The Economist (1994b) Schools Brief: Investing in People' (26 March) pp. 114–15.

The Economist (1996) 'Training and Jobs: What Works?' (6 April) pp. 21–3.

Turner, P. *et. al.* (1992) 'Training – A Key to the Future', *Employment Gazette* (August).

Chapter 15

Welfare I: Income and Wealth Inequality

Paul Marshall

■ 15.1 Introduction

Even at the crudest level no assessment of the well-being of a society can have much credibility unless it takes some account of the distribution of income as well as its aggregate total. (Morris and Preston, 1986)

This quotation has survived successive editions of this book because it captures so well the fact that the overall view of a society's 'welfare' must be informed by the way in which aggregate income is shared among its constituent members rather than by the size of the total itself. Following the reforms to the 'Welfare State' introduced by the Conservative government in the mid-1980s, a different Conservative cabinet embarked on a comprehensive review of social policy spending in 1993, concerned, in particular, with a public sector deficit (borrowing requirement) of £50 billion. In addition, an Independent Commission on Social Justice, which had been initiated by the Labour Party but established as independent of political parties, reported in 1995 on its investigations into the relationships between economic and social factors and the need for reforms to ensure that these relationships foster prosperity coupled with fairness. Needless to say, recent debate has echoed old arguments over issues relating to concepts of 'fairness', 'equity' and 'social justice'.

However, even for a simple economy, measuring the distribution of economic gains is very difficult; for a large, developed, mixed economy, in which both public and private sectors exert their influences on income distribution, the complications of measuring distribution patterns are endless. The study from which the quotation is taken is of income distribution in the UK, and covers a period during which there were major structural changes to the economy, several exogenous shocks (including the oil price hike of the early 1970s) and major social and political upheavals, including three changes of government. Nevertheless, as the quotation underlines, if we are interested in measuring economic welfare, and its tendency to change over time, we must take account of the **distribution of the gains from economic processes** no matter how complicated or dynamic they might be.

In the case of a mixed economy like the UK, the role of government is a crucial influence upon the distribution of income and wealth, and this will be emphasised in the course of this chapter, particularly in relation to government's objective of reducing inequality. Within the government spending section of the national accounts are many items which relate to programmes aimed at improvements in individual welfare. The range of such programmes is considerable, spanning subsidies to both production (for example, farm income support programmes) and consumption (for example, household income maintenance programmes). Indeed, such is the range that any overview must be selective. For present purposes, the selection concentrates on issues which lie at the heart of government aims to reduce inequalities in the distribution of income and wealth, issues which are often subsumed under the heading of 'social policy'. Why governments need to finance and/or provide such programmes, and to **what extent they should** do so, are extremely difficult questions to answer, and this chapter can do little more than shed some light on the policy debate.

For economists, the issues to be discussed concern individual 'welfare' – whether welfare is maximised for everyone through the market system or whether market-determined incomes require alteration by state action and, if so, how the alteration is to be achieved. Clearly, the welfare of individuals depends upon a multitude of things and not simply on the acquisition of material goods and services; it is the search for an understanding of the characteristics of, and the influences exerted by, this multitude that forms the basis of enquiry in social science. Within social science, it is Economics which has concentrated on the material aspects of well-being, but it is difficult to maintain a strict divorce between Economics and other disciplines when trying to analyse the causes of the distribution of material consumption.

15.1.1 The Efficiency/Equity Trade-off

As an analytical concept, and as an aim of government policy, **efficiency** holds centre stage throughout this book, reflecting the main preoccupation of economists. But questions of welfare relate often to **equity** as well as to efficiency, and

here lies a problem for both the analyst and the policy maker: **it is rare for an efficiency objective to be achieved without an inequality being created**. Indeed, to recognise the reality of the problem of managing a mixed economy is to see it as a search for acceptable **trade-offs** between equity and efficiency. What the trade-offs look like is a major question for research into the evaluation of government expenditure programmes. What the trade-offs **should** look like is part of a normative debate which manifests itself in the varying policies advanced from different political standpoints. Thus, for some observers, the question of equity should be at the forefront of political debate and should be the primary consideration in the formation of government expenditure plans. This argument may stem from altruism, but it may also be based on pragmatism; if 'the system' creates too much inequality it may invite violent political upheaval, or even revolution! On the other hand, some observers argue that efficiency should be always the main criterion for judging public expenditure programmes since only if the economy is efficient in every respect can the income available for redistribution be maximised; in other words, reducing inequality depends on reducing inefficiency! The issue of the trade-off will recur throughout this chapter, and is often illustrated by the characteristics of the social policies implemented by different governments.

15.1.2 The Concept of Inequality

Using the term 'inequality' in the present context is intended as a comment upon the extent to which the rewards of the market place, supplemented and modified by government tax/transfer programmes, are distributed equally throughout the population. To measure inequality in this way is very difficult both for reasons of practical computation and for reasons of principle. Practical difficulties loom large when choosing appropriate data from which to analyse distributions. In the UK, for example, official estimates of income distribution are often derived from Inland Revenue returns whereby the definition of 'income' is that used for the purposes of income taxation.

Since income defined for tax purposes may exclude some important sources of income (for example capital gains, imputed income from home production and property ownership, fringe benefits and certain government transfers), measures of distribution based on this definition may be inaccurate.

But even if comprehensive measures of income were available, and distributions were to be computed accurately, there remains a difficult issue of principle – namely, how to **judge** distributions as 'equal' or 'unequal'. Certainly, we know what an equal distribution of incomes looks like – one in which **every income unit** (individual or household) has the **same income as any other unit**. We might be tempted to say, therefore, that any distribution in which at least one income unit has more or less than each of the other units is unequal. However, this is not very helpful when looking at a world of many distributions in which the **degree** of inequality differs; it is this very question of degree which makes the measurement problem so difficult to resolve. If we are interested in comparing distributions at a point in time, or assessing changes in inequality over time, the problem becomes acute.

The crux of the problem lies in the fact that, while it is always possible to describe different patterns of income distribution, it is often not possible to describe different patterns of **inequality** without invoking a value judgement. Suppose, for example, that a change in government policy makes the top 10 per cent of income recipients slightly better off, the next 80 per cent much better off and the bottom 10 per cent slightly worse off. Has the policy change effected a more equal distribution of income? How is the small loss suffered by the bottom 10 per cent of income recipients to be weighed against the large gain to the majority of the population? What comment can we make about a change which has made the bottom 10 per cent of income recipients worse off while raising the incomes received by the top 10 per cent?

Clearly, for an observer to describe one pattern of income distribution as more or less equal than another, reference must be made to an accepted concept of **social justice**, a rule by which any pattern of shares may be judged. Later on, we shall concentrate on **poverty** as an important manifestation of inequality, and this issue of social justice takes on more obvious relevance when we try to make judgements about government measures to improve the relative positions of individuals or households at the bottom of the income distribution. But we must not lose sight of the fact that a comparison of distributions may involve comparisons of gains and losses – that is, altered distributional positions for different percentile groupings – in which case judgements about which is more equal or even, perhaps, 'preferred', cannot be made on any objective criteria. The history of 'Welfare Economics' has been written in terms of a search for an objective criterion by which to judge the outcome of economic processes but the question of social justice does not reside exclusively within the domain of academic reasoning. Indeed, the very question of a trade-off between equity and efficiency, discussed earlier and to be returned to later, lies (again) at the heart of real-world government decisions affecting the distribution of income. Both government expenditures and methods of raising revenue affect income distribution; a government implementing policies to promote efficiency at the expense of equity will be more likely to create inequalities than a government opting to sacrifice efficiency gains for equity goals.

15.1.3 The Measurement of Inequality

The Lorenz curve is used for **comparative** analysis – for example, comparing income distributions between countries at some point in time or between different points in time in a given country The curve shows cumulative percentage income shares: the bottom 10 per cent of the population (income units) receive x per cent of income, the bottom 20 per cent receive y per cent, where y is greater than x, and so on. When there is perfect equality – when every n per cent of the population receives n per cent of total income – the Lorenz curve is a 45° line or **line of income equality**. Such a line thus operates as a yardstick by which to gauge the inequality in any given distribution. If there is inequality, the Lorenz curve lies below the 45° line, and the more unequal the distribution the further away from the 45° line lies the Lorenz curve. **Figure 15.1(a)** shows two hypothetical Lorenz curves with the distribution in year *t* represented as more equal than that in year *t* − 50.

It is possible to draw unambiguous conclusions from **Figure 15.1(a)** because one Lorenz curve lies completely outside the other. But let us examine **Figure 15.1(b)** where the two Lorenz curves cross. Are we still able to judge which of the two distributions is more equal? The Lorenz curves show that, for all percentile groups up to the bottom 40 per cent, their share in total income was higher in year *t* − 50 than in year *t*, but above this point shares were higher in year *t*. A measure of inequality which gives a greater weight to improvements in the share of total income enjoyed by the lower income groups would register *t* − 50 as the year of greater equality; a measure of inequality which gives a greater weight to improvements in upper income group shares would yield a preference for year *t*.

The same problem arises when using the Gini coefficient. This numerical measure of inequality is based on the relationship between the Lorenz curve and the line of income equality; it measures the ratio of the area between the Lorenz curve and the diagonal (the line of income equality) to the total area beneath the diagonal. In **Figure 15.2**, the Gini coefficient is measured as the ratio $A/(A + B)$.

It can be seen from **Figure 15.2** that when the Lorenz curve follows the diagonal, when incomes are equally distributed, the Gini coefficient has a value of 0 ($A = 0$). At the other extreme, when all income is held by one individual ($B = 0$), the Gini coefficient has a value of 1. Thus, for purposes of comparison, the nearer the Gini coefficient is to 0 the more equal the distribution may be considered to be. However, when two Lorenz curves cross, how can we draw an unambiguous conclusion regarding relative inequalities? Consider **Figure 15.1(b)** again: the Gini coefficient suggests that incomes are more equally distributed in year *t*, but this obscures the fact that, from the viewpoint of the bottom four deciles, year *t* − 50 is more equal.

It would seem, then, that when measuring the degree of inequality in income distribution we cannot avoid introducing value judgements about the 'desired' state of distribution. Any two obser-

Figure 15.1 *Hypothetical Lorenz Curves and the Measurement of Inequality*

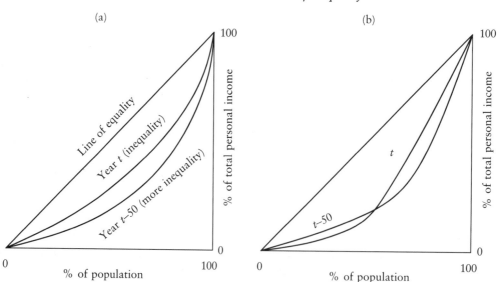

(a)

(b)

Figure 15.2 *Measuring the Gini Coefficient From the Lorenz Curve*

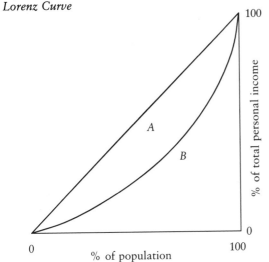

vers with different views on the weight which should be given by society to improvements in the position of the lower income groups could place two different interpretations on any decrease in the value of the Gini coefficient between two points in time. Only if the Gini coefficient is used in conjunction with the original data on percentile shares is an adequate comparative picture likely to emerge.

▌ *15.2* The Distribution of Personal Incomes in the UK

The official estimates of the distribution of personal incomes in the UK are published by the Office for National Statistics (ONS – formerly the CSO) and illustrate the problems referred to so far. Note that the estimates are of the shares of total personal income which accrue to income units. Although analysing the distribution of incomes among capitalists, labourers and rentiers still has its uses, in the modern economy the distinctions between factors of production are rather blurred When analysing the share and causes of the pattern of income shares, it is important to distinguish market-determined influences from the effects of government policies

and also to identify the rich and varied social and demographic factors at work. In the 1970s, the Royal Commission on the Distribution of Income and Wealth (the Diamond Commission) identified four major forces: changes in the age structure of the population; changes in the activity rates of various sectors of the population; changes in marital patterns; and changes in education patterns. Not surprisingly, the Commission concluded that alterations to the pattern of income distribution were often attributable to some combination of these separately identified factors (Diamond Commission, 1975).

The task of the analyst in this area is complicated by the measurement problems discussed earlier and also by the fact that official data change through time, both in terms of definition and also in terms of what information is gathered and published. Thus, until the mid-1980s, analysts could rely on the regular publication of data relating to incomes both before and after income tax. Since earnings form the major component of personal incomes, such data were very useful in analysing patterns in market-determined incomes and the extent to which a progressive personal tax system modified inequality in the distribution of personal incomes However, such estimates contributed little towards measuring the impact of social policies and, in particular, the effects of social security programmes. Recent official estimates do take account of transfers and benefits as well as taxes, and a clearer picture has emerged about the impact of 'Welfare State' arrangements on the pattern of personal income distribution. **Table 15.1** presents the official estimates for the period from the end of the 1940s until the middle of the 1980s.

What do the data suggest? If the period since the Second World War has been one of rising prosperity for the UK, how has this prosperity been shared out among the population? The data show clearly that pre-tax income has not been shared equally at any point in time. To the extent that pre-tax incomes reflect a market-determined set of rewards, this is to be expected. But what about shares over time – have pre-tax incomes become more or less equally shared? The data suggest that we cannot draw unambiguous con-

Table 15.1 *Cumulative Distribution of Personal Income Before and After Income Tax, UK, 1949–85, selected years*

Quantile Group	1949	1959	1967	1975–76	1984–85
(a) Before Income Tax					
Top 1%	11.2	8.4	7.4	5.7	6.4
Top 10%	33.2	29.4	28.0	26.2	29.4
Top 50%	76.3	76.9	76.0	76.2	77.7
Bottom 50%	23.7	23.1	24.0	23.8	22.3
(b) After Income Tax					
Top 1%	6.4	5.3	4.9	3.9	4.9
Top 10%	27.1	25.9	24.3	23.1	26.5
Top 50%	73.5	74.8	73.2	73.4	75.1
Bottom 50%	26.5	25.2	26.8	26.6	24.9

Sources: Diamond Commission, *Report No. 1*, Table 15; *Economic Trends*, No. 409, November 1987, Table A, p. 84; *Social Trends*, 18 (1988 edn).

clusions about changes in the degree of inequality over time, the main reason being that the percentile groupings at different points in the distribution have fared differently at different points in time. Of course, we must bear in mind that the individual income units also differ within each percentile grouping at different points in time: for example, the units comprising the top 10 per cent group in 1985 are not the same as those in the same percentile group in 1955. In other words, the data do not tell us anything about upward and downward mobility within the distribution.

There is much more mobility than is popularly believed. As can be seen from **Table 15.2**, for Great Britain between 1991 and 1993 roughly 17 per cent of adults moved either up or down more than one decile (and many others moved a single decile). Extending this over the period of a decade would demonstrate that those stuck at the bottom of the pile are often there temporarily because they are having an unusually bad year (as often happens to the self-employed); they are young; or they are old (see also Brittan, 1995; *The Economist*, 27 May 1995, p. 36; Goodman and Webb, 1994). This is confirmed by an OECD study

Table 15.2 *Adults Moving Between Different Household Income[1] Groupings, 1991 to 1993, GB (%)*

	Income fell 4 or more deciles	Income fell 2–3 deciles	Income stable[2]	Income rose 2–3 deciles	Income rose 4 or more deciles
1991 income grouping					
Lowest decile	–	–	67.2	19.1	13.7
2nd decile	–	–	76.3	14.8	8.9
3rd decile	–	12.1	64.8	14.1	9.1
4th decile	–	14.0	62.1	16.4	7.4
5th decile	5.0	14.2	59.9	15.1	5.8
6th decile	8.4	12.0	59.3	18.1	2.1
7th decile	8.6	14.7	63.3	13.4	–
8th decile	12.2	15.7	62.5	9.6	–
9th decile	10.7	16.8	72.5	–	–
Highest decile	11.9	12.3	75.8	–	–
All deciles	5.7	11.3	66.3	12.1	4.6

Notes:
[1] Equivalised disposable income has been used for ranking the adults.
[2] Income did not change, of it fell by one decile or increased by one decile.

Source: Social Trends, 26 (1996 edn), Chart 5.19.

covering the period 1986–1991 (see *The Economist*, 20 July 1996, p. 84).

However, if we do accept that inequality is reflected in the shares enjoyed by different percentile groupings, looking at these shares over time suggests that the degree of inequality was subjected to opposing forces until the 1980s. Over the 30–year period, from the end of the 1940s to the end of 1970s, the share of pre-tax income enjoyed by the top percentiles of income recipients fell: the share of the top 1 per cent fell, from just over 11 per cent to just over 5 per cent, while the share of the top 10 per cent fell from just over 33 per cent to just over 26 per cent. This suggests that incomes were becoming more equally distributed. Yet, during the same period, the share enjoyed by the bottom percentiles also fell, with recovery in the 1960s and early/mid-1970s proving insufficient to regain the share enjoyed at the end of the 1940s, suggesting that incomes became more unequally distributed over the period.

How are we to weigh these opposing forces? It would appear that the Lorenz curves at different points of time are crossed, and that we cannot make a clear judgement about overall inequality without reference to a specific concept of social justice – the very problem discussed earlier. The only firm conclusion which might be drawn from the data is that whatever redistribution of pre-tax incomes took place over the period, it did so from the top to the middle. Similar difficulties face us when trying to assess the changing degree of inequality after the 1970s – that is, some percentile groupings fared better than others in the overall distribution of incomes. However, the estimates do suggest that there was no reduction in the degree of inequality in the distribution of pre-tax incomes; indeed the share of the top half of the distribution increased while the share of the bottom half decreased.

☐ *15.2.1 Trends in Factor Incomes*

To explain the causes of the observed changes in the distribution of pre-tax incomes over the period in question requires an understanding of highly-complicated and interrelated forces. Not all of these forces are economic, although for present purposes we shall look in more detail at the distribution of factor market incomes. Social and demographic factors also play their part in altering income shares over time. For present purposes, we shall let the observation rest there, although we shall return in Chapter 16 to the age factor when we consider the incidence of poverty and the problem of inter-generational finance of social security arrangements. Several relevant observations on activity rates (for example, the labour force participation of married women) have also been made in Chapter 13).

So far as economic forces are concerned, we can usefully begin with a closer look at factor market patterns. When a mixed economy allocates resources, it determines rewards to factors of production in both private and public sectors while the state's tax-transfer mechanism provides income maintenance for those who are eligible. We shall leave the distribution of state transfers until later, and concentrate first on factor incomes as an indication of how rewards are shared out on the supply side of the economy (the many determinants of this distribution are discussed in most other chapters of this book). There are at least two important questions to address: how are the total rewards from economic processes shared out among the various factors of production and, if one type of reward dominates, what forces help to determine its distribution? The answer to the first question offers a guide to answering the second. To understand the forces which determine the distribution of incomes, we need to know the dominant source of income; an increase in the share going to capital is likely to have an impact on the overall distribution which is different from that resulting from an increase in the share enjoyed by labour. Furthermore, if one component of income accounts for, say, more than half the rewards in an economy, then any change in the dispersion of that component will result in a change in the overall dispersion of incomes.

Researchers into the distribution of incomes have seen **changes in earnings** as a major indicator of both the overall state of the economy and the prevailing degree of inequality. Lydall, for example, discerned a trend towards equality in the distribution of incomes, from the immediate post-war years until the later 1950s, and argued that this trend owed much to post-war economic expansion and the improving fortunes of labour (Lydall, 1959). According to Lydall, the sustained high level of employment during the period meant that earned income rose faster than any other form of personal income, and that such a trend would be a major force towards equality. However, as calculated by Nicholson, this pattern changed during the period 1957–63 with the rate of growth of employment income slowing down relative to that of self-employment (and, within employment income, the rate of growth of wages slowed down relative to that of salaries). During this period rent, dividends and interest became the most rapidly-growing sector of personal income. The result, according to Nicholson, was a slowing down in any trend towards equality (Nicholson, 1967).

According to official estimates the downward slide in the share of labour income continued into the 1970s, when it steadied before falling again over the next twenty years, from 77 per cent in 1971 to 67 per cent in 1994. In part, this trend reflects the high unemployment of the 1980s and 1990s which, in turn, is reflected partly in the growth of the proportion of total income which is accounted for by social security benefits. **Table 15.3** shows the relative shares of the main com-

ponents of total household income in the UK for the period from the early 1970s to the early 1990s.

As well as the share going to earnings being on the decline, wages and salaries are subject to forces which prevent an equal distribution of earnings among earners. Between the sexes there is considerable inequality: in the first place, the top male earners have consistently earned more than the top female earners; secondly, the difference between the highest female earnings and the lowest male earnings has been consistently less than that between highest and lowest female earnings. For example, in 1987, the gross weekly earnings figure for the highest female decile (full-time) was only about 15 per cent higher than the median for men (full-time), while the median for women was only some 70 per cent of that for men; five years later, in 1992, this inequality had worsened, with weekly gross earnings for the highest female decile only some 9 per cent higher than the median for men and the median for women only some 65 per cent of that for men. Such inequalities have persisted despite legislation on equal pay and opportunities and sex discrimination (see Chapter 13). Another significant inequality persists between manual and non-manual earners (regardless of sex), with non-manual earnings consistently outstripping manual earnings in all deciles within the two distributions.

Table 15.3   *Percentage Shares of Main Components in Total Household Income, UK, 1971–94[1]*

	1971	*1976*	*1981*	*1986*	*1991*	*1994*
Wages and salaries[2]	68	67	64	59	58	57
Income from self-employment[3]	9	9	9	10	10	10
Rent, interest and dividends	6	6	6	7	9	6
Private pensions, annuities, etc.	5	5	6	8	10	11
Social security benefits	10	11	13	13	11	13
Other current transfers[4]	2	2	2	3	2	3

Note:
[1] Figures to nearest whole numbers.
[2] Includes Forces' pay and income in kind.
[3] After deducting interest payments, depreciation and stock appreciation.
[4] Mostly other government grants.
Source: Social Trends, 26 (1996 edn), Table 5.2.

The share of personal income going to **rents**, **dividends** and **interest** behaved more erratically during the period from 1960. Throughout the 1960s, this share fell steadily before 'hitting bottom' in the early 1970s. However, it climbed again during the 1980s, reaching 9 per cent in 1990, although currently it is back at the level of 1980. The most marked increase in share is that shown by social security benefits although that has been essentially static since 1980. We shall return to this pattern in the following chapter.

Of course, looking at the shares accruing to the major components of personal income cannot 'explain' changes in inequality. There is much more to the story than this. However, the broad categories which we have considered do give some strong indications of what is happening to the degree of inequality associated with the overall distribution of personal incomes. In particular, it is difficult to avoid the conclusion that during the 1980s, the increased share in income enjoyed by the highest percentiles in the distribution resulted, in part, from an increased concentration of earned income due to a rise in the proportions of the population who were unemployed or retired.

15.2.2 The Upward Trend of Inequality in Recent Times

To the extent that changes in the pattern of inequality of income distribution represent changes in the distribution of economic and social welfare, it is necessary to gauge all elements which affect net income and, hence, potential individual/household expenditure on goods and services. One important element in these calculations is the extent to which government influences the pattern of personal income distribution. When considering UK governments in this respect, for the period since 1945, we must concentrate on two things: the effect of progressive income taxation and the effect of Welfare State transfers. A progressive tax structure smooths out the dispersion of incomes after tax and works towards a more equal distribution. Many Welfare State benefits, in principle, are transfers of income both in cash and in kind to the poorest percentiles in the distribution and, hence, a force towards reducing inequality. The pattern which emerges, particularly towards the end of the period in question and as we approach the start of the next millennium, is that while the State's tax/transfer mechanism affords protection to those individuals and households at the bottom of the distribution of personal incomes, **it has not prevented a widening of the disparity between the top and bottom percentile groupings in the population of income recipients.**

Table 15.1 presents official estimates of the distribution of personal income **after income tax**, for the period up to 1985. Taking first the period from the end of the 1940s up to the end of the 1970s, two observations can be made. First, income tax does indeed reduce the income dispersion at any point in time. Second, over time, the post-tax dispersion of income alters in roughly the same directions as the pre-tax dispersion. In other words, the redistribution of post-tax income has been from the top of the distribution towards the middle rather than towards the bottom. It would thus appear to be the case that, for the period in question, income tax was progressive and a force for equality but that its progressivity altered little over time.

What about the period after 1979? The most obvious point to make is that for the first time since the Second World War, the share of post-tax income enjoyed by the top 10 per cent of the distribution increased. The share of the top 50 per cent of the distribution also rose steadily after the end of the 1970s. For the most part, these trends are a reflection of the same patterns emerging in the distribution of pre-tax incomes. However, an additional factor is that successive governments post-1979 set out to reduce the burden of direct taxation, either by raising tax thresholds or by reducing tax rates, and since 1979 both these changes have been implemented on several occasions. Raising the tax threshold takes some income earners out of the income tax net, but it does nothing positive to improve the relative positions of those whose earned incomes are initially too low to be liable for income tax. Reducing the standard rate of income tax affects only taxpayers, and cannot be considered a force to reduce inequality in post-tax income distribution. It must be noted also that the 1980s saw a massive reduction in higher rates of income tax – from 83 per cent to 40 per cent on earned income (although few paid the highest rates in practice).

However, if government policy is to have a direct effect on inequality in personal income distribution, this is most likely to be seen as a result of programmes of social security and income maintenance. The details of the Welfare State and its impact on households at the bottom of the income distribution are discussed in the following chapter, but for the moment we can consider the pattern of distribution which emerges for the UK after accounting for the government's tax/transfer programmes, as defined in the official series. The adoption of new methodologies of both definition and measurement in the production of estimates of income distribution have assisted in confirming that the distribution

Table 15.4 *Household Income Definitions used by ONS in Estimates of Income Distribution*

Income Concept	Definition
Original income	Earnings *plus* Occupational pensions *plus* Annuities, *plus* Investment income *plus* Other income
Gross income	Original income *minus* Cash benefits
Disposable income	Gross income *minus* Income tax *minus* NICs
Post-tax income	Disposable income *minus* Indirect taxes
Final income	Post-tax income *plus* Benefits in kind (Education, NHS, Travel subsidies, Housing subsidy and Welfare foods)

Source: Economic Trends (January 1992), p. 128.

Figure 15.3   *Stages of Redistribution*

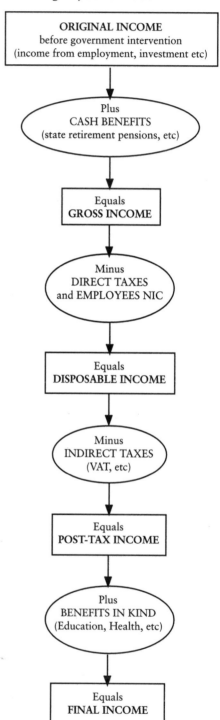

Source: Economic Trends, No. 494, p. 35.

of personal incomes has become more unequal in recent times.

The wider and more comprehensive impact of government activity on income distribution in the UK is gauged by the ONS in terms of the difference between 'original income' and 'final income'. The definitions of these two concepts and the stages between them are summarised in **Table 15.4** and **Figure 15.3**.

It should be noted that, in addition to being based on a sample of households, the figures published by the ONS are based on an assumed incidence of taxes and benefits and a corresponding imputation process. It follows that the ONS estimates are somewhat less than 'hard facts' about 'final' income distribution. However, as estimates, they do enable an informed impression to be gained about the redistributive effects of government tax/transfer programmes. Another important feature of the ONS estimates is that in 1990 the estimates were produced using 'equivalence' scales. The figures reported that year related to 1987 and were 'equivalised' in that household incomes were adjusted for both household size and composition to estimate an equivalent standard of living; that is, to recognise that a household of five adults needs a higher income than a single person living alone in order to enjoy the same standard of living (although not one five times higher because of scale economies in house sharing). It is argued that using

'equivalised' income puts all households on an equal footing regardless of size or composition and, hence, provides a better means of comparison.

□ *15.2.3 'Unadjusted' Estimates*

Table 15.5 shows the distribution pattern suggested for the decade 1976–86 by the ONS's 'unadjusted' estimates; that is, without accounting for equivalence. Such a series was not available in official publications prior to the 1970s and this run of estimates is the culmination of CSO researches to the middle of the 1980s.

The estimates in **Table 15.5** suggest an important observation: while the combined impact of taxes and benefits works to reduce inequality at any point in time, it has not prevented a widening of the gap between the top and the bottom over time. At any point in time the distribution of original income in **Table 15.5** shows a pattern which is similar to that of the distribution of pre-tax incomes but the dispersions in the shares of disposable and final incomes are much less marked. For example, in 1986 the top fifth enjoyed 50.7 per cent of original income but only 42.2 per cent and 41.7 per cent of disposable and final income respectively, while the negligible share in original income enjoyed by the bottom fifth rose to 5.9 per cent for both disposable and

Table 15.5   *Cumulative Distribution of Original, Disposable and Final Household Income, UK. 1976–86 (%)*

Quintile Group	Original Income			Disposable Income			Final Income		
	1976	1981	1986	1976	1981	1986	1976	1981	1986
Top 20% (a)	44.4	46.4	50.7	38.1	39.4	42.2	37.9	38.6	41.7
Top 40%	71.0	73.3	77.6	62.2	63.5	66.3	61.9	62.6	65.6
Top 60%	89.8	91.3	94.0	80.4	81.2	83.2	79.9	80.5	82.6
Bottom 40%	10.2	8.7	6.0	19.6	18.8	16.9	20.1	19.5	17.3
Bottom 20% (b)	0.8	0.6	0.3	7.0	6.7	5.9	7.4	7.1	5.9
Gap (a)−(b)	43.6	45.8	50.4	31.1	32.7	36.3	30.5	31.5	35.8

Source: Social Trends, 19 (1989 edn), Table 5.18.

final income. However, the estimates suggest also that the dispersions in both disposable and final incomes were wider in 1986 than ten years previously. In 1976, the gap in original income shares was 43.6 percentage point between top and bottom fifths, the disposable income gap was 31.1 points and that for final income was 30.5; the respective gaps for 1986 were 50.4, 36.3 and 35.8.

Thus, the CSO estimates suggest that, for the decade in question, despite tax/transfer arrangements softening underlying inequalities, there was a trend towards greater inequality so far as the extremes of the income distribution were concerned. This conclusion was supported by a study of the longer period from 1968 to 1983, undertaken by Morris and Preston (1986) using the raw data from the Family Expenditure Survey rather than the published group data. Using the tax and benefit model of the Institute for Fiscal Studies, which adopts income definitions similar to those of the CSO, Morris and Preston concluded that both the Lorenz curve and the Gini coefficients gave reliable results for the period studied and that there was 'a clear cut rise in inequality over the 1968–83 period'.

□ 15.2.4 'Equivalised' Estimates

Whilst it can be argued that equivalence measures offer better comparisons across households in terms of living standards, the effects on distribution patterns are not dramatic because the majority of households either stay in the same quintile grouping in the distribution, or move only to the next one. However, the distribution of equivalised income is less unequal than that calculated on the unadjusted basis because in the latter there are a disproportionately high number of single person households in the bottom quintile group and these tend to have the lowest absolute incomes. **Table 15.6** shows the 'equivalised shares'. Once again, as with the unadjusted estimates, the dispersion at a point in time is generally reduced although the post-tax distribution shares reflect the effect of benefits on the bottom quintile. Over time, the degree of inequality represented by the percentage points gap between the top and bottom quintiles appears to have increased until 1990, after which it fell back somewhat as a result of changes at both ends of the distribution.

Table 15.6 *Cumulative Distribution of 'Equivalised' Incomes, UK, 1977–95 (%)*

Quintile Group	Equivalised Original Income Share				Equivalised Gross Income Share				Equivalised Disposable Income Share				Post-Tax Equivalised Income Share			
	1977	1983	1990	1994/5	1977	1983	1990	1994/5	1977	1983	1990	1994/5	1977	1983	1990	1994/5
Top 20% (a)	43	47	51	51	37	37	44	43	36	38	43	41	37	39	45	43
Top 40%	69	73	76	76	61	62	67	66	59	61	66	64	60	61	68	65
Top 60%	87	90	91	91	79	79	83	83	77	78	82	80	77	78	83	81
Bottom 40%	14	11	9	8	22	20	18	18	24	23	18	20	23	22	16	18
Bottom 20% (b)	4	3	2	2	9	8	7	7	10	10	7	8	9	9	6	7
gap (a)−(b)	39	44	49	49	28	31	37	36	26	28	36	33	28	30	39	36

Note: The table does not include trends in final income because equivalisation is not appropriate for this measure
Source: Social Trends, 22, Table 5.19; Economic Trends, No 471; Economic Trends, No 506.

☐ *15.2.5 Recent Estimates*

Following the 1991 Budget, the IFS model was used to estimate the cumulative effect of tax and benefit changes since 1979 on household disposable incomes. The model showed that while the combined changes had, on average, produced gains, the distribution of these gains was uneven and the top 10 per cent of income earners had gained a weekly rise while the bottom 50 per cent had actually lost on average over the period.

Further evidence that inequality increased in more recent times was offered by Jenkins (1991), who calculated that most of the real income growth during the 1980s took place in the upper income bands with little gain being enjoyed by those in the lower bands. Jenkins claimed that 'in 1967 the richest 10 per cent had an income almost 10 times that of the poorest band. In 1978, the ratio was just more than 10, but in 1988, it was almost 18'. In his updating of the work of the Royal Commission, Stark (1990) also added fuel to the argument that income inequality worsened over the 1980s. According to Stark, the income of the top 10 per cent increased by 40 per cent while the bottom 40 per cent suffered a decrease of up to 8 per cent.

Subsequently, and making use of yet another new official series, 'Households Below Average Income' (HBAI – see the following chapter), Jenkins and Cowell (1994) estimated that those in the top 5 per cent of the population enjoyed almost 30 per cent of the income growth of the 1980s. Moreover, while the shares enjoyed at the top of the distribution increased, those accruing to the percentiles at the bottom fell. This trend has also shown up quite markedly in the official estimates. The data published in the 1995 edition of *Social Trends* (Table 5.19) show very clearly how the trend of shares moves from being negatively inclined for the bottom 20 per cent, through horizontal for the middle percentiles, to being positively inclined for the top 20 per cent for the period covering the 1980s and into the early 1990s. It should be noted that the data relate to 'net equivalised income before housing costs'. If data referring to 'after housing costs' are used, the resulting pattern of inequality is even more marked.

Furthermore, as shown in **Figure 15.4**, whereas the trend lines for those earning below average income all remained fairly constant between 1961 and 1983, the subsequent decade saw those at the bottom end of the distribution clearly losing touch with those on above-average incomes, reflecting, in part, changes in the labour market discussed in Chapter 13.

Yet more evidence has been provided by the estimates of Goodman and Webb (1994), also using the HBAI methodology but basing their findings on detailed analysis of the Family Expenditure Survey for the 30–year period between 1961 and 1991. Goodman and Webb confirm that there has been a continually rising trend of inequality since 1977, and point out that this has been the longest sustained period of inequality since the beginning of the 1960s. The features underlined by Goodman and Webb echo comments made earlier in this chapter, for example on the declining contribution of earnings and the rising contribution of social security benefits, and also set part of the agenda for the next chapter, for example in respect of the ageing of the population and the growth in the numbers of lone parents.

One final factor to consider, as ever, is experience overseas. Although widening inequality has by no means been universal, not having transpired in Italy, Portugal and Spain, it has occurred across a wide range of economies, from New Zealand to Sweden. It therefore follows that other factors than government policy are partly responsible, including the tendency for the well-educated and skilled to prosper at the expense of the ill-educated and unskilled.

 ## 15.3 The Concentration of Wealth

In the view of many observers, the distribution of wealth shares within a society gives a more accurate picture of the degree of inequality, because

Figure 15.4　*Percentage of People Whose Income is Below Various Fractions of Average Income[1], UK*

Note:
[1] Before housing costs.
Source: Social Trends, 26 (1996 edn), Chart 5.17.

the full extent of individuals' economic power is determined ultimately by their potential command over available resources and this must reflect ownership of assets as well as current income. It is thus held that any society which aims for social justice will be concerned about both wealth and income shares. Unfortunately, when it comes to measuring wealth shares, obstacles are met which are even bigger than those encountered in the estimation of income distributions. This is true even though wealth and income are but different dimensions of a common set of means by which individuals satisfy their wants. Wealth refers to the stock of means available, while **income** refers to the **flow** of means from the given stock. Another term for wealth is 'net worth' which underlines the fact that wealth relates to a **net stock** – the difference between a set of assets and a set of liabilities.

15.3.1 The Definition and Measurement of Wealth

Given that any stock of means is measured by the total (capitalised) value of the various items within the stock, the essential preliminary step in empirical work is to determine which assets are to be included in the definition of the wealth stock. Some researchers see the crux of the problem in the relationship between 'value' and 'ownership', the key concept being that of 'marketability'. An individual may own the right to an income flow from a given asset, yet he or she may not be able to realise the market value of that asset because it is **non-transferable**. A prime example of this is the state pension – the asset has a value to its owner because it bestows income, but the pension right cannot be traded in the market-place. Should such rights be included in the calculation of a comprehensive wealth stock? Less difficult to handle in empirical work are those assets which confer income benefits upon their owner and are disposable at an **exchange price** – cash, bank deposits, company shares, government bonds, dwellings and so forth. Clearly, such assets must be included in any definition of personal wealth.

Official measures of wealth distribution in the UK represent **estimates** of wealth holdings since the Inland Revenue does not undertake a regular survey of such holdings in the way that it does for personal incomes. This is because the UK fiscal system does not include a comprehensive wealth tax; it does include capital taxes but those relate to disposals or transfers of assets rather than holdings. This means that estimates of holdings are made from too narrow a definition of wealth since transfers of 'capital', as defined for tax purposes, exclude some forms of wealth. Prior to the 1960s, no official estimates of wealth distribution appeared in government statistical publications, but since then such estimates have been published annually. From 1962 to 1978, the Inland Revenue published annual estimates of both total wealth holdings and the distribution of those holdings based on the 'estate multiplier' method, whereby the estates of persons who die in a given year are used as the sample base for estimating the wealth of the living in that year. From the mid-1970s, the CSO published their estimates of wealth holdings based on calculations of the aggregates of assets *minus* liabilities owned by individuals – the so-called 'balance-sheet' approach. From 1978 the Inland Revenue combined these two approaches to produce a new annual series which is also published by the ONS in *Social Trends*.

Needless to say, the methods adopted by government statisticians are disputed by other researchers, and a comprehensive survey must include these alternative estimates. For present purposes, we shall confine ourselves to official estimates. For estimates of wealth distribution prior to the 1960s, we shall refer to the calculations of Professor Jack Revell who pioneered the balance-sheet approach, later taken up by the CSO. This was the line taken by the Diamond Commission in the mid-1970s and, following the Commission, we can present the trends in wealth concentration in two distinct periods with 1960 as the watershed. **Table 15.7** presents the various estimates of the distribution of **marketable wealth** – that is, excluding pension rights (both state and occupational).

The patterns in **Table 15.7** suggest that over the course of the twentieth century there has been a marked reduction in the shares of marketable

Table 15.7 *The Distribution of Marketable Wealth in Great Britain, 1911–60, and the UK, 1966–93*[1]

Quantile Group	% Share of Wealth, GB			% Share of Wealth, UK			
	1911–13	*1936–8*	*1960*	*1966*[2]	*1976*	*1986*	*1993*[3]
Top 1%	69	56	42	33	21	18	17
Top 5%	87	78	75	56	38	36	36
Top 10%	92	88	83	69	50	50	48
Top 25%				87	71	73	72
Top 50%				97	92	90	92

Notes:
[1] Figures to nearest whole number.
[2] Using 'estate multiplier' method.
[3] 1993 figures are based on probate and are not strictly comparable.

Source: Diamond Commission, *Report No. 1*, Cmnd 6171, Table 41 for figures for Great Britain only; *Social Trends*, 26 (1996 edn), Table 5.21 for UK figures.

wealth enjoyed by the top percentiles in the distribution, yet wealth remains concentrated in the hands of a minority of wealth-holders. From the beginning to the end of the period, that is by the start of the 1990s, the share of the top 10 per cent fell from over 90 per cent to around 50 per cent; however, in 1993, over 90 per cent of marketable wealth was still owned by the wealthiest 50 per cent of holders of marketable wealth. It should be noted also that although the rate of decline in wealth shares at the top of the distribution increased between 1960 and 1980, it slowed considerably during the 1980s. Indeed, a significant feature of the 1980s pattern is that the share of the wealthiest one per cent remained constant at around 18 per cent. It should be noted also that, between 1982 and 1989, the Gini coefficient for wealth rose by two percentile points, from 64 to 66, and although no firm conclusions can be drawn from such a small change, it does lend support to the view that there has been little redistribution of wealth in the UK over the past two decades.

15.3.2 The Distributional Impact of Pension Rights

It should be pointed out that the inclusion of pension rights in the definition of wealth reduces significantly the shares enjoyed by the top percentiles. However, the relative changes in share diminish in size in moving from the top to the fiftieth percentile suggesting that the redistributive effect of including pension rights has its biggest impact on the wealthiest percentiles in the distribution rather than across the distribution as a whole. Indeed, from the mid-1970s through to the 1990s, the share of wealth holdings, inclusive of pension rights, enjoyed by the top 50 per cent stayed above 80 per cent.

One likely explanation of this trend is that, since the middle of the 1970s, state pensions have become relatively less important in the composition of aggregate wealth and, because the inclusion of state pension rights reduces the inequality of wealth distribution, this relative decline has led to some increase in inequality in the distribution

of personal wealth including pension rights (see Stewart, 1991). In 1976, marketable wealth accounted for 54 per cent of aggregate personal wealth, and in 1989 it accounted for 60 per cent, having declined steadily to 51 per cent by 1984 and then climbed back during the second half of the 1980s. Occupational pension rights rose from 10 per cent to 20 per cent between 1976 and 1986 and then fell back to 18 per cent by 1989. Over the same period, state pension rights fell from 37 per cent to 22 per cent.

15.3.3 Other Patterns of Accumulation

(a) Property Ownership

The official estimates of wealth distribution in the UK have been required to account for the effects of including pension rights because the growth and spread of such rights, in particular those relating to occupational and other forms of private pension, has been a significant feature of the accumulation pattern in the UK. However, pension rights have not provided the only significant change in the pattern and composition of wealth holdings in the UK in recent times. A full analysis of the determinants of accumulation requires an understanding of relative **savings functions** in the community – the relative propensities to save out of incomes generated by differing property regimes and the relative influences of earnings and profits, and so on. In the space available we cannot discuss such issues in depth, but we can assume that, other things remaining unchanged, an increase in the spread of property ownership over time will lead to a break-up of concentration in property incomes and, to the extent that such returns constitute a significant component of wealth holdings, should be a force to reduce inequality in wealth holdings overall.

We have already discussed the housing market in some detail in Chapter 3. In 1971, the value of dwellings, net of mortgage debt, accounted for 26 per cent of the net wealth of the personal sector in the UK, whereas by 1993 this proportion was at 30 per cent, having fallen from 43 per cent in 1988.

However, the increasing importance of dwellings in the composition of total net wealth is most clearly appreciated by comparison with the trends in the proportion of wealth held in the form of financial assets.

That a combination of increased owner occupation and rising property values will have a significant impact on the overall distribution of wealth has been recognised in official publications through separate estimations, inclusive and exclusive, of the effects of including dwellings in the calculations of wealth holdings. Taken at face value, the official estimates could seem to bear out the prediction that removing the value of dwellings (net of mortgage debt) from 'marketable wealth' renders the distribution of marketable wealth more unequal than the distribution pattern which emerges when the value of dwellings is included, given that the moderately wealthy accumulate a much higher proportion of their wealth in housing than the very wealthy. **Figure 15.5** depicts the comparison.

At face value, the pattern suggested by **Figure 15.5** seems fairly clear, with the share of total marketable wealth enjoyed by the top percentiles being significantly reduced by the inclusion of housing in each of the two years on display and with the reduction increasing between the two years. Thus, by 1992, the share of the wealthiest 10 per cent is reduced by 16 percentage points if the value of dwellings is included in the estimate of marketable wealth. Note, however, that the gap was 18 percentage points in 1991.

(b) Financial assets

The influence on the overall pattern of wealth ownership exerted by financial assets is rather uncertain and it is likely that forces of accumulation have pulled in different directions. Between 1971 and 1993, the proportion of wealth accounted for by building society shares stayed around 8 per cent, according to the ONS. During the same period, the proportion of wealth held in the form of national savings and bank deposits fell quite markedly, from 13 per cent to 9 per cent. The combined effect of these opposing trends on the overall concentration of wealth will depend upon the extent to which they represent switching among 'popular' assets, compared with changes in relative patterns of ownership.

Figure 15.5 *Comparison of Wealth Distribution With and Without Property Values, 1976 and 1992*

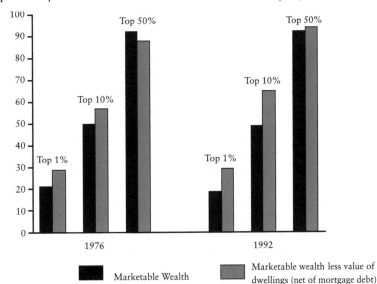

Source: Social Trends, 25 (1996 edn), Table 5.23.

Nor do the trends exhibited by stocks and shares suggest an obvious influence on concentration. Following the stock market collapse of the early 1970s, with a 42 per cent fall in share prices in 1974 (much greater than in any one of the previous 14 years), the proportion of wealth accounted for by stocks and shares fell dramatically. Between 1971 and 1976, the proportion of total wealth values accounted for by stocks and shares fell from 20 per cent to 8 per cent and by 1987 it had fallen to 5.5 per cent. During the early to mid 1980s this trend changed direction and the proportional value of stocks and shares climbed back to 8 per cent by 1986. Stocks and shares became a more popular form of wealth holding during this period and the proportion of the adult population owning shares increased from 6 per cent in 1984 to over 20 per cent by the beginning of 1988. This trend was fuelled by government policy as well as exhortation and the transfers from public to private ownership in the mid-1980s were very heavily over-subscribed. It is true, of course, that such trends do not tell us anything about the relative values of individual shareholdings, and this is essential to understanding the real impact of market stocks such as the stock market crash of Autumn 1987. On the other hand, the impact of that crash is a likely contributor to the halt in the recovery of stocks and shares as a proportional component of overall wealth which is a feature in the official data for the end of the 1980s – the proportion of 8 per cent still held in 1989.

15.4 Inheritance, Wealth Concentration and Taxation

While some influences on wealth concentration might be noticeable over a relatively short time period, as in the case of changes in wealth composition, others, like certain biological, social and demographic factors, operate over very lengthy time periods. The complex set of all the relationships which ultimately determines a person's wealth are a mixture of genetic endowments, material inheritance, educational opportunities, social and economic environments, marital status and so forth. These influences are, in turn, deter-mined in large part by social and cultural norms regarding modes of inheritance, marital patterns, etc. Strong influences on the long-term distribution of wealth are exerted by the extent to which the rich marry the rich and the poor marry the poor, and by differential fertility – if the rich have fewer children than the poor then concentration increases and vice versa. These are very important considerations, but we do not have the space here to discuss them further. However, one socio-demographic factor which we must look at more closely is that of inheritance patterns. One custom which works strongly against the dispersion of wealth is that of **primogeniture**, strictly the passing on of wealth to the first-born child (although, historically, this has been interpreted as the first-born son). If inheritance was not an important determinant of the degree of wealth concentration then such a custom would assume less importance. However, available evidence suggests that inheritance is a major factor in the self-perpetuating cycle of wealth determination.

Much of this evidence has been produced by the work of Harbury and his collaborators. Harbury's original work (Harbury, 1962) examined the relationship between estates left by the wealthiest wealth holders and the estates left by their fathers and, using a sample of the large estates left in the years 1956 and 1957, concluded that around two thirds of rich sons had fathers who were among the wealthiest 0.25 per cent of wealth holders. In later studies, Harbury and collaborators argued that although inheritance was declining as a determining factor in wealth concentration, it remained the single most important determinant. For example, Harbury and McMahon found that 50 per cent of sons leaving over £1 million had fathers who had done the same (Harbury and McMahon, 1973) while Harbury and Hitchens found that 58 per cent of those who had died wealthy had themselves inherited large fortunes (Harbury and Hitchens, 1976).

15.4.1 Wealth Taxation

If inheritance is such an important determinant of wealth concentration, and if government had a serious commitment to reducing inequality, one might expect that the fiscal system would be used to discourage the concentration of inheritances. So far in the UK, however, this has not been the case. Until 1974, Estate Duty was the main tax on wealth in the UK. Unfortunately, estate duty was not a notable success in reducing inequalities, partly because it was never applied properly to discretionary trusts, and partly because the rules permitted exemption of gifts *inter vivos* unless such transfers took place within seven years prior to the donor's death. However, perhaps the greatest fault of estate duty as a means of reducing wealth inequality lay in the principle of taxing the value of an estate rather than the value of an inheritance. It is not large estates *per se* which perpetuate inequalities but the fact that they are passed on as large inheritances, and the most efficient way to promote equality by taxing wealth is to tax inherited receipts. Furthermore, if its rates structure is progressive, an inheritance tax offers an incentive to donors to disperse their wealth more widely than they would in the face of an estates tax. In 1974, the Estate Duty was replaced by the Capital Transfer Tax. This represented an improvement in that the new tax was levied on a cumulative basis, not just on wealth at death but also on gifts and bequests *inter vivos*. However, the Capital Transfer Tax was still based on the estate principle and not levied on receipts on transfer, and thus did not provide the additional incentive to disperse wealth that is offered by an inheritance tax.

The Finance Act of 1986 brought in yet another change, with Capital Transfer Tax being replaced by the Inheritance Tax. As in the cases of Estate Duty and Capital Transfer Tax, the new levy was hedged by a long list of wealth exemptions. Further, although the tax is cumulative, no tax is payable on the first part of the cumulative total, an exemption which is increased in April of each year in line with the rise in the Retail Prices Index. Finally, once again (despite its name) the Inheritance Tax is levied on the value of a gift or an estate and not the amount received or inherited; the main charge under the tax arises on transfers made by an individual on death, or within seven years of death. As with its predecessors, there is no incentive provided under this tax for a wider dispersal of inheritances.

Bibliography

Atkinson, A. B. (1972) *Unequal Shares* (London: Penguin).

Atkinson, A. B. (1996) *Incomes and the Welfare State* (Cambridge: CUP).

Brittan, S. (1995) 'Redistribution, Yes, "Equality", No', *Financial Times* (16 February) p. 20.

Department of Social Security (1994) *Households Below Average Income* (London: HMSO).

Diamond Commission (Royal Commission on the Distribution of Income and Wealth) (1975) *Report No. 1*. Cmnd 6171 (London: HMSO); (1975) *Report No. 4*. Cmnd 6626 (London: HMSO).

Goodman, A. and S. Webb (1994) 'For Richer, For Poorer: The Changing Distribution of Income in the UK, 1961–91', *Fiscal Studies*, 15 (4).

Harbury, C. D. (1962) 'Inheritance in the Distribution of Personal Wealth', *Economic Journal* (December) .

Harbury, C. D. and D. M. Hitchens (1976) 'The Inheritance of Top Wealth Leavers', *Economic Journal*, 86.

Harbury, C. D. and P. C. McMahon (1973) 'Inheritance and the Distribution of Personal Wealth in Britain', *Economic Journal*, 83.

Jenkins, S. (1991) 'Living Standards and the Diverging "Thatcher" Effect', *The Guardian* (15 April) p. 13.

Jenkins, S. P. and F. A. Cowell (1994) 'Dwarfs and Giants in the 1980s: Trends in the UK Income Distribution', *Fiscal Studies*, 15 (1).

Johnson, P., G. Stark and S. Webb (1991) 'A Decade of Taxation Gains and Losses', *Financial Times* (20 March) p. 23.

Lydall, H. F. (1959) 'The Long Term Trend in the Size Distribution of Income', *Journal of the Royal Statistical Society* (Series A, 122, Part 1).

Morris, N. and I. Preston (1986) 'Taxes, Benefits and the Distribution of Income 1968–83', *Fiscal Studies* (November).

Nicholson, R. J. (1967) 'The Distribution of Personal Income', *Lloyds Bank Review* (January).

Office of National Statistics (1995) 'The Effects of Taxes and Benefits on Household Income, 1994/95', *Economic Trends*, No. 506, pp. 21–59.

Social Security Select Committee (1991) *Low Income Statistics: Households Below Average Income Tables 1988*, First Report 1990–91, House of Commons.

Stark, T. (1990) *Income and Wealth in the 1980s* (London: Fabian Society).

Stewart, I. (1991) 'Estimates of the Distribution of Personal Wealth II: Marketable Wealth and Pension Rights of Individuals 1976 to 1989', *Economic Trends*, No. 457.

The Economist (1994) 'For Richer, For Poorer' (3 November) pp. 19–21.

Wilkinson, M. (1993) 'British Tax Policy 1979–90: Equity and Efficiency', *Policy and Politics*, 21 (3) pp. 207–217.

Chapter 16

Welfare II: Poverty and Income Maintenance

Paul Marshall

■ 16.1 Introduction

While the discussion of distribution and inequality in **Chapter 15** referred mainly to a summary index, the Gini coefficient, important occasional use was made of the comparison between *extremes* in the distribution. We turn now in more detail to this question of extremes as we consider poverty as a manifestation of inequality. However, while 'poverty' is indeed a reflection of 'inequality', the two concepts are quite separate and have different meanings. It is a tautology to state that where incomes are unequally distributed, the poorest members of the population will be found at the bottom of the distribution. It may anyway be the case that these poor individuals are rich indeed when compared with those in the bottom percentile (or even the top percentile) of the income distribution in some other population. In other words, we might judge, say, the bottom 20 per cent of any population to be 'poor', but this may be true in only a relative sense, rather than an absolute one.

▢ 16.1.1 'Absolute' versus 'Relative' Definitions

The issue of **relative versus absolute** makes it difficult to identify the poor. If we could rely on an absolute (objective) measure we could estimate poverty simply by counting the individuals (or the households) who do not possess the means of achieving the absolute minimum standard of living. An absolute yardstick can also be applied over time and, hence, offers the means of checking whether or not the incidence of poverty is changing. So why not rely on an absolute measure of poverty? To answer this question, we must consider carefully what exactly is meant by this term. Such a measure would attempt to define a minimum level of subsistence for the chosen income unit (individual or household) and to determine the level of income necessary to guarantee that such a minimum can be enjoyed. Thus, 'the poor' would be those units with incomes short of the minimum level. It should be easy to appreciate that defining absolute subsistence is difficult and not particularly helpful in the formulation of social policy.

One obvious criticism of absolute measures is that any population is likely to be heterogeneous in terms of minimum requirements. Compare, for example, the basic food requirements of an 18-year-old male who is tall and heavy and whose occupation is felling trees, with those of a retired female schoolteacher who is small and light. But a more fundamental problem is that poverty is usually defined with reference to prevailing social norms and available 'life styles'; that is by comparing the differing living standards enjoyed by different units in the population. Of course this, in turn, causes further difficulties for empirical measurement. What is the minimum living standard for the UK in the 1990s? For example, should every household be expected to own a television set? Many social observers have wrestled with the problems of defining a minimum relative living standard (and, hence, standards of 'relative deprivation') but none has yet derived a definition which has proved universally acceptable.

16.1.2 Income or Expenditure? Individual or Household?

Another difficult theoretical issue which has very serious implications for empirical work is the question of whether poverty should be defined by reference to **income or expenditure**. Some researchers argue that individuals' incomes indicate whether or not they are poor because incomes determine consumption potential. Other researchers argue that this is not the case, and that consumption is determined by expenditure which, in turn, is determined not only by income but also by wealth (past savings) and by borrowing – an individual who can dip into past savings and/or can borrow is less constrained in current spending then someone who depends solely on current income to finance current expenditure.

There is also the issue as to whether the reference unit for determining living standards should be the **individual** or the **household** (see, for example, Ramprakash, 1994, p. 118). Some researchers argue that choosing the individual as

the basic reference unit loses sight of the fact that many individuals live in a household where incomes are pooled and shared, thus permitting some household members to have access to a higher level and range of consumption than that determined by individual income. On the other hand, it can be argued that households vary in size, age and gender structure, with a consequent variable network of dependants, and that such dependency must be recognised when calculating real incomes or expenditures and, therefore, real poverty.

Given the variety of approaches which might result from such differences, it is not surprising that empirical research has not used a consistent database, nor even used a consistent definition of the income unit. In their famous comparative study of 1953 and 1960, Abel-Smith and Townsend (1965) used the Family Expenditure Survey and based their findings on expenditure data for 1953 and income data for 1960. Since 1972, the Department of Social Security has also used the FES for its own 'official' estimates of the numbers in poverty. However, later studies by the DSS adopt the 'family', which usually means 'tax unit' or 'budget unit' and constitutes a narrower income/expenditure unit than that of the 'household' adopted by Abel-Smith and Townsend. Since broader units, like households, offer greater access to shared resources than do narrower definitions like the tax unit, it is not surprising that the extent of poverty is relatively greater when measured across the narrower units.

Nor do the problems for researchers end here. For example, another difficult question to answer is whether or not poverty is manifested by individuals' **total** expenditure or by their **specific** expenditures – the actual goods and services purchased. Some researchers have emphasised the need to consider specific expenditures (or, strictly, consumption of specific commodities) and, historically, state welfare programmes have subsidised consumption of specific goods – for example, milk and orange juice. The difficulties for social commentators raised by such considerations are akin to those raised by the concept of **merit goods**, namely that attempts by government to subsidise specific consumption can interfere with individuals' exercise of free choice. For example, a wealthy individual might choose to eat a diet which, taken in isolation, would identify him as poor.

□ *16.1.3 Poverty Estimates*

However, even if all empirical research were to adopt **either** income **or** expenditure and also the same definition of income or expenditure unit, they could still produce very different estimates of the scale and incidence of poverty, depending on the yardstick adopted as the 'poverty line' (see, for example, Ramprakash, 1994, p. 119). Such yardsticks vary according to the degree of 'relativity' built into the measurement. The deficiencies of the absolute standard, combined with the desire to maintain a consistent yardstick, have resulted in most of the major postwar studies adopting the state's minimum standard when trying to measure the full extent of poverty in the UK. An additional and important argument advanced for using this reference standard concerns the desire to test the efficacy of government policies in fighting poverty – in the words of Atkinson (1969), 'the success of Government policy is being judged in the light of its own minimum standards'. Within the framework of a parliamentary democracy, this approach seems to be the only possible way in which self-imposed standards, and hence the consensus view on relative life styles, might be judged in terms of success in limiting the numbers falling below these standards.

The 'official' poverty line was the one adopted by Abel-Smith and Townsend (1965) in their survey. Their empirical investigation was based on the FES and measured poverty against National Assistance, the prevailing minimum available under the state's income maintenance arrangements. The investigation undertaken by Abel-Smith and Townsend was the first national survey of poverty, and it produced an estimate of 3.8 per cent of the population living in poverty; that is with incomes below the level set for National Assistance. Such a finding came as a rude shock to a nation lulled into believing that postwar prosperity,

coupled with 'welfare state' maintenance arrangements, had eradicated poverty from the social landscape. Further empirical work by Atkinson (1969) suggested that the proportion of the population in poverty was still around 3.5 per cent at the end of the 1960s.

The pressure exerted by private researchers was not matched by any government response until 1974, when an official data series on 'Low Income Families' (LIF) was first published (covering 1972), and a comprehensive review of the empirical evidence on poverty had to await a report from the Royal Commission on the Distribution of Income and Wealth published in 1978. The official series, following the practice adopted by Abel-Smith and Townsend, measured 'low incomes' by reference to 'Supplementary Benefit' (SB) which had replaced 'National Assistance' as the state minimum. The series produced estimates relating to categories of 'low income', defined as below 140 per cent of the appropriate SB level, and it came to be used extensively by social commentators, both public and private. This series of LIF statistics was superseded in 1988 by a new one, produced biennially, based on 'average income' (the 'Households Below Average Income', or HBAI series). In addition to the difference in the definition of 'low income', estimates in the new series are based on the broader household rather than the family or benefit unit used by the old series. The major significance of this 1988 change is the move away from measuring 'poverty' against the minimum standard of income established by the state's income maintenance programme (for an excellent comparative analysis of the LIF and HBAI series see Giles and Webb, 1993; for a strong critque of HBAI see Pryke, 1995).

The latest official data in the SB-based series relate to 1985, but estimates by Johnson and Webb (1990) have extended the series to 1987 and shown that, over the whole period covered by the series, from 1972 to 1987, both the numbers of families and the number of persons (in families) living below the SB level increased. Not only has there been a steady increase in the numbers of families and persons below supplementary level, but the percentage changes during the 1980s were higher than those for the 1970s. Between 1972 and 1979, the increase in the number of families below SB was over 16 per cent and that for persons below SB the increase was nearly 20 per cent. Between 1979 and 1987, there was approximately a 20 per cent increase in the number of families below SB level and the number of persons below SB increased by almost 36 per cent during the same period. Indeed, by the relative standards applying during the period, such estimates suggest that 'poverty' has persisted stubbornly since the 1960s – on the basis of these official estimates just over 5 per cent of the population was living below the SB level in 1987. The new 'average income' benchmark suggests also that (relative) poverty remains a significant feature of the UK's socio-economic structure. In a detailed comparison of the 'old' and the 'new' measures, as applied to data for 1983, Johnson and Webb (1990) concluded that, on the old basis of assessing incomes, around 10 per cent of the population would have had incomes below half the average in 1983, and although the new methodology reduces this proportion, it remained significant at 8 per cent at the end of the 1980s.

In 1996, Oppenheim and Harker published new findings on behalf of the Child Poverty Action Group which confirmed the poverty trends measured by others. Using the two main approaches referred to so far, supplementary benefit/income support as the poverty line and half average income (after housing costs), Oppenheim and Harker calculated the figures shown in **Table 16.1**.

It should be noted here that measuring poverty in terms of income net of housing costs is itself contentious (see *The Economist*, 7 October 1995; Pryke, 1995). While it might be argued that housing is an essential element in individual/household budgeting, it can be contended that actual housing costs to an individual or household are often determined by the exercise of personal choice. However, it is certainly the case that housing costs form a higher proportion of the income of poorer households than of richer households (see, for example, Goodman and Webb, 1994). Whatever view prevails in regard to the definition of poverty, it would seem that in relative terms and irrespective of the definition of the 'poverty line', poverty has grown quite markedly in recent times.

16.1.4 The Origins of the Present System

For most of the postwar period, anti-poverty legislation in the UK has built on the foundations laid down in the Beveridge Report (Cmd 6404) of 1942, subject to occasional modification. There was no attempt at a comprehensive overhaul of the Beveridge system until the Conservative Government's White Paper in 1985 and the subsequent reforms embodied in the 1986 Social Security Act (implemented fully only in 1988). The primary aim of the Beveridge Plan was to eradicate all want by concentrating on its causes: loss of work through unemployment or sickness, cessation of work through retirement and the drain on household resources created by large numbers of dependants. The main instrument of the system was a comprehensive programme of social (or 'national') insurance, offering flat-rate benefits to the unemployed and the sick and flat-rate retirement pensions, financed mainly by weekly contributions from those covered by the

Table 16.1   *Poverty in the 1990s According to Two Methods of Estimation*

Income Support 'Poverty Line'		Half Average Income 'Poverty Line'	
1979	1992	1979	1992
6% of pop'n *below* 14% of pop'n *on or below*	8% of pop'n *below* 25% of pop'n *on or below*	9% of pop'n *below*	25% of pop'n *below*

Source: Oppenheim and Harker (1996) p. 24.

scheme. This programme was supported by Family Allowances (later to become Child Benefits) payable on behalf of all children except the first born. As a minimum income guarantee, the programme included National Assistance (later Supplementary Benefit and then Income Supplement) for those whose needs could *not* be met by the insurance scheme. The insurance benefits were intended to be sufficient to satisfy subsistence needs, and the role of National Assistance was anticipated to be minimal.

The optimism underlying the anticipation of such a minimal role for National Assistance was founded on an assumption that full employment would prevail. This optimism was reflected also in the fact that Family Allowance was not to be payable for the first child in a family since the family wage in a fully-employed economy would be sufficient to support one child. It must be remembered that the Beveridge scheme was introduced at a time when government believed that management of aggregate demand would in future ensure that the evil of mass unemployment did not return. This new-found faith in demand management was to be enshrined in the famous White Paper (Cmd 6527) of 1944. It is worth

remembering also that the years 1945–50 witnessed the introduction of other 'social welfare' programmes to complete a massive frontal attack on the main causes of deprivation; in particular the Education Act 1944 and the National Health Service Act 1946 were meant to add significant firepower to the state's armoury. **Table 16.2** summarises the flurry of state activity in the 1940s which provided the foundations for what came to be known as the 'Welfare State'.

16.2 Socio-economic Changes and the Incidence of Poverty

Although not intended by Beveridge, the social security system in the UK grew steadily such that, by the 1990s, it was the largest item of public expenditure, accounting for almost one third of the total. Over this same period the importance of social security benefits as a component of personal incomes grew dramatically, from less than 10 per cent in the mid-1950s to over 20 per cent by the mid-1980s. According to its critics, this relative growth of the social security system is further testimony to its failure, brought about by its

Table 16.2 *The 1940s Foundations of the Welfare State*

Social Security	*Beveridge Report* (1942) *Social Insurance White Paper* (1944): accepted most of Beveridge's recommendations *Family Allowance Act* 1945 *National Insurance Act* 1946 (Based on 1944 White Paper) *National Insurance (Industrial Injuries) Act* 1946 *National Assistance Act* 1948
Employment	*Employment Policy White Paper* (1944): committed government to maintaining a high (and stable) level of employment through deficit spending when necessary
Health	*National Health Service White Paper* (1944): set plans for comprehensive health care for all, free of direct user charge and financed out of general taxation *National Health Service Act* 1946 (Based on 1944 White Paper)
Education	*Educational Reconstruction White Paper* (1943): set out plans for comprehensive national system of primary, secondary and further education, primary and secondary education to be free of direct user charge and financed out of general taxation *Education Act* 1946 (based on 1943 White Paper)

intrinsic nature and by the fact that its basic philosophy has been interpreted differently by successive governments.

So large a scheme, covering so many categories of want through state discretion, is likely to be slow to adapt to changes in the social and economic structure. The postwar period has seen many demographic changes and, in particular, proportional increases in the dependent sectors of the population as well as changes in the scale and incidence of unemployment and changes in the occupational wage structure. One result of the many changes unforeseen by Beveridge has been the heavy dependency upon the role of the so-called 'safety net' of National Assistance/Supplementary Benefit/Income Support. The Beveridge intention that the safety net would play a minimal role has not been realised. In terms of demographic and structural changes, the three most significant ones have been in the number of aged people, family composition and the level and incidence of unemployment.

☐ 16.2.1 Poverty and Old Age

The population of the UK, like that of the rest of Europe and other parts of the developed world, has been getting older and is expected to continue doing so well into the foreseeable future. In the UK at the beginning of the 1950s, the proportion of the population aged 65 and over was just under

11 per cent, but by the middle of the 1980s it had risen to just under 15 per cent. Projections published by the OECD, and reproduced in **Table 16.3**, suggest that by the middle of the next century the elderly populations of the UK and several other developed countries will have doubled their proportional sizes.

The projections in **Table 16.3** suggest severe implications for future income maintenance arrangements (and for the health care of the elderly) in the light of their performance in the face of the ageing of the population to date. One vivid representation of the burden placed on the system so far is that around 16 per cent of the social security budget in the mid-1980s would not have been required if the benefit at the time had been payable to the number of pensioners alive in the early 1950s (Dilnot, Kay and Morris, 1984). This is not to say that the burden of the elderly had been completely unanticipated by Beveridge. Indeed, the Report envisaged that over the 'transitional period' up to 1965, social security costs would rise by some 25 per cent due to the increasing burden of retirement pensions. However, over the course of the transitional period the cost of retirement pensions, in real terms, was twice as high as Beveridge had envisaged.

Poverty among old people is not a new feature of society, but it has been a notorious contributor to total domestic poverty over the course of the twentieth century. The famous surveys of poverty in York undertaken by Rowntree found that old age was the major cause of poverty in under 5 per

Table 16.3   *Projections of the Elderly Population, UK and Selected Countries (% of Population Aged 65 and Over)*

	UK	US	Japan	Canada	France	W. Germany	Italy
1980[1]	14.9	11.3	9.1	9.5	14.0	15.5	13.5
1985[1]	15.1	11.9	10.2	10.4	13.0	14.8	12.9
2000	14.5	12.1	15.2	12.8	15.3	17.1	15.3
2020	18.7	17.2	22.9	20.0	21.2	23.5	20.7
2040	26.4	25.3	29.2	29.2	29.7	34.1	29.1
2050	28.7	29.0	33.1	33.0	34.0	36.2	31.0

Note:
[1] Actual.
Source: Financial Times, 6 July 1988, using OECD Demographic Data Files.

cent of poor households in 1899 whereas, in 1951, old age was estimated to be the cause of poverty in two-thirds of poor households. Rowntree's explanation of this trend included the increase in the relative size of the aged population and the increased tendency for the aged to live alone rather than with their families. As we have seen, the proportion of old people in the population has increased markedly since Rowntree's last survey.

Income sources for the aged are based less on market earnings than is the case with younger age groups. Labour market activity rates for pensioner households have fallen dramatically since the beginning of the twentieth century, and retirement pensions, both state and private, have become the main source of income for such households. Some indication of how this reliance on pension income affects living standards for old people can be taken from a comprehensive survey of poverty in the early 1970s which found a 17 per cent risk of poverty for the elderly compared with only 2.5 per cent for other adults (the risk for old people living alone was calculated to be as high as 30 per cent) and that, in total, elderly households accounted for approximately 42 per cent of the poverty among the sample (Fiegehen, Lansley and Smith, 1977).

While the risk factor remains high for old people, recent government estimates suggest that old age has diminished as a factor in poverty since the beginning of the 1970s. The rewards of occupational pension schemes, and the returns from other forms of savings, have meant that recently-retired pensioners have come to rely less on social security benefits than other pensioners, (although any associated relief on the burden on taxpayers has had to be balanced against a growing proportion of pensioners in the population). New legislation to combat poverty introduced in the mid-1980s gave more emphasis to the burden of pensions on taxpayers than to the burden of poverty on pensioners, against the background of a fall in the proportion of pensioners in the poorest fifth of the population from 35 per cent to 19 per cent between 1971 and 1982. Nevertheless, such an estimate still suggests that roughly one in five of the poorest fifth were pensioners at the start of the 1980s.

Evidence that pensioners still figure very significantly as a low income group is provided also by the new 'average income' method of counting low income families, introduced in 1988. As calculated by Johnson and Webb (1991), nearly 80 per cent of individuals in pensioner households in 1983 had ('household equivalised') incomes below the average, compared with 61 per cent of all individuals. It should be noted also that, despite the government's switch of emphasis in its 1985 Green Paper, in that same year 27 per cent of persons in receipt of Supplementary Benefit were in pensioner families and nearly 40 per cent of individuals with incomes below the Supplementary Benefit level were in pensioner families. More recent data suggest that retirement continues to be an important determining factor in the incidence of poverty: in 1993, almost 40 per cent of households in the bottom quintile of the income distribution in the UK were retired households according to *Social Trends* (1995, Table 5.16), while the calculations for CPAG estimated that 22 per cent of the poor (recall the working definition of 'living below 50 per cent of average income after housing costs') were made up from single pensioners and pensioner couples (Oppenheim and Harker, 1996, Figure 2.3).

☐ *16.2.2 Family Poverty*

The other major component of the dependency sector of the population is children. Various surveys of poverty in the years before the Second World War had identified the number of children in a family as a major determinant of family poverty. In recent years, concern has arisen again over this issue. Despite a fall in the proportion of households with dependent children from 39 per cent to 32 per cent over the period 1971–85, the proportion of couples with children, together with single parents, rose from 48 per cent to 58 per cent among the poorest fifth of the population over roughly the same period (1971–82). One estimate has claimed that between £1.5 and £2 billion of social security expenditure in the mid-1980s was due to trends in the number of children wholly or partly within the social security system's responsibility (Berthoud, 1985). The estimates made by Oppenheim and Harker (1996, Figure 2.6) put 33 per cent of children in poverty in 1992/93, a more than three-fold growth over the 10 per cent of 1979. The increase in the number of single parents has been a particular cause for concern. According to official estimates, the rise in divorces, the increasing incidence of illegitimate births and fewer illegitimate children being put forward for adoption all contributed to the proportion of people living in one-parent families with children doubling from 2.5 per cent in 1961 to 5 per cent by 1985. It must be said that the one-parent family was a problem identified by Beveridge, but its increase on such a scale was not anticipated – by 1991 the number of single-parent families in receipt of special state assistance (one-parent family benefit and/or Income Support) had reached 1.27 million (Bradshaw, 1991), and the Oppenheim and Harker calculations for 1992/93 estimate lone parents as making up 17 per cent of the poor (*op. cit.*, Figure 2.3).

16.2.3 Lower Earnings and Unemployment

The Beveridge Report paid a lot of attention to the problems created by unemployment, taking account of the history of the labour market and, in particular, the 1930s. However, in this one respect, the experience of the first three decades after Beveridge seemed to suggest that full employment was the norm and unemployment was, indeed, a contingency. The reality after 1970 was to shatter this illusion as unemployment rose to over 13 per cent by 1984, including a dramatic increase in the numbers of long-term unemployed which swelled the numbers in receipt of Supplementary Benefit following the exhaustion of rights to Unemployment Benefit. While almost 80 per cent of household income came from employment in 1961, the proportion had fallen to around 60 per cent by 1991 (Goodman and Webb, 1994, Figure 21).

The significance of unemployment as a factor in calculating low incomes is underlined by Johnson and Webb (1990) in their survey of low in-

comes for the period from 1979 to 1987. They observe that the most notable change in the composition of the low income group during this period was the two-thirds increase in the number of families receiving Supplementary Benefit, and they point out that this reflects, in part, not only the increase in unemployment over the period but also the increase in the proportion of long-term unemployed who had lost their eligibility for Unemployment Benefit. Thus, in 1979, some 50 per cent of the unemployed were receiving Supplementary Benefit but by 1987 the proportion had increased to 61 per cent. The new official low income series also underlines the significance of unemployment – of those individuals living in households where the 'head' was unemployed in 1981, 75 per cent had incomes below 80 per cent of the average and 42 per cent had incomes below half the average; by 1985 these proportions had risen to 84 per cent and 47 per cent respectively. According to the CPAG definition, 16 per cent of the poor in 1992/93 were unemployed (Oppenheim and Harker, 1996, Figure 2.7).

However, unemployment has not been the sole economic cause of poverty among families. Another problem which Beveridge failed to anticipate was the high incidence of **low earnings** among households in poverty after the Second World War. Beveridge virtually took it for granted that earnings in a fully-employed labour market would be sufficient to support a dependent spouse and one child. Yet the general increase in living standards which has pushed up the poverty line has left behind certain groups in low-paid employment. In 1987, there were 370 000 families (940 000 persons including children) with incomes below Supplementary Benefit level despite the family head being in full-time employment.

16.3 The Response From the System

16.3.1 Poverty Among the Aged

How well has the system copied with these social and economic pressures? Given the numbers remaining in poverty, particularly in specific groups of dependants, the UK's social security programme has been found wanting. Some observers have blamed successive governments for failing to implement fully the Beveridge proposals, while others have emphasised that the cause of the problem lies in the nature of social insurance programmes. One important principle of the Beveridge scheme which has not been adhered to consistently is that National Insurance benefits should be at least equal to the basic poverty standard. On this principle was based the expectation that National Assistance (now Income Support) would be a genuine 'safety net'. Yet for long periods throughout the post-Beveridge years, this principle was not adhered to in the categories of pensioners and children. Many pensioner households have had to rely on a flat-rate state retirement pension which has not been maintained at all times at a level above the state minimum. Hence, those pensioner households totally dependent on the state retirement pension have required supplementation to their flat-rate benefit, and even in the early 1980s more than one-fifth of pensioners were supported by Supplementary Benefit.

The most important determinant of the system's response to changes in the socio-economic structure has been the fact that benefit levels and eligibility conditions have been at the discretion of government. Social security budgeting has had to take its place in the ranking of expenditure priorities, set against available government revenues. Thus, as a matter of policy, the value of the basic state retirement pension, as a proportion of net average earnings, fell from around 32 per cent in 1982 to around 22 per cent in 1996 (see Atkinson, *Times Higher Education Supplement*, 12 April 1996). At this point, it should be recalled that the Beveridge perception of social security was one of insurance against contingencies like unemployment and sickness, and against loss of earnings on retirement, with earmarked benefits for children and all supported by National Assistance for those not catered for within the insurance scheme. The Beveridge programme of income maintenance was thus founded on a relationship between the principles of 'contribution' for the insurance part and 'eligibility' (or means-testing) for the assistance part.

This has given rise to two difficulties for governments. In the first place, social insurance is not very flexible; because its benefits depend on past contributions it reacts slowly to socio-economic change. Secondly, the relationship between contribution record and means-testing for supplementation is very difficult to maintain.

To try and resolve the first difficulty, successive UK governments added on several new measures to the fundamental, Beveridge-based, social security programme. Inevitably, this increased the scheme's complexity. Significant steps were taken to modify provision in the three main areas outlined earlier: retirement, family size and low earnings. The increase in the number of pensioners was to put pressure on the social security system in terms of both the increasing costs of providing Beveridge-style retirement pensions and the need to make adequate provision for pensioners as living standards rose for the population as a whole. The year 1961 saw the introduction of a graduated pension, financed by a graduated contribution (a scheme which was extended to earnings-related supplements to unemployment benefit, sickness benefit and maternity allowances in 1966). Those employees with occupational pension rights considered by the authorities to be 'adequate' were permitted to 'contract out' of the graduated pensions scheme, another significant factor leading, by the end of the 1960s, to a situation wherein the cost of benefits had risen significantly in relation to the size of the potential 'tax base'. From 1969 onwards, graduated contributions financed more and more of the flat-rate benefits.

However, the major change in state pension arrangements was to come in the Social Security Pensions Act 1975 and its implementation in April 1978. This legislation introduced the State Earnings Related Pension Scheme (SERPS) under which retirement pensions were to comprise an earnings-related addition to the basic flat-rate benefit (once again, provision was made for adequate occupational pension schemes to be 'contracted out' of SERPS). Early fears about the full cost of SERPS led to a proposal for its abandonment in a government Green Paper published only seven years after its introduction. However, the ensuing White Paper of 1986 retained SERPS with modifications designed to reduce its long-term cost.

16.3.2 Insurance or 'Pay As You Go'?

In respect of pensions, the second difficulty referred to earlier links closely with the first since the problem of the ever-increasing cost of pensions has arisen mainly because public preoccupation has been with the income maintenance aspect of pensions rather than with the principle of insurance. It is difficult to see how this could be otherwise in a state-provided scheme. To try and appreciate this point it might help to rehearse the arguments for state involvement in provisions for retirement.

Microeconomic theory depicts the individual as maximising the satisfaction which he or she derives from consuming goods (including leisure) and services, according to taste and subject to various constraints. The rational individual, interested in lifetime utility, will attach relative weights to present and future consumption levels according to the time-preference pattern of consumption, and attempt to maximise satisfaction subject to both present and expected future constraints. Given that individuals do behave in this way, a state programme of compulsory provision for old age may distort the individual's 'optimal' (from the point of view of personal time-preference) allocation of consumption between time periods. The individual with positive time preference is forced to increase future consumption at the expense of the present, and even the individual who places a greater weight upon future consumption is satisfied only if the level of state provision accords with his or her own expectations and desires.

The counter-argument is that the time preferences of most individuals are such that they make inadequate provision for old age for two main reasons: widespread myopia, intensified by the difficulties of decision-making which takes account of the distant future; and a lack of means by which to plan a consumption pattern over more than one time period. Even if the state could mitigate the latter part of the problem by providing those without means with a margin of saving over current consumption, this would be fruitful only if the first part of the problem could be solved.

Thus, given that individuals are improvident, or find the calculus of optimisation concerning future income streams, investment yields, family circumstances, likelihood of employment and so on beyond their mental powers, the state assumes a paternalistic role via the compulsory purchase of annuities so as to protect the individual. If the individual does not want this protection – for example, if he or she has a very strong positive time preference for consumption – the state justifies its interference on the grounds of social costs. While concern for others might lead society to help the myopic and improvident, it does not prevent society from taking steps to ensure that the need for such aid is minimised. Furthermore, it is reasonable to expect that the working population at any point in time might wish to minimise the likelihood of their children having to support the retired population at some future date and demand that individuals be compelled to make proper provision for their retirement needs.

It must be admitted that even if a case exists for compulsory insurance, itself debatable, it is by no means obvious that this requires the compulsory purchase of state annuities. But assuming that this method of protection is adopted, should a state scheme be organised, as far as possible, on an insurance basis? The pension problem is an inter-generational one. If we accept that the sole rationale for intervention is to protect a future generation of tax-payers (the assumption we made above), then the state has a duty to organise its scheme on a funded basis, that is to ensure its actuarial soundness. To protect current policy-holders against the possibility of receipts being less than adequate to cover benefit payments at some future date, a reserve fund would be accumulated on behalf of all insured persons. To create such a reserve, premiums would be set at a sufficiently high level; if the individual wants the promise of a higher level of benefit, or more comprehensive coverage than is allowed by the original contract, he or she must be prepared to pay a higher premium. In this way, then, a reserve is accumulated for each individual, and it follows that an increase in the number of people insured must mean an increase in total reserves.

However, if we modify the rationale of intervention to one of protecting all generations, including current taxpayers, then the state has no need to organise its scheme on a funded basis (even assuming it could do so), but can make use of its coercive powers to establish the programme on a 'pay-as-you-go' basis, whereby current beneficiaries are supported by current contributions. In other words, an 'acceptable' tax/transfer plan can be devised. This argument is based on two assumptions: that the scheme is financed by compulsory contributions and that future governments maintain the compulsion. Given these conditions, we can view social 'insurance' as a form of social contract whereby the young are prepared to support the old on the guarantee that a future generation of taxpayers will do the same for them when they grow old.

But what happens if the age structure of the population changes? In particular, what happens if the proportion of the retired population increases significantly? In order to maintain the same level of pension per head of the retired population the contributory costs on the active population must rise. If this situation persists, and these costs continue to rise, the contract is very much weakened and is likely to be modified by government action. This problem appears even with real incomes growing over time if pension levels are to be determined relative to current living standards. In other words, the insurance system collapses into the government's general tax/transfer programme with a consequent burden on public finances.

The consequences of accepting the provision of income maintenance for retired people as part of a state tax/transfer mechanism are many. One important feature at the time of inception is that pensions can be paid immediately – that is, contributions do not have to grow on a funded basis before an individual enjoys the fruits of entitlement. But the most important, if obvious, conse-

quence is that pension arrangements as part of a wider tax/transfer mechanism are decided by government and become the subject of political as well as financial constraints – this problem is 'writ large' for the economies of those countries mentioned earlier in the OECD report, a problem which has been referred to as the 'pensions time bomb'. This can raise difficult problems in respect of inequality – what should be the 'reasonable' level for state pension benefits given the benefits enjoyed by those in receipt of occupational pensions and how should state retirement transfers compare with, say, transfers to the temporarily sick or unemployed? For example, if the value of the state pension is maintained in relation to average earnings then a rising 'dependency ratio' of pensioners to taxpayers will require the latter to face rising tax rates. In the UK government policy has been to allow the basic pension to grow in line with the general level of prices rather than earnings, but whereas this relieves pressure on tax rates it causes the *relative* income of pensioners to decline over time.

These questions have been discussed constantly in the debate over pensions in the UK. At the same time, eligibility for retirement pension has been, and continues to be, based on contribution records. From the very start, the post-Beveridge scheme of national insurance was not funded on an actuarial basis. Even in its early years, current contributions from employees and employers comprised a very large proportion of the total current receipts of the National Insurance Fund, and by the mid-1960s this proportion had risen to 80 per cent with contributions from interest income and exchequer grants having fallen dramatically.

Clearly, the social security system has moved a long way from the insurance principles recommended in the Beveridge Report. As one research report puts it:

in introducing full-rate pensions straight away, the Government acknowledged a funding deficiency to be met from general taxation. When the time came to pay the subsidy on any substantial scale, the pledge was abandoned and a 'pay as you go' basis adopted. The National

Insurance Fund was reduced to meaningless accounting and the actuarial link between contribution and benefits abandoned.
(Dilnot, Kay and Morris, 1984).

Yet, as the same report points out, 'contribution records' are still the basis of eligibility (at substantial administrative cost). Whether or not this is because governments still believe (as Beveridge did) that individuals are more willing to pay 'contributions' than 'taxes' is debatable. Of course, if governments do believe this to be so they might also believe that their capacity for raising revenue without generating too much political 'heat' is enhanced.

16.3.3 Poverty Among Families With Children

In the area of family poverty too there have been major changes. We have mentioned the long-term decline in the real value of Family Allowances. In 1957 child tax allowances were reintroduced (first used in 1909 but removed when the Family Allowance was introduced) whereby deductions could be allowed from income for tax purposes at rates varying according to the age of the child. While such allowances offered indirect help to families with children, their distributional consequences differed from those of direct benefits. To see this more clearly, consider the situation after 1968 when Family Allowances became classified as taxable income and hence subject to reclamation by the Inland Revenue (the 'claw-back' principle). This clawing-back meant that the real value of the Family Allowance rose as family income fell. Tax allowances, on the other hand, increased in value as family income rose because of the rate structure of income tax. This meant that families with incomes so low as to be unaffected by income tax did not receive any real benefit from the tax allowances, and the benefits enjoyed by taxpaying families favoured the higher income groups.

Both tax allowances and Family Allowance were merged in the Child Benefit Act 1975 which introduced a **flat-rate benefit** on behalf of each child in a family and paid at a higher rate for one-parent families, the latter in recognition of the growth in single parenthood. Child Benefit, like the Family Allowance, is a 'universal' benefit – that is, payable to every family unit with children irrespective of the income of that family unit. As such, it remains a contentious issue and we shall return to it shortly when considering the vexed question of how to make social security more efficient.

The other main cause of family poverty discussed earlier was that of earnings too low to support a spouse and child, contrary to the assumption of the Beveridge Report. This problem was brought to governments' attention on several occasions by various lobbies, in particular by the Child Poverty Action Group. A response was offered by the Conservative Government of 1971 when it introduced Family Income Supplement (FIS), a means-tested benefit specifically aimed at those families where the family head was in full-time employment but whose earnings were below the 'prescribed amount'. FIS was welcomed with great optimism, but its effects were disappointing and it was replaced in 1988 by **Family Credits**.

There were many other modifications and additions to the social security over the post-Beveridge period. We cannot enter into the details of the main 'piecemeal' changes, but we should note here that help with housing costs was another major source of help offered to low-income families. Rate rebates were introduced in 1968, and a national scheme of rent rebates and allowances was introduced in 1972 following years of development in local authority schemes in the 1950s and 1960s. In 1983, **Housing Benefit** was introduced to replace these earlier arrangements. The other major change to note is the extension of the principle of earnings-related income maintenance, not only from the supplement offered under the 1961 graduated pension scheme to the subsequent pension arrangements discussed previously, but also to other national insurance benefits in 1966 and 1975. By the time of the Thatcher government's reforms of the mid-1980s, the social security system offered a complex array of 30 separate benefits with differing structures and rationales and costing over £2 billion annually to administer.

□ *16.3.4 The Problem of 'Take-up'*

We turn now to a question which has so far only been hinted at. While the pressures on the social security system go some of the way to explain why so many individuals have had to rely on the safety net of benefit supplementation, they do not explain why so many have fallen **below the poverty line**. The main reason why so many fall below this line is because they are not in receipt of full income supplementation even when entitled to it. This is the infamous problem of low 'take-up' thought, by most commentators, to be due to two causes: the complexity of the social security system and the stigma which attaches to receipt of means-tested benefits. The complexity of the system was underlined earlier. Not only is there a plethora of benefits for claimants to consider, but there is also a detailed and, for many claimants, difficult application procedure. Part of the difficulty lies in the detail required in order to assess the means and needs of claimants, but this very enquiry is also considered to be degrading by many potential claimants. As a consequence, many eligible individuals refrain from claiming means-tested benefits.

A government inquiry in 1965 found that one-third of pensioners were ignorant of the availability of National Assistance, while 30 per cent of married couples and 20 per cent of single men and women indicated that pride prevented them from applying for supplementary help. Family Income Supplement at the end of the 1970s was being taken up by only 50 per cent out of those eligible while, at the same time, the take-up rate for Supplementary Benefit was around 74 per cent and that for Rent and Rates Rebates in the region of 70 per cent, all according to government estimates. In 1987, Fry and Stark published a comparison of their own estimates of Supplementary Benefit take-up and those of the DHSS for a period covering the end of the 1950s to the middle of the 1980s (Fry and Stark, 1986). Their findings, reproduced in **Table 16.4**, underline the fact that take-up of the 'bottom line' income support for the period in question was well short of 100 per cent.

Low take-up of means-tested benefits creates two serious problems for income maintenance programmes. One obvious consequence is that income support is not being given to many of the households most in need of it. A second consequence, creating a problem for the longer term, is that low take-up rates affect the accuracy of policy planning because they influence the outcome of benefit expenditure by the government. For example, a reduction in universal benefits and an increase in selective or 'targeted' (means-tested) benefits should, in principle, result in a more equal distribution of final incomes but, if

Table 16.4   *Estimates of Supplementary Benefit Take-up*

| Study | Year | Take-up rate | | |
		Pensioners	Non-pensioners	All
DHSS	1977	0.72	0.79	–
DHSS	1979	0.65	0.78	0.70
DHSS	1981	0.67	0.75	0.71
Fry and Stark	1984	0.87	0.81	0.83
Fry and Stark[1]	1984	0.66	0.78	0.74

Note:
[1] Estimates on 'DHSS basis'.

Source: Fry and Stark (1986).

the former type of benefit has a high take-up rate and the latter a low one, the move towards equality is lessened. This is a problem we shall return to later.

□ 16.3.5 The Social Security 'Traps'

Another reason advanced to explain high numbers remaining in poverty, even during a time of economic growth for the country as a whole, relates to the implicit taxation of earned income in a social security system which relies on means-tested benefits for basic income support. This implicit taxation arises from the interaction among means-tested benefits and between them and the income tax system. As the number of means-tested benefits rose over the decades following the Beveridge Report, this was to become an increasing problem .

The various means-tested benefits and the social security programme are, in fact, examples of the principle of 'negative (income) taxation' in the sense that rules governing the receipt of benefit include elements of tax as well as welfare payment. These separable elements emerge from both the direction of the **total** resource flow involved and the nature of the impact at the **margin** of economic activity. Taking the case of a family unit of given size, we can demonstrate this point by assuming eligibility for weekly benefit to be determined by the amount of weekly income earned by the unit from other sources, say from earned income. Thus, at the margin, the net flow of resources is from the private sector to the government. In other words, the family unit is being taxed on **additional earnings**. However, the total flow of resources remains in the opposite direction to that of a tax since the net overall effect of the scheme is a supplement to the income of the family unit.

We may also note at this stage that the structure of means-tested benefits, as in this example, usually bears the other hallmarks of a taxation scheme. Benefit is paid to, or withheld from, a defined tax unit (say, head of household plus dependants); is determined by reference to a defined base (say, earned income); and the benefit

payable in any period depends on income received by the tax unit from the base source during that same period. There is, however, one feature of means-tested social security benefits which does set them apart from usual tax conventions: the marginal rate of tax applied to low levels of income is often very high because state supplements to income are a substitute for a lack of income from other sources within the tax base. Hence, as other income rises, the supplement is withdrawn. The rationale for this may lie in the philosophy behind the system (only those who have a genuine need for state help can receive it) and/or a lack of resources in society to permit a more generous redistribution of resources towards the lower income groups.

The propensity for claimants to incur high marginal tax rates is increased by interaction between the benefits system and the income tax. The so-called **poverty trap** usually operates when an increase in earnings offers only a small increase in final income because of simultaneous lower benefit receipt and higher taxes and/or National Insurance Contributions; in its most extreme form it has affected families in work such as to make them *worse-off* through the earning of an extra £1 of income. While the withdrawal of means-tested benefits has placed claimants on high marginal rates of (implicit) tax throughout the post-Beveridge period, the piecemeal additions to the benefit system served to intensify the problem. In particular, the introduction of FIS and its resulting interaction with housing subsidies was to become the main reason for poor households facing marginal rates of tax in excess of 100 per cent: the numbers of families in this severe form of the poverty trap was estimated by the Treasury and Civil Service Committee in 1982 to have increased from 15 000 in early 1974 to 105 600 by the end of 1981. A detailed analysis of how this trap operated in 1994/95 is provided by Parker (1995, Table 2.5) who argues that insufficient progress has been made to eradicate it over the past decade (*ibid.*, Table 3.2) with some one million adults currently involved.

The **unemployment trap** operates when low-earning households find that they are either financially better-off depending on state benefits than in paid employment, or that the difference in living standards offered by the two choices is so small that the incentive to find paid work is very weak. This particular problem was considered to be severe by the 1970s in the case of the short-term unemployed. It has been estimated that, in 1978, about 21 per cent of the heads of working families would have received more than 90 per cent of their weekly income if, instead, they had been unemployed for a short time (Dilnot, Kay and Morris, 1984). This was probably due to the availability of earnings-related benefit supplements and the fact that tax rebates were received during unemployment of short duration. In 1982, Unemployment Benefit was made taxable and earnings-related benefit supplement was abolished earlier in the same year. This was followed by a series of other, less significant changes (Parker, 1995, Table 2.1). Parker argues that the Conservative government effectively reduced both out-of-work living standards and work incentives, thereby transforming an unemployment trap into an **income support trap**, 'which is more damaging because it reduces the incentive to save as well as to work, and may well also jeopardise family solidarity'. Four other 'traps' are identified by Parker, who argues that the way to resolve the problem is to get rid of dependence on work-tested and means-tested benefits.

16.3.6 Fairness, Incentives and Supply-side Effects

High marginal rates of tax on the poor are considered to be undesirable for reasons of equity as well as efficiency. When a tax system, like that of the UK, is based on a principle of 'ability to pay' supported by a progressive rates structure, it is absurd as well as unfair for the tax system to combine with the social security programme and impose higher marginal rates of tax on low income groups than on higher income groups. While most observers agree about the inequity of the system's regressive rates structure, there is less agreement on the extent to which means-testing creates genuine disincentives to effort. Government preoccupation with the question of

work disincentives has been a constant feature of social security in the UK, although this concern has been dressed up in different language from time to time. Hence, 'less eligibility' was the principle behind the nineteenth century Poor Law condition that state aid to the unemployed should be less than the lowest earnings rate; the principle supported the 'wages stop' of the post-Beveridge Unemployment Benefit programme; and the need to minimise the 'disincentive to effort' became an essential ingredient of government policies based on supply-side economics during the 1970s and 1980s.

The increasing government pre-occupation with supply-side economics has encouraged several investigations by economists into household reactions to changes in the relative costs of work and leisure. These have concentrated more on changes in the marginal rate of taxation, and less on the average rate which affects disposable incomes and is more significant when considering Keynesian demand-side policy. The likely outcome to a change in marginal rates of tax is clearly an empirical question, but one which has proved difficult to answer, and research into labour supply reactions has unearthed evidence of both incentives and disincentives arising from alterations in the marginal net income of households. However, so far as the poverty trap is concerned, since the effective marginal tax rates can be so high it is difficult to assume that disincentives to effort do not exist in and around the trap, and government concern has accordingly centred on how many individuals are actively caught in the trap.

In looking at the unemployment trap, empirical work has tended to concentrate on the estimation of the **replacement rate** – that is, the ratio of net income out of work to net income in work, for various household categories. Our earlier reference to relative returns from working and living on state benefit before and after 1978 took account of replacement rates. The estimate quoted there of the proportions affected by high replacement rates was but one of several attempts to measure the supply-side disincentives of the benefit system before and after the 1978 changes. As with the poverty trap, estimation of the impact of the unemployment trap have proved difficult, and there is by no means a consensus on the issue of whether or not the benefit system has induced unemployment. A correlation between benefit/income rates and unemployment for the period up to the end of the 1970s has been calculated by Hemming (1984) which suggests that, on the whole, both increased from 1948 to the end of the period. In particular, a large increase in the benefit/income ratio after the introduction of the earnings-related supplement in 1966 is worthy of note.

16.3.7 The Conservative Reforms of the 1980s

As part of its comprehensive reappraisal of the relative roles of public and private sector in the mixed economy, and in its determination to ensure that government spending is 'efficient', the Conservative government turned its attentions to issues of social security in the mid-1980s. A White Paper in 1985 and the resulting parliamentary debate led to the Social Security Act 1986, which introduced several major changes to the benefit side of social security arrangements, with full implementation of these reforms taking place in April 1988. What we observe in both the debate and the subsequent reforms is clear recognition of the list of problems discussed earlier, with added emphasis on the efficiency/equity trade-off referred to at the outset of **Chapter 15**. The main defects of the system, as identified by the 1985 White Paper, were deemed to be its complexity, its failure to give proper support to those most in need, the problems created by the poverty and unemployment 'traps' and the burden of costs on future generations of taxpayers. In addition, the White Paper emphasised the government's concern about the restrictions on individual choice on the matter of pensions.

The response to the problems identified in the White Paper was set out in the 1986 Act, and centred on changes to the income-related benefits. The Green Paper had, in fact, proposed the abolition of SERPS, but this met with stiff opposition and the Act, instead, set out modifications aimed

at reducing its cost for future generations. Supplementary Benefit was replaced by **Income Support**; Family Income Support was replaced by **Family Credit**; and a new **Housing Benefit** replaced the previous two-part scheme (one for recipients of Supplementary Benefit and one for all others on low incomes). But these changes were not in name only. The new system rationalised the relationship between these three main income-related benefits and established their entitlements on the same basis for the first time. At the same time, the changes represented a shift in resources towards Income Support and Family Credit and away from Housing Benefit which, in effect, meant a **shift of emphasis in the system towards families with children and away from pensioners**. Income Support could continue to be the main benefit for those not in full-time work, offering a benefit of a personal allowance plus increases for dependants. Under the new benefit there would be no additions for specific needs whether 'one-off' or longer-term. Instead, such needs would be met out of a new Social Fund. Like its predecessor, Family Credit was designed to offer supplements to low-income families in full-time work and with children to support. It was also designed to be more extensive in its coverage than was FIS.

The issue of whether or not the provisions in the 1986 Act would be likely to achieve the objective laid down in the earlier White Paper initially provoked a mixed response. It was true that the social security system was *simplified*, but it was *not made simple*. In particular, the reforms offered no structural alterations which might improve take-up – even the White Paper's optimistic forecasts had been limited to an assumed take-up rate of 60 per cent for Family Credit. In respect to helping those most in need, initial estimates suggested that the majority of couples with children and single parents were made better off by the reforms while about three quarters of pensioners were either unaffected or made worse off. Finally, on the question of the social security traps, the position was ambiguous. The unemployment trap should have been eased and the extreme form of the poverty trap was virtually eliminated (no more marginal tax rates of 100 per cent or greater). However, the extension of cover offered under the Family Credit arrangements was to face many more individuals than previously with marginal tax rates around 80 per cent (Dilnot and Webb, 1988).

The reforms of the mid-1980s were aimed to combine with the income and wealth creating effects of the freer market economy encouraged by the government's general economic programme of the period following 1979, a programme which came to be labelled 'Thatcherism'. This combination should have provided a major force for the eradication of poverty – the *'trickle down'* effect of wealth creation supported by a more efficient social security system. Unfortunately, the expected result was not forthcoming by the beginning of the 1990s. On the contrary, as we saw in the previous chapter's discussion on income distribution, the signs were suggesting an increase in inequality.

So far as the absolute position of the poor was concerned, researchers were unable to find any evidence of a significant improvement. According to one estimate (Jenkins, 1991) average real incomes for the poorest 10 per cent of households were about the same in 1988 as they had been 20 years previously, and were actually lower than they had been 10 years previously. Townsend was also to argue that the real incomes of the poorest two deciles had fallen over the decade 1979–89 (Townsend, 1991), and even though Johnson and Webb were to modify Townsend's findings, showing that by removing an inconsistency in Townsend's income definition the real incomes of the poorest two deciles had risen by 5 per cent, the same authors could not escape the conclusion that, so far as the poorest groups were concerned, 'it is clear that even on a consistent definition of income their living standards have grown only slowly over the last decade' (Johnson and Webb, 1991).

Given the recent history of the UK economy, and the changes in both structure and magnitude of income maintenance programmes, it is little wonder that social security benefits became the fastest-growing component of personal incomes over the period covered by Goodman and Webb's (1994) analysis. The authors summarised the causes of the pattern as rising numbers entitled to benefits; rising housing costs adjusted for inflation; the introduction of new benefits; and changes in benefit levels.

■ 16.4 A European Perspective

How does the UK poverty picture compare with that in the rest of Europe? To answer this question properly and fully would require us to reconsider all of the methodological issues raised so far in order to attempt any comments about the pattern of poverty across a population totalling some 400 million individuals (for details see Ramprakash, 1994).

One attempt which caused considerable controversy on publication, but which did give rise to real concern about the UK's record on poverty *vis-à-vis* its European partners, was the EC report on the second anti-poverty programme, published in April 1991 (EC, 1991). The stark conclusion of this report was that, in 1985, the UK had the fifth highest 'poverty rate' in Europe behind Portugal, Ireland, Spain and Greece, and that the percentage in poverty (both individuals and households) in the UK had risen between 1980 and 1985, the two reference dates used in the report. Not only did such findings give cause for concern to policymakers, but they also created considerable controversy because they were based on *relative* measures and, hence, emphasised inequalities in income distribution rather than poverty in any *absolute* sense.

Estimating for both individuals and households, the EC report measured poverty in relation to both national and Community criteria. Using expenditure, rather than income, as the guide, the report defined as 'poor' by the *national* criterion, any individual or household spending less than 50 per cent of the national average for any given period. Using a Community criterion, an individual or household was classified as 'poor' when spending less than 50 per cent of average Community spending (measured by a purchasing power standard) for any given period. In each case, 'adult equivalent' scales were used to take account of differences in household size and composition.

□ 16.4.1 Using a National Criterion

The Overall Picture

The picture presented by using a national criterion was a depressing one, suggesting that in 1985 some 50 million persons in the Community (about 16 million households) were poor, and that this represented very little change in the total number of poor in the Community since 1980. The findings suggested, however, that there had been changes in the proportions of poor found in individual countries, with some faring better and some worse between the two years. **Figure 16.1** presents a clear and stark impression of the relative changes in numbers of poor persons experienced by eleven of the twelve members over the five-year period (there were no survey returns for Luxembourg) with the biggest increase in numbers seen to be in the UK.

Figure 16.1   *Changes in the Number of Poor Persons in the Community, 1980–85[1]*

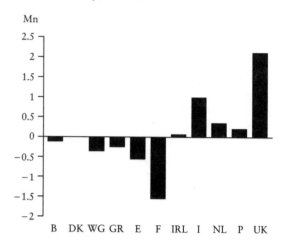

Note:
[1] National criteria.
Source: EC (1991).

Table 16.5   *Poverty among Children and the Elderly in the Community*

	Children			Elderly		
	Poverty Index (National Poverty Rate = 100)		Variation in the Absolute Number of Poor (%)	Poverty Index (National Poverty Rate = 100)		Variation in the Absolute Number of Poor (%)
	1980	1985		1980	1985	
Belgium	113	114	−20.3	175	181	−17.7
Denmark	110	114	−5.4	238	255	12.1
F.R. of Germany	110	138	3.5	136	141	−8.1
Greece	96	103	−16.5	145	153	−2.9
Spain	106	107	−14.5	157	125	−21.7
France	108	124	−6.6	159	136	−31.2
Ireland	122	143	23.8	163	73	−50.5
Italy	114	97	−14.4	132	129	1.5
Netherlands	136	155	25.6	44	46	31.9
Portugal	112	112	−2.3	139	139	8.1
United Kingdom	138	132	12.2	163	119	−7.1

Source: EC (1991).

High-risk Groups

These comprise predominantly children and the elderly. The findings of the EC report emphasised yet again that the very young and the very old are particularly vulnerable to poverty. We saw earlier how these distinct groupings have emerged time and again from UK studies, and the evidence from across Europe confirms that throughout the Community chilren and the aged form consistently high-risk groups in relation to poverty. **Table 16.5** gives data from the report which show that, with the exceptions of Greece in 1980 and Italy in 1985, the index of poverty among children was positive everywhere in both years and, with the exception of the Netherlands, the poverty index for the elderly was positive everywhere in both 1980 and 1985. **Table 16.5** shows also that in most countries (exceptions being Italy and the UK) the poverty index either stayed the same or worsened for children between 1980 and 1985, while for the elderly it either stayed the same or worsened in six of the eleven countries surveyed over the same period.

As a final point in relation to **Table 16.5** we should remind ourselves that insofar as the ageing of the European populations is a contributor to the large number of poor persons also being elderly persons, the problem is unlikely to diminish.

The EC Report also highlighted the other socio-economic groups most vulnerable to poverty, and again we can see the parallels between the UK picture, as discussed earlier in the chapter, and the rest of the Community. In particular, we can observe the prevalence of poverty among single parent (particularly female) households and among households with low educational attainment and/or low economic activity of the household head.

16.4.2 Using a Community Criterion

Using average household, or individual, income or expenditure as the poverty yardstick for each member state produces 12 different poverty lines (only 11 in the 1991 report, given no returns for Luxembourg). What happens to the picture if we apply just one Community poverty line; that is if poverty is defined with reference to some notion of a Community average income or expenditure for households and individuals? The question is addressed in the 1991 report by referring to any household (or individual) as being 'poor' if expenditure is less than 50 per cent of the Community average household expenditure (per adult equivalent) for the period in question. As with the measures for individual countries, this poverty line was calculated by reference to data from national family budget surveys. The survey suggests that the fundamental extent and causes of poverty changes only slightly but the distribution of Community poverty changes dramatically.

Table 16.6, taken from the EC report, suggests that, measured against a Community poverty line, overall poverty fell slightly between 1980 and 1985 and that it fell slightly also for the high-risk groups of children and the elderly across the whole of the Community. That Community-wide poverty was reduced during the period 1980–85 was welcome news for the makers of European social policy, but the size of the reduction was not impressive and begged questions about the efficiency of the Community's general social programme. We shall address some aspects of this shortly, but first we should also consider the dramatic changes in the geographical distribution of poverty which result from adopting a poverty line. **Figure 16.2** gives a very clear impression of how the geographical distribution of poverty

Table 16.6 *Community Poverty Incidence, 1980 and 1985*

	1980		1985	
	%	million	%	million
Households	14.8	16.4	14.4	16.2
Persons	16.8	52.9	15.9	51.3
Children	19.7	13.5	19.4	12.3
Elderly (65+)	22.5	9.9	19.6	8.5

Source: EC (1991).

Figure 16.2   *Percentage of Poor Community Households Located in Each Member Country*

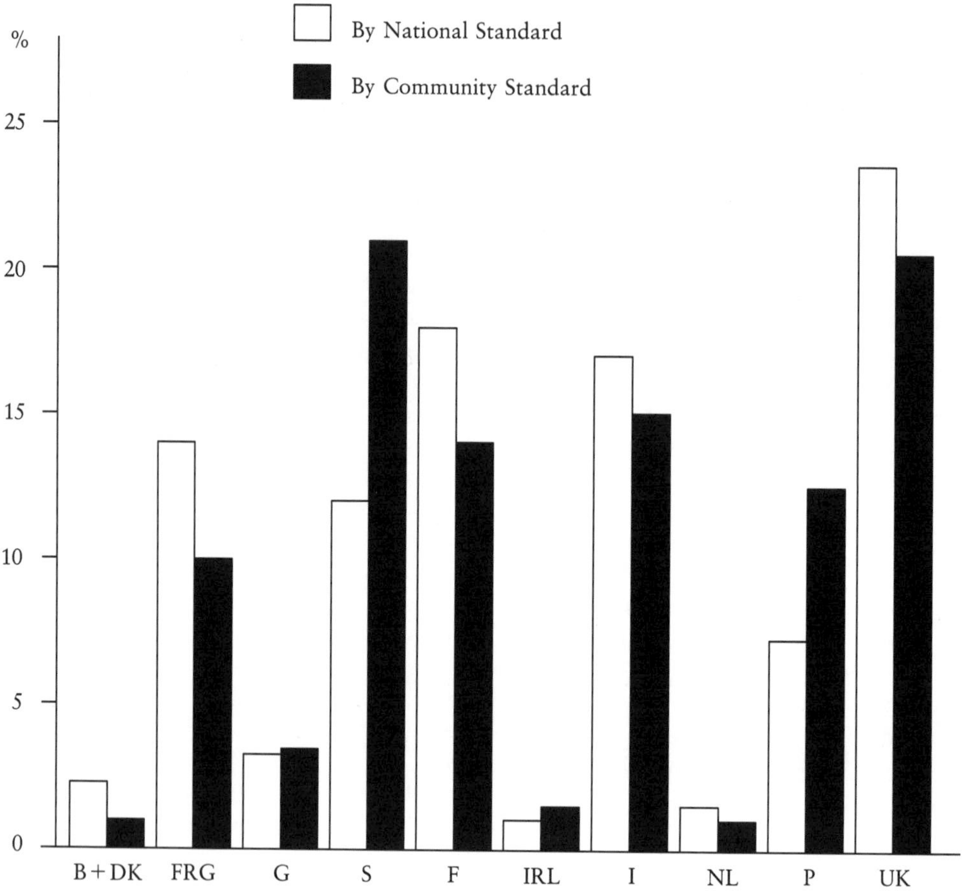

□ By National Standard

■ By Community Standard

Source: EC (1991).

responds to changing the poverty line from a national to a Community criterion.

From the viewpoint of the UK, the initial comparison is not very favourable. Using the national poverty line as the criterion, the UK had the biggest share of the Community's poor in 1985 at 23.5 per cent, with France next at about 18.3 per cent followed by Italy (17.1 per cent), West Germany (14.3 per cent) and Spain (11.9 per cent). National poverty lines obviously do not take account of relative living standards outside national boundaries and, as we saw early in this chapter, a cohort of 'poor' according to a national poverty line might appear (relatively) rich according to

some other nation's poverty line. So how does adopting the Community poverty line change poverty rankings? As **Figure 16.2** illustrates, the UK is overtaken by Spain but the gap is very narrow and remains potentially embarrassing for UK policy-makers. The proportion of the Community's poor who are resident in the UK does fall, but it also falls in Italy, France and West Germany whereas only Spain suffers an increase (a fairly dramatic one in fact, from 11.9 to 20.9 per cent).

It could be argued, however, that measuring poverty distribution on the basis of population percentages is very unfair to countries with large populations because this increases the likelihood of larger numbers in poverty. Thus, to counteract the population effect, the EC report offered a picture of the geographical distribution of poverty that results from assuming the Community's population to be equally distributed. One obvious effect of this is to offer a picture as if some of the households from the more densely populated and more industrial countries had been relocated into previously less dense and more agrarian countries. As one would expect, the poverty percentage now rises dramatically in countries like Portugal and Ireland and falls dramatically in the UK, France and Italy.

16.4.3 Community Action to Combat Poverty

Every Community country has adopted some form of the mixed enterprise economy and, in line with this, some variant of the 'welfare state' model of social policy whereby markets reward individuals and households according to the market value of their productivity and the state offers income supplementation when market earnings are low and also when there are no market earnings as in the case, for example, of children, the retired and those whose skills are obsolete. Hence, as we saw earlier in the case of the UK, researching all the reasons for a country's poverty profile requires analysis of both market patterns, state tax-transfer programmes and labour market legislation. Clearly, we cannot begin here to explore the details of each of the member states. However, we can at least offer some comment on the collective action taken so far by the Community to combat the considerable poverty in its midst.

The Community programme to combat poverty is piecemeal, but it is possible to single out three main prongs of attack on both inequality and poverty, namely:

- the collective commitment by member states to develop *social* as well as economic policy;
- the European Social Fund;
- the Anti-Poverty Programme.

The Commitment to Social Policy

Article 2 of The Treaty of Rome specifies an objective of an accelerated raising of the standard of living across the Community – that is, it makes it clear that the Community's objectives are social as well as economic. To this end, the Community has developed policies and provided finance for projects relating to: unemployment; training; equal opportunities (to include policies relating to regions as well as gender); improving working conditions; families and the elderly; immigrants; handicapped people; and social security and public health. Many of these areas have received significant funding for many years.

The European Social Fund

Many of the real commitments to the development of social policy are made through this Fund, representing a massive injection of finance mainly into the improvement of labour market returns. The list of commitments made under the Social Fund is large but its three major categories are:

- training and employment of young people (under-25s) – about 75 per cent of the Fund's resources are put to this end;
- helping disadvantaged regions via a geographical concentration of the Fund's activities, with targeted regions so far including all of Greece, Ireland and Portugal and specific areas of Italy, Spain and Northern Ireland;
- helping specific adult groups – for example, the long-term unemployed; women returning to work; handicapped people who are capable of work in the labour market; immigrant workers; individuals suitable for retraining for new technologies; and persons working in the promotion of employment (for example, in vocational training and recruitment). By the second half of the 1980s the expenditure in these various areas was accounting for 7 per cent of the Community budget and covered some 2.5 million people (approximately 85 per cent of them under 25 years of age were benefiting from the Social Fund).

The Specific Anti-poverty Programme

In addition to its efforts on the supply side of the European market-based economies, the Community also addressed the issue of poverty created by absence of any access to labour markets. There were two major programmes launched, each one concerned primarily with the gathering of information about poverty and inequality and with measuring poverty incidence. The initial programme for the period 1975–80, very much concerned with gathering information about poverty, was superseded in 1984 by a new programme of more specific Community action for the period up to 1988 coupled with further research into and measurement of the incidence of poverty. The EC report referred to earlier was part of the culmination of this research. The various projects under the second programme were to concentrate on testing new methods of helping the poor, on the dissemination and exchange of knowledge about the extent and incidence of poverty and on the evaluation of projects. In terms of target areas, the distribution of activities can be seen from the pie chart published by the Community in 1987, and reproduced as **Figure 16.3**.

16.5 The Future of Social Security

What emerges from both the findings of the EC report and the nature of the categories within the Community's anti-poverty programme is an awareness of what has been labelled by some observers as the 'new poverty'. As we have seen in previous sections of this chapter, what might be termed the 'old poverty' was concentrated mainly in two broad categories: dependent children (and their families), and old people. Both of these categories remain at the core of the poverty problem in both the UK and throughout the Community, but a new category of poor has emerged who are more diverse in nature and belong perhaps to what is regarded as society's periphery rather than its core: immigrant workers (who usually earn low wages and suffer intermittent unemployment); single parents; ethnic minorities

Figure 16.3   *Community Anti-poverty Programme*[1]

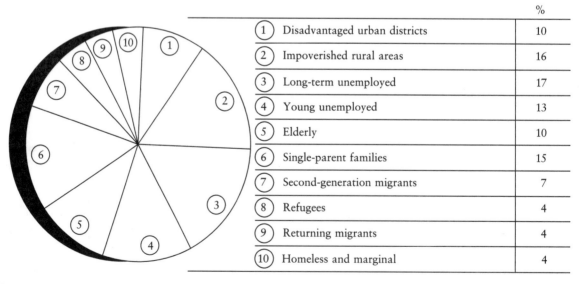

		%
(1)	Disadvantaged urban districts	10
(2)	Impoverished rural areas	16
(3)	Long-term unemployed	17
(4)	Young unemployed	13
(5)	Elderly	10
(6)	Single-parent families	15
(7)	Second-generation migrants	7
(8)	Refugees	4
(9)	Returning migrants	4
(10)	Homeless and marginal	4

Note:
[1] Excluding Spanish and Portuguese projects selected in 1987.
Source: Commission of the European Communities, DG V.

(who might suffer the additional burdens of prejudice and discrimination); the mentally and physically handicapped; and longer-term unemployed young people. As the 'service economy' emerged throughout the 1970s and 1980s, there was rapid growth throughout the Community in both part-time working and in home-based work and small-scale self-employment, and many of these opportunities offered no more than relatively low, and often temporary, returns for labour.

According to one eminent poverty analyst, the sufferers of the 'old poverty' were a large proportion of the working class who were able 'to mobilise particularly through labour and socialist movements, to form alliances with the liberal middle class, and to build the defences which eventually came to be called the Welfare State' (Donnison, 1991). The same observer sees no similar socio-political solution to the problems of the 'new poor' because they are so diverse and scattered and, therefore, do not form a cohesive political lobby – indeed, they 'share nothing but their exclusion from the mainstream of society'.

Whether or not one agrees with this socio-political analysis, it is clearly being recognised to some extent in the categorisation of aid objectives within the European Social Fund. But so far as social policy in individual countries is concerned, the 'new poverty' adds yet another dimension to an already difficult policy agenda – if households or families comprise low earners who find only intermittent employment to supplement, say, one mainstream household income, then both the poverty and the employment traps discussed earlier pose severe disincentive effects unless combined incomes lift the whole family or household well above state assistance levels.

It is not surprising, therefore, to find that the issue of 'universal' versus 'selective' benefits remains at the centre of debate on social security. The UK government has placed **efficiency** at the forefront of economic objectives, and increasingly blurred the distinctions between economic and social issues. Since universal benefits are made available to all, regardless of means, they are deemed to be a less efficient means of income redistribution than selective benefits which, by

definition, are targeted on those recipients most in need. This issue underpinned the 1986 reforms, but the argument has continued and lies at the heart of the debate over social security spending which was fuelled by the 1993 review of social security spending. As Atkinson (1996) has stated, 'the economics of the Welfare State is now centre-stage, entering debates about the macro-economy and about the wealth of nations. Reform of the Welfare State is one of the key policy issues of the 1990s'.

Proposals for resource switching, and consequent denial of fundamental Beveridge principles such as providing a flat-rate benefit for all families with children, are seen by many as a significant denial of 'universality' as a cornerstone of the social security system. However, the 1988 reforms opened the door for 'selective' arrangements which followed soon after with the freezing of universal child benefits and renewed 'benefit targeting' of needy families (special benefit rises of up to 9.3 per cent in 1988). Future tax/transfer support of the aged could be modified along similar lines. Bearing in mind the burden on future generations of working taxpayers of providing income support to a disproportionally growing retired population, many of whom will be enjoying the fruits of their occupational pension schemes, the demand by voters for more selective measures to concentrate transfers on the 'genuinely needy' within the retired population is likely to grow. Increased awareness that the UK state pension scheme has not been 'as of right' but 'pay as you go' is likely to fuel such demands.

The debate over selectivity in the social security system brings us back, full circle, to the efficiency/equity trade-off. On the one hand there is a concern for efficiency and the removal of disincentives in tax/transfer programmes while, on the other, there is a concern for the welfare of the poor. A problem for Party image-makers in the 1990s is how to present a (prospective) government as a (potentially) 'caring' administration as well as one which is concerned with efficiency and increased incentives. The solution to the problem for the future lies in persuading the electorate that 'targeting' is a synonym for 'cost-effective caring'. The Report of the Commission on Social Justice

(1994) offered the ultimate in eclecticism on this matter.

So to persuade the electorate is conditional upon achieving two related objectives, namely finding a way to much simpler means-testing and improving markedly the take-up of available benefits. One way to reach these goals which has received a lot of attention from economists, and which enjoys a degree of consensus among political opinions, is to introduce some form of *truly comprehensive negative income tax* which would follow the principles outlined earlier but would combine social security benefits and income tax payments in a single system of centrally administered redistribution. To date, no government has gone that far in its legislaion (although a variant was proposed in a Green Paper published by the Heath-led Conservative Government of 1972) and Mr Fowler's overhaul of the mid-1980s fell a long way short of such radicalism. The concept of a 'Citizen's Income', along social dividend lines, appeared briefly on centre-stage in the Report of the Commission on Social Justice, but only in terms of a list of its *pros* and *cons*, with the latter tipping the balance (see also Parker, 1995, Part Five). To date, the concept of a 'European Social Dividend' available to all (subject to means) and operating across national boundaries has not appeared as a serious item on the politico-economic agenda for a Europe approaching the start of a new millennium.

Bibliography

Abel-Smith, B. and P. Townsend (1965) *The Poor and the Poorest* (London: Bell & Sons).

Atkinson, A. (1972) *Unequal Shares* (London: Penguin).

Berthoud, R. (1985) 'Mr Fowler's Examination', *Catalyst* (Autumn).

Bradshaw, J. (1991) 'Social Security Expenditure in the 1990s', *Public Money and Management* (Winter).

Cmd 6404 (1942) *Social Insurance and Allied Services* (The Beveridge Report) (London: HMSO).

Cmd 6527 (1944) *Employment Policy* (London: HMSO).

Commission on Social Justice, the Report of 1996, *Social Justice: Strategies for National Renewal* (London: Vintage).

Diamond Commission (1975) *Report No.1.* Cmnd 6171 (London: HMSO).

Diamond Commission (1976) *Report No.4.* Cmnd 6626 (London: HMSO).

Dilnot, A., J. Kay and C. Morris (1984) *The Reform of Social Security* (Oxford: Clarendon Press).

Dilnot, A. and S. Webb (1988) 'The 1988 Social Security Reforms', *Fiscal Studies* (August).

Donnison, D. (1991) 'Squeezed and Broken on the Brink', *The Times Higher Education Supplement*, 19 April, p. 13.

EC (1991) *Final Report on the Second European Poverty Programme* (Brussels: Commission of the European Communities).

Fiegehen, G., P. Lansley and A. Smith (1977) *Poverty and Progress in Britain, 1953–73* (Cambridge: CUP).

Fry, V. and G. Stark (1986) 'The Take-Up of Supplementary Benefit: Gaps in the 'Safety Net'?', *Fiscal Studies* (November).

Giles, C. and S. Webb (1993) 'A Guide to Poverty Statistics', *Fiscal Studies*, 14 (2) pp. 74–97.

Goodman, A. and S. Webb (1994) 'For Richer, For Poorer: the Changing Distribution of Income in the UK, 1961–91', *Fiscal Studies*, 15 (4).

Hemming, R. (1984) *Poverty and Incentives* (Oxford: Oxford University Press).

Jenkins, S. (1991) 'Living Standards and the Diverging 'Thatcher' Effect', *The Guardian* (15 April) p. 13.

Jenkins, S. and F. Cowell (1994) 'Dwarfs and Giants in the 1980s: Trends in the UK Income Distribution', *Fiscal Studies*, 15 (1).

Johnson, P. and S. Webb (1990) *UK Poverty Statistics: A Comparative Study* (London: Institute for Fiscal Studies).

Morris, N. and I. Preston (1986) 'Taxes, Benefits and the Distribution of Income 1968–83', *Fiscal Studies* (November).

Nicholson, R. (1967) 'The Distribution of Personal Income', *Lloyds Bank Review* (January).

Nolan, B. (1989) 'An Evaluation of the New Official Low Income Statistics, *Fiscal Studies*, 10 (4).

Oppenheim, C. and Harker, L. (1996) *Poverty: the Facts* (London: Child Poverty Action Group).

Parker, H. (1995) *Taxes, Benefits and Family Life: The Seven Deadly Traps* (London: IEA).

Pryke, R. (1995) *Taking the Measure of Poverty* (London: IEA).

Ramprakash, D. (1994) 'Poverty in the Countries of the European Union: A Synthesis of Eurostat's Research in Poverty', *Journal of European Social Policy*, 4 (2) pp. 117–28.

Social Security Select Committee (1991) *Low Income Statistics: Households Below Average Income Tables 1988*. First Report 1990–91, House of Commons.

The Economist (1996) 'The Poor: Consumers Like the Rest of Us' (24 February) pp. 30–1.

Townsend, P. (1991) *The Poor are Poorer: A Statistical Report on Changes in the Living Standards of Rich and Poor in the United Kingdom 1979–1989* (Statistical Monitoring Unit, University of Bristol).

Chapter 17

Industry and Policy I: Theory and Competition Policy

Keith Hartley and Nick Hooper

17.1 Introduction: The Policy Issues

Industrial policy focuses on firms, industries and markets and their performance. Continued concern about the relatively poor performance of the UK economy in world markets has resulted in governments formulating various policies to 'improve and solve' the problem. Inevitably, the various policy solutions have some impact on firms, industries and their efficiency and so might be classified as part of industrial policy. For example, education policy affects the supply of skilled labour and its productivity for firms and industries; social security and taxation policy affects the willingness to work and the incentives to effort and enterprise; and road building affects industry's transport costs and its access to product and factor markets. Policies with a more direct impact on industry are those which affect ownership, industrial structure, the behaviour of firms and their performance. In the UK, these issues have been a source of continuing controversy between the major political parties. During the 1970s and 1980s, controversy ranged over policy towards manufacturing industry and the

size of the public sector, reflecting concern about crowding-out, de-industrialisation and the decline of the UK's manufacturing base. The Labour governments of the 1970s favoured interventionist policies in the form of an industrial strategy, state ownership, a policy of 'picking winners' and an extensive system of subsidies to firms, industries and regions. In contrast, the Conservative governments of the 1980s emphasised supply-side policies aimed at making markets work better through a smaller public sector and reduced state intervention reflected in privatisation, contracting-out, deregulation, the withdrawal of industrial and regional subsidies and more emphasis on competition policy and support for small firms. This policy aimed to replace a culture of dependency on the state with an enterprise culture based on profitability and lower personal taxation, offering greater incentives for managers, workers, shareholders and new businesses.

The policy agenda in the 1990s has departed from that of previous decades. Changes in the electorate, in political parties and in their leaders meant a search for new solutions to the UK's continuing economic problems reflected in its growth, inflation, unemployment and balance of payments performance. Events in Eastern Europe and the former Soviet Union in the late 1980s and early 1990s raised serious doubts about the efficiency and performance of centralised planning, state ownership and collectivist solutions to economic problems. These changes were also associated with the end of the Cold War and the superpower arms race and its replacement with disarmament and the search for a Peace Dividend in nations of the former Warsaw Pact and NATO. For Russia, the tasks of disarmament and conversion of its military-industrial complex at the same time as it was attempting the transition from a centrally-planned to a market economy created major adjustment problems. The European Union is also experiencing change with the 1992 Single Market programme, the addition of new members (Austria, Finland and Sweden in 1995) and progress towards Monetary Union. The Conservative government re-elected in 1992 remained committed to a free enterprise economy with further privatisation (British Coal, British Energy, British Rail, HMSO), market-testing and competing for quality, together with more 'hiving-off' of state agencies. The end of the Cold war resulted in disarmament and reduced defence spending with the government leaving defence contractors to make commercial decisions about conversion and diversification into civil markets. Critics of such policies, including New Labour, do not believe that these measures will improve the long-run competitiveness of UK industry.

New Labour is no longer committed to universal state ownership and the re-nationalisation of the privatised utilities, but rather stresses the importance of firms and industries which are recognised as world-class competitors in sectors characterised by high technology (R&D intensive) and high value-added processes and skills. Examples given by New Labour of such sectors include British Aerospace, GEC and the UK defence industrial base. New Labour also argues that industry needs more investment, more research and development, a greater use of the latest technology and an improved quality of its labour force through more and better education, training and retraining. The privatised utilities may be subject to a windfall profits tax and tougher regulation.

New Labour also supports regional development agencies and the creation of a Defence Diversification Agency for defence firms and communities seeking assistance to move from defence to civil markets.

The different attitudes of Labour and Conservative governments of the 1970s and 1980s towards industrial policy reflected alternative views about the role, extent and appropriate form of state intervention in the economy. At one extreme, interventionists favoured an active role with governments intervening throughout the economy at both the industry and firm level, including the possibility of state ownership where major firms and industries were performing badly as reflected in labour productivity, exports and excessive profitability or losses (leading, for example, to the nationalisation of the car company British Leyland in 1975 and of the airframe and shipbuilding industries in 1977). The other extreme takes a laissez faire approach to industrial policy where everything is left to market forces. However, between these extremes there is a view which recognises that, if left to themselves, private markets may fail to work properly and that government might have to intervene to correct for market failure and improve the operation of markets.

Economists can contribute to debates about industrial policy by subjecting myths, emotion, special pleading and alternative policy solutions to economic analysis, critical evaluation and empirical evidence. **The central question to be addressed is whether economic theory offers any guidelines for a public policy towards industry.** Typically, economists focus on **efficiency issues** whilst recognising that public policies have **equity implications** in terms of their impacts on the distribution of income and wealth in society and that distributional issues are a further source of controversy.

The debates between the political parties confirm the diversity of interpretations and definitions of industrial policy. Broadly, these debates can be grouped around themes concerned with industry structure, firm behaviour and performance, ownership and subsidies. This chapter outlines the contribution of economic theory to industrial policy (theory which is also relevant to Chapters 18 and 19); it considers the importance of manufacturing and analyses policies on industry structure and performance in the form of competition policy. Chapter 18 analyses ownership and policies on privatisation, regulation and competitive tendering. Chapter 19 deals with policies towards subsidies, R&D and the role of government purchasing.

◼ *17.2* UK Manufacturing: Does it Matter?

Any analysis of industrial policy needs to start with a definition of an industry. Economists define an industry as a group of firms producing similar products with the boundary of an industry determined by a gap in the chain of substitutes (measured by the cross elasticity of demand). On this basis, all sectors of the UK economy can be regarded as industries (for example, the agricultural, banking, construction, fishing, tourist and transport industries). However, the focus of industrial policy is usually on the manufacturing sector and its importance to the UK economy. Manufacturing industry is defined to embrace those firms which produce a physical product (comprising divisions 2 to 4 of the International Standard Industrial Classification 1980 – for example aerospace; chemicals; electrical and

mechanical engineering; motor vehicles; and paper, printing and publishing).

Concern has been expressed over the competitiveness and continuing decline of the UK's manufacturing base (deindustrialisation). Questions have been raised as to whether deindustrialisation can seriously damage your wealth. It has been suggested that manufacturing industry is vital to the prosperity of the UK and that 'A strong manufacturing sector is of fundamental importance to the UK and poor performance in manufacturing would have an impact far beyond the manufacturing sector' (HC 41–I, 1994, p. 124). However, many of the arguments about manufacturing need to be subject to critical scrutiny, distinguishing special pleading, emotion and myths from the economic logic of the arguments, their analytical basis and the availability of any supporting empirical evidence. For example, with some of the arguments that 'manufacturing matters', there is a danger of concluding that *only* manufacturing matters, or that only physical production is a real wealth creator, so ignoring the potential economic contribution of knowledge, ideas and the services sector.

The concerns about manufacturing have been reflected in trends in various statistical indicators, especially the shift away from manufacturing towards services (see **pp. 33–6**), the productivity gap between the UK and its major international competitors (see **pp. 82–3**), the trade balance in

Table 17.1   *Manufacturing and Productivity*

	Percentage shares of manufacturing in GDP			1991: UK = 100		
	1970	*1980*	*1990*	*Labour Costs*	*Productivity*	*Unit Labour Costs*
UK	28.7	23.2	18.9	100	100	100
France	29.9	24.2	21.0	114	139	82
Germany	38.4	32.8	31.2	124	140	89
Italy	27.1	27.8	22.4	128	121	106
Japan	36.0	29.2	28.9	98	150	65
USA	25.2	21.8	18.9	115	175	66

Source: HC 41-I (1994).

manufactured goods (which moved into deficit in 1983 for the first time since the Industrial Revolution), the decline in the UK's share of world trade in manufactures (see **p. 218**) and competition from the low-wage countries of South-East Asia (Hong Kong, South Korea, Singapore and Taiwan).

The UK's experience is not unique and, over the period 1970–90, the share of manufacturing in national output declined in all the major industrial nations while that of services increased. By 1990, the share of manufacturing in GDP was similar in the UK, France and the USA, although the share was much higher in Germany and Japan. However, over the period, the decline in manufacturing's share of both GDP and employment was much greater in the UK than in the other major industrial nations (**Table 17.1**).

The UK experienced a relative economic decline during the 1960s and 1970s (for example, the UK fell from second place in terms of real income per person in Europe in 1950 to tenth by 1979). Data for the 1980s suggest an improved UK productivity performance in relation to previous periods and in relation to the productivity gap with Europe (see **pp. 86–8**). For example, German labour productivity was 51 per cent above that of the UK in 1979 but it was only 10 per cent higher in 1993; and over the same period, French labour productivity was 35 per cent and 10 per cent higher, respectively, than in the UK. This productivity improvement can be interpreted as the UK performing a belated 'catching-up' process reflecting supply-side policies, particularly policies towards trade unions and industrial relations. It has also been claimed that the UK has a competitive advantage in its low labour costs relative to other major industrial nations. This may, however, be misleading since typically in manufacturing, the employment component of total costs is small (about 25 per cent); the UK cannot compete on labour costs with Pacific Rim nations; and low UK labour costs can be offset by low productivity so that unit labour costs are not necessarily lower.

It has been argued that the decline in the UK manufacturing sector should not be a cause for concern because it can be offset by the expansion of other sectors of the economy, especially services. There are, however, doubts that services could substitute for a substantial part of the UK's manufacturing industry because:

- of their past failure to do so and the magnitudes involved – each 1 per cent decline in the export of UK manufactures requires in excess of a 2.5 per cent rise in the export of services to compensate;
- the interdependence between manufacturing and services means that poor performance in manufacturing will adversely affect the services sector;
- of the claim that technical progress in manufacturing offers greater prospects of high-wage jobs able to raise living standards compared with the part-time, low-wage jobs characteristic of parts of the services sector.

A concern with the decline of UK manufacturing has resulted in a variety of proposals to reverse this trend, some of which require action by industry (private market solutions) whereas others require government policy initiatives. The range of solutions which have been proposed to 'solve' this UK economic problem have included:

- **greater accumulation of both physical and human capital**: reflecting low investment in UK manufacturing and the relatively low skill level (human capital) of the workforce, especially at craft and technician levels (*Economic Journal*, 1996);
- **improved innovation**: reflecting the view that research and development (R&D) contributes to the competitiveness both of individual firms and the economy, and that the UK's relatively low R&D spending has adversely affected its long-term growth rate (HC 41–I, 1994; see also Chapter 19);
- **the City and industry**: reflecting criticisms of the City's attitudes towards industry concerned with short-termism with its emphasis on high internal rates of return, high dividends and short payback periods leading to a failure to undertake long-term investments;
- **finance for small firms**: reflecting worries about 'too little' finance for small firms resulting from

the emphasis of UK banks on collateral (security) in their lending decisions rather than assessing business prospects and the human capital attributes of the entrepreneur;

- **improved management**: reflecting alleged management failings including an inability to attract enough high quality people into management in the manufacturing sector (especially for medium-size firms and compared with the City) and the relatively low proportion of managers with an engineering and technical background leading to a poor understanding of science and technology among management;

- **UK macroeconomic and industrial policy**: reflecting a 'Cambridge' view which focuses on the damaging impact on UK manufacturing of an overvalued exchange rate, high interest rates and an ineffectual industrial policy;

- **a reform of UK institutions**: reflecting the view that historical and institutional factors have resulted in a set of institutions which are resistant to change – because the UK was not occupied and won World War II, there was a continuity of institutions and interest groups which failed to adapt and respond to the new post-1945 market opportunities.

17.3 Theory and Industrial Policy

17.3.1 Introduction

The continuing controversy over UK manufacturing – whether manufacturing matters and proposals for solving the problem – provides a classic example of the contribution which economics and economists can make to debates about public policy in general and industrial policy in particular. For example, if historical and institutional factors explain the UK's economic performance, why have individuals and groups failed to respond to the opportunities and incentives to replace poor institutions with better ones (why has institutional competition not occurred – see *Economic Journal*, 1996)?

Questions about the proper role of government in the economy dominate policy debates. In relation to industry, it has to be asked whether there are any economic arguments for government intervention, and if so, to what extent should the state intervene and in what form? The methodology of economic policy provides a framework for analysing industrial policy issues. The approach requires economists to seek answers to three questions, namely:

- **What is the policy problem** and what are governments trying to achieve? Usually, the underlying problem worrying policy-makers can be deduced from the government's stated objectives (and vice versa). For example, in 1993, the Conservative government aimed to improve living standards and the quality of life through improved competitiveness (Cmnd 2563, 1994; Cmnd 2867, 1995).

- **Why is there a problem?** Economists use their theories to explain the causes of problems which are worrying governments. For example, British industry's declining international competitiveness might result from a structure of too many small firms unable to undertake the necessary R&D and thus obtain the scale economies required to compete in world markets, or it might reflect a comparative advantage in areas other than manufacturing. Alternatively, it might be due to general inefficiency reflecting the motivation and attitudes of managers and workers (a culture of dependency rather than enterprise), or it might reflect interest rate and exchange rate policy. The choice between these alternative theories depends on which best explains the facts.

- **What can be done to solve the problem?** Usually, there are alternative policy solutions. To improve the performance of UK manufacturing industry might require an industrial strategy; better management; improvements in education and training; more innovation; more investment; or a competition policy. Private monopolies could be controlled through nationalisation, by creating contestable markets (see below) or by state regulation of prices or profits. Governments might promote technical progress through subsidising R&D, by training more scientists or through placing contracts with

UK firms for advanced technology equipment (such as computers, Eurofighter 2000, nuclear power stations and space satellites). Theories can be used to predict the likely effects of alternative policy solutions, with governments having to choose between the alternatives. Such choices will reflect the governing party's values and ideology, its possible interest in maximising the welfare of the community and its immediate concern with votes and re-election.

Economic theory approaches industrial policy issues from the starting point of Paretian welfare economics. It is assumed that society aims to maximise welfare by achieving an **optimum allocation of resources** (that is, a Pareto optimum which occurs where it is impossible to make one person better off without making someone else worse off). In a private enterprise economy, the Paretian model suggests that properly-functioning competitive markets are socially desirable since perfectly competitive markets result in a Pareto optimum allocation of resources. On this basis, market forces determine the optimum size of the manufacturing sector. The model provides some broad guidelines for industrial policy. State intervention is required whenever markets are failing to work properly (that is, where there are substantial departures from the competitive ideal). **This approach suggests that industrial policy is a means of correcting for major market failures.** The obvious focus is on the operation of product markets, although it has to be recognised that failures can occur in markets for capital, labour, money, foreign exchange and resources.

There are two general sources of market failure, namely **imperfections** in the form of monopolies, oligopolies, restrictive practices and entry barriers, and **beneficial or harmful externalities**, including public goods (for example, defence). Externalities mean that, left to themselves, private competitive markets might provide too little of some socially desirable activities such as information and basic R&D and too much of some socially undesirable products such as pollution, noise and traffic congestion. Here, however, economists have to be careful in distinguishing between the **technical issues** concerned with the

causes of market failure, and the **policy issues** concerned with the choice of the most appropriate solution. For example, even if imperfections are identified as the main source of market failure, governments have to choose between such alternative policies as increased competition, reduced tariff barriers and the state regulation of monopoly prices and profits. Similarly, externalities might be corrected through taxes and subsidies, public ownership or legislative changes in property rights allowing the courts to determine compensation for the victims of spillovers. As a further example of alternative solutions, a Pareto optimum allocation of resources can be achieved through either a perfectly competitive private enterprise economy or by direct controls and commands in a centrally-planned, state-owned economy.

17.3.2 The Structure-Conduct-Performance Paradigm

In examining the causes of market failure and the range of policy solutions, industrial economists use their standard tool kit, namely, the structure–conduct–performance framework. This states that industrial performance depends ultimately upon industry structure where the variables in the model are structure, conduct and performance.

Structure

Structure comprises the number and size distribution of firms in an industry and the opportunities for the entry of new firms. There are two extremes – **perfect competition** and **monopoly** – with the intermediate and often typical cases of **monopolistic competition** and **oligopoly**. With this approach, industry concentration is determined by economies of scale, the size of the market (the number of firms of optimal scale it will support) and entry barriers. Perfectly competitive markets are characterised by free entry, with large numbers of relatively small firms each operating at optimal scale.

Conduct

Conduct embraces the pricing, advertising, marketing, R&D and product differentiation aspects of firm behaviour (in other words price and non-price competition), as well as the possibilities for collusion and restrictive agreements.

Performance

Performance is measured by technical and allocative efficiency. In this context, **a concern with a Pareto optimum allocation of resources requires that prices equal marginal cost throughout the economy.** Applied to a private enterprise competitive economy, the result would be firms which are technically efficient so that X-inefficiency (organisational slack resulting in above-minimum average cost) is absent and, in the long run, normal profits (that is, profits at a level which neither induces entry nor exit) would be earned. On this basis, the efficiency of an economy's industries might be measured by such performance indicators as profitability, and by inter-firm and international comparisons of labour productivity and total factor productivity. However, the Pareto approach is static, and a society interested in growth will be concerned with the dynamic aspects of industrial performance as reflected in innovation and technical progress (see the taxonomy in **Table 17.2**).

The model in **Table 17.2** runs from industry structure to conduct to performance with the

Table 17.2   *A Taxonomy of Industrial Policy*

Industry Features	Main Characteristics	Examples of Industrial Policy Options
Structure	Number of firms Size of firms Entry conditions	Monopoly, mergers and restrictive practices policies in UK and EU Tariff policy; government contracts
Conduct	Pricing Advertising Marketing Product differentiation Research and development Collusion and restrictive agreements	Monopoly and restrictive practices policy Regulation of prices and advertising Consumer protection policy Regulation of new products and standards Restrictive practices policy
Location	Regional Towns Inner cities Rural areas	Subsidies to firm and labour Location of industry policy Local authority planning controls Tourism policy; subsidies to rural industry and to agriculture

Ownership	Firm behaviour
	– profit maximisation
	– non-profit objectives
		Nationalisation of firms and industries
		Privatisation with or without:
		  a competition
		  b regulation

Performance	Efficiency – technical – allocative Profitability Growth	Monopoly, merger and competition policy State regulation of profits Industrial strategy; R&D and technology policy

relationships depending on the assumptions about firm behaviour (that is, its objectives). The standard assumption is that firms are **profit maximisers**. On this basis, the neo-classical model shows that, for given demand and cost conditions, monopoly leads to a higher price and a lower output than perfect competition. Also, since monopoly prices exceed marginal costs, Paretian welfare economics concludes that there will be a misallocation of resources and hence a market failure: monopoly is regarded as socially undesirable (see **Figure 17.1**). Estimates of the losses of consumer benefit due to monopoly have ranged from extremely small to up to 7 per cent of gross corporate product in the UK and up to 13 per cent of gross corporate output in the USA. However, the analysis can be modified to allow for a trade-off between the cost savings from mergers and economies of scale and the loss of consumer benefits due to monopoly. Alternative approaches have also emerged involving contestability, transaction costs, game theory and the Austrian critique, all of which are discussed in the sections which follow. Further complications arise from the theory of second-best which shows the limited applicability of the Paretian model.

☐ *17.3.3 Trade-Offs*

Let us consider a competitive industry and ask whether such an industry should be monopolised through mergers? If we assume that a merger leads to economies of scale which would not otherwise be available to a competitive industry, then a merger to monopolise a competitive industry will result in cost savings. Thus, there will be a trade-off between the cost savings from scale economies and the loss of consumer benefit (surplus) due to the monopolisation of the competitive industry. Logically, the merger should be allowed to proceed if the additions to producer profits (surplus) exceed the loss of consumer benefits (surplus) as shown in **Figure 17.1**.

This trade-off analysis is not, however, without its critics. It uses a modified form of Paretian welfare function which allows a comparison of gains and losses, but distributional issues cannot

Figure 17.1 *Mergers, Scale Economies and Competition*

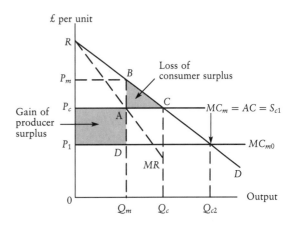

be ignored so that we must ask whether the same or different weights should be attached to changes in producer and consumer benefits. Moreover, after the merger has taken place, a profit-maximising monopolist will expand output (beyond OQ_m in **Figure 17.1**) so raising producer profits and reducing the loss of consumer surplus, resulting in an even stronger case for the merger. Nevertheless, the merger will continue to be associated with a misallocation of resources, with price greater than the new marginal costs. In the circumstances, consumers could in principle bribe the monopolist to produce at the new competitive price and output (Q_{c2} at P_1 in **Figure 17.1**): the monopoly would be no worse off since it would be compensated for its lost profits and consumers would be substantially better off. Such socially desirable compensation does not occur because substantial transaction costs make it too costly to negotiate this solution between the consumers and the monopolist. Finally, once the merger has occurred, competitive pressures will be absent allowing the firm to become technically inefficient which results in a departure from cost-minimising behaviour.

☐ *17.3.4 Contestable Markets*

The concept of contestable markets represents a further modification to the standard structure-performance paradigm. A contestable market is one where there is the possibility and threat of entry by domestic and foreign firms, and therefore the **threat of rivalry**. A perfectly contestable market is one which has no entry barriers, where entry and exit are easy and costless, and which may or may not be characterised by economies of scale or economies of scope (that is, economies which result from the range or scope of a multi-product firm's activities). In contestable markets, potential entrants are attracted by opportunities for profits. 'Hit and run behaviour' is evident since new entrants are not at a cost disadvantage compared with established suppliers, and the absence of sunk (irrevocable) costs means that exit is costless. One of the major features and policy implications of this approach is that a contestable market need not be populated by a large number of firms (as in perfect competition). In fact, a contestable market may contain only one or a small number of firms. Thus, with contestable markets, economists no longer have to assume that efficient outcomes occur only where there are large numbers of firms as in perfect competition. **Contestability rather than structure determines performance**.

☐ *17.3.5 Transaction Costs*

Economic activity and exchange is a transaction process in a world of imperfect information and knowledge. Producers do not have complete knowledge of production possibilities and market opportunities. Similarly, individuals as consumers lack information on the price and quality of goods and services on offer, and as workers they will have only limited information on the wages, employment conditions and career prospects available in the labour market. Further costs are incurred in completing a transaction or doing business. For instance, after searching the market for a new car, costs are incurred in negotiating a price, and then policing, monitoring and enforcing a contract. After all, if producers and consumers were perfectly informed, and there were no transaction costs, then markets would not fail since all opportunities for mutually advantageous

trade and exchange would be fully exploited. In other words, transaction costs impede and, in some cases, completely block the formation of markets.

Transaction costs have been defined as the costs of running the economic system, and include all the costs involved in planning, bargaining, modifying, monitoring and enforcing an implicit or explicit contract (Williamson, 1981, p. 1544). On this approach, the modern corporation, other economic institutions and organisational arrangements reflect efforts to economise on transaction costs rather than to pursue anti-competitive practices and create monopolies. Two assumptions are central to transaction cost economics; **bounded rationality and opportunism** (or self-interest). Bounded rationality recognises that economic agents have a limited capacity to handle information and to solve complex problems. Opportunism recognises that self-interest-seeking individuals will affect transactions by hoarding valuable information, distorting data and sending misleading messages. As a result, all contracts are incomplete and the possibility of opportunism means that it cannot be assumed that economic agents will reliably fulfill their promises (hence the need to screen economic agents for reliability).

Transaction cost economics offers some distinctive explanations and interpretations of economic organisations, *inter alia* that:

- transactions will be organised in markets unless market exchange creates substantial transaction cost penalties. On this basis, firms will be substituted for markets if it becomes too costly to use markets compared with the costs of managing a firm. Indeed, compared with conventional micro-economics which focuses on prices and quantities, transaction cost economics examines the features of transactions and maintains that the details of organisation matter.

- it explains decisions by firms to undertake activities in-house or to buy-in, as reflected in the extent of integration (for example, vertical integration being preferred to incomplete short-term contracts).

- it explains the internal organisation of modern

corporations in the form of hierarchies, internal government and divisions. An example is the multi-divisional, or M-form, organisation which resembles a mini-capital market compared with the centralised, unitary or U-form structure. The success of the M-form was due to its ability to economise further on transaction costs.

- it explains non-standard and unfamiliar forms of economic organisation such as conglomerates, multinationals and franchising. Transaction cost economics has also been applied to the economics of family organisation dealing with families as firms and analysing different contractual relationships (for example, marriage contracts).

This approach accepts that whilst firms seek to economise on transaction costs, they might also aim to become monopolists. However, the transactions school believes that monopolising behaviour is the exception. In advocating transaction cost economics, it has been suggested that it is the only hypothesis that is able to provide a discriminating rationale for the succession of organizational innovations that have occurred over the past 150 years and out of which the modern corporation has emerged (Williamson, 1981, p. 1564). However, critics claim that transaction costs are so general that they can be used to rationalise almost anything, and that the approach does not offer any testable and refutable predictions. The critics suggest that we have a simple proposition without any predictive content: firms are used whenever they are cheaper, all costs considered – and markets are used whenever they are cheaper, all costs considered. However, the notions of imperfect information and contestability are elements in the Austrian critique.

☐ 17.3.6 Game Theory

Many real world markets do not resemble the perfectly competitive model. Instead, many markets are imperfectly competitive, often comprising small numbers of relatively large firms. Such oli-gopoly industries are characterised by **interdependence**, and game theory attempts to explain how oligopolies respond to their rivals' actions. Game theories focus on equilibrium outcomes which occur when each firm selects the best strategy, given the strategy of its rivals. Unlike perfect competition and monopoly, there is no single theory of oligopoly. Examples of oligopolies include the UK banking, brewing, car, cigarette, newspaper and pharmaceutical industries. Competition in such industries often takes non-price forms such as advertising, 'free gifts', brand proliferation, research and development and the availability of spare capacity to deter new entrants (although price wars, predatory pricing and collusion are not unknown). These developments in the New Industrial Economics use modern game theory to explain strategic competition and interaction between large firms. Whilst the approach has the appeal of being more realistic, Austrian economists are critical of its dependence on equilibrium outcomes.

☐ 17.3.7 The Austrian Critique

The Austrian economists (such as Hayek, Schumpeter and Kirzner) are critical of neo-classical economics and the structure-conduct-performance paradigm, with its underlying emphasis on perfect competition and equilibrium. They assert that actual economies consisting of real world firms and industries are never in equilibrium (that is, never at a state of rest). Instead, economies are characterised by **ignorance** and **uncertainty**, which leads to continuous change and continuous market disequilibrium. Faced with an unknown and unknowable future, Austrian economists view human choices by market agents as subjective. Ignorance and uncertainty create opportunities for profits and it is the entrepreneur's task to discover these profitable opportunities. To the Austrians, competition means continuous rivalry (contestability) with entrepreneurs searching for opportunities to make money before anyone else – all of which occurs in a world of ignorance and uncertainty where there is no such thing as perfect information and knowledge. To the Austrians, trial and error price adjustments, and trial and error advertising and product variations are simply a **search and discovery process** – they are methods of trying to obtain market information in situations where knowledge is imperfect and costly to acquire. But conventional theory regards these actions by a businessman as evidence that he possesses some monopoly power. In other words, the competitive process which we witness in the high street seems alien to our model of a perfectly competitive equilibrium. In the high street, the trial and error price cuts made by businessmen are simply examples of the way they try to gain information on their profit-maximising price (they are searching for profits).

The public policy implications of the Austrian approach concern two major issues in particular. In the first place, they concern the role of **profits**. At any given moment, profits may seem to be monopolistic resulting from output restrictions – the monopoly problem. Austrians, however, regard high profits as temporary since rival entrepreneurs will be attracted into the relatively profitable activity. Austrians suggest that monopoly control regulations should involve an assessment of profits over the **long run** (whatever that might be). They believe that any public policy which minimises the rewards of entrepreneurship will **reduce** future entrepreneurial effort, with adverse effects on the competitive process.

Secondly, they concern **industrial organisation**. Austrians believe that policy-makers should avoid making statements either about the most efficient form of industrial organisation or about the wastes of advertising, product differentiation and duplication. Austrians claim that no one has sufficient knowledge and competence to judge which form of market structure is the most efficient for meeting **tomorrow's** consumer needs (some of today's sunrise industries will almost certainly become tomorrow's dinosaurs and smokestack industries). Entrepreneurs do not have perfect foresight, but they do have a greater motivation than politicians and bureaucrats to meet new and unexpected consumer demands – namely, their desire to seek out profitable opportunities. Critics claim, however, that the Austrian approach ignores completely the costs and time

required for an economy to adjust and respond to free market forces, and that such costs and time might be unacceptable to society and to vote-conscious governments. Austrian economics is also criticised for being vague, indeterminate and imprecise.

☐ *17.3.8 The Theory of Second-best*

There is a further problem in using the Paretian model. It requires that all the conditions for an optimum are satisfied simultaneously throughout the whole of the economy. For example, optimality requires that all markets be perfectly competitive throughout the economy. However, consider the case where perfect competition exists in only a limited section of the economy, but not everywhere. Assume also that there is a constraint in the form of at least one private market which is monopolistic and which can **never** be made perfectly competitive. In these circumstances, it does not follow that policy efforts to introduce perfect competition into some, but not all, of the private markets will necessarily move the economy towards an optimum position. It might, but it might also either leave welfare and/or efficiency unchanged or affect them adversely. Thus, given a constraint such that the rules for optimum resource allocation cannot be satisfied throughout the economy, it becomes necessary to resort to a next-best or **second-best** solution, in which efforts are made to make the best of the existing situation. A second-best solution is likely to involve a complete departure from the conditions required for optimum resource allocation. In the example given above, the second-best policy rule might require the departure from perfect competition in those markets where it already exists. Similar examples apply to other Paretian-type, piecemeal policy recommendations involving proposals for more marginal cost pricing, more centralisation or more free trade.

Given the importance of **constraints** or **distortions** preventing the achievement of a first-best or Pareto optimum, questions arise about their nature. Constraints can be policy-created, such as a government's support for 'national champions' or domestic monopoly defence contractors, or its desire to protect newly-privatised state industries from competition. But such policy-created constraints can always be removed by changing public policy! Presumably, therefore, governments are reluctant to change policy because of the likely effects on their popularity. If so, an alternative theory of industrial policy is required which embraces voters and political parties, and which recognises the role of the political market place.

☐ *17.3.9 A Public Choice Approach*

Traditionally, state intervention in an economy was rationalised on grounds of market failure. Governments and bureaucracies were assumed to formulate policies to correct such market failures. Government was regarded as a black box and was not analysed using the same self-interest, maximising and exchange concepts which had been applied extensively to households, firms and markets in capitalist economies. Instead, elected politicians and bureaucracies were assumed, somewhat simplistically, to pursue the public interest and to implement the will of the people. By way of contrast, public choice analysis is concerned with collective non-market decision-making. It applies neo-classical concepts of exchange and self-interest to the political market place of voters, political parties, governments, bureaucracies and interest groups.

Voters are assumed to act like consumers and to maximise their expected benefit or utility from the policies offered by rival politicians and political parties. Similarly, political parties resemble firms and seek to maximise votes. Parties compete in market structures ranging from small to large numbers of rivals, where new parties can enter or threaten to enter the market. The majority party forms the government and obtains the entire market. Its policies will be implemented through bureaucracies which are monopoly suppliers of information and services, aiming to maximise their budgets. In the UK, the Department of Trade and Industry has a central role in policy towards industry, together with support for regions, inner cities and industrial innovation. Other Depart-

ments with an involvement in industrial policy include Defence (R&D and equipment procurement); Environment (environmental protection); the Home Office (fraud); Transport (civil aviation and bus and rail services); the local authorities (for example industrial estates); and the state regulatory agencies (for example, the Office of Telecommunications (OFTEL), Office of Fair Trading (OFT), and Office of Gas Supply (OFGAS)).

In the course of formulating and implementing policies, governments and bureaucracies are lobbied by pressure groups pursuing their own self-interest by trying to influence policy in their favour (so introducing contestability into the political market). With the intention of safeguarding or improving their incomes, producer groups of management, professional associations and trade unions lobby governments for contracts (to buy British), subsidies, laws to licence and restrict entry and for protection from foreign competition. Producer groups are willing to allocate resources in their efforts to persuade governments to create or protect monopoly rights – sometimes referred to as rent seeking and rent protection. For example, producers in a competitive industry will seek to obtain monopoly profits by persuading the government to introduce economic regulation of their industry, perhaps by pointing to the wastes and duplication of competition and to the fragmented nature of competitive industries. Presumably, they would be willing to invest resources in order to capture monopoly profits. At the limit, they would spend P_mBAP_c in **Figure 17.1**, so that the social cost of monopoly is the sizeable area P_mBCP_c.

It happens that not all the lobbying costs are wasted. Politicians and officials may receive payments in kind in the form of expenses-paid trips or free meals. In some cases, the market may be provided with valuable information. Nevertheless, the producer group and rent-seeking approach to government explains public policies in terms of **wealth transfers**. Government is a mechanism for promoting exchanges of wealth or rents, the aim being to take wealth from some groups and to transfer it to other groups. On this view, industrial policy is about which firms, industries and regions gain from policy and about who loses and who has to pay. Such wealth transfers and rent-seeking occurs in a political market place where the rules and constraints on behaviour are determined by the constitution, which is itself the result of exchanges within the political market.

When the various agents in the political market place are recognised, it is perhaps not surprising that governments often seem to ignore obvious opportunities for making people better off. Many economists are fond of advocating public policies which expand the opportunities for consumer choice by promoting competition and mutually advantageous trade and exchange both within and between nations. But if such policies are socially desirable, why do governments frequently ignore them? Why the use of tariffs to protect British industry, regulations to prevent entry and, on occasions, a preference for buying defence equipment from higher cost domestic firms? Policies and changes which appear so attractive to economists often fail to recognise the influence of the different agents in the political market place and their impact on policy formulation. **Figure 17.2** presents a framework for identifying and mapping the various linkages within the political market. It takes the example of government policy towards cigarette smoking and shows the agents which will try to influence and modify government policy in their favour.

The economics of politics and bureaucracies provides predictions which are relevant to explaining UK industrial policy (Downs, 1957; Niskanen, 1971), namely that:

Figure 17.2   *Linkages[1] in the Political Market: The Example of Smoking*

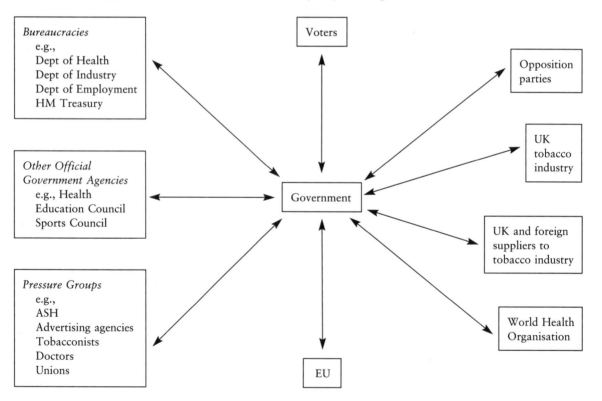

Note:
[1] For simplicity, most of the linkages shown by the arrows focus on the government. Other inter-relationships are possible.

- In a two-party democracy, both parties will agree on any issues which are strongly favoured by a majority of voters. As a result, party policies will be more vague, more similar to those of the other party (consensus politics) and less directly linked to an ideology than in a multi-party system.
- Political parties will attempt to differentiate their policies, but movements towards the political extremes of total laissez faire or complete collectivism are likely to be constrained by the potential loss of moderate voters.
- Government is more attentive to producers than consumers when it formulates policies. Producer groups dominate both because they can afford to invest in the specialised information needed to influence government and also because they have the most to gain from influencing public policy in their favour. As a result, government policies tend to favour producers more than consumers.
- Bureaucracies aiming to maximise their budgets will be inefficient in supplying a given output and will overspend. Their budgets are likely to be too large as they exaggerate the demand for their services and underestimate the costs of their preferred activities. This affects the way in which information is presented to politicians. In bidding for a larger budget, a bureaucracy can stress how the funds will contribute to social benefits in the form of, say, jobs, high technology and exports.

The public choice approach shows that the form and extent of state intervention as reflected in industrial policy cannot be divorced from the motives and behaviour of politicians, bureaucracies and interest groups. The traditional market failure analysis suggested that state intervention was needed to correct market failure and to improve the operation of markets. By way of contrast, the public choice approach recognises that governments and state intervention can also fail.

These approaches to analysing aspects of industrial policy will now be applied to a set of issues which dominate current debates: should governments regulate the economy and is competition policy an effective regulatory instrument?

Alternatively, should policy focus on ownership choosing between private or public ownership (see Chapter 18)? Can firm behaviour and performance be sufficiently influenced by subsidies? Governments can also affect industrial performance directly through their public purchasing policies (Chapter 19). In some cases, the absence of a policy or doing nothing is a conscious policy decision. The rest of this chapter will show how economists can contribute to debates about competition policy.

▋ 17.4 The Economics of Regulation and Regulatory Policy

□ 17.4.1 The Issues

Since 1960, there have been numerous examples of regulation. They have included employment legislation embracing contracts; employment protection; equal opportunities; health and safety at work and training and redundancy. At various times there have been controls on prices, wages and profits in such forms as minimum wages; equal pay; rent control; price regulation schemes (for example, NHS drugs); profit rules on government contracts; and price freezes for the nationalised industries. The structure, conduct and performance of industry has been regulated by monopolies, mergers and restrictive practices policy. Regulation has also taken the form of government licensing of entry as with patents; public houses; taxis; television companies; road and air transport; and new pharmaceutical products. Finally, output is regulated through such forms as pollution controls and safety standards, as in the case of food products and passenger transport (for example, speed restrictions; vehicle testing; airliner safety).

The 1980s were characterised by a mix of both regulation and deregulation, which can be linked to a broad interpretation of privatisation (see Chapter 18). The privatisation of public monopolies such as telecommunications, gas, electricity and water resulted in the creation of industry-specific regulatory agencies. At the same time, the Conservative government **deregulated** some markets such as bus transport, financial services, and Sunday trading. All of this raises general issues concerning the rationale for regulation, the likely response of firms to regulatory constraints on their behaviour and the calculation of the costs and benefits of regulation. In addressing such issues it is useful to start with a classification system.

☐ *17.4.2 The Forms of Regulation*

Regulation takes various forms, and a distinction can be made between **voluntary self-regulation** and **government regulation** via laws and regulatory agencies. The professions and the Stock Exchange, together with codes of conduct for advertisers (such as cigarette companies) and the media are examples of voluntary self-regulation. In contrast, government regulations can be general or specific. General regulations such as competition policy affect all firms in the economy, whilst specific regulations can be aimed at one sector such as telecommunications or gas and/or relate to specific aspects of firm behaviour such as advertising, prices or profits. For example, the Review Board for Government Contracts regulates profit rates on all non-competitive government contracts, whilst the Medicines Act 1968 regulates the introduction of new pharmaceutical products into the UK market. In these various forms, regulations affect aspects of structure through entry conditions, as well as conduct (advertising, R&D) and performance (prices, profits). Whatever its form, the central issue is **why regulation is needed**.

☐ *17.4.3 The Rationale for Regulation*

Economic theory suggests that regulation is a means of correcting for market failure, thereby improving the operation of markets. State regulation might, for example, be a means of controlling private monopoly power or, alternatively, a means of controlling harmful externalities. **An alternative public choice view suggests that government regulation benefits producers rather than consumers.** Firms will devote resources to lobbying governments to introduce favourable policies such as regulating entry, on the pretext of protecting consumers from 'cowboy' operators and from 'cheap, inferior and unsafe foreign products'. Regulators will have only limited information about producers. The possibility arises of new or existing regulatory agencies being **captured** by the industry and persuaded to act in favour of producers rather than consumers. Senior officials in the regulatory agency might seek employment in their regulated industry (for example, defence; pharmaceuticals).

Firms also have an incentive to persuade the regulatory agency that its required standards can be met voluntarily, claiming that excessively high standards will lead to bankruptcy with implications for plant closures, unemployment and a government's popularity. Alternatively, firms might accept the costs of government regulations in return for more beneficial policies elsewhere such as restrictions on new entry. Certainly, firms are unlikely to be passive-mechanistic agents, but will seek to change regulations and to adapt to them. This in turn requires an explanation of how firms are likely to respond to different regulatory rules.

☐ *17.4.4 The Response of Firms*

Regulation can take various forms such as licence requirements; certification; entry fees; inspection systems and fines for breaching regulations; the auctioning of rights; and controls on prices and profits. In choosing between these alternatives, policy-makers need to know what they are trying to achieve, and how firms are likely to respond to different regulatory instruments.

At the outset, it has to be recognised that regulators do not have perfect information about producers in the regulated industry. For example, a regulator trying to enforce cost-based prices incorporating an average profit rate, does not know whether a firm's costs reflect efficient behaviour or X-inefficiency. In these circumstances, regulators have to formulate incentives which will change firm behaviour in certain socially desirable directions, but some incentives can give unexpected and undesirable results. A state-determined limit on profits might, for example, induce a firm to pursue objectives other than maximum profits, so substituting expenditure on staff or other discretionary items such as luxury offices, for profits. Alternatively, if the profit controls take the form of a maximum rate of return earned on capital, the regulated firm may use increasingly capital-intensive production methods. Regulatory controls on advertising may encourage a firm to expand its unregulated marketing inputs, for example by employing more salesmen or introducing new sponsorship schemes (as with sports sponsorship). In other words, firms may respond to regulatory constraints by seeking alternative ways of making money, thereby raising questions about the effectiveness of regulation.

17.4.5 The Desirability of Regulation

Some governments, politicians and civil servants are fond of proposing regulation – they seem to believe that all regulation is good and that more is desirable regardless of cost. However, regulation is not costless, so it is necessary to examine the likely **costs and benefits** and to assess any evidence, particularly on costs and benefits at the **margin**, in order to enable a choice to be made about the **optimal amount** of regulation.

Regulation involves substantial transaction costs in negotiating, monitoring and enforcing regulatory rules. Staff are needed by the regulatory agency and costs are imposed on producers in responding to the regulator's requirements. For example, a monopoly inquiry involves substantial inputs by members of the inquiry team and corresponding inputs by the monopolist. Specialist witnesses will also be hired by both parties, and the monopolist might devote resources to a public relations campaign and to lobbying politicians. There are also possible indirect costs which need to be included in the analysis. For example, regulatory requirements for the introduction of new drugs into the NHS might lead to longer development periods, so delaying the introduction of new pharmaceutical products. There might also be adverse effects on innovation with fewer new drugs being marketed, and firms might shift their R&D activities to foreign locations where there are fewer regulatory restrictions. In the meantime, delays in the introduction of new drugs can have harmful effects on patients in the form of prolonged suffering and death which might have been avoided by the earlier use of the new product. Questions then arise as to whether the delays are beneficial insofar as they protect consumers from the unforeseen and possibly harmful side effects of new drugs: a classic trade-off situation.

A cost–benefit analysis of regulation must also take account of its potential benefits. Regulatory agencies which aim to remove market failures will introduce policies to correct for externalities or to change the structure, conduct or performance of markets with the ultimate objective of improving consumer welfare. But can society assess the output or performance of a regulatory agency? Various performance indicators have been suggested, not all of which can be easily related to consumer satisfaction. For example, agencies are likely to emphasise the number of inquiries and reports; the number of licences issued; the number of inspections; the number of prosecutions; and the size of the regulatory authority. The Director-General of Fair Trading will refer to the number of monopoly inquiries; the number of merger investigations; reports issued; and the number of cases brought before the Restrictive Practices Court. Similarly, in regulating the introduction of new drugs, the Medicines Division of the Department of Health will eagerly report the number of licences awarded; the time taken to process applications; the introduction of any new testing requirements; inspection and enforcement activities; and the number of statutory orders.

The various performance indicators **appear** impressive, indicating a lively, active and vigorous regulatory authority. However, many of the indicators measure inputs or intermediate output, rather than **final output**: they do not indicate the effects on consumers and how highly consumers might value such effects. Supporters of regulation will obviously claim that it results in substantial social benefits. However, a regulatory agency aiming to maximise its size or budget will exaggerate the social benefits of its activities (such as improved product safety) and under-estimate or ignore the costs of regulation. A regulatory agency will also favour independent fund-raising powers in the form of, say, licence fees which enable it to finance inefficiency, labour hoarding and discretionary activities such as luxury headquarters and offices. Some of these arguments about regulation will now be applied to UK competition policy which is a classic example of a general form of regulatory policy.

■ *17.5* Competition Policy

□ *17.5.1 The Economic Rationale*

Competition policy is a classic example of general regulatory arrangements applying to all firms in the UK economy. It embraces policy towards monopolies, mergers and restrictive practices. In this context, standard economic theory offers some clear policy guidelines suggesting that monopoly and other imperfections result in market failure and hence are socially undesirable (see **Figure 17.1**). Theory defines monopoly as a single seller of a product with no close substitutes. This model indicates that policy-makers need to focus on structural characteristics, the resulting performance reflected in the relationship between price and marginal cost and whether excessive profits are earned in the long run. However, theory also recognises that small numbers of firms constituting an oligopoly can have market power and that groups of firms acting together through collective agreements (cartels) can behave like a monopolist. As a result, policy needs to focus on mergers creating oligopoly or monopoly situations; on the conduct of firms in relation to entry barriers (for example, advertising); and on collective agreements which restrict competition in an industry. How far have such guidelines from economic theory influenced UK competition policy?

□ *17.5.2 UK Practice*

UK competition policy is based on various pieces of legislation dating from 1948, concerned with monopolies, mergers, restrictive practices, resale price maintenance (RPM) and consumer protection. Monopolies and mergers may be referred for investigation by the Monopolies and Mergers Commission (MMC) whilst restrictive practices including RPM are the subject of legal procedures in the Restrictive Practices Court (see **Table 17.3**). Specific reference to consumer protection was first incorporated in the 1973 Fair Trading Act.

Current policy towards monopolies and mergers is based on the Acts of 1973 and 1980. The 1973 Fair Trading Act created an Office of Fair Trading (OFT) with a Director-General and cases **selected for investigation** referred to the MMC. Where a monopoly situation appears to exist, both the Director-General of Fair Trading and the Secretary of State for Trade and Industry can refer cases to the MMC (see **Figure 17.3**). A monopoly is defined as one firm or a group of firms acting together (called a complex monopoly) accounting for **at least 25 per cent** of the relevant **local** or **national** market. Selected mergers are referred to the MMC by the Secretary of State for Trade and Industry. Mergers **may be** investigated where they involve a 25 per cent or more market share or **at least £70 million worth of assets are taken over** (the asset test was £30 million until 1994). These definitions are interesting. The market share criterion contrasts with the economists' definition of monopoly as a single seller. Whilst the policy definition embraces oligopoly, it also implies that, as the number of similar-sized firms declines from 5 to 4, a market changes from competition to a monopoly situation constituting a policy-relevant imperfection. Moreover, the value of assets taken over figure for mergers introduces an absolute size of firm criterion into the policy definition of monopoly. This contrasts with the economists' emphasis on market share. However, an absolute size criterion allows vertical and conglomerate mergers to be investigated. It might also reflect a public choice perspective, whereby large size can create dominant producer groups capable of influencing

Table 17.3 *Major Competition Policy Measures*

Legislation	Agencies	Features
Monopolies and Restrictive Practices Act 1948	Monopolies Commission	Monopoly = one-third or more of a market
Restrictive Trade Practices Act 1956	Registrar and Restrictive Practices Court	Restrictive agreements illegal but exemptions (gateways); if agreement passes through a gateway it still has to satisfy a public interest criterion
Resale Prices Act 1964	Restrictive Practices Court	RPM declared illegal subject to exemptions (gateways) and ultimate public interest test
Monopolies and Mergers Act 1965	Board of Trade mergers panel Monopolies Commission	Mergers to be reviewed involving one-third or more market share, or where value of assets taken over exceeded £5 million
Restrictive Trade Practices Act 1968	Registrar and Restrictive Practices Court	Amendment of 1956 Act to incorporate information agreements
Fair Trading Act 1973	Director-General of Fair Trading Monopolies and Mergers Commission Consumer Protection Advisory Committee	Replaced 1948 and 1965 Acts Monopoly = 25 per cent or more of a local or national market Mergers to be reviewed involving one-quarter or more market share or value of assets taken over exceeded £15 million (increased to £70 million in 1994) Public interest defined to include competition Reference to consumer protection
Restrictive Trade Practices Act 1976	Director-General of Fair Trading Restrictive Practices Court	Consolidated previous legislation (1956, 1968) with an extension to services Agreements registered with Director-General of Fair Trading
Resale Prices Act 1976	Director-General of Fair Trading Restrictive Practices Court	Consolidated previous legislation (1964), banning RPM

Table 17.3   *Major Competition Policy Measures (cont'd)*

Legislation	Agencies	Features
Competition Act 1980	Director-General of Fair Trading Monopolies and Mergers Commission	Deals with anti-competitive practices and extended monopoly control to public sector bodies and nationalised industries
EU Articles 85 and 86 of Treaty of Rome	Directorate General for Competition (European Commission) European Court of Justice	Applies only where trade between member states is affected Article 85 deals with restrictive practices and allows exemptions Article 86 originally applied to monopolies; but extended to prohibit mergers
EU merger regulation 1989	Directorate General for Competition (European Commission) European Court of Justice	Aggregate world-wide turnover above ECU 5 billion and other requirements

government purchasing and regulatory policies: hence, large firms might be undesirable.

The procedure for UK merger policy (**Figure 17.4**) allows for **confidential guidance** and **pre-notification**. One or more parties to a merger can ask for confidential guidance on the chances of it being referred to the MMC once it is in the public domain. In 1995, there were 107 requests for confidential guidance compared with 76 in 1994 (**Table 17.4**). There is also a statutory procedure to allow the parties to a merger to pre-notify the OFT of the details. In such cases, unless the Director-General of the OFT requests extra time to consider the proposals, the Secretary of State must announce a decision within 20 working days of the OFT receiving the completed form. Where the Director-General requests an extension, only one extension of 15 working days is allowed (before 1994, two extensions were allowed of 10 and 15 working days). This procedure is designed to obtain faster clearance of mergers involving no public interest issues. Also, where a proposed or completed merger might lead to the

loss of competition, the merging parties can give a binding undertaking for the divestment of part of the merged company's business as an alternative to a MMC reference. For completed mergers, the Secretary of State loses the power to make a MMC reference six months after the merger becomes public.

In its investigations, the MMC has to determine whether a monopoly or proposed merger operates or is likely to operate **against the public interest**. In the case of both monopolies and mergers which are contrary to the public interest the MMC can recommend appropriate action to be taken, but cannot itself enforce a remedy. Only the relevant Secretary of State can enforce remedies against monopolies and can choose to prohibit a merger or to allow it to proceed unconditionally or subject to conditions. However, the Secretary of State is not bound to follow the recommendations of the MMC. For the first time, the 1973 Act defined the public interest to include the desirability of maintaining and promoting competition. However, the public interest

Figure 17.3 *Procedures Under the Fair Trading Act and the Competition Act*

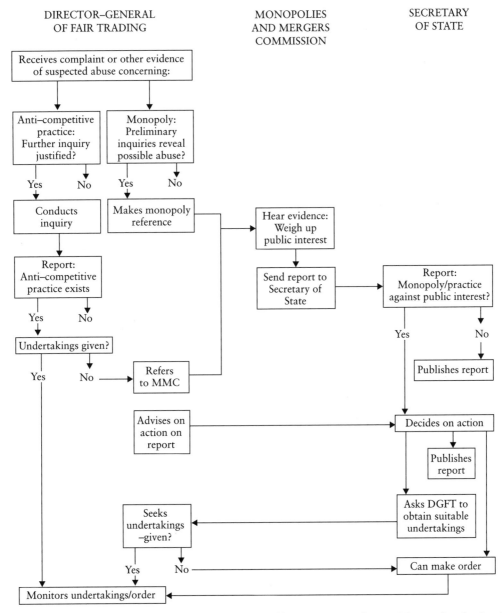

Source: House of Commons Trade and Industry Committee. *Fifth Report: UK Policy on Monopolies.* Session 1994–95. HC 249.I, p. x.

definition is wide-ranging. It includes a concern with consumer interests in relation to price, quality and variety; encouraging cost reductions, technical progress and new entry; a consideration of the international competitive position of UK producers; and promoting a balanced distribution of industry and employment. It is not at all obvious that some of these elements such as

Figure 17.4   *Merger Procedures*

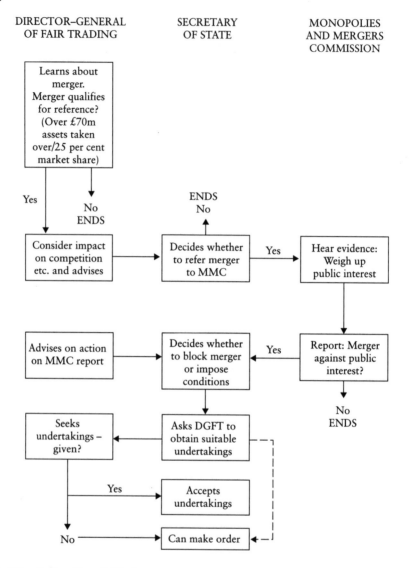

Source: DTI, *Competition Policy: How it Works.*

a balanced distribution of industry – itself an ambiguous term – are the proper concern of competition policy. Moreover, the MMC retains substantial discretion since it is allowed to take into account any factors which it deems to be relevant in determining the public interest! This is, in fact, a distinctive feature of UK policy towards monopolies and mergers.

Whilst standard economic theory suggests that competition is socially desirable, UK policy has not condemned monopolies and mergers as undesirable. **A discretionary cost-benefit approach is adopted, with each case examined on its merits.** Policy recognises that monopolies and mergers involve a trade-off between the costs of reduced competition, including X-inefficiency,

Table 17.4 *Number of Mergers Examined and References to the MMC, 19981–95*

Year	Total numbers of cases examined	Found not to qualify and proposal abandoned	Qualifying cases Nos	Qualifying cases % change	Confidential guidance cases	Pre-notified cases[1]	References to the Commission Recommended by Director-General	References to the Commission Recommended but not made	References to the Commission Made but not recommended	References to the Commission Total references	References as % of qualifying cases
1981	n/a	n/a	164	– 9.9	15	–	8	–	–	8	4.9
1982	n/a	n/a	190	+15.9	32	–	9	–	1	10	5.3
1983	n/a	n/a	192	+ 1.1	37	–	10	2	1	9	4.7
1984	n/a	n/a	259	+34.9	43	–	5	1	–	4	1.5
1985	n/a	n/a	192	–25.9	34	–	6	–	–	6	1.9
1986	524	211	313	+63.0	55	–	15	2	–	13	4.2
1987	478	157	321	+ 2.5	40	–	6	–	–	6	3.1
1988	456	150	306	– 4.7	45	–	11	–	–	11	3.6
1989	427	146	281	– 8.2	32	–	14	–	–	14	5.0
1990	369	108	261	– 7.1	22	51	21	–	4	25[2]	11.3
1991	285	102	183	–29.9	15	38	8	1	–	7[3]	4.2
1992	200	75	125	–31.7	21	9[4]	10	2	–	10[5]	9.6
1993	309	112	197	+57.6	46	13	5	2	–	3	2.0
1994	381	150	231	+17.3	76	7	8	–	–	8	5.2
1995	473	198	275	+19.0	107	12	11	2	–	9	3.3

Notes:
[1] The prenotification procedure was introduced under provisions of the Companies Act 1989.
[2] The figure counts the four acquisitions by South Yorkshire Transport Ltd as one reference, and excludes divestments in lieu of reference: 1, Rank/ Mecca; and 2, Hillsdown Holdings/Strong and Fisher.
[3] This figure excludes divestments in lieu of reference: 1, International Marine Holdings Inc/Benjamin Priest Group plc; 2, Trafalgar House plc/The Davy Corporation; and 3, Williams Holdings plc/Racal Electronics plc.
[4] One other merger notice was withdrawn.
[5] This figure excludes three divestments in lieu of reference: Redland plc/Steetley plc; Bowater plc/Assets of Pembridge Investments plc (DRG Packaging); Schlumberger Ltd/Assets of the Raytheon Company (Seismographic Service Group). It includes The Gillette Company/Parker Pen Holdings Ltd reference.
Source: Annual Reports of the Director General of Fair Trading.

and the potential benefits through scale economies and technical progress (**Figure 17.1**). Moreover, existing UK monopolies and mergers policy might be rationalised on second-best grounds. The standard welfare economics case for competition has to be modified where governments accept as policy-created constraints the continued existence of monopolies in parts of the economy. Alternatively, a public choice approach would explain current policy, with its wide-ranging public interest criterion and a reluctance to act against monopolies, as reflecting the influence of producer groups.

UK policy towards restrictive practices and RPM has taken a different approach. The Restrictive Practices Act 1976 and the Resale Prices Act of 1976 consolidated the prior legislation of 1956, 1964 and 1968. Restrictive practices legislation applies to the supply of both goods and services. It is concerned with agreements which restrict prices (pricing cartels), conditions of sale and quantities to be supplied, and which lead firms to exchange information on prices and costs. Restrictive agreements have to be registered, and are presumed to be illegal and against the public interest unless the parties can establish a case for exemption before the Restrictive Practices Court. To be exempted, an agreement has to pass through one or more of eight **gateways**. For example, it has to be shown that an agreement protects the public against injury; that it provides substantial benefits to the public as purchasers, consumers or users; that it acts as a countervailing power against the anti-competitive practices of third parties; or that its removal would result in serious and persistent local unemployment or a substantial reduction in exports. Once again, some of these gateways such as the concern with employment and exports are rather odd aims for competition policy. However, even if an agreement passes through the gateways, it still has to satisfy the tailpiece or public interest test. The Court has to determine whether, both currently and in the future, the benefits to the public on balance outweigh the detriments or costs. The Resale Prices Act 1976 controls RPM in the same way as restrictive agreements. There is a general presumption that RPM is contrary to the public interest unless a supplier can gain exemption through one or more of five gateways. RPM would be allowed if its abolition would substantially reduce the quality and variety of goods for sale; if there would be a substantial reduction in the number of retail outlets; if there is likely to be a long-run increase in retail prices; or where there might be dangers to health or a substantial reduction in necessary point-of-sale sales or after-sales services. Once through a gateway, it is still necessary to satisfy the tailpiece where the Court has to consider the balance of benefits and detriments.

The Competition Act 1980 complemented existing legislation and takes a different approach from that of the 1976 Acts. It is concerned with the anti-competitive practices of individual firms supplying goods or services which have the effect of restricting, distorting or preventing competition. Examples include price discrimination, predatory pricing, exclusive supply and rental-only contracts, all of which are aspects of a firm's **conduct**. The 1980 Act also extended monopoly control to include the nationalised industries and other public sector bodies (for example, the bus companies, and water authorities). The 1980 procedure requires the Director General of Fair Trading to investigate alleged anti-competitive practices. Where such a practice exists, the Director-General can require the firm to cease the practice or it can be referred to the MMC which will apply the 1973 public interest test.

These four pieces of legislation (Acts of 1973, two Acts in 1976 and the Act of 1980) form the basic framework of UK competition policy. There has been some additional and peripheral legislation. The Deregulation and Contracting-Out Act of 1994 extends the scope for companies to offer undertakings as an alternative to an MMC investigation, so resulting in speedier solutions to competition problems and allowing faster deregulation. In addition the regulatory agencies for the privatised utilities can refer aspects of their industry's operations for investigation by the MMC (for example, 1994 references included South West Water and Scottish Hydro-Electric). The Director General of Fair Trading can also review the rules made by specialist regulators under the Financial

Services Act, the Court and Legal Services Act, the Broadcasting Act and the Companies Act.

As a member of the European Union (EU), the UK is also subject to European competition law, reflected in Articles 85 and 86 of the Rome Treaty which are enforced by the European Commission. Article 85 prohibits restrictive agreements and practices which prevent, restrict or distort competition within the EU and which affect trade between member states. Examples include price-fixing, price discrimination, market-sharing and limitations of production, technical progress and investment. As in the UK, agreements may be exempted where they improve production, distribution or technical progress, subject to the requirement that these benefits must not be outweighed by other detriments associated with reduced competition. The European Commission has the power to impose **heavy fines** on the guilty parties to a restrictive agreement (fines of up to ECU 1 million or 10 per cent of annual world turnover, whichever is the greater).

Article 86 originally applied to monopolies but was extended to mergers. It deals with situations where trade between member states might be affected by one or more enterprises taking improper advantage of a dominant position (usually defined as having over 40 per cent share of the market). Examples of improper practices include the imposition of inequitable purchase or selling prices (unfair pricing), or limiting production, markets or technical developments. However, questions arise as to what constitutes a firm with a dominant position. In the case of mergers, the position is clearer. Under the 1989 regulation, the European Commission can control and prohibit mergers which have an EU dimension. These are defined as mergers where the **aggregate worldwide turnover** of the firms involved is above ECU 5 billion (approximately £3.5 billion), and **EU-wide turnover** for at least two of the firms involved is above ECU 250 million (approximately £175 million), unless two-thirds of that turnover is within one member state. Such mergers must be notified and will be prohibited if they create or strengthen a dominant position so that effective competition is impeded. All other mergers falling outside this regulation will be dealt with by national governments. Firms and member states can appeal to the European Court of Justice against decisions of the European Commission. Clearly, European competition policy and its relationship with national policy will be an important issue for the future development of the European Union.

Three issues are likely to dominate the evolution of an EU competition policy required for achieving a genuinely free internal market. First, there is likely to be a continued concern with the Community's merger regulations and their potential conflict with national merger policy. Indeed, the 1989 EU regulation on mergers reflected unanimous voting with some countries objecting to limits lower than the ECU 5 billion threshold. A Commission proposal for the end of 1996 is a reduced threshold with a world-wide turnover of ECU 2 billion and an EU turnover of ECU 100 million (CMLR, 1996). Second, the European Commission has become increasingly concerned about the competition implications of state subsidies and other forms of government protectionism (for example, the level of state aid to some European airlines). Third, the European Commission is likely to become more actively involved in policy towards cartels and restrictive policies, particularly in the services sector and in markets dominated by state-owned industries. For example, the Commission has focused on creating a **level playing field** (see also Chapter 19), taking action against agreements, concerted practices, abuse of dominant positions, government subsidies (for example, for R&D and specific industries), dumping and mergers which are incompatible with the Single Market. In a radically changed environment (due, for example, to the Single European Market, recession and technical change), the European Commission has to distinguish between two types of firm and group behaviour: First, behaviour which contributes to the development and restructuring of European industry (for example, co-operation and mergers which increase competition); and second, behaviour which prevents adjustment by partitioning markets and strengthening dominant positions (such as anti-competitive behaviour; state-aid and subsidies).

17.5.3 The Results of Competition Policy

Any evaluation of UK competition policy needs to focus on final output indicators in terms of the effects of policy on market structure, conduct and, ultimately, performance reflected in improvements in consumer welfare. Such an appraisal requires a model of structure, conduct and performance which holds constant all other relevant influences and identifies the contribution of competition policy. Other influences such as newly-industrialising nations, international trade, membership of the EU, technical progress, oil price shocks and the general level of aggregate demand and expectations in the UK economy cannot be ignored.

Confirmation of the continued need for competition policy affecting monopolies, mergers and restrictive practices can be obtained from the annual reports of the OFT and the reports of the MMC. By 1995, the MMC had issued some 100 reports on UK monopoly situations. Examples included the supply of beer (tied houses); the gas industry; cigarettes; soap and detergents; postal franking machines; animal waste; credit card services; the supply of petrol; cross channel ferries and travel agency services for tour operators. There have also been investigations of professional services (for example of architects, surveyors and solicitors) and such public sector activities as British Rail commuter services, some water authorities and the National Coal Board. In 1994, seven monopoly reports were published by the MMC covering activities such as films, recorded music, contraceptives, ice cream and private medical services. Various monopoly situations and practices have been found to be against the public interest.

In its judgements, the MMC assesses monopolies in terms of their policies and their effects on prices; advertising; marketing; new entrants, innovation and, ultimately, profitability. For example, in 1989, the MMC found that certain restrictions on advertising by the professions acted against the public interest and the Director General of Fair Trading was asked to seek assurances

that the professions would modify their behaviour. Similarly, the 1989 report on the supply of beer (Cmnd 651) found that six brewers produced 75 per cent of beer sold and owned 75 per cent of all tied houses. An earlier 1969 report on the supply of beer (Cmnd 216) had already concluded that the tied-house system operated against the public interest. In its 1989 report, the Commission found a **complex monopoly** situation in brewing (mainly through tied houses) which restricted competition and was against the public interest. Unusually for the Commission, it recommended a series of **structural** changes to achieve a more competitive regime. These included a ceiling of 2000 on the number of tied premises owned by a brewer; allowing tied tenants to sell a 'guest' draught beer; and also allowing them to buy nonalcoholic and low alcohol drinks as well as wines and some other drinks from the lowest-cost suppliers.

In 1994, the MMC found that complex monopoly situations existed in sectors such as ice cream, recorded music, films and private medical services. However, in the cases of ice cream and recorded music (for example, the price of CDs), the MMC concluded that the complex monopoly did not operate against the public interest. In the case of ice cream, it was estimated that Birds Eye, Mars and Nestlé accounted for 88 per cent of the market in 1992, but the MMC found no evidence that the monopoly inhibited competition or choice, nor that it adversely affected prices, innovation or efficiency. In contrast, the MMC found that the complex and scale monopoly in films was associated with two practices which operated against the public interest: the practice whereby aligned distributors normally first offered their films to MGM and Odeon cinemas and the lengthy exhibition periods required as a condition of supply.

The concern of UK monopoly policy with prices, entry, profitability and consumers has a possible economic basis in models of perfect competition and contestable markets. But such models do not provide operational guidelines for determining when prices are too high and profits become excessive. Are prices too high if they result in abnormal profits, and, if so, how is it possible to distinguish abnormal from normal profits? Austrian economists would adopt a different approach suggesting that market power is usually transitory and that so-called monopoly profits are the temporary reward of successful entrepreneurship. To the Austrians, an innovating monopolist generates a **social gain** represented by the firm's profits and the resulting consumer surplus: without the innovation a new product such as a microcomputer would never have been produced so there is no question of a deadweight loss due to a departure from the perfectly competitive output. Such contrasting interpretations of monopoly makes life extremely difficult and complicated for governments which have to determine a monopoly policy.

Critics of UK monopoly policy claim that it is **slow and ineffective.** Some MMC enquiries have taken 2–3 years, although recently enquiries have been completed in one year or less. Few reports are issued in any one year (for example, seven in 1994) and, to date, the total number of monopoly investigations represents only a small part of the UK's monopoly and oligopoly industries (although the presence of the MMC might of itself have a deterrent effect). Moreover, governments are often reluctant to take effective remedial action against monopolies, preferring to rely on informal undertakings, which may reflect pressure from producer groups and the possibility that the regulatory agency has been captured by producers. In addition, the remedies secured after an investigation apply only to the firms involved so that they have only limited impact on the conduct of other firms in other markets. Thus, the system has only a limited deterrent effect. The result is that UK monopoly policy has not achieved any major changes in either the structure or the conduct of monopoly industries which have been investigated.

Even the 1989 MMC recommendations for structural change in the brewing industry were modified by successive Secretaries of State. Clearly, the brewers represent a powerful producer group which lobbied the government to modify, or not to implement or to delay the recommendations of the MMC. In the event, the MMC's recommendations were modified, such

that brewers with more than 2000 pubs were required to dispose of either their brewery business or to sell or place at 'arm's length' **half** of the pubs they owned above the 2000 ceiling (for example Bass, with 7300 pubs, had to sell 2658 rather than 5300). At the same time, the brewers have responded to the new regulatory requirements in ways which are to their benefit and which might conflict with the aims of the MMC's 1989 Report. For example, Grand Metropolitan and Courage agreed to a pubs-for-breweries exchange with Grand Met ceasing to make beer and a new jointly-owned company running the pubs. At the same time, Courage entered into an agreement to supply beer to Grand Met's pubs. In fact, a number of brewers and companies running pubs have entered into long-term supply agreements. Some brewers have stopped brewing and retained their pubs (such as Greenalls). Elsewhere, pubs have been sold and then converted to private houses; and there have been instances where brewers, when disposing of surplus pubs, have tried to restrict the future use of pubs sold to private individuals for use as private dwellings only (a practice which OFT found to be a breach of the 1989 Order). Allegations have also been made that sales representatives of the big brewers have intimidated tenants not to take a guest beer or have made it difficult to stock a guest beer (for example, threatening rent increases or eviction). Subsequent events have confirmed that regulation has produced unexpected and, in some respects, undesirable outcomes. The 1989 MMC Report expected its proposals to result in lower beer prices and to prevent increased concentration and possibly lead to new entry. Evidence suggests that the regulatory intervention has resulted in higher prices and that industry concentration has increased significantly since the 1989 MMC Report. In 1989, there were six major brewers; by 1996 there were only three major brewers (Bass-Carlsberg-Tetley; Scottish & Newcastle–Courage; Whitbread).

Cases continue to arise and are not diminishing. A variety of anti-competitive practices have been investigated under the 1980 Competition Act. This Act allows the OFT and the Director-General to investigate complaints. Where the Director-General identifies anti-competitive practices he must report on whether an MMC investigation is required. However, instead of an MMC reference, the Director-General can accept undertakings which remedy the anti-competitive practices. A firm can be investigated under the 1980 Act if its UK annual turnover is £10 million or more and it has 25 per cent or more market share or belongs to a group whose turnover and market shares exceed these levels.

Under the 1980 Act, Black and Decker's policy of refusing to supply retailers who sold its products below a particular price was found to be anti-competitive and against the public interest. In 1994, the Director-General reported on Fife Scottish Omnibuses (a subsidiary of Stagecoach Holdings) following complaints from its main rivals that it ran loss-making commercial bus services. Fife Scottish was found to have acted anti-competitively and gave satisfactory assurances to the Director-General without a reference to the MMC. Also in 1994, the OFT reported on allegations that price cuts by *The Times* and *Daily Telegraph* newspapers represented predatory pricing aimed at eliminating specific competitors such as *The Independent*. The Director-General concluded that since the price cuts did not appear to be targeted at any specific newspaper a formal investigation would not be justified.

The government's initiatives on privatisation, deregulation, contracting-out and public purchasing policy will continue to create new demands on the UK's competition agencies. An example occurred with the 1993 MMC reports on the gas industry (Cm 2314–2317). The Reports recommended that the privately-owned British Gas should be split into two companies (separating trading from transport and storage) and that competition should be introduced over a 10-year period.

Mergers are also contributing to major structural changes in the UK economy with substantial numbers of mergers being of the horizontal and conglomerate types. Between 1990 and 1994, the annual rate of mergers within the UK varied between some 400 and 800 per annum, and in 1994, almost 90 per cent of qualifying mergers were of the horizontal type. However, relatively few qualifying mergers, often under 5 per cent, are actually referred to the MMC. For example, in 1994, the OFT examined 381 proposed or completed mergers and eight references were made to the MMC. Of those referred, not all are found to be contrary to the public interest. For example, between 1965 and 1992, there were 176 merger references, of which only 61 were declared to be against the public interest. Moreover, the Secretary of State does not always accept the recommendations of the MMC. In 1995, it reported on the competing bids by British Aerospace (BAe) and GEC for the warship builder VSEL. The MMC found that the proposed merger between BAe and VSEL might not be expected to operate against the public interest but that the proposed merger between GEC and VSEL was against the public interest. In the event, the Secretary of State allowed both bids to proceed, with the result that GEC acquired VSEL.

By the mid-1980s, there was concern over the continued merger boom, allegations of asset stripping and especially the size of some acquisitions and their controversial nature (for example GEC–Plessey and Nestlé–Rowntree). As a result, the government reviewed its merger policy and published the results in 1988 (DTI, 1988). The 1988 review confirmed the earlier findings of poor, disappointing or inconclusive post-merger performance (for example with respect to profitability). Such evidence was used to suggest that mergers were failing to provide economic benefits. Nevertheless, the government review reaffirmed its view that 'the vast majority of mergers raise no competition or other objections, and are rightly left free to be decided by the market' (DTI, 1988, p. 7). The 1988 review also confirmed that the main, though not the only, factor in determining whether a merger should be referred to the MMC should be its **potential effects on competition within the UK**. In fact, evidence from MMC merger reports between 1970 and 1990 showed that bidding firms had a significantly better chance of success if the MMC decided that competition was likely to increase or remain unchanged. However, to allow for a few exceptional cases (such as foreign ownership of UK companies or the level of any state ownership in the acquiring company), an open-ended public interest criterion was retained in the legislation.

At the European level, a 1991 case showed how the European Commission's merger control regulation was applied to the creation of a dominant position defined to embrace actual and potential competition from firms located within and outside what was then the European Community. The case involved a bid by Aerospatiale (France) and Alenia (Italy) for the de Havilland Aircraft Company of Canada. The Commission found that the acquisition would have given de Havilland and ATR (the French–Italian venture) 50 per cent of the world market and 67 per cent of the EC market for 20–70 seat commuter aircraft. This would have created a dominant position and the Commission rejected the proposed merger. In 1994, the Commission received 95 notifications of qualifying mergers and 83 of these were cleared at the first stage; seven cases were investigated in more detail (lasting up to four months) and on three of these, the Commission reached an adverse view, and one merger was prohibited.

Restrictive practices legislation has been extremely effective in removing certain restrictive agreements which were the basis for the widespread cartelisation of UK industry in the 1950s. By 1994, almost 12,000 agreements had been registered, over 70 per cent of which were goods agreements. A substantial number of agreements have been abandoned, and many have been modified to remove any anti-competitive effects. In 1994, the Director-General found that 1261 out of 1280 agreements which were registered in the year did not contain significant restrictions on competition. Interestingly, it is possible that restrictive practices legislation, originally introduced in 1956, might have contributed to the high rate of merger activity in the 1960s. Nevertheless, evidence shows that the UK legislation resulted in new entry, increased competition, lower prices and generally contributed to its main objective of improving industrial efficiency (Cmnd 331, 1988).

Similarly, legislation was effective against resale price maintenance. In 1960, RPM applied to about 20–25 per cent of consumer expenditure; by 1979, it was restricted to net books and medicines, representing under 2 per cent of consumer expenditure, and by 1996 both these exceptions were under pressure. Effectively, the net book agreement was abandoned in 1995 and the Director-General has recently applied to the Court for the reversal of its earlier decision on the agreement. The overall result of the RPM legislation was improved efficiency in retailing and lower prices, although the effects were smaller than expected and some groups such as small independent retailers and their customers had to bear the costs of the change. Nevertheless, the Resale Prices Act has made a major contribution to increased competition in retailing to the general benefit of consumers.

At the European level, application of Article 85 to restrictive agreements resulted in the Commission adopting 17 decisions in 1994, some involving fines. For example, cement producers were fined a record total of ECU 248 million for agreeing to exchange price information and protect their home markets. In contrast, a 1996 Commission decision approved a co-operation agreement between Lufthansa and SAS designed to create a long-term alliance subject to the condition that other airlines would be permitted to operate services between Germany and Scandinavia.

By the late 1980s, however, there were serious doubts about the effectiveness of UK restrictive practices legislation in tackling cartels. A government review suggested that 'the Act must now appear a relatively weak piece of legislation' (Cmnd 331, 1988, p. 29). It is criticised because potential colluders are unlikely to be detected (for example, secret price-fixing agreements amongst ready-mixed concrete companies in 1991); whether an agreement is registerable depends on its form, not upon its effect; penalties for ignoring the law are not sufficiently heavy to act as a deterrent; it catches trivia by including agreements which do not restrict competition; there are too many exemptions, and the whole registration process is costly and a waste of resources.

Eventually, in August 1996, the Government published a draft Bill for reforming UK competition law entitled **Tackling Cartels and the Abuse of Market Power**. The draft Bill has a number of distinctive features in that:

- It introduces a **prohibition** on anti-competitive agreements (such as cartels and agreements to restrict competition). This will replace the Restrictive Trade Practices Act of 1976 and 1977 and the Resale Prices Act 1976.
- The new prohibition will apply to agreements which 'have, or are likely to have, a significant effect on competition' (that is, preventing, restricting or distorting competition in the UK). Vertical agreements can be excluded from the scope of the prohibition.
- There will be a minimum threshold of £20 million based on the turnover of the parties to the agreement.
- Agreements which breach the prohibition will be allowed **exemption** where they provide certain countervailing benefits. Exemption is possible where the agreement contributes to improving production or distribution or promoting technical or economic progress while allowing consumers a fair share of the resulting benefit.
- The Director-General of Fair Trading will have the prime role of investigation, enforcement, giving negative clearance and issuing exemptions. Decisions by the Director-General can be reviewed by a new **Tribunal** which will replace the existing Restrictive Practices Court. Appeal to the High Court against the decisions of the Tribunal will be possible on limited grounds.
- To enforce the prohibition, the Director-General will be given adequate powers of investigation (such as to enter premises to inspect and take documents).
- Breaches of the prohibition can result in **financial penalties** of up to 10 per cent of a company's UK turnover or £350,000, whichever is the higher (up to a maximum penalty of £1.5 million).
- There will be further consultation on whether prohibition should also apply to the abuse of dominant market positions. In the meantime, there are proposals to strengthen the Fair Trading Act and Competition Act by introducing stronger investigatory powers and allowing the Director-General to impose interim orders forbidding particular anti-competitive practices

(for a discussion see *Financial Times*, 20 August 1996, p. 10).

☐ *17.5.4 The Single European Market*

In addition to competition policy within the UK market, a major change has occurred which will affect competition and contestability within the EU. Whilst there are no tariffs between member states of the EU, there were, until 1992, a number of substantial and costly non-tariff barriers. Physical, technical and fiscal barriers meant that the EU consisted of 12 fragmented national markets, separated by frontier controls, public procurement practices and different product and technical standards, all of which hindered trade in goods and services between member states. The EU aimed to remove these various barriers and to create a single internal market by 1992 (see Chapter 11).

It was estimated that the Single European Market would result in potential gains of over ECU 200 billion, equivalent to 5.3 per cent of Community GDP in 1988 (Cecchini, 1988, p. 84). Such gains would result from lower costs due to the abolition of frontier barriers, removing the barriers to entry into national markets (for example, for public procurement), exploiting scale economies and a general increase in competitive pressures in both goods and services markets. Nevertheless, the estimated benefits from abolishing non-tariff barriers could not realistically be achieved in 1993, and currently, for example, cross-frontier trade is hindered by administrative formalities and border controls (red tape and delays); public procurement protects national industries from foreign competition; and divergent technical regulations, standards and certification procedures mean costly market fragmentation (as in the case of financial services and telecommunications).

Critics claim that the likely benefits have been exaggerated, that they are based on a simple perfectly competitive model which will never be achieved and that most of the worthwhile economies of scale have been exploited. Further potential gains also remain available from opening-up national defence equipment markets, an area currently outside the remit of the EU. Moreover, efforts to exploit any potential scale economies within the EU will probably require mergers, leading to possible conflicts with competition policy: the price of efficient scale might be monopoly which will benefit producer groups rather than consumers.

■ *17.6* Conclusions

Proposals have been put forward for major reforms of UK competition policy. There are suggestions that the current UK approach of investigating each case on its merits should be replaced by the prohibition approach. The 1996 draft Bill represents a move towards prohibition for cartels and restrictive agreements. Concern has also been expressed about three types of cases which might be possible candidates for prohibition: First, intellectual property rights (such as copyright) where laws which encourage creativity and innovation involve exclusivity and possible monopoly power; second, vertical restraints such as refusal to supply by a dominant firm (for example, newspaper distribution); and third, predatory pricing which is defined as the deliberate acceptance of losses aimed at eliminating rivals with the expectation of future abnormal profits. There are, of course, problems in distinguishing predatory pricing from low prices reflecting reduced market demand or attempts to market a new product or to attract new customers to an existing product. Also, in the time taken to investigate predatory pricing, rivals can be eliminated. Finally, suggestions have been made for the creation of a single competition authority combining the OFT and the MMC (Carsberg, 1996).

Inevitably, changes in competition policy will involve gainers and losers. Similar worries about potential gainers and losers from policy changes have dominated the debate about UK privatisation policy. Indeed, privatisation involves issues of ownership, monopoly, regulation and market competition. The chapter which follows examines the relative merits of public versus private ownership and the role of ownership in enterprise performance.

Bibliography

Beesley, M. (1993) *Major Issues in Regulation* (London: Institute of Economic Affairs).

Blackaby, F. (ed.) (1979) *De-industrialisation* (London: Heinemann).

Carsberg, Sir Bryan (1996) *Competition Regulation the British Way*, IEA Occasional Paper 97 (London: IEA).

Cecchini, P. (1988) *The European Challenge 1992* (London: Wildwood House).

Cmnd 216 (1969) *Report on the Supply of Beer* (Monopolies Commission) (London: HMSO).

Cmnd 331 (1988) *Review of Restrictive Trade Practices Policy* (Department of Trade and Industry) (London: HMSO).

Cmnd 651 (1989) *The Supply of Beer* (MMC) (London: HMSO).

Cmnd 727 (1989) *Opening Markets – New Policy on Restrictive Trade Practices* (London: HMSO).

Cm 2314 (1993a) *Gas* (MMC) (London: HMSO).

Cm 2315 (1993b) *British Gas plc* (MMC) (London: HMSO).

Cm 2316 (1993c) *Gas and British Gas plc* (MMC) (London: HMSO).

Cm 2317 (1993d) *Gas and British Gas plc* (MMC) (London: HMSO).

Cmnd 2563 (1994) *Competitiveness: Helping Business to Win* (London: HMSO).

Cmnd 2867 (1995) *Competitiveness: Forging Ahead* (London: HMSO).

Cmnd 475 (1996) *Annual Report of the Director General of Fair Trading* (London: HMSO).

Common Market Law Reports (1996) 'Green Paper on Review of Merger Regulation', *Common Market Law Review Antitrust Reports* (April) pp. 455–7.

Department of Trade and Industry (1988) *Mergers Policy* (London: HMSO).

Downs, A. (1957) *An Economic Theory of Democracy* (New York: Harper and Row).

Economic Journal (1996) 'Controversy: De-industrialisation and Britain's Industrial Performance Since 1960', *Economic Journal* (January) pp. 170–218.

Galbraith, J. K. (1992) *The Culture of Contentment* (London: Penguin).

Gowland, D. and S. James (1991) *Economic Policy After 1992* (Aldershot: Dartmouth).

HCP 41–1 (1994) *Competitiveness of UK Manufacturing Industry*, House of Commons Trade and Industry Committee (London: HMSO).

Niskanen, W. A. (1971) *Bureaucracy and Representative Government* (London: Aldine Atherton).

Peacock, Sir Alan and Bannock, G. (1991) *Corporate Takeovers and the Public Interest* (Aberdeen: Aberdeen University Press).

Williamson, O. E. (1981) 'The Modern Corporation: Origins, Evolution, Attributes', *Journal of Economic Literature* (December) pp. 1537–68.

Chapter 18

Industry and Policy II: Privatisation

Peter Curwen and Keith Hartley

18.1 Introduction: The Policy Debate

Privatisation is a policy which embraces debates about the importance of ownership as a determinant of enterprise performance. Questions also arise as to who gains and who loses from the policy. In theory, consumers are supposed to benefit, but other possible beneficiaries include top managers, shareholders and the financial institutions advising on privatisation policy. The pay of top managers in the privatised utilities has been a source of criticism (Curwen, 1994a) raising questions about the effectiveness of shareholders in exercising control over their companies. Further concern has been expressed about the extent of competition in the privatised utilities sector (including mergers) and the effectiveness of the regulatory arrangements. Proposals have been tabled for a tougher regulatory regime to operate more in the interests of consumers and, especially by the Labour Party, for a 'windfall tax' on the profits of the privatised utilities.

The chapter starts by considering the economic arguments for state ownership (see Curwen, 1986 for a detailed review of the previous decades) and presents of a framework for classifying the various forms of privatisation. The aims of privatisation policy are assessed and related to models of enterprise performance. There follows a review of the UK privatisation programme and its consequences, including the role of regulation and deregulation. The chapter concludes with an evaluation of competitive tendering and other aspects of 'privatising choice'.

18.2 The Nationalised Industries

Until the 1980s, the UK economy consisted of a mix of publicly and privately-owned firms and industries. Within the public sector, public corporations, including nationalised industries, are state-owned bodies accountable to government but with a substantial degree of independence and the activities of which, in the case of nationalised industries, are financed largely by the consumers of their goods and services rather than by the taxpayer. These industries have been the focal point of continuing debate between the political parties, with Labour governments traditionally preferring state ownership of the means of production. Since 1945, UK industries such as aerospace, airlines, coal, gas, electricity, rail, shipbuilding, steel and telecommunications have at various times been state-owned, as too have individual firms such as British Leyland, British Petroleum, Rolls-Royce and Royal Ordnance. However, since 1979, a substantial number of nationalised industries and state-owned companies have been privatised, raising debates about whether ownership is an important determinant of enterprise performance.

Various economic arguments have been used to explain and justify nationalisation. After 1945, much emphasis was placed on the need to control private monopoly power; to plan and control the commanding heights of the economy; to include social costs and benefits into decision-making, and to improve industrial relations by removing the traditional conflict between labour and capital. In the 1970s, state ownership of firms such as British Leyland and Rolls-Royce was justified as a rescue operation to save strategically and economically important companies and to prevent substantial job losses. Nationalisation, however, is not without its problems. Objectives have to be specified; pricing, investment and financial rules are required; and performance has to be monitored. Problems have often arisen because of the lack of clearly specified objectives or because of changing and conflicting aims, resulting from the need to balance a concern with economic efficiency, technical efficiency, anti-inflationary pricing policies, social objectives and financial targets.

Economists seeking economically efficient solutions are fond of proposing **marginal cost pricing rules** for nationalised industries, requiring them to set price equal to long-run marginal cost. However, 'marginal cost' has to be defined and measured, and difficulties arise where state industries are monopolies not subject to competitive pressures. In such circumstances, the lack of contestability is likely to be associated with organisational slack and X-inefficiency: marginal cost is whatever the Chairman of the nationalised indus-

try says it is! Moreover, in decreasing cost industries, marginal cost pricing will be associated with losses. In such circumstances, losses are consistent with an economically-efficient solution and are not an indication of inefficiency. However, marginal cost pricing is further criticised on second-best grounds. Where prices do not equal marginal cost throughout the economy, the appropriate second-best pricing rule for a nationalised industry is likely to require a departure from strict marginal cost pricing (see Chapter 17).

Actual pricing policies for the UK nationalised industries have varied from a requirement to break-even (that is, average cost pricing), to marginal cost pricing or to a requirement to act commercially. Marginal cost pricing was introduced following a 1967 White Paper. In a 1978 White Paper a further element was introduced requiring nationalised industries to aim at a **real rate of return** on their new investment programmes of 5 per cent (8 per cent from 1993). The required rate of return is reviewed periodically and is related to the return achieved by private companies thereby ensuring that the nationalised industries do not divert resources away from more valuable alternatives. Also, since 1976, the nationalised industries and most other public corporations have been subject to **external financing limits** (EFLs) which control the amount of finance, whether grants or borrowing, which an industry may raise during the financial year to supplement its income from normal trading.

Since 1979, the government has been concerned about the efficiency and losses incurred by the nationalised industries and has sought to reduce the size of this sector through denationalisation or privatisation. By 1989, the government's major aim for the nationalised industries was to 'ensure their effectiveness and efficiency as commercial concerns and to strengthen them to the point where they can be transferred to the private sector or, where necessary, remain as successful businesses within the public sector', and this remains the case today (see Cm 2821, p. 60). As successful public sector businesses, they are expected to minimise the burden on the taxpayer (via subsidies), earn an economic return on their assets and improve their commercial performance. In other words, the remaining nationalised industries are to act commercially. If such an objective is interpreted as profit maximisation, it will promote technical efficiency but, in the absence of competition, it will not produce allocative efficiency.

During the 1980s, as shown in **Table 18.2**, a substantial number of nationalised industries were privatised. In 1979, the nationalised industries accounted for some 11 per cent of GDP and employed over 1.8 million people; by 1993, the corresponding figures were 2.3 per cent and some 400 000 employees (*ibid.*, p. 61). During this period, the productivity of the nationalised industries increased substantially, reflecting efficiency improvements, reductions in overmanning and the incentive of possible privatisation. Between 1979 and 1992, average annual productivity growth of the nationalised industries was 3.9 per cent, exceeding that for both manufacturing (3.5 per cent) and the economy as a whole (1.9 per cent). By 1993, the remaining UK nationalised industries were British Nuclear Fuels (now renamed BNFL), British Coal, British Rail, British Waterways, Caledonian MacBrayne (services to remote islands), Highlands and Islands Airports, the Civil Aviation Authority, London Transport, Nuclear Electric and the Post Office, together with such public corporations as the BBC, the Commonwealth Development Corporation and the Urban Development Corporations. However, the privatisation has since taken place of Railtrack and most other parts of British Rail, London buses, British Coal, and British Energy (but leaving Magnox Electric in public hands), such that there are no longer any substantial sectors left to privatise other than the Post Office.

18.3 Privatisation: A Classification System

The distinction between government (public) and private finance and provision can be used to classify the different forms of UK privatisation policy. Such a classification system is shown in **Figure 18.1** which provides a useful starting point for analysis and also allows the rival advocates of private and state ownership to contemplate hor-

izontal, vertical and diagonal movements between the boxes. Inevitably, **Figure 18.1** is only a broad classification system. For instance, state-owned enterprises selling products to private markets may also receive subsidies, and there are privately-owned schools and hospitals. In addition, monopolies transferred from the public to the private sector are subject to regulatory constraints. In the case of airports, and the privatised utilities, namely, electricity, gas, telecommunications and water, the regulatory agencies impose a pricing rule known as RPI-X, where RPI is the retail prices index and X is a percentage figure. This rule imposes a ceiling on the annual increase in a firm's prices (in respect of specific packages of services) which will always be X per cent below the general inflation rate. Even so, the early 1990s financial results of the major privatised utilities led to public criticism of excessive profits and over-charging reflecting their monopoly power. Critics have also pointed to the deliberate and substantial under-pricing of some privatisations, where the beneficiaries were the financial institutions (underwriters).

18.4 Objectives of Privatisation Policy

Privatisation policy has been associated with various objectives, some of which are in conflict. Consumers are expected to benefit from rivalry, more choice, greater efficiency and innovation. The policy is also aimed at reducing the size of the public sector through denationalisation, and reducing public sector borrowing (for proceeds from privatisation see **Table 18.2**; Cm 3201, 1996; and *Statistical Supplements to the FSBR*, section 5). Furthermore, it has been associated with a desire for wider share ownership. Suggestions have also been made that the real purpose of the policy is to reduce the monopoly power of trade unions. There are conflicts between some of these objectives. For example, reducing the size of the public sector and maximising Treasury income from selling public assets can be achieved by transferring monopoly power from the public to the private sector without increasing rivalry. It

Figure 18.1   *Classifying Privatisation*

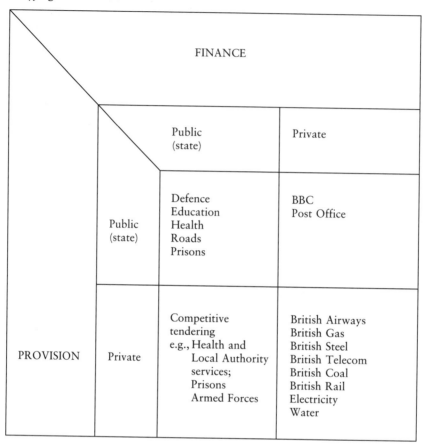

is, of course, likely that the actual extent and form of privatisation policy will reflect the influence of agents in the political market place – namely, governments seeking votes and established interest groups (managers and workers) trying to protect their positions, especially their income and on-the-job leisure.

The debate about privatisation in its wider aspects raises the general question of whether ownership is an important determinant of economic performance. The 1980s Conservative governments claimed that following privatisation, productivity and profitability in the newly-privatised companies increased dramatically (as in the case, for example, of British Aerospace, Jaguar and the National Freight Consortium). The official explanation offered is that:

the overwhelming majority of employees have become shareholders in the newly privatised companies. They want their companies to succeed. Their companies have been released from the detailed controls of Whitehall and given more freedom to manage their own affairs. And they have been exposed to the full commercial disciplines of the customer. Even former monopolies now face increased competition'.

(Conservative Manifesto, 1987, p. 36).

This suggests a model in which improvements in economic performance depend not only upon ownership, but also on competition and managerial freedom (for example, in respect of internal organisation and employment contracts). Others would add the external environment as a further variable in the model in the form of, for example, the Thatcher effect via Rayner scrutinies, Financial Management Initiatives and the withdrawal of subsidies providing a shock effect throughout the public and private sectors (Dunsire *et al.*, 1988). Some of these complex and sometimes inter-dependent issues can be simplified into a two variable model showing the impact of ownership and market structure on efficiency. A framework is shown in **Table 18.1**, where the following hypotheses on enterprise performance or efficiency can be formulated:

1. *D* is superior to *A*, where *D* represents private ownership and a competitive product market.
2. *D* is superior to *C* – neo-classical economics favours competition.
3. *D* is equal to, or superior to, *B* – does ownership matter? One review of the evidence suggests that under competition, private firms are likely to be superior (Kay and Thompson, 1986, p. 16).
4. *B* is superior to *A*, reflecting the role of competition.
5. *C* is superior to *A*, reflecting the policing role of private capital markets.

6. *B* could be superior, inferior or equal to *C* (inconclusive) depending on the relative strengths of competition and ownership.

Testing hypotheses about the effects of ownership and market structure on enterprise performance and efficiency is not without its problems. Indicators are required to measure enterprise performance and, ultimately, economic efficiency. Some crude performance indicators are readily available such as profitability, labour productivity and international competitiveness, and tests can be undertaken to determine whether performance improves following a change from public to private ownership, *ceteris paribus*. It should be borne in mind that an increase in profitability might reflect the exercise of market power by a newly-privatised monopolist, and higher labour productivity could reflect investment in new equipment. Moreover, empirical tests of performance before and after an ownership change need to allow for what would have happened without the change, and the distinct possibility that a transfer of ownership will result in the pursuit of different objectives.

Table 18.1 *Ownership and Market Structure: A Taxonomy*

	Monopoly	Competition
Public Ownership	A 1. Absence of competition induces technical inefficiency 2. No fear of going bankrupt 3. Government intervention distorts decision-making 4. Potential for allocative efficiency (price = marginal cost)	B 1. Market forces promote greater technical efficiency 2. Still no fear of bankruptcy 3. Government intervention still distorts decision-making 4. Potential for allocative efficiency
Private Ownership	C 1. Fear of bankruptcy 2. No government intervention 3. Pressure exerted by shareholders 4. Allocative efficiency unlikely	D 1. Competition induces technical efficiency 2. Fear of bankruptcy 3. No government intervention 4. Pressure exerted by shareholders 5. Allocative efficiency

18.5 The Privatisation Programme

The privatisation programme in the UK officially began with the election of the first Thatcher government in 1979, and has accordingly been in operation for the better part of two decades. The concept of privatisation was not original to the UK, nor was it first conceived in 1979, but there can be no doubt that the UK has been at the forefront in the development of strategies for transferring assets and services from public to private sectors, and that the perceived success of its programme has spawned a host of imitators throughout the world.

Public–private transfers or their reverse are, naturally, linked to political philosophies, so the swing to the right in British politics in 1979, which in good part reflected dissatisfaction with the performance of public enterprise, understandably gave rise to a concerted attempt to shrink not merely the public enterprise sector but the welfare state in general. It is nevertheless of interest to note that pre-1980 Conservative administrations had made virtually no progress in unwinding the postwar programme of nationalisation. Prior to 1979, denationalisation, as it was then called, amounted only to some tinkering with British Steel, road haulage and Thomas Cook, and this was counter-balanced by the nationalisation of British Leyland and Rolls-Royce in the early-1970s at a time when the Heath government was as ideologically committed to the free market as the Thatcher government of 1979.

Privatisation inevitably poses a threat to vested interests, especially trade unions, and a government may initially feel insufficiently sure of itself to take these on (as in the case of Mrs Thatcher and the coal miners). In addition, the Opposition will invariably threaten to renationalise at the earliest opportunity, which may well discourage potential investors (leading to allegations of capital market failure). It is further evident that, whereas the government would prefer to dispose of industries that are unprofitable and hence a drain upon public resources, it is only the profitable ones which can be readily sold off and even

they may require their debts to be written off or pension funds to be topped up.

The sale of profitable concerns necessarily deprives the government of an ongoing stream of income, so there are longer-term losses to set against any immediate revenue from sales. There is finally the problem of setting aside the time in a busy legislative programme to create the legal instruments needed to effect public-private transfers. These are initially going to need to be devised on a case-by-case basis, and a good deal of experimentation is likely to prove necessary before a workable format for a particular political/economic environment is hit upon.

It is evident from the above that the Thatcher governments of the 1980s assigned a high priority to the achievement of its privatisation programme, yet this alone was not a sufficient condition for success as is evident from experience in countries such as France. The advantage enjoyed by Mrs Thatcher was that she did not need the support of other political parties to push through the programme. Throughout the 1980s, the Thatcher administrations possessed an absolute majority in Parliament, and hence were able to steamroller through their privatisation programme.

18.5.1 Coverage of the Programme

Inspection of the 1979 Manifesto which first officially introduced the programme indicates that even at that early stage it consisted of more than 'denationalisation' (the selling off of industrial assets). For this reason, the programme is generally referred to as one of 'privatisation', although it might more appropriately be described as 'rolling back the frontiers of the state' because it has evolved over the years to encompass a whole range of practices, most notably:

- The disposal of state-owned industrial assets to private sector individuals/organisations via either a public offer for sale or a trade sale/management buy-out.
- The disposal of other state-owned assets such as land and buildings (for example, council houses).

- The cessation of state controls over the private provision of goods and services (deregulation).
- The contracting-out of services previously performed by central and local government agencies.
- The imposition of 'user charges' and fees in respect of services previously supplied at zero cost.
- The introduction of initiatives which seek to stimulate competitive outcomes in the absence of market prices.

Throughout the 1980s, the programme consisted primarily of asset sales, with varying amounts of deregulation thrown in for good measure. Over the past six years, the programme has switched direction as a result of the comparative scarcity of assets for disposal.

In effect, the UK government was obliged to create its programme of industrial asset sales from the ground floor upwards, which accounts in good part for the time it took to achieve sales on any scale. The key decisions related to which specific assets were to be transferred, how the new organisations were to be structured and the legal form of the transfers. The organisations, once privatised, obviously had to be legally independent, although they could nevertheless remain dependent upon government contracts, possibly involving subsidies, for much of their business.

In certain cases, for historical reasons, a number of public enterprises were already structured as public limited companies (PLCs) and could be sold off without any need for structural changes. This explains why the earliest sales included British Aerospace, British Petroleum and Cable & Wireless. However, in certain cases, an existing organisation needed to be split up, as was true when Britoil was created through separation from the rest of the British National Oil Corporation. In other cases, the 'public interest' (and hence loss-making) obligations needed to be split off from the provision of profitable goods and services. In the example of the water industry, this resulted in the creation of the National Rivers Authority to which was ceded ownership and responsibility for the upkeep of rivers while the provision of water and sewerage services to customers was left for the commercial water authorities. British Telecom, by way of contrast, was obliged to maintain uneconomic call boxes in rural areas.

From a legal perspective, in order to be privatised, a public enterprise needs to be converted into a PLC under the relevant Companies Act, in the process acquiring a shareholder in the form of the government. The government can subsequently sell all or part of its shareholding to private individuals, firms or institutions via an offer for sale/tender. In certain cases, the government has created a single 'golden' or 'special' share which, while nominally worth £1, serves to impose potentially wide-ranging restrictions upon a privatised concern.

Where an organisation is already a PLC, potential shareholders can be supplied with a properly constituted financial track record to guide their investment decisions. However, a public enterprise which has never been a PLC presents a host of difficulties which can, as in the case of British Airways, cause its privatisation to be delayed for a period of years. For example, a set of accounts needs to be created in accordance with private sector accounting standards, debts may need to be written-off (or, as in the case of British Gas, created) in order to generate an appropriate level of gearing (debt to equity) or the pension fund may need to be topped up (as in the case of BT). Furthermore, it may be necessary to operate the new company for several years while still in public ownership in order to provide a track record in its restructured form.

Finally, if the new company looks to be under-capitalised in relation to its future investment needs, additional shares may need to be created via a rights issue, either directly to the public at the time of privatisation (as in the case of British Aerospace) or to the government which subsequently sells on the shares.

☐ 18.5.2 Public Offers

The full list of privatisations executed via a public offer of shares is set out in **Table 18.2**. Altogether, up to the end of 1996, a total of 43 companies were sold off either in their entirety or via a series

Table 18.2   *Privatisations via Public Offer of Shares 1979–96*

		% sold[0]	Company £mn	Government £mn
Amersham International	February 1982	100.0	6	65
Anglian Water	December 1989	98.4	−61[14]	768[15]
Associated British Port Holdings	February 1983	51.5	56[16]	−34[17]
	April 1984	48.5	–	52
BAA	July 1987	95.6	–	1281
British Aerospace	February 1981	51.6	100	50
	May 1985	59.0	188	363
British Airways	February 1987	97.5	–	900
British Energy	July 1996	87.8	−700[14]	2108[15]
British Gas	December 1986	96.6	−2286[14]	7720[15]
British Petroleum	October 1979	5.2	–	290
	September 1983	7.2	–	566
	November 1987	36.8	1515	5370
British Steel	December 1988	100.0	–	2425
British Telecommunications	December 1984	50.2	1290[16]	2626[17]
	December 1991	25.9	–	5240
	July 1993	20.7	–	5335
Britoil[1]	November 1982	51.0	−88[18]	641[19]
	August 1985	49.0	–	449
Cable & Wireless	October 1981	49.4	35	189
	December 1983	22.3	–	275
	December 1985	31.1	331	602
Eastern Electricity[2]	December 1990	97.6	a	a
East Midlands Electricity	December 1990	97.5	a	a
Enterprise Oil	July 1984	100.0	–	392
Jaguar[3]	August 1984	100.0	297	0
London Electricity	December 1990	97.5	a	a
Manweb[4]	December 1990	97.5	a	a
Midlands Electricity	December 1990	97.7	a	a
National Power	March 1991	60.9	a	a
	March 1995	38.3	a	a
Northern Electric[12]	December 1990	97.5	a	a
Northern Ireland Electricity	June 1993	96.5	–	362
Northumbrian Water[6]	December 1989	98.4	123	34
North West Water[7]	December 1989	98.4	330	524
Norweb[7]	December 1990	98.4	a	a
PowerGen	March 1991	59.5	a	a
	March 1995	36.6	a	a
Railtrack	May 1996	98.0	–	1950
Rolls-Royce	May 1987	96.7	283	1080
Scottish Hydro-Electric	June 1991	96.6	a	a
Scottish Power	June 1991	96.4	a	a

Table continued opposite

Table 18.2 continued

		% sold[0]	Company £mn	Government £mn
Seeboard[8]	December 1990	97.5	a	a
Severn Trent	December 1989	98.4	361	488
Southern Electric	December 1990	97.5	a	a
Southern Water[9]	December 1989	98.4	46	347
South Wales Electricity[10]	December 1990	97.5	a	a
South Western Electricity[11]	December 1990	97.0	a	a
South West Water	December 1989	97.4	266	27
Thames Water	December 1989	97.4	−12[14]	934[15]
Welsh Water[13]	December 1989	98.4	276	70
Wessex Water	December 1989	98.4	81	165
Yorkshire Electricity	December 1990	97.5	a	a
Yorkshire Water	December 1989	97.8	89	383
Regional Electricity[a]	December 1989		−2 815[14]	7 907[15]
Nat. Power/PowerGen[a]	March 1991		−768[14]	2 954[15]
Nat. Power/PowerGen[a]	March 1995		−	3 594
Scottish Hydro/Power[a]	June 1991		−626[14]	3 481[15]
TOTAL			−1 683	61 973

Notes:
[0] Of the total issued including any new shares issued at the time of the sale.
[1] Taken over by BP in February 1988.
[2] Renamed Eastern Group in October 1994. Taken over by Hanson in January 1996.
[3] Technically, the money had been given to Jaguar's parent company, BL, but an equivalent sum was deducted from loan aid previously promised to BL. Jaguar was taken over by Ford in November 1989.
[4] Taken over by ScottishPower in October 1995.
[5] Taken over by Avon Energy of the USA in June 1996.
[6] Taken over Lyonnaise des Eaux in December 1995.
[7] Taken over by North West Water in October 1995. Together called United Utilities.
[8] Taken over by Central and South West of the USA in April 1996.
[9] Under offer by ScottishPower.
[10] Renamed Swalec in November 1993. Taken over by Hyder in January 1996.
[11] Taken over by Southern Company of the USA in February 1996.
[12] Under offer by CE Electric of the USA.
[13] Renamed Hyder in April 1996.
[14] Debt injection at time of sale.
[15] Including debt repayment.
[16] Debt extinguished prior to sale.
[17] Net of extinguishing debt prior to sale.
[18] Debt repayment prior to sale.
[19] Including debt repayment prior to sale.

[a] No breakdown for individual companies is available.

of tranches. As a consequence of the latter, the total number of sales amounted to 54. However, on some occasions, a group of related companies were sold simultaneously, so the actual number of occasions on which shares were sold was 30.

This has been a very substantial programme, and in financial terms has raised more revenue than any other. According to our own estimates, which allow for the role played by debt in every case, the total revenue raised so far is roughly £62 billion. However, this takes no account of the fairly large sums raised through means other than public offers (see *Statistical Supplements to the FSBR*, section 5), so the total figure for all privatisation is in excess of £70 billion. The first financial year in which £1 billion was raised was 1983–84. In 1984–85, £2 billion was raised, largely from BT, and in 1986–87, £4.4 billion was raised (BT and British Gas). The peak years were 1988–89 (£7.1 billion – BP, Gas and Steel), 1991–92 (£7.9 billion – Electricity, Water and BT) and 1992–93 (£8.2 billion – BT and Electricity). Revenue has subsequently fallen away but the odd billion is still rolling in.

One of the stated objectives of the programme was to expand the number of individual shareholders in the UK. Financial intermediaries such as pension funds and unit trusts are particularly well developed in the UK, and most individuals invest in shares indirectly through intermediaries rather than hold shares as such. The public offers were accordingly biased towards the small shareholder in a variety of ways such as the use of a clawback facility (see below).

- *Subscriptions* The smallest number of applications was 8000 for the ABP offer in 1984 which was in the form of a tender. The largest number was 4.5 million for British Gas in 1986. The number of times each issue was subscribed was also highly variable. As a basic rule of thumb, one-half of the shares on offer were acquired by the general public post-clawback, so the extent of over-subscription has to take clawback into account.

  In certain cases, essentially the tender issues such as Britoil in 1982 and Enterprise Oil, the issues were under-subscribed and the under-

writers were left with the shares. The only offer for sale under-subscription was BP in 1987 when, due to the market crash, only 0.03 per cent of the shares were bought by individuals. On the other hand, the British Airways offer was 32 times subscribed pre-clawback (23 times post-clawback) and the tiny ABP offer in 1983 was 34 times subscribed (see Curwen, 1994b for details).

- *Value of Combined Offers* In calculating the value of individual flotations it must be borne in mind that typically one-half of the revenue from the combined offers was forthcoming from institutions. In addition, the use of tranches meant that the money was not always paid in a single financial year, and the value of the money has changed over the years due to inflation.

  The largest sum raised was £7.9 billion from the Regional Electricity Companies, but from a single company it was £6.9 billion from BP in 1987 (of which part went to the company). In practice, British Gas raised £7.7 billion overall for the government because £2.3 billion of debt was created in addition to the £5.4 billion from the sale itself. By way of contrast, ABP left the government with a *de facto* loss in 1983.

- *Arrangements for Small Investors* On 29 occasions, some involving multiple sales, small investors were permitted to pay by instalments, most commonly two but sometimes three. In the majority of cases the first instalment was set at £100, but it was set much higher where there was a greater degree of risk, as for Rolls-Royce, in order to discourage 'widows and orphans'.

  A commonly-used method to encourage small investors to hold on to their shares was to offer a loyalty bonus at the end of a three-year period, invariably on the basis of one bonus share for every 10 or 15 held continuously during that period up to a stated maximum which usually varied between 150 and 500 shares. In cases involving utilities, customers received twice the rate of bonus given to non-customers. In certain cases, small investors were offered alternatives in the form either of bill vouchers or a discount on the second and/or final instalment.

- *Clawback* The early flotations involved a straightforward procedure. A specified share of the offer for sale or tender was allocated to the general public, to institutions in the UK, to overseas institutions and to employees/pensioners. If the general public over-subscribed their share then their subscriptions were heavily cut down so as to bring into equivalence their aggregate allocations and the number of shares set aside for them.

   This frequently resulted in undesirably small allocations, but the Treasury was unwilling to to allocate an initially much larger share to the general public for fear of alienating the institutions. It accordingly hit upon the concept of clawback whereby if the public over-subscribed their allocation by more than a specified number of times, then part of the allocation initially set aside for domestic and overseas institutions would be transferred across to the public allocation. In the majority of cases from 1987 onwards, the clawback threshold was exceeded, often by a wide margin.

- *Employee Arrangements* A considerable effort was expended to conjure up offers which would appeal to employees, and this was generally successful. In the majority of cases, employees were offered some free shares, but these were typically worth less than £200 even after adjustments for length of service, and generally much less. Almost invariably, free shares were accompanied by an offer of matching shares whereby if an employee bought one share then the Treasury would provide one, and sometimes two, matching share(s). The value of the incentive obviously depended upon the cost of the shares, but rarely exceeded £500. Employees also had priority in the public offer.

- *Special Shares* Special (or golden) shares have been introduced on 24 occasions (some involving multiple sales) as well as in respect of two trade sales (Sealink and VSEL). On a further three occasions, restrictions similar to those forming part of a Special Share were introduced. The Special Share has accordingly been a characteristic of the privatisation programme. Eight types of restriction can be identified. The most commonly used among these were a restriction on the issue of new voting shares and a restriction on the proportion of the total shares which could be held by a single shareholder. This was normally set at 15 per cent, and if exceeded the owner was obliged to dispose of the excess holding. Other frequently used restrictions were in respect of the proportion of shares held by foreigners; special voting rights or provisions; disposal of assets; winding up or dissolution; appointment of a British Chief Executive; and government appointed directors.

In the majority of cases the Special Shares were of indefinite duration with the government reserving the right to terminate them at a time of its choosing. In other cases, either a minimum or maximum duration was specified, again with the right to early termination in the latter case. Less commonly, a termination date alone was specified. Some Special Shares have been redeemed. Amersham's lapsed at the end of the minimum specified period in 1988 and that of Enterprise Oil terminated in December 1988. In the case of Britoil, the Special Share was retained after its takeover by BP but eventually abandoned in July 1990, whereas in the case of Jaguar it was waived at the end of October 1988 subsequent upon the takeover bid by Ford.

☐ 18.5.3 Other Asset Sales

Although most commentary has inevitably focused upon the major offers for sale discussed above, it should be recognised that they are numerically in the minority where privatisations are concerned despite accounting for the vast majority of all revenue raised. In fact, the majority of disposals have taken the form either of trade sales, whereby the privatised company is acquired by another concern without a flotation, or of buyouts by management and/or employees, occasionally in conjunction with other parties.

The disposal of a self-sufficient part of a public enterprise has sometimes been on such a scale as to merit inclusion in the list of major privatisations, for example Enterprise Oil (hived off from

British Gas). In all such cases, a public offer for sale was involved. However, legislation authorising the private sale of subsidiaries and assets was also passed in the form of, for example, the Transport Act 1981 (for British Rail) and the Transport Acts 1982 and 1985 (for the National Bus Company) which involved only trade sales or buy-outs.

In the case of the Post Office, Section 62(3) of the British Telecommunications Act 1981 empowered the Secretary of State to make such disposals, which have so far taken the form of Giroleasing in February 1990 and the Girobank in July 1990.

Trade Sales

Trade sales have been less common than buy-outs, but more controversial. The best-known buy-out was that of the National Freight Company (now NFC) in February 1982, which has always been regarded as a major success story. The best-known trade sales, on the other hand, have included not only the successful disposal of Wytch Farm by British Gas in May 1984 but also the disposal of part of Royal Ordnance to BAe which was the subject of investigation by the European Commission. More recently, most of the Coal industry and railways have been disposed of in this way.

Many of the disposals by the British Technology Group (previously the NEB) also took the form of trade sales, including ICL, Fairey, Ferranti and Inmos. British Rail sold its hotels and Sealink in this way, as did British Airways in respect of International Aeradio in March 1983 and of British Helicopters in September 1986. The Post Office sold the Girobank in July 1990 to the Alliance and Leicester Building Society for £112 million, one of the rare trade sales which genuinely netted in excess of £100 million for the Treasury prior to coal and railway disposals.

Altogether, some 40 trade sales have taken place. Many of the companies have subsequently been resold and most have disappeared from view. Although most have attracted little attention in the media, partly because the government has made little attempt to publicise them, they are indicative of how much more far-reaching the privatisation programme has been than is evident from the public offers for sale.

Buy-outs

So far there have been roughly 200 buy-outs of companies undergoing privatisation. Management buy-outs have been the most common form, but some buy-outs have been by employees (not all of whom typically invest). On a number of occasions the vendor has retained a stake, for example British Steel in Sarclad. On other occasions, managers from outside companies have engaged in a buy-in.

The buy-out of National Freight involved an entire state-owned enterprise. However, in the early 1980s, buy-outs were a commonplace feature of the industries such as steel, shipbuilding and cars as they disposed of peripheral activities prior to the flotation of the core parts of their business. In addition, there have been cases of the break-up of one entity into many pieces (for example, National Bus) and the return to private hands of companies temporarily taken into the public sector in order to restore their fortunes (National Enterprise Board/British Technology Group). Individual coal mines and parts of the railways have also been sold off in this way.

Council Housing

Some small-scale sales of council houses took place during the 1970s, but prior to the 1980 Housing Act, which gave tenants the statutory right to buy their properties, such sales were at the discretion of local councils which mostly refused to sell either through political conviction or disinterest.

In order to ensure a favourable reception for the properties on offer, the government came up with a substantial discount off their market value. Discounts were set initially at a minimum of 30 per cent for tenants of three years' standing, with the rate rising by 1 per cent for each additional year of tenancy up to a maximum of 50 per cent.

These were subsequently increased in 1983 and 1986 when sales began to flag. Revenue from sales peaked at over £5 million in 1983–84, but it inevitably fell away once the most attractive properties were sold and many of the remaining tenants were unable to raise a mortgage. Over the period since 1990, the decline in house prices has discouraged purchasers and sales have been insignificant. However, the transfer of some 5 per cent of the housing stock from public rental to private ownership can reasonably be viewed as one of the outstanding features of government policy in the 1980s.

◼ 18.6 Consequences

◻ 18.6.1 Widening Share Ownership

As noted previously, while most UK households hold shares indirectly via institutions, direct holdings have long been uncommon except among the very wealthy. The government set out explicitly to change this pattern of behaviour, commencing with the offer for sale for British Aerospace in 1981. Ostensibly, this would have the virtue of enhancing interest in the conduct of privatised concerns on the part of shareholder-consumers, thereby making them more responsive to the marketplace. The more cynical view was that it would induce more households to vote Conservative.

The consequences are open to interpretation. Most obviously, whereas only 7 per cent of the general public owned shares directly in 1979, this figure had grown to 20 per cent by 1990. On the other hand, half of this increase represented individuals who held nothing but the shares of privatised concerns and whose holdings were often rather trivial in value. Furthermore, a good deal of 'stagging' (selling within a few days of receipt of certificates) was noticeable, indicating that the shares had been acquired for purely speculative reasons, and there was a tendency for further disposals to occur when second instalments fell due. From the perspective of the companies themselves this meant, firstly, that their share registers tended to shrink rapidly post-privatisation but, secondly, that they often remained saddled with huge numbers of small shareholders with commensurately high administrative costs.

Since 1990, even allowing for the additional sales, there has been a noticeable reduction in direct shareholdings. Probably, by the year 2000, considerably fewer than 10 million individuals will hold shares directly.

◻ 18.6.2 Privatisation and the PSBR

The Public Sector Borrowing Requirement (PSBR) is the sum of expenditures by central government, local authorities and public corporations not covered by tax revenue. The PSBR rose to particular prominence in the period post-1979 when its consequences for the growth of the money supply, and hence inflation, formed a key element of the monetarist doctrine in fashion at that time.

That the primary purpose of the initial privatisation programme was to raise revenue in order to shrink the PSBR (by virtue of calling it 'minus expenditure') was, naturally, never admitted by the authorities, although it was accepted to be the case by almost everyone else. It should be borne in mind in this regard that the revenue from the sale of a public enterprise occurs on a once-and-for-all basis. However, assuming that the sale is of a profitable concern, the government is forgoing the stream of profits that it would have received in future years. Hence, these two factors need to be traded off one against the other, and if the discounted stream of profits exceeds the revenue raised by the sale then in the longer term the PSBR will be adversely affected.

During the fiscal years 1979–80 to 1983–84 inclusive the PSBR, excluding privatisation receipts, remained in excess of 3 per cent of GDP, and the sales of industrial assets, which at that time were quite modest, made little difference to these magnitudes. However, subsequent upon the first BT offer, late in 1984, privatisation receipts began to pick up sharply at precisely the time when the PSBR, excluding such receipts, was on a steeply falling trend. Hence, in 1986–87, asset sales generated revenue equal to more than half the size of that year's PSBR, and the following year it was not only considerably larger but also sufficient to create a debt repayment when netted out against the gross figure for the PSBR.

During the ensuing two years, the PSBR turned into a debt repayment exclusive of privatisation receipts, and increasingly little was heard about the revenue-raising virtues of privatisation. However, the PSBR has reappeared once again in something akin to its old glory such that privatisation receipts are once again more than welcome. Nevertheless, from a presentational viewpoint the government now treats these receipts as a means by which tax cuts can be financed without the need to cut public expenditure.

18.6.3 The Effect Upon Trade Unions

During the 1970s, the view was commonly held in right-wing circles that the trade unions had usurped excessive economic and political power and hence needed to be 'put in their place'. In seeking to achieve this, privatisation was seen as an appropriate vehicle since it would shift the industrial relations climate markedly in favour of management who would have an incentive to dismiss unproductive workers and hold down wages.

That public enterprise was overstaffed, relatively unproductive and, at certain points in the business cycle, overpaid by the standards of the private sector, was undeniable. Nevertheless, the unions were extremely strong in the public enterprise sector, and the coal miners had taken on the role of pacesetters in the annual wage round. The first Thatcher government was accordingly unwilling to seek outright confrontation, although it subsequently became persuaded that its position was sufficiently secure for an ultimately successful confrontation with the coal miners to be engineered.

From that point onwards, it appeared that even though the public enterprise unions ostensibly had much to lose through privatisation, they were powerless to prevent it happening. Certainly, they resorted to strike action on a much smaller scale than might have been expected. On the whole, they appeared to take the pragmatic view that if privatisation was indeed inevitable, then their best policy was to protect their interests through negotiation rather than outright opposition.

It is difficult in practice to draw general conclusions concerning the experience of the unions post-privatisation. Clearly, the fluctuating state of the economy was itself a major factor explaining trends in pay and employment. Furthermore, in several cases such as British Steel, the rationalisation process largely took place before the companies were officially privatised, indicating that, even if many of the companies had remained in public ownership, they could not have expected to remain altogether immune from the pressures of the changing marketplace. This is particularly exemplified in the case of the coal industry which was cut back to fifteen pits while in public ownership.

The employment news during the 1990s has been generally, though not invariably, bad, and even companies such as BT have been forced by the pressure of competition to shed jobs in a manner which did not happen post-privatisation. Terms and conditions of employment have also been vulnerable to deterioration, but here again it is difficult to separate out the direct consequences of privatisation from factors such as the recent severe recession and changes in the competitive climate faced by privatised concerns which would have affected them irrespective of ownership.

18.6.4 Efficiency

In a free market, competitive pressures should, at least in theory, guarantee a high level of efficiency. Take those pressures away and 'organisational slack' may well appear. For example, both politicians and managers will seek out opportunities to promote their own interests. Furthermore, pressure groups such as trade unions will press for excessive manning and wage levels.

According to property rights theory, the fact that private companies are obliged to raise funds in the capital markets results in the acquisition of shareholders who will press for greater efficiency and hence profitability. Public enterprise, on the other hand, not merely has access to subsidised public funds but can use them wastefully, secure in the belief that the government will permit neither bankruptcy nor takeover by a private concern to occur. Under such circumstances, improved efficiency goes unrewarded and inefficiency goes unpunished. Privatisation is accordingly needed in order both to remove political interference and to introduce the disciplines of the private capital markets (see **Table 18.1**).

However, whether this hypothesis is correct is open to question. There is considerable evidence that countries such as Japan and Germany, where hostile takeovers have historically been rare, have until recently outperformed the UK and USA where such bids are commonplace. On the other hand, the experience of the 1990s so far indicates to the contrary.

Certainly, there is insufficient reason to suppose that privatisation is a necessary condition for improved efficiency since quite a number of concerns have been made significantly more efficient whilst remaining in public ownership. For this reason, many commentators prefer to emphasise the virtues of competition irrespective of ownership. Despite this, many companies have been privatised with monopoly powers intact in order to maximise their value to the Exchequer.

One obvious difficulty which must be acknowledged here is that efficiency is not a wholly clear-cut concept. Profitability may seen to offer a useful measure, but it is necessary to adjust for differing degrees of competition which presents serious practical difficulties. In any event, so much 'tidying up' of balance sheets took place prior to many privatisations that any form of 'before and after' financial comparisons are bound to be suspect.

Many studies have tried to overcome the measurement problems by concentrating upon costs and productivity (Curwen, 1986), but here the difficulty is not so much the ambiguity inherent in the concepts as the provision of valid comparisons, either between companies before and after privatisation or between equivalent private and public concerns. In the former case there is only a small sample set available, either within or outside the UK, and there are problems in adjusting for differing periods of time, macroeconomic conditions and any restructuring that preceded privatisation. In certain cases, there is also the need to adjust for a post-privatisation regulatory regime. Not surprisingly, the assessment has almost invariably been cautious, frequently emphasising that an element of enhanced competition post-privatisation is a necessary condition to ensure that there is an improvement in efficiency (Marsh, 1991).

Where public corporations have been compared with their nearest equivalent private counterparts the latter have come out on top more often than not. Nevertheless, few studies exist which have attempted to test the effect of ownership in a truly competitive environment. Where multi-sectoral and multi-country comparisons have been conducted, excluding sectors such as posts and railways, the results mostly support the hypothesis that in competitive environments, privately-owned industrial companies outperform their public counterparts both in terms of productivity and profitability, a conclusion that is unaffected by adjustments to allow for differences in size and industry structure (for comprehensive recent studies see Parker, 1994 and 1995).

■ 18.7 Deregulation and Regulation

□ 18.7.1 Deregulation

Deregulation, or liberalisation, simply means that an industry which has previously been able to protect itself from competition, either because it has been given a statutory monopoly or because it has been successful in erecting barriers to entry, is exposed to competitive forces through the government in effect changing the rules of the game. By so doing, the government hopes to make an industry behave much as it would have done had it been privatised, but without actual transfer from public to private sector needing to take place.

Liberalisation can operate in conjunction with asset transfers, provide a preliminary step on the route to denationalisation or provide an alternative to it. The government has never been altogether clear which option to adopt. The majority of economists favour the third, but the government has in practice opted primarily for the other two. In particular, this was evident during the first term of office when BT and coaching services were deregulated (Curwen, 1986, pp. 259–77).

Other early deregulation included the White Paper on *Buses* (Cmnd 9300, July 1984) which introduced competition into the market for short-distance bus journeys (Curwen, 1986, pp. 279–84). The Energy Act 1983 saw the introduction of more liberal rules regarding electricity generation. The basic proposal was that Electricity Boards would be encouraged to buy 'at a fair price' any surplus electricity generated by industrial concerns and those involved in combined heat and power schemes. The Oil and Gas (Enterprise) Act 1982 required British Gas to provide a common carrier facility to any other enterprises which wished to enter the gas supply business. Modest liberalisation also occurred without any subsequent transfer of ownership, as in the case of the Post Office (express mail and other services) and British Coal (opencast mining). In addition, Cable TV was deregulated in 1984 and various initiatives launched to reduce the regulatory burden on industry.

The most interesting recent developments have involved the energy industry where attempts are being made to rectify mistakes made at the time of privatisation. Thus, for example, the Regional Electricity Companies (RECs) lost their local monopolies in 1998 in one fell swoop, the year when full competition is due to be introduced into the domestic energy sector. What is especially interesting about this is that whereas the electricity industry was probably privatised in too fragmented a form, and is currently in the process of restructuring itself, as shown in **Table 18.3**, British Gas (BG) retained too much monopoly power and is having to be broken up. Since 1991, BG has been obliged by the competition authorities to surrender a large part of its industrial and commercial markets to new suppliers which are mostly subsidiaries of large oil companies. A trial run for the domestic market deregulation, due to

become fully operational in 1998 at the end of a staged introduction, is under way (see *Financial Times*, 14 May 1996, p. 8).

Since privatisation, the UK electricity and water companies have been characterised by substantial restructuring. Mergers and acquisitions have been of the horizontal, vertical and conglomerate type, including mergers between electricity and water companies and the foreign acquisition of UK utilities. (see **Table 18.3**).

☐ *18.7.2 Regulation*

We have noted that the favoured method for disposing of assets owned by the state was to sell them off to private individuals and institutions. In certain cases, the companies were released into a competitive environment which could be relied upon to force the companies to be efficient and to prevent them from earning excessive profits. In the majority of cases, however, the privatised companies retained part, and sometimes nearly all, of the monopoly powers which they possessed whilst in public ownership, and they clearly could not be left entirely free to exercise these monopoly powers to the detriment of consumers.

There were, in principle, a number of ways for dealing with this problem. For example, it was possible to use a system of taxes and subsidies both to induce additional production of what consumers wanted at acceptable prices and also to penalise them if they produced too little at excessive prices. A second alternative was to rely upon existing regulatory bodies. The Monopolies and Mergers Commission was the key body in this respect (Curwen, 1986, p. 285) but it was widely accepted that such an organisation did not have the resources to monitor individual concerns. It was accordingly felt that the answer was to create new specialist regulatory agencies, along the lines of the MMC, with specific responsibilities for monitoring prices, costs, profits and any other relevant factors in the privatised utilities.

The use of regulatory agencies has always been a preferred alternative to public ownership in the USA, and it was accordingly argued that the UK should copy their example. In principle, by

Table 18.3 *Restructuring Electricity and Water*

Bidder	Target	Bid Value	Date	MMC Referral
Trafalgar House	Northern Electric	£1.20 bn	Dec. 1994 Abandoned 4 Aug. 1995	No: 14 Feb. 1995
Lyonnaise des Eaux	Northumbrian Water	£823 mn	March 1995	Automatic. 26 July 1995: OK if prices cut.
Southern Company USA	South Western Electricity	£1.07 bn	July 1995	No: 31 Aug. 1995
Hanson	Eastern Group	£2.50 bn	July 1995	No: 31 Aug. 1995
ScottishPower	Manweb	£1.10 bn	July 1995	No: 31 Aug. 1995
PowerGen	Midlands Electricity	£1.95 bn	Sept. 1995	Yes: 23 Nov. 1995 April 1996: OK subject to conditions[1]
North West Water	Norweb	£1.83 bn	Sept. 1995[2]	No: 2 Nov. 1995
National Power	Southern Electric	£2.80 bn £2.50 bn	Oct. 1995 April 1996[3]	Yes: 23 Nov. 1995 April 1996: OK subject to conditions[1]
Welsh Water[4]	Swalec	£1.04 bn	Nov. 1995	No: 24 Jan. 1996
Central & South West USA	Seeboard	£1.60 bn	Nov. 1995	No: 8 Jan. 1996
Wessex Water	South West Water	£n/a	March 1996	Automatic[6]
Severn Trent	South West Water	£n/a	March 1996	Automatic[6]
General Public Utilities/Cinergy USA[5]	Midlands Electricity	£1.73 bn	May 1996	No: 6 July 1996
ScottishPower	Southern Water	£1.56 bn	May 1996	Automatic 19 July 1996: OK subject to conditions
Southern Electric	Southern Water	£1.60 bn	May 1996 Abandoned 20 June 1996	Automatic
CE Electric USA[7]	Northern Electric	£766 mn	October 1996	
Dominion Resources USA	East Midlands Electricity	£1.30 bn	November 1996	

Notes:
[1] However, the President of the Board of Trade blocked the bids on 24 April 1996.
[2] Agreed by shareholders and renamed United Utilities in October 1995.
[3] The original offer lapsed when it was referred. The new offer was different because of changed circumstances, but was held to be worth 8.6% more on a like-for-like basis.
[4] Renamed Hyder on 1 April 1996.
[5] Trading as Avon Energy.
[6] The President of the Board of Trade blocked both bids on 25 October 1996 in line with the MMC's recommendation.
[7] A partnership of CalEnergy and Peter Kiewit.

subjecting regulated concerns to a regime whereby they are obliged to submit, for example, proposals for price increases to the regulatory body, monopoly power is kept under control. In the context of pricing, it is common in the USA for a formula along the lines of 'yielding a fair and reasonable return taking into account the level of costs' to be introduced.

It may be argued that the regulatory bodies in the USA show up well in respect of protecting the rights of individuals, but they are open to criticism on a whole variety of grounds. The bulk of research indicates that regulation in the USA has been unnecessarily costly, inefficient and slow to operate. The regulation of prices has come in for particular criticism. For the most part, prices are fixed in relation to costs, with the obvious consequence that, since higher costs can be passed on in higher prices, there is very little incentive to be efficient and minimise costs. In addition, if the permitted rate of return on capital is fixed too high in relation to the cost of borrowing funds for investment, then the regulated concern will prefer to buy more and more machinery and substitute capital for labour on an undesirable scale.

Fierce criticism has also been directed at the tendency for regulated concerns to 'capture' their regulatory agencies in the sense that the latter become so involved in the affairs of the concerns that they end up protecting the concerns' interests against external attack, and even acting as their spokesmen. As a consequence, monopoly power can end up being jealously guarded by the regulatory agency in the face of potential new entry. Some critics even go so far as to argue that the agencies often did not need to be captured since it was effectively agreed between the politicians responsible for the regulatory agency and the regulated concern that the protection of the latter's monopoly powers would be in their mutual self-interest. Certainly, it is undeniable that regulatory agencies are unlikely to be left alone to get on with their job.

There is considerable dispute as to the success or otherwise of the relevant regulatory bodies in the UK (see, for example, the annual assessments by the IEA, most recently Beesley (Ed.), 1996). The key bodies are known respectively as OF-

TEL, OFGAS, OFWAT, OFFER, OFRail and the CAA. Most are overseen by a Director-General who is typically in post for several years before moving on, and who has, for better or worse, considerable personal power.

The central plank of the regulatory system is concerned with prices. The original price cap formula was devised by Professor Littlechild for BT, and subsequently adopted for gas, electricity and water. It took the form of *RPI minus X*, where RPI stands for the Retail Prices Index, the conventional measure of inflation, and X represents an efficiency factor. The value of X is set in advance for a period of at least one year.

There is no X factor for water. Instead, the water privatisation introduced a *k* factor, which was to be *added to* the RPI. In addition, the gas privatisation introduced a Y factor, where Y represents permissable cost pass-throughs which relate primarily to matters outside the control of the relevant company.

The principle underlying the X factor is to force a company to pass on to its customers some of the efficiency gains accruing from privatisation whilst simultaneously providing it with an incentive to reduce its costs. This arises because, if it can reduce its costs by more than the X factor which is pre-set, it gets to keep the difference for itself. Unfortunately, the principle is flawed when put into practice. The price formula must periodically be reviewed, and a new formula agreed between the company and its regulator subject to an appeal by the company to the MMC. However, each renegotiation is necessarily influenced by what the company has recently achieved, and if profitability appears to be excessive, the formula will almost certainly be tightened up, as for BT. The end result is very similar to rate of return regulation, which as noted above reduces the incentive to reduce costs in the first place.

Regulators are required to work towards their own abolition by creating conditions conducive to greater competition. It is hardly surprising that this is strongly resisted by the companies, and there are no prospects for abolition in the foreseeable future. As Vickers concludes (1991, p. 29), 'regulatory economics in Britain is only at the end of the beginning'.

■ *18.8* Privatising Choice

18.8.1 Introduction to Competitive Tendering

Competitive tendering, or contracting-out, is potentially a vast area covering the possible use of private contractors for a whole range of public sector services. Contracting-out is one element of the current government's privatisation policy. It is concerned with the central or local government **financing** of services which could be **supplied** by private contractors. By the late 1980s, it was the focus of major policy initiatives in local government, the NHS, defence and other parts of central government. Cleaning, catering, laundry, refuse collection, maintenance and security services are popular examples. With its emphasis on better value for money, government policy aims to extend the use of private contractors by public bodies where this will increase their economy, efficiency and effectiveness. The policy has recently been extended to, for example, prisons and prison escort services.

Contracting-out can be viewed as an aspect of public procurement policy since it involves the public sector purchasing goods and services from private firms. As such, the debate about contracting-out is not new. For example, within the NHS, there is a tradition of buying pharmaceutical products, high-technology medical equipment and buildings from private firms. Similarly, within defence there is a long tradition of buying weapons and equipment from private firms.

Consideration now needs to be given to the basic policy problem: how do public bodies such as NHS hospitals assess the efficiency of their direct labour departments and in-house services? The starting point is that direct labour departments are usually monopoly suppliers of services protected from possible public and private sector rivals. In the absence of competition from rival departments and from private contractors, there are no alternative sources of information and no alternative cost yardsticks to assess the efficiency of a public agency. Here, efficiency is defined to embrace two aspects. In the first place, it is con-

cerned with the lowest-cost method of supplying a **given** quantity and quality of service. Secondly, it is also concerned with the lowest-cost method of supplying **different** levels of service. This second aspect of efficiency enables a local authority or hospital to determine whether its existing level of service is worthwhile. For example, a lower level of service might be so much cheaper that the extra cost of the existing provision is deemed not to be worthwhile.

Contracting-out is offered as a solution to the problem of public sector monopolies which are criticised as inefficient bureaucracies responding to the wishes of producer groups rather than consumers. To its supporters, competitive tendering, or even the threat of rivalry (contestability) means improved efficiency and cost savings. It allows public procurement agents to recontract with different suppliers and for different levels of service. Competition between rival suppliers leads to the introduction of new ideas, the latest management techniques and modern equipment, thereby resulting in major changes in established and traditional methods of working. New equipment might replace labour; manning levels can be reassessed; and part-time workers might replace full-timers. Successful firms in a competition are also subject to the incentives and penalties of a fixed price contract so that there is no open-ended financial commitment as can arise with in-house units.

The opponents of contracting-out claim that it leads to a poor quality and unreliable service. Examples are given of dirty streets, schools and hospital wards, and of penalty clauses being imposed on contractors. Proposals for privately-managed prisons have been condemned because of fears of lower standards and conditions in prisons, with discipline determined by profit-conscious managers with incentive to 'encourage' returners. Private contractors are also believed to be less reliable than in-house units. For example, it is suggested that they are less able to respond to emergencies; they are liable to default and bankruptcy; and the award of a contract to a private firm leads to industrial relations problems and strikes. On the issue of cost savings, critics claim that these are short-lived. Low bids can be used to buy into an attractive new contract and eliminate the in-house capacity, so that the public authority loses its bargaining power. As a result, it becomes dependent on a private monopoly which, in the long run, means higher prices, a lack of dynamism and a poor quality service. Competitive tendering involves substantial transaction costs which are often ignored by the supporters of contracting-out. Moreover, critics claim that any cost savings from contracting-out are achieved at the expense of the poorly-paid members of society, so that the policy cannot avoid equity issues and debates about the distribution of income. The various arguments are summarised in **Table 18.4**.

The arguments for and against provide extensive opportunities for critical analysis and evaluation. Some of the arguments obviously represent special pleading by those interest groups most likely to gain or lose from the policy. However, many of the arguments for and against contracting-out can be resolved by empirical testing. UK studies suggest, for a given level of service, potential annual cost savings of some 25 per cent over a range of hospital and local authority activities and of 20 per cent for refuse collection. Similarly, a study of Australian cleaning contracts confirmed price reductions of some 20 per cent due to competitive tendering with either no effect on quality or occasionally an improvement in quality. Whilst private contractors require longer hours, shorter holidays and withdraw sickness benefits and pension rights, most of the cost savings from contracting-out reflect productivity improvements (see, for example, Domberger *et al.*, 1996; Hartley and Huby, 1985; Szymanski and Wilkins, 1993).

If society wants improved efficiency, then privatisation and contracting-out are not sufficient: competition is also required. However, competitive tendering is likely to be associated with contractors lobbying for public sector business and for entry barriers to protect their existing markets and profits. Inevitably, there will be opposition from established interest groups likely to lose from the policy. Opponents of the policy can impose delays by insisting upon discussions with all interested parties; the timing of any change can be inappropriate; administrative time might be unavailable to prepare the tender documents and to undertake the necessary comparative studies, especially in an era of manpower cuts; and an authority might be reluctant to face a confrontation with the trade unions leading to major industrial relations problems. There is a more fundamental worry. With competitive tendering, choices about the quantity and quality of service provision are ultimately made by elected representatives whose preferences are unlikely to reflect the diversity of preferences of large numbers of individual consumers in properly functioning markets.

Table 18.4   *Contracting-out: The Arguments*

The Case For Contracting-out	*The Case Against Contracting-out*
1. Public sector in-house monopolies are inefficient bureaucracies	1. Private contractors offer a poor quality and unreliable service
2. Competition allows regular recontracting by public procurement agents	2. Private contractors are liable to default, bankruptcy, and are less able to respond to emergencies
3. Competition leads to new ideas, modern equipment and changes in traditional methods of working	3. Contractors use low bids to buy into attractive contracts and eliminate the in-house capacity so that public authority becomes dependent on a private monopoly
4. Successful firms in competition are subject to incentives and penalties of a fixed price contract	4. Private contractors achieve cost savings by cutting jobs, reducing wages and worsening working conditions

18.8.2 Competitive Tendering in the Local Authorities

Competitive tendering in the local authorities dates back over a decade. However, it was initially of little significance, and progress awaited the passing of the Local Government Act 1988 (Carnaghan and Bracewell-Milnes, 1993, pp. 27–8). This required all tiers of local government to adopt competitive tendering for a wide range of services previously supplied by monopoly Direct Service Organisations (DSOs).

The 1988 Act was concerned with refuse collection, building cleaning, street cleaning, grounds maintenance, schools and welfare catering, sports and leisure management and vehicle maintenance. The Act applied to contracts above a specified value, fixed their length and the minimum number of tenders to be achieved, and sought to outlaw anti-competitive practices. It did not forbid the use of DSOs as such, but required them to be operated commercially.

The Local Government Act 1992 extended compulsory competitive tendering (CCT) to local authority white-collar services, operative in principle as from April 1994. For example, CCT for construction-related and legal services commenced in October 1995 and for housing management in April 1996. A complicating factor is the existence, since 1 July 1993, of the European Union public procurement directives which oblige local authorities to put out their largest contracts to tender across the Union (Carnaghan and Bracewell-Milnes, 1993 p. 38).

The eventual scale of competitive tendering is accordingly hard to estimate (for recent amendments see *Municipal Journal*, 24 May 1996, p. 15 – but note that the Labour Party is committed to reform). The private sector has had variable success in winning contracts. Many local authorities have yet to award a single contract to a private company, but those that have offered refuse-collecting contracts have awarded them to private companies in the great majority of cases although the proportion is much lower for all other services (see, for example, *Municipal Journal*, 1994, pp. 115, 143, 148).

Just how big a saving has been achieved is hotly disputed, although there can be no doubt that some savings have been forthcoming, and at the very least DSOs have been obliged to examine their working practices if only to hold at bay the pressure for privatisation (Carnaghan and Bracewell-Milnes, 1993, Chapter 4).

18.8.3 Competitive Tendering in the NHS

Compulsory competitive tendering in the NHS was introduced in 1983, and was therefore a fairly early Thatcherite initiative (Carnaghan and Bracewell-Milnes, 1993, pp. 116–25). As such, it was inevitably somewhat speculative, and in practice, as noted by the National Audit Office, it has not been a conspicuous success. The explanation for this can be found, in particular, in the discretion allowed to those responsible for the contracts, since they were enabled, for example, to reject low private sector bids on the grounds that an acceptable quality of provision could not be delivered at the tendered price.

They were also in a position to discourage private contractors, for example by the insertion of stiff penalty clauses in contracts. Furthermore, the Department of Health has shown little inclination to insist upon a re-tender, leaving contractors free to bend the rules. Ironically, the change in the law resulted in a reduction in the number of laundry service contracts being awarded externally, and hospital canteens effectively remain a no-go area for private contractors. In any event, where private contractors have won tenders, they have usually taken on the existing workforce, albeit on less-attractive terms than previously. Hence, although savings have been made (Parker and Hartley, 1990), they have undoubtedly been more modest than was anticipated a decade ago.

18.8.4 Market-testing

Despite the widespread introduction of competitive tendering into local authority circles, its central government equivalent, 'market-testing', met with strong resistance in the corridors of White-hall. It had its origins in the *Competing for Quality* document issued in November 1991. Within a year, a White Paper had been issued by William Waldegrave which contained a hugely ambitious masterplan. Instead of the original £25 million of services to be market-tested in 1992, some £1.5 billion were to be market-tested in 1993. Unfortunately, this plan took insufficient account both of the administrative implications of such a figure and of the absence of the wholehearted support of the affected parties.

Projected savings are claimed to be of the order of 25 per cent. Given that the savings achieved in respect of local authority tendering are typically in the 5 to 10 per cent range, this seems a mite optimistic. Certainly, given the labour-intensive nature of most of the services identified for market-testing, such savings can only be forthcoming through redundancies, thereby guaranteeing the wholehearted opposition of most of the civil service.

The enhanced programme clearly failed to elicit the desired response since, in June 1993, the Prime Minister was called upon to warn a number of Departments about their slow progress. At the time, the DTI, the Department for Education, the Scottish Office and the Department of Transport had failed to complete a single exercise. When the deadline was reached at the end of September 1993, William Waldegrave was obliged to admit that some £800 million of the overall £1.5 billion programme was still outstanding. Furthermore, savings were running at only 14 per cent of the value of the work compared to the 25 per cent predicted.

Arguably the most revealing statistic was that in-house teams had won 57 per cent of the bids by value, and 91 of the 150 contracts awarded where there was a competition between the existing staff and outside contractors. As was clearly noted, no private contractor had spare skilled personnel, and it was invariably necessary to transfer most of the existing workforce to the new contractor. These would often be unco-operative because there would be the expectation of subsequent redundancies.

A complicating factor in all cases of competitive tendering is the European Community *Acquired Rights Directive* of 1977. This protects workers' pay and conditions when they change employers, and has been translated into the *Transfer of Undertakings (Protection of Employment) Regulations* 1981 under UK national law. The government originally claimed that the TUPE regulations applied only to transfers within the private sector. However, it has been forced to accept that the European Court of Justice has, through recent rulings in cases such as Dr Sophie Redmond Stichting vs Bartol (1992) and Rask vs ISS Kantineservice (1993), extended the scope of TUPE to cover contracting-out of many, though by no means all, public services. This led the government to amend TUPE in the Trade Union Reform and Employment Rights Act 1993.

It is evident that hopes of major savings through market-testing are likely to be confounded if they are unavailable in respect of labour costs, and this has undoubtedly influenced the attitude of prospective private sector contractors. At one point, it also appeared to be the case that it would not be possible to offer less favourable pension rights when employees were transferred, in accordance with the provisions of the Employment Protection (Consolidation) Act 1978, effectively cutting off a further source of savings. However, a test case at the Employment Appeal Tribunal in July 1993 established that pensions were not covered by the Acquired Rights Directive.

☐ *18.8.5 Executive Agencies*

In the meantime, the reshaping of the civil service proceeds apace. In the quest to introduce the entrepreneurial spirit into the corridors of power, the *Next Steps* initiative was introduced in 1988 in order to create quasi-autonomous executive agencies. The Home Civil Service agencies (109 at end-1995), in conjunction with the equivalent bodies within Customs and Excise (23 at end-1995) and the Inland Revenue (27 at end-1995), will eventually employ 80 per cent of all civil servants compared to the 67 per cent actually employed at end-1995 (Cm 3164).

Agencies, run by Chief Executives, are not fully autonomous since the Treasury and spending departments are understandably reluctant to release their control over such a significant slab of public spending. Civil servants are themselves unhappy about the employment implications of agencies, in particular about the limitations which these may impose upon their careers.

Agencies have responsibilities, aims and objectives set out in a framework document. Key performance targets are set annually by Ministers and performances against these targets are published. Agencies are heavily involved in market-testing activities. Indeed, some have become so commercially-minded that they operate like private sector concerns. At the end of 1993, the government announced that it intended to privatise as many as possible of the agencies. The DVOIT (vehicle licensing), HMSO and AEA Technology have been sold off, and plans are well advanced to dispose of, among others, ADAS, and the Occupational Health and Safety Agency. Potential privatisation candidates are generally identified during the course of the obligatory five-yearly reviews.

18.8.6 User Charges

User charges have long been familiar to the general public in the form of prescription charges which have been in continuous use since 1968. Resistance to health service charges has always been strong, so it is unsurprising that the Conservative government preferred to switch to softer, but less remunerative alternatives. Some alternatives involved charges to the public, such as entry fees to museums and historical sites, and to private concerns for weather forecasts and agricultural testing. Although demand has been discouraged, it has stood up better than might have been expected and the government has been pleased with the amount of revenue raised.

The agency programme has involved the sale of a wide array of services, and some agencies such as the Ordnance Survey have become largely self-financing. Many services are sold by one agency to another via a system of internal markets. Where an agency is fully self-financing, it can be converted into a trading fund similar to the Royal Mint before being subject to a privatisation feasibility study.

18.8.7 Public/Private Co-operative Ventures

Shortly after its election in 1979 the government pondered the thorny question as to how to encourage capital investment without recourse to public expenditure. Its solution was the introduction of the *Ryrie rules* which contained a 'non-additionality' principle such that private funding would replace, rather than be additional to, public spending. Unfortunately, it was also determined that the price tendered by private concerns would have to undercut that fixed by public sector organisations, even though the latter had access to finance at below- market level interest rates. As a result very little was achieved.

With the railways and road building programme remaining a severe drain on public investment funds, the Treasury was obliged to scrap the Ryrie rules in 1989, and this was shortly followed by a Department of Transport document entitled 'New Roads by New Means' which authorised private sector involvement in toll roads.

The 1992 Autumn Statement went further in stating that where private concerns were responsible for government-approved projects and were able to recoup the cost through charges at the point of use, the Treasury would not apply a value-for-money test against a theoretical public sector alternative. In the Autumn Statement, the then government asserted that in principle it was happy to invite private sector participation in joint ventures provided there was a 'sensible' sharing of risks. What was proposed was that the government would specify its contribution in terms of money and risk and invite participation via open competition. However, the private sector would have to accept the risks involved (see *Financial Times Survey*, 10 November 1995, p. 30) yet these were often difficult to assess, especially where public funding had previously been the norm, so private concerns were likely to be hesitant.

In September 1993, Chancellor Clarke listed 78 joint projects under what is known as the **Private Finance Initiative** (PFI). However, 43 of these were merely proposals. Among the most important were the Heathrow express rail link, the Paddington–Liverpool St Cross Rail link and the modernisation of the West Coast railway line. However, of the £5 billion total for PFI projects listed at the end of 1995 (*ibid.*, p. 29), over half was accounted for by the Channel Tunnel rail link.

The government's line on risk is that it must be borne by the private sector but that, provided the project offers value for money, it has no objection to a high rate of profit being earned. Unfortunately, voters may object to, for example, sizeable bridge or road tolls which end up in the coffers of private concerns. In practice, the private sector has not yet undertaken any significant partnership projects in the absence either of a subsidy or the public sector accepting some element of risk.

□ *18.8.8 The Citizen's Charter*

In July 1991, the government published a White Paper entitled *The Citizen's Charter* (Cm 1599). It was described as 'the most comprehensive programme ever to raise quality, increase choice, secure better value and extend accountability. It will ensure that quality of service to the public and the new pride it will give to those who work in the public services will be a central theme of government policy for the 1990s.'

In excess of 80 proposals were put forward for improving the quality of public services. Some involved privatisation, as in the case of British Rail, while others were concerned with recognising achievement, as in the case of the award of a chartermark. At the heart of the White Paper lay the promise that the public should not merely expect to be kept informed about the kind of service to which they were entitled, but also to be provided with the means to take remedial

action should that service not be of an acceptable quality.

There are currently 40 main Charters, but the Charter programme will essentially be seen either as success or failure depending upon how it deals with the treatment of parents and schools, rail passengers and NHS patients. For example, the Parent's Charter is concerned with the provision of information on the performance of individual pupils and schools. In November 1992, the initial GCSE exam league tables were published, and were immediately criticised both for inaccuracy and for failing to take account of different pupil capabilities when entering different schools. A revised Charter was published in 1994 (see Cm 2970, pp. 4–6).

Rail passengers have most to gain directly from the Passenger's Charter since British Rail is obliged to pay compensation where trains fail to meet reliability and punctuality targets. On the other hand, the targets are adjusted to take account of the previous record on a given line, they can be 'captured' by the suppliers of the services, and compensation is not particularly generous when measured against the potential loss which might arise when a journey is seriously delayed (*ibid.*, pp. 14–15).

The Patient's Charter (revised in January 1995) promised, in particular, that no one should have to wait more than two years for treatment once they were on a hospital waiting list. In March 1991, there were in excess of 50 000 such patients, but these no longer remained a year later (*ibid.*, pp. 7–10). This was countered by the criticism that the time was only recorded after entering a list, so it could be reduced by delays in so doing, and that all that had happened was an expansion of the queue waiting between one and two years. On the other hand, things had improved somewhat compared to previously.

The first report on the Charter in November 1992 claimed that roughly 90 per cent of the targets set in July 1991 either had been met or were on course to be met, with British Rail as the main source of failures. The second report, in March 1994, listed more than one hundred new commitments to raise service standards, among them compensation for council tenants who improve their homes, and yet more were listed in 1995 (Cm 2970). Nevertheless, the Charter programme has been widely criticised on the grounds that, for example, many charters either specify no standards at all or standards that are so vague that they leave customers in the dark; with most services there is no financial compensation when things go wrong; and few charters are audited independently.

■ *18.9* Conclusions

This chapter has provided little more than an overview of the UK privatisation programme; to cover it in any detail would require a book. The asset sales which initiated the programme have now been copied throughout both the developed and developing world. A major transfer of economic activity from the public to the private sector has undoubtedly been successfully executed in the UK, although commentators are apt to forget the extensive problems that beset many disposals and which have recurred elsewhere.

It is particularly worthy of note that the assumption that major companies/industries can simply be transferred wholesale into private hands without any subsequent governmental control has for the most part proven to be illusory. Deregulation has dragged regulation in its wake to such an extent that it is arguable whether privatised industries are more or less subject to central control post-privatisation.

For the most part, the evidence indicates that performance has improved post-privatisation, although this has by no means been an invariable rule. On the other hand, this can sometimes be ascribed to the policies pursued pre-privatisation as the companies were made ready for sale.

There have also been extensive problems in switching into the 'privatising choice' phase of the programme. Perhaps more importantly, the general public has remained largely ignorant of what is happening, or holds negative views in relation to, for example, the Citizen's Charter. It is accordingly unlikely that the Conservative government will be remembered for privatising

choice, although other countries are showing considerable interest in following the path being beaten out in the UK.

Bibliography

Beesley, M. (Ed.) (1996) *Regulating Utilities: A Time for Change?* (London: IEA).

Bishop, M. and J. Kay (1988) *Does Privatization Work?* (London Business School).

Carnaghan, R. and B. Bracewell-Milnes (1993) *Testing the Market: Competitive Tendering for Government Services in Britain and Abroad.* Research Monograph 49 (London: IEA).

Chancellor of the Exchequer (1996) *Public Expenditure: Statistical Analyses 1996–97*, Cm 3201 (London: HMSO).

Curwen. P. (1986) *Public Enterprise* (Brighton: Wheatsheaf).

Curwen, P. (1994a) 'Directors' Pay in Privatized Companies', *Public Money and Management*, 14 (1).

Curwen, P. (1994b) *Privatization in the UK – The Facts and Figures* (London: Ernst & Young).

Domberger, S. *et al.* (1996) 'The Determinants of Price and Quality in Competitively-Tendered Contracts', *Economic Journal*, 105 (433) pp. 1454–70.

Dunsire, A. (1990) 'The Public/Private Debate: Some United Kingdom Evidence', *International Review of Administrative Sciences*, 56 (1) pp.63–78.

Dunsire, A., K. Hartley, D. Parker and B. Dimitriou (1988) 'Organizational Status and Performance', *Public Administration* (Winter) pp. 343–58.

Foster, C. (1993) *Privatisation, Public Ownership and the Regulation of Natural Monopoly* (Oxford: Blackwell).

Graham, C. and T. Prosser (1991) *Privatising Public Enterprises: Constitutions, the State and Regulation in Comparative Perspective* (Oxford: OUP).

Hartley, K. and M. Huby (1985) 'Contracting-out in Health and Local Authorities', *Public Money* (September) pp. 23–6.

Hartley, K., D. Parker and S. Martin (1991) 'Organisational Status, Ownership and Productivity', *Fiscal Studies*, 12 (2) pp. 46–60.

Holmes, D. and P. Curwen (1995) 'Returns to Small Shareholders from Privatization – Reprise', *The Review of Policy Issues*, 1 (3) pp. 53–60.

Marsh, D. (1991) 'Privatisation Under Mrs Thatcher. A Review of the Literature', *Public Administration*, 69 (4) pp. 459–80.

Parker, D. (1990) 'The 1988 Local Government Act and Compulsory Competitive Tendering', *Urban Studies*, 27 (5) pp. 653–68.

Parker, D. (1991) 'Privatisation Ten Years On: A Critical Analysis of its Rationale and Results', *Economics*, XXVII (4) pp. 155–63.

Parker, D. (1994) 'Privatisation and Business Restructuring: Change and Continuity in the Privatised Industries', *The Review of Policy Issues*, 1 (2) pp. 3–28.

Parker, D. (1995) 'The Impact of UK Privatisation on Labour and total Factor Productivity', *Scottish Journal of Political Economy*, 42 (2) pp. 201–20.

Parker, D. and K. Hartley (1990) 'Competitive Tendering: Issues and Evidence', *Public Money and Management* (Autumn) pp. 9–16.

Parker, D. and K. Hartley (1991) 'Organisational Status and Performance: the Effects on Employment', *Applied Economics*, 23 (2) pp.403–416.

Prosser, T. (1986) *Nationalised Industries and Public Control: Legal, Constitutional and Political Issues* (Oxford: Blackwell).

Szymanski, S. and S. Wilkins (1993) 'Cheap Rubbish? Competitive Tendering and Contracting-Out in Refuse Collection – 1981–1988', *Fiscal Studies*, 14 (3) pp. 109–30.

Thompson, S., M. Wright and K. Robbie (1990) 'Management Buy-Outs From the Public Sector: Ownership Form and Incentive Issues', *Fiscal Studies*, 11 (3) pp. 71–88.

Uttley, M. and N. Hooper (1992) 'The Political Economy of Competitive Tendering', in T. Clarke and C. Pitelis (eds) *The Political Economy of Privatization* (London: Routledge).

Vickers, J. (1991) 'Government Regulatory Policy', *Oxford Review of Economic Policy*, 7 (3) pp. 39–62.

Vickers, J. and G. Yarrow (1988) *Privatisation: An Economic Analysis* (Boston: MIT Press).

Walsh, K. (1995) *Public Services and Market Mechanisms* (London: Macmillan Press).

Wright, M. and T. Buck (1992) 'Privatisation Under Mrs Thatcher: An Extension to the Debate', *Public Administration*, 70 (2) pp. 287–91.

The Citizen's Charter: The Facts and Figures. Cm 2970, September 1995 (London: HMSO).

Next Steps: Agencies in Government – Review 1995. Cm 3164, February 1996 (London: HMSO).

Public Expenditure. Statistical Supplement to the Financial Statement and Budget Report 1995–96. Cm 2821, February 1995 (London: HMSO).

The Government's Guide to Market Testing. August 1993 (London: HMSO)

The Strategic Management of Agencies – Full Report of Case Studies. September 1995 (London: HMSO).

Chapter 19

Industry and Policy III: Subsidies, Technology and Government Purchasing

Keith Hartley and Nick Hooper

■ 19.1 Introduction

Competition and privatisation are not the only instruments of industrial policy. Governments have available a range of other instruments which can affect the performance of firms and industries. These include subsidies which can also be used as instruments of regional and technology policy and as a means of correcting for beneficial externalities (a source of market failure). The UK Department of Trade and Industry (DTI) is responsible for policy towards firms, industries, regions, science and technology, with a budget of £3,275 million in 1995–96. Government is also a major buyer of goods and services and its purchasing or procurement policy can also affect industry performance. This chapter shows how economists analyse this range of policy instruments, starting with subsidy policy.

■ 19.2 Subsidy Policy

□ 19.2.1 A Classification System

At their simplest, subsidies are payments by government to producers which are designed to reduce prices. Such a definition can be modified to allow for payments to firms and industries to ensure their survival or to prevent contraction. More generally, subsidies are a means of affecting the **allocation and use of resources** in the economy, thereby interfering in the operation of markets. The issue is, however, whether such interference is desirable.

Over time, governments in the UK have offered various subsidies to firms, industries, regions and factors of production. Subsidies have been used to achieve specific policy objectives such as maintaining or increasing employment, assisting the balance of payments through export promotion and import-saving and encouraging growth through supporting high technology. At times, the range of industrial subsidies has been bewildering, and so extensive that questions have arisen as to whether there are any economic activities in the UK which should not qualify for a subsidy!

As a starting point in analysing subsidies, a classification system is required. Subsidies can be classified in at least three related ways, namely, general or specific, applying a production function approach or by using a location dimension.

General and Specific Types

General schemes offer subsidies to all firms satisfying certain conditions which might relate to investment, location, employment, size of firm or type of activity (for example agriculture, manufacturing or tourism). General schemes have been the traditional method of subsidising UK industry. They are automatic and aim to influence industry decisions and hence the operation of markets without involving substantial transaction costs. In contrast, specific or discretionary schemes are designed for an individual firm or project with subsidies being used to prevent bankruptcy and plant closure or to promote reorganisation, re-equipment and restructuring. Alternatively, specific subsidies might be offered for the development of a new high technology project such as a supersonic airliner or a new generation of computer. In principle, specific schemes aim at fine tuning by setting the subsidy at the minimum level required to influence a firm's decisions. However, this approach involves substantial transaction costs. It requires detailed information about a firm's costs and its efficiency, and it assumes that civil servants will be motivated to negotiate the minimum subsidy. Further costs will be incurred in bargaining, monitoring and policing. Critics claim that public servants may be influenced in their decisions by the prospect of employment in industry or that specific subsidies result in an undesirable cosiness between civil servants and the firms with which they

negotiate. The example of the abandoned De Lorean sports car project shows the potential costs to the taxpayer of unsuccessful subsidies and the opportunities for possible fraud and misuse of public funds.

The Production Function Approach

A distinction can be made between subsidies for outputs and those for factor inputs. Farmers, for example, receive output subsidies. Factor inputs can also be subsidised, the aim being to encourage and increase the use of relatively cheap (subsidised) factors. Input subsidies embrace capital, labour and technology. Examples include incentives to invest in new plant and machinery, to substitute labour for capital and to increase research and development.

The Geographic or Location Dimension

Subsidies in their general and specific forms, for inputs and outputs, can be tied to specially designated areas of the country embracing development areas, intermediate areas, enterprise zones, free ports and inner cities.

During the 1960s and 1970s, UK expenditure on subsidies increased substantially from under 2 per cent of GDP at market prices and roughly 4 per cent of government expenditure in 1965 to corresponding figures of almost 4 per cent and roughly 7–8 per cent, respectively in 1975. The Conservative government post-1979 took a different attitude towards a general and massive subsidy policy, as reflected in the declining trend in government subsidies between 1987 and 1993. As a further indication of that government's industrial policy, the annual level of real spending by the DTI declined substantially during the late 1980s, whilst privatisation proceeds were much greater than the DTI's budget. In view of the major contrasts between the 1970s and 1980s, questions have to be asked about the economic logic of UK subsidy policy.

19.2.2 Economic Theory and Subsidies

A **market failure approach** suggests that subsidies are required whenever there are substantial and beneficial externalities or social benefits. Alternatively, subsidies might be required to cover the **losses associated with marginal cost pricing** applied to a decreasing cost industry. Whilst a number of UK firms and nationalised industries have received subsidies to reduce losses and to prevent closure, usually these have not been associated with marginal cost pricing and decreasing costs. Instead, subsidies have more often been justified on grounds of social benefits. The argument is that private markets, if left to themselves, will provide too little of some socially desirable activities and subsidies are required to correct this market failure. Typically, governments have used the social benefits argument to justify subsidies to protect jobs, to promote high technology and to support the balance of payments, all of which are deemed to be in the national or public interest. Economists need to assess these arguments critically, subjecting them to economic analysis and empirical evidence.

The methodology of economic policy can be applied to subsidy policy, although critics might claim that it is a counsel of perfection. The objectives of policy have to be clearly stated. The causes of the policy problem have to be identified, and it needs to be shown that subsidies are the most appropriate and efficient solution from the available alternatives. For example, with regional policy, the aim might be to increase employment in the high-unemployment areas of the country. However, this might conflict with the objective of promoting a reallocation of resources from declining to expanding regions and encouraging firms to locate in their most efficient areas. Questions then arise about the causes of local unemployment. Is it, for example, due to wages failing to reflect local labour market conditions; do firms elsewhere lack information about local labour supplies; are there infrastructure deficiencies which raise the costs to firms locating in the area; is the housing market impairing labour mobility; or is the capital market failing to finance worthwhile human investments in mobility and training? From this analysis of causes, it does not follow that subsidies to firms in high unemployment areas are the only, or even the most appropriate and efficient solution.

19.2.3 State Aid

Almost every day, the media report some dispute or other concerning the award of state aid somewhere in the EU. This is hardly surprising since a firm or industry which operates with little or no state aid is bound to resent any award of state aid to its competitors – a particular problem for the UK where privatised companies are largely left to fend for themselves while their competitors, as for example in the case of airlines and steel, are kept from bankruptcy only by virtue of subsidies.

Article 92 of the Treaty of Rome bans 'any aid granted by a member state or through resources in any form whatsoever which distorts or threatens to distort competition by favouring certain undertakings or the production of certain goods'. However, aid can be exempted from this ban where it is:

- of a social character and given to individuals in a non-discriminatory manner;
- related to national disasters;
- concerned with German unification.

And it may be acceptable where it is related to specific activities or areas and where the EU as a whole can be seen to benefit.

The definition of subsidies as used by the EU (see CEC, 1991, p. 13) is:

all forms of specific transfers from the government sector which directly or indirectly benefit enterprises, for which the government receives no equivalent compensation in return and which are granted with the purpose of changing market outcomes.

Not all subsidies fall within the compass of the EU. Those that do are known as **State aids**, and include direct transfers to firms; grants; credit on preferential terms; tax concessions; equity investments which would not be undertaken by a commercial investor; provision of public goods or services at below market prices; and public procurement at above market prices. They may be received directly by the party to be assisted or indirectly via either higher output prices or lower input prices generated via subsidies to other economic actors. They may be paid to producers or to consumers; linked to gross output, intermediate inputs or primary inputs; and directed at traded or non-traded goods.

Table 12.2 (see **p. 303**) details state aid to the manufacturing sector during 1988–90 and 1990–1992 (the latest years available and hence confined to the EU 12) using three different measures. During the period 1988–90 some 40 per cent of EU aid went to manufacturing, with total expenditure showing a clear downwards trend in real terms during the subsequent two-year period. The modest reduction in terms of the percentage of value added nevertheless represented a significantly lower figure compared to the mid-1980s.

Leaving aside the particular problems of the old East Germany, it is evident that the main problems in relation to value added are to be found in Greece, Italy, Belgium and Portugal, although the latter shows up much better in terms of aid per person employed. The UK was the best performer in terms of value added both in 1988–90 and 1990–92, although Spain improved considerably to run it close in the latter period, with the position reversed in terms of aid per person employed.

Despite its size, the UK's total aid bill in 1990–92 amounted to roughly half that of France, a third that of West Germany and a quarter that of Italy. These three countries (together with East Germany) accounted for nearly 80 per cent of total EU aid in 1990–92 and obviously contributed to the difficulties discussed previously with achieving sufficient convergence to make EMU a reality. In 1990–92, 89 per cent of UK state aid to manufacturing took the form of grants, the highest figure in the EU. Grants are easy to legislate for and very flexible, but it is notable that the UK provided only 6 per cent of aid in the form of tax reductions compared to 37 per cent in Germany.

Table 19.1 classifies state aid, somewhat arbitrarily, in terms of sector and function. It shows that roughly 40 per cent of aid went on horizontal objectives in 1990–92, roughly 10 per cent on aid to specific sectors and 50 per cent on regional aid. Whereas the UK matched this profile closely in 1988–90, it was relatively heavy on sectoral aid during 1990–92 and relatively light on regional aid. The UK provided a relatively large share of its aid to SMEs and for trade/export. In practice, as can be seen, there was tremendous variability between EU states, so the UK pattern was not particularly atypical.

19.2.4 Regional and Regeneration Policy

Markets are changing continuously and the results of change are reflected in the expansion and decline of different regions in the UK. Traditionally, high unemployment areas in northern England, Scotland, Wales and Northern Ireland were associated with the decline of the UK's traditional smokestack industries such as coal, shipbuilding, steel and textiles. Sunrise industries such as electronics have developed elsewhere. However, the recession of the early 1990s signalled a change in the traditional north-south differential in regional unemployment rates, with the South-East and especially East Sussex, Kent and Greater London experiencing substantial increases in unemployment. Also, in the 1990s, cuts in defence budgets meant that UK and other EU regions dependent on defence industries and military bases were vulnerable to job losses (such as Barrow and Rosyth). Interestingly, however, the last major statement by any government on regional policy was contained in a White Paper of 1983 (Cmnd 9111 – *Regional Industrial Development*).

The regional policy problem arises because markets do not adjust instantly, and because private markets do not consider the social costs and benefits of their activities (externalities). Successive UK governments have thus intervened to correct regional imbalances by seeking to reduce the regional differentials in unemployment rates. However, problems have arisen because the

Table 19.1 State Aid to the Manufacturing Sector, 1990–92: Breakdown of Aid According to Sector and Function %

Sectors/Function	B	DK	D	GR	E	F	IRL	I	L	NL	P	UK	EUR 12
Horizontal Objectives	82	68	21	64	50	71	31	30	34	72	34	45	38
Research and Development	13	31	9	1	17	27	4	3	12	26	3	7	10
Environment	0	15	1	0	3	0	0	0	0	5	0	1	1
S.M.E.	26	1	4	12	10	11	7	9	16	20	1	15	9
Trade/Export	16	8	1	15	1	30	20	9	0	2	0	15	9
Economisation of Energy	7	11	2	0	2	1	0	3	0	14	1	0	2
General Investment	12	0	0	3	6	1	0	2	5	3	18	6	2
Other Objectives	7	2	4	32	10	0	0	5	0	2	10	0	4
Particular Sectors	2	30	8	6	34	18	0	8	0	10	55	25	12
Shipbuilding	1	24	2	0	12	1	0	1	0	4	37	2	2
Other Sectors	1	6	6	6	22	16	0	7	0	6	19	23	9
Regional Objectives	16	2	72	30	16	11	69	62	66	18	11	30	50
Regions under 92(3)c	16	2	5	0	3	7	0	4	66	18	0	20	6
Regions under 92(3)a	0	0	36	30	14	5	69	58	0	0	11	10	43
Berlin/Zonenrand			31										
TOTAL	100	100	100	100	100	100	100	100	100	100	100	100	100

Source: CEC (1995) Table 6.

objectives of regional policy have often been social and political rather than economic. Budget-conscious government Departments can offer schemes to solve regional unemployment which will be supported by producers likely to benefit and by governments attracted by the likely favourable effects on votes.

In England, regional policy is delivered primarily through ten Government Offices in the Regions (otherwise known as Integrated Regional Offices) which coordinate various government Departments and work with local Training and Enterprise Councils, business and other local partners. The IROs aim to maximise the competitiveness, prosperity and quality of life in the regions. In 1996, the Conservative government's main regional policy instrument administered by the DTI was **Regional Selective Assistance** (RSA – for a full analysis see House of Commons Trade and Industry Committee, 1995, pp. xxxvii–xlii). This is a discretionary scheme and is designed to support projects which create new employment or safeguard existing jobs, which attract foreign investment or which increase regional and local competitiveness and help areas adversely affected by economic change. In 1994–95, spending on RSA was £113 million and for 1995–96 the corresponding figure was £104 million. The DTI claimed that, in 1994–95, each £1 million of RSA grant attracted £8.5 million of capital investment which was expected to create or safeguard 230 jobs. RSA is demand-led rather than cash-limited, so projects do not compete against each other. Technically, there is a cost-per-job limit, although it has been ignored on occasion. There are also EU-imposed limits (known as Net Grant Equivalent) on the percentage of fixed capital costs which the public sector contribution may cover.

The DTI also seeks to obtain the UK's fair share of EU structural Funds for training and economic development in high unemployment areas (for details see House of Commons Trade and Industry Committee, 1995, pp. xvii–xxii), although once it has obtained access to these funds it shows some reluctance actually to spend them especially outside Northern Ireland (see *Financial Times*, 29 July 1996). At the regional level, the main funds are the European Regional Development Fund (ERDF) which provides support for investment, infrastructure and small firms in the most disadvantaged regions; and the European Social Fund (ESF) which supports vocational training and recruitment aid. In 1993, the EU agreed a new regional initiative, known as KONVER, which provides funds to those areas of the EU particularly dependent on, and especially vulnerable to, cuts in defence spending (disarmament). KONVER funds aim at the diversification and conversion of defence-dependent regions and support takes such forms as training, the promotion of innovation and technology transfer, assistance to small firms and the conversion of sites previously used by the armed forces (including environmental improvements).

Areas eligible for regional funds are known as **Assisted Areas** and they embrace Intermediate and Development Areas. The current Assisted Areas map, defining those areas of Great Britain eligible for regional funds, was introduced in 1993 (see House of Commons Trade and Industry Committee, 1995, p. xiii). The previous Assisted Areas map dated from 1984 (*ibid.*, p. xii) and the new map represented the government's assessment of those areas currently facing structural unemployment problems. The criteria for Assisted Area status included current unemployment rates, the persistence of unemployment rates above the national average and long-term unemployment, together with estimates of a future jobs gap, inner-city and urban problems, distance from the main markets, activity rates and known problems not reflected in unemployment rates. New areas which became eligible for regional aid in 1993 included the South-East (for example, East Kent, inner areas of London, south-eastern coastal towns); coalfield areas in the Midlands and Yorkshire affected by pit closures; and areas subject to closures or manpower reductions at defence establishments or major defence suppliers. As a result, the Assisted Areas covered 34 per cent of the working population of Great Britain, slightly less than in 1984. Government support is also available for inner cities, enterprise zones and free ports.

Critics of current UK regional policy condemn its free market approach, with reductions in special support for the regions and an emphasis on improving the operation of product and factor (including labour) markets throughout the economy. They claim that there will be too little government assistance and financial support to solve the regional problem, and they also assert that there is a need for more policy instruments. In particular, supporters of an interventionist policy favour **Industrial Development Certificates** (IDCs) as a means of controlling new factory buildings and extensions, thereby influencing the location decisions of firms. Originally, IDCs were used to reduce congestion in London and the South-East and to promote activity in the Assisted Areas; but they were no longer used after 1982.

Nonetheless, whether an interventionist or laissez-faire approach is preferred, there remain some outstanding issues for regional policy. Questions arise about the aims of policy and the potential conflicts between efficiency and social objectives; about whether policy is simply transferring jobs between different parts of the country; and ultimately, about the beneficiaries from the policy. Regional policy is not, however, the only form of support for UK industry. The DTI also offers selective assistance to individual firms and industries (for example, aerospace; shipbuilding; chemicals and biotechnology; telecommunications); it has a variety of measures for supporting small firms (for example, one-stop-shops; consultancy; loan guarantees); it encourages business to develop a positive and competitive response to environmental issues; and there is a major programme of support for industrial innovation (see President of the Board of Trade *et al.*, 1994 and 1995).

Regional policy, which assists companies, can be contrasted with regeneration policy which assists areas. It is operated by the DoE and sets out to 'improve the competitiveness of firms, the job prospects and quality of life of local people, and the social and physical environment' (President of the Board of Trade *et al.*, 1994, para. 12.1). In 1993, 20 separate programmes formerly administered by five different Departments were brought together in the Single Regeneration Budget. This now encompasses the Urban Programme, Urban Development Corporations, English Partnerships, the Business Start-Up Scheme and Regional En-terprise Grants, and is increasingly disbursed by a process of competitive bidding by local partnerships. It now dwarfs regional policy spending as illustrated in **Figure 19.1**, which reflects the fact that disparities within regions have become more of a problem than disparities between regions which have narrowed considerably since the turn of the decade (see **Figure 13.11, p. 352**). Traditional regional policy measures have never provided much of a solution to the former problem because manufacturing companies have been unwilling to move into inner-city locations where the worst intra-regional disparities are to be found.

19.2.5 Externalities and Environmental Policy

Externalities mean that left to themselves, private markets will fail to work properly by under-providing some socially desirable activities (for example, basic research, street lighting and information) and over-providing some socially undesirable activities (for example, pollution, noise and litter). Basically, externalities arise where there are benefits and costs outside of private market decisions and transactions: hence, private decision-makers will ignore any wider implications of their behaviour (in other words, there is a missing market for the externality). Using this approach, economists analyse environmental issues as an externality. Examples of environmental problems include noise, air and water pollution, ozone depletion and the greenhouse effect (global warming). Other examples are deforestation, acid rain, accidents at nuclear power stations and chemical plants, traffic congestion, the 'over-crowding' of local beauty spots (such as the English Lake District), the depletion of natural resources and the noise from low flying military aircraft. In 1996, the UK government announced targets for cutting motor vehicle pollution over the next few years and a classic example of blanket controls was the control of pollutants from domestic coal fires (via smoke-free zones and smokeless fuel).

Figure 19.1   *Government Expenditure on Regeneration and Regional Preferential Assistance (in real terms, 1993–94 prices)*

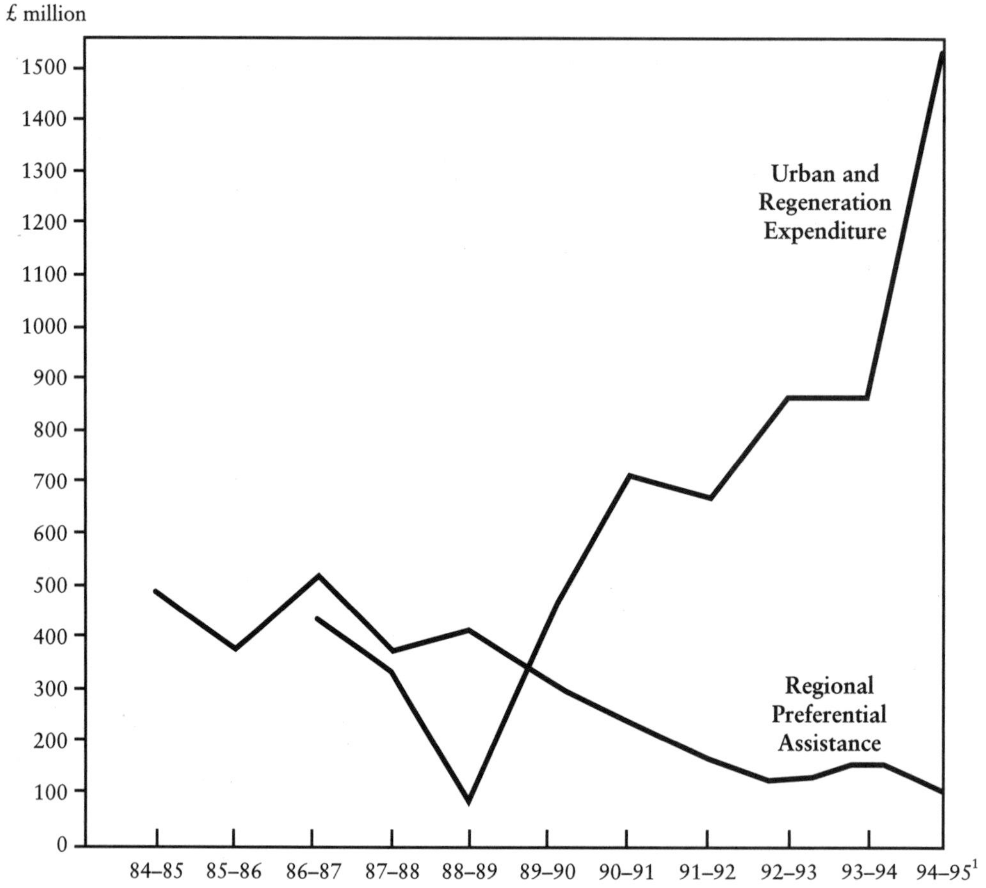

£ million

Notes

[1] Estimates.

Up to 1993–94, urban and regeneration policy includes City Challenge (introduced 1992/93), Urban Programme, City Grants, Derelict Land, UDCs and Docklands Light Railway, Manchester Regeneration, Inner City Task Forces, City Action Teams (introduced 1989/90), ERDF and New Towns (net); in 1994–95 it includes the whole of the Single Regeneration Budget. Regional preferential assistance includes RDG, RSA, REG (introduced 1988/89) and English Estates.

Source: House of Commons Department of Trade and Industry Committee (1995) p. xxiii

Subsidies can contribute to correcting market failure by increasing the output of socially-desirable activities (beneficial externalities). Government might, for example, support basic research into new, cleaner, environmentally-friendly production methods or offer subsidies to firms and households using environmentally-friendly fuels. Alternatively, it might be necessary to use taxation to reduce the output of harmful externalities (for example, pollution from motor vehicles). In addition to subsidies and taxes (market incentives), externalities can be corrected by other policy measures such as public ownership, or by legislative changes in property rights allowing the courts to determine compensation for the victims of spillovers, or by regulations imposing limits or complete bans on certain socially unde-sirable activities (for example, airport opening hours). However, environmental problems are not created solely by industry. Consumers also create harmful externalities through, for example, their use of motor cars (with implications for the location of homes, schools and shops) and their tourist activities with their possible destruction of the natural environment. All of these environmen-tal issues raise questions about the appropriate policy response and whether environmental issues are the proper concern of the DTI or the Depart-ment of the Environment (DoE) or, ultimately, consumers themselves. Conflicts between these Departments are also likely if the DoE favours 'tough' environmental policies (for example, to-wards motor vehicle pollution) which the DTI views as being 'bad' for competitiveness and growth.

☐ *19.2.6 Technology Policy*

Government support for science, technology and R&D is designed to improve the efficiency, com-petitiveness and innovative capacity of the UK. But why is state intervention required? Here, the argument is that R&D is risky; it may take a long time to produce marketable reults; and the bene-fits are likely to extend far beyond a single inno-vating firm. On this basis, it is argued that, if left to themselves, **private markets will fail to provide the socially desirable amount of R&D** and will encourage the hoarding of valuable ideas, so re-sulting in too little innovation and its dissemina-tion, with adverse effects on economic growth. Such market failure reflects at least three factors: First, a belief that capital markets will fail to finance large-scale, risky and long-term projects (for example, supersonic airliners); Second, the costs of establishing property rights in valuable ideas; and third, the possibility that the pursuit of profits might lead to the hoarding of valuable ideas and a failure to generate the socially desir-able transfer of knowledge throughout the econ-omy.

Persuasive though these arguments appear, they are often long on emotion and short on economic analysis, critical content and empirical evidence. For example, what might appear to be market failures in research and scientific activity might simply reflect the diversity of solutions adopted by firms to economise on transaction costs. Simi-larly, it is not sufficiently convincing evidence of a capital market failure to claim that it failed to provide funds for high-technology projects such as Concorde. In these cases, the capital market might be working properly and judging that the projects are likely to be unprofitable. After all, the UK capital market has funded large-scale, long-term and risky projects such as the Channel Tun-nel and the North Sea oil fields. Nor does it follow that state intervention will take an impar-tial long-term view, independently of the political market including a government's need to be re-elected and a maximum term of office of five years. In fact, public choice analysis predicts that governments can also fail.

Once governments decide to intervene in re-search and scientific markets, they are faced with a **complex choice set**. Decisions are needed on support for basic or applied research and technol-ogy transfer; on training the appropriate number and mix of different types of scientists and engi-neers; and on whether to offer support in the form of cash incentives (such as subsidies), tariff pro-tection, patent legislation, or public procurement. Further choices are required on whether to sup-port key high-technology industries such as aero-space, electronics and telecommunications and, if so, whether to favour **small or large firms and a competitive, oligopolistic or monopoly industry structure**. Here, the evidence suggests that an industry with many moderate-to-large firms of relatively similar size will be the most technically progressive, and that a market structure inter-mediate between monopoly and perfect competi-tion would promote the highest rate of inventive activity (Kamien and Schwartz, 1982, p. 3). In 1995, the top UK companies for R&D spending were Glaxo, SmithKline Beecham, Unilever, Ze-neca, Shell, General Electric, Wellcome, BT, Rolls-Royce and ICI.

Some of the results of UK government policy on civil and defence R&D are shown in **Table 19.2**. Defence is a major user of government R&D

funds, particularly in the aerospace and electronics industries. However, the large share of defence in government spending on science and technology led the Ministry of Defence in 1987 to admit that defence R&D may crowd-out valuable investment in the civil sector, so impairing industry's ability to compete in international markets for civil high-technology products. Interestingly, though, between 1987 and 1993, there was no dramatic shift in the relative shares of government spending on military and civil R&D. The defence share of total government funding for R&D declined from 0.47 per cent of GDP in 1987 to 0.36 per cent in 1993, but total government funding for both civil and defence purposes declined from 1.04 per cent of GDP in 1987 to 0.86 per cent in 1993.

The DTI has a major programme of assistance for industrial innovation and technology support.

In recent years, policy has changed from support for near-market R&D to support for long-term research collaboration, management best-practice, technology-transfer and measures for small firms. The DTI has encouraged collaborative programmes, involving European firms (Eureka), as well as collaboration between government, industry and higher-education and between scientists and business (for example, the Technology Foresight Programme). It has also promoted technology transfer where the market may be slow to adapt (for example, IT and modern materials). In 1995, DTI merged with the Office of Science and Technology (OST) and OST expenditure on science in 1995–96 was £1309 million. In addition, the DTI has provided further support for specific sectors, namely aircraft, aero-engine and civil space-research programmes together with launch aid for civil aerospace projects. Interestingly, both

Table 19.2   *Gross Expenditure on Civil & Defence R&D in the UK, 1993, £mn*

Sectors Providing the Funds	Sectors Carrying out the Work[1]				
	Government	Higher Education	Business Enterprise	Private Non-profit	Totals
Civil					
Government	1 043	1 540	390	151	3 124
Higher Education	4	100	–	–	104
Business Enterprise	136	156	6 218	240	6 749
Private Non-profit	32	283	–	96	411
Abroad	23	151	1 103	26	1 303
Sub-total	1 238	2 230	7 710	513	11 692
Defence					
Government	556	16	739	11	1 322
Higher Education	–	–	–	–	–
Business Enterprise	67	20	324	–	411
Private Non-profit	19	–	–	–	19
Abroad	13	–	295	–	308
Sub-total	654	36	1 359	11	2 060
Total Civil + Defence	1 893	2 266	9 069	524	13 752

Note:
[1] Columns do not include Abroad sector.

Source: OST (1995) *Forward Look* (London: HMSO).

the defence and DTI R&D programmes offer substantial public sector support to the UK aerospace industry. For example, by 1996, launch aid payments on the Airbus 320, 330 and 340 airliners totalled some £700 million with further payments of almost £400 million for support of the Rolls-Royce RB211 engine series. In return, by 1996, the levies received on these projects totalled £423 million. In evaluating government support for civil aircraft programmes, one study concluded that between 1945 and 1975 the net effect of aerospace launch aid has been a net loss of national welfare (Gardner, 1976, p.149). In contrast, a 1993 Parliamentary Report recommended that the government increase its funding towards aerospace research and technology to a level which is sufficient to maintain the UK industry's technology competitiveness (HC 563, 1993).

☐ *19.2.7 European Collaboration*

The trend towards the rising costs of some advanced technology projects means that the minimum entry costs are so high that it is necessary for a number of large firms or even nations to combine. Even before the completion of the Single European Market, there were some notable examples of European government involvement in collaborative programmes. These included Airbus, Concorde, the European Centre for Nuclear Research, ESPRIT (an IT programme), the European Space Agency and a series of joint defence ventures mainly involving military aircraft, helicopters and missiles such as the three-nation Tornado and the four-nation Eurofighter 2000 combat aircraft. For such projects, European collaboration reflects the fact that independence based on small national markets is too costly. For example, the total development costs on Eurofighter 2000 so far amount to some £13.6 billion at 1995–96 prices, with the UK paying a 33 per cent share. The total production order for all four nations so far is some 600 aircraft, with the UK ordering about 250.

Europe's high-technology industries such as aerospace, defence, electronics and telecommunications are frequently criticised for the wasteful duplication of costly R&D programmes and for the relatively short production runs resulting from a dependence on a small domestic market. International collaboration is often presented as the appropriate solution leading, so it is claimed, to the eventual creation of European-wide high technology industries capable of competing with Japan and the USA in world markets. Supporters of European collaboration in high technology claim a variety of benefits, including:

- Cost savings for both R&D and production.
- The sharing of risks and costs allows projects to be undertaken which would be too costly on an independent national basis (for example, space satellites and supersonic airliners).
- The creation of a European industry able to compete in world markets for high-technology products, so avoiding the EU becoming a bloc of metal bashers.
- A set of general economic and political benefits in the form of domestic jobs, the balance of payments, rivalry in ideas and the creation of a united Europe through reducing national barriers and prejudice.

The simple economics of collaboration are shown in **Figure 19.2**. Consider the case of a two-nation collaborative military aircraft project based on equal sharing of R&D costs and a pooling of national orders. In the ideal case, each nation bears only 50 per cent of the development costs compared with an independent national venture and gains from the doubling of output which, through learning economies, will reduce unit production costs by about 10 per cent.

Collaboration, however, has some disadvantages and costs leading to departures from the ideal model. Where governments are involved, substantial transaction costs arise as each partner nation seeks to establish property rights in the joint programme. Bargaining between partner governments, their bureaucracies and customers (such as the armed forces), together with lobbying from producer groups of scientists and contractors, can lead to substantial inefficiencies. Work might be shared on political, equity and bargaining criteria (for example, based on national orders: *juste retour*) and not on the basis of efficiency and competition. Each partner will demand its fair share of high-technology work. Also, there might be substantial administrative costs in the form of duplicate organisations, frequent committee meetings, delays in decision-making and excessive government involvement in monitoring and policing international contracts. As a result, collaborative programmes involving governments might lead to higher costs and take longer to develop than a national project. For example, the European Space Agency has been criticised for inefficiency in its management and staffing levels; for continuing to procure on a cost-plus basis rather than using competitively-determined fixed-price contracts; and for allocating 96 per cent of its work on the basis of *juste retour* rather than competitive bidding (DTI, 1995).

The Airbus civil airliner is often quoted as one of the successes of European collaboration. Airbus entered the Boeing-dominated market for jet airliners and achieved a market share of 27 per cent by the early 1990s, but this market penetration was at a cost in terms of subsidies. One study has estimated that the net welfare effect of Airbus market entry is negative for Europe, suggesting that the Airbus project has actually decreased European welfare (Klepper, 1990). Government involvement in collaboration also raises wider issues of public purchasing, and we must accordingly turn to consider the likely effects of government purchasing on industrial performance.

■ 19.3 Public Purchasing

19.3.1 Scope of Government Procurement

Government purchasing is big business. In 1993–94, central government procurement spending was about £40 billion, with a further £20 + billion of purchasing by the NHS. Government purchases range from standard items such as banking services, clothing, paper clips, furniture, motor cars, office equipment and accommodation, to more complex products such as bridges, computers, space satellites, nuclear power stations and Trident submarines. Such purchases have the potential for influencing industrial performance. Defence and Health are the major spending departments, purchasing from industries such as aerospace, electronics, ordnance, shipbuilding, pharmaceuticals and medical equipment.

Government purchasing from private and state-owned enterprises involves **choices about a product, a contractor and a contract**. Decisions are required on the type of goods and services to be purchased, the selection of a contractor and the choice of a contract. Often such choices provide scope for governments to pursue wider economic and social objectives and not simply the acquisition of goods and services. Considerations of the national interest might lead a government to purchase from higher-cost domestic suppliers so as to protect a nation's key strategic industries, its technology, jobs and the balance of payments. The

Figure 19.2   *The Economics of Collaboration*

a   R&D Costs

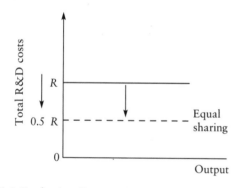

b   Unit Production Costs

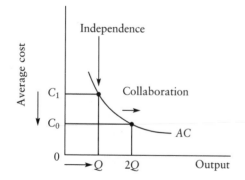

pursuit of such wider ends makes it difficult for Parliament and independent analysts to determine whether public procurement is giving good value for money. However, privatisation results in the transfer of purchasing from the public to the private sector where commercial criteria rather than wider public interest considerations dominate procurement choices.

The range and complexity of public procurement choices can be illustrated by considering two limiting models. At one extreme, the government as the buyer knows what it wants, the products exist and they are being traded in competitive-type markets. In these circumstances, the state acts as a competitive buyer, specifies its requirements, invites competitive tenders and awards a fixed price contract to the lowest bidder. Problems arise at the other extreme where the government is the only buyer, is uncertain about its requirements and the product does not yet exist (as is often the case for high-technology products such as defence equipment and telecommunications). Moreover, the domestic market might contain only one or relatively few actual or potential suppliers. The government as the major, or only, buyer might have to select a contractor and to write a contract for a project which either does not exist, might involve a major jump in the state of the art and where the contractor requires a cost-based contract with a substantial proportion of the risks borne by the state. Contracts for such advanced technology projects are often associated with cost overruns, time slippages and major modifications and sometimes with cancellations (for example, the Nimrod AEW project in 1986) leading to allegations of waste, incompetence and contractor inefficiency.

Where a government Department is a major buyer, as with defence equipment and the NHS, its procurement choices and contracting policies can have a decisive effect on an industry's size, structure, entry and exit, technical progress, efficiency, prices and profitability. For example, non-competitive government contracts, as with some defence equipment and pharmaceuticals for the NHS, are subject to state regulatory constraints. A Review Board for Non-Competitive Government Contracts and a Pharmaceutical Profit Regulation Scheme are designed to ensure that government contractors receive a reasonable rate of return on capital, where 'reasonable' usually means a profit rate similar to the average return earned by British industry. However, firms respond and adapt to regulatory constraints. The possibility of post-costing and renegotiation of excessive profits provides firms with an inducement to sacrifice profits for expenditures which give satisfaction (utility) to the company's managers, such as company cars, luxury offices and the hoarding of scientists.

For many years, there have been continued debates about whether co-ordinated government purchasing might improve industrial performance through, for example, exploiting the economies of scale associated with combining and standardising orders from different state agencies. Since 1979, the emphasis has been on achieving better value for money from public purchasing. Government Departments have been subject to Rayner scrutinies, budgets have been cash limited, civil service manpower has been reduced and functions traditionally undertaken in-house have been contracted-out to private firms. Also, in 1984, an official review concluded that government procurement was costing the taxpayer too much, mainly due to administration costs and because the prices paid were often higher than necessary. There followed the 1984 Government Purchasing Initiative which, by 1995, was credited with value for money savings of over £2 billion. At the same time, defence has been the focus of a major initiative in the form of its competitive procurement policy which was launched officially in 1984.

More recently, in 1995, the government introduced a new strategy for government procurement known as *Setting New Standards* (Cmnd 2840, 1995). This new initiative reflected the development of policies for market testing, contracting-out and internal markets which has led to government Departments undertaking more of their business through procurement rather than direct, in-house provision. The prime objective of government procurement is to achieve best value for money defined to embrace whole life cost and quality and not solely short-term lowest price. Competition remains the main means of achieving value for money, but there is a recognition that it might be mutually beneficial to avoid an 'unnecessarily adversarial approach' and that government Departments might develop a long-term formal partnership agreement with suppliers. Such long-term partnership agreements might be used where the market is highly specialised or where a Department's requirements are complex and continuously developing (as in the case of defence equipment). The 1995 procurement initiative also recognised that tendering is costly for suppliers and that in general, between three and six bids will be sufficient to provide 'genuine competition' (in the past, some Departments invited as many as 30 bidders – see Cmnd 2840, 1995, p. 13). These initiatives appear sensible, but limiting competition to three to six suppliers creates opportunities for collusive tendering, and the move to long-term partnership agreements removes competitive pressures from suppliers and allows the emergence of a 'cosy relationship' between buyer and seller with the possibility of X-inefficiency.

Evidence suggests that there is substantial scope for improving the efficiency of public procurement, not only in the UK but throughout the EU. As the only or major buyer, the government will be lobbied to 'buy British', thereby preventing foreign firms bidding for UK government contracts. In fact, protectionism and support for domestic industries (national champions) have often characterised public procurement throughout the EU. The creation of the Single European Market in 1992 enabled public procurement for civil goods and services to benefit from increased competition, free trade and economies of scale. There are, however, problems of creating a **level playing field** for public procurement in the Single European Market.

19.3.2 *Public Purchasing in the Single Market: A Level Playing Field?*

Before the creation of the SEM, public procurement in member states was characterised by government protectionism, preferential purchasing, limited information on contracts, a preference for restricted or negotiated contracts and support for national champions. Examples of protected sectors included defence, energy, transport and telecommunications where state support was justified in terms of strategic factors, high technology or the maintenance of employment in declining industries. In these sectors, governments as buyers were the source of anti-competitive behaviour in markets.

For **civil** goods and services, estimates suggested that opening-up or liberalising public procurement markets as part of the Single Market initiative would result in substantial economic benefits reflected in savings of 0.5 per cent of Community GDP and the creation of 350 000 jobs. These estimated savings arose from increased competition and from the successful firms obtaining greater economies of scale. Although the estimated benefits appear attractive, there remain problems of creating a level playing field in EU public procurement markets.

A level playing field refers to the need for something called 'fair competition'. Here problems arise because firms losing-out in any competition are likely to claim that the winning bid represented 'unfair competition'. More fundamental problems arise over the meaning of the term 'fair competition'. Unlike the economist's textbook model of perfect competition, real world competition is characterised by rivalry and contestability occurring in economies dominated by ignorance and uncertainty. No one can predict accurately the future (not even economists!) and markets are always changing so that they never reach the state of equilibrium so beloved of economic textbooks. In the real world, competition means continuous rivalry as firms search for profitable market opportunities ahead of their rivals.

A firm needs to take risks, and if it is successful and discovers a new product or process before its rivals and consumers are willing to pay for the discovery, then the innovating firm will make money until its rivals discover a superior product. This suggests that playing fields will never be level but will always be changing. Indeed if governments interpret a level playing field to mean uniformity and standardisation, then it is likely to be rejected by consumers who want diversity. For example, does a level playing field mean that the English Lake District should have a Mediterranean climate?

An alternative interpretation of a level playing field requires all the participants to abide by the agreed rules of the game. Competition becomes 'unfair' if governments, firms or buyers fail to observe the agreed rules. For example, bribes and criminal activity can influence the award of contracts. Within EU public procurement markets, there are several sources of 'unfair competition' resulting in a failure to achieve a level playing field. These include:

- Subsidies to private firms.
- Favourable financial arrangements for state-owned enterprises.
- Governments as buyers behaving anti-competitively. For example, governments have opportunities for discretionary behaviour in interpreting the **most economically advantageous tender** which embraces delivery, running costs, security of supplies, etc, as well as price.
- Failure to comply with 'need to advertise' contracts in the *Official Journal of the European Communities* and to announce the results of competitions.
- Differences in the definition of the public sector, in the diversity of public purchasing arrangements and in the range of activities undertaken 'in-house' and by contract. For example, in some countries, decentralised public purchasing might mean that the size of public contracts falls below the relevant thresholds for EU procurement rules. Elsewhere, some public sector activities performed 'in-house' are not subject to competitive tendering.
- The possible creation of cartels and collusive tendering.
- The costs to firms of appealing against 'unfair competition'. There are legal and reputation costs and, even if successful, the award of damages might not make the exercise worthwhile.

Data are not always available to enable the Commission to monitor the application of its public procurement rules and to assess the extent of openness in public procurement markets in each member state. For example, countries differ in the coverage of their industrial statistics, the degree of detail shown by their statistics and in the extent to which such statistics show the details of public procurement. Up-to-date information is often not available, so that the Commission can only use historic data (for example, input-output tables). Also, the Commission has only limited staff and resources for investigating non-compliance with its directives on public procurement. Some of this work is extremely time-consuming as it requires a careful study of large numbers of public contracts in each member state to ensure that their announcement and awards have complied with the rules.

Research by economists has found evidence of:

- Preferential public purchasing within EU states for industries such as electricity and gas; pharmaceuticals; medical equipment; railway rolling stock; shipbuilding and telecommunications. Casual empiricism also suggests that when purchasing motorcars, national governments and police forces favour their national car industries.
- A higher proportion of open tendering and a decline in negotiated contracts. Nonetheless, there were substantial differences between member states. In 1992, open competition accounted for 39 per cent of all advertised contracts in the UK compared with 80 per cent in The Netherlands and 11 per cent in Italy.
- Differences between the location and ownership of firms obtaining contracts. In 1992, for example, 99.5 per cent of UK public contracts were awarded to companies based in the UK, but only 64 per cent of these contracts were awarded to UK-owned companies. This suggests that public markets might be more open than appears to be the case from some of the data.

Problems nevertheless remain. Governments as buyers are likely to seek 'loopholes' in the EU legislation; suppliers may acquire their major rivals in other member states so creating monopolies and oligopolies; and firms will seek opportunities to thwart the rules. Further possibilities for cost-savings could be achieved by extending the Single Market to include the procurement of defence equipment. Estimates suggest cost-savings of at least 10 per cent from 'opening-up' national defence markets to competition. But, of course, defence markets are the classic example of protectionism where 'national security' considerations dominate procurement choices. Nonetheless, the UK's experience with the procurement of defence equipment illustrates the benefits of a competitive procurement policy.

19.3.3 A Competitive Procurement Policy: the Case of Defence

The Ministry of Defence (MoD) is the largest single customer for the products of British industry, with its purchases ranging from simple items such as batteries, cars and furniture to highly complex equipment such as missiles, submarines and advanced combat aircraft. For 1995–96, expenditure on defence equipment totalled £8.7 billion. About 80 per cent of the MoD's defence equipment is purchased directly from UK industry; a further 10 per cent benefits domestic industry through its participation in collaborative programmes and the remaining 9 per cent is imported. Within the UK, MoD is a major purchaser of the outputs of the aerospace, electronics, shipbuilding and ordnance industries. In 1994–95, the leading UK defence equipment contractors, which were each paid over £250 million by the MoD, were British Aerospace (including Royal Ordnance), GEC, Rolls-Royce, Vickers Shipbuilding and Engineering (VSEL) and Hunting.

R&D also forms a substantial part of the defence equipment programme through which it can have a major impact on technical progress in specific sectors of the UK economy, particularly aerospace, electronics and shipbuilding. Also, it is often claimed that there are additional economic benefits associated with spin-off and technology transfer from defence to the civil sector of the economy. However, the Conservative government announced that necessary investment in defence R&D may crowd-out valuable investment in the civil sector and that restraints on government-funded defence R&D spending were required to free resources for civil work. Such a proposition needs to be carefully assessed, particularly the evidence on crowding-out and whether the UK's commitment to defence R&D has affected adversely its international competitiveness. Furthermore, where there is evidence of these adverse effects, it is necessary to discover whether they have arisen because, in the past, cost-plus defence contracts have tended to reduce a firm's innovative drive, and whether the situation has changed now that the MoD operates a competitive procurement policy (see below). Issues also arise as to what happens to the resources released from defence R&D -- whether they are used in civil technology or elsewhere in the civil sector in the UK; whether they remain unemployed or whether they emigrate. It is evident that, in the long run, reduced defence R&D sends out clear signals to the labour market about future employment prospects in military technology work.

Traditionally, MoD procurement policy was characterised by support for UK industry, by non-competitive cost-plus or cost-based contracts, and by contractors bearing none of the risks of the project. Defence contractors were often criticised for cost escalation, delays, labour hoarding, inefficiency and project failures. In 1984, the MoD introduced a new competitive procurement policy in an effort to change the traditional dependency relationship in which defence business was regarded as 'lucrative, not very competitive and a cosy relationship' (HC 392, 1988, p. vixxv). The MoD became a more demanding customer, introducing and extending competition and encouraging new entrants, especially small firms. Risks were shifted from the MoD to industry, with a greater use of firm or fixed-price contracts rather than cost-plus contracting. In 1988, a further extension of competition occurred when the MoD announced that it was more willing to purchase equipment from overseas sources where they are likely to offer greater value for money.

The published results of the new competition policy are impressive. In 1979–80, 30 per cent of MoD contracts by value were awarded on a competitive basis and 22 per cent were cost-plus a percentage fee contracts; by 1994–95, the corresponding figures were 73 per cent and 1 per cent, respectively. At the outset of the new policy, a target was announced for achieving cost savings of 10 per cent on the total equipment budget. Some of the actual results of competition have been impressive, with cost savings ranging from 10 per cent to 70 per cent, all of which might be taken as indicators of monopoly pricing and/or inefficiency in UK defence industries. In 1987–88, for example, the median cost saving on a group of 13 equipment projects was 40 per cent, giving total savings of over £100 million. Similarly, there are examples where competition resulted in savings of over £400 million from 10 projects originally expected to cost £2.4 billion. Estimates by the MoD in 1994 resulted in a claim that competition had reduced procurement costs by over £1 billion per year (over 10 per cent of the equipment budget) and was a major factor in improving the competitiveness of the UK defence industry, enabling it to win export orders in excess of £6 billion in 1993 (HC 390, 1994).

Competition policy as implemented by the MoD is not without its problems and it is subject to both constraints and conflicts. A potential constraint arises if the MoD or the government is unwilling to impose the ultimate sanction on poor performance by a major contractor – namely, bankruptcy. Until 1988, there was a further constraint in that domestic monopolies dominated the high technology and costly equipment programmes. These comprised British Aerospace (aircraft, missiles, ordnance and small arms), Rolls-Royce (aero-engines), Westland (helicopters), GEC (torpedoes), VSEL (nuclear-powered submarines) and Vickers (tanks). However, the 1988 announcement of the MoD's willingness to buy from overseas meant that the threat of competition increased the contestability of those UK defence markets dominated by domestic monopolies. But conflicts arise between competition policy, leading to foreign purchases, and support for the UK defence industrial base which

appears to offer attractive wider economic and social benefits in the form of security, independence, jobs, technology and an improved balance of payments. The role of defence industrial factors was formally recognised in a 1996 government statement on Defence Procurement and Industrial Policy. Within the framework of value for money and competition, the government recognised the need to give 'full consideration to defence industrial factors in procurement decisions' (HC 209, 1996, p. xii). These defence industrial factors were defined to include the retention in the UK of 'essential military capabilities' and the value to the armed forces of industrial back-up. The focus is on defence-based factors rather than the wider industrial or economic objectives often associated with debates about the UK defence industrial base.

19.3.4 The UK Defence Industrial Base and the Peace Dividend

The debate in 1985–86 over the future of the Westland helicopter company was a classic example of the arguments about the need for a defence industrial base (DIB). It was claimed that the UK needed a strong DIB for strategic objectives and for national economic benefits. The strategic benefits included security of supply in times of tension and war (an insurance policy), the need for equipment designed specially for national requirements and the capability to respond to emergencies (such as the Falklands crisis and Gulf conflict). There are also claimed to be national economic benefits in the form of employment, foreign exchange savings and earnings and the development of high technology, including spin-offs to the civil sector. Certainly, defence sales are a major source of industrial employment, accounting for 395 000 jobs in 1994. The result is a significant pressure group which will seek to persuade governments to spend more on defence equipment and to buy British. Large producers with domestic monopolies will use their political influence and lobbying to oppose foreign purchases (of, for example, Boeing AWACS and other American equipment). Stress will be placed on job losses, possibly in marginal constituencies, the loss of a vital defence capability and the dangers of depending on foreigners.

Many of the arguments for a DIB are vague and emotive and are used to rationalise and justify the **status quo**. Costs are ignored. Informed public choice on the appropriate or optial size and composition of the UK's DIB needs answers to three questions. First, what is meant by the DIB and why is it needed? Second, what is the minimum size and composition of the DIB? For example, should it comprise only an R&D capability in certain key technologies (and if so, which?) and what would be the costs and benefits if the current DIB was reduced by, say, 10 per cent or 20 per cent? Third, how much are the Armed Forces willing to pay for retaining key UK industrial capabilities for military objectives? Any wider economic benefits such as jobs and advanced technology should be charged to other government Departments (for example Trade and Industry). Indeed, the point has to be made that there are usually alternative ways of achieving employment, technology and balance-of-payments objectives.

Buying British is not costless. It can mean paying more for equipment, (perhaps, an extra 25 per cent or more), and waiting longer for delivery. The result is smaller defence forces and less protection. Ultimately, it is necessary to ask what the defence budget is buying: protection for UK citizens or protection for UK defence industries? Each option involves different sets of costs and benefits and, once again, choices cannot be avoided (Hartley and Hooper, 1993).

Major changes have occurred since 1990 as UK defence contractors have adjusted to disarmament and substantial reductions in British defence spending (the Peace Dividend). Faced with a reduced demand for new equipment (cancellations; fewer new projects; the stretching-out of programmes; shorter production runs), defence firms have responded by seeking new military and civil markets at home and overseas. Mergers have occurred both nationally and internationally (for example, GEC's acquisition of VSEL; British Aerospace and the French Matra company merging their missile business); and, of course, there

have been job losses, plant closures and exits from the industry. For example, between 1990 and 1994, employment in UK defence industries declined from 550 000 to 395 000. The question then arises as to whether governments should leave the adjustment process to market forces or whether they should intervene either to encourage a re-allocation of resources from declining defence industries to expanding sectors or more directly to assist the conversion of defence plants to civil activities (swords to ploughshares). The Labour Party has proposed a Defence Diversification Agency which would assist defence firms and communities to shift from defence to civil markets. Whichever policy option is chosen, the required re-allocation of resources from defence to civil activities will involve time and substantial adjustment costs: any peace dividend will not be an instant free gift. On this basis, disarmament can be viewed as an investment process involving short-run costs and the prospect of long-run benefits (the Peace Dividend).

Bibliography

Cecchini, P. (1988) *The European Challenge 1992* (London: Wildwood House).

Cmnd 2840 (1995) *Setting New Standards: A Strategy for Government Procurement* (London: HMSO).

Commission of the European Communities (1991) 'Fair Competition in the Internal Market: Community State Aid Policy', *European Economy*, 48.

Commission of the European Communities (1995) *Fourth Survey on State Aid in the European Union in the Manufacturing and Certain Other Sectors*. 564/95 (Brussels: CEC).

DTI (1995) *UK Space Policy: a discussion document* (London: DTI).

Gardner, N. (1976) 'Economics of Launching Aid', in A. Whiting (ed) *The Economics of Industrial Subsidies* (London: HMSO).

Gowland, D. and S. James (1991) *Economic Policy After 1992* (Aldershot: Dartmouth).

Hartley, K. and N. Hooper (1993) 'The Economic Consequences of the UK Government's Decision on the Hercules Replacement, *Research Monograph Series 2* (York: Centre for Defence Economics).

House of Commons (1996) *Government Reply to the First Reports from the Defence and Trade and Industry Committees Session 1995–96 on Aspects of Defence Procurement and Industrial Policy*, HC 209, 210 (London: HMSO).

House of Commons Defence Committee (1988) *Business Appointments*, HC 392 (London: HMSO).

House of Commons Trade and Industry Committee (1993) *British Aerospace Industry*, HC 563 (London: HMSO).

House of Commons Trade and Industry Committee (1995) *Fourth Report: Regional Policy*. Session 1994–95. HC 356-I (London: HMSO)

Kamien, M. I. and N. L. Schwartz (1982) *Market Structure and Innovation* (Cambridge: Cambridge University Press).

Klepper, G. (1990) 'Entry into the Market for Large Transport Aircraft', *European Economic Review*, 34 (4) pp. 775–803.

National Audit Office (1994) *Ministry of Defence: Defence Procurement in the 1990s*, HC 390 (London: HMSO).

President of the Board of Trade *et al.* (1994) *Competitiveness: Helping Business to Win.* Cm 2563 (London: HMSO).

President of the Board of Trade *et al.* (1995) *Competitiveness: Forging Ahead.* Cm 2867 (London: HMSO).

Chapter 20

Macroeconomic Policy

Peter Curwen

■ 20.1 Introduction

Putting together a book of this kind is, as noted in the preface, a bit like constructing a jigsaw puzzle which comes in a completely blank box where the first problem to be addressed is ensuring that the section of the overall picture visible on each piece of the jigsaw is as clear as possible. We have addressed this task in the chapters up to this point. None of these chapters has been entirely self-contained because it is not possible to view inflation, unemployment or any other element of what is ultimately an interacting system entirely in isolation. Of necessity, therefore, anyone who has read through the entire text up to this point will have learned a good deal about the overall picture, but not enough to put the jigsaw together without a certain amount of additional assistance.

In the course of this chapter many of the threads which run through earlier chapters will therefore be pulled together with a view to explaining the evolution of macroeconomic policy in the UK. It is important in this context to remember the significance of the term 'evolution' because one of the difficulties in assembling the jigsaw is that the size and shape of the pieces is constantly evolving. Just as you are about to put the final pieces into place you discover that they do not fit the remaining spaces because some part

of the overall system no longer functions as it did a short time ago. Our purpose is accordingly both to examine, albeit briefly, some of the models of macroeconomic management which have been adhered to at various times and with varying degrees of conviction by UK governments, and also to examine the empirical assessments of how these models have performed in practice.

This chapter necessarily contains a more wide-ranging historical perspective than most others, but in common with them it concentrates upon the evolution of theory and practice over the past two decades. To retain the continuity of the narrative it is assumed that the reader has indeed read all or most of the preceding chapters, or at least those concerned with the elements of the schematics which appeared in Chapter 2. In that context, it is worth reminding ourselves of certain of the salient points raised in that analysis, namely the existence of trade-offs between objectives; the fact that policy instruments are inter-dependent (for example, the budgetary stance has implications for the money supply); and the possibility that something which has instrumental status at one point in time, such as the exchange rate, can at another point in time acquire objective status. These factors would be confusing enough in a pure economic world. Unfortunately, this book being concerned with political economy, we need to allow for the fact that the addition of the political cycle into the analysis means that, *inter alia*, logic and consistency has never been the hallmark of UK macroeconomic policy.

This does not mean, of course, that governments do not now understand most of the principles relating to how an advanced economy functions. It is interesting to note in this context that the macroeconomic strategies of Majorite Conservatism and 'New Labour' are remarkably similar – irrespective of who wins in 1997, there will be no sudden U-turns in policy which is why, for example, the stock market remains buoyant and the exchange rate is rising at the end of 1996 even though the odds are heavily in favour of a change in government. The most obvious ongoing problem is the temptation for the existing government, like most of its predecessors, to try and bribe the voters even though it knows perfectly well that this is incompatible with the smooth running of the economy, thereby creating unnecessary burdens for its successors.

Among the well-understood principles are elements such as 'Tinbergen's rule' which states that there need to be at least as many independent instruments as there are objectives. However, the waters are muddied somewhat if the objectives are defined less rigorously. Thus, for example, it is evident that fixing two objectives as, say, price stability and 'full' employment may require instruments to be used in such a focused manner that some other objective such as the balance of payments or the rate of growth falls well short of the values which would independently be chosen. If, however, the former objectives are redefined as 'an acceptable rate of inflation' and 'a modest level of unemployment' then it should simultaneously be possible to improve both the balance of payments position and the rate of growth.

It is reasonable to view the situation in late 1996 as broadly compatible with this line of argument. True, there is some inflation, a balance of payments deficit and quite a lot of unemployment, but none of these individually is particularly alarming either in terms of recent history, overseas experience or both. Hence, despite the best endeavours of certain commentators, any talk of 'crisis' is simply being disregarded. This can be compared with earlier periods when, for example, huge store was set by the state of the balance of payments and imbalances on a scale which would today be shrugged aside were sufficient to bring down governments.

■ 20.2 Crisis and Credibility

The concept of 'crisis' is well-known to the student of postwar UK macroeconomic policy, and this can be seen as an adjunct to the concept of 'credibility'. Here again it is worth observing that the present Conservative government is seen as economically credible (its main problem is that it is simultaneously seen as irredeemably 'sleazy') because it has set itself reasonable objectives and largely achieved them (see discussion of MTFS below). In so doing, it has clearly learned something from the unpleasant experiences of its predecessors, as has 'New Labour' which is seen as economically credible precisely because it also intends to continue with existing policies.

The issue of credibility is particularly interesting because it can be used to explain the behaviour of governments in the immediate postwar period. On the face of it, these governments were amazingly successful by modern standards. In particular, as previously noted, unemployment was extremely low, and it is hardly surprising that many critics of UK governments in recent times have advocated a return to the Keynesian model, arguing that if it worked then it ought to work equally well now.

However, the key issue is whether it was the then governments' policies *per se* or their credibility that really mattered. What governments did at the time was to declare that their primary objective was 'full' employment and that they would take immediate remedial action whenever the economy moved away from the attainment of this objective. This sent out a clear message to companies in the private sector that the level of demand would be maintained, and hence that it would be safe, and indeed expedient, to invest in building up capacity for future sales. This investment, in turn, ensured that demand remained high and hence that expectations were fulfilled, leading to yet more investment.

In such a climate, companies could be expected to take a long-term view of their prospects, and hence their employees not merely regarded their jobs as secure but anyway worried little about losing them since they could walk along to the nearest factory and get others quite easily. This, in turn, meant that they were willing and able to take on long-term commitments, most notably in the form of a mortgage (traditionally of 25–year duration).

This promoted both the building of houses and the production of consumer goods to fill them, which further stimulated the economy. In response, employers took to hoarding labour, afraid that if they laid off workers in response to what they all 'knew' would be a temporary downturn in demand, given that the government was effectively underwriting full employment, they would be unable to replace them with equivalent workers when demand picked up again because these had all been hired by their competitors.

One side-effect of this policy was that workers would sometimes end up 'sweeping the factory floor' in the absence of any more useful work to be done, but they would still be employed and they would still be paid. Unemployment was, in effect, hidden from public view at such times.

What would have happened had governments in the period through to the mid-1960s not underwritten unemployment cannot be known for certain. What is certain, however, is that people at the time *believed* that the (Keynesian) instruments in use at the time, essentially fiscal instruments supplemented by adjustment of hire purchase conditions and bank lending, were effective in maintaining full employment. So what, it may reasonably be asked, could go wrong?

There can be no single, simple answer to such a question. In the first place, it is evident from our schematic model that an economy such as that of the UK, unwisely confident in the superiority of its (over)long-established methods of production and ironically having suffered what might reasonably be seen as too little damage to its exhausted physical capital during World War II, would end up importing so many manifestly superior products from overseas that its balance of payments would become a severe problem. If it was also committed to a fixed exchange rate and unwilling to fall back on direct controls, the only remaining instruments would be those already in use to promote full employment which would now have to be redirected to restricting, rather than expanding, demand – otherwise known as **stop–go** or perhaps more appropriately, as **go–stop**. This would adversely affect the credibility of the full-employment commitment.

Secondly, despite the superiority of imports, the home market would be so buoyant under conditions of full employment that domestic producers would still find ready buyers and hence see little point in improving their products. This, in turn, would ensure that imports would continue to erode market share.

Thirdly, trade unions would note that employers were reluctant to fire workers, and become increasingly aggressive, demanding higher wages and other concessions. Employers in their turn, confident that demand would be maintained, would see the opportunity to pass on these higher wages to consumers in the form of higher prices, generating inflation and yet more opportunities for importers.

Finally, commentators would begin to question whether the policy of full employment could survive these pressures, and in so doing further undermine the policy's credibility. Sooner or later credibility would become so damaged by these pressures that behaviour would no longer be conditioned by the assumption that full employment would continue to be the norm and, just as the belief in full employment was self-fulfilling, so the lack of belief in full employment would become self-fulfilling.

□ 20.2.1 The Golden Age

It is tempting to look back on the 1950s and early 1960s as some kind of golden age when everyone had a job and all was well in the world. Not only was there full employment but the economy was growing fairly rapidly (albeit, rather ominously, much more slowly than competing economies) and people were becoming manifestly more prosperous with an increasing trend to home and car ownership. Even inflation, although on a rising trend, was sufficiently subdued in most years so as not to be a direct cause for concern.

On the whole, the range of policy instruments seemed to be perfectly adequate for the task of demand management. The emphasis was upon adjustment of tax rates rather than of public expenditure because of the relative ease with which the former could be flexed in the short run. Monetary policy played a subservient role, mainly through controls on credit which could bite quickly and effectively in a world of pervasive controls. To appreciate this point, credit must be carefully distinguished from the concept of money, the former being a liability (that is, owed to a lender) whereas the latter is an asset. This freed up interest rates to protect the exchange rate which had to be held within pre-ordained limits. Most of the time the exchange rate was not under pressure, and hence interest rates could remain quite low which helped reduce the cost of servicing the national debt. Since demand management appeared to be adequate for the purpose, little attention was paid to supply-side issues. The ease with which the economy could be managed was greatly assisted both by the regularity of the business cycle (recessions could be expected to be short, even if not sweet) and the rapid growth of other economies which provided ample export markets for successful UK companies.

Nevertheless, the limited range of instruments was clearly only adequate to deal with a limited range of objectives, namely employment and the balance of payments. Once inflation crept into the frame in the mid-1960s something else was clearly needed. On the one hand, this stimulated an ill-fated attempt to use economic planning as a measure on the supply side, encompassing the setting up of the National Economic Development Council (NEDC), the creation of a Department of Economic Affairs and a National Plan. On the other hand, there was an attempt to deal with inflationary pressures through a series of prices and incomes policies, as detailed below, initially through the agency of a National Board for Prices and Incomes.

□ 20.2.2 Credibility on the Wane

It is possible to argue that credibility began to die the death during the latter half of the 1960s, a period during which Harold Wilson and the Labour Party were in power. The core problem was the balance of payments which at the time appeared to be in serious trouble. We have had cause to remark, earlier in the book, about the dangers of over-reacting to short-term disturbances, and in retrospect, with a much revised set of data in front of us, it is hard to appreciate why the situation after Wilson took power in 1964 was seen as a crisis (that of November 1964 being followed by others in July 1965 and July 1966). However, Wilson was forced to respond with severe deflationary action which was ultimately unsuccessful, leading to a devaluation in November 1967.

The economy failed to respond with immediate effect, so further deflationary fiscal policies were put into effect, ceilings were imposed on bank lending and import controls were temporarily introduced. This package was rewarded with an approximate return to the economic situation prevailing during the early 1960s. However, with credibility seriously damaged, crisis was to remain the order of the day as successive governments under Heath, Wilson and Callaghan spent the 1970s coping with the fall-out of the golden years. Unlike its main competitors, the UK had done very little during this period to improve its competitiveness, and now this began to take its toll in no uncertain fashion.

It is of considerable interest that it was during the early years of the decade that Heath's government embarked upon an experiment with freeing up markets generally known as the 'Selsdon' philosophy. However, this was to prove a damp squib by Thatcherite standards (Heath, significantly, has long been regarded as a 'wet' Tory), as a sharp upturn in unemployment resulted in Spring 1972 in the infamous 'dash for growth' Barber Budget. Furthermore, faced by the possibility of the bankruptcy of the British car industry, the government acted entirely against the grain of its principles in accepting the need to subsidise 'lame ducks'.

Bearing in mind that there were already renewed signs of growth and that inflation was already well above its long-term trend, the 1972 Budget was a somewhat risky affair. This risk was compounded by the introduction of a new system of monetary controls known as **Competition and Credit Control (CCC)**. Prior to 1971, the primary emphasis of monetary policy was to restrict the availability of loans from banks and of hire purchase contracts on the grounds that, whereas the interest rate was thought to be the key monetary variable, investment appeared in practice to be influenced more by the availability than by the nominal cost of credit. As usual, given the existence of willing lenders and willing borrowers, market forces tried to reassert themselves through the setting up of secondary banks whose activities fell outside the remit of Bank of England controls (the process known as 'disintermediation'), and the government sought through CCC to switch from a system which tried to control the growth of lending to one which tried to control the growth of deposit-taking.

All banks, whether joint stock or otherwise, were obliged to observe a uniform minimum reserve ratio on a daily basis. **Eligible reserve assets**, which approximated to those previously counted as liquid assets, were to be held to the extent of a minimum (reserve asset ratio) of 12.5 per cent of **eligible liabilities**, which consisted of sterling deposits, excluding those with an original maturity of over two years, and net of inter-bank transactions and sterling certificates. All banks were obliged to place Special Deposits with the Bank of England on request. Calls for Special Deposits, which would be deducted from a bank's reserve assets, would be expressed as a uniform percentage for all banks, normally of eligible liabilities. The London clearing banks alone were required to maintain an average balance at the BoE of 1.5 per cent of eligible liabilities.

Because they were previously operating what was in effect an interest rate cartel, the London and Scottish clearing banks were also required to abandon their long-standing agreements on interest rates. Each bank was henceforth to express its lending rates in relation to a **base rate** determined by itself according to its own view of the market.

However, in the light of the possibility that the banks might bid up interest rates sufficiently high as to attract funds away from the building societies, the authorities reserved the right to keep interest rates within specified limits.

These arrangements permitted the BoE to squeeze the liquidity of the banks either by calling for Special Deposits, which in turn would oblige banks to limit their lending in order to keep their now reduced eligible reserve assets above the minimum ratio with eligible liabilities, or via 'open market operations' (OMOs) whereby the Bank used attractive interest rates to induce banks to exchange eligible reserve assets for longer-dated, and hence 'ineligible' government securities, which would also have the effect of reducing the reserve asset ratio. It should be noted that, because the ratio was set at 12.5 per cent, a reduction of £1 in assets would reduce liabilities by £8 – in other words, it would squeeze the amount of money in circulation quite sharply provided banks were close to their minimum reserve asset ratio. This operated after October 1972 in conjunction with a **Minimum Lending Rate (MLR)** which replaced the previous Bank Rate. The key point about the MLR was that it was determined by the average price (and hence the interest rate) that the discount houses, which were committed to purchasing the entire issue, offered for Treasury Bills (short-dated government securities), and was automatically set above that level. In principle, therefore, the MLR followed the market whereas the Bank Rate had been used to signal interest rate changes directly to the market. In practice, however, the MLR could also be raised unilaterally so that the CCC system was one which relied primarily upon controlling the supply of money in circulation combined with an element of direct control over interest rates.

The CCC system rapidly fell into disrepute for a variety of reasons such as its narrowness of scope (secondary banks remained outside the system and grew rapidly at the expense of clearing banks); the existence of plentiful quantities of eligible reserve assets in the form of Treasury Bills as the government sought to finance its rapidly expanding PSBR; and a failure of political will when confronted by the need to raise interest rates sharply in order to control the money supply. As shown in **Figure 20.1**, there was a sharp surge in the ratio of broad money to GDP (see below for discussion of definitions of the money supply) and this period was particularly characterised by the first of a series of speculative booms in the housing market which we observed in **Figure 3.12**.

The year 1972 was also characterised by the decision to float sterling as the Bretton Woods exchange rate system began to collapse at the seams. Naturally, sterling floated downwards, so inflationary pressure was generated through the rising price of imports. There was already growing pressure in this respect because raw material prices were beginning to rise sharply, a tendency which accelerated further with the subsequent decision by OPEC to quadruple oil prices. Supply-side shocks on this scale would have taxed a much healthier economy than the UK. The government responded in a variety of ways which included higher interest rates and a prices and incomes policy. These steps were ill-received and led to the three-day week (during which output

remained at roughly its previous 5-day level) and a miners' strike. The government foolishly made this an issue of confidence, went to the polls and lost. Whether the incoming Labour government relished the thought of tackling its inherited problems is, of course, another matter.

20.2.3 Prices and Incomes Policies

In the light of the above, it is helpful to make a few comments on prices and incomes policies at this juncture. As noted in Chapter 2, prices and incomes policies have the obvious virtue that, since they operate on the supply side of the economy, they can be introduced at times when demand is running at a high level to sustain employment in order to deal with the inflationary consequences of that demand. They would appear to be particularly useful where the main causal factor in the inflationary process is believed to be the behaviour of trade unions.

Figure 20.1   *Ratio of M4 to GDP*

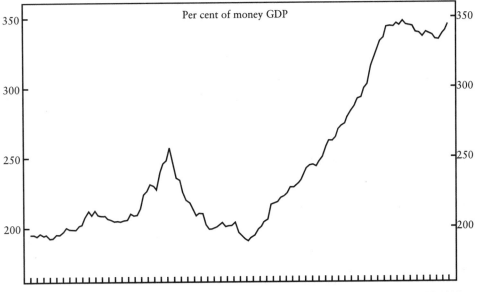

Source: FSBR 1996–97, Chart 2.3.

Various attempts were made to restrain prices and incomes during the period up to the mid-1960s. Controls were introduced in 1948–50; debatably in 1956; in 1961 (in the form of a 'pay pause'); and in 1962–64 (in the form of 'guideposts' for prices and incomes). During 1964, the National Board for Prices and Incomes was established to supersede the National Incomes Commission and advance warning of wage and price changes was required. In July 1966, prices and incomes were 'frozen' for six months, and this was followed by a further six months of 'severe restraint'. Between 1968 and 1972, there was no official policy as such, but wage and price increases were supposedly determined by reference to such criteria as productivity increases.

The statutory 1972–4 policy commenced with a ninety-day standstill on prices, charges for services, pay, dividends, and rents. Phase I lasted until the end of March 1973 when the Counter-Inflation Act was introduced which set up a Price Commission and a Pay Board. Phase III, introduced in October 1973, critically introduced a threshold such that if the RPI rose by 7 per cent above its level in October 1973 within the ensuing 12–month period then workers were entitled to 40p plus a further 40p for every percentage rise above 7 per cent. By April 1974 the first threshold had been breached, and by October twelve increments had become payable. Not surprisingly, any idea of continuing compulsion was abandoned at this point and a voluntary policy known as the 'Social Contract' was introduced. In any event, it would have been much more difficult for the incoming Labour government to have continued with compulsory restrictions upon its natural supporters, the trade unions, than its predecessor even though Heath's government was ideologically committed to free markets – including non-interference in free wage bargaining.

A retrospective examination of these various attempts at prices and incomes policies indicates clearly that success was forthcoming only where the trade union movement was both willing to support the policy and had sufficient clout to keep its individual members in line (as in 1948–50). However, it is important to bear in mind that even if such policies work in the short term, those affected are likely to try (usually successfully) to recover lost ground once the policies are weakened/lifted, and that the more desperate does the need for such policies become, the more desperately do people subject to them strive to avoid their effects.

20.2.4 Money Supply in the Ascendent

In addition to its experiment with prices and incomes policy, the government also restructured CCC through the introduction of the 'supplementary special deposits' scheme (popularly known as the 'corset'). This operated as a form of tax on the growth of interest-bearing eligible liabilities (IBELs) since any growth above a pre-determined limit would result in the excess being transferred to the Bank of England where it would earn no interest. However, this inevitably led to avoidance in the form of companies issuing their own bills which were then guaranteed by the banks.

Nevertheless, taken in conjunction with the brutal increase in interest rates during late 1972 and early 1973 (as shown in **Figure 20.2**), the ratio of broad money to GDP did fall back sharply again as shown in **Figure 20.1**. Furthermore, the Labour government began to address the escalating crisis in the realisation that the methods which had apparently served its predecessors so well during the 1950s and 1960s would no longer suffice. True, it felt it necessary to cling on to the failed experiment with prices and incomes policies, albeit in a voluntary rather than compulsory format (the 'Social Contract'), but this was introduced as a weapon in its battle to control inflation which had, at least for the time being, to be given a priority over unemployment. That being so, the use of expansionary demand management, for example through increased public expenditure, was to be set aside despite the government's left-wing credentials. This change in attitude is usually associated with the (in)famous speech made by the then prime minister, James Callaghan, at the 1976 Labour Party Conference when he announced that:

Figure 20.2 *Interest Rates 1970–73*

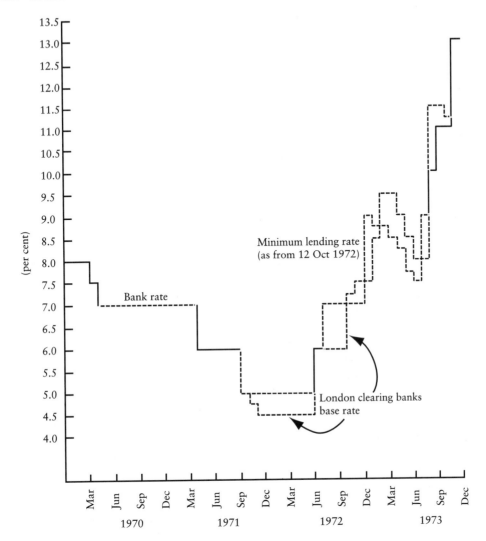

We used to think that you could just spend your way out of a recession, and increase employment, by cutting taxes and boosting government spending. I tell you in all candour that that option no longer exists, and that in so far as it ever did exist, it worked by injecting inflation into the economy.

By this time confidence was at a low ebb and sterling was on the slide, reaching an all-time low against the dollar in October 1976. The government turned to the IMF for help and this body has often been demonised as responsible for the introduction of so-called 'monetarist' doctrines in the UK. We will have much more to say about monetarism in what follows, but for the moment it suffices to note that the virtues of holding back the growth in the money supply had already been accepted within the terms of CCC and that the IMF was concerned with a somewhat different concept known as Domestic Credit Expansion (DCE – see below). It can be argued, however, that the DCE limits imposed by the IMF represented the first formal use of monetary targets insofar that the government sent a Letter of Intent to the IMF which accepted the need to emphasise monetary policy (in practice, via a higher MLR, a call for supplementary special deposits and prioritising bank lending).

An important aspect of this new emphasis upon the money supply was that it broke down some of the artificial barriers which had previously been erected between fiscal and monetary policy. In effect, it was now accepted that if the government ran a budget deficit then it could either be financed by attracting existing private money away from other uses, in which case no new money would be created, or by selling securities to banks as assets which would then provide the collateral for paying cash to the government in return – a sophisticated method of printing new money. If there was a link between money and inflation, then prioritising inflation control meant restricting monetary growth which in turn meant reducing the PSBR through fiscal means.

This linkage was important because the government was in the awkward position of having to sell its policies to both the financial markets and its natural supporters who tended to have rather different perceptions of how it should proceed. It was convenient to divert part of the blame for expenditure cuts onto the 'gnomes of Zurich' consequent upon the IMF loan, but this would not win an election. Could the economy therefore be reflated without fuelling inflation? Arguably so, if a prices and incomes policy could be made to stick. The government accordingly increased its expenditure and announced a 5 per cent guideline for pay rises in the 1978–79 pay round. The electorate were not amused as they expected prices to rise much faster than this. Ford awarded their workers 17 per cent in November 1978 and the 'Winter of Discontent' was set in motion. In May 1979, the Labour government was unceremoniously replaced by Mrs Thatcher's first administration.

□ 20.2.5 Targeting Money

As indicated above, Keynesian demand management policies involved short-term discretionary interventions using primarily fiscal instruments. Whilst they were originally devised to regulate the level of employment, they could, of course, be used to regulate anything provided that it was demand-driven, including inflation and the balance of payments.

Let us suppose, therefore, that the level of demand is altered whether through a fiscal or monetary instrument, but that its effects upon objectives are either heavily watered down as it passes along a line of intermediate targets, or that there are considerable time lags involved in the process or both. Then either we will not get anything like the desired impact or it will appear much too late to be useful. Indeed, a worst case scenario would be where the instrumental change is initiated because the economy is in recession, but only affects objectives when the economy has begun to grow again. In such circumstances, its deflationary intent would become an inflationary outcome.

For this reason, it became increasingly advocated that discretionary changes should be minimised and replaced wherever possible by simple rules. For example, it is evident that an increase in the money supply, its velocity of circulation remaining unaffected, will alter either real output or the price level or both. If, for example, output is forecast to be growing at 5 per cent, and it is thought desirable that prices should remain unchanged, then a sensible rule would be that the amount of money in circulation be increased by 5 per cent so that there is just enough extra money to buy the extra goods available at existing prices.

Whilst this precise relationship may be difficult to bring about, if only because of the difficulty in producing accurate forecasts, the end result should still be no more than very modest levels of inflation. Thus, it becomes possible to replace a target set for the objective (the price level) by a target set for the intermediate variable (the money supply), setting aside the usual qualifications (the *ceteris paribus* principle) relating to such matters as the value of the exchange rate.

The resultant rule, to the effect that the growth of the money supply should be set equal to the assumed long-run (that is, through an entire business cycle) growth of output, has much to commend it in principle, and it can then be extended to other related rules such as 'balance the budget' or even 'balance the budget by reducing both tax revenue and public expenditure' since this will also serve to reduce distortions at the microeconomic level. This, in turn, could lead to a belief in the virtues of privatisation and the freeing up of as many microeconomic markets as possible.

■ 20.3 Monetarism

These ideas are generally lumped together under the title of 'monetarism', although all so-called monetarists do not by any means agree on everything, even on the most appropriate definition for 'money'. Monetarism is no longer 'fashionable' among UK policy-makers, but it was certainly influential in relation to the policies pursued by the Thatcher governments during the period 1979–85. As we noted in Chapter 1, monetarism's rise to prominence reflected the loss of faith in the Keynesian model and in particular the breakdown in the Phillips Curve relationship after 1968 (see **pp. 101–3**).

□ 20.3.1 What is Money?

One of the most obvious difficulties to be addressed is the need for a clear-cut definition of what is meant by 'money'. In a simple sense, the answer is that there will a change in the money supply if there is a change in the amount of currency held by the non-bank private sector and/or in bank deposits. However, this leaves considerable leeway in interpretation and over the years the authorities have resorted to a wide array of alternatives, of which a selection is represented in **Figure 20.3**. Until the end of July 1989, the UK definitions were M0; non-interest bearing M1 (nib M1); M1; M2; M3; M3c; M4 and M5. M1, M3 and M3c were subsequently

dropped, but were replaced by M4c. Then, in August 1990, M4c and M5 were replaced by data for a range of liquid assets outside M4. M3H was introduced in August 1992 in order to provide a broad monetary aggregate similar to that used elsewhere in the EU. The definitions were rationalised and clarified in December 1992. The Bank of England made it clear that many of the definitions were produced so as to satisfy outside demand (for example from econometricians requiring consistent runs of data). Only three mattered for policy purposes: M0, M2 and M4. M0 consists almost entirely (over 99 per cent) of notes and coin. M2 is notes and coin in circulation plus private sector retail deposits, whereas M4 includes these and wholesale deposits as well. M4 is effectively a modernised version of sterling (£)M3, reflecting institutional changes.

The main reason for this multiplicity of definitions is that it is not clear in practice which institutions are banks (see **p. 112**). Given that a building society is (increasingly) similar, but not identical, to a bank, it is treated as a bank for some definitions but not for others. The Abbey National Building Society's conversion to a bank on 12 July 1989 triggered an alteration in definitions of money because it caused a huge switch of assets from the building society to the banking sector. This switch was, however, a purely statistical artefact with virtually no economic significance.

There are similar difficulties over the definition of a deposit. As a concept, it is an 'almost perfectly liquid' claim on a bank. However, it is unclear whether a 7-day account is 'almost perfectly liquid', or, indeed, whether such a term can be applied to funds which can be obtained instantly, but subject to the payment of a penalty.

A final point relates to the use of DCE rather than the money supply *per se*. It is possible to break down the supply of money into a domestic (DCE) component and an overseas component. The latter is closely related to the state of the balance of payments current account. If a surplus exists, then money will flow in to settle the outstanding debts, and vice versa. If money flows in, then this will enable UK residents to buy more imports, assuming the exchange rate remains

Figure 20.3   *Relationships between the Monetary Aggregates and their Components*[1]

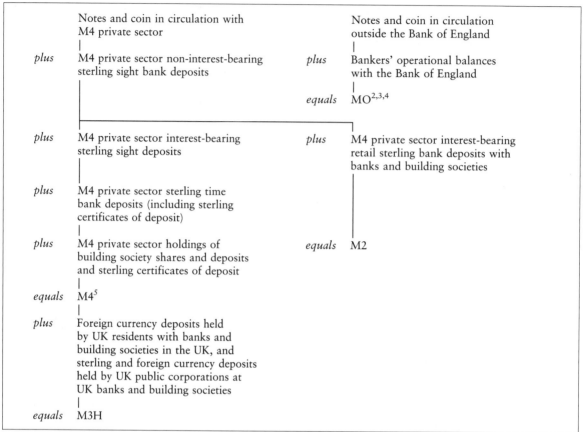

Notes:

[1] The Abbey National Building Society was authorised under the Banking Act 1987 as from the date of its conversion to a public limited company on 12 July 1989. From the end of July onwards its assets were transferred into the category of retail banks and ceased to be included in the building societies category. The amount of assets transferred (£32 billion) were such as to cause a major discontinuity in the series which included bank deposits but excluded building society deposits (namely M1, M3 and M3$_c$) and these were accordingly terminated as of June 1989. In aggregate M2, M4 and M5 were unaffected as there were equal and offsetting changes in the bank and building society contribution to each aggregate. There was a small but easy to adjust for statistical break in M0 due to the appearance of bankers' deposits at the Bank of England placed by the Abbey National, and an insignificant break in nib M1. The disappearance of M3$_c$ was compensated for by the creation of a new definition M4$_c$ which included certain deposits in currencies other than sterling placed with UK banks and building societies by the rest of the UK private sector.

    The term 'non-bank private sector' is used throughout this text to refer to the sector comprising UK residents other than the public sector and banks. The increasingly blurred distinction between banks and building societies has resulted in the increased use of the term 'M4 private sector' to indicate that both banks *and* building societies are excluded.

    In the light of the statistical discussion paper (Bank of England, 1990a) and the subsequent responses to it, the August 1990 *Bank of England Quarterly Bulletin* (pp. 336–7) announced the Bank's intention of replacing the monetary aggregates M4$_c$ and M5 by data for a range of liquid assets outside M4. These were also discussed in the May 1991 *Quarterly Bulletin* (pp. 263–6).

    As a consequence the definition of 'broad' money is now confined to M4, and has its base 'notes and coin in circulation with the M4 private sector' as shown in the Figure.

[2] M0 is calculated on a weekly averaged basis. All other aggregates are calculated at end-months.

[3] The stock of M0 outstanding at the end of June 1991 was £18 million while that of M4 was £445 billion.

[4] Bank of England equations suggest that a 1 per cent increase in consumption will raise M0 by 0.2 per cent in the current quarter and by 1 per cent in the long run. A permanent 1 per cent increase in interest rates will lower M0 by 0.1 per cent in the current quarter, and in the long run will lower the growth of M0 by 0.5 per cent per annum.

[5] Over the last decade M4 deposits have grown broadly in line with total gross wealth. See *Bank of England Quarterly Bulletin* (August 1990), pp. 381–2.

Source: Bank of England.

roughly constant. Thus, the current account will tend towards equilibrium and attention can be directed towards internal equilibrium by setting a target for DCE. This approach was favoured by the IMF during the 1970s, and it would obviously be relevant to a situation where the UK rejoined the ERM with a view to full monetary union.

20.4 The Medium Term Financial Strategy

The Keynesian model which drove macroeconomic policy during the early postwar period could be characterised as interventionist and as operating with short time horizons. In other words, it was designed to deal with an existing problem as quickly as possible. This approach was formally thrown out by Mrs Thatcher after the 1979 election although, as we have seen, her predecessor had effectively already started down that route.

The core proposition underlying the new Conservative approach was that the economy would only thrive in a non-inflationary environment. In other words, inflation would become the primary objective and be tackled through variations in aggregate demand which would be regulated via the money supply. This, of itself, would result in an improvement in the job market because decisions could now be taken on the assumption of stable prices. Meanwhile, (un)employment would also be tackled on the supply side in order to reduce the natural rate of unemployment (see pp. 359–60).

Such an approach could not be expected to yield immediate results; a longer time horizon was needed, albeit one constrained by the electoral cycle. Thus was born the idea of a **Medium Term Financial Strategy** (MTFS). The macroeconomic element would comprise control of inflation via the money supply, which in turn would require careful control over the size of the PSBR for reasons noted above. The microeconomic element would involve the range of supply-side measures discussed on **pp. 23–4**.

The first version of the MTFS was published in March 1980, and is set out in **Table 20.1** which

indicates its rolling nature; in March each year the targets would be amended in the light of what had happened the previous year and a further year added on the end. The table indicates actual outcomes as well as targets which were set in relation to at least one measure of the money supply with associated projections for the PSBR.

An important aspect was the manner in which the target ranges were reduced over successive

Table 20.1 *MTFS, Target Ranges[1] and Outcomes (%)*

	1979/80	1980/81	1981/82	1982/83	1983/84
Money Supply: M0 (% change)					
Outcome	10	$6\frac{1}{2}$	0	$3\frac{1}{2}$	$6\frac{1}{4}$
Money Supply: M1 (% change)					
March 1982	*	*	*	8–12	7–11
March 1983	*	*	*	*	7–11
Outcome	*	*	*	11	11
Money Supply: £M3 (% change)					
June 1979	7–11	*	*	*	*
March 1980	*	7–11	6–10	5–9	4–8
March 1981	*	*	6–10	5–9[2]	4–8[2]
March 1982	*	*	*	8–12	7–11
March 1983	*	*	*	*	7–11
Outcome	$16\frac{1}{4}$	$19\frac{1}{2}$	$12\frac{3}{4}$	10	$9\frac{3}{4}$
Money Supply: PSL$_2$ (% change)					
March 1982	*	*	*	8–12	7–11
March 1983	*	*	*	*	7–11
Outcome	*	*	*	9	$12\frac{1}{3}$
PSBR (% of GDP)					
June 1979	$4\frac{1}{2}$	*	*	*	$2\frac{1}{4}$
March 1980	$4\frac{3}{4}$	$3\frac{3}{4}$	3	*	$1\frac{1}{2}$
March 1981	5	6	$4\frac{1}{4}$	$3\frac{1}{4}$	2
March 1982	*	$5\frac{3}{4}$	$4\frac{1}{4}$	$3\frac{1}{2}$	2
March 1983	*	*	$3\frac{1}{2}$	$2\frac{3}{4}$	$2\frac{3}{4}$
Outcome	$4\frac{3}{4}$	$5\frac{1}{2}$	$3\frac{1}{2}$	$3\frac{1}{4}$	$3\frac{1}{4}$

Notes:
[1] Targets are set for a 14-month period commencing in February.
[2] 'Illustrative range'.

Source: FSBR, 'Red Book', for each year.

years. The purpose of this was to affect expectations about the future course of inflation. If people believed that the government would bring the rate of inflation down year by year, they would in theory adjust their behaviour in line with this expectation, for example by reducing wage demands.

As can be seen in **Table 20.2**, the initial definition chosen for the money supply was £M3 in preference to the narrow definition M0. At this time, as shown in **Figure 20.1**, broad money was beginning to grow again in relation to GDP, and the government wanted to hold its growth within a 7–11 per cent range (see **Table 20.1**). It therefore chose to push bank base rates up to an unprecedented 17 per cent (see **Figure 20.4**), but £M3 grew by over 16 per cent in 1979–80 so it became necessary to continue the medicine as well as to operate a tight fiscal policy. One side-effect was that sterling rose sharply, producing the unfortunate combination of difficulties in export markets and competition from imports worsening the recession at home.

One of the most interesting policy quirks was the decision to switch the emphasis from direct taxation, via a reduction in the basic rate from 33 per cent to 30 per cent and in the top rate from 86

per cent to 60 per cent, to indirect taxation via an increase in VAT to 15 per cent. Although the primary objective was to reduce inflation, it was evident that doubling VAT would cause retail prices to rise. This triggered a debate about the difference between a one-off stimulus to prices and an ongoing, but smaller stimulus. This was, as usual, left unresolved if only because it was difficult to assess the extent to which inflationary expectations would be affected over the longer term even assuming the direct effects of the VAT increase were short-lived.

It may also be noted that attempts to introduce market principles into the bloated public corporation sector had equally perverse consequences. Since public corporations were heavily subsidised, market prices meant higher prices and hence a further stimulus to inflation. These two policies certainly looked to be a classic case of first having to make things worse before they can be made better.

As can be seen, this policy combination nevertheless failed to bring £M3 down into its target range; indeed, it grew even faster during 1980–81 than the previous year whereas narrow money was behaving much better. The PSBR was also coming in above target. Fiscal policy was tight-

Figure 20.4 *Bank Base Rates, 1979–96*

Source: Barclays Bank Review.

ened in 1981 and an attempt to ease policy via lower interest rates was short-lived. The raising of excise duties and the non-indexation of income tax allowances in 1981 in the face of growing unemployment can reasonably be seen as a politically courageous but necessary act if prosperity was to return, although at the time it caused consternation in the ranks of those whose sympathies still lay with the principles of Keynesianism.

This period revealed one of the obvious difficulties with monetary targeting, namely that since broad money contained a variety of different elements, switching between them might not affect the aggregate at all but might affect what the money was used for, and particularly the probability that it would be spent and hence affect output and prices. More significantly, perhaps, it became clear that trade-offs between objectives would remain the order of the day

As shown in **Table 20.1**, the government needed to respond to the fact that £M3 remained obstinately outside its target range, and in March 1982 it decided to target a measure of narrow money, M1, although the target was set fairly high. Further, it could hardly continue with interest rates at their penal levels (although they were actually negative in real terms), so they were brought down during 1981 and 1982 in frequent but small steps, as shown in **Figure 20.4**. They were then kept roughly stable until the middle of 1984 while the emphasis in the 1983 Budget and beyond was upon cutting taxes both in recognition of the obstinacy with which unemployment continued to grow and in line with the principles of the supply-side model.

From 1979 to 1982 the government pursued a determinedly monetarist path. From 1983 to 1985 this was watered down somewhat but not abandoned. Disappointment with the performance of its chosen measures of the money supply led to a period of experimentation with a variety of other measures such as M0 and PSL$_2$, as shown in **Table 20.2**. Money GDP was also targeted as part of the MTFS, the implication being that if prices were rising then output would have to fall somewhat to keep the lid on money GDP growth.

1983 was an election year, so it may not seem unduly surprising that interest rates were held

down and the fiscal position eased somewhat. However, inflation was by now in its third successive year of decline (a trend by no means confined to the UK) and the government felt that it had some cause to congratulate itself that the medicine had worked – not that the ever-growing band of the unemployed felt inclined to join in, but they were in the minority and those who had survived the recession were now in the mood to spend, spend, spend as money incomes soared above the now reduced rate of inflation.

The mid-1980s will always be associated with the tenure of Nigel Lawson as Chancellor of the Exchequer. Things began inauspiciously as a combination of an upturn in inflation, continuing unemployment and a rampant dollar caused a loss of confidence in sterling which in turn boosted import prices and hence inflation. Interest rates were pushed up as shown in **Figure 20.4**, but following Mrs Thatcher's free-market principles, when sterling came under further pressure because of a weakness in oil prices (foreigners persisted in exaggerating the importance of oil for the UK economy) it was initially allowed to find its own level.

This level was very low indeed – $1.04 at its lowest ebb – and even Mrs Thatcher cavilled at the prospect of a pound worth less than a dollar, so interest rates were pushed up further. The government took note of the adverse consequences of such volatility in the exchange rate, and in November 1985 the monetarist strategy bit the dust. What was clearly needed was sufficient stability in the exchange rate to control any inflationary impact. Such stability would only be forthcoming if the exchange rate was 'managed'. This indicated the need to peg sterling to a stable currency – most obviously the German mark – although this was 'unofficial' in the sense that sterling remained outside the Exchange Rate Mechanism (ERM). The chosen value for the DM fluctuated between 3.0 and 3.2 to £1.

It is of interest that this action was paralleled on a wider stage in the form of the 'Plaza Accord' of October 1985. However, fashionable or not, it clearly implied the need to redirect monetary policy to control of the exchange rate rather than concentrating upon money supply control via the interest rate. As shown in **Table 20.2**, £M3 was

Table 20.2 MTFS, Target Ranges[1] and Outcomes (%)

	1984/85	1985/86	1986/87	1987/88	1988/89	1989/90	1990/91	1991/92	1992/93	1993/94	1994/95	1995/96	1996/97
Money Supply: M0 (% change)													
March 1984	4–8	3–7[2]	2–6[2]	1–5[2]	0–4[2]								
March 1985		3–7	2–6[2]	1–5[2]	0–4[2]								
March 1986			2–6	2–6	2–6								
March 1987				2–6	1–5	1–5							
March 1988					1–5	1–5	1–5						
March 1989						1–5	0–4	0–4	–1–3				
March 1990							0–4	0–4	0–4				
March 1991							0–4	0–4	0–4				
March 1992								0–4	0–4	0–4			
March 1993										0–4[3]	0–4[3]	0–4[3]	0–4[3]
Nov. 1994											0–4[3]	0–4[3]	0–4[3]
Nov. 1995												0–4[3]	0–4[3]
Nov. 1996													0–4[3]
Outcome[4]	5½	3½	4	5	7½	5¾	2½	2¼	5	6½	6½		
Money Supply: £M3 (% change)													
March 1984	6–10	5–9[2]	4–8[2]	3–7[2]	2–6[2]								
March 1985[6]		5–9	4–8[2]	3–7[2]	2–6[2]								
March 1986			11–15										
Outcome[4]	9½	14¾	18	22	22								
Money Supply: M4 (% change)													
March 1993									4–8[7]	3–9[3]	3–9[3]	3–9[3]	3–9[3]
Nov. 1994											3–9[3]	3–9[3]	3–9[3]
Nov. 1995												3–9[3]	3–9[3]
Nov. 1996													3–9[3]
RPI excl. MIPs (% change)													
March 1993										1–4	1–4	1–4	1–4
Nov. 1994											1–4	1–4	1–4
Nov. 1995												1–4	1–4
Nov. 1996													1–4
Outcome									4¾	3	2¼	3	

Table 20.2 *MTFS, Target Ranges[1] and Outcomes (%) (cont'd)*

	1984/85	1985/86	1986/87	1987/88	1988/89	1989/90	1990/91	1991/92	1992/93	1993/94	1994/95	1995/96	1996/97	1997/98
PSBR (% of GDP)														
March 1984	2¼	2	2	1¾	1¾	*	*	*	*	*	*	*	*	*
March 1985	3¼	2	2	1¾	1¾	*	*	*	*	*	*	*	*	*
March 1986	3	2	1¾	1¾	1½	1½	*	*	*	*	*	*	*	*
March 1987	*	1½	1	1	1	1	1	*	*	*	*	*	*	*
March 1988	*	*	1	−¾	−¾	0	0	*	*	*	*	*	*	*
March 1989	*	*	*	−¾	−3	−2¾	−1¾	−1	−½	*	*	*	*	*
March 1990	*	*	*	*	*	−1¼	−1¼	−½	0	*	*	*	*	*
March 1991	*	*	*	*	*	−1½	−¼	1¼	2	*	*	*	*	*
March 1992	*	*	*	*	*	*	*	2¼	4½	4¾	3½	2½	¾	*
March 1993	*	*	*	*	*	*	*	*	5¾	8	6½	5½	4½	3¾
Nov. 1994	*	*	*	*	*	*	*	*	*	*	5	3	1¾	¾
Nov. 1995	*	*	*	*	*	*	*	*	*	*	*	4	3	2
Nov. 1996	*	*	*	*	*	*	*	*	*	*	*	*	3½	2½
Outcome	3	1½	1	−¾	−3	−1½[7]	−¼[8]	2½	5¾	7¾	5¼	4½	*	*
Money GDP (% change)														
March 1985	6¾ (8¼)[9]	8½ (7)[9]	6¾	5¾	5	*	*	*	*	*	*	*	*	*
March 1986	*	9½ (8¼)[9]	6¾	6½	6	5½	*	*	*	*	*	*	*	*
March 1987	*	*	6	7½	6½	6	*	*	*	*	*	*	*	*
March 1988	*	*	*	*	7½	6½	6	5½	6	5½	*	*	*	*
March 1989	*	*	*	*	11	7¾	6	6	5½	*	*	*	*	*
March 1990	*	*	*	*	*	8½	7½[8]	6¾[8]	6¼[8]	*	*	*	*	*
March 1991	*	*	*	*	*	*	7¼[8]	6[8]	7½[8]	*	*	*	*	*
March 1992	*	*	*	*	*	*	*	5	6½	6¾	6¾	6	5¼	*
March 1993	*	*	*	*	*	*	*	*	3¼	4¾	7	6½	5½	4¾
Nov. 1994	*	*	*	*	*	*	*	*	*	*	6	6¼	5¼	5
Nov. 1995	*	*	*	*	*	*	*	*	*	*	*	5	6	5½
Nov. 1996	*	*	*	*	*	*	*	*	*	*	*			

Notes:
1 Targets are set for a 14–month period.
2 'Illustrative range'.
3 'Monitoring range'.
4 Data taken from source cited. Slightly different figures are cited elsewhere. Outcomes relate to a 12-month period.
5 Old definition including public sector deposits.
6 New definition excluding public sector deposits.
7 2nd half only.
8 Adjusted for distortions arising from the abolition of domestic rates.
9 Adjusted for coal strike.

Source: *FSBR*, 'Red Book', for each year, of which the most recent are those for 1996–7, HC30 (Nov. 1995) and 1997–98, HC90 (Nov. 1996).

fully targeted for the last time in March 1985, lapsing after November to the status of being 'monitored' (perhaps just as well in view of the outcomes, which bore no relation to the targets). By 1987, only M0 remained as a targeted definition of money although interestingly that seemed to go hand in hand with its emergence above its target range (see **Figure 20.5**). This suggested to some that the money supply would only behave itself if you did not target it.

The period from 1986 to 1988 is popularly known as the 'Lawson boom', although it was never as popular among commentators as it was among the general public. This was because the economy grew very rapidly and earnings grew even faster. This led to a surge in real consumption as households 'shopped till they dropped', taking out unprecedented amounts of credit on the back of the additional collateral supplied by soaring house prices which in many cases doubled in value during this period (with houses increasingly being remortgaged to release further cash). As shown in **Figure 20.4**, interest rates fell unstea-

dily but significantly from their peak in early 1985, being pushed down further in response to the stock market crash in October 1987 in order to ensure that firms could borrow cheaply to tide them over any short-term liquidity crisis. With interest rates now largely directed at the exchange rate, and no measure of broad money being targeted, monetary policy was slackened, as shown in **Figures 20.1** and **20.5**. On a more positive note, unemployment turned the corner and now began to fall very sharply, further boosting consumer confidence. In addition, the PSBR, responding to fiscal drag, was evolving into a PSDR.

There were similarities with the early 1970s situation discussed above, with the same consequences, including an alarming deterioration in the current balance as imports were sucked in and an upturn in inflation. Could this have been prevented? Mrs Thatcher, among others, felt that interest rates were undesirably low and that the money supply was being insufficiently targeted. Chancellor Lawson was more preoccupied with holding down the value of sterling, but even he

Figure 20.5   *Monetary Growth*

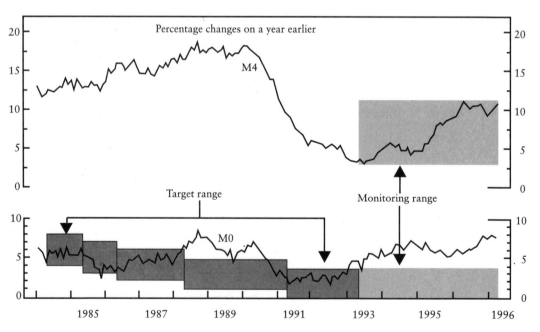

Source: FSBR 1997–98, chart 3.24.

could hardly ignore the message sent out by **Figure 20.5** that narrow money had shifted well outside its target range and needed to be reined back sharply. This meant that the exchange rate target would have to be sacrificed, albeit temporarily, in the cause of monetary tightening. As shown in **Figure 20.4**, interest rates began their upwards march in the Spring of 1988, initially in a series of small, frequent steps but subsequently in more protracted leaps and bounds.

By the end of the decade, with interest rates seemingly stuck at 15 per cent, the good times were at an end. M0 was being dragged back into its target range, and the M4 measure of broad money had turned sharply downwards, stabilising its ratio to money GDP for the first time in over a decade, as shown in **Figure 20.1**. An element of stability was not unwelcome after what could best be described as a roller coaster decade. However, at the end of the day, it remained very difficult to determine the extent to which macroeconomic policy had been either success or failure. Objectives had been re-prioritised towards inflation and later the exchange rate, necessitating a somewhat different approach in terms of instruments and intermediate targets. Fiscal measures had remained important, although now directed towards money supply control and the supply side, and interest rates had come to the fore although this had exposed the trade-off between achieving internal and external objectives when over-emphasising a single instrument.

It is possible to view the Lawson boom as the pay-off for the very strict fiscal and monetary policies pursued at the beginning of the decade – a kind of virtue rewarded. On the other hand, the boom in effect served merely to recover lost ground (see **pp. 84–5**) and it could hardly be argued that there had been a coherent use of policy instruments throughout the decade, what with the rise and rather rapid demise of monetarism (though Milton Friedman and others denied that it had ever been implemented as intended and hence that it could not be held to have 'failed').

The path of unemployment presented particular difficulties. Its lengthy rise through to 1986 had been hugely costly in both economic and social terms, but it had fallen so sharply after

1986 that the UK looked to have evolved a set of labour market policies which made continental Europe's approach, which generated much less unemployment prior to 1986, look decidedly pedestrian and likely to generate more unemployment in the longer term.

Understandably, the 1980s was not a decade which treated everyone equally well, especially in terms of wealth (through home ownership), and this inevitably colours how the decade is viewed. However, the more critical question was whether the economy was more resilient in 1990 than in 1980, and that was to be tested by the onset of a severe recession which was partly a direct consequence of the policy tightening in response to the over-heated economy of the late 1980s.

In many ways, little seemed to have altered between 1980 and 1990. During 1990, the current account was seriously in deficit; inflation was rapidly approaching double figures; unemployment was on the rise; the PSBR had returned; and growth was moving into negative territory. In other words, the forecast 'soft landing' had turned out to be extremely 'hard', the 1980s' reforms of the economy notwithstanding. This meant that inflation had to be given pride of place among the objectives (there was considerable disagreement about the relevance of the current account deficit (see **Chapter 9**)).

☐ *20.4.1 Entering the ERM*

What neither Mrs Thatcher nor Chancellor Lawson realised at the time, nor lesser players such as Foreign Secretary Howe, was that **Europe** was to be the issue which was to fracture the Conservatives during the 1990s. One aspect of this concerned the issue of UK entry into the Exchange Rate Mechanism which took place in October 1990. As noted above, the pound had shadowed the DM unofficially during the Lawson boom, and he and his supporters believed that, if anything, this should have been done rather earlier on the grounds that it would have sent out a clear signal that the UK intended to pursue the kind of policies that would have allowed sterling to remain at a relatively fixed level in relation to Europe's strongest currency. In other words, the UK would have had to keep inflation down to Germanic levels and this would have coloured the attitude of all players in the economy, including wage bargainers, as appeared to have been the case in much of continental Europe.

Mrs Thatcher, and her adviser, Sir Alan Walters, responded that the policy of shadowing the DM had led to a considerable reduction in interest rates and a considerable expansion of the money supply, thereby inevitably storing up inflationary pressures for the future. However, it was also apparent that, with the Single European Market about to transpire at the end of 1992 (in theory, at least), and the possibility of full economic and monetary union pencilled in for some time before the end of the decade, the UK would look to be even less of a good European than it was already perceived to be on the continent if it turned its back irrevocably on the ERM, and even Mrs Thatcher had seen the wisdom in 1989 of agreeing to join even if the terms were unspecified. In fact, the terms turned out to be an obligation to remain in the 'wide band' (see pp. **282–4**), which at least gave the UK some additional control over its domestic affairs compared to membership of the narrow band (which would, however, constitute a prerequisite for full EMU).

Entering the ERM officially, even in the wide band, inevitably enhanced the government's credibility – but only modestly. Thus it was that interest rates, which had been jacked up to protect what was widely seen as an excessively high 'shadow rate' against the DM, had to be kept high to protect what was now widely seen as an excessively high wide band. Enhanced credibility did permit a small reduction at the time of ERM entry, as shown in **Figure 20.4**, because among other things it denoted a determination to control inflation through holding down import price rises, but the subsequent reductions can more readily be attributed to the need to respond to an deepening recession and clear evidence that inflation was anyway on a downwards path (see **Figure 4.6**). As shown in **Figure 20.5**, broad money was rising more slowly by the end of 1990 than it had been for the past decade, so those

who continued to believe in a causal relationship between the money supply and inflation felt strongly that the government should have moved faster and more resolutely in reducing interest rates.

A more widely held view was that the fierceness of the Lawson boom was not a particularly good justification for the fierceness of the response. In retrospect, it is inevitably easy to see the signs of the looming recession and to be dismayed at the government's failure to adjust its policy stance in good time. However, it turned out initially to be a uniquely anglo-saxon recession (since continental Europe remained quite buoyant due, *inter alia*, to German reunification), and the Conservatives were arguably as much concerned with internal dissentions as with the state of the economy.

☐ 20.4.2 Into the 1990s

The MTFS is set out in the annual Financial Statement and Budget Report (FSBR), popularly known as the 'Red Book' on account of its cover. In the early 1990s, the FSBR typically reiterated the government's determination to hold down inflation and to direct monetary policy (essentially the interest rate) primarily at holding sterling within the wide band of the ERM. Fiscal policy was to be set so as to balance the Budget over the 'medium term' (see *Financial Market Trends*, 64, June 1996). In other words, it was not to play a Keynesian short-term counter-cyclical role, and the PSBR would accordingly be allowed to fluctuate with the economic cycle. **Table 20.2** demonstrates this cyclical pattern, with the PSDRs of the late-1980s Lawson boom degenerating rapidly into the PSBRs of the early 1990s recession. There was to be no repeat of the sharp tightening of fiscal policy which had occurred a decade earlier; on the other hand, there was no desire for the expenditure side of the equation to spiral out of control at a time of necessarily falling tax revenues.

How, then, was the economy to recover? With difficulty might come the reply. Holding down inflation (not too difficult in a climate of rapidly rising unemployment) would generate a positive environment for future growth and help with expectations; some fiscal slackening would occur; and interest rates would be carefully and gradually reduced (see **Figure 20.4**). Despite the high exchange rate, the economy was reasonably competitive (what survived of manufacturing was by now resilient enough to weather a (not too protracted) recession. However, the recession, albeit shallower than that of a decade earlier, did prove to be more protracted. We have referred to this matter in Chapter 2 (see **pp. 38–43**). Essentially, the problem was that the private sector was excessively indebted, and felt the need for a breathing space to restore its finances. This caused, in particular, a dramatic collapse in house prices in real terms (and a first-ever reduction in money terms – see **pp. 60–2**) with an associated collapse in housing-related consumption.

This was not helped by interest rate policy. Superficially, base rates had fallen a long way – from 15 to 10 per cent by early 1992 – but even the latter figure was way above the rate of inflation after mid-1990 so it was hardly likely to set off renewed investment, especially with private individuals saving rather than spending as before. The need to keep the pound within the ERM was the problem here, so that came into question.

The other potentially significant explanation for the ongoing recession is most simply expressed as 'insecurity'. Recessions always do engender insecurity, but it is possible that this recession was unusual in that it affected not merely, or even primarily, the industrial heartlands in the north but also the service-driven areas in the South which had largely been untouched on prior occasions.

☐ *20.4.3 ERM and Out*

The story of how sterling was driven out of the ERM has been recounted in detail in Chapter 11, and does not warrant repetition here. However, the issue can also usefully be set within the context of the MTFS. Given the need to maintain a high exchange rate, as noted above, the authorities felt unable to reduce interest rates below 10 per cent, yet significantly positive real interest rates were clearly inappropriate during a prolonged recession. Whilst M0 was happily remaining within its target range, this was not particularly meaningful nor, in a recession, particularly helpful, and the MTFS basically was otherwise an empty shell. Not surprisingly, the financial markets didn't need to be told that the interest rate was being used to achieve two incompatible objectives, and that either interest rates would have to come down to reflate the economy or stay high to protect sterling.

Technically, if the Bundesbank had been willing to countenance much lower interest rates, those in the UK could also have fallen without posing a threat to sterling, but the Germans understandably felt disinclined to put their own anti-inflationary credibility on the line, so the UK was left to sink or swim. The financial markets speculated on the need to reflate and from then on there simply was no way of holding sterling in the ERM.

Once the die was cast, the government pretended it was all quite deliberate and, more plausibly, that it was all for the best. The MTFS was beefed up in March 1993 with a target range for underlying inflation (RPIX). It is of interest, firstly, that in targeting RPIX the government was reverting to a traditional objective (the exchange rate having started out as an instrument) and, secondly, that it sought to enhance the credibility of the MTFS by inviting the Bank of England to act as a reviewer through the publication of a separate quarterly *Inflation Report* to be appended to the *Bank of England Quarterly Bulletin*. If the Governor of the Bank of England didn't like what he saw, he would henceforth be able to express this view in public, although the last word, as ever, would be that of the Chancellor.

This modest attempt at more open policy-making was enhanced by the invitation to 'seven wise men' with widely differing beliefs to advise the Chancellor. The reason for this was a recognition that the one instrument/one objective model of the late 1980s needed to be broadened out to take account of other factors. Hence, for example, the inflation target was to be supported by the addition to the MTFS of a measure of broad money in the guise of M4, although this was to be 'monitored' rather than targeted, and indeed M0 was itself switched from targeted to monitored mode (see **Table 20.2** and Hudson and Fisher, 1994, p. 82). In judging the outlook for inflation, such indicators as the exchange rate, asset prices and house prices were also to be taken into account.

Freed from the constraint of the ERM, the authorities were able to concentrate on escaping from the recession. This can be considered in terms of the fiscal/monetary policy mix. As indicated in **Table 20.2** and **Figure 20.4**, the monetary stance had been loosened somewhat after 1990, but interest rates could now be reduced further after the temporary blip at the time sterling fell out of the ERM. Meanwhile, the fiscal stance, which had loosened considerably in the period commencing in 1990, could be left fairly loose as well. However, combined with a lower exchange rate, such policy loosening did raise the spectre of a renewed bout of inflation, so it could be pushed only so far, and indeed the fiscal stance had to be tightened again somewhat in 1994 to prevent too rapid an escalation in the debt/GDP ratio. In this respect, the government was surprisingly subtle in that it announced this tightening in the 1993 Budget but with its effects largely delayed until the 1994–95 financial year.

Those who still adhere to the view that 'money matters' have become alarmed recently because of the growth rates of both narrow and broad money as shown in **Figure 20.5**. In part, this is explained by a downturn in M0 velocity – the number of times units of money are used within a given time period – which contrasts sharply with experience pre-1990 when financial innovations meant that, for example, far less cash needed to be held and M0 velocity accordingly rose steadily (see Breedon and Fisher, 1994; Janssen, 1996), and it is generally accepted that broad money figures must be treated with increasing care because of its fluctuating velocity (see, for example, King, 1994a, p. 266). However, if broad money does indeed retain predictive power concerning inflation (in which case it would need to be targeted once again) there will be a noticeable upturn in RPIX during 1997 if not before (and there was, for example, a very sharp upturn in November 1996,

partly due to the annual estimation procedure explained on **pp. 92–3**).

20.5 Conclusions

As Mervyn King neatly expressed it (King, 1994, p. 263) 'policy is a matter of trial and error – some would say errors by the authorities and trials of the private sector'. Nevertheless, the authorities have no problem explaining the point of the exercise; in a word 'stability' (Governor of the Bank of England, 1996). But stability of what, exactly? As we have seen above, the government remains resolved to keep inflation below a predetermined level, depending on where the economy is in the cycle. This is rationalised as follows (*ibid.*, p. 327):

> A forward-looking approach to inflation targeting does therefore necessarily take account of what is happening or likely to happen to the real side of the economy – output and employment – because this influences the outlook for inflation itself. In focusing on inflation over the medium and longer term, we are in fact using it as a barometer, if you like, of the prospective balance between aggregate demand and the supply capacity of the economy. In this sense it is not in fact so far removed from stabilising output and employment around their trend rates, except that instead of seeking to estimate those trends directly – which as I say is a hazardous process – we monitor the prospect for inflation as evidence of an emerging imbalance between them.

Should the Conservatives be replaced by a Labour government in 1997, there is every reason to expect more of the same. Indeed, 'New Labour' has many times promised that it will behave conservatively and responsibly. So much for the principles.

It is interesting, however, that whilst almost all other advanced countries would go along with the desirability of stability in the medium/long term, there is still no consensus on the optimal method of achieving low inflation. In Germany, as in

Japan and Switzerland, monetary targets remain in vogue. Some EU member states which are in the narrow band of the ERM and aspire to full EMU see the exchange rate as a critical element in the equation. The UK and a number of other countries such as Australia, Canada, Italy and Spain target inflation. The US Federal Reserve informally targets money GDP.

This indicates a choice between objectives and intermediate variables such as the money supply. The money supply and the exchange rate have a patchy record, not only in the UK (which wasn't alone, for example, in falling out of the ERM), which tends to damage the credibility of most countries that favour them. This suggests that inflation targeting has some merit, a matter we addressed in section 4.4.2, whilst the fact that this is compatible with short-term output instability inclines some to favour targeting money GDP. On the other hand, a surge in growth would necessitate a reduction in inflation if a target for money GDP is to be met.

This, in turn, suggests that policy must be flexible with built-in overrides to take account of the likes of supply-side shocks. However, the absence of simple rules means that the Chancellor can allow himself to be swayed by political considerations. This has led to the Bank of England being able to express its views via public meetings between the Chancellor and the Governor, a monthly game which has probably done little for credibility in recent times because of the Governor's consistent pleas for higher interest rates and the Chancellor's fairly consistent refusal to grant them until very recently, and then in such a way as to make it fairly certain that they will have to rise further.

Critics of the current approach argue that an upturn in interest rates would be extremely, and unnecessarily damaging. They point out that the growth of manufacturing output generally moves inversely with interest rates and that, as shown in **Figure 20.6**, real interest rates are already too high by international standards. They believe that, whereas in the USA the Federal Reserve Board has stated its mission as 'achieving the highest rate of sustainable growth compatible with price stability', and delivered a much superior economic

Figure 20.6 *Real Interest Rates*

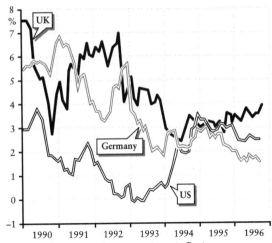

Note: Three-month rates minus inflation.

performance as a consequence (resulting in Clinton's easy second term election victory), the UK government has become fixated on inflation because the markets blame it if inflation rises but not if unemployment rises. They argue further that what is needed to restrain inflation is a tighter fiscal stance, either through higher taxes, lower spending, or both (for a forthright expression of these views see, for example, Kaletsky in *The Times*, 1 November 1996). Since the government is obviously going to ease the fiscal stance in the run-up to the 1997 election, higher interest rates will become inevitable if a Lawson-style 'Clarke boom' is to be avoided.

On the other hand, it can be argued that there is nothing obviously wrong with the way macroeconomic policy is currently handled in the UK since the economy is growing and the pound is strong. The Governor of the Bank of England has recently stated (*ibid.*, p. 328) that 'stability in the broader macroeconomic sense that I have described, including steady growth and lower unemployment – is closer than it has been for a very long time'. It is certainly difficult to argue that policy is 'inept' if judged by the standards of the past three decades, as 'New Labour' know perfectly well. Rather, it can be argued that the impending election is causing 'political' considerations to rear their usual ugly heads, and hence that things can only improve once that is out of the way irrespective of who is elected. However, it is debatable whether the monthly Treasury/Bank game is particularly helpful, and it is evident that any commitment by an incoming government to eventual full EMU, or even to the preliminary step of attempting to stabilise sterling within the pre-1992 narrow band (at the time of writing it is highly volatile, albeit ironically on an upwards trend partly because the UK is not having to fiddle the books to meet the Maastricht criteria), would require more emphasis to be placed on the exchange rate.

Bibliography

Bank of England (1980) 'Methods of Monetary Control', *Bank of England Quarterly Bulletin* (December).

Bank of England (1982) 'The Role of the Bank of England in the Money Market', *Bank of England Quarterly Bulletin* (March).

Bank of England (1990a) 'Monetary Aggregates in a Changing Environment: A Statistical Discussion Paper', *Discussion Paper 47* (March).

Bank of England (1990b) 'The Determination of the Monetary Aggregates', *Bank of England Quarterly Bulletin* (August).

Bank of England (1991) 'Liquid Assets Outside M4', *Bank of England Quarterly Bulletin* (May).

Blackaby, F. (ed.) (1978) *British Economic Policy 1960–74* (London: Heinemann).

Breedon, F. and P. Fisher (1994) 'The Determination of M0 and M4', *Bank of England Quarterly Bulletin* (February).

Chancellor of the Exchequer (1995) *Financial Statement and Budget Report 1996–97*, HC 30 (London: HMSO).

Chancellor of the Exchequer (1996) *Financial Statement and Budget Report 1997–98*, HC90 (London: The Stationery Office).

Governor of the Bank of England (1996) 'Economic Growth and Employment Through Stability', *Bank of England Quarterly Bulletin* (August).

Haldane, A. (1995) 'Rules, Discretion and the United Kingdom's New Monetary Framework', *Bank of England Working Paper Series No 40* (November).

Hudson, S. and P. Fisher (1994) 'Monetary Policy in the United Kingdom', *Economics and Business Education*, 2 (2).

Janssen, N. (1996) 'Can We Explain the Shift in M0 Velocity? Some Time-Series and Cross-Section Evidence', *Bank of England Quarterly Bulletin* (February).

Kasman, B. (1992) 'A Comparison of Monetary Policy Operating Procedures in Six Industrial Countries', *Federal Reserve Babk of New York Quarterly Review* (Summer).

King, M. (1994a) 'The Transmission Mechanism of Monetary Policy', *Bank of England Quarterly Bulletin* (August).

King, M. (1994b) 'Monetary Policy Instruments: The UK Experience', *Bank of England Quarterly Bulletin* (August).

Pepper, G. (1992) 'Controls and Distortions: Monetary Policy in the 1970s', *National Westminster Bank Quarterly Review* (February).

Pepper, G. (1993) 'Monitoring the Money Supply and Distortions to Monetary Data', *National Westminster Bank Quarterly Review* (February).

The Economist (1995) 'How Low Can They Go?' (2 December).

Index